W9-AFA-658

DESTINATION TOMORROW

Jack Carpenter

DESTINATION TOMORROW

Cover:
INDIANA: *The American Dream I*
Courtesy The Museum of Modern Art

Jack Carpenter

State University of New York
at Stony Brook

DESTINATION TOMORROW

WM. C. BROWN COMPANY PUBLISHERS
Dubuque, Iowa

Library of Congress Catalog Card Number: 76—183799

ISBN 0—697—03813—0

Second Printing, 1972

Printed in the United States of America

Contents

Preface xi

SECTION 1 THE HEALTH OF THE NATION—DIAGNOSING THE ILLS

Charles A. Reich
Consciousness III: The New Generation 3

Peter L. Berger and Brigitte Berger
The Blueing of America 14

Arnold Beichman
Six "Big Lies" About America 21

Milton Mayer
The Children's Crusade 31

Benjamin DeMott
The Way It Is: Some Notes on What We Feel 40

Questions and Quotations for Discussion and Writing Assignments 53

SECTION II SOME OLD WOUNDS—BLACK, RED, AND SORE

Frederick Douglass
July 4, 1852 63

Frederick Douglass
Learning to Read 64

Jesse Jackson (Interviewed by David Frost)
When Whites Are Unemployed, It's Called a Depression 72

Al Calloway
An Introduction to Soul 78

Vine Deloria, Jr.
Indians Today, the Real and the Unreal 82

Edward Abbey
What About the Indians? 91

Rollo May
The Man Who Was Put in a Cage 99

Questions and Quotations for Discussion and Writing Assignments 104

SECTION III WHAT DO WOMEN WANT?

Walt Whitman
A Woman Waits for Me 113

Lucy Komisar
The New Feminism 115

Richard Brautigan
15% 124

Marlene Dixon
Why Women's Liberation? 125

Walter Karp
The Feminine Utopia 138

Germaine Greer
Love: The Ideal 149

Edward Field
The Bride of Frankenstein **157**

William Carlos Williams
The Knife of the Times **159**

Questions and Quotations for Discussion and Writing Assignments **161**

SECTION IV LOVE, MARRIAGE, FAMILY—COUPLES, COUPLING, AND COMMUNES

William Blake
The Garden of Love **169**

Rollo May
Paradoxes of Sex and Love **170**

Germaine Greer
Altruism **187**

Richard Brautigan
As the Bruises Fade, the Lightning Aches **190**

Richard Brautigan
The Moon Versus Us Ever Sleeping Together Again **191**

Walt Whitman
The Dalliance of the Eagles **192**

Alvin Toffler
The Fractured Family **193**

Interviews by John Kronenberger—Is the Family Obsolete? **208**
Alvin Toffler, Author, "Future Shock" **208**
Shirley MacLaine, Actress **209**
Erich Segal, Author, "Love Story" **210**
Margaret Mead, Anthropologist **211**
Betty Friedan, Feminist **212**

Gary Snyder
Why Tribe **214**

Herbert A. Otto
Communes: The Alternative Life-Style 217

Questions and Quotations for Discussion and Writing Assignments 229

SECTION V A PLACE TO LIVE—SODOM, GOMORRAH, OR THE HOG FARM?

William Blake
London 239

Robert Cowley
Does Your Room Look Like the Collyer Brothers'? 240

Robinson Jeffers
Return 245

Robinson Jeffers
Signpost 246

Wendell Berry
Some Thoughts on Citizenship and Conscience in Honor of Don Pratt 247

Joseph Wood Krutch
Birds and Airplanes 258

Smohalla Speaks 263

Edward Abbey
Episodes and Visions 265

Paul Ehrlich
Eco-Catastrophe! 279

Questions and Quotations for Discussion and Writing Assignments 289

SECTION VI DOORS OF EDUCATION, DOORS OF PERCEPTION

Neil Postman and Charles Weingartner
Crap Detecting 298

Peter Marin
The Open Truth and Fiery Vehemence of Youth: A Sort of Soliloquy 308

Jerzy Kosinski
Children of TV 327

Carlos Castaneda
From the Teachings of Don Juan: A Yaqui Way of Knowledge 329

Gary Snyder
Passage to More Than India 344

Questions and Quotations for Discussion and Writing Assignments 350

SECTION VII THE GOOD LIFE—MAKING IT WITH STYLE

Michael Lydon
The Second Coming of Bo Diddley 361

Peter Schrag
The Age of Willie Mays 380

Peter Fonda and Dennis Hopper (Interviewed by David Frost)
Are We All Pushers? 390

Nora Ephron
Mush 397

Questions and Quotations for Discussion and Writing Assignments 408

SECTION VIII UTOPIA OR APOCALYPSE?

Gerald Clarke
Putting the Prophets in Their Place 415

Isaac Asimov
The Next 100 Years 420

Alan Watts
The Future of Ecstasy 426

Kurt Vonnegut, Jr.
Harrison Bergeron 439

Frederik Pohl
Day Million 445

Questions and Quotations for Discussion and Writing Assignments 449

Preface

Happy the man, and happy he alone,
He who can call today his own;
He who, secure within, can say,
Tomorrow, do thy worst, for I have liv'd today.
JOHN DRYDEN

Tomorrow to fresh wood, and pastures new.
JOHN MILTON

When we were kids, "tomorrow" puzzled us: we waited for it, but when it finally came, it was always "today." We sensed then, even before we understood, that the future is an abstract concept, that only today is real; and yet, we were human and could not stop ourselves from dreaming about and planning for the "fair adventure of tomorrow."

Although *Destination Tomorrow* contains much material about man's fate on this little spaceship we call Earth, it is not a doomsday book about the future and the shocks that await us there. It is a book of readings about basic human experiences, the kind of experiences that we face today and will face again each tomorrow. Today our problems seem to be new problems; our ideas, new ideas; even our feelings seem different from those others have felt before us. Yet if we look closely at contemporary social concerns, dilemmas, needs, and desires, if we strip away their "now" language and "relevant" packaging, we discover that they are not original. We want to love, to live meaningful lives, to find freedom and order, to have a sense of happiness, ease, and health, to find a good place in which to live and grow.

Some "prophets" insist that television and other forms of electronic communication are altering the character of human experience; others point out that new knowledge in genetics, behavioral science, and mind-control drugs may radically change man's nature and thrust him into a "brave new world" where freedom and dignity are obsolete luxuries or faint memories. This book hopes to show that through the study of present forms of experience (loving, learning, governing, feeling), future forms will be made more comprehensible. Ideally, readers of this book will discover that the *timely* merely conceals the *timeless* and that the best preparation for even a science-fiction future is self-knowledge, awareness of what it means to be human.

The readings in this anthology are by important contemporary thinkers who are also fine and exciting writers, not strident peddlers of political fads, not pontificators, not brow-beaters. I have grouped the readings into eight sections, each dealing with a compelling area of human experience, and have supplemented the essays with poems, stories, and photographs. Providing students with several selections and various modes of expression on the same general subject—the family, for example—opens up the possibility for a great number of stimulating discussions and writing assignments. By reading and discussing several selections on the same subject, the student acquires a body of information and ideas about which he can write richly-detailed, probing themes.

The eight sections of this book provide ample materials for a standard semester, allowing approximately two weeks for each unit. It is not necessary for the sections in *Destination Tomorrow* to be studied in the order presented, though there is a progression from the first section to the eighth with each successive section complementing those that precede it. At the end of each section are provocative questions designed to guide the student's reading, activate class discussions, and stimulate writing assignments. Along with the questions are insightful quotations from famous and not-so-famous people regarding the major ideas posed by the readings. My experience has convinced me that students and teachers enjoy reading such quotations, using them as springboards in discussions, writing about them, comparing them—even collecting them. I encourage my students to seek out pertinent, pungent sayings and to jot them down in a commonplace book or notebook for future use and amusement. I explain to them that almost every writer keeps such a book, drawing from it ideas and materials for his own writing.

I have tried to make *Destination Tomorrow* a lively and engrossing collection, one that will interest students by challenging and even occasionally amusing them. I hope that through it they will discover that reading and writing are essential human actions.

My thanks to the many colleagues and students who helped shape this book, especially to Mrs. Rose Williams and Ronald Overton, who assisted in the preparation of the manuscript. And finally, a word about my wife, Melinda. What can I say except that without her imaginative contributions this book would not exist.

SECTION I The Health of the Nation—Diagnosing the Ills

A nation, like an individual citizen, can be sick or healthy, or various stages in between. There are indicators or symptoms of the health of America today—drug abuse, unemployment, the war in Asia, civil disobedience, Jesus freaks, sexual liberation, black power, women's liberation, divorce rates, a deteriorating environment, plastic Christmas trees, flag decals, and on and on. The real trick is to take these often unrelated, or seemingly unrelated, symptoms and from them construct a sound diagnosis of what is wrong with the patient.

Most Americans are amateur diagnosticians; if you want to know what is ailing America, just ask your barber or hairdresser. One citizen looks at college students with their long hair, strange clothes, drugs, bold sexuality, and concludes that the nation is going to pot, led by a bunch of degenerate "commie weirdos." Another citizen, looking at the same students, sees the most morally adventurous group of young people in the history of the nation, searchers after new values, new truths—a great bunch of kids. Obviously, diagnosing a nation's health—usually called social or cultural criticism—is not an exact science; rather, it is a mode of analysis, argument, and persuasion. Everyone can recognize the symptoms, but interpreting them takes sensitivity, wisdom, judgment, and a strong dose of humanity. Many critics make their diagnosis before they see the patient; prejudice precedes examination—and that is not good medicine.

For the serious-minded, for those deeply concerned about understanding what the nation is about and where it is going, unsophisticated, prejudiced diagnoses will not do. In these difficult, confusing times we do not need facile generalizations that divide us; we need bold, incisive, but sincere social criticism. Such criticism should inform us of the subtle differences between fads and forces, between the superficial and the serious. It should probe beneath the surfaces of slogans, bumper stickers, and decals, to find what uneasiness and frustration motivate people to wear ideas like chips on shoulders. It should expose the shoddy in government, in business, in fashion, in the arts, and in other social criticism. Above all, it should provide a view of the fears, customs, conceits, and abuses of the nation; by so doing, it will help us understand ourselves.

Three Signs. Courtesy of Lester Lefkowitz.

Charles A. Reich

Consciousness III: The New Generation

Beginning with a few individuals in the mid-nineteen-sixties, and
gathering numbers ever more rapidly thereafter, Consciousness III has
sprouted up, astonishingly and miraculously, out of the stony soil of
the American Corporate State. So spontaneous was its appearance that
no one, not the most astute or the most radical, foresaw what was coming or recognized it when it began. It is not surprising that many people
think it a conspiracy, for it was spread, here and abroad, by means 1
invisible. Hardly anybody of the older generation, even the FBI or
the sociologists, knows much about it, for its language and thought are
so different from Consciousness II as to make it virtually an undeci-
pherable secret code. Consciousness III is, as of this writing, the greatest secret in America, although its members have shouted as loudly as
they could to be heard.

We must pause over the origins of Consciousness III, lest it seem
too improbable and too transitory to be deemed as fundamental as
Consciousness I and Consciousness II. One element in its origin has
already been described: the impoverishment of life, the irrationality,
violence, and claustrophobia of the American Corporate State. But how
did this corporate machine, seemingly designed to keep its inhabitants
perpetually on a treadmill, suddenly begin producing something altogether new and unintended? The new consciousness is the product 2
of two interacting forces: the promise of life that is made to young
Americans by all of our affluence, technology, liberation, and ideals,
and the threat to that promise posed by everything from neon ugli-
ness and boring jobs to the Vietnam War and the shadow of nuclear
holocaust. Neither the promise nor the threat is the cause by itself;
but the two together have done it.

Editor's Note: In *The Greening of America* Charles Reich defines Consciousness I as the human spirit or attitude of the frontier—rugged individualism; it is "the traditional outlook of the American farmer, small businessman and worker who is trying to get ahead." Consciousness II is the spirit of the socialized, organization man.

The promise comes first. We have all heard the promise: affluence,
security, technology make possible a new life, a new permissiveness, a
new freedom, a new expansion of human possibility. We have all heard
it, but to persons born after World War II it means something very
different. Older people learned how to live in a different world; it is
really beyond them to imagine themselves living according to the new
promises. The most basic limitations of life—the job, the working day, 3
the part one can play in life, the limits of sex, love and relationships,
the limits of knowledge and experience—all vanish, leaving open a life
that can be lived without the guideposts of the past. In the world that
now exists, a life of surfing *is* possible, not as an escape from work, a
recreation or a phase, but as a *life*—if one chooses. The fact that this
choice is actually available is the truth that the younger generation
knows and the older generation cannot know.

The promise is made real to members of the younger generation
by a sense of acceptance about themselves. To older generations, particularly Consciousness II people, great issues were presented by striving
to reach some external standard of personal attractiveness, popularity,
ability at sports, acceptance by the group. Many lives, including some
outstanding careers, were lived under the shadow of such personal
issues; even late in life, people are still profoundly influenced by them.
Of course the new generation is not free of such concerns. But to an
astonishing degree, whether it is due to new parental attitudes, a less 4
tense, less inhibited childhood, or a different experience during school
years, these are not the issues which plague the younger generation.
If the hero of *Portnoy's Complaint* is the final and most complete example of the man dissatisfied with the self that he is, the new generation says, "Whatever I am, I am." He may have hang-ups of all sorts,
insecurities, inadequacies, but he does not reject himself on that account. There may be as many difficulties about work, ability, relationships, and sex as in any other generation, but there is less guilt, less
anxiety, less self-hatred. Consciousness III says, "I'm glad I'm me."

The new generation has also learned lessons from technology, by
being born with it, that the older generation does not know even though
it invented technology. It is one thing to know intellectually that there
is a Xerox machine that can copy anything, a pill that can make sexual 5
intercourse safe, or a light motorcycle that can take two people off
camping with ten minutes' preparation, but it is quite another thing
to live with these facts, make use of them, and thus learn to live *by*
them.

These experiences and promises are shared to some extent by the
youth of every industrial nation, and the new consciousness is, as we 6
know, not limited to the United States. But Consciousness III, the specifically American form, is not based on promise alone. A key word in
understanding its origin is *betrayal.*

Older people are inclined to think of work, injustice and war, and
of the bitter frustrations of life, as the human condition. Their capacity

for outrage is consequently dulled. But to those who have glimpsed the
real possibilities of life, who have tasted liberation and love, who have
seen the promised land, the prospect of a dreary corporate job, a ranch-
house life, or a miserable death in war, is utterly intolerable. Moreover,
the human condition, if that is what it is, has been getting steadily
worse in the Corporate State; more and more life-denying just as life 7
should be opening up. And hovering over everything is the threat of
annihilation, more real and more terrifying to the young than to anyone else. To them, the discrepancy between what could be and what
is, is overwhelming; perhaps it is the greatest single fact of their existence. The promise of America, land of beauty and abundance, land of
the free, somehow has been betrayed.

They feel the betrayal in excruciatingly personal terms. Between
them and the rich possibilities of life there intervenes a piercing insecurity—not the personal insecurity their parents knew, but a cosmic
insecurity. Will the nation be torn apart by riots or war? Will their
lives be cut short by death or injury in Vietnam? Will the impersonal 8
machinery of the state—schools, careers, institutions—overwhelm them?
Above all, will they escape an atomic holocaust (they were, as many
people have pointed out, the generation of the bomb). Insecurity sharp-
ens their consciousness and draws them together.

Parents have unintentionally contributed to their children's condemnation of existing society. Not by their words, but by their actions,
attitudes, and manner of living, they have conveyed to their children
the message "Don't live the way we have, don't settle for the emptiness
of our lives, don't be lured by the things we valued, don't neglect life 9
and love as we have." With the unerring perceptiveness of the child,
their children have read these messages from the lifeless lives of their
"successful" parents, have seen marriages break up because there was
nothing to hold them, have felt cynicism, alienation, and despair in
the best-kept homes of America. And will have none of it.

Kenneth Keniston, in *Young Radicals,* found that one of the most
telling forces in producing the political ideals of the new generation
is the contrast between their parents' ideals (which they accept) and 10
their parents' failure to live these same ideals. Keniston found that
young radicals show a *continuity* of ideals from childhood on; they
simply stayed with them while their parents failed to.

We might add to this that our society, with its dogmatic insistence
on one way of seeing everything, its dominating false consciousness,
and its ever-widening gap between fact and rhetoric, invites a sudden
moment when the credibility gap becomes too much, and invites cata- 11
clysmic consequences to the consciousness of a young person when that
occurs. For so vehemently does the society insist that its "truth" be
accepted wholly and undeviatingly down the line, and so drastic are
the discrepancies once seen, that a single breach in the dike may bring
a young person's entire conversion. All that is needed is to participate
in one peace demonstration and find *The New York Times*' report of it

inexcusably false, and the whole edifice of "truth" collapses. Such "conversions" are constantly seen on campuses today; a freshman arrives, his political views are hometown-Consciousness I, and suddenly he is radicalized. The fabric of manufactured "truth," spread taut and thin, breaches, and one breach leaves it irrevocably in tatters.

If a history of Consciousness III were to be written, it would show a fascinating progression. The earliest sources were among those exceptional individuals who are found at any time in any society: the artistic, the highly sensitive, the tormented. Thoreau, James Joyce, and Wallace Stevens all speak directly to Consciousness III. Salinger's Holden Caulfield was a fictional version of the first young precursors of Consciousness III. Perhaps there was always a bit of Consciousness III in every teen-ager, but normally it quickly vanished. Holden sees through the 12
established world: they are "phonies" and he is merciless in his honesty. But what was someone like Holden to do? A subculture of "beats" grew up, and a beatnik world flourished briefly, but for most people it represented only another dead end. Other Holdens might reject the legal profession and try teaching literature or writing instead, letting their hair grow a bit longer as well. But they remained separated individuals, usually ones from affluent but unhappy, tortured family backgrounds, and their differences with society were paid for by isolation.

Unquestionably the blacks made a substantial contribution to the origins of the new consciousness. They were left out of the Corporate State, and thus they had to have a culture and life-style in opposition to the State. Their music, with its "guts," contrasted with the insipid white music. This way of life seemed more earthy, more sensual than that of whites. They were the first openly to scorn the Establishment and its values; as Eldridge Cleaver shows in *Soul on Ice*, and Malcolm 13
X shows in his autobiography, they were radicalized by the realities of their situation. When their music began to be heard by white teenagers through the medium of rock 'n' roll, and when their view of America became visible through the civil rights movement, it gave new impetus to the subterranean awareness of the beat generation and the Holden Caulfields.

The great change took place when Consciousness III began to appear among young people who had endured no special emotional conditions, but were simply bright, sensitive children of the affluent middle class. It is hard to be precise about the time when this happened. One chronology is based on the college class of 1969, which entered as freshmen in the fall of 1965. Another important date is the 14
summer of 1967, when the full force of the cultural revolution was first visible. But even in the fall of 1967 the numbers involved were still very small. The new group drew heavily from those who had been exposed to the very best of liberal arts education—poetry, art, theatre, literature, philosophy, good conversation, Later, the group began to include "ordinary" middle-class students. In time there were college

athletes as well as college intellectuals, and lovers of motorcycles and skiing as well as lovers of art and literature. But the core group was always white, well educated, and middle class.

Among today's youth, the phenomenon of "conversions" is increasingly common. It is surprising that so little has been written about these
conversions, for they are a striking aspect of contemporary life. What
happens is simply this: in a brief span of months, a student, seemingly
conventional in every way, changes his haircut, his clothes, his habits,
his interests, his political attitudes, his way of relating to other people,
in short, his whole way of life. He has "converted" to a new consciousness. The contrast between well-groomed freshman pictures and the
same individuals in person a year later tells the tale. The clean-cut, 15
hard-working, model young man who despises radicals and hippies can
become one himself with breathtaking suddenness. Over and over again,
an individual for whom a conversion seemed impossible, a star athlete,
an honor student, the small-town high school boy with the American
Legion scholarship, transforms himself into a drug-using, long-haired,
peace-loving "freak." Only when he puts on a headband and plays un-
expectedly skillful touch football or basketball, or when a visitor to his
old room back home catches sight of his honor society certificate, is
his earlier life revealed.

As the new consciousness made youth more distinct, the younger
generation began discovering itself as a generation. Always before,
young people felt themselves tied more to their families, to their
schools, and to their immediate situations than to "a generation." But
now an entire culture, including music, clothes, drugs, began to distinguish youth. As it did, the message of consciousness went with it. 16
And the more the older generation rejected the culture, the more a
fraternity of the young grew up, so that they recognized each other
as brothers and sisters from coast to coast. That is its history up to
this writing; let us now try to describe the content of Consciousness
III.

A few warnings are needed. First, in attempting to describe Consciousness III systematically and analytically, we are engaging in an
intellectual process which Consciousness III rejects; they have a deep
skepticism of both "linear" and analytic thought. Second, we shall be
talking about an idealized consciousness, and not about something that
is to be seen in all aspects in any one person. The members of the 17
new generation have their doubts, hang-ups and failings too, and Consciousness III may coexist with earlier patterns and values. Third, Consciousness III itself is just in an early stage of development, and probably
the elements of it would have to be described differently in one or two
years.

The foundation of Consciousness III is liberation. It comes into
being the moment the individual frees himself from automatic acceptance of the imperatives of society and the false consciousness which 18
society imposes. For example, the individual no longer accepts unthink-

ingly the personal goals proposed by society; a change of personal goals is one of the first and most basic elements of Consciousness III. The meaning of liberation is that the individual is free to build his own philosophy and values, his own life-style, and his own culture from a new beginning.

Consciousness III starts with self. In contrast to Consciousness II, which accepts society, the public interest, and institutions as the primary reality, III declares that the individual self is the only true reality. Thus it returns to the earlier America: "Myself I sing." The first commandment is: thou shalt not do violence to thyself. It is a crime to
allow oneself to become an instrumental being, a projectile designed 19
to accomplish some extrinsic end, a part of an organization or a machine. It is a crime to be alienated from oneself, to be a divided or schizophrenic being, to defer meaning to the future. One must live completely at each moment, not with the frenzied "nowness" of advertising, but with the utter *wholeness* that Heidegger expresses. The commandment is: be true to oneself.

To start from self does not mean to be selfish. It means to start from premises based on human life and the rest of nature, rather than premises that are artificial products of the Corporate State, such as power or status. It is not an "ego trip" but a radical subjectivity designed to find genuine values in a world whose official values are false 20
and distorted. It is not egocentricity, but honesty, wholeness, genuineness in all things. It starts from self because human life is found as individual units, not as corporations and institutions; its intent is to start from life.

Consciousness III postulates the absolute worth of every human being—every self. Consciousness III does not believe in the antagonistic or competitive doctrine of life, Competition, within the limits of a sport like tennis or swimming, is accepted for its own pleasure, although even as athletes III's are far less competitive (and sometimes, but not always, poorer athletes as a result). But III's do not compete "in real life." They do not measure others, they do not see others as something to struggle against. People are brothers, the world is ample for all. In
consequence, one never hears the disparagements, the snickers, the 21
judgments that are so common among I's and II's. A boy who was odd in some way used to suffer derision all through his school days. Today there would be no persecution; one might even hear one boy speak, with affection, of "my freaky friend." Instead of insisting that everyone be measured by given standards, the new generation values what is unique and different in each self; there is no pressure that anyone be an athlete unless he wants to; a harpsichord player is accepted on equal terms. No one judges anyone else. This is a second commandment.

Consciousness III rejects the whole concept of excellence and comparative merit that is so central to Consciousness II. III refuses to evaluate people by general standards, it refuses to classify people, or analyze them. Each person has his own individuality, not to be com-

pared to that of anyone else. Someone may be a brilliant thinker, but
he is not "better" at thinking than anyone else, he simply possesses his
own excellence. A person who thinks very poorly is still excellent in
his own way. Therefore people are in no hurry to find out another
person's background, schools, achievements, as a means of knowing him; 22
they regard all of that as secondary, preferring to know him unadorned.
Because there are no governing standards, no one is rejected. Everyone is entitled to pride in himself, and no one should act in a way
that is servile, or feel inferior, or allow himself to be treated as if he
were inferior.

It is upon these premises that the Consciousness III idea of community and of personal relationships rests. In place of the world seen
as a jungle, with every man for himself (Consciousness I) or the world
seen as a meritocracy leading to a great corporate hierarchy of rigidly
drawn relations and manoeuvers for position (Consciousness II), the
world is a community. People all belong to the same family, whether
they have met each other or not. It is as simple as that. There are no
"tough guys" among the youth of Consciousness III. Hitchhikers smile
at approaching cars, people smile at each other on the street, the
human race rediscovers its need for each other. "I felt lonesome, so I
came looking for some people," a III will say. Something in the makeup
and pride of a I or II will keep him from "confessing" that "weakness"
in quite such an open way. But III does not want to stand head and
shoulders above the crowd. III values, more than a judgeship or executive title, the warmth of the "circle of affection" in which men join
hands. In personal relations, the keynote is honesty, and the absence of
socially imposed duty. To be dishonest in love, to "use" another person,
is a major crime. A third commandment is: be wholly honest with others,
use no other person as a means. It is equally wrong to alter oneself 23
for someone else's sake; by being one's true self one offers the most;
one offers them something honest, genuine, and, more important, something for them to respond to, to be evoked by. A work of art is not
valued because it changes itself for each person who views it, it retains
its own integrity and thus means something unique and marvelous to
those who see it. Being true to oneself is, so Consciousness III says,
the best and only way to relate to others. Consciousness III rejects most
of what happens between people in our world: manipulation of others,
forcing anyone to do anything against his wish, using others for one's
own purposes, irony and sarcasm, defensive stand-offishness. III also
rejects relationships of authority and subservience. It will neither give
commands nor follow them; coercive relations between people are
wholly unacceptable. And III also rejects any relationships based wholly
on role, relationships limited along strictly impersonal and functional
lines. There is no situation in which one is entitled to act impersonally,
in a stereotyped fashion, with another human being; the relationship
of businessman to clerk, passenger to conductor, student to janitor must
not be impersonal.

But to observe duties toward others, after the feelings are gone,
is no virtue and may even be a crime. Loyalty is valued but not artificial duty. Thus the new generation looks with suspicion on "obligations" and contractual relations between people, but it believes that
honesty can produce far more genuine relationships than the sterile
ones it observes among the older generation. To most people, there is
something frightening about the notion that no oath, no law, no prom- 24
ise, no indebtedness holds people together when the feeling is gone.
But for the new generation that is merely recognition of the truth
about human beings. Moreover, getting rid of what is artificial is essential to make way for what is real, and Consciousness III considers
genuine relationships with others, friendship, companionship, love, the
human community, to be among the highest values of life.

The premise of self and of values based on human life leads
directly to a radical critique of society. Many people are puzzled by
the radicalism of Consciousness III—have they been infiltrated by communists, are they influenced by "a few left-wing agitators," have they
been reading Marx? It does indeed seem astonishing that naïve young
people, without political experience, should come up with a critique of
society that seems to have escaped the most scholarly as well as the 25
most astute and experienced of their elders. But there is no mystery,
no conspiracy, and very little reading of Marx. Older people begin by
assuming that much of the structure of the Corporate State is necessary and valid; starting there they never get very far. The young people
start with entirely different premises, and all is revealed to them.

What Consciousness III sees, with an astounding clarity that no
ideology could provide, is a society that is unjust to its poor and its
minorities, is run for the benefit of a privileged few, is lacking in its
proclaimed democracy and liberty, is ugly and artificial, that destroys
environment and self, and is, like the wars it spawns, "unhealthy for 26
children and other living things." It sees a society that is deeply un-
truthful and hypocritical; one of the gifts of the young is to see through
phoniness and cant, and Consciousness III sees through the Establishment verities of our society with corrosive ease.

Consciousness III sees not merely a set of political and public
wrongs, such as a liberal New Dealer might have seen, but also the
deeper ills that Kafka or the German expressionists or Dickens would
have seen: old people shunted into institutional homes, streets made
hideous with neon and commercialism, servile conformity, the competi-
tiveness and sterility of suburban living, the loneliness and anomie of 27
cities, the ruin of nature by bulldozers and pollution, the stupid mindlessness of most high school education, the coarse materialism of most
values, the lovelessness of many marriages, and, above all, the plastic,
artificial quality of everything; plastic lives in plastic homes.

All of Consciousness III's criticisms of society were brought into sharpest focus by the Vietnam War. For the war seemed to sum up the evils of our society: destruction of people, destruction of environ-

ment, depersonalized use of technology, war by the rich and powerful against the poor and helpless, justification based on abstract rationality, hypocrisy and lies, and a demand that the individual, regardless of his conscience, values, or self, make himself into a part of the war machine, an impersonal projectile bringing death to other people. Those who said 28
they could not go believed that compulsory service in a war they hated would be so total a destruction of their genuine values that even if they did return to the United States, they could never return to the ranks of the genuinely living.

The initial premise of self leads not only to a critique of society, it also leads, in many representatives of Consciousness III, to a deep personal commitment to the welfare of the community. This may sound contradictory to those who wrongly equate the premise of self with selfishness, and it may seem to contradict the premise that the individual, not society, is the reality. But there is no contradiction. It is quite true that the individual does not accept the goals or standards 29
set by society. But of course, he recognizes that society has a vast influence on the welfare of people everywhere, including his own desire to be an independent being. Mostly he sees this influence as bad, but he also sees how much better things could be. And therefore, for the sake of the welfare of individuals, he is committed to the improvement of society. It is the manner of commitment that differs from II.

There is one essential qualification to what we have said: dedication to the community is not to include means that do violence to the self. A Consciousness III person will not study law to help society, if law is not what he wants to do with his life, nor will he do harm to others in order to promote some good, nor will he deny himself the experiences of life for any cause. The political radical of Consciousness 30
III is thus very different from the radical of the Old Left, the communist, socialist, or civil libertarian ready to dedicate himself and his life to the cause, puritanical, sour, righteous. To the new consciousness, to make himself an object to serve the cause would be to subvert the cause.

Subject to this qualification, the key to the Consciousness III commitment lies in the concept of full personal responsibility. In the case of Consciousness II, commitment to society means commitment to reform in the general direction already established by society (equality, better education), the notion of "reform" merely meaning that the "liberal" is somewhat ahead of where society is at. And the commitment has limits; the liberal enjoys his high status, his elegant house, his security, and comfort, and fights his battle from that position. Con- 31
sciousness III feels that, if he is to be true to himself, he must respond *with himself*. He may take a job, such as teaching in a ghetto school, which offers neither prestige nor comfort, but offers the satisfaction of personal contact with ghetto children. He must live on a modest scale to retain the freedom that his commitment demands. He must take risks. And at the same time, he must be wholly himself in what he

does. He knows that he is an agent of change, whether he plays music or works in a ghetto, so long as he affirms himself in his work, and so long as his work expresses the full responsibility of his feelings.

It is this notion of personal responsibility which makes the new generation, when it finds itself excluded from the decision-making process, demand a part in that process. For the liberal, it is sufficient to say, "I oppose air pollution, but in my job I have nothing to do with it, no responsibility in that direction, all I can do is try to influence those who do." That, to Consciousness III, is not being responsible; if one is not part of the decision-making process, responsibility requires that one gain such power.

It is this same personal responsibility that makes the young student feel himself to be an adult, not a person getting ready for life. By attempting to be fully alive *now*, young people grow more serious, more thoughtful, more concerned with what is happening in the world. Many adults of the older generation have smooth baby faces, the faces of men interested only in the Sunday ball games, the nearest skirt, or the bowling league, as if they were permanent juveniles, as if they never, not once in their lives, faced their world and took its concerns on themselves, or accepted the responsibilities of full consciousness. The faces of Consciousness III seem to have lived more, even in their short years. A look at a college classbook of today, compared with one of fifteen years ago, tells the difference. That is one reason why the people of Consciousness III have a sense of each other as a generation with something in common.

During the Columbia confrontation, a group of Columbia varsity athletes were invited to an alumni meeting to receive awards, then disinvited when they asked to make statements on the campus situation. The alumni didn't want to think of athletes having political views. The athletes, fencers who had won a national championship and basketball players who had won the Ivy League championship, then picketed the alumni meeting in a driving rain in their varsity C blazers, until the alumni finally let them in and let them speak (*The New York Times,* May 25, 1968). It wasn't the athletes' "job" to picket in the rain; they could have signed a letter if they wanted to express themselves. But they were not the smooth-faced, ever-juvenile jocks of American expectations. They were serious adults. And they thought it essential, if they were to be *whole* as selves, to make a *personal* response, and thereby, as Sartre's Orestes did in *The Flies,* assume responsibility that "was not theirs," and thus achieve a full existence. It is interesting that journalists, in writing about the new generation, tend to use the term "a youth" with some of its older meaning—not merely a young man, but the hero of a story—a person who possesses the qualities of boldness, action, and moral purpose. It is as if young people have recaptured courage, and the ability to take action, and thus recovered a measure of power over their fate.

Because it accepts no imposed system, the basic stance of Consciousness III is one of openness to any and all experience. It is always in a state of becoming. It is just the opposite of Consciousness II, which tries to force all new experience into a pre-existing system, and to assimilate all new knowledge to principles already established. Although we can attempt to describe the specific content of Consciousness III at a given moment, its lasting essence is constant change, and constant growth of each individual.

Peter L. Berger
and Brigitte Berger

The Blueing of America

A sizable segment of the American intelligentsia has been on a
kick of revolution talk for the last few years. Only very recently this
talk was carried on in a predominantly Left mood, generating fantasies
of political revolution colored red or black. The mood appears to have 1
shifted somewhat. Now the talk has shifted to cultural revolution.
Gentle grass is pushing up through the cement. It is "the kids," hair
and all, who will be our salvation. But what the two types of revolution talk have in common is a sovereign disregard for the realities of
technological society in general, and for the realities of class and power
in America.

Only the most religious readers of leftist publications could ever
believe that a political revolution from the Left had the slightest prospects in America. The so-called black revolution is at a dividing fork,
of which we shall speak in a moment. But as to the putatively green
revolution, we think that the following will be its most probable result:
It will accelerate social mobility in America, giving new opportunities 2
for upward movement of lower-middle-class and working-class people,
and in the process will change the ethnic and religious composition of
the higher classes. Put differently: far from "greening" America, the
alleged cultural revolution will serve to strengthen the vitality of the
technological society against which it is directed, and will further the
interests of precisely those social strata that are least touched by its
currently celebrated transformations of consciousness.

The cultural revolution is not taking place in a social vacuum, but
has a specific location in a society that is organized in terms of classes.
The cadres of the revolution, not exclusively but predominantly, are
the college-educated children of the upper-middle class. Ethnically, they 3
tend to be Wasps and Jews. Religiously, the former tend to belong to
the main-line Protestant denominations, rather than to the more funda-
mentalist or sectarian groups. The natural focus of the revolution is
the campus (more precisely, the type of campus attended by this population), and such satellite communities as have been springing up on

its fringes. In other words, the revolution is taking place, or minimally has its center, in a subculture of upper-middle-class youth.

The revolution has not created this subculture. Youth, as we know
it today, is a product of technological and economic forces intimately
tied to the dynamics of modern industrialism, as is the educational system within which the bulk of contemporary youth is concentrated for
ever-longer periods of life. What is true in the current interpretations
is that some quite dramatic transformations of consciousness have been
taking place in this sociocultural ambience. These changes are too
recent, and too much affected by distortive mass-media coverage, to
allow for definitive description. It is difficult to say which manifestations are only transitory and which are intrinsic features likely to persist over time. Drugs are a case in point. So is the remarkable upsurge
of interest in religion and the occult. However, one statement can be
made with fair assurance: the cultural revolution has defined itself in
diametric opposition to some of the basic values of bourgeois society, 4
those values that since Max Weber have commonly been referred to as
the "Protestant ethic"—discipline, achievement and faith in the onward-
and-upward thrust of technological society. These same values are now
perceived as "repression" and "hypocrisy," and the very promises of
technological society are rejected as illusionary or downright immoral.
A hedonistic ethic is proclaimed in opposition to the "Protestant" one,
designed to "liberate" the individual from the bourgeois inhibitions in
all areas of lfe, from sexuality through aesthetic experience to the manner in which careers are planned. Achievement is perceived as futility
and "alienation," its ethos as "uptight" and, in the final analysis, inimical to life. Implied in all this is a radical aversion to capitalism and
the class society that it has engendered, thus rendering the subculture
open to leftist ideology of one kind or another.

Its radicalism, though, is much more far-reaching than that of
ordinary, politically defined leftism. It is not simply in opposition to
the particular form of technological society embodied in bourgeois capitalism but to the very idea of technological society. The rhetoric is 5
Rousseauean rather than Jacobin, the imagery of salvation is intensely
bucolic, the troops of the revolution are not the toiling masses of the
Marxist prophecy but naked children of nature dancing to the tune of
primitive drums.

When people produce a utopia of childhood it is a good idea to
ask what their own childhood has been like. In this instance, the answer
is not difficult. As Philippe Ariès has brilliantly shown, one of the major
cultural accomplishments of the bourgeoisie has been the dramatic 6
transformation of the structure of childhood, in theory as well as in
practice. Coupled with the steep decline in child mortality and mor-
bidity that has been brought about by modern medicine and nutrition,
this transformation is one of the fundamental facts of modern society.
A new childhood has come into being, probably happier than any previous one in human society. Its impact, however, must be seen in con-

junction with another fundamental fact of modern society—namely, the
increasing bureaucratization of all areas of social life. We would see
the turmoil of youth today as being rooted in the clash between these
two facts—paraphrasing Max Weber, in the clash between the new
"spirit of childhood" and the "spirit of bureaucracy." However one may
wish to judge the merits of either fact, both are probably here to stay.
Logically enough, the clash almost invariably erupts when the gradu-
ates of the new childhood first encounter bureaucracy in their own life
—to wit, in the educational system.

We cannot develop this explanation any further here, though we
would like to point out that it is almost exactly the opposite of the
Freudian interpretations of the same clash provided, for example, by
Lewis Feuer or Bruno Bettelheim: Rebellious youth is not fighting
against any fathers; on the contrary, it is outraged by the *absence* of
parental figures and familial warmth in the bureaucratic institutions
that envelop it. The point to stress, though, is the transformation of
childhood, born of the bourgeoisie, today affects nearly all classes in 7
American society—*but it does not affect them equally.* As, for example,
the work of John Seeley and Herbert Gans has demonstrated, there exist
far-reaching differences between the childrearing practices of different
classes. The transformation, and with it the new "spirit of childhood,"
developed most fully and most dramatically in the upper-middle class—
that is, in the same social context that is presently evincing the manifestations of "greening."

To say this is in no way to engage in value judgments. If value
judgments are called for, we would suggest calibrated ones. Very few
human cultures (or subcultures) are either wholly admirable or wholly 8
execrable, and the intellectuals who extoll this particular one are as
much *terribles simplificateurs* as the politicians who anathematize it. In
any case, our present purpose is to inquire into the probable consequences of the cultural changes in question.

The matrix of the green revolution has been a class-specific youth
culture. By definition, this constitutes a biographical way station. Long-
haired or not, *everyone*, alas, gets older. This indubitable biological
fact has been used by exasperated over-thirty observers to support
their hope that the new youth culture may be but a noisier version of
the old American pattern of sowing wild oats. Very probably this is
true for many young rebels, especially those who indulge in the external
paraphernalia and gestures of the youth culture without fully entering 9
into its new consciousness. But there is evidence that for an as yet
unknown number, the way station is becoming a place of permanent
settlement. For an apparently growing number there is a movement
from youth culture to counter-culture. These are the ones who drop
out permanently. For yet others, passage through the youth culture
leaves, at any rate, certain permanent effects, not only in their private
lives but in their occupational careers. As with the Puritanism that
gave birth to the bourgeois culture of America, this movement too has

its fully accredited saints and those who only venture upon a *halfway covenant.* The former, in grim righteousness, become sandal makers in Isla Vista. The latter at least repudiate the more obviously devilish careers within "the system"—namely, those in scientific technology, business and government that lead to positions of status and privilege in the society. They do not drop out, but at least they shift their majors —in the main, to the humanities and the social sciences, as we have recently seen in academic statistics.

The overall effects of all this will, obviously, depend on the magnitude of these changes. To gauge the effects, however, one will have to relate them to the class and occupational structures of the society. For those who become permanent residents of the counterculture, and most probably for their children, the effect is one of downward social
mobility. This need not be the case for the halfway greeners (at least 10
as long as the society is ready to subsidize, in one way or another, poets, T-group leaders and humanistic sociologists). But they too will have deflected from those occupational careers (in business, government, technology and science) that continue to lead to the higher positions in a modern society.

What we must keep in mind is that whatever cultural changes may be going on in this or that group, the personnel requirements of a technological society not only continue but actually expand. The notion that as a result of automation fewer and fewer people will be required to keep the technological society going, thus allowing the others to do their own thing and nevertheless enjoy the blessings of electricity, is in contradiction to all the known facts. Automation has resulted in changes in the occupational structure, displacing various categories of
lower-skilled labor, but it has in no way reduced the number of people 11
required to keep the society going. On the contrary, it has increased the requirements for scientific, technological and (last but not least) bureaucratic personnel. (The recent decline in science and engineering jobs is due to recession, and does not affect the long-term needs of the society.) The positions disdained by the aforementioned upper-middle-class individuals will therefore have to be filled by someone else. The upshot is simple: *There will be new "room at the top."*

Who is most likely to benefit from this sociological windfall? It will be the newly college-educated children of the lower-middle and working classes. To say this, we need not assume that they remain untouched by their contact with the youth culture during their school years. Their sexual mores, their aesthetic tastes, even their political
opinions might become permanently altered as compared with those 12
of their parents. We do assume, though, that they will, now as before, reject the anti-achievement ethos of the cultural revolution. They may take positions in intercourse that are frowned upon by Thomas Aquinas, they may continue to listen to hard rock on their hi-fi's and they may have fewer racial prejudices. But all these cultural acquisitions are, as it were, functionally irrelevant to making it in the technocracy. Very

few of them will become sandal makers or farmers on communes in Vermont. We suspect that not too many more will become humanistic sociologists.

Precisely those classes that remain most untouched by what is considered to be the revolutionary tide in contemporary America face *new prospects of upward social mobility.* Thus, the "revolution" (hardly the word) is not at all where it seems to be, which should not surprise anyone. The very word *avant-garde* suggests that one ought to look behind it for what is to follow—and there is no point asking the *avant-gardistes,* whose eyes are steadfastly looking forward. Not even the Jacobins paid attention to the grubby tradesmen waiting to climb up over their shoulders. A technological society, given a climate of reasonable tolerance (mainly a function of affluence), can afford a sizable number of sandal makers. Its "knowledge industry" (to use Fritz Machlup's term) has a large "software" division, which can employ considerable quantities of English majors. And, of course, the educational system provides a major source of employment for nontechnocratic personnel. To this may be added the expanding fields of entertainment and therapy, in all their forms. All the same, quite different people are needed to occupy the society's command posts and to keep its engines running. These people will have to retain the essentials of the old "Protestant ethic"— discipline, achievement orientation, and also a measure of freedom from gnawing self-doubt. If such people are no longer available in one population reservoir, another reservoir will have to be tapped.

There is no reason to think that "the system" will be unable to make the necessary accommodations. If Yale should become hopelessly greened, Wall Street will get used to recruits from Fordham or Wichita State. Italians will have no trouble running the RAND Corporation, Baptists the space program. Political personnel will change in the wake of social mobility. It is quite possible that the White House may soon have its first Polish occupant (or, for that matter, its first Greek). Far from weakening the class system, these changes will greatly strengthen it, moving new talent upward and preventing rigidity at the top (though, probably, having little effect at the *very* top). Nor will either the mechanics or the rewards of social mobility change in any significant degree. A name on the door will still rate a Bigelow on the floor; only there will be fewer Wasp and fewer Jewish names. Whatever other troubles "the system" may face, from pollution to Russian ICBMs, it will not have to worry about its being brought to a standstill by the cultural revolution.

It is, of course, possible to conceive of such economic or political shocks to "the system" that technological society, as we have known it in America, might collapse, or at least seriously deteriorate. Ecological catastrophe on a broad scale, massive malfunction of the capitalist economy, or an escalation of terrorism and counter-terror would be cases in point. Despite the currently fashionable prophecies of doom

for American society, we regard these eventualities as very unlikely.
If any of them should take place after all, it goes without saying that
the class system would stop operating in its present form. But whatever else would then be happening in America, it would *not* be the 15
green revolution. In the even remoter eventuality of a socialist society
in this country, we would know where to look for our greeners—in
"rehabilitation camps," along the lines of Castro's Isle of Pines.

We have been assuming that the children of the lower-middle and
working classes remain relatively unbitten by the "greening" bug—at
least sufficiently unbitten so as not to interfere with their aspirations
of mobility. If they too should drop out, there would be literally no
one left to mind the technological store. But it is not very easy to
envisage this. America falling back to the status of an underdeveloped 16
society? Grass growing over the computers? A totalitarian society, in
which the few remaining "uptight" people run the technocracy, while
the rest just groove? Or could it be Mongolian ponies grazing on the
White House lawn? Even if the great bulk of Americans were to become "beautiful people," however, the rest of the world is most unlikely
to follow suit. So far in history, the uglies have regularly won out over
the "beautiful people." They probably would again this time.

The evidence does not point in this direction. The data we have
on the dynamics of class in a number of European countries would suggest that the American case may not be all that unique. Both England 17
and western Germany have been undergoing changes in their class
structures very similar to those projected by us, with new reservoirs of
lower-middle-class and working-class populations supplying the personnel requirements of a technological society no longer served adequately
by the old elites.

What we have described as a plausible scenario is not terribly
dramatic, at least compared with the revolutionary visions that intellectuals so often thrive on. Nor are we dealing with a process unique
in history. Vilfredo Pareto called this type of process the "circulation 18
of elites." Pareto emphasized (rightly, we think) that such circulation
is essential if a society is going to survive. In a Paretian perspective,
much of the green revolution would have to be seen in terms of de-
cadence (which, let us remark in passing, is not necessarily a value
judgment—some very impressive flowerings of human creativity have
been decadent in the same sociological sense).

But even Marx may, in a paradoxical manner, be proven right in
the end. It may be the blue-collar masses that are, at last, coming into
their own. "Power to the people!"—nothing less than that. The "class 19
struggle" may be approaching a new phase, with the children of the
working class victorious. These days we can see their banner all over
the place. It is the American flag. In that perspective, the peace emblem
is the old bourgeoisie, declining in the face of a more robust adversary. Robustness here refers, above all, to consciousness—not only to a
continuing achievement ethos, but to a self-confidence not unduly wor-

ried by unending self-examination and by a basically intact faith in the possibilities of engineering reality. Again, it would not be the first time in history that a declining class leaned toward pacifism, as to the "beautiful things" of aesthetic experience. Seen by that class, of course, the blue-collar masses moving in suffer from considerable aesthetic deficiencies.

"Revolutionary" America? Perhaps, in a way. We may be on the eve of its blueing.

Arnold Beichman

Six "Big Lies" About America

The culture of a free society becomes seriously corroded when
lies circulate freely as truths; when an unsupported assertion is accepted 1
as a statement of fact rather than as something to be proved, when the
line between possibility and certainty becomes invisible.

In political discourse, one expects lies and half-truths; politicians
are not, after all, philosopher-kings. In culture, however, when lies
begin to be accepted as worthy of debate by our enormously powerful
social critics and literary intellectuals a crisis in values follows. Culture
cannot long withstand perversions of truth. When culture becomes poli- 2
tics, revolutionary politics in particular, there can be no criterion for
truth and its inseparable companion, rationality, for then every man
is his own judge of truth with the right, if he so chooses, to force his
truth on the refractory. As André Malraux once wrote: "The path that
leads from moral reasoning to political action is strewn with our dead
selves."

America today is a country about which more lies are told by
Americans than were ever dreamed of in Moscow, Peking or Havana.
There is nothing new about this. The earlier highwater mark of such
lying came in the nineteen-thirties when leading American intellectuals
transformed a nauseating tyrant (see Robert Conquest's "The Great
Terror" for confirmation of my description) into a democratic socialist 3
and the personification of a free culture—far superior, of course, to
"capitalist" culture. Within the memory of many, there were young
people in English-speaking democracies who swore they would not fight
for king or country—famed Oxford pledge—while at the same time they
demanded a system of collective security against Fascism, but without
rearmament.

What is new is that lying through the perversion of language or
distortion of visible fact is now widely accepted as normal, so long as
these derelictions are created by "progressives" around "progressive" 4
issues. Take a little lie: the misuse of the phrase "underground press"
to describe the left-radical-counterculture newspapers, all of which are

obtainable on most 42d Street newsstands or on street corners from the East Village to Haight-Ashbury. The phrase "underground press" formerly defined publications which had to circulate secretly, from hand to hand, because they were against a repressive government, against a ruthless establishment, determined to punish publishers of such publications. There was an underground press in Czarist Russia, as there is one today in Communist Russia. An underground press existed in France during the Nazi occupation. It didn't sell at any kiosks in Paris any more than a *samizdat* paper, like Chronicle of Current Events, sells at kiosks in Moscow.

Our "underground" newspapers and books are sold openly and widely with full instructions on how to make a Molotov cocktail or how
to make false claims for "lost" travelers' checks so you can live in the 5
U. S. on "no dollars a day." About the worst fate that can befall the publisher of our "underground" papers is bankruptcy. Why, then, is it the fashion to refer to this press as the "underground press" when so clearly it is not?

Or take the word "blind," a oneway adjective which is attachable only to unprogressive political positions. Robert Heilbroner, the economist, likes to talk about "blind anti-Communism," but no true progressive could ever say, for example, "blind anti-Fascism." On the contrary, one must *always* condemn a Fascist dictatorship, but one need condemn
a Communist dictatorship only once a year—say, on the anniversary 6
of the second invasion of Czechoslovakia— or during some particularly horrendous event. To keep harping about Communism makes you a "blind anti-Communist." To praise Communist revolutions as a significant modernizing force is to be an unsentimental realist, a scholar; to be doubtful is to be "blind" to reality.

My concern here is not to catalogue little lies but to discuss Big
Lies about America, the Big Lies which are now common currency 7
among so many American social critics and their followers:

I. America Is Either Already a Fascist Country or on the Road to Fascism.

This is all agreed, among the social critics I am discussing, but there is some dispute as to how soon before American Fascism becomes *real* Fascism. This isn't as absurd as it sounds. After all, if a polemicist
announces over the radio, television, in a newspaper or magazine or 8
in a best-selling book that America is a Fascist country, it might be considered zany to make such a statement. So you get around this problem in rationality by distinguishing between "Fascism" and "real Fascism," without ever making it clear what the distinction might be.

Charles Reich in "The Greening of America" tells us that America is at "the brink of an authoritarian or police state." He tells us that

"today [in America] both dissent and efforts at change are dealt with
by repression." The Harvard Crimson a few months ago announced
with dramatic precision that America will be living under "real Fascism
. . . before three years are over." Prof. Herbert Marcuse has said that 9
"as far as I'm concerned, one can speak with complete justification of
an incipient Fascism" in America. A few sentences later in the same
interview he disclosed the existence in America of "preventive Fascism."

Prof. Philip Slater of Brandeis has written that "liberals will be
given the choice, during the next decade or so, between participating
in some way in the new culture and living under a Fascist regime."
Mel Wulf, legal director of the American Civil Liberties Union, has 10
as his formulation sentences like: "Though we are not yet a Fascist
state in general . . ." or, "Though we are not now a police state in
general. . . ."

The usefulness of this charge that America is now or is about to
go Fascist is that it is such a Big Lie that no evidence is needed to
prove it; or better yet, *everything* is evidence, whatever is handiest.
Recently the handy evidence was found, of all places, in Prime Minister
Trudeau's Canada, following last fall's assassination of the Quebec
Labor Minister by terrorists. Trudeau's "police-state" measures meant
—I heard this charge made in a lovely Central Park West cooperative
apartment—that America was next. You didn't have to prove that Tru- 11
deau's decrees were Fascist; the mere declaration that they were Fascist meant there was no need to prove they were. What is more,
to call them Fascist was to imply that these decrees were permanent
and that, therefore, Canada had embarked on the road to Fascism.
Thus, a correspondent for The New Republic, writing from Montreal
as a self-described "draft-refusing" American said: "The morning of
Oct. 16 . . . the country chosen as a refuge and whose government all
praised for its tolerance had suddenly, without warning, become a
police state."

And since America is Canada's overbearing next-door neighbor and 12
since Canada dare not sneeze without first obtaining America's imperial
permission, be assured that Fascism's next stop is America.

Thus by constant reiteration that America is pre- or proto-Fascist
America becomes Fascist and all the scholarly qualifiers, like "incipient"
or "preventive" or "not yet a Fascist state in general" get blurry and
redundant. In this atmosphere, any unpleasant or awful event in America can be transformed into living documentation that we now live in
Amerika. Such demonology can so easily turn a doubtful future into 13
the undoubted present—I think, therefore it is. This sort of "noncogni-
tive" cognition was ably defined by George Lukacs, the eminent Hun-
garian Marxist: "It is the Stalinist tendency to exclude everywhere so
far as possible any sort of mediating concepts and to bring into direct
connection the crudest matters of fact with the most abstract theoretical positions."

Take this question: Does anybody really think that President Nixon, Vice President Agnew and Dr. Kissinger would dare impose a Fascist regime on America or that they are contemplating such a *coup d'état?* There are intellectuals who regard it as highly reactionary or at best naive to ask such a question, since it implies there is possible doubt as to such a conspiracy. Not to believe that the nation's leaders, the Pentagon and the military-industrial complex are planning a Fascist takeover is to demonstrate that one has been brainwashed into a state of political cretinism. And to demand some proof of such conscious (or "unconscious") plotting is to place oneself solidly in *their* camp. Were I to argue that Fascism means something specific or were I to suggest that there is a huge difference between being a Republican incumbent President desperately anxious to be re-elected and being an "incipient" Fascist, the grudging concession might be: "Well, maybe Nixon hasn't got there yet, but give him time and you'll see." While it is permissible to add up every act of injustice in America as proof of the existence of Fascism, to use a similar "ethical calculus" about other countries, where acts of injustice are systemic, not episodic, to prove their "Fascism" would be impermissible.

The more scholarly and objective way to pin the "Fascist" label on America is to blur the distinction between this country and the U.S.S.R. For example, the historian Howard Zinn has written: "When the United States defines the Soviet sphere as 'totalitarian' and the West as 'free,' it becomes difficult for Americans to see totalitarian elements in our society, and liberal elements in Soviet society. Moralizing in this way, we can condemn the Russians in Hungary and absolve ourselves in Vietnam."

Let Zinn's Russian peers try to organize a Moscow version of a "March on Washington," or demand an end to Soviet occupations of foreign territory or an end to discrimination against ethnic minorities and he'll see the difference between "totalitarian elements" in America and totalitarian elements in the Soviet Union. But Zinn knows all this —and still he'll keep repeating this same old equation about: U. S. totalitarian elements = Soviet liberal elements.

The greatest purveyor of the canard about Fascist America is the mythopoeic Professor Marcuse, whose phrases, "repressive tolerance" and "the democratic educational dictatorship of free men," remind me of Robespierre's defense of the Terror: "The revolutionary government is the despotism of liberty against tyranny." When one begins to turn culture into revolutionary politics, the rhetoric of paradox is a most useful weapon, like the New Left phrases "creative disorder" (i.e.—preventing a pro-Vietnam war meeting from taking place at Harvard) or "creative vandalism" (i.e.—destroying 10 years of a professor's research during a building occupation). In the same category is Tom Hayden's description of student revolutionaries as "guerrillas in the field of culture."

II. America Is Guilty of Genocide.

If one argues that genocide is something like what happened at
Auschwitz or Katyn Forest, the argument shifts: America is guilty of
cultural genocide, ethnic genocide, psychic genocide—all of which are
ipso facto as bad as physical genocide. If it is argued that China's overwhelming of Tibet, Stalin's seizure of the Baltic countries and the dispersal of their populations, and Soviet counterrevolutionary invasions 18
of East Germany, Hungary, Poland and Czechoslovakia might be considered acts of cultural or ethnic genocide, and that the Kremlin's suppression of Russian intellectual life is metaphorical genocide, the retort
may be that all this is "cold war" propaganda. If the debater is too
young to have experienced the cold war, the answer may be: "So
what? Russia is bad but America is worse."

Usually, the rebuttal is that the debater knows nothing about Russia, China or Cuba and is interested only in America and her infamies;
to start talking about Russia or other foreign countries, about which the
debater knows only what he reads in an untrustworthy press, is diver-
sionary. Yet often a little later the same debater who had just proclaimed his ignorance of the U.S.S.R., China and Cuba evidences a lot 19
of knowledge about the Greek dictatorship, which America is said to
be supporting with enthusiasm; he's an expert on Franco Spain, going
back to 1936, and on Thailand, Brazil, the Dominican invasion and all
other military dictatorships allied to American "imperialism." Any knowledge of "people's dictatorships" has either escaped his notice or is regarded as irrelevant to America's genocidal crimes.

This kind of moral standard is easily acquired if you believe that
Fascist-militarist dictatorships, unlike Communist or "Third World" or
"socialist" dictatorships, are unprogressive, backward-looking and anti-
historical. Thus Conor Cruise O'Brien said in a recent essay: "It is not 20
enough to say that an underdeveloped country has the right to be non-
aligned; it is necessary to recognize its right to 'go Communist' if that
is the tendency of the political and social forces inside the country
itself."

But supposing the political and social forces wanted to go Fascist,
theocratic, anarchic or, heaven forbid, capitalist; or if after they went 21
"Communist," the people decided they had been wrong and wanted
to throw out "Communism"—what then? Obviously that would be a
C.I.A.-inspired plot.

The same kind of moral standard is visible in cultural-exchange
programs. Were the White House to negotiate some huge exchange
program with the Greek colonels, it would confirm the State Depart- 22
ment's Fascist sympathies. To expand cultural exchanges with Moscow,
even after the Czech invasion, is a good thing. Were America to threat-
en cancellation of such exchanges because of Czechoslovakia, it would
mean that the White House wants to revive the cold war.

III. The Bomber Left in America Is a Moral Force.

The Bomber Left may be guilty. But the guilt is pardonable because (1) America is a violent country, (2) violence is the Bomber Left's agonizing answer to the need for a moral response to America's counter-revolutionary refusal to "change"* and (3) nobody, except by accident, ever gets hurt during a bombing. So the bomb becomes an abstraction destroying another abstraction: a computer center at Wisconsin (where a student was killed); a faculty club at the University of California, Santa Barbara, where a custodian was killed; a hall at Pomona College, Claremont, Calif., where a secretary was blinded and otherwise severely injured opening a time-bomb package. Political frustration ascribed to the Bomber Left usually evokes among *avant-garde* social critics deep sorrow; a similar indulgence for the "Goldwater Right" is unthinkable; any violence arising out of despair on the "Wallace Right" is, by *avant-garde* convention, backward-looking and contemptible. Violence on the Bomber Left† is an aberrant yet progressive step toward the New Jerusalem. Thus Bomber Left violence becomes nonviolence while Bomber Right violence (where is it?) becomes Fascist violence. The Bomber Left is made up of victims of American society; the Bomber Right *is* American society.

Today the most popular question on any sociology or political science examination is: "Discuss political violence pro and con." For some academicians and literary intellectuals—these "officer candidates without an army," as Friedrich Engels called student revolutionaries in Czarist Russia—"violence" has become the "in" word, there being no other way.

Carl Oglesby, former head of Students for Democratic Society, has written: "The rebel is an incorrigible absolutist who has replaced all 'problems' with the one grand claim that the entire system is an error, all 'solutions' with the single irreducible demand that change shall be total, all diagnoses of disease with one final certificate of death. To him, total change means only that those who now have all the power shall no longer have any, and that those who now have none—the people, the victimized—shall have all."

*Prof. Douglas Dowd of Cornell has written: "Violence on the left by the people who are trying to change things has to be understood for what it is. It is in the first place being practiced by people who have tried many other kinds of things, whether you're speaking of Weathermen now or bombers. They are serious, committed people and the other characteristic is that they're desperate. They've given up the idea that a movement can get any place *without* violence."

†A similar indulgence of the radical left is granted by some of our social critics when the radical left obviously violates civil liberties. For example, Prof. Warner Berthoff of Harvard's English department defended the breaking up of a pro-Vietnam war meeting at Harvard last March with these words: "Like those on the platform, those in the audience [i.e., those who broke up the meeting] came to say something. They said it. In the circumstances of a political rally, wherever it happens to be staged, the right to shout down speakers is embraced by the same principle of freedom of speech and expression as protects the speakers in their efforts to make themselves heard."

With such alternatives in so final a form, there can be only one
next step. This apocalyptic rage so afflicts an important sector of the
student-academic-intellectual left that as sharp a critic of American
society as Prof. H. Mark Roelofs of New York University has been 26
moved to say: "The radical not in communion with the society he would
remake is condemned to inanity and to thinking and talking in a fantasy
world of his own devising."

Yet it is this fantasy world, born out of what Nietzsche described
as "the weariness that wants to reach the ultimate with one leap," which
has seized the imagination of young men and women and which has 27
persuaded them that there is no way out but destruction, the way
described by Bakunin and Nechaeyev in their "Catechism of the Revolutionist."

"The revolutionist is a doomed man. He has no personal interests,
no affairs, no sentiment, attachments, property, not even a name of his 28
own. Everything in him is absorbed by one exclusive interest, one
thought, one passion—the revolution. . . . Day and night he must have
one thought, one aim—inexorable destruction."

IV. The American Worker Is a "Honky" Who Revels in Racial Discrimination, Imperialist Wars, Fascism, Anti-Intellectualism, "Blind" Anti-Communism and Other Political Blood Sports.

Instead of producing a race willing and capable of serving High
Culture, these latter-day industrial troglodytes, say the critics, have 29
created a disgusting life style far inferior to the thousand-dollar-hi-fi-stereo-Fiat-Spider-Triumph-"Easy Rider"-acid head-Progressive Labor-pot life style of their opposites. Surprisingly, these same critics, while condemning the dollar imperialism of the American worker, find it intolerable that there should be any poverty in America. Presumably should this poverty be finally eliminated, the newly affluent workers would then become in the eyes of their putative liberators—such as Marcuse, Oglesby, Reich, Dowd—reactionary, racist, imperialist and puritanical honkies impatient to become high-priced hard hats.

This lie about the American worker is an old élitist one which goes
back to Alexander Hamilton, who said: "Take mankind in general, they
are vicious." This contempt was more recently expressed by Prof.
Andrew Hacker of Cornell, who was absolutely ecstatic that he could
announce America's approaching "terminal hour." Its doom was in- 30
evitable because even if America "could end poverty and bigotry, diffuse its pyramids of power, and suppress its imperial tendencies, there is no reason to believe that such a society would contain a greater quotient of talented people." He also announced that "the egos of 200 million Americans have expanded to dimensions never before considered appropriate for ordinary citizens." As George Orwell said in another

connection, "You have to belong to the intelligentsia to believe things like that: No ordinary man could be such a fool."

V. Our Political System Is an Utter Fraud, Particularly the Two-Party System.

This lie is generally circulated by American academicians who insist that a one-party state is not to be condemned out of hand, that if the one-party system has a "socialist" cachet, it might even be a useful modernizing vehicle. I am not suggesting there is anything particularly sacred about a two-party or multiparty state, nor that such a state is beyond reform. What I am arguing is that a one-party state is a far greater threat to freedom than a two-party or multiparty state.

C. Wright Mills in one of his essays bemoaned the fact that neither in the U. S. nor the Soviet Union "are there nationally responsible parties which debate openly and clearly the issues which the world now so rigidly confronts. The two-party state is without programatic focus and without organizational basis for it. We must recognize that, under some conditions, the two-party state can be as irresponsible as the one-party state." Now, the late Columbia sociologist was no enraptured admirer of the Soviet Union, yet it is humbuggery to talk about how, "under some conditions," a two-party state can be as "irresponsible" as a one-party state. Can a mild adjective like "irresponsible" apply with equal force to the one-party and two-party states?

If the two-party system or multiparty system has any merit at all it is this simple idea: that no men or group of men will ever become infected by the idea that it is upon them and their party alone that a nation depends; that, ultimately, they are so indispensable that it would be treason for them to surrender power, election or no election, to a democratic opposition. It is one of the curiosities of modern American political thinking that the very intellectuals who mock the two-party or multiparty state as a fiction are among the staunchest supporters of one-party states elsewhere in the world, so long as these states boast a Marxist-Leninist-Maoist inspiration. Or if they are not the staunchest supporters they are tolerant of Communist one-party systems or "African" one-party systems, where elections always end up with 99 per cent plus for the incumbent one-party regime. Fascist one-party states never benefit from this tolerance, nor do boring no-party states in Africa like Tubman's Liberia or Houphouët-Boigny's Ivory Coast. Since these countries are avowedly nonsocialist, their one-party (or no-party) regimes are definably reactionary, not progressive like Fidel Castro's Cuba.

Perhaps the American two-party system is faulty. It is possible, however, to build a better two-party system out of an already existing two-party system; it is difficult to build any kind of multiparty system

out of a one-party system.* Why not then a genuine two-party or multi-party system for all modernizing as well as modernized countries?
Why not a kind word for our two-party state, imperfect as it is and 34
one which may, a year hence, become a three-party or four-party system? Why is a one-party "socialist" state preferable to an imperfect two-party state?

VI. America Is on the Way Down While Other Countries are on the Way Up.

All the countries of the world, particularly those which go by the name "revolutionary" or "people's democracies," are privileged, apparently, to have their faults and virtues judged by the standards of
history. America, according to the critics we are discussing, is the one 35
country which may be judged by the standards of sociology. This double standard of judgment, of course, makes it impossible ever to grant America the benefit of the doubt or the credit for good intentions.

To view a nation through history is to allow the possibility of a melioristic future. To judge a nation by sociology is to inhibit comparison of its hopeful present with an inglorious past. To believe that
anything can improve here without a violent revolution (I insist on the 36
adjective "violent" since everybody today is for revolution, especially President Nixon) is, according to these critics, to demonstrate a benighted chauvinism. What this adds up to is that whatever America does, for whatever reason, America is wrong.

Unlike the other 143 countries in the world, only America is to be judged by the exacting and unattainable standards of a Utopia. If there is full, high-wage employment in America for a decade, then capitalism is merely buying off the workers so that they won't rebel. When unemployment comes, that's the *real* capitalism. If—so goes this view—the Gross National Product rises and consumer income with it, it merely reflects the materialism of American civilization. If the G.N.P.
falls slightly, it's the beginning of the end, thank God. If President 37
Nixon loses two Supreme Court nominations and one SST vote, it doesn't mean much because, after all, has anything really changed? It's better to vote for Nixon than for Hubert Humphrey because, as President, Nixon will bring Fascism to America much faster than a practitioner of "repressive tolerance" like Humphrey, and then. . . . (The same political strategy in Weimar Germany was expressed by the German Communist party as "*Nach Hitler, kommen wir*": After Hitler, we will come). Besides, whatever Nixon does as President would be no worse than anything Humphrey might do.

*Nikolai Bukharin, the Soviet theoretician, once said: "We might have a two-party system [in Russia], but one of the parties would be in office and the other in prison." Bukharin was later executed by Stalin.

Racism, tribalism, communalism and religious hate burden India, Pakistan, Sudan, Japan, Ceylon, Australia, Britain, Yugoslavia, Algeria with its Berbers, Spain with its Catalans and Basques, Latin America and its Indians, the U.S.S.R. and China and their repressed minorities, and on and on. The world crackles with hate, with racial and nationalistic passions—but only America, in the view of the critics we have been following, is racist. (What distinguishes America from the rest of the world is that we, its citizens, happen to be ashamed of our racism, while most everybody else is busy explaining the rationale of racial and religious discrimination and why it's impossible to abolish it overnight.)

Thus, having neatly caricatured the country and most of its 200 million inhabitants, we can all await the revolution, *we* intellectuals, *we* culture critics, *we* who have helped bring the Day of America's judgment nearer.

Amerika—Fascist, genocidal, materialistic, violent, paranoid, honky, insensitive, undemocratic, counterrevolutionary, hopeless . . . did ever a country since Nazi Germany so deserve to be utterly destroyed?

Milton Mayer

The Children's Crusade

I am of two minds about this country's present convulsions. My
heart is in the highlands with the hellers. But my head tells me . . .
It's an old head, mine, without much wool on the top of it in the place 1
where the wool ought to grow. Let me tell you what it is like to be
old in the United States of America at the tail end of the nineteen-sixties.

My generation accepted the precepts of its parents, and they were
the same precepts our parents had accepted from theirs. We violated
the precepts, naturally; but we accepted them. The new generation
rejects them. We were wrong and the new generation is right. Our pre- 2
cepts were good precepts, but still the new generation is right. They
are right because preceptorial is as preceptorial does. We were—and,
of course, are—pious frauds. They are impious Abelards.

That's the one big change. Another one is this: except for the rem-
nantal remains of Gopher Prairie, the America of my youth is vanished
without a trace; *Spurlos versunken.* In its perfectly splendid isolation,
the rest of the world, being out of sight, was out of mind. My father 3
didn't know whether Korea was in the Caribbean or the Mediterranean,
or whether the Congo was a Spanish dance, a Hindu god, or a chocolate
bar; he didn't care, and he didn't have to care.

It was an unjust America, of course. Blacks were Negroes, Negroes
were niggers, and niggers were ineducable and would therefore always
be menial. Jews knew their place and did not take forcible possession of
the boardroom of the college or country club that refused to practice
participatory democracy. It was an uncouth America, but a generous
America and a visionary America. Its golden door was open and the 4
lamp was bright beside it. Its very existence was a terror to tyranny
everywhere, lest its spirit be infectious. In its pre-scientific and anarchic
ardor it cultivated the techniques, if not the arts and institutions, of
peace. In the first eight years of my life in Chicago, I never once saw a
soldier. America was still, as it was intended to be, a refuge from chau-

Reprinted, with permission, from the September, 1969 issue of *The Center Magazine,* a publication of the Center for the Study of Democratic Institutions in Santa Barbara, California.

vinistic horrors. If someone had told my father that he had to take a loyalty oath, he would have said, "What do you think this is—Russia?"

Gone, all gone now, to be replaced by the garrison state and the last best hope of preserving the status quo ante all over the world. If, then, you can understand what it is to be old in this country at the tail end of the nineteen-sixties, you will be able to understand why I am 5
of two minds about the present convulsions: on balance, the changes I have seen in my time have been for the worse. I am afraid. But about certain aspects of the situation I am of one mind.

First: The revolution of the young blacks, formerly Negroes, is nothing but the Jim Crow branch of the American Children's Crusade. What the American Negroes are saying to the American whites is what the American young are saying to the American old: "I don't dig you. I don't love you. I don't honor you. I don't obey you." Whether it's 6
Vietnam and "Hell, no, we won't go," or the ghetto and "Hell, no, we won't stay," the message is the same. The parochial concern of the Negro should not obscure the common cause against an America whose promises were made with its fingers crossed.

Second: The revolution of the young Americans—white, black, red, or pink—is nothing but the American branch of the world revolution of the rising generation—and the American branch is behind the times. The French branch has pulled down de Gaulle. The Spanish and Japanese branches have driven Franco and Sato up the wall. The Italian branch has made it impossible to govern Italy. The German branch has 7
paralyzed Prussianism, and the Czech branch has immobilized communism. In our characteristic American provincialism we suppose that we have something special going here. The only thing that is special, indeed unique, is the elders' effort to persuade the young to call themselves kids in the hope that they won't take themselves seriously.

Third: The revolution is overdue—the revolution which Jeremiah and Jefferson invoked when they said that God's justice would not sleep forever. The evils that were containable under kings are no longer containable under politicians. A world that spends more on war than it does on health and education combined is not susceptible of reform. It 8
calls for revolution. But revolution is not the same thing as rebellion. The aftermath of the Russian Revolution instructs us that revolution is not a matter of systems but of men; as the men are, so will the revolution be.

John Locke never heard of law and order, but he had heard of divine right. "When men are miserable enough," said Locke, "they will rebel, cry up divine right how you will." I think he should have said "desperate enough" instead of "miserable enough." The difference between submissive misery and desperate rebellion is hope. And the dif- 9
ference between rebellion and revolution is intelligence. The young everywhere, black, white, poor, rich, have the desperate certitude of hope along with the adolescent possibility of intelligence. The young don't need God *or* the big battalions on their side. All they need is the

actuarial table, and they've got it. My object here is to persuade them to win a revolution instead of a rebellion—to make their victory stick. No revolution—not the French, not the American, and not the Russian —has ever stuck.

What is wanted is intelligence. That the status quo is unintelligent is superbly self-evident. But the revolution against it is not *ipso facto* intelligent. If it strikes with the wrong weapons at the wrong people for the wrong reasons, it will prove to have been unintelligent. If it assumes
that there is nothing wrong with power and that a transfer or redistri- 10
bution of power will improve the human condition, it will prove to have been unintelligent. He who says, "This ruler is a fool, but when I am a ruler I will not be a fool" is already a fool. It is not power that corrupts, but the unintelligent belief that power is not necessarily corrosive.

The revolution has to be intelligent, and the Negro's revolution has to be especially intelligent because he is its natural leader and is fighting in an exposed position. If he acts unintelligently he will go down faster than the white revolutionary whose pallor restrains (though it
does not disable) the counter-revolution. To ask the Negro to be more 11
intelligent than the white is only to ask him to use the intelligence he already has. But if all he has learned through his suffering is how to burn, baby, burn, he hasn't learned anything more than the white man, whose technological triumph consists of burning babies.

There is nothing the young can do to disrupt the American college campus that hasn't been done by their elders. They should not connive with their elders in its disruption. They should revolutionize it—revolutionize it intelligently on the intelligent ground that it has forfeited
its legitimacy and prostituted its independence. A university fifty per 12
cent of whose budget is provided by the producers of overkill is monopolized by them and every one of its procedures tainted. (The Supreme Court once held that control of six per cent of the market for automobile magnetos was enough to constitute a monopoly in the industry.)

If the Negro does not use his superior intelligence, he is lost, because an ignorant little man cannot beat an ignorant big one. Whitey has overkill; blackie has underkill. The inference is inescapable. Along
toward the end of 1941—but prior to December 7th of that year—Pro- 13
fessor Morris Cohen listened while a Jewish colleague said, "I just want to bash in a few Nazi heads before I die." Somebody turned to Cohen and said, "And what do you think?" "I think," said Cohen, "that bashing heads is for the ninety-six per cent—not for the four per cent."

Even the ninety-six per cent cannot win that way now. It took the winners of the First World War fifteen years to realize that they had lost it. It took the winners of the Second World War only five. What keeps the winners of the third world war from launching it is the suspicion that they have lost it in advance of its launching. They can't bash in a few Russian or American heads without being bashed back. Their unintelligent alternative, as every schoolboy knows, is a balance of ter-

ror which is ruinous in any terms and in its own terms unreliable. Their
only hope is to save their faces: It is an open secret that the Americans
will agree to surrender to the Vietcong if the Vietcong will agree to
proclaim an American victory. Old whitey seems to be at the end of the 1
road. The inventor of the lynching bee at Calvary, the auction block
at Charleston, and the shoot-out at Verdun seems to have no more
inventions.

The young—above all, those who are non-Caucasian and therefore
preconditioned to use their intelligence—are called upon to go out and
turn the world upside down. Like the Apostles of Jesus, they do not
need any baggage. They do not need black studies, because intelligence
is not absorbed through the epidermis. They do not need black dormi- 1
tories, because intelligence is not contracted by sleeping with people.
They do not need black awareness, because intelligence is aware of
itself and everything else. They need the intelligence they acquired in
the course of their suffering, nothing more.

It is not enough for them to do their thing; the thing has to be the
sensible thing to do. The sensible thing to do is not to demand a debased education on the ground that a debased education is what the 1
young, and especially the Negro young, are fit for. The sensible thing
to do is to demand a good education plus the compensatory qualifica-
tions of which they have been deprived.

A good education is not vocational training. The purpose of education is human freedom. We don't want Dow Chemical or R.O.T.C. off
the campus; we want everything off the campus that has nothing to do
with education for human freedom. That takes care not only of Dow
Chemical and R.O.T.C. but also the placement office, home economics,
physical education, business administration, journalism, speech, fraternities, and all the other goodies with which the old have tricked out 1
higher learning in the hope of keeping the young quiet in a rest home
for rich adolescents. We don't want war research off the campus; we
want everything off the campus that has nothing to do with education
for human freedom—including war research and industrial and commercial and labor research. We don't want theology, law, medicine, and
engineering off the campus, but across the street where we can take
advantage of pure research without diverting it from its purity.

Their motto has to be the motto of my alma mater, and it has to be
properly parsed. The motto of my alma mater is, "Let knowledge grow 1
more and more, that human life may be enriched." My alma mater
abandoned the enrichment for the knowledge, the end for the means,
and achieved the first self-sustaining nuclear chain reaction; the enrichment of human life in Hiroshima astonished the world.

Education has always presupposed authority—the rightful authority, 1
in respect of teaching, of those who know over those who don't know.
It has lost its authority because its practitioners have lent themselves to
the production and perpetuation of deadly error. Authority stripped of
its rightfulness is authoritarianism. The young are right in repudiating

authoritarianism. But they are mortally wrong if they think that they will improve their situation by replacing their elders' authoritarianism with their own.

Their intelligence, as it rejects authoritarianism, rejects the struggle for Negro rights as such and for student rights as such. Such a struggle is self-interested and is therefore no different in principle from the self-interest that disgraces their elders. There is no such category as Negro rights or student rights because there is no such category as
Negro or student. Either there are human rights or there are none. 20
Either we are first of all men, and only then black men or white men, or we are nothing. Because blacks are men, they are not to be badgered. Because they are men, they are not to be manipulated. Because they are men, they are not to be conscripted or enslaved. When the Negro was a slave, and the white man called him a black, he said, "I am a man."

The Negro does not have to be superhuman or saintly. He has only to be intelligent. What was good about Martin Luther King was his intelligence. He would not lift a finger to save one man or one country.
His race was the one race, man, without regard to the amount of mel- 21
anin in his skin. He knew the perdurable agony of man in his own person. Persecution was his teacher, and he learned from his teacher how to speak for man.

Who else will speak for man? Not whitey. Whitey has battened on partiality—on racism, on nationalism, on the exploitation of his brother, black and white. Whoever fights for partiality is playing whitey's game
and playing into whitey's hands, perpetuating the intolerable separation 22
of man into species. Separatism is for the birds; there is only one surviving species of the class *Homo,* and that is *Homo sapiens.* Whoever speaks for man must refuse to let any man be segregated by anybody —even by himself.

Just as there must be one world or none, so there must be one culture or none. That culture is man's. Asian and African and European studies in America are justified only by the American's ignorance of Asia, Africa, and Europe; that is, they are not justified at all. The black culture of the African-descended American, like the Irish culture of the
Irish-descended American, is an atavism that denies the common man- 23
hood and asserts a tribalism which is always and everywhere barbarian. If I cannot understand the writings of Eldridge Cleaver because of any skin color, then Eldridge Cleaver cannot understand the writings of Shakespeare because of his. Everybody, and not just the Nazis, will burn the books.

What is wanted here is unanswerable argument. Attack education for its present debasement, and you are unanswerable. Assert your right to live without killing, and you are unanswerable. Demand justice and
not advantage, and you are unanswerable. Call upon the church, not 24
for five hundred million dollars in special reparations for the Negro but for five hundred billion dollars in general justice for the poor, and you are unanswerable. But call policemen "pigs" and you are answerable

by those who remember the Nazis calling the Jews *Schweinehunde*. Call public officials "fascists" and you are answerable by those who remember fascism. Call for power and you are answerable by those who remember the Caesars and the Hapsburgs and the Romanovs. Call for black faculties and black curricula and you are answerable by those who call for humanistic faculties and humane curricula. Call for separatism and you will have on your side—though they kill you—the supremacists who have the necessary overkill to maintain the separatism you call for. Do you want separate but equal opportunity? You will get the separate opportunity and suffer the inequality that follows ineluctably from the separation of the minority from the majority.

The Negro racist, like the white racist, bases his racism on dignity. But men cannot shoot or burn or brawl their way to dignity; if they could, the American white man would be the most dignified man on earth. Does it make the young feel good to occupy an administration building and horrify the straights and terrify the timid and license the governor to turn on the tear gas? Do they want to feel good or to be intelligent? Do they want a rebellion or a revolution? Dignity is not a matter of feeling good—of the mumbo-jumbo of "black is beautiful" or "America the beautiful." America is no more beautiful than Africa and black is no more beautiful than blue.

I wish that the young could make their demands negotiable, but I don't see how they can if they make them intelligent. I don't see how overkill can be negotiated. I don't see how a ghetto or nerve gas research or the C.I.A. can be negotiated. But properly non-negotiable objectives cannot be achieved by throwing a rock through a window on the ground that the owner of the window understands nothing but force. He understands force, all right, and he has it. His level of intelligence has to be raised to the point where he can comprehend that the travesty of the campus and the ghettos and the battlefield is finished. A generation which elects a Lyndon Johnson or a Richard Nixon has no visible intention to negotiate. It will pay lip service to negotiation, provided that the shape of the table is right and as long as it doesn't have to stop doing the only thing it knows how to do. Harvard University had three hundred years to clean house on the basis of negotiable demands. The people who rightfully deplore the claim of the riotous young to amnesty have amnestied themselves since the world began. There may be those who recall Cain's general demurer to the complaint that he had failed to discharge his responsibility to his brother.

Old whitey may be unintelligent and out of steam, but he still has his pristine cunning. If he is persistently pushed he will propose gradualism, by which he means gradually wearing blackie down. Whitey isn't wicked. He is unconcerned. His unconcern is not immoral. It is unintelligent. By power possessed, he cannot understand what Paul meant by saying that we are all members one of another. He cannot understand what Jesus meant by saying that he who takes the sword will perish by it. He cannot understand what the prophet meant by proclaiming the greater damnation of those who devour widows' houses and make long prayers for a pretense. He didn't mean to be like this. Power benighted him, and he walks in the noonday as in the night. If I may paraphrase an eminent Harvard alumnus—a hundred generations of people like us is enough. If the new generation turns out to be the hundred and first, it is lost.

The old have torn down Vietnam and kept the ghettos in their place,
and now they say that the young want to tear things down without having anything to put in their place. The old are not competent to complain, and the complaint is an empty one anyway. The young don't have
to have anything to put in the place of the present shambles. The Lord
God Jehovah did not tell their ancestors and mine what to put in the 28
place of Sidon and Tyre; he told them, "You shall walk in My path and
I will show you My way." It is easy to think up the right thing. What is
hard is to stop doing the wrong one. The Lord did not tell their ancestors and mine to do good. He told them, "Cease to do evil—learn to do
good." They need only to be intelligent.

If they are intelligent, the totalitarian spirit—which unintelligently
obeys all laws—will call them anarchists. But they should not be dis-
mayed. True, anarchy is the second worst condition of human society.
The worst is tyranny. He who, like the intelligent founders of this republic, will not have tyranny, must take his chances on anarchy. The
Nuremberg decision of the International Military Tribunal in 1946
requires anarchy of the soldier who is ordered to perform inhuman 29
acts. Disorder is no worse than injustice, which is the institutionalization
of disorder. When the laws are rooted in violence and maintained by
violence, they must not be obeyed. Socrates was right, not wrong, when
he said, "Men of Athens, I love you, but I shall obey God rather than
you." John Brown was right. Mohandas Gandhi was right. Martin Luther
King was right. And Thomas Aquinas was right seven centuries ago
when he said that an unjust law is no law and does not bind a man
in conscience.

There is a higher law. The higher law does not have to be very
high to be higher than the Selective Service Act or the Internal Revenue
Act, only more intelligent. The young should study the German experience of the nineteen thirties, when the most literate nation on earth, 30
mistaking literacy for intelligence, elevated ignorance to power and cut
its own head off. They should study the German experience and learn
that neither the government nor the majority is by definition a good
judge of justice. Civil disobedience may be treasonable. It is not necessarily unpatriotic. A patriot will set his country right if he can, but in
no case will he contribute to its continued delinquency.

I am one of the elders of whom I speak. The young terrify me. They 31
terrify me because I have mine, which I got by the exercise of the good
precepts I learned from my parents plus being white and landing on my
feet every time I fell on my face. The young do not terrify me with
their popguns; I have ten machine guns for every one of their popguns.

They terrify me because they show some small sign of social maturity, of civic responsibility and human concern. Their elders, like me, are nice people, but they did not mature. The young have seen them playing cops and robbers at home and overkill in their worldwide playpen. Television reveals the infantilism of the adults' attention span. They cannot talk; they can sit mesmerized, or they can shout or mumble. They made the young mumble, "One nation, indivisible," and after they had mumbled it a few thousand times, some subversive told them that five per cent of the American people have twenty per cent of the nation's income and twenty per cent have five per cent of it, and they began to become what their elders call cynical; that is, intelligent. The day the young complete the process their elders will fall off the stage of history; they won't even have to be pushed.

The President of Notre Dame says that "we need a rebirth of academic, civic, and political leadership—a sharing of those youthful ideals and dreams, whether they are impossible or not." The President of Notre Dame is right. But whose fault is it that we need such a rebirth? How did we come to be so needy, with so rich a heritage and so profligate a land? How are we to be reborn? What does "a sharing of those youthful ideals and dreams" mean? What have the elders got to offer as their share? Not youth or ideals or dreams.

The ideals of the elders are money, fame, and power, and they dream of bigger and better sugarplums. They are starved for soul food, and chicken every Sunday has not filled them. They are obese, but unfilled. Now they have run out of time. They have run out of time to choose to free the Negroes or to fight a civil war to enslave them. All they can do now is cry up the divine right of law and order and shudder for themselves as they see it in action and observe the lawlessness and disorder it brings in its train.

Our black brethren are freeing themselves impatiently. For three centuries they waited patiently—so patiently that whitey, who takes impatience for manliness, took them for sheep who look up to be fed and look down when they aren't. They waited at the end of the line, and no matter how short the line got they were still waiting. They waited at the back of the bus, and no matter how empty the bus was they were still at the back. Their patience is beginning to be exhausted.

Whitey had no intention of living up to his profession that all men are created equal. As this country's sovereign he could not and can not pass the buck for its derelictions. What the country was was his doing; was, and is. His tragic flaw was his possession by power and the consequent corruption of his intelligence. He did not understand that no man can free another because no man can enslave another. Whitey wanted blackie to act like a freedman. But blackie isn't a freedman; no man is. He is a free man, and a free man because he is a man. Therein lies his dignity—not in the grace of his master—and he loses it not by being in chains but by chaining himself to the humiliating values of his master. Whoever would want to be and do and have what the American white man is and does and has is not a man but a slave and, like the American white man, an unhappy slave at that.

The only hope of the old is the intelligence of the young. Their
intelligence may be undeveloped, but it is not yet corrupted. They are
still young. They have been forced by the American educational process
to undertake their own education. They are not to be put down or put
off, because they have been set to wondering. What set them to wondering was, I suppose, the two victorious world wars their elders waged 36
and lost in the process of winning them. Coming in the wake of these
wingless victories, they would have had to be catatonic epileptics not
to have wondered. Wonder is the beginning of wisdom. The young are
wising up. All they have not to do is what e. e. cummings called up-grow
and down-forget.

Their intelligence tells them that the only solution to racialism is
miscegenation. There was a time when an Irishman could not be elected
President. There was a time when a Catholic could not be elected President. There was even a time when a fighting Quaker couldn't be elected
President. The change in our national attitude was the result of what
we Dixiecrats call mixing. Hybrid corn and hybrid pigs are of higher
quality than the original stocks, and there is no evidence whatever that 37
hybrid man is not. Since seventy per cent of all the Americans "blacks"
are part "white" and millions of American "blacks" have passed unknow-
ingly into the so-called white race, the racist who says he wouldn't want
his daughter to marry a Negro—or a white man—has no way of knowing whether she does or doesn't and neither has she or her fiancé.
As long as pigmentation provides our society with the one discernible
other, and as long as whitey is ineducable by anthropology, psychology,
and theology, the only solution is to make indiscernible others of us all.

Five hundred years would do it. But then five hundred years of
education for freedom would make intelligent human beings of us and it
wouldn't matter anymore what color we were. But we have run out of 38
time. It isn't the future that's dark—it's the present. If the young do not
bring light to the world, if they spurn a little suffering undergone for
the sake of intelligence, the wave of the present will roll over them and,
like their elders, they will be heard of no more.

Benjamin DeMott

The Way It Is: Some Notes on What We Feel

Hard times, confusing times. All at once—no warnings or trendy
winks from the past—we've become New People, putting demands to
ourselves and to life in the large for which precedents don't exist. And
because the scale of our transformation causes inward ruptures, harries 1
us into feelings and expectations that have no names, our nerves are
shaky, we shuttle between nostalgia and a manic optimism—behave
always as though out at some edge.

If we grasped our situation, had a clear concept of where we
were and why, we might suffer less. But where can we turn for clari-
fication? Among a thousand wonders, the period is remarkable for the
absence of a fully humane genius among those who represent us to
ourselves. Vast step-ups of production schedules have occurred in the
art-and-culture-commentary industries, and substantial talents breathe
among us, pump hard, fight for and win wide audiences. Yet no image 2
or vocabulary adequate to the truth of the age comes forth. The need
is for perspective and comparative evaluation, acts of consideration and
assessment, and we've been offered instead—the notion of "blame" is
irrelevant: the work produced probably could not have been otherwise,
given the time—discrete patches of intensity, special pleading and description, and virtually no interpretation worth the name.

Wife-swapping (John Updike), protest marches (Norman Mailer),
exotic theatrical and cinematic entertainments (Susan Sontag), acid-
tripping and radical chic (Tom Wolfe)—these and a hundred other
"characteristic phenomena" are evoked in exacting, often exciting detail
and with superlative attentiveness to personal response. But the place 3
of the phenomena in moral history, the interrelationships among them,
the chief forces and principles determining the nature of the emergent
new sensibility, are left undefined. Often, in fact, the pitchman's cant
and jargon—copywriters' tags like *The Scene . . . getting it all together
. . . encounter group . . . enter the dialogue . . . a piece of the action*

. . . *with it* . . . *Now generation*—appear to contain better hints to our truth than does any novel, essay or play.

And from this failure of art and intellect to nourish and illuminate, many problems flow. One is our readiness to accept "explanations" of ourselves that actually deepen the general confusion. There is, for instance, the hugely popular delusion that the central development of our time has been the widening of the gap between youth and everybody else. The yearly periodical indices disclose that three to four 4
times as many words are now being written about youth as were written a decade ago. And the statistic reflects the growth of a superstition that the story of the age may simply be the simultaneous appearance of two ages, two worlds—one belonging to young people and the other to the rest of us—and that the prime influence on behavior and feeling in both worlds is the attitude of each toward the other.

A handy formula: it provides a means of organizing events, tastes, gestures. But if the order thus established is convenient, it's also primitive: you buy it only at the cost of blindness to the essential unity of the period. The college senior demanding the "restructuring" of his commencement ceremonies, the company president struggling to "involve" minor line executives in top-echelon decisions, the guerrilla-theater propagandist sneering at old-style radicals for being "hung up on words and argufying"—these clearly aren't the same man. Yet ignor- 5
ing the connections among their apparently disparate behaviors, pretending that the task of cultural inquiry amounts to finding out "what the young are thinking," as though the latter lived not among us but on remote, inaccessible islands, is a mistake. This is an age; what's happened, baby, has happened to men as well as babes; we can indeed say "we," and the sniffish fear of doing so continues to cost us to this day.

One other expensive delusion demands notice—namely, the view that our newness is a function of an unexampled fury of sensation-hunting. Easy to adduce evidence supporting this theory, to be sure. Contemporary man has been a tripper in many senses; recent years saw incredible expansions of air travel, motel chains, tourist agencies. The manufacture, on demand, of variety goes on without pause—*Hair, Che, Dionysus, Commune,* Breslin, Millett, Reich, Barbados, Eleuthera, the
Algarve, Arthur, Electric Circus, Max's Plum, Beatles, Doors, Led Zep- 6
pelin, topless, bottomless, bare. . . . And it's undeniable that the age has created vehicles and instruments of sensation on an order of arousal power never before legitimized by the consent of an entire society. But we nevertheless simplify ourselves, enshroud our lives in a mist of moralizing, if we accept as an adequate perspective what in fact is no more than a style of self-laceration. We are not, in the broad mass, pure sensationalists, snappers-up of unconsidered kicks; without denying the chaos and the extravagance, it can still be claimed that the age has more dignity, promise and intellectual complication than any such formula allows.

Wherein lies the complication? If we aren't out for sensation alone, what are we after? Where is our center, what are our growing points, what actually has been happening in our lives?

Best to answer flatly: major changes have been occurring in our sense of self, time and dailiness. For one thing, we've become obsessed with Experience. (We behave, that is to say, as though we're determined to change our relation to our experience, or to have our "usual" experiences in new ways.) For another, we've come to relish plurality of self. (We behave as though impatient or bitter at every structure, form, convention and practice that edges us toward singleness of view or "option," or that forces us to accept this or that single role as the whole truth of our being.) For yet another, we seem to be striving to feel time itself on different terms from those hitherto customary. (We're anxious to shed ordinary, linear, before-and-after, cause-and-effect 7
understandings of events even in our personal lives. We feel distaste for inward response that's insufficiently alive to The Moment, or that glides over each instant as a betweenness—in another minute it'll be time to go to work, go to dinner, write our brother, make love, do the dishes—rather than living into it, inhabiting it as an occasion, without thought of antecedents or consequences.) And finally, we've conceived a detestation of the habitual. (We are seeking ways of opening our minds and characters to the multiplicity of situations that are echoed or touched or alluded to by any one given situation. We hope to replace habit—"the shackles of the free," in Bierce's great definition—with a continually renewed alertness to possibility.)

As goes without saying, labeling and categorizing in this manner is presumptuous: the congeries of inexpressible attitudes and assumptions in question is dense, intricate, tightly packed—more so than any confident arbitrary listing can suggest. And, as also should go without saying, the vocabulary used here to name the assumptions isn't much favored by any of us who're just "getting through the days" called the seventies. We don't tell ourselves, "We must change our relation to our experience." We don't say, "I must find a new way of having my experience." We live by no abstract formulas, we simply express our preferences. We perhaps say, in planning a political meeting: "Let's 8
not have so many speeches this time." We perhaps say, when serving on a parish committee to reinvigorate a WASP church: "Let's have a different kind of service at least once. . . . Once a month, maybe." We perhaps say at conferences: "When do we break into small groups?" We perhaps say, if we're a girl and boy preparing for a costume party (a girl in a midi did in fact say, Halloween night, at Hastings Stationery in Amherst, Massachusetts, over by the greeting cards, to her date), "Look, why don't we change clothes? I'll go in your stuff, you wear my midi." And it's clearly a jump from innocuous jokes of this sort to the solemn apparatus of historical statement.

On occasion, though, we ourselves do grow more explicit or theoretical. Certain exceptional situations—or community pressures—have

drawn from some of us flat declarations that our aim is to change our relation to our experience. Middle-class drug users do say aloud, for example, that they use drugs, pot or acid, in order to create simultaneously a wholly new sense of personal possibility and to alter the inner landscape of time so that experience can be occupied, known in its own
moment-to-moment quality, texture, delight, rather than as a backdrop 9
for plans, intentions, anxieties. And if the majority is vastly less explicit than this about its intentions, if the unity of our purposes escapes most of us, we nevertheless do venture forth, time and time over, old, young, middle-aged, in situations of striking range, and do the thing itself—arrange, that is, to have our experience in new ways.

Some of our contrivances are mainly amusing—fit matter for *New Yorker* cartoons. They take the form of homely efforts at energizing recreation or casual relations with others, or at injecting the values of surprise—or even of moderated risk—into commonplace situations. The long-hair fad, feminization of costume and behavior, cosmetics for men, Unisex, etc.: here is an attempt to create a new way of having the experience of masculinity (or femininity). If freedom is most real when most on trial, then masculinity will be most piquantly masculine when set in closer adjacency to its "opposite": let me have my sexuality as
conscious choice rather than as taken-for-granted, unopposable, uncon- 10
frontable bio-cultural conditioning. Or again: the taste of the sons and daughters of the middle class for tattered clothes, worn jeans, torn shoes, soul music, coarse language, rucksacks, thumbing—or for stripping to bare skin, as at Woodstock—is expressive of a yearning to have the experience of middle-class life in a fresh way, with an allusion to the life of the field hand or the workingman or the savage, and with a possibility vivid at every moment, at least in one's own fantasy, of being taken for something that (by objective definition) one isn't.

And there are countless comparable efforts—tentative, self-conscious, touching and hilarious by turns—to transform or ventilate familiar patterns of experience. The intimidated young grow beards and find a new way to have the experience of intimidation—as intimidators rather than as the intimidated. Men slightly older, stockbrokers or editors, grow beards and live for a moment, in a passing glance met on the street or subway, as figures momentarily promoted to eccentricity, individuality, mystery. The fashionably decorous find a new way of combining the experience of being fashionable with that of displaying sexual fury and
abandon—The Scene, the pounding, raging discotheque. The experi- 11
ence of the theatergoer and moviegoer is complicated and "opened to possibility" by the invention of participatory theater and the art-sex film. (The routine moviegoing experience occurs in a new way at sex documentaries because of nervous consciousness among patrons of their adjacency to each other; the experience of theatergoing occurs in a new way at *Hair* or La Mama or the Living Theater or the Performance Group because of nervous consciousness among the audience of its relations with the players.) Even the most ordinary activities—driving

a car—are touched by the energizing spirit. And here as elsewhere risks are offered at a variety of levels. The timid can participate, while motoring, in the decal dialogue—flags vs. flowers, hardhats vs. hippies, on windshields and hoods. (The politicization of tourism.) The more daring can affix risqué bumper stickers and thereby possess an idea of themselves not merely as traveling or politicking but as, at any given moment, escalating to Don Juanism.

Predictably, the influence of the new impulses and assumptions has produced—even among "safe" middle-class people—behavior that's empty, ugly or pathetic: frivolous sexual indulgence, promiscuity, group sexual "experiments," attempts to restore lyric quality to humdrum domesticity by the gaudy device of The Affair. And predictably the influence of the new taste is easiest to read in the exotic trades and professions. The intellectual journalist seeks to change his relation to his work by crossing his objective function as a noter of external events with an enterprise in self-analysis—scrutiny of the unique intricacies of his own response to the occurrences "covered." Painters and sculptors for their part aim at altering their own and their audience's experience as gallery-goers by impacting that experience with the experience of the supermarket or with that of the toyshop or hobbyist's tool table. Directors like Julian Beck and Richard Schechner show actors how to alter the terms of their experience: no longer need the actor imitate another person, play a "role," learn a part. He can simultaneosly act and be: by presenting his own nature, using his own language, setting forth his own feelings in a dynamic with an audience, establishing relations in accordance with momentary shifts of personal feeling, and thereby foreclosing no possibility within himself. And similar opportunities stem from the new terms of relatedness between performers and audience throughout the worlds of showbiz and sports—witness the example of the surprising intimacies of the new sports heroes or a dozen rock stars with their fans.

But it's not only in exotic worlds of work or leisure that men labor to invent new ways of having familiar experience. That effort has touched American culture in scores of unlikely places, from the condominium and the conglomerate to priestly orders and women's liberation cells and books by George Plimpton. And because the "movement," to speak of it as that, is universal, the economic consequences are overwhelming. The desire to combine plain locomotion with adventure, "engagement with reality," recreated the family wagon as Mustang or Camaro and sold 10 million sports cars. Corporations able to manufacture, for people immured in seemingly unchangeable situations, a means of moving toward an alternative experience, expand immensely—witness the growth of Avon Products, which sells the possibility of Fatal Womanhood to housewives unable to "get out." Everywhere the consumer pursues the means and images of another life, a different time, a strange new window on experience. And the supplier's ingenuity is breathtaking, as attested by Tom Wolfe's account of the marketing of

militancy among the rich, or his inventory of the contents of the novelist
Ken Kesey's "house":

"Day-Glo paint . . . Scandinavian-style blonde . . . huge floppy
red hats . . granny glasses . . . sculpture of a hanged man . . . Thun- 14
derbird, a great Thor-and-Wotan beaked monster . . . A Kama Sutra
sculpture . . . color film . . . tape recorders. . . ."

The range of materials manufactured in this country to meet the
demand for self-transformation and extension of role has become so
extraordinary, indeed, that a wholly new kind of mail-order catalogue
has lately begun to appear. One such—the 128-page *Whole Earth Cata-* 15
logue (1969-71)—lists thousands of commercially produced products of
use to ordinary men bent on moving beyond the limits of their training,
job or profession in order to participate (by their own effort) in the
life styles of others—farmers, geologists, foresters, you name it.

None of this would matter greatly, of course—much of it would
seem eligible for only satiric regard—if it could be neatly separated
from the major political events of recent years. But as is often true 16
of alterations of sensibility, the new feeling for "possibility" and the
new dream of plural selves can't be thus separated. Throughout the
sixties these forces had measureless impact on public as well as upon
private life, and their influence has lately been intensified.

To speak of the influence with appropriate balance is difficult:
political acts have political content—indefensible to propose some latter-
day version of the old-style Freudian "medical egotism" which substituted chatter about neuroses and psychoses for political explanations
of the course of national affairs. For that reason it needs to be said 17
aloud once more—about, say, the teachers and students who participated
in the first teach-ins against the Vietnam war in 1964 and '65, or in
the strike against the Cambodian invasion in 1970, ventures whose consequences for men and nations still can't be fully accounted—that these
were not trivial men acting out quirkish desires to escape into the
Enveloping Scene, or into The Unpredictable. They were passionately
concerned to alter what they regarded as a senseless, perilous, immoral
course of adventurism.

But true as this is, the current behavior of teachers and students
does have psychocultural as well as political ramifications. The "politically concerned" member of an American faculty knew in former
days what his prescribed role was: to observe, to make amusing remarks. He might examine (ironically, in asides) the substance of his 18
frustration or impotence—shrug it off in a glancing commentary in his
classes, nothing more. During the teach-ins and in the earlier Cuban crisis,
he and many of his students stepped beyond these limits, reached out
toward another self. No longer a teacher in the orthodox form, nevertheless he still taught; no longer a disseminator or accumulator of knowledge in the conventional frame, he still pursued understanding. He
passed through the conventional frame with his students, advanced
from the warehouse of reported experience-graphs, charts, texts—and

appeared now as a grappler with immediacy, a man bidding for influence in the shaping of public policy even in the act of teaching, laboring to possess the teacher's experience in a new way.

And precisely this determination figured at the center of the major political event of this age. It is the black man's declaration of his sense of possibility that, more than any other single force, is shaping these years. Whipped, lynched, scourged, mocked, prisoned in hunger, his children bombed, his hope despised, the American black was the archetypal "limited self": no movement feasible, seemingly, save from despair to a junkie's high. The glory and terror of our age is the awakened appetite for new selfhood, new understandings of time, new ground for believing in the pliancy of experience, on the part of 20 million black Americans. Their grasp of the meaning of "open" experience lends a color of dignity even to the most trivial venture in self-extension elsewhere in the culture. And nothing is more striking than that they truly are demanding multiplicity, will not trade off blackness for whiteness, will not substitute one simplicity for another. The aim is to add a new self and participate in a new life with no sacrifice of the old.

Everywhere in the culture, in sum, the same themes sound: the will to possess one's experience rather than be possessed by it, the longing to live one's own life rather than be lived by it, the drive for a more various selfhood than men have known before. Few efforts to summarize those themes convey the energy, excitement and intensity of the longing. ("There is is an increased demand by all parts of the citizenry," says the Teachers College for Research and Education in American Liberties, in mild voice, "for participation in decision-making in all areas of public and private institutional life.") Few men can contemplate the new demands without contradictory responses, fear and trembling among them. But whatever the response, the unity of sensibility lies beyond denial. Young, old, black, white, rich and poor are pursuing the dream of a more vital experience. Propelled often by the belief that if we know the good, then we must act the good, we're moving from passive to active; from "package to prove." And at the root of our yearning stand the twin convictions: that we can be more, as men, than we're permitted to be by the rule of role and profession, and that the life of dailiness and habit, the life that lives us, precedes us, directs us to the point of suppressing moral conscience and imagination, is in truth no life at all.

Fine, fine, says a voice: it's a way of describing a cultural change. But why the change in the first place? All that mid-century agonizing about Conformity, Silent Generation, etc. And then this sudden outbreak, this demand (if you will) for more life, more selves, the open sense of time and the rest: how and why is it happening? Surely not a simple cyclical process. . . .

For philosophers of the media the question holds no mysteries. Nothing more natural, they consider, than for people to ask more of themselves now: men are more, as men, than they used to be. Through

the centuries we've been extending ourselves steadily, touching and comprehending life at ever-greater distances from our immediate physical environment. Lately we press a button and a world of hot events pours into our consciousness—at peace we know war; in the clean suburb we know the blighted ghetto; sober and rational we watch doomed men turn on; law-abiding and confident, we watch the furtive
cop collect his grease. As we hold the paper in our hands we know that 22
somewhere on earth an excitement yet undreamed is tracked for us: hijackers whirled across the sky are tied to us with umbilical cables. And the knowledge quickens our belief in a fascinating otherness that could be, that will be, momentarily ours. Why would we rest content in mere is-ness? What can our experience be but a ceaseless prodding by the demons of Possibility?

Nor do the philosophers stop here. Marshall McLuhan argues that, because of its low-definition picture, TV has restructured the human mind, remade mental interiors in the Kantian sense, creating new aptitudes, new schema of perception, which in turn foster generalized enthusiasm for "involvement and participation" throughout the culture.
. . . "TV has affected the totality of our lives, personal and social and 23
political," he writes. "If the medium is of high definition, participation is low. If the medium is of low intensity, the participation is high. . . . In 10 years the new tastes of America in clothes, in food, in housing, in entertainment and in vehicles [will] express the new pattern of . . . do-it-yourself involvement fostered by the TV image."

A match for the ingenuity of this sort of explanation is found in the writings of some who propose existential philosophy as a Key Influence on the age. Since the philosophy asserts the precedence of the
person over the culturally fixed function or situation (so runs the argu- 24
ment), and since its themes are well diffused, is it not reasonable to feel its presence in the new insistence on a man's right to break free of the constraints of special social or professional roles?

Perhaps—but the likelihood is strong in any case that the engulfing public events of recent years have had a share more to do with our new attitudes and psychology than the line count in the boob tube or the essays of Merleau-Ponty. A powerful lesson taught by the Vietnam war from the mid-sixties onward, for example, was that bureaucrats, diplomats, generals and presidents who allow themselves to be locked into orthodox, culturally-sanctioned patterns of thought and assumption
make fearful mistakes. Men came to believe that it was because General 25
Westmoreland was a general, a military man to the core, that he could not admit to scrutiny evidence that challenged his professional competency. No event in American history cast sterner doubt on the efficacy of the limited professional self—on the usefulness of clear-eyed, patent-haired, inhumanly efficient defense secretaries, technicians, worshipers of military "intelligence"—than the disasters that followed every official optimistic pronouncement about Vietnam from the middle sixties onward.

Because men of authority were inflexible, locked into Chief-Executivehood, because they couldn't bring themselves to believe in the upsurges of The Scene that destroy careful, sequential, cause-and-effect narratives, human beings by the tens of thousands were brutally slaughtered. What good therefore was the perfected proficiency that took a man to the top? We had begun learning, in the fifties, to say the phrase "The Establishment" in a tone of contempt. In those early days the chief target was a certain self-protectiveness, caution—and snootiness—in the well placed. But the war showed The Establishment forth as a particular style of intellectual blindness and emotional rigidity: those black suits, high-rise collars, unctuous assurances, fabled undergraduate distinctions at Harvard and Yale, 19-hour days, those in-group back-patting sessions, at length came to appear, in the eyes of people at every level of life, as a kind of guarantee of self-loving self-deception. Lead us not into that temptation, so went the general prayer: give us back our flexibility.

And the prayer for variousness, for a way out of "structured experience," has been hugely intensified by the national traumas through which we've passed. In the moments of national shame and grief and terror—the killing of the Kennedys, of Martin Luther King, Malcolm X —a new truth came belatedly but fiercely home. Our fixities weren't objectionable simply because they were fixities: they carried within them, unbeknown to the generations that kept faith with them, a charge of human unconcern and viciousness that positively required a disavowal of the past—flat rejection of past claims to value, principle or honor. For the seed of our traumas, whether assassinations or riots, seemed invariably to lie in racism, in a willful determination to treat millions of human beings as less than human. The contemplation of the deaths of heroes, in short, opened a door for us on our own self-deceit and on the self-deception practiced by our fathers. Neither they nor we had told it like it was. And they were apparently all unaware that because of their fantasies and obliviousness millions suffered. They spoke of goodness, of social and family values, of man's responsibility to man, they spoke of community, fidelity, ethics, honor before God, and never obliged themselves to glance at the gap between their proclamations and the actualities their uncaringness created. Their way of inhabiting doctor-dom, lawyer-dom, sober citizenhood, their ways of having the experience of respectable men, shut them in a prison of self-love and unobservance: who among us could bear so airless, priggish, mean a chamber?

Had we had no help in ascertaining the relevant facts, had the discoverers and representatives of the Black Experience not written their books, we might have been slower to ask such questions. Dr. King's dream might have moved us less, and lived less vividly in memory, had James Baldwin not written *The Fire Next Time*, or had there been no successors—no Cleaver, no LeRoi Jones—or had we been unprepared by the earlier struggles, marches and rides.

But what matters here is that the discovery of the Black Experience has filled us with a sense that, if we are connected with the history that shaped that experience, then the connection should be broken. Let us no longer dress or act or feel as our predecessors had done, let us no longer be educated passively in lies as we had been, let us no longer listen politely to the "authorities" sanctimoniously assuring us that history is "important" or that the greater writers "must be mastered" or 29
that truth is tradition or that virtue equals a stable self. Our obligation to the past, the credibility of those who spoke of the dignity of the departed—blind men, crude unbelievers in the human spirit—these are vanishing, leaving us freer of the hand of the past than any before us have been. Faith of our fathers—what God could sponsor that faith? How can we be men and go on living in the old ways in the old house?

And then over and beyond all this, though entangled with it in subtle potent ways, there has arisen an unprecedented outcry against human dailiness itself. The outcry I speak of isn't rationalized as an 30
onslaught against moral obliviousness. It appears also to be beyond politics, domestic or foreign, and without philosophical content. Its single thrust is the claim that middle-class life is unredeemable not by virtue of its being evil but because it is beyond measure boring.

Consider recent literary patterns. The last decade opened with pronouncements by Norman Mailer against the dreariness of safe, habitual life and for violence and brutality, even when practiced by mindless 31
teen-agers murdering a helpless old man, as an escape from deadly dailiness. A few years later, a chorus of sick comics and "black-humor" novelists were being applauded for social commentary issuing directly from professed disgust with every aspect of habit-ridden middle-class life.

And, arguably more important, whenever middle-class experience was represented at any length and with any care in our period, the artist obdurately refused to include a detail of feeling that would hint at imaginative satisfactions—or openings of possibility—feasible within the middle life. Teaching a toddler to swim, for instance—a familiar cycle. Coaxed and reassured, my child at length jumps in laughing from poolside, absolute in trust of my arms; a second later she discovers that by doing my bidding she can "stay up," move; watching in delight, 32
I'm touched and freshened. I see I'm trusted and worth trusting, emulated and worth emulating. . . . What a drag, says mod fiction, what sentimentality, how trivial. . . . In the domestic pages of John Updike's *Couples*, no mother is radiated by the beauty of her child bathing in the tub. No father learns, with a lift of pride, of his son's meeting a hard responsibility well and tactfully. The insistence on boredom, weariness, repetitiveness, burdensomeness is unrelenting; crankiness, leftovers, nagging, falsity, insufferable predictability—these are presented as the norms of the workaday-weekend cycle. Grown men join together for a recreational game of basketball in Mr. Updike's novel—but, although the author is superb at rendering sensation, he creates no plea-

sure of athletic physicality, nor even the act of slaking decent thirst. Everywhere his talk assures the reader There Must Be More Than This, nowhere in the texture of dailiness can he find a sudden, sweet increment of surprise, a scene that permits "modest, slow, molecular, definitive, social work," or any other hope for renewal:

> Foxy . . . was to experience this sadness many times, this chronic sadness of late Sunday afternoon, when the couples had exhausted their game, basketball or beachgoing or tennis or touch football, and saw an evening weighing upon them, an evening without a game, an evening spent among flickering lamps and cranky children and leftover food and the nagging half-read newspaper with its weary portents and atrocities, an evening when marriages closed in upon themselves, like flowers from which the sun is withdrawn, an evening giving like a smeared window on Monday and the long week when they must perform again their impersonations of working men, of stockbrokers and dentists and engineers, of mothers and housekeepers, of adults who are not the world's guests but its hosts.

Whether writers of this commitment and assumption are creators of the age less than they are its victims can't be known. Whether their voices would have sufficed to persuade us of the uselessness of sequential, predictable, "closed-self" ways of having our experience, had there been no war and no black rebellion, we can't be certain. It's clear, though, that a man who seeks in the popular literature of this age, an image of his life that allows for possibility and freshening within the context of dailiness, and without loss of stable selfhood, isn't able to find it: in our world, so says the official dictum, it's quite impossible to breathe.

But, says another voice, is it impossible? Or, asking the question in a different way, can we truly survive if we persist in our present direction? Suppose we continue on our present course, pressing for new selves and new ways of experiencing. Will we be nourishing a growing point for humanness? Can a humane culture rise on any such foundations?

For pessimists several reminders are pertinent. One is that the taste for Immediate Experience and Flexible Selves is deeply in the American grain. The belief in the power of unmediated experience to show men where they err—and how to cope—was powerful on the American frontier, and survives in the writings of virtually every major American thinker in our past. Again and again in the pages of Thoreau, Emerson, William James, Peirce and Dewey "pure" Experience is invoked as teacher, and again and again these sages set forth a demand for Openness. Habit, routinized life, fixed manners, conventions, customs, the "usual daily round"—these block us off from knowledge and also from concern for the lives of those different from ourselves. Therefore (our native sages concluded) therefore, shake free of the deadening job or ritual, escape into the grace of wholeness, fly in the direction of surprise and the unknown—in that direction lie the true beginnings of a man.

And there is far more to the return to the ideal of open experience than the ineluctable American-ness of the thing. The return is itself a symbol of an awakened awareness of the limits of reason and of the danger that constant interventions of intellect between ourselves and
experience hide from us the truth of our natural being, our deep con- 36
nectedness with the natural world that the technological mind has been poisoning. And, more important than any of this—for reasons already named—there is a moral and spiritual content to the rejection of the structures of the past which, though now increasingly deprecated, has unshakable vigor and worth.

There are, however, immense problems. The immediate-experience, multiple-selves cause contains within it an antinomian, anti-intellectual ferocity that has thus far created fears chiefly about the safety of institutions—universities, high schools, legislatures, churches, political conventions. But the serious cause for alarm is the future of mind. The
love of the Enveloping Scene as opposed to orderly plodding narra- 37
tives, fondness for variety of self rather than for stability, puts the very idea of mind under extraordinary strain. It is, after all, by an act of sequential reasoning that Norman O. Brown and many another characteristic voice of our time arrived at their critique of the limits of consecutive thought. Once inside the scene, utterly without a fixed self, will our power to compare, assess and choose survive?

Within the past few years men have begun thinking purposefully on these problems, aware that "planning" would necessarily henceforth be in bad odor, yet unconvinced that the future could be met with any hope whatever minus the resources of intellect. One question addressed was: Can society be reorganized in a manner that will accommodate the appetite for self-variousness and possibility—without insuring the onset of social chaos? (Among the most brilliant suggestions were those advanced by Professors Donald Oliver and Fred Newmann in a *Harvard Education Review* paper [1967] that looked toward the invention of a world in which men may move freely at any point in their
post-pubescent lives into and away from the roles of student, appren- 38
tice and professional.) Another question addressed was: Can society be so organized as to permit genuine simultaneities of role? Is it possible to create situations in which we can simultaneously engage our resources as domestic man, political man, inquiring man? (The most imaginative effort in this direction now in progress is a two-year-old Office of Education venture in educational reform—Triple T, Training of Teachers-Trainers. The scheme has enlisted scholars, professional instructors in pedagogy and a significant segment of laymen and minority group representatives—barbers to bankers—in cooperative planning and carrying out of experimental teaching programs in dozens of local communities around the nation.)

These are small beginnings—but already some significant truths have appeared. It is clear that men on the conservative side, "defenders of orthodox values" (professional, social or academic), need to be disabused of the wishful notion that heroic, do-or-die Last Stands for tradition are still feasible. The movement of culture—what's happening—has happened so irreversibly, the changes of assumption and of cultural texture are so thoroughgoing, that the idea of drawing a line—thus far and no farther—is at best comic. The option of Standing Pat has been foreclosed; there is no interest on the part of the "opposition" in face-to-face struggle; when and if traditionalists march forth to an imagined Fateful Encounter, they'll find only ghosts and shadows waiting.

And on the radical side, it's clear that the task is somehow to establish that the reason for rehabilitating the idea of the stable self, and the narrative as opposed to the dramatic sense of life, is to insure the survival of the human capacity to have an experience. For as John Dewey put it years ago:

> Experiencing like breathing is a rhythm of intakings and outgivings. Their succession is punctuated and made a rhythm by the existence of intervals, periods in which one phase is ceasing and the other is inchoate and preparing. [We compare] the course of a conscious experience to the alternate flights and perchings of a bird. The flights are intimately connected with one another; they are not so many unrelated lightings succeeded by a number of equally unrelated hoppings. Each resting place in experience is an undergoing in which is absorbed and taken home the consequence of prior doing, and, unless the doing is that of utter caprice or sheer routine, each doing carries in itself meaning that has been extracted and conserved. . . . If we move too rapidly, we get away from the base of supplies—of accrued meanings—and the experience is flustered, thin and confused. If we dawdle too long after having extracted a net value, experience perishes of inanition.

Despite the cultural revolution, we possessed until very recently, a poet of "perchings," a believer in human rhythms who was capable of shrewd distinctions between caprice and routine, and firm in his feeling for the ordinary universe—and for the forms of ordinary human connectedness. Randall Jarrell (1914-1965) could write of ordinary life that it was a matter of errands generating each other, often a tiresome small round, the pumping of a rusty pump, water seeming never to want to rise—and he could then add that within the round, to alert heads, came a chance to act and perceive and receive, to arrive at an intensity of imaginative experience that itself constitutes an overflowing and a deep release:

> . . . sometimes
> The wheel turns of its own
> weight, the rusty

Pumps pumps over your
  sweating face the clear
Water, cold, so cold! You cup
  your hands
And gulp from them the
  dailiness of life.

The shadow over us just now is that we seem too disposed to dis-
believe in that nourishment—almost convinced it can't be real. But we
nevertheless possess some strength, a possible way forward. We know 42
that within the habitual life are a thousand restraints upon feeling, concern, humanness itself: our growing point is that we have dared to
think of casting them off.

Questions and Quotations for Discussion and Writing Assignments

I

1. Charles Reich thinks America is changing because of a revolution in consciousness. All of the outward signs—bell-bottoms, jeans, beards, and beads—are fads, passing fashion, he says, but they do signal "a growth of awareness, a change of values, a renewal of knowledge, and a step toward liberation." Do you agree? Can there be a revolution without radical struggle?
2. What, in Reich's view, created Consciousness III? What two forces interacted to cause this change in consciousness?
3. Is it really possible, as Reich says, to live your life as a "surfer"?
4. A key word in understanding the origins of Consciousness III is "betrayal." How, in Reich's opinion, has America been betrayed? How do young people feel about this betrayal?
5. What contributions to Consciousness III have been made by black people?
6. What are the three commandments of Consciousness III? Do they sound familiar—old words to a new tune?
7. Charles Reich is very optimistic about young people; as he describes them, they are alive, good, kind, generous, loving, etc. Is his picture of young people true or is it overly simple? Do young people "rip off" from each other?
8. Is Reich's picture of people over thirty accurate and fair?
9. How did the Vietnam War bring all of "Consciousness III's criticisms of society" into "sharp focus"?
10. How will the Consciousness III person relate to society? Will he withdraw from it or participate in it?
11. After having read Reich's article carefully and after having thought seriously about the young people you know, do you believe that a new consciousness does exist or is it merely the child of Reich's optimistic good nature?

12. What is the meaning of the title, "The Blueing of America"?
13. Peter and Brigitte Berger believe that both the political and cultural revolutions show a strong "disregard for the realities of technological society in general, and for the realities of class and power in America." What are the differences between a political revolution and a cultural one? Do they react differently to the "realities of technological society" and to "the realities of class and power in America"? What, according to the Bergers, are these realities?
14. Almost all the writers in this section express the view that the cultural revolution "has defined itself in diametric opposition to some of the basic values of bourgeois society," as the Bergers put it. Citing examples from your reading and from your own experience, explain what is meant by middle-class or bourgeois values. Then give examples of how the cultural revolution diametrically opposes these values.
15. What is the "counter-culture"? (Television newsmen, movie stars with long hair, English teachers, clergymen—all use the term, but few try to define it.) How strong or significant is the counter-culture on or near your campus? How do people who are into the counter-culture make a living—that is, if they do? Is the very phrase "make a living" anathema to counter-culture people?
16. Is Arnold Beichman simply trying to make the truth known or does he have a political purpose in writing his article, "Six 'Big Lies' About America"? Is his essay neutral and objective or biased and prejudiced?
17. Where do the "six lies" come from? Who spreads them?
18. What are "creative disorder" and "creative vandalism"? Are they ever justified?
19. In discussing lie number IV, Beichman describes the young critics of American workers who spread this lie; these young critics have a "thousand-dollar-hi-fi-stereo-Fiat-spider-Triumph-'Easy Rider'-acid head-Progressive Labor-pot life style," he writes. Hasn't he used the same kind of generalization and twisting of evidence in this description as that used by the people he is criticizing?
20. Beichman supports the two-party system. Why? Does it offer to American voters significantly different political perspectives?
21. What distinctions does Milton Mayer make betwen revolution and rebellion? Why does he place so much emphasis on the necessity for intelligence in the handling of power? What are his examples of how a revolution can "go down" if it isn't intelligent?
22. What does Milton Mayer mean by an "unanswerable argument"? What examples of unanswerable arguments does he offer? Would he agree with Arnold Beichman's list of the six "Big Lies" about America? With a part of the list?
23. What is Mayer's attitude toward "black studies" and other ethnic "culture" studies?
24. What, in Mayer's view, is the purpose of education? How have the universities been perverted in seeking their goals?

25. Mayer says that the unintelligent obey all laws, and, though he doesn't think highly of anarchy, he states that there are times when laws must be broken. What times? When should men disobey laws and become anarchists?
26. Throughout his essay Mayer speaks of "whitey" as the force against which the children's crusade must march. What is his attitude toward "whitey"? How does he describe or define "whitey"?
27. One popular explanation for the problems people over thirty have in communicating with those under thirty is summarized in the phrase "Generation Gap." What is Benjamin DeMott's opinion of this explanation? Why does he call it a "popular delusion"? What other popular explanations of why we live in difficult, confusing times does DeMott reject as being too simple?
28. DeMott writes that we have made at least four very important changes "in our sense of self, time, and dailiness." What are these four changes? (The four points are the structural cornerstones of his essay.)
29. One of DeMott's most intriguing insights is that today we desire to "have our experience in new ways." What does he mean? What examples does he give? Is it truly possible to change the way we have our experiences? With drugs perhaps? Or through mystical means? Is there a difference between an experience and a sensation?
30. According to DeMott, a wide range of products and materials are "manufactured in this country to meet the demand for self-transformation and extension of role. . . ." He calls the desire for new roles a dream of "plural selves." What examples of these products and materials for role extension does he give? Why, in your opinion, do some students wear the shoes or boots of the construction worker or cowboy, the vest and headband of an Indian, or the overalls of a farmer? Is it possible by trying to be many selves that we become nobodies, people with costumes but no real sense of self?
31. How can "the life of dailiness and habit, the life that lives us," as DeMott says, direct and suppress our "moral conscience and imagination"?
32. What, according to DeMott, have we learned from the war in Vietnam about the mental attitudes of "professionalism," specifically the professionalism of bureaucrats, diplomats, generals, and presidents?
33. One powerful point DeMott makes is that we seem to have become disenchanted with middle-class life, not because it is evil, but "because it is boring beyond measure." Is his observation correct? What is middle-class life? What is the evidence that people are becoming bored with it?
34. **Written Assignment:**
    a. Compile a list of bumper stickers or slogans that express opinions about the health of the nation—"America, Love It or Leave It," "Leagalize Dope," etc. A good list should provide an interesting index to the wide range of feelings, emotions, and tensions of the American people struggling to make their positions known. Be prepared to discuss your list in class.

b. Write an essay in which you explain the purpose and meaning of some of these slogans. You may wish to write about slogans that contradict each other, or you may write about ones that express similar attitudes or common concerns. As you organize your paper, keep in mind that slogans unite some people while alienating others. So consider what groups of people will be offended by the slogans and who will support them.

c. Write 10 bumper stickers that express your personal feelings about important areas of American life. Remember that slogans, in order to be effective, must be succinct and memorable. Be prepared to explain to the class how your slogans will affect various groups of people. What group of people do you want your slogans to influence? Can a bumper sticker influence anyone who does not already believe in the idea expressed by the sticker? Is it possible that stickers serve only as badges or symbols of belief, not as ways of communicating ideas?

II

1. Nor can we usefully consider our present system without confronting the consequences of capitalism within our individual selves. Corroding competition ("the pursuit of loneliness," in Philip Slater's words), the repression of women, of true masculine identity, and of the artistic, spiritual and feeling elements in all of us, all derive from our alienated concepts of work, from the obsession that we must brutalize ourselves and one another lest all motivation lapse.

   CHARLES A. REICH

2. Everywhere we look at present we see something new trying to be born. A pregnant, swollen world is writhing in labor, and everywhere untrained quacks are officiating as obstetricians. These quacks say that the only way the new can be born is by a Caesarean operation. They lust to rip the belly of the world open.

   ERIC HOFFER

3. "To save this town, we had to destroy this town."

   American Army Officer explaining how his unit saved a Vietnamese town.

4. This is the patent age of new inventions
   For killing bodies, and for saving souls,
   All propagated with the best intentions.

   LORD BYRON

5. Long hair and bare feet and unhomogenized peanut butter are not ultimate statements about society; they are, it must be repeated, metaphors. They stand for values now neglected or abused, such as personal autonomy and rediscovery of the natural.

   CHARLES A. REICH

6. MY COUNTRY, RIGHT OR WRONG—"An empty phrase, a silly phrase. . . . Each man must, for himself alone, decide what is right

and what is wrong, and which course is patriotic and which isn't. You cannot shirk this and be a man. To decide it against your convictions is to be an unqualified and inexcusable traitor, both to yourself and to your country, let men label you as they may. . . . Only when a Republic's *life* is in danger should a man uphold his government when it is in the wrong. There is no other time.

"This Republic's life is not in peril. This nation has sold its honor for a phrase. . . . The stupid phrase needed help and it got another one: 'Even if the war be wrong, we are in it and must fight it out; WE CANNOT RETIRE FROM IT WITHOUT DISHONOR.' Why, not even a burglar could have said it better. An inglorious peace is better than a dishonorable war."

MARK TWAIN denouncing the U. S. occupation of the Philippines in 1901

7. No one is fool enough to choose war instead of peace. For in peace sons bury fathers, but in war fathers bury sons.

HERODOTUS

8. Many of the people who were most hostile toward the machine have lived all their lives in an automated world where they had but to press a button or tinkle a bell and have squadrons of servants—animated machines—do their bidding.

ERIC HOFFER

9. The best case for democracy, and the best reason for having faith in the freedom of learning and teaching which it fosters, is that in the long history of civilization humanity has proved stronger than hate, and falsehood less enduring than truth.

CARL L. BECKER

10. All social progress is laid to discontent.

ABRAHAM LINCOLN

11. If you will help run our government in the American way, then there will never be danger of our government running America in the wrong way.

OMAR N. BRADLEY

12. Time is running out for us. The United States is fast becoming the sort of society our ancestors fled.

GORE VIDAL

13. I approve all instantaneous violence because it comes from a provocation, it's provoked by the evil deeds of others; but I am against all planned, advocated, reasoned violence.

JONAS MEKAS

14. And they came and said to him, "Teacher, we know that you are true, and care for no man; for you do not regard the position of men, but truly teach the way of God. Is it lawful to pay taxes to Caesar, or not? Should we pay them, or should we not?" But knowing their hypocrisy, he said to them, "Why put me to the test? Bring me a coin, and let me look

at it." And they brought one. And he said to them, "Whose likeness and inscription is this?" They said to him, "Caesar's." Jesus said to them, "Render to Caesar the things that are Caesar's, and to God the things that are God's."

MARK 12: 14-17

15. There are similarities between absolute power and absolute faith: a demand for absolute obedience, a readiness to attempt the impossible, a bias for simple solutions—to cut the knot rather than unravel it, the viewing of compromise as surrender. Both absolute power and absolute faith are instruments of dehumanization. Hence, absolute faith corrupts as absolutely as absolute power.

ERIC HOFFER

16. . . . art is always more radical and more diametrically opposed to oppression than any politics.

JONAS MEKAS

17. Since primitive times, virtually all religious or social systems have attempted to maintain themselves by forbidding free criticism and analysis either of existing institutions or of the doctrine that sustains them; of democracy alone is it the cardinal principle that free criticism and analysis by all and sundry is the highest virtue.

CARL L. BECKER

18. We cannot retreat from organized society, but we can begin searching for ways to make certain that organizations reflect both the requirements of technology and what we are learning about from our youth—the needs of nature and man.

CHARLES A. REICH

19. He who says, "This ruler is a fool, but when I am a ruler I will not be a fool" is already a fool.

MILTON MAYER

20. There is no such category as Negro rights or student rights because there is no such category as Negro or student. Either there are human rights or there are none.

MILTON MAYER

21. That government is best which governs least.

HENRY DAVID THOREAU

22. A politician on a campaign tour began his speech one night like this: "Ladies and gentlemen, it is truly one of the high points of my career to be in your great city of insert-the-name."

23. The dictionary of law is written by the bosses of order. Our moral dictionary says no hoisting from each other. To steal from a brother or sister is evil. To *not* steal from the institutions that are the pillars of the Pig Empire is equally immoral.

ABBIE HOFFMAN

24. Stealing is stealing, even if you call it revolution. It isn't the way to strike a blow against capitalism or anything else. Besides, it corrupts a movement and it corrupts the people in it. They even steal from one another.

    SEYMOUR MARTIN LIPSET

Related Readings:

BERRY, WENDELL, "Some Thoughts on Citizenship and Conscience in Honor of Don Pratt," page 247.

SECTION II Some Old Wounds—Black, Red, and Sore

Two deep, racial wounds scar our history as Americans, festering wounds that seem far from healed. Until these wounds are healed, America is not one indivisible nation.

Our forefathers seized this continent from the Indians who were already here, killed many of them, and herded the rest onto reservations. Then these Christian ancestors brought slaves to work the land they had "discovered." The slaves have been freed, and the Indians can leave the reservations, but, as the readings in this section disclose, this nation has not made full restitution for the sins of its forefathers. Blacks and Indians are discriminated against in the 1970's, though with greater subtlety than in the past. Blacks are frozen out of the labor market and shunted into ghettos, which are like modern reservations. The difference in their status from that of the Indians is the Indians own their reservations and most ghetto property does not belong to the local black residents. Indians can grab a piece of the American pie if they are willing to become imitators of white men, forsaking their own traditions, trading their culture in on the new white model. If they are not willing "to learn to become dark-brown white men with credit cards and crew-cut sensibilities" (Edward Abbey), they can become roadside red men, lifting a few bucks from the tourists, provided they are not overcome with shame.

Is there real hope for curing the old wounds, for fulfilling the promise of freedom and equality to all men? As blacks and Indians develop pride in their ancient cultures and great traditions, as they find authentic, not imitation, identities, the tensions wind tight between them and some white Americans, but the tensions result from strong feelings and not from apathy. No longer can white Americans pretend that "the others" are invisible; white America must see and contend with proud people who have different colored skins and different values. Some Americans, especially young ones, are waking up to the fact that black culture has much to teach them about living with grace, energy, and style; they are also aware that Indians can teach them how to live in peace with the environment. Indians have lived in harmony with the land for hundreds of years, leaving no terrible scars and no wastes.

Yes, there is hope—some.

Kids Running Past Hole in Fence. Courtesy of Susan Lazarus.

Frederick Douglass

July 4, 1852

What, to the American slave, is your Fourth of July? I answer:
a day that reveals to him, more than all other days in the year, the
gross injustice and cruelty to which he is the constant victim. To him,
your celebration is a sham; your boasted liberty, an unholy license;
your national greatness, swelling vanity; your sounds of rejoicing are
empty and heartless; your denunciation of tyrants, brass-fronted im-
pudence; your shouts of liberty and equality, hollow mockery; your 1
prayers and hymns, your sermons and thanksgivings, with all your religious parade and solemnity, are, to Him, mere bombast, fraud, deception, impiety, and hypocrisy—a thin veil to cover up crimes which would
disgrace a nation of savages. There is not a nation of savages. There
is not a nation on the earth guilty of practices more shocking and bloody
than are the people of the United States at this very hour.

Go where you may, research where you will, roam through all the
monarchies and despotisms of the Old World, travel through South
America, search out every abuse, and when you have found the last, 2
lay your facts by the side of the everyday practices of this nation, and
you will say with me that, for revolting barbarity and shameless hypocrisy, America reigns without a rival.

Excerpt from a speech delivered in Rochester, New York, on July 4, 1852.

Frederick Douglass

Learning to Read

Established in my new home in Baltimore, I was not very long in perceiving that in picturing to myself what was to be my life there, my imagination had painted only the bright side; and that the reality had its dark shades as well as its light ones. The open country which had been so much to me, was all shut out. Walled in on every side by towering brick buildings, the heat of the summer was intolerable to me, and the hard brick pavements almost blistered my feet. If I ventured out on to the streets, new and strange objects glared upon me at every step, and startling sounds greeted my ears from all directions. My country eyes and ears were confused and bewildered. Troops of hostile boys pounced upon me at every corner. They chased me, and called me "Eastern-Shore man," till really I almost wished myself back on the Eastern Shore. My new mistress happily proved to be all she had seemed, and in her presence I easily forgot all outside annoyances. Mrs. Sophia was naturally of an excellent disposition—kind, gentle, and cheerful. The supercilious contempt for the rights and feelings of others, and the petulance and bad humor which generally characterized slaveholding ladies, were all quite absent from her manner and bearing toward me. She had never been a slaveholder—a thing then quite unusual at the South—but had depended almost entirely upon her own industry for a living. To this fact the dear lady no doubt owed the excellent preservation of her natural goodness of heart, for slavery could change a saint into a sinner, and an angel into a demon. I hardly knew how to behave towards "Miss Sopha," as I used to call Mrs. Hugh Auld. I could not approach her even as I had formerly approached Mrs. Thomas Auld. Why should I hang down my head, and speak with bated breath, when there was no pride to scorn me, no coldness to repel me, and no hatred to inspire me with fear? I therefore soon came to regard her as something more akin to a mother than a slaveholding mistress. So far from deeming it impudent in a slave to look her straight in the face, she seemed ever to say, "look up, child; don't be afraid." The sailors belonging to the sloop esteemed it a great privilege to be the bearers of parcels or messages to her, for whenever

From the book *Life and Times of Frederick Douglass.*

they came, they were sure of a most kind and pleasant reception. If little Thomas was her son, and her most dearly loved child, she made me something like his half-brother in her affections. If dear Tommy was exalted to a place on his mother's knee, "Feddy" was honored by a place at the mother's side. Nor did the slave-boy lack the caressing strokes of her gentle hand, soothing him into the consciousness that, though motherless, he was not friendless. Mrs. Auld was not only kind-hearted, but remarkably pious; frequent in her attendance of public worship, much given to reading the Bible, and to chanting hymns of praise when alone. Mr. Hugh was altogether a different character. He cared very little about religion; knew more of the world and was more a part of the world, than his wife. He set out doubtless to be, as the world goes, a respectable man, and to get on by becoming a successful ship-builder, in that city of ship-building. This was his ambition, and it fully occupied him. I was of course of very little consequence to him, and when he smiled upon me, as he sometimes did, the smile was borrowed from his lovely wife, and like all borrowed light, was transient, and vanished with the source whence it was derived. Though I must in truth characterize Master Hugh as a sour man of forbidding appearance, it is due to him to acknowledge that he was never cruel to me, according to the notion of cruelty in Maryland. During the first year or two, he left me almost exclusively to the management of his wife. She was law-giver. In hands so tender as hers, and in the absence of the cruelties of the plantation, I became both physically and mentally much more sensitive, and a frown from my mistress caused me far more suffering than had Aunt Katy's hardest cuffs. Instead of the cold, damp floor of my old master's kitchen, I was on carpets; for the corn bag in winter, I had a good straw bed, well furnished with covers; for the coarse corn meal in the morning, I had good bread and mush occasionally; for my old tow-linen shirt, I had good clean clothes. I was really well off. My employment was to run of errands, and to take care of Tommy; to prevent his getting in the way of carriages, and to keep him out of harm's way generally. So for a time every thing went well. I say for a time, because the fatal poison of irresponsible power, and the natural influence of slave customs, were not very long in making their impression on the gentle and loving disposition of my excellent mistress. She regarded me at first as a child, like any other. This was the natural and spontaneous thought; afterwards, when she came to consider me as property, our relations to each other changed, but a nature so noble as hers could not instantly become perverted, and it took several years before the sweetness of her temper was wholly lost.

The frequent hearing of my mistress reading the Bible aloud, for she often read aloud when her husband was absent, awakened my curiosity in respect to this *mystery of reading*, and roused in me the desire to learn. Up to this time I had known nothing whatever of this wonderful art, and my ignorance and inexperience of what it could do for me, as well as my confidence in my mistress, emboldened me to ask her to teach me to read. With an unconsciousness and inexperience equal to my own, she readily consented, and in an incredibly short time, by her kind assistance, I had mastered the alphabet and could spell words of three or four letters. My mistress seemed almost as proud of my progress as if I had been her own child, and supposing that her husband would be as well pleased, she made no secret of what she was doing for me. Indeed, she exultingly told him of the aptness of her pupil, and of her intention to persevere in teaching me, as she felt her duty to do, at least to read the Bible. And here arose the first dark cloud over my Baltimore prospects, the precursor of chilling blasts and drenching storms. Master Hugh was astounded beyond measure, and probably for the first time proceeded to unfold to his wife the true philosophy of the slave system, and the peculiar rules necessary in the nature of the case to be observed in the management of human chattels. Of course he forbade her to give me any further instruction, telling her in the first place that to do so was unlawful, as it was also unsafe; "for," said he, 'if you give a nigger an inch he will take an ell. Learning will spoil the best nigger in the world. If he learns to read the Bible it will forever unfit him to be a slave. He should know nothing but the will of his master, and learn to obey it. As to himself, learning will do him no good, but a great deal of harm, making him disconsolate and unhappy. If you teach him how to read, he'll want to know how to write, and this accomplished, he'll be running away with himself." Such was the tenor of Master Hugh's oracular exposition; and it must be confessed that he very clearly comprehended the nature and the requirements of the relation of master and slave. His discourse was the first decidedly anti-slavery lecture to which it had been my lot to listen. Mrs. Auld evidently felt the force of what he said, and like an obedient wife, began to shape her course in the direction indicated by him. The effect of his words *on me* was neither slight nor transitory. His iron sentences, cold and harsh, sunk like heavy weights deep into my heart, and stirred up within me a rebellion not soon to be allayed. This was a new and special revelation, dispelling a painful mystery against which my youthful understanding had struggled, and struggled in vain, to wit, the white man's power to perpetuate the enslavement of the black man. "Very well," thought I. "Knowledge unfits a child to be a slave." I instinctively assented to the proposition, and from that moment I understood the direct pathway from slavery to freedom. It was just what I needed, and it came to me at a time and from a source whence I least expected it. Of course I was greatly saddened at the thought of losing the assistance of my kind mistress, but the information so instantly derived to some extent compensated me for the loss I had sustained in this direction. Wise as Mr. Auld was, he underrated my comprehension, and had little idea of the use to which I was capable of putting the impressive lesson he was giving to his wife. He wanted me to be a slave; I had already voted against that on the home plantation of Col. Lloyd. That which he most loved I most hated; and the very determination which he expressed to keep me in ignorance only rendered me the more resolute to seek intelligence. In learning to read, therefore, I am not sure that I do not owe quite as much to the opposition of my master as to the kindly assistance of my amiable mistress. I acknowledge the benefit rendered me by the one, and by the other, believing that but for my mistress I might have grown up in ignorance.

Growing in Knowledge.

I lived in the family of Mr. Auld, at Baltimore, seven years, during which time, as the almanac makers say of the weather, my condition was variable. The most interesting feature of my history here, was my learning to read and write under somewhat marked disadvantages. In attaining this knowledge I was compelled to resort to indirections by no means congenial to my nature, and which were really humiliating to my sense of candor and uprightness. My mistress, checked in her
benevolent designs toward me, not only ceased instructing me herself, 3
but set her face as a flint against my learning to read by any means. It is due to her to say, however, that she did not adopt this course in all its stringency at first. She either thought it unnecessary, or she lacked the depravity needed to make herself forget at once my human nature. She was, as I have said, naturally a kind and tender-hearted woman, and in the humanity of her heart and the simplicity of her mind, she set out, when I first went to live with her, to treat me as she supposed one human being ought to treat another.

Nature never intended that men and women should be either slaves or slaveholders, and nothing but rigid training long persisted in, can perfect the character of the one or the other. Mrs. Auld was singularly deficient in the qualities of a slaveholder. It was no easy matter for her to think or to feel that the curly-headed boy, who stood by her side, and even leaned on her lap, who was loved by little Tommy, and who loved little Tommy in turn, sustained to her only the relation of a chattel. I was more than that; she felt me to be more than that. I could talk and sing; I could laugh and weep; I could reason and remember; I could love and hate. I was human, and she, dear lady, 4
knew and felt me to be so. How could she then treat me as a brute without a mighty struggle with all the noblest powers of her soul. That struggle came, and the will and power of the husband was victorious. Her noble soul was overcome, and he who wrought the wrong was injured in the fall no less than the rest of the household. When I went into that household, it was the abode of happiness and contentment. The wife and mistress there was a model of affection and tenderness. Her fervent piety and watchful uprightness made it impossible to see her without thinking and feeling "that woman is a Christian." There was no sorrow nor suffering for which she had not a tear, and there was no innocent joy for which she had not a smile. She had bread for

the hungry, clothes for the naked, and comfort for every mourner who came within her reach. But slavery soon proved its ability to divest her of these excellent qualities, and her home of its early happiness. Conscience cannot stand much violence. Once thoroughly injured, who is he who can repair the damage? If it be broken toward the slave on Sunday, it will be toward the master on Monday. It cannot long endure such shocks. It must stand unharmed, or it does not stand at all. As my condition in the family waxed bad, that of the family waxed no better. The first step in the wrong direction was the violence done to nature and to conscience, in arresting the benevolence that would have enlightened my young mind. In ceasing to instruct me, my mistress had to seek to justify herself *to* herself, and once consenting to take sides in such a debate, she was compelled to hold her position. One needs little knowledge of moral philosophy to see where she inevitably landed. She finally became even more violent in her opposition to my learning to read than was Mr. Auld himself. Nothing now appeared to make her more angry than seeing me, seated in some nook or corner, quietly reading a book or newspaper. She would rush at me with the utmost fury, and snatch the book or paper from my hand, with something of the wrath and consternation which a traitor might be supposed to feel on being discovered in a plot by some dangerous spy. The conviction once thoroughly established in her mind, that education and slavery were incompatible with each other, I was most narrowly watched in all my movements. If I remained in a separate room from the family for any considerable length of time, I was sure to be suspected of having a book, and was at once called to give an account of myself. But this was too late: the first and never-to-be-retraced step had been taken. Teaching me the alphabet had been the "inch" given, I was now waiting only for the opportunity to "take the ell."

Filled with the determination to learn to read at any cost, I hit upon many expedients to accomplish that much desired end. The plan which I mainly adopted, and the one which was the most successful, was that of using my young white playmates, with whom I met on the streets, as teachers. I used to carry almost constantly a copy of Webster's spelling-book in my pocket, and when sent on errands, or when play-time was allowed me, I would step aside with my young friends and take a lesson in spelling. I am greatly indebted to these boys—Gustavus Dorgan, Joseph Bailey, Charles Farity, and William Cosdry.

Although slavery was a delicate subject, and very cautiously talked about among grown up people in Maryland, I frequently talked about it, and that very freely, with the white boys. I would sometimes say to them, while seated on a curbstone or a cellar door, "I wish I could be free, as you will be when you get to be men." "You will be free, you know, as soon as you are twenty-one, and can go where you like, but I am a slave for life. Have I not as good a right to be free as you have?" Words like these, I observed, always troubled them; and I had

no small satisfaction in drawing out from them, as I occasionally did,
that fresh and bitter condemnation of slavery which ever springs from
nature unseared and unperverted. Of all conscience, let me have those
to deal with, which have not been seared and bewildered with the
cares and perplexities of life. I do not remember ever to have met
with a *boy* while I was in slavery, who defended the system, but I do
remember many times, when I was consoled by them, and by them 6
encouraged to hope that something would yet occur by which I would
be made free. Over and over again, they have told me that "they believed I had as good a right to be free as *they* had," and that "they did
not believe God ever made any one to be a slave." It is easily seen that
such little conversations with my play-fellows had no tendency to
weaken my love of liberty, nor to render me contented as a slave.

When I was about thirteen years old, and had succeeded in learning to read, every increase of knowledge, especially anything respecting the free states, was an additional weight to the almost intolerable burden of my thought—"*I am a slave for life.*" To my bondage I could see no end. It was a terrible reality, and I shall never be able to tell how sadly that thought chafed my young spirit. Fortunately, or unfortunately, I had earned a little money in blacking boots for some gentlemen, with which I purchased of Mr. Knight, on Thames street, what was then a very popular school book, viz., "The Columbian Orator," for which I paid fifty cents. I was led to buy this book by hearing some little boys say they were going to learn some pieces out of it for the exhibition. This volume was indeed a rich treasure, and every opportunity afforded me, for a time, was spent in diligently perusing it. Among much other interesting matter, that which I read again and again with unflagging satisfaction was a short dialogue between a master and his slave. The slave is represented as having been recaptured in a second attempt to run away; and the master opens the dialogue with an upbraiding speech, charging the slave with ingratitude, and demanding to know what he has to say in his own defense. Thus upbraided and thus called upon to reply, the slave rejoins that he knows how little anything that he can say will avail, seeing that he is completely in the hands of his owner; and with noble resolution, calmly says, "I submit to my fate." Touched by the slave's answer, the master insists upon his further speaking, and recapitulates the many acts of kindness which he has performed toward the slave, and tells him he is permitted to speak for himself. Thus invited, the quondam slave made a spirited defense of himself, and thereafter the whole argument for and against slavery is brought out. The master was vanquished at every turn in the argument, and appreciating the fact he generously and meekly emancipates the slave, with his best wishes for his prosperity. It is unnecessary to say that a dialogue with such an origin and such an end, read by me when every nerve of my being was in revolt at my own condition as a slave, affected me most powerfully. I could not help feeling that the day might yet come, when the well-directed answers made by the slave to the master, in this instance, would find a counterpart in my own experience. This, however, was not all the fanaticism which I found in the Columbian Orator. I met there one of Sheridan's mighty speeches, on the subject of Catholic Emancipation, Lord Chatham's speech on the American War, and speeches by the Great William Pitt, and by Fox. These were all choice documents to me, and I read them over and over again, with an interest ever increasing, because it was ever gaining in intelligence; for the more I read them the better I understood them. The reading of these speeches add much to my limited stock of language, and enabled me to give tongue to many interesting thoughts which had often flashed through my mind and died away for want of words in which to give them utterance. The mighty power and heart-searching directness of truth penetrating the heart of a slave-holder, compelling him to yield up his earthly interests to the claims of eternal justice, were finely illustrated in the dialogue, and from the speeches of Sheridan I got a bold and powerful denunciation of oppression and a most brilliant vindication of the rights of man. Here was indeed a noble acquisition. If I had ever wavered under the consideration that the Almighty, in some way, had ordained slavery and willed my enslavement for his own glory, I wavered no longer. I had now penetrated to the secret of all slavery and all oppression, and had ascertained their true foundation to be in the pride, the power, and the avarice of man. With a book in my hand so redolent of the principles of liberty, with a perception of my own human nature and the facts of my past and present experience, I was equal to a contest with the religious advocates of slavery, whether white or black, for blindness in this matter was not confined to the white people. I have met many good religious colored people at the south, who were under the delusion that God required them to submit to slavery and to wear their chains with meekness and humility. I could entertain no such nonsense as this, and I quite lost my patience when I found a colored man weak enough to believe such stuff. Nevertheless, eager as I was to partake of the tree of knowledge, its fruits were bitter as well as sweet. "Slaveholders," thought I, "are only a band of successful robbers, who, leaving their own homes, went into Africa for the purpose of stealing and reducing my people to slavery." I loathed them as the meanest and the most wicked of men. And as I read, behold! the very discontent so graphically predicted by Master Hugh had already come upon me. I was no longer the light-hearted gleesome boy, full of mirth and play, as when I landed in Baltimore. Light had penetrated the moral dungeon where I had lain, and I saw the bloody whip for my back, and the iron chain for my feet, and my *good kind* master, he was the author of my situation. The revelation haunted me, stung me, and made me gloomy and miserable. As I writhed under the sting and torment of this knowledge I almost envied my fellow slaves their stupid indifference. It opened my eyes to the horrible pit, and revealed the teeth of the frightful dragon that was ready to pounce upon me; but alas, it opened no way for my escape. I wished myself a beast, a bird, anything rather than a slave. I was wretched and gloomy beyond my ability to describe. This everlasting thinking distressed and tormented me; and yet there was no getting rid of this subject of my thoughts. Liberty, as the inestimable birthright of every man, converted every object into an asserter of this right. I heard it in every sound, and saw it in every object. It was ever present to torment me with a sense of my wretchedness. The more beautiful and charming were the smiles of nature, the more horrible and desolate was my condition. I saw nothing without seeing it, and I heard nothing without hearing it. I do not exaggerate when I say it looked at me in every star, it smiled in every calm, breathed in every wind, and moved in every storm. I have no doubt that my state of mind had something to do with the change in treatment which my mistress adopted towards me. I can easily believe that my leaden, downcast, and disconsolate look was very offensive to her. Poor lady! She did not understand my trouble, and I I could not tell her. Could I have made her acquainted with the real state of my mind and given her the reasons therefor, it might have been well for both of us. As it was, her abuse fell upon me like the blows of the false prophet upon his ass; she did not know that an angel stood in the way. Nature made us friends, but slavery had made us enemies. My interests were in a direction opposite to hers, and we both had our private thoughts and plans. She aimed to keep me ignorant, and I resolved to *know,* although knowledge only increased my misery. My feelings were not the result of any marked cruelty in the treatment I received; they sprung from the consideration of my being a slave at all. It was *slavery,* not its mere *incidents* I hated. I had been cheated. I saw through the attempt to keep me in ignorance. I saw that slaveholders would have gladly made me believe that they were merely acting under the authority of God in making a slave of me and in making slaves of others, and I felt to them as to robbers and deceivers. The feeding and clothing me well could not atone for taking my liberty from me. The smiles of my mistress could not remove the deep sorrow that dwelt in my young bosom. Indeed, these came in time but to deepen my sorrow. She had changed, and the reader will see that I had changed too. We were both victims to the same overshadowing evil, *she* as mistress, I as slave. I will not censure her harshly.

Jesse Jackson

When Whites Are Unemployed, It's Called a Depression

Interviewed by David Frost

FROST: What is your most precious memory of the late Martin Luther King? Is there one particular moment that you spent with him that you cherish more than any other?

JACKSON: I guess I would have to say at least two moments. One would have to be growing up in South Carolina and not expecting anything except the conditions as they were. We just accepted the fact that we were to go to the inferior schools, we were to sit in the back of the bus, we were to pass by the water fountains and act as if we were not thirsty, or go downtown to see a movie and not really see it. We had accepted our lot, and at that time the only answer was that we were academically and biologically inferior. And here began to arise a man out of the even deeper South, the cradle of the Confederacy, with a Ph.D., who was far more intelligent and articulate than his adversaries, and who fought in such a way that nobody could argue with his program for black liberation. People could only argue with the timing and how he applied his techniques. So the experience of a redefinition of myself came as a small child. Thus, I grew up in the generation that had the privilege to operate in the shadows of Dr. King.

And perhaps some of the other, more precious moments would have to do with the many staff meetings we had where he would not only lay out programs in terms of where we were going, but he had time to talk with us personally about our own futures and careers and involvements. The experiences were too great and too many to tie it down to one single experience, to say the least. But in the midst of a conversation with him when the assassin's bullet struck him down was the most traumatic moment that I've ever experienced; but other than that, it would be very difficult to tie down one particular experience.

FROST: Mrs. Coretta Scott King said she would like a fuller investigation into the person or persons responsible for the assassination of Martin Luther King. Are you convinced it was one man, James Earl Ray?

JACKSON: It just couldn't have been one man. But the reascn I have not personally been so caught up in pursuing who did it, the real issue—and I think it's the way Dr. King would perhaps have dealt with it—is not *who* killed Dr. King. *What* killed Dr. King? In terms of the atmosphere, it's obvious that the plan, the man being able to escape, where they found the man, and other bits and pieces of evidence indicate that far more people were involved. So it was a broader conspiracy, but there was a certain atmosphere—there *is* a certain atmosphere—in the nation that gives sanction to ambush and assassination of people who are not in the tide of agreeing with America yum-yum and some of her policies now that are in conflict with the best interests of mankind. I mean, we look at a nation of two hundred million people, and the top 1 percent of the population controls more than 26 percent of the wealth, and the bottom 20 percent less than 5.4 percent of the wealth. A nation that would come up nine years ago with two programs—one to go to the moon and one to rid the nation of poverty—and nine years later 54 billion dollars have been spent to get two men to the moon, to get two boxes of rocks of moon dust, and only 5.7 billion for forty million hungry people, twenty-eight million of whom are white. The nation is caught up in this kind of absurd contradiction, and we find that the federal budget just last year was 157 billion dollars, and 108 billion was spent for past, present, and future wars—70 percent. And only 19 billion for health, education, and welfare collectively. So a nation that's 70 percent inclined toward killing and only 12 percent inclined toward healing indeed has some real sicknesses and some major adjustments to make, and to speak out against that nation is really to speak in its best interest and for its health. But a climate is set now that when you do speak out for the nation and against its sickness, you simply fall prey to those who are so sick that they want to be quiet in the face of this atrocity.

FROST: If you think there's that sort of mood in the land, do you fear for your own life?

JACKSON: Certainly one with a wife and children has to take it into consideration. However, one cannot really significantly involve himself in this movement of human liberation unless he really comes to grips philosophically, personally, and religiously, existentially, with money, jail cells, and death. If one can get the power to move on in spite of the monetary temptations not to move on, if one can move on in spite of jail cells that are put in your path as tyranny, if one can move on in spite of the likelihood of an early death, then one stands in a position to create new power alternatives. I mean, those of us who are Christians have a real choice between following Methuselah, who lived nine hundred years about nothing, and Jesus, who died at thirty-three about something and perhaps could have lived to have been as old as Methuselah. So in one of Dr. King's last speeches, in which he spoke of the quality of life, and it's not so much how old you are but how well you've lived the life that you had a chance to live, and given the fact that so many boys are dying at eighteen, about far less than liberating people, it just does not really matter.

FROST: How old are you now?

JACKSON: I was twenty-eight last week.

FROST: Hold old do you think you'll live to be?

JACKSON: That's a very difficult thing to say, except, needless to say, those of us in the movement are so aware of the fact that death is almost imminent for those that persistently speak out on major issues, I guess the only difference is that at one time in my life I perhaps would have projected working on a certain job twenty years, and then where I was going to work out a retirement program. And now it's day to day.

But if I lived day to day in fear, my fear would make me die a thousand deaths. And I can't spend my energy on dying. I have to spend my energy on living. So I really don't take it that much into account.

FROST: What would you say is the most frightening experience that has happened to you in your life?

JACKSON: Perhaps most frightening was the point at which I became sensitive to the black-white conflict and the absolute dominance and military power of whites and the instilled fear that blacks have developed as a part of their—

FROST: What was the moment when that happened?

JACKSON: Well, I was about five years of age and went down the street to a store. We used to play with this white fellow who owned the local store. His name was Jack. And all of us used to run in and out and buy our candy and our Mary Jane and our cookies. And he'd play with us, and his people owned the store, and he worked. So this particular day I went into the store, and I was in a big hurry, so I whistled. I said, "Jack," I said, "I got to have my candy now." I whistled. He wheeled around and drew a .45 in my face and cocked the guard and cursed and told me to never whistle at him again, that that was not my place. The store was full of black people, but nobody acted as if they heard or saw Jack. And the first thing went into my mind was, "I can't tell my parents. Because if I tell them, they probably would be killed too." Which means that psychologically, even at five years of age, a certain realization of black fear and intimidation in the face of white military suppression, the fact that my parents were subjected at a certain angle to it, and that I had to live in the face of it set a certain indelible imprint upon my mind. But it was only when I began to get closer with Dr. King personally and philosophically that I began to deal with what all black people in America face at one level or another. You just don't say certain things in the South and live. You just don't say certain things and get a chance to work. You just don't do certain things and live to be twenty-one. And when James Meredith started to march against fear in Mississippi and many people reacted by saying that it was a useless march, James Meredith was dealing with a very basic reality of black people in America living under that kind of tyranny where fear is instilled very early. And rather than coming to grips with that fear and using courage as an antidote, we live much of our lives escaping that fear.

So he was asked while in the South, "Why don't you drink the water downtown?" He said, "Because I'm not thirsty." They said, "Why don't you eat downtown?" He said, "Well, I ate before I left home." "Why don't you go to the movies?" "I'm not interested." Which are lies that come in the face of the fear. That fear usually starts at a very early age and you become so comfortable in the face of it until you walk by the water fountains, and you aren't thirsty, and you walk by the food, and you really don't get hungry because you close off that portion of your mind.

If there's anything new now, it's that we're moving up now, and we're moving up so much so until courage has told fear to get behind, and we're moving on. And so our theme song, Billy Taylor's *I Wish I Knew How It Felt to Be Free*, becomes a different kind of song than *Trouble Don't Last Always, Sometimes I Feel Like a Motherless Child* or sad and sorrowful songs that were sounding pitiful. Now there's a yearning to be free against a yearning to just survive.

FROST: Jesse, what would you say is the state of your movement now? I mean, you're carrying on with Operation Breadbasket, aren't you, and you're getting into new things as well.

JACKSON: When I grew up in the South we used to talk about how long we could work and how hard we could work without giving out. Now we talk about getting independent. For a long time, we spoke of the movement in purely moral and social terms. We thought that where we lived was a ghetto based upon a social presupposition and that we were based or judged on whether we were good or evil, moral or immoral. The fact is that what is known as the ghetto—called that by the sociologists—is really a colony that is built upon an economic prerogative rather than a social one. So blacks really are seen as economic entities, rather than moral agents. We're seen as profits or losses, assets or liabilities.

And when one looks at the structure of the colony, it is there for four very basic purposes. One, we represent the margin of profit of every major business in the nation. Economically, we have a position of power, once it's collected, that's greater, relative to the American economy, than China, Russia, or the European Common Market.

We are the chief labor base. We are called lazy often, but we know better. I mean, we make cotton king and we hold tobacco road. And hew out the sides of mountains. And we've wanted to work so bad we've shined other people's shoes and cleaned other people's houses when our own was unkept. So we know that saying that we are lazy is just a rich man's scapegoat for not really dealing with the fact of a basic redistribution of wealth that's necessary if peace is to come to the nation.

Thirdly, we have been the soldiers in the time of war, died disproportionately in every major war. But fourthly, we have been that community that has stood between white America and real true bloody revolution. What I mean is that whites who cannot compete in mainstream white America usurp the executive jobs in the area where we live. The car distributorships—white. The banks, insurance companies, the construction companies, the construction workers, the builders, the school principals, the police.

My real thought is that when we're unemployed, we're called lazy; when the whites are unemployed it's called a depression, which is the psycho-linguistics of racism.

(*Laughter*)

Now, what is beginning to happen if one watches the construction confrontations around the nation, blacks who've been lazy have got a movement going and saying, "We want to work." And the whites are fighting, interestingly enough, over the right to work in the community where we live, and yet will not let us live in the community where they live. Because of the confusion, many whites think eliminating blacks will be the solution to their problems. And many blacks in response think eliminating whites will be their solution. But the real solution is the expansion of the economy at the base, where the law of supply and demand is not used to exploit people, and both groups can have a job and income, where neither will be eliminated.

FROST: I read one quote of yours where you were saying that instead of conflict between the poor black and the poor white, they should get together, and there should be a conflict between the haves and the have-nots. Can you see that happening? Can you see a sort of alliance of poor people, black and white?

JACKSON: Well, it's really happening by negation rather than affirmation. That is, we're backing into that relationship rather than going on into it because we really see it clearly.

Racism as a form of skin worship, and as a sickness and a pathological anxiety for America, is so great, until the poor whites—rather than fighting for jobs or for education—fight to remain pink and fight to remain white. And therefore they cannot see an alliance with people that they feel to be inherently inferior. But because of the tremendous job shortage at the base of the economy now, they're having to come together—the poor are—in spite of themselves. We took this tour around Illinois last year and found these poor white mothers who were caught in the same bind that poor black mothers were caught in, and in that their drive to survive is stronger than their drive to be moral, ethical, or white. The survival is really melting us into a new kind of relationship.

Kids with Dog. Courtesy of Jerry Newirth.

Al Calloway

An Introduction to Soul

Soul is sass, man. Soul is arrogance. Soul is walkin' down the street in a way that says, "This is me, muh-fuh!" Soul is that nigger whore comin' along . . . ja . . . ja . . . ja, and walkin' like she's sayin', "Here it is, baby. Come an' get it" Soul is bein' true to yourself, to what is *you*. Now, hold on: soul is . . . that . . . uninhibited . . . no, *extremely* uninhibited self . . . expression that goes into practically every Negro endeavor. That's soul. And there's swagger in it, man. It's exhibitionism, and it's effortless. Effortless. You don't need to put it on; it just comes out.—*Claude Brown*

When I walk on Eighth Avenue, man, I see rhythms I don't see downtown. *Polyrhythms.* You look at one cat, he may be doin' bop, bop-bop bop, bop-bop, and another one goin' *bop*-de-bop, *de*-bop. Beautiful, man. Those are *beautiful* people. Yeah. But when I go downtown to Thirty-fourth Street, everybody's walkin' the same, you dig? They don't put themselves into it. Their walk tells you nothing about who they are. *Polyrhythms.* That's what it is. Like a flower garden in a breeze. The roses swing a little bit from side to side, kind of stiff, not too much. The lilacs swing wide, slow, lazy, not in a hurry. A blade of grass wiggles. It's cause they're all different and they're bein' themselves. Polyrhythms, like on Eighth Avenue. That's soul.—*Al Calloway*

Soul Is Motion and Sound.

It is stomping and clapping with the gospel music of the First Tabernacle of Deliverance (Spiritual), American Orthodox Catholic Church on Harlem's One Hundred Twenty-fifth Street, and boogalooing the Funky Broadway to the Memphis gospel soul blues of Otis Redding while walking down the street. Soul is "Doin' the Thing" with the church-oriented funky jazz of Horace Silver and just *moving* back down home with John Lee Hooker's gutbucket folk blues. Soul is being natural, telling it like it is. In the plantation fields and later the church, black

people were allowed to keep *some* form of their self-expression going. The beautiful simple poetry of spiritual work songs like *Steal Away*—let's sneak back to the "Good Ship Jesus" and sail all the way home—is part of the blues of today, just as the spiritual ecstasy in a Yoruba Temple in West Africa is akin to what is felt in the soul-stirring Sanctified and Baptist churches of America's black ghettos. When Mahalia Jackson sings, the gospel and the blues of Bessie Smith become the *essence* of soul. Ray Charles throws his head back and shouts, "Oh, yeah!" and transmits an inner feeling of goodness. When you've heard it like that, you *know* you have been moved. Then he comes in with, "Don't it make you want to feel all right," and it's like everything has been unraveled and you just lay in there and groove. Ray Charles turns 3
you on. So does Aretha Franklin and "Mister Soul" James Brown. On a warm day in Harlem one can see and feel an infinite variety of rhythms. People stand on tenement stoops and on the sidewalks and sway to jukebox music here, WLIB and WWRL radio there. Some get caught up in front of record shops and just soul dance like they want to. All around you, Watusi, Boston Monkey, Shing-a-ling, Karate, Boogaloo, The Pearl, the Funky Broadway. Storefront-church tambourines ring and two young men in red shirts walk down the street, one playing a sheepskin drum and the other a cowbell or a fife. A saxophone riffs, a trumpet wails, and then there's the shout. The black poet LeRoi Jones calls it "Ka'ba. . . . Our world is full of sound/our world is more lovely than anyone's. . . ."

Soul Heroes.

At Forty-third Street and Langley Avenue, on Chicago's South Side, amid the many storefront churches and dilapidated tenements, stands a soulful monument to African-American folk heroes past and present. Last summer, Billy Abernathy, his wife, and at least a score of other artists and draftsmen within the black community formed the Organization of Black American Culture (O.B.A.C.) and got the building's owner, who happens to be black, to consent to the creation of the revolutionary and historical hand-painted mural. Folk heroes who have made great contributions to the worlds of music, sports and literature adorn the Wall: men like Marcus Garvey, Malcolm X and Stokely Carmichael; men who have steered large masses of black people away from 4
the "assimilation complex" bag that DuBois talked about and guided them to the positive course of *digging* themselves. The Wall is blessed with Dr. DuBois' image too. The great innovators of American music, Charlie Parker, Thelonious Monk, Max Roach, Ornette Coleman and the late John Coltrane, share a large portion of the Wall, along with Sassy Sarah Vaughn and Nina Simone. The mighty men, Muhammad Ali and Wilt Chamberlain, are there because they do their thing with a lot of style, and that's important. The real genius of the Wall is that it

generates African-American self-pride. No matter what happens to Chicago, the Wall is sure to stand.

The Nitty–Gritty of Soul.

There's a little piece of real estate in Harlem called Harlem Square, and on and about its four corners the curious, the intellectual and the political meet and exchange ideas. The center of activity there is one of Harlem's landmarks, Michaux's National Memorial African Bookstore. Marcus Garvey, Adam Clayton Powell Jr., Malcolm X and other soul heroes were heard by thousands at many a mass rally that took place in front of Michaux's. Inside the bookshop, every inch of available space is jammed with books by and about black folk. In the back room, where some of the soul heroes sat and wrote their speeches, the walls are crowded with photographs, paintings and drawings of great people of color. Every wall is a wall of respect. It is in Michaux's bookstore ("The House of Common Sense and Home of Proper Propaganda") that you learn about African musicians long ago who mastered the art of circular breathing and the simultaneous playing of instruments made out of elephant tusks and antelope horns. When you *see* the blind soul brother Roland Kirk playing his Manzello (the first saxophone), tenor sax and Stritch at the same time, and frequently blowing long sheets of sound without a breath, you are witnessing soul, baby.—One thing is certain: soul would be nowhere without the great savior, soul food. Black people brought to the Americas a tradition of how to make good food. Being close to the earth was their nature, and it was not difficult for them to find beans and greens that were good and to make good bread out of corn and crackling. It was a good thing that they knew this too, because *the man* would work them in the fields from sunup till dusk and sometimes they had other chores after that. On top of which they had to go all out for self, or the plantocracy would have starved them to death. When it came down to the hog, the planters didn't know anything except ham, bacon, spareribs and chops. The rest of it was no good, or so they thought, and the slaves copped it. They came up with pig tails, pig knuckles, ham hocks, hog maws, pig ears, snout, neck bones, chitlins, tripe and sowbelly. By the time fried or smothered chicken (The Gospel Bird) became a delicacy for special Sundays, black people were making candied yams, sweet-potato pie and fruit cobblers from the vegetables and fruits that they grew in their little patches or gathered from around. Traditionally, black people have congregated at the church for social and spiritual life, because church organization was (is) the only form allowed them. So when the sisters get together with those pots you can bet your life the food's going to be good. If you go into the Victory Restaurant on One Hundred Sixteenth Street in Harlem, you'll dig Bishop Shelton's sisters, with their natural hair and little caps and no makeup and floor-length gowns, serving soul food from eight in the morning till midnight. A plate of knuckles, black eyes and rice, a thick slice of corn bread, a glass of lemonade and a small home-made sweet potato pie, and you're straight. If you really want to dig deep, get into Adam Powell's bag and cop a mess of chitlins and greens and soak them down with hot sauce. Soul food is why it is still chic to have a soul sister in the kitchen. Everybody digs the way she makes steaks, lobsters, roasts and *mmm* those rolls, pies and cakes.

The Style of Soul.

It is about nurturing creativity, being aesthetic in thought and action as much as possible. It permeates one's entire existence. In Harlem, as in all of America's urban black communities, the style is seen in the way a soul brother selects and wears his vines (suit, coat, tie, shirt, etc.). The hat and shoes are most important. If they are *correct*, it is certain that his whole thing is beautiful. You know that he's a cat who cares about himself. His hat will be a soft beaver, felt or velour, blocked in whatever way he may feel at any given time. He buys the best hat and while he's in his crib playing tunes and laying with his woman he may just let his hands go all over the hat like a potter does his clay. Thus, he creates his thing. A soul brother's shoes are always pointy-toed and so shiny that he can almost adjust his hat while looking at them. The Sixties have ushered in a "new" mood among a significant number of soul brothers and sisters, causing a clean break with "anything other than what you really are." As reflected in manner of dress, a little stingy hat without the brim called a *ziki* is worn, or a free-form *fila* which is like a soft bag. The *kufe*, a small round headpiece, is also what's happening. Some soul brothers have gone all the way into a 6
West African thing and are wearing *shokotos* (pants). The style of soul is getting back into the African folk bag. At the House of Ümoja (which means *unity* in Swahili), one of the many African shops in Harlem, soul brothers wear pieces of ivory in their ears and ornament their noses with gold like the Yorubas of West Africa. Wilt Chamberlain wears an African medallion around his neck and so does Jimmy Brown. Lew Alcindor wears *dasikis* and so does LeRoi Jones.—Soul is what, forever, has made black people hip. And it is what has enticed whites to imitate them without understanding it. Among black people, soul is a congenital understanding and respect for each other. It is the knowledge that one is but a segment of all that is, which is spatial, particled, like the colors in a rainbow; yet like when its colors are all rolled into one it is a deep purple haze . . . like morning . . . like dusk. It makes you humble, peaceful. That is why, above all, soul is wise and weary. It is the self-perception that informs you how and when to groove in your own way while others groove in theirs, and it is the sophistication that knows better than to ask, "Understand me," and settles instead for, "Don't mess with me; I'm in my own thing, baby."

Vine Deloria, Jr.

Indians Today, the Real and the Unreal

Indians are like the weather. Everyone knows all about the weather, but none can change it. When storms are predicted, the sun shines. When picnic weather is announced, the rain begins. Likewise, if you count on the unpredictability of Indian people, you will never be sorry.

One of the finest things about being an Indian is that people are always interested in you and your "plight." Other groups have difficulties, predicaments, quandaries, problems, or troubles. Traditionally we Indians have had a "plight."

Our foremost plight is our transparency. People can tell just by looking at us what we want, what should be done to help us, how we feel, and what a "real" Indian is really like. Indian life, as it relates to the real world, is a continuous attempt not to disappoint people who know us. Unfulfilled expectations cause grief and we have already had our share.

Because people can see right through us, it becomes impossible to tell truth from fiction or fact from mythology. Experts paint us as they would like us to be. Often we paint ourselves as we wish we were or as we might have been.

The more we try to be ourselves the more we are forced to defend what we have never been. The American public feels most comfortable with the mythical Indians of stereotype-land who were always THERE. These Indians are fierce, they wear feathers and grunt. Most of us don't fit this idealized figure since we grunt only when overeating, which is seldom.

To be an Indian in modern American society is in a very real sense to be unreal and ahistorical. In this book we will discuss the other side —the unrealities that face *us* as Indian people. It is this unreal feeling that has been welling up inside us and threatens to make this decade the most decisive in history for Indian people. In so many ways, Indian people are re-examining themselves in an effort to redefine a new social structure for their people. Tribes are reordering their priorities to account for the obvious discrepancies between their goals and the goals whites have defined for them.

Indian reactions are sudden and surprising. One day at a conference we were singing "My Country 'Tis of Thee" and we came across the part that goes:

Land where our fathers died 7
Land of the Pilgrims' pride . . .

Some of us broke out laughing when we realized that our fathers undoubtedly died trying to keep those Pilgrims from stealing our land. In fact, many of our fathers died because the Pilgrims killed them as witches. We didn't feel much kinship with those Pilgrims, regardless of who they did in.

We often hear "give it back to the Indians" when a gadget fails
to work. It's a terrible thing for a people to realize that society has set 8
aside all non-working gadgets for their exclusive use.

During my three years as Executive Director of the National Congress of American Indians it was a rare day when some white didn't visit 9
my office and proudly proclaim that he or she was of Indian descent.

Cherokee was the most popular tribe of their choice and many people placed the Cherokees anywhere from Maine to Washington
State. Mohawk, Sioux, and Chippewa were next in popularity. Occa- 10
sionally I would be told about some mythical tribe from lower Pennsylvania, Virginia, or Massachusetts which had spawned the white standing before me.

At times I became quite defensive about being a Sioux when these white people had a pedigree that was so much more respectable than mine. But eventually I came to understand their need to identify as
partially Indian and did not resent them. I would confirm their wildest 11
stories about their Indian ancestry and would add a few tales of my own hoping that they would be able to accept themselves someday and leave us alone.

Whites claiming Indian blood generally tend to reinforce mythical beliefs about Indians. All but one person I met who claimed Indian
blood claimed it on their grandmother's side. I once did a projection 12
backward and discovered that evidently most tribes were entirely female for the first three hundred years of white occupation. No one, it seemed, wanted to claim a male Indian as a forebear.

It doesn't take much insight into racial attitudes to understand the real meaning of the Indian-grandmother complex that plagues certain whites. A male ancestor has too much of the aura of the savage warrior, the unknown primitive, the instinctive animal, to make him a respectable member of the family tree. But a young Indian princess? Ah, there 13
was royalty for the taking. Somehow the white was linked with a noble house of gentility and culture if his grandmother was an Indian princess who ran away with an intrepid pioneer. And royalty has always been an unconscious but all-consuming goal of the European immigrant.

The early colonists, accustomed to life under benevolent despots, projected their understanding of the European political structure onto the Indian tribe in trying to explain its political and social structure. European royal houses were closed to ex-convicts and indentured servants, so the colonists made all Indian maidens princesses, then proceeded to climb a social ladder of their own creation. Within the next generation, if the trend continues, a large portion of the American population will eventually be related to Powhattan.

While a real Indian grandmother is probably the nicest thing that could happen to a child, why is a remote Indian princess grandmother so necessary for many whites? Is it because they are afraid of being classed as foreigners? Do they need some blood tie with the frontier and its dangers in order to experience what it means to be an American? Or is it an attempt to avoid facing the guilt they bear for the treatment of the Indian?

The phenomenon seems to be universal. Only among the Jewish community, which has a long tribal-religious tradition of its own, does the mysterious Indian grandmother, the primeval princess, fail to dominate the family tree. Otherwise, there's not much to be gained by claiming Indian blood or publicly identifying as an Indian. The white believes that there is a great danger the lazy Indian will eventually corrupt God's hard-working people. He is still suspicious that the Indian way of life is dreadfully wrong. There is, in fact, something *un-American* about Indians for most whites.

I ran across a classic statement of this attitude one day in a history book which was published shortly after the turn of the century. Often have I wondered how many Senators, Congressmen, and clergymen of the day accepted the attitudes of that book as a basic fact of life in America. In no uncertain terms did the book praise God that the Indian had not yet been able to corrupt North America as he had South America:

> It was perhaps fortunate for the future of America that the Indians of the North rejected civilization. Had they accepted it the whites and Indians might have intermarried to some extent as they did in Mexico. That would have given us a population made up in a measure of shiftless half-breeds.

I never dared to show this passage to my white friends who had claimed Indian blood, but I often wondered why they were so energetic if they did have some of the bad seed in them.

Those whites who dare not claim Indian blood have an asset of their own. They *understand* Indians.

Understanding Indians is not an esoteric art. All it takes is a trip through Arizona or New Mexico, watching a documentary on TV, having known *one* in the service, or having read a popular book on *them*.

There appears to be some secret osmosis about Indian people by which they can magically and instantaneously communicate complete knowledge about themselves to these interested whites. Rarely is physi-

cal contact required. Anyone and everyone who knows an Indian or
who is *interested,* immediately and thoroughly understands them.

You can verify this great truth at your next party. Mention Indians
and you will find a person who saw some in a gas station in Utah, or who
attended the Gallup ceremonial celebration, or whose Uncle Jim hired 21
one to cut logs in Oregon, or whose church had a missionary come to
speak last Sunday on the plight of Indians and the mission of the church.

There is no subject on earth so easily understood as that of the
American Indian. Each summer, work camps disgorge teen-agers on 22
various reservations. Within one month's time the youngsters acquire
a knowledge of Indians that would astound a college professor.

Easy knowledge about Indians is historical tradition. After Columbus "discovered" America he brought back news of a great new world
which he assumed to be India and, therefore, filled with Indians. Almost at once European folklore devised a complete explanation of the 23
new land and its inhabitants which featured the Fountain of Youth,
the Seven Cities of Gold, and other exotic attractions. The absence of
elephants apparently did not tip off the explorers that they weren't in
India. By the time they realized their mistake, instant knowledge of
Indians was a cherished tradition.

Missionaries, after learning some of the religious myths of tribes
they encountered, solemnly declared that the inhabitants of the new
continent were the Ten Lost Tribes of Israel. Indians thus received a 24
religious-historical identity far greater than they wanted or deserved.
But it was an impossible identity. Their failure to measure up to Old
Testament standards doomed them to a fall from grace and they were
soon relegated to the status of a picturesque species of wildlife.

Like the deer and the antelope, Indians seemed to play rather than
get down to the serious business of piling up treasures upon the earth 25
where thieves break through and steal. Scalping, introduced prior to
the French and Indian War by the English,[1] confirmed the suspicion

[1]Notice, for example the following proclamation:

"Given at the Council Chamber in Boston this third day of November 1755 in the twenty-ninth year of the Reign of our Sovereign Lord George the Second by the Grace of God of Great Britain, France, and Ireland, King Defender of the Faith—By His Honour's command / J. Willard, Secry. / God Save the King

"Whereas the tribe of Penobscot Indians have repeatedly in a perfidious manner acted contrary to their solemn submission unto his Majesty long since made and frequently renewed.

"I have, therefore, at the desire of the House of Representatives . . . thought fit to issue this Proclamation and to declare the Penobscot Tribe of Indians to be enemies, rebels and traitors to his Majesty. . . . And I do hereby require his Majesty's subjects of the Province to embrace all opportunities of pursuing, captivating, killing and destroying all and every of the aforesaid Indians.

"And whereas the General Court of this Province have voted that a bounty . . . be granted and allowed to be paid out of the Province Treasury . . . the premiums of bounty following viz:

"For every scalp of a male Indian brought in as evidence of their being killed as aforesaid, forty pounds.

"For every scalp of such female Indian or male Indian under the age of twelve years that shall be killed and brought in as evidence of their being killed as aforesaid, twenty pounds.

that Indians were wild animals to be hunted and skinned. Bounties were set and an Indian scalp became more valuable than beaver, otter, marten, and other animal pelts.

American blacks had become recognized as a species of human being by amendments to the Constitution shortly after the Civil War. Prior to emancipation they had been counted as three-fifths of a person in determining population for representation in the House of Representatives. Early Civil Rights bills nebulously state that other people shall have the same rights as "white people," indicating there *were* "other people." But Civil Rights bills passed during and after the Civil War systematically excluded Indian people. For a long time an Indian was not presumed capable of initiating an action in a court of law, of owning property, or of giving testimony against whites in court. Nor could an Indian vote or leave his reservation. Indians were America's captive people without any defined rights whatsoever.

Then one day the white man discovered that the Indian tribes still owned some 135 million acres of land. To his horror he learned that much of it was very valuable. Some was good grazing land, some was farm land, some mining land, and some covered with timber.

Animals could be herded together on a piece of land, but they could not sell it. Therefore it took no time at all to discover that Indians were really people and should have the right to sell their lands. Land was the means of recognizing the Indian as a human being. It was the method whereby land could be stolen legally and not blatantly.

Once the Indian was thus acknowledged, it was fairly simple to determine what his goals were. If, thinking went, the Indian was just like the white, he must have the same outlook as the white. So the future was planned for the Indian people in public and private life. First in order was allotting them reservations so that they could sell their lands. God's foreordained plan to repopulate the continent fit exactly with the goals of the tribes as they were defined by their white friends.

It is fortunate that we were never slaves. We gave up land instead of life and labor. Because the Negro labored, he was considered a draft animal. Because the Indian occupied large areas of land, he was considered a wild animal. Had we given up anything else, or had anything else to give up, it is certain that we would have been considered some other thing.

Whites have had different attitudes toward the Indians and the blacks since the Republic was founded. Whites have always refused to give non-whites the respect which they have been found to legally possess. Instead there has always been a contemptuous attitude that although the law says one thing, "we all know better."

Thus whites steadfastly refused to allow blacks to enjoy the fruits of full citizenship. They systematically closed schools, churches, stores, restaurants, and public places to blacks or made insulting provisions for them. For one hundred years every program of public and private white

America was devoted to the exclusion of the black. It was, perhaps, embarrassing to be rubbing shoulders with one who had not so long before been defined as a field animal.

The Indian suffered the reverse treatment. Law after law was passed requiring him to conform to white institutions. Indian children were kidnapped and forced into boarding schools thousands of miles from their homes to learn the white man's ways. Reservations were
turned over to different Christian denominations for governing. Reser- 33
vations were for a long time church operated. Everything possible was done to ensure that Indians were forced into American life. The wild animal was made into a household pet whether or not he wanted to be one.

Policies for both black and Indian failed completely. Blacks eventually began the Civil Rights movement. In doing so they assured themselves some rights in white society. Indians continued to withdraw from 34
the overtures of white society and tried to maintain their own communities and activities.

Actually both groups had little choice. Blacks, trapped in a world
of white symbols, retreated into themselves. And people thought com- 35
parable Indian withdrawal unnatural because they expected Indians to behave like whites.

The white world of abstract symbols became a nightmare for Indian people. The words of the treaties, clearly stating that Indians
should have "free and undisturbed" use of their lands under the pro- 36
tection of the federal government, were cast aside by the whites as if they didn't exist. The Sioux once had a treaty plainly stating that it would take the signatures or marks of three-fourths of the adult males to amend it. Yet through force the government obtained only 10 percent of the required signatures and declared the new agreement valid.

Indian solutions to problems which had been defined by the white society were rejected out of hand and obvious solutions discarded when they called for courses of action that were not proper in white society.
When Crow Dog assassinated Spotted Tail the matter was solved under 37
traditional Sioux customs. Yet an outraged public, furious because Crow Dog had not been executed, pressured for the Seven Major Crimes Act for the federal government to assume nearly total criminal jurisdiction over the reservations. Thus foreign laws and customs using the basic concepts of justice came to dominate Indian life. If, Indians reasoned, justice is for society's benefit, why isn't our justice accepted? Indians became convinced they were the world's stupidest people.

Words and situations never seemed to fit together. Always, it
seemed, the white man chose a course of action that did not work. 38
The white man preached that it was good to help the poor, yet he did nothing to assist the poor in his society. Instead he put constant pressure on the Indian people to hoard their worldly goods, and when they failed to accumulate capital but freely gave to the poor, the white man reacted violently.

The failure of communication created a void into which poured the white do-gooder, the missionary, the promoter, the scholar, and every conceivable type of person who believed he could help. White society failed to understand the situation because this conglomerate of assistance blurred the real issues beyond recognition.

The legend of the Indian was embellished or tarnished according to the need of the intermediates to gain leverage in their struggle to solve problems that never existed outside of their own minds. The classic example, of course, is the old-time missionary box. People were horrified that Indians continued to dress in their traditional garb. Since whites did not wear buckskin and beads, they equated such dress with savagery. So do-gooders in the East held fantastic clothing drives to supply the Indians with civilized clothes. Soon boxes of discarded evening gowns, tuxedos, tennis shoes, and uniforms flooded the reservations. Indians were made to dress in these remnants so they could be civilized. Then, realizing the ridiculous picture presented by the reservation people, neighboring whites made fun of the Indian people for having the presumption to dress like whites.

But in the East, whites were making great reputations as "Indian experts," as people who devoted their lives to helping the savages. Whenever Indian land was needed, the whites pictured the tribes as wasteful people who refused to develop their natural resources. Because the Indians did not "use" their lands, argued many land promoters, the lands should be taken away and given to people who knew what to do with them.

White society concentrated on the individual Indian to the exclusion of his group, forgetting that any society is merely a composite of individuals. Generalizations by experts universalized "Indianness" to the detriment of unique Indian values. Indians with a common cultural base shared behavior patterns. But they were expected to behave like a similar group of whites and rarely did. Whites, on the other hand, generally came from a multitude of backgrounds and shared only the need for economic subsistence. There was no way, therefore, to combine white values and Indian behavior into a workable program or intelligible subject of discussion.

One of the foremost differences separating white and Indian was simply one of origin. Whites derived predominantly from western Europe. The earliest settlers on the Atlantic seaboard came from England and the low countries. For the most part they shared the common experiences of their peoples and dwelt within the world view which had dominated western Europe for over a millenium.

Conversely Indians had always been in the western hemisphere. Life on this continent and views concerning it were not shaped in a post-Roman atmosphere. The entire outlook of the people was one of simplicity and mystery, not scientific or abstract. The western hemisphere produced wisdom, western Europe produced knowledge.

Perhaps this distinction seems too simple to mention. It is not.
Many is the time I have sat in Congressional hearings and heard the
chairman of the committee crow about "our" great Anglo-Saxon heritage
of law and order. Looking about the hearing room I saw row after row 45
of full-blooded Indians with blank expressions on their faces. As far
as they were concerned, Sir Walter Raleigh was a brand of pipe tobacco that you got at the trading post.

When we talk about European background, we are talking about
feudalism, kings, queens, their divine right to rule their subjects, the 46
Reformation, Christianity, the Magna Charta and all of the events that
went to make up European history.

American Indians do not share that heritage. They do not look
wistfully back across the seas to the old country. The Apache were not
at Runnymede to make King John sign the Magna Charta. The Chero- 47
kee did not create English common law. The Pima had no experience
with the rise of capitalism and industrialism. The Blackfeet had no
monasteries. No tribe has an emotional, historical, or political relationship to events of another continent and age.

Indians have had their own political history which has shaped the
outlook of the tribes. There were great confederacies throughout the
country before the time of the white invader. The eastern Iroquois 48
formed a strong league because as single tribes they had been weak
and powerless against larger tribes. The Deep South was controlled
by three confederacies: the Creeks with their town system, the Natchez,
and the Powhattan confederation which extended into tidelands Virginia. The Pequots and their cousins the Mohicans controlled the area
of Connecticut, Massachusetts, Rhode Island, and Long Island.

True democracy was more prevalent among Indian tribes in pre-
Columbian days than it has been since. Despotic power was abhorred 49
by tribes that were loose combinations of hunting parties rather than
political entities.

Conforming their absolute freedom to fit rigid European political
forms has been very difficult for most tribes, but on the whole they
have managed extremely well. Under the Indian Reorganization Act
Indian people have generally created a modern version of the old tribal 50
political structure and yet have been able to develop comprehensive
reservation programs which compare favorably with governmental
structures anywhere.

The deep impression made upon American minds by the Indian
struggle against the white man in the last century has made the contemporary Indian somewhat invisible compared with his ancestors. 51
Today Indians are not conspicuous by their absence from view. Yet
they should be.

In *The Other America*, the classic study of poverty by Michael
Harrington, the thesis is developed that the poor are conspicuous by 52
their invisibility. There is no mention of Indians in the book. A century ago, Indians would have dominated such a work.

Indians are probably invisible because of the tremendous amount of misinformation about them. Most books about Indians cover some abstract and esoteric topic of the last century. Contemporary books are predominantly by whites trying to solve the "Indian problem." Between the two extremes lives a dynamic people in a social structure of their own, asking only to be freed from cultural oppression. The future does not look bright for the attainment of such freedom because the white does not understand the Indian and the Indian does not wish to understand the white.

Edward Abbey

What About the Indians?

What about the Indians? There are no Indians in the Arches
country now; they all left seven hundred years ago and won't be back
for a long time. But here as elsewhere in the canyonlands they left a
record of their passage. Near springs and under overhanging cliffs, good 1
camping spots, you may find chipping grounds scattered with hundreds
of fragments of flint or chert where the Anasazi hunters worked their
arrowpoints. You may find shards of pottery. At other places you will
see their writing on the canyon walls—the petroglyphs and pictographs.

Petroglyphs are carved in the rock; pictographs are painted on the
rock. Whether in one form or the other they consist of representations
of birds, snakes, deer and many other animals, of human, semihuman 2
and superhuman figures, and of designs purely abstract or symbolic.
In some places you find only petroglyphs, in other places only pictographs, in some places both. The explicitly representational often comes
side by side with the highly abstract.

In style the inscriptions and paintings range from the crude and
simple to the elegant, sophisticated and subtle. They seem to include
the work of different cultures and a great extent of time: on a wall
of rock near Turnbow Cabin is pictured a man on horseback, which 3
must have been made after the arrival of the Spanish in North America;
on another rock wall a few miles southwest of Moab is the petroglyph of
what appears to be a mastodon—a beast supposedly extinct more than
twenty thousand years ago.

Whether crude or elegant, representational or abstract, very old
or relatively new, all of the work was done in a manner pleasing to
contemporary taste, with its vogue for the stylized and primitive. The
ancient canyon art of Utah belongs in that same international museum 4
without walls which makes African sculpture, Melanesian masks, and
the junkyards of New Jersey equally interesting—those voices of silence
which speak to us in the first world language. As for the technical competence of the artists, its measure is apparent in the fact that these
pictographs and petroglyphs though exposed to the attack of wind, sand,

rain, heat, cold and sunlight for centuries still survive vivid and clear. How much of the painting and sculpture being done in America today will last—in the merely physical sense—for even a half-century?

The pictures (to substitute one term for the petroglyph-pictograph combination) are found on flat surfaces along the canyon walls, often at heights now inaccessible to a man on foot. (Because of erosion.) They usually appear in crowded clusters, with figures of a later date sometimes superimposed on those of an earlier time. There is no indication that the men who carved and painted the figures made any attempt to compose them into coherent murals; the endless variety of style, subject and scale suggests the work of many individuals from different times and places who for one reason or another came by, stopped, camped for days or weeks and left a sign of their passing on the rock.

What particular meaning, if any, have these pictures on the canyon walls? No one has a definite answer to that question but several possible explanations come to mind when you see them, in their strange and isolated settings, for the first time.

They could be the merest doodling—that is an easy first impression. Yet there's quite a difference between scribbling on paper and on sandstone. As anyone knows who has tried to carve his name in rock, the task requires persistence, patience, determination and skill. Imagine the effort required to inscribe, say, the figure of a dancer, with no tool but a flint chisel and in such a way as to make it last five hundred years.

Perhaps these stone walls served as community bulletin boards, a form of historical record-keeping, a "newspaper rock" whereon individuals carved and painted their clan or totemic signatures. Or the frequently repeated figures of deer, beaver, bighorn sheep and other animals might represent the story of successful hunting parties.

While many of the pictures may have had for their makers a religious or ceremonial significance, others look like apparitions out of bad dreams. In this category belong the semihuman and superhuman beings with horned heads, immensely broad shoulders, short limbs and massive bodies that taper down to attenuated legs. Some of them have no legs at all but seem to rise ghostlike out of nothing, floating on air. These are sinister and supernatural figures, gods from the underworld perhaps, who hover in space, or dance, or stand solidly planted on two feet carrying weapons—a club or sword. Most are faceless but some stare back at you with large, hollow, disquieting eyes. Demonic shapes, they might have meant protection and benevolence to their creators and a threat to strangers:

Beware, traveler. You are approaching the land of the horned gods. . . .

Whatever their original intention, the long-dead artists and hunters confront us across the centuries with the poignant sign of their humanity. I was here, says the artist. We were here, say the hunters.

One other thing is certain. The pre-Columbian Indians of the
Southwest, whether hunting, making arrowpoints, going on salt-
gathering expeditions or otherwise engaged, clearly enjoyed plenty of
leisure time. This speaks well of the food-gathering economy and also
of its culture, which encouraged the Indians to employ their freedom 12
in the creation and sharing of a durable art. Unburdened by the necessity of devoting most of their lives to the production, distribution, sale
and servicing of labor-saving machinery, lacking proper recreational
facilities, these primitive savages were free to do that which comes as
naturally to men as making love—making graven images.

But now they are gone, some six or seven hundred years later,
though not as a race extinguished: their descendants survive in the
Hopi, Zuñi and other Pueblo tribes of Arizona and New Mexico. What
drove the ancient ones out of the canyonlands? Marauding enemies?
Drouth and starvation? Disease? The fear born of nightmares, the nightmares that rise from fear? A combination of these and other causes?
The old people have left no record of disaster on the mural walls of
the canyons; we can do no more than make educated guesses based on
what is known about climatic changes, tribal warfare and Indian village
life in the Southwest. Their departure from the high plateau country
may have been gradual, an emigration spread out over many years, or 13
it may in some places have been a sudden, panicky flight. In almost
all of the cliff dwellings valuable property was abandoned—arrow-
heads, pottery, seed corn, sandals, turquoise and coral jewelry—which
suggests that something happened which impelled the inhabitants to
leave in a great hurry. But other explanations are possible. Personal
property would have been buried with the dead, to be later dug up
by pillagers and animals or exposed by erosion. Or the departing Indians, having no domesticated animals except dogs, may simply have
been unable to carry away all of their possessions. Or the abandoned
articles may have been under a curse, associated with disease and
death.

Today, outside the canyon country and particularly in Arizona and
New Mexico, the Indians are making a great numerical comeback, out-
breeding the white man by a ratio of three to two. The population of
the Navajo tribe to take the most startling example has increased from
approximately 9500 in 1865 to about 90,000 a century later—a multipli-
cation almost tenfold in only three generations. The increase is the 14
indirect result of the white man's medical science as introduced on the
Navajo reservation, which greatly reduced the infant mortality rate and
thereby made possible such formidable fecundity. This happened despite the fact that infant mortality rates among the Indians are still
much higher than among the American population as a whole. Are
the Navajos grateful? They are not. To be poor is bad enough; to be
poor and multiplying is worse.

In the case of the Navajo the effects of uncontrolled population
growth are vividly apparent. The population, though ten times greater

than a century ago, must still exist on a reservation no bigger now than it was then. In a pastoral economy based on sheep, goats and horses the inevitable result, as any child could have foreseen, was severe overgrazing and the transformation of the range—poor enough to start with—from a semiarid grassland to an eroded waste of blowsand and nettles. In other words the land available to the Navajos not only failed to expand in proportion to their growing numbers; it has actually diminished in productive capacity.

In order to survive, more and more of the Navajos, or The People as they used to call themselves, are forced off the reservation and into rural slums along the major highways and into the urban slums of the white man's towns which surround the reservation. Here we find them today doing the best they can as laborers, gas station attendants, motel maids and dependents of the public welfare system. They are the Negroes of the Southwest—red black men. Like their cousins in the big cities they turn for solace, quite naturally, to alcohol and drugs; the peyote cult in particular grows in popularity under the name of The Native American Church.

Unequipped to hold their own in the ferociously competitive world of White America, in which even the language is foreign to them, the Navajos sink ever deeper into the culture of poverty, exhibiting all of the usual and well-known symptoms: squalor, unemployment or irregular and ill-paid employment, broken families, disease, prostitution, crime, alcoholism, lack of education, too many children, apathy and demoralization, and various forms of mental illness, including evangelical Protestantism. Whether in the *favelas* of Rio de Janeiro, the *barrios* of Caracas, the ghettos of Newark, the mining towns of West Virginia or the tarpaper villages of Gallup, Flagstaff and Shiprock, it's the same the world over—one big wretched family sequestered in sullen desperation, pawed over by social workers, kicked around by the cops and prayed over by the missionaries.

There are interesting differences, of course, both in kind and degree between the plight of the Navajo Indians and that of their brothers-in-poverty around the world. For one thing the Navajos have the B.I.A. looking after them—the Bureau of Indian Affairs. The B.I.A. like everything else is a mixture of good and bad, with policies that change and budgets that fluctuate with every power shift in Washington, but its general aim over the long run has been to change Indians into white men, a process called "assimilation." In pursuit of this end the little Indians are herded into schools on and off the reservation where, under the tutelage of teachers recruited by the B.I.A. from Negro colleges deep in the Bible Belt, the Navajo children learn to speak American with a Southern accent. The B.I.A., together with medical missions set up by various churches, also supplies the Navajos with basic medical services, inadequate by national standards but sufficient nevertheless to encourage the extravagant population growth which is the chief cause, though not the only cause, of the Navajos' troubles.

A second important difference in the situation of the Navajo Indians
from that of others sunk in poverty is that the Navajos still have a home
of their own—the reservation, collective property of the tribe as a whole.
The land is worn out, barren, eroded, hopelessly unsuited to support a
heavy human population but even so, however poor in economic terms, 19
it provides the Navajo people with a firm base on earth, the possibility
of a better future and for the individual Navajo in exile a place where,
when he has to go back there, they have to take him in. Where they
would not think of doing otherwise.

Poor as the land is it still attracts the avarice of certain whites in
neighboring areas who can see in it the opportunity for profit if only
the present occupants are removed. Since the land belongs to the tribe
no individual within the tribe is legally empowered to sell any portion
of it. Periodic attempts are made, therefore, by false friends of the 20
Navajos, to have the reservation broken up under the guise of granting
the Indian "property rights" so that they will be "free" to sell their
only tangible possession—the land—to outsiders. So far the tribe has
been wise enough to resist this pressure and so long as it continues
to do so The People will never be completely separated from their
homeland.

Retaining ownership of their land, the Navajos have been able to
take maximum advantage through their fairly coherent and democratic
tribal organization of the modest mineral resources which have been
found within the reservation. The royalties from the sale of oil, uranium,
coal and natural gas, while hardly enough to relieve the Indians' general poverty, have enabled them to develop a tribal timber business, to 21
provide a few college scholarships for the brainiest (not necessarily the
best) of their young people, to build community centers and finance
an annual tribal fair (a source of much enjoyment to The People),
and to drill a useful number of water wells for the benefit of the old
sheep and goat raising families still hanging on in the backlands.

The money is also used to support the small middle class of officials and functionaries which tribal organization has created, and to
pay the costs of a tribal police force complete with uniforms, guns,
patrol cars and two-way radios. These unnecessary evils reflect the
influence of the Bureau of Indian Affairs and the desire on the part
of the more ambitious Navajos to imitate as closely as they can the 22
pattern of the white man's culture which surrounds them, a typical and
understandable reaction. Despite such minor failures the Navajos as a
tribe have made good use of what little monetary income they have.
It is not entirely their fault if the need remains far greater than tribal
resources can satisfy.

Meanwhile the tribal population continues to grow in geometric
progression: 2 . . . 4 . . . 8 . . . 16 . . . 32 . . . 64, etc., onward and
upward, as the majority of The People settle more deeply into the 23
second-class way of life, American style, to which they are fairly accustomed, with all of its advantages and disadvantages: the visiting case-

worker from the welfare department, the relief check, the derelict automobiles upside down on the front yard, the tarpaper shack next to the hogan and ramada, the repossessed TV set, the confused adolescents, and the wine bottles in the kitchen midden.

Various solutions are proposed: industrialization; tourism; massive federal aid; better education for the Navajo children; relocation; birth control; child subsidies; guaranteed annual income; four-lane highways; moral rearmament. None of these proposals are entirely devoid of merit and at least one of them—birth control—is obviously essential though not in itself sufficient if poverty is to be alleviated among the Navajo Indians. As for the remainder, they are simply the usual banal, unimaginative if well-intentioned proposals made everywhere, over and over again, in reply to the demand for a solution to the national and international miseries of mankind. As such they fail to take into account what is unique and valuable in the Navajo's traditional way of life and ignore altogether the possibility that the Navajo may have as much to teach the white man as the white man has to teach the Navajo.

Industrialization, for example. Even if the reservation could attract and sustain large-scale industry heavy or light, which it cannot, what have the Navajos to gain by becoming factory hands, lab technicians and office clerks? The Navajos are *people,* not *personnel*; nothing in their nature or tradition has prepared them to adapt to the regimentation of application forms and time clock. To force them into the machine would require a Procrustean mutilation of their basic humanity. Consciously or unconsciously the typical Navajo senses this unfortunate truth, resists the compulsory miseducation offered by the Bureau, hangs on to his malnourished horses and cannibalized automobiles, works when he feels like it and quits when he has enough money for a party or the down payment on a new pickup. He fulfills other obligations by getting his wife and kids installed securely on the public welfare rolls. Are we to condemn him for this? Caught in a no-man's-land between two worlds the Navajo takes what advantage he can of the white man's system—the radio, the pickup truck, the welfare—while clinging to the liberty and dignity of his old way of life. Such a man would rather lie drunk in the gutters of Gallup, New Mexico, a disgrace to his tribe and his race, than button on a clean white shirt and spend the best part of his life inside an air-conditioned office building with windows that cannot be opened.

Even if he wanted to join the American middle class (and some Indians do wish to join and have done so) the average Navajo suffers from a handicap more severe than skin color, the language barrier or insufficient education: his acquisitive instinct is poorly developed. He lacks the drive to get ahead of his fellows or to figure out ways and means of profiting from other people's labor. Coming from a tradition which honors sharing and mutual aid above private interest, the Navajo thinks it somehow immoral for one man to prosper while his neighbors go without. If a member of the tribe does break from this pattern, through luck, talent or special training, and finds a niche in the affluent society, he can also expect to find his family and clansmen camping on his patio, hunting in his kitchen, borrowing his car and occupying his bedrooms at any hour of the day or night. Among these people a liberal hospitality is taken for granted and selfishness regarded with horror. Shackled by such primitive attitudes, is it any wonder that the Navajos have not yet been able to get in step with the rest of us?

If industrialism per se seems an unlikely answer to the problems
of the Navajo (and most of the other tribes) there still remains industrial tourism to be considered. This looks a little more promising, and
with the construction of new highways, motels and gas stations the
tribe has taken steps to lure tourists into the reservation and relieve 27
them of their dollars. The chief beneficiaries will be the oil and auto-
motive combines far away, but part of the take will remain on the
reservation in the form of wages paid to those who change the sheets,
do the laundry, pump the gas, serve the meals, wash the dishes, clean
the washrooms and pump out the septic tanks—simple tasks for which
the Navajos are available and qualified.

How much the tourist industry can add to the tribal economy,
how many Indians it may eventually employ, are questions not answerable at this time. At best it provides only seasonal work and this on
a marginal scale—ask any chambermaid. And whether good or bad in
strictly pecuniary terms, industrial tourism exacts a spiritual price from
those dependent upon it for their livelihood. The natives must learn
to accustom themselves to the spectacle of hordes of wealthy, outland- 28
ishly dressed strangers invading their land and their homes. They must
learn the automatic smile. They must expect to be gaped at and photographed. They must learn to be quaint, picturesque and photogenic.
They must learn that courtesy and hospitality are not simply the customs of any decent society but are rather a special kind of commodity
which can be peddled for money.

I am not sure that the Navajos can learn these things. For example, 29
the last time I was in Kayenta I witnessed the following incident:

One of the old men, one of the old Longhairs with a Mongolian
mustache and tall black hat, is standing in the dust and sunlight in
front of the Holiday Inn, talking with two of his wives. A big car rolls
up—a Buick Behemoth I believe it was, or it may have been a Cadillac
Crocodile, a Dodge Dinosaur or a Mercury Mastodon, I'm not sure
which—and this *lady* climbs out of it. She's wearing golden stretch pants, 30
green eyelids and a hiveshaped head of hair that looks both in color
and texture exactly like 25¢ worth of candy cotton. She has a camera
in her hands and is aiming it straight at the old Navajo. "Hey!" she
says. "Look this way." He looks, sees the woman, spits softly on the
ground and turns his back. Naturally offended, the lady departs without
buying even a postcard.

But he was an old one. The young are more adaptable and under the pressure to survive may learn to turn tricks for the tourist trade. That, and a few coal mines here and there, and jobs away from the reservation, and more welfare, will enable the Navajos to carry on through the near future. In the long run their economic difficulties can only be solved when and if our society as a whole is willing to make an honest effort to eliminate poverty. By honest effort, as opposed to the current dishonest effort with its emphasis on phoney social services which benefit no one but the professional social workers, I mean a direct confrontation with the two actual basic causes of poverty: (1) too many children and—(here I reveal the secret, the elusive and mysterious key to the whole problem)—(2) too little money. Though simple in formula, the solution will seem drastic and painful in practice. To solve the first part of the problem we may soon have to make birth control compulsory; to solve the second part we will have to borrow from Navajo tradition and begin a more equitable sharing of national income. Politically unpalatable? No doubt. Social justice in this country means social surgery—carving some of the fat off the wide bottom of the American middle class.

Navajo poverty can be cured and in one way or the other—through justice or war—it will be cured. It is doubtful, however, that the Navajo way of life, as distinguished from Navajos, can survive. Outnumbered, surrounded and overwhelmed, the Navajos will probably be forced in self-defense to malform themselves into the shape required by industrial econometrics. Red-skinned black men at present, they must learn to become dark-brown white men with credit cards and crew-cut sensibilities.

It will not be easy. It will not be easy for the Navajos to forget that once upon a time, only a generation ago, they were horsemen, nomads, keepers of flocks, painters in sand, weavers of wool, artists in silver, dancers, singers of the Yei-bei-chei. But they will have to forget, or at least learn to be ashamed of these old things and to bring them out only for the amusement of tourists.

A difficult transitional period. Tough on people. For instance, consider an unfortunate accident which took place only a week ago here in the Arches country. Parallel to the highway north of Moab is a railway, a spur line to the potash mines. At one point close to the road this railway cuts through a hill. The cut is about three hundred feet deep, blasted through solid rock with sides that are as perpendicular as the walls of a building. One afternoon two young Indians—Navajos? Apaches? beardless Utes?—in an old perverted Plymouth came hurtling down the highway, veered suddenly to the right, whizzed through a fence and plunged straight down like helldivers into the Big Cut. Investigating the wreckage we found only the broken bodies, the broken bottles, the stain and smell of Tokay, and a couple of cardboard suitcases exploded open and revealing their former owners' worldly goods—dirty socks, some underwear, a copy of *True West* magazine, a comb, three new cowboy shirts from J. C. Penney's, a carton of Marlboro cigarettes. But nowhere did we see any eagle feathers, any conchos of silver, any buffalo robes, any bows, arrows, medicine pouch or drums.

Some Indians.

Rollo May

The Man Who Was Put in a Cage

What a piece of work is man! how noble in reason! how infinite in faculty! in form and moving how express and admirable! . . . The paragon of animals!
—SHAKESPEARE, HAMLET

We have quite a few discrete pieces of information these days
about what happens to a person when he is deprived of this or that
element of freedom. We have our studies of sensory deprivation and
of how a person reacts when put in different kinds of authoritarian
atmosphere, and so on. But recently I have been wondering what 1
pattern would emerge if we put these various pieces of knowledge
together. In short, what would happen to a living, whole person if his
total freedom—or as nearly total as we can imagine—were taken away?
In the course of these reflections, a parable took form in my mind.

THE STORY BEGINS with a king who, while standing in reverie at the
window of his palace one evening, happened to notice a man in the 2
town square below. He was apparently an average man, walking home
at night, who had taken the same route five nights a week for many
years. The king followed this man in his imagination—pictured him
arriving home, perfunctorily kissing his wife, eating his late meal, inquiring whether everything was all right with the children, reading the paper, going to bed, perhaps engaging in the sex relation with his wife or perhaps not, sleeping, and getting up and going off to work again the next day.

And a sudden curiosity seized the king, which for a moment banished his fatigue: "I wonder what would happen if a man were kept 3
in a cage, like the animals at the zoo?" His curiosity was perhaps in
some ways not unlike that of the first surgeons who wondered what
it would be like to perform a lobotomy on the human brain.

So the next day the king called in a psychologist, told him of his idea, and invited him to observe the experiment. When the psychologist demurred saying, "It's an unthinkable thing to keep a man in a cage," the monarch replied that many rulers had in effect, if not literally, done so, from the time of the Romans through Genghis Khan down to Hitler and the totalitarian leaders; so why not find out scientifically what would happen? Furthermore, added the king, he had made up his mind to do it whether the psychologist took part or not; he had already gotten the Greater Social Research Foundation to give a large sum of money for the experiment, and why let that money go to waste? By this time the psychologist also was feeling within himself a great curiosity about what would happen if a man were kept in a cage.

And so the next day the king caused a cage to be brought from the zoo—a large cage that had been occupied by a lion when it was new, then later by a tiger; just recently it had been the home of a hyena who died the previous week. The cage was put in an inner private court in the palace grounds, and the average man whom the king had seen from the window was brought and placed therein. The psychologist, with his Rorschach and Wechsler-Bellevue tests in his brief case to administer at some appropriate moment, sat down outside the cage.

At first the man was simply bewildered, and he kept saying to the psychologist, "I have to catch the tram, I have to get to work, look what time it is, I'll be late for work!" But later on in the afternoon the man began soberly to realize what was up, and then he protested vehemently, "The king can't do this to me! It is unjust! It's against the law." His voice was strong and his eyes full of anger. The psychologist liked the man for his anger, and he became vaguely aware that this was a mood he had encountered often in people he worked with in his clinic. "Yes," he realized, "this anger is the attitude of people who—like the healthy adolescents of any era—want to fight what's wrong, who protest directly against it. When people come to the clinic in this mood, it is good—they can be helped."

During the rest of the week the man continued his vehement protests. When the king walked by the cage, as he did every day, the man made his protests directly to the monarch.

But the king answered, "Look here, you are getting plenty of food, you have a good bed, and you don't have to work. We take good care of you; so why are you objecting?"

After some days had passed, the man's protests lessened and then ceased. He was silent in his cage, generally refusing to talk. But the psychologist could see hatred glowing in his eyes. When he did exchange a few words, they were short, definite words uttered in the strong, vibrant, but calm voice of the person who hates and knows whom he hates.

Whenever the king walked into the courtyard, there was a deep fire in the man's eyes. The psychologist thought, "This must be the way people act when they are first conquered." He remembered that he had also seen that expression of the eyes and heard that tone of

voice in many patients at his clinic: the adolescent who had been unjustly accused at home or in school and could do nothing about it; the college student who was required by public and campus opinion to be a star on the gridiron, but was required by his professors to pass courses he could not prepare for if he were to be successful in 10
football—and who was then expelled from college for the cheating that resulted. And the psychologist, looking at the active hatred in the man's eyes, thought, "It is still good; a person who has this fight in him can be helped."

Every day the king, as he walked through the courtyard, kept reminding the man in the cage that he was given food and shelter and taken good care of, so why did he not like it? And the psychologist noticed that, whereas at first the man had been entirely impervious to 11
the king's statements, it now seemed more and more that he was pausing for a moment after the king's speech—for a second the hatred was postponed from returning to his eyes—as though he were asking himself if what the king said were possibly true.

And after a few weeks more, the man began to discuss with the psychologist how it was a useful thing that a man is given food and shelter; and how man had to live by his fate in any case, and the part of wisdom was to accept fate. He soon was developing an extensive theory about security and the acceptance of fate, which sounded to the psychologist very much like the philosophical theories that Rosenberg and others worked out for the fascists in Germany. He was very 12
voluble during this period, talking at length, although the talk was mostly a monologue. The psychologist noticed that his voice was flat and hollow as he talked, like the voice of people in TV previews who make an effort to look you in the eye and try hard to sound sincere as they tell you that you should see the program they are advertising, or the announcers on the radio who are paid to persuade you that you should like highbrow music.

And the psychologist also noticed that now the corners of the man's mouth always turned down, as though he were in some gigantic pout. Then the psychologist suddenly remembered: this was like the middle-aged, middle-class people who came to his clinic, the respectable bourgeois people who went to church and lived morally but who were always full of resentment, as though everything they did was con- 13
ceived, born, and nursed in resentment. It reminded the psychologist of Nietzsche's saying that the middle class was consumed with resentment. He then for the first time began to be seriously worried about the man in the cage, for he knew that once resentment gets a firm start and becomes well rationalized and structuralized, it may become like cancer. When the person no longer knows whom he hates, he is much harder to help.

During this period the Greater Social Research Foundation had a board of trustees meeting, and they decided that since they were expending a fund to keep a man supported in a cage, it would look better if representatives of the Foundation at least visited the experiment. So a group of people, consisting of two professors and a few graduate students, came in one day to look at the man in the cage. One of the professors then proceeded to lecture to the group about the relation of the autonomic nervous system and the secretions of the ductless glands to human existence in a cage. But it occurred to the other professor that the verbal communications of the victim himself might just possibly be interesting, so he asked the man how he felt about living in a cage. The man was friendly toward the professors and students and explained to them that he had chosen this way of life, that there were great values in security and in being taken care of, that they would of course see how sensible his course was, and so on.

"How strange!" thought the psychologist, "and how pathetic; why is it he struggles so hard to get them to approve his way of life?"

In the succeeding days when the king walked through the courtyard, the man fawned upon him from behind the bars in his cage and thanked him for the food and shelter. But when the king was not in the yard and the man was not aware that the psychologist was present, his expression was quite different—sullen and morose. When his food was handed to him through the bars by the keeper, the man would often drop the dishes or dump over the water and then would be embarrassed because of his stupidity and clumsiness. His conversation became increasingly one-tracked; and instead of the involved philosophical theories about the value of being taken care of, he had gotten down to simple sentences such as "It is fate," which he would say over and over again, or he would just mumble to himself, "It is." The psychologist was surprised that the man should now be so clumsy as to drop his food, or so stupid as to talk in those barren sentences, for he knew from his tests that the man had originally been of good average intelligence. Then it dawned upon the psychologist that this was the kind of behavior he had observed in some anthropological studies among the Negroes in the South—people who had been forced to kiss the hand that fed and enslaved them, who could no longer either hate or rebel. The man in the cage took more and more to simply sitting all day long in the sun as it came through the bars, his only movements being to shift his position from time to time from morning through the afternoon.

It was hard to say just when the last phase set in. But the psychologist became aware that the man's face now seemed to have no particular expression; his smile was no longer fawning, but simply empty and meaningless, like the grimace a baby makes when there is gas on its stomach. The man ate his food and exchanged a few sentences with the psychologist from time to time; but his eyes were distant and vague, and though he looked at the psychologist, it seemed that he never really *saw* him.

And now the man, in his desultory conversations, never used the
word "I" any more. He had accepted the cage. He had no anger, no 18
hate, no rationalization. But he was now insane.

The night the psychologist realized this, he sat in his apartment
trying to write a concluding report. But it was very difficult for him
to summon up words, for he felt within himself a great emptiness. He
kept trying to reassure himself with the words, "They say that nothing 19
is ever lost, that matter is merely changed to energy and back again."
But he could not help feeling that something *had* been lost, that something had gone out of the universe in this experiment.

He finally went to bed with his report unfinished. But he could
not sleep; there was a gnawing within him which, in less rational and
scientific ages, would have been called a conscience. Why didn't I tell the
king that this is the one experiment that no man can do—or at least why
didn't I shout that I would have nothing to do with the whole bloody
business? Of course, the king would have dismissed me, the founda- 20
tions would never have granted me any more money, and at the clinic
they would have said that I was not a real scientist. But maybe one
could farm in the mountains and make a living, and maybe one could
paint or write something that would make future men happier and
more free. . . .

But he realized that these musings were, at least at the moment,
unrealistic, and he tried to pull himself back to reality. All he could
get, however, was this feeling of emptiness within himself, and the 21
words, "Something has been taken out of the universe, and there is left
only a void."

Finally he dropped off to sleep. Some time later, in the small hours
of the morning, he was awakened by a startling dream. A crowd of
people had gathered, in the dream, in front of the cage in the courtyard, and the man in the cage—no longer inert and vacuous—was shouting through the bars of the cage in impassioned oratory. "It is not only 22
I whose freedom is taken away!" he was crying. "When the king puts
me or any man in a cage, the freedom of each one of you is taken away
also. The king must go!" The people began to chant, "The king must
go!" and they seized and broke out the iron bars of the cage, and
wielded them for weapons as they charged the palace.

The psychologist awoke, filled by the dream with a great feeling
of hope and joy—an experience of hope and joy probably not unlike
that experienced by the free men of England when they forced King
John to sign the Magna Charta. But not for nothing had the psycholo- 23
gist had an orthodox analysis in the course of his training, and as he
lay surrounded by this aura of happiness, a voice spoke within him:
"Aha, you had this dream to make yourself feel better; it's just a wish
fulfillment."

"The hell it is!" said the psychologist as he climbed out of bed. 24
"Maybe some dreams are to be acted on."

Questions and Quotations for Discussion and Writing Assignments

I

1. In Chapter X of the *Life and Times of Frederick Douglass,* the former slave explains how he learned to read. Why did Douglass's master react violently to the boy's acquisition of such a simple skill?
2. How does Douglass describe his mistress, Mrs. Sophia? How does slave-owning change her? What generalization about the effects of owning slaves does Douglass draw from his observation of Mrs. Sophia? How can a slave owner be, as Douglass says, a "victim" of slavery?
3. What does Douglass mean when he says, "It was *slavery,* not its mere *incidents* I hated"?
4. Explain Jesse Jackson's remark that he is less interested in *who* killed Dr. Martin Luther King than in *what* killed him.
5. Jesse Jackson says that black ghettos are "built upon an economic imperative rather than a social one." Define the two phrases "economic imperative" and "social imperative." In Jackson's view, what changes must be made if ghettos are to be abolished?
6. What does Jesse Jackson mean when he says that the black community "has stood between white America and real true bloody revolution"?
7. Does Jackson think an alliance between black people and poor white people is possible? What could force such an alliance to come about?
8. In defining "soul," Al Calloway makes his points with vivid examples and descriptive details rather than reasoned argument or a dictionary-type definition. Why? Which of his examples or details seem most helpful in conveying the idea of "soul"? Which seem least effective?
9. Is "soul" the same thing as "style"?
10. Al Calloway writes that "the Sixties have ushered in a 'new' mood among a significant number of soul brothers and sisters, causing a clean break with 'anything other than what you really are.' " In a philosophical sense is it ever possible to be "anything other than what you really are"? What does Calloway mean?
11. He also writes that "soul" is too sophisticated to ask, "understand me"; instead, soul says, "Don't mess with me; I'm doing my own thing, baby." What is the difference between these two attitudes?
12. What is Vine Deloria's tone in the opening paragraphs of "Indians Today"? Is it angry, calm, ironic, satiric, cynical, humorous, or what? The way he uses the words "plight," "transparency," and "real" provides some clues to his tone. Can you find this same tone at other points in the essay?
13. What, according to Deloria, causes many whites to claim an Indian heritage—especially an Indian grandmother?
14. How, in Deloria's view, were the attitudes of whites toward blacks and Indians different?

15. Deloria writes that "Indians continued to withdraw from the overtures of white society and tried to maintain their own communities and activities." Are Deloria and Calloway saying essentially the same things about the quest for identity among Indians and black people?
16. What is Deloria's attitude toward "Indian experts"? What varieties of "Indian experts" does he mention?
17. What, according to Deloria, do Indians want?
18. At the beginning of "What About the Indians?" Edward Abbey writes about petroglyphs and pictographs. Does this discussion provide an intriguing and interesting introduction to his article? What effect on the reader is he trying to achieve with this discussion?
19. What is meant by the term "assimilation" as Abbey uses it?
20. What are the two chief problems of the Navajos? How can these problems be solved?
21. At the conclusion of "What About the Indians?" Abbey tells of the deaths of two young Indian boys in an automobile wreck. What point does he wish to make about this accident? How does the list of items found in the wreckage help make this point?
22. In Rollo May's parable of "The Man Who Was Put in a Cage," the prisoner's life in the cage is divided into distinct stages, each marked by changes in his attitudes. What are these stages?
23. Why does the king put the man in the cage? What does the parable say about people who have absolute power?
24. Is May's parable effective? Does it make you want to break up the cages and release the prisoners? Does it give you a desire to be free? What people today, other than those in federal penal institutions, are kept in cages?
25. The "moral" of May's parable is: "When the king puts me or any man in a cage, the freedom of each one of you is taken away also." How do you interpret this moral?
26. One major point made by May's parable is that men will relinquish many of their freedoms if they are made secure. How is the man in the cage made secure? Can anyone—black man, Indian, teenager, or adult—be free if he is dependent on a paternal figure for food, shelter, or clothing?

II

1. We hold these truths to be self-evident, that all men are created equal, that they are endowed by their Creator with certain unalienable Rights. . . .

   THE DECLARATION OF INDEPENDENCE

2. A wise man of Athens was asked when injustice would be abolished. "When those who are not wronged feel as indignant as those who are.

   ARTHUR MEE'S BLACKOUT BOOK

3. The tragedy of life is not so much what men suffer, but rather what they miss.

THOMAS CARLYLE

4. If I cannot understand the writings of Eldridge Cleaver because of my skin color, then Eldridge Cleaver cannot understand the writings of Shakespeare because of his.

MILTON MAYER

5. It is maintained that a society is free only when dissenting minorities have room to throw their weight around. As a matter of fact, a dissenting minority feels free only when it can impose its will on the majority: what it abominates most is the dissent of the majority.

ERIC HOFFER

6. The same man that was colonizing our people in Kenya was colonizing our people in the Congo. The same one in the Congo was colonizing our people in South Africa, and in Southern Rhodesia, and in Burma, and in India, and in Afghanistan, and in Pakistan. They realized all over the world where the dark man was being oppressed, he was being oppressed by the white man; where the dark man was being exploited, he was being exploited by the white man.

MALCOLM X

7. I for one believe that if you give people a thorough understanding of what confronts them and the basic causes that produce it, they'll create their own program, and when the people create a program, you get action.

MALCOLM X

8. One of the things that made the Black Muslim movement grow was its emphasis upon things African. This was the secret to the growth of the Black Muslim movement. African blood, African origin, African culture, African ties. And you'd be surprised—we discovered that deep within the subconscious of the black man in this country, he is still more African than he is American.

MALCOLM X

9. Nothing is more certainly written in the book of fate than that these people are to be free; nor is it less certain that the two races, equally free, cannot live in the same government. Nature, habit, opinion have drawn indelible lines of distinction between them. It is still in our power to direct the process of emancipation and deportation, peaceably, and in such slow degree that the evil will wear off insensibly, and their place be, *pari passu*, filled up by free white laborers. If, on the contrary, it is left to force itself on, human nature must shudder at the prospect held up.

THOMAS JEFFERSON

10. It follows, from what has been stated, that it is a great and dangerous error to suppose that all people are equally entitled to liberty. It is a reward to be earned, not a blessing to be gratuitously lavished on all

alike;—a reward reserved for the intelligent, the patriotic, the virtuous and deserving;—and not a boon to be bestowed on a people too ignorant, degraded and vicious, to be capable either of appreciating or of enjoying it.

John C. Calhoun

11. The white tenant lives adjoining the colored tenant. Their houses are almost equally destitute of comforts. Their living is confined to bare necessities. They are equally burdened with heavy taxes. They pay the same high rent for gullied and impoverished land.

    They pay the same enormous prices for farm supplies. Christmas finds them both without any satisfactory return for a year's toil. Dull and heavy and unhappy, they both start the plows again when "New Year's" passes.

    Now the People's Party says to these two men, "You are kept apart that you may be separately fleeced of your earnings. You are made to hate each other because upon that hatred is rested the keystone of the arch of financial despotism which enslaves you both. You are deceived and blinded that you may not see how this race antagonism perpetuates a monetary system which beggars both."

    Thomas E. Watson

12. The old code of equity law under which we live commands for every wrong a remedy, but in too many communities, in too many parts of the country, wrongs are inflicted on Negro citizens for which there are no remedies at law. Unless the Congress acts, their only remedy is in the street.

    John F. Kennedy

13. Our nation is moving toward two societies, one black, one white—separate and unequal.

    from the Report of the National Advisory Commission on Civil Disorders

14. White people cannot, in the generality, be taken as models of how to live. Rather, the white man is himself in sore need of new standards, which will release him from his confusion and place him once again in fruitful communion with the depths of his own being.

    James Baldwin

15. Negro blood is sure powerful—because just *one* drop of black blood makes a colored man.

    Langston Hughes

16. The Negro was willing to risk martyrdom in order to move and stir the social conscience of his community and the nation . . . he would force his oppressor to commit his brutality openly with the rest of the world looking on. . . .

    Martin Luther King

17. Indian-hating still exists; and, no doubt, will continue to exist, so long as Indians do.

    Herman Melville

18. The most common trait of all primitive peoples is a reverence for the life-giving earth, and the native American shared this elemental ethic: the land was alive to his loving touch, and he, its son, was brother to all creatures . . . During the long Indian tenure the land remained undefiled save for scars no deeper than the scratches of cornfield clearings or the farming canals of the Hohokans on the Arizona desert.

    STEWART UDALL

19. The lake is our church. The mountain is our tabernacle. The evergreens are our living saints. . . . They give us food, drink, physical power, and understanding.

    TAOS INDIANS

20. Something's happening these days. We better all be aware of it. Self-styled historians are deliberately tarnishing Custer—casting innuendos on him and on the men who fought here. It may be part of a scheme to undermine our traditions and our beliefs in the American army.

    NATIONAL PARK SERVICE HISTORIAN,
    CUSTER BATTLEFIELD NATIONAL MONUMENT

21. Custer Died For Your Sins.

    Bumper Sticker

22. The American Indian is the vengeful ghost lurking in the back of the troubled American mind. Which is why we lash out with such ferocity and passion, so muddied a heart, at the black-haired young peasants and soldiers who are the "Viet Cong." That ghost will claim the next generation as its own. When this has happened, citizens of the USA will at last begin to be Americans, truly at home on the continent, in love with their land.

    GARY SNYDER

23. Civilization or death to all American savages.

    Toast of MAJ. GENERAL JOHN S. SULLIVAN
    and his officers (July 4, 1779)

Related Readings:

SMOHALLA SPEAKS, page 263.
CASTANEDA, CARLOS, Selections from *The Teachings of Don Juan: A Yaqui Way of Knowledge,* page 329.
LYDON, MICHAEL, "The Second Coming of Bo Diddley," page 361.
SCHRAG, PETER, "The Age of Willie Mays," page 380.
MAYER, MILTON, "The Children's Crusade, page 31.

SECTION III What Do Women Want?

One of mankind's sacred trusts, generation after generation, is the transmittal of human values, the kindling of the spark of human awareness leading to the shock and recognition of the responsibilities of being unique. Although cultural values differ from society to society, there is still a body of transmitted information that aspires to truth: a functional and sometimes ennobling way to endure the world. And yet, as William Faulkner said, when accepting the Nobel Prize, "I believe that man will not merely endure: he will prevail. He is immortal, not because he alone among creatures has an inexhaustible voice, but because he has a soul, a spirit capable of compassion and sacrifice and endurance."

Today, man seems less likely to prevail than ever before. He makes war on his fellows, his cities are rotting, his refuse pollutes the waterways and oceans of his planet, his life is encrusted with things that he cannot barter for happiness. The peculiarities of language serve me well here. Although the brotherhood of man encompasses females, it is the masculine pronoun that pervades this parade of horribles. And yet women, mothers, who generally exert some moral influence within the confines of their households, can be said to shape the direction of mankind through their children. Have women permitted their store of tenderness, emotion, compassion, and empathy to be negated because these qualities are "feminine" and connote weakness? Have women abstained, remained passively silent in matters of national policy because they felt intellectually incapable of moving in man's sphere of influence?

Surely, the answer to these questions is a qualified no. Responsibility must be equally divided between those who made it happen and those who permitted it to happen. There is small consolation, however, in the moral salve that men are active, women passive. This passivity, this relinquishing of concern, this lesser self-image demands that women begin to reconcile themselves to participatory life. It will be a difficult task to persuade women to lay aside their dependence and assume active and equal status because women have always been able to get "results" through the manipulation of men. This hallowed compromise is unsatisfactory primarily because it is so dishonest. There is a politician's saying that "if you can't stand the heat, get out of the kitchen." The heat of making responsible decisions, standing independent and apart from men, has driven women into the kitchen. If women do in fact have power as individuals, strong and competent characters of their own, then the ideal of reflected glory, the role of submissive spouse must be put aside as degrading and destructive of their humanity. And it is because of her stunted humanity that woman has turned her eyes toward liberation.

The purpose of the Women's Liberation Movement is sometimes narrowly defined (as it was when women sought only the vote): it is a matter of economics (seeking freedom from the inequity of doing equal work for unequal pay). Women's Lib is more often monstrously defined as having no purpose: it is crazy and lazy (seeking freedom from the burdens of home and family); it is simply disruptive (reflecting the jealousy and bitterness of ugly women who could not get a man). These definitions are being answered, however slowly. On the basis of one man, one vote, woman is man's political equal. Legislation may eliminate economic discrimination in employment, social security inequities, and income tax penalties. Social equality may stem, in part, from day-care centers, free contraception and abortion on demand, equal opportunities at all levels of employment and in all fields of endeavor. It is in the larger, more significant field of cultural equality that the most difficult problems lie, for we have swallowed an image of woman that is less than human—a mindless, frivolous, sexual being in an attractive package who may be had for a promise and who will serve faithfully the man who gives her identity through *his* life and striving. The image is hollow, the being herself is false.

It is in the service of destruction that Women's Liberation labors: the destruction of this inhuman being. The question is not how to release women from the bondage of raising children, but how best to raise children that are whole, self-confident human beings. The question is not how to free women from a double sexual standard, but how to encourage human relationships that are genuine sharings, based on mutual respect. The question is not how to keep women from competing with men in a man's world, but how to free the creative and sympathetic energies of women and direct them to the solution of today's overwhelming problems.

Our society, the world's society, desperately needs mitigation. Yet half our population, half our power and productivity, sits quietly in the chimney corner surrounded by ashes. Cinderella's fairy godmother took her out of the scullery, dressed her up, gave her some status symbols, and the Charming Prince was her reward. Was that any way to treat a nice girl who could talk to mice and birds? To let her marry a prince who didn't recognize her without her make-up? Well, American women can expect no such miraculous godmother (Betty Friedan notwithstanding), want no such easy freedom, seek no such romantic ending. Our gilded coach may turn into a pumpkin pie, our coachmen may lead us by a circuitous route, our Prince may not exist. But in rags and tatters, with or without glass slippers, we must go to the ball, because that's where the action is.

MELINDA CARPENTER

Walt Whitman

A Woman Waits for Me

A woman waits for me, she contains all, nothing is lacking,
Yet all were lacking if sex were lacking, or if the moisture of the right
man were lacking.

Sex contains all, bodies, souls,
Meanings, proofs, purities, delicacies, results, promulgations,
Songs, commands, health, pride, the maternal mystery, the
seminal milk,
All hopes, benefactions, bestowals, all the passions, loves, beauties,
delights of the earth.
All the governments, judges, gods, follow'd persons of the earth,
These are contain'd in sex as parts of itself and justifications of itself.

Without shame the man I like knows and avows the deliciousness of
his sex,
Without shame the woman I like knows and avows hers.

Now I will dismiss myself from impassive women,
I will go stay with her who waits for me, and with those women that
are warm-blooded and sufficient for me.
I see that they understand me and do not deny me,
I see that they are worthy of me, I will be the robust husband
of those women.

They are not one jot less than I am,
They are tann'd in the face by shining suns and blowing winds,
Their flesh has the old divine suppleness and strength,
They know how to swim, row, ride, wrestle, shoot, run, strike, retreat,
advance, resist, defend themselves,
They are ultimate in their own right—they are calm, clear,
well-possess'd of themselves.
I draw you close to me, you women,
I cannot let you go, I would do you good,
I am for you, and you are for me, not only for our own sake, but for
others' sakes,
Envelop'd in you sleep greater heroes and bards,

They refuse to awake at the touch of any man but me.
It is I, you women, I make my way,
I am stern, acrid, large, undissuadable, but I love you,
I do not hurt you any more than is necessary for you,
I pour the stuff to start sons and daughters fit for these States,
    I press with slow rude muscle,
I brace myself effectually, I listen to no entreaties,
I dare not withdraw till I deposit what has so long accumulated
    within me.

Through you I drain the pent-up rivers of myself,
In you I wrap a thousand onward years,
On you I graft the grafts of the best-beloved of me and America,
The drops I distil upon you shall grow fierce and athletic girls, new
    artists, musicians, and singers,
The babes I beget upon you are to beget babes in their turn,
I shall demand perfect men and women out of my love-spendings,
I shall expect them to interpenetrate with others, as I and you
    interpenetrate now,
I shall count on the fruits of the gushing showers of them, as
    I count on the fruits of the gushing showers I give now,
I shall look for loving crops from the birth, life, death, immortality,
    I plant so lovingly now.

Lucy Komisar

The New Feminism

A dozen women are variously seated in straight-backed chairs,
settled on a couch, or sprawled on the floor of a comfortable apartment on Manhattan's West Side. They range in age from twenty-five 1
to thirty-five, and include a magazine researcher, a lawyer, a housewife,
an architect, a teacher, a secretary, and a graduate student in sociology.

They are white, middle-class, attractive. All but one have college
degrees; several are married; a few are active in social causes. At first, 2
they are hesitant. They don't really know what to talk about, and so
they begin with why they came.

"I wanted to explore my feelings as a woman and find out what
others think about the things that bother me." Slowly, they open up, 3
trust growing. "I always felt so negative about being a woman; now
I'm beginning to feel good about it."

They become more personal and revealing. "My mother never
asked me what I was going to be when I grew up." "I never used to
like to talk to girls. I always thought women were inferior—I never *liked* 4
women." " I've been a secretary for three years; after that, you begin
to think that's all you're good for." "I felt so trapped when my baby
was born. I wanted to leave my husband and the child."

Repeated a hundred times in as many different rooms, these are
the voices of women's liberation, a movement that encompasses high 5
school students and grandmothers, and that is destined to eclipse the
black civil rights struggle in the force of its resentment and the consequence of its demands.

Some of us have become feminists out of anger and frustration over
job discrimination. When we left college, male students got aptitude
tests, we got typing tests. In spite of federal law, most women still are
trapped in low-paying, dead-end jobs and commonly earn less than
men for the same work—sometimes on the theory that we are only 6
"helping out," though 42 per cent of us support ourselves or families.

Others have discovered that the humanistic precepts of the radical
movement do not always apply to women. At a peace rally in Wash-

ington last year, feminists were hooted and jeered off the speakers' platform, and white women working in civil rights or antipoverty programs are expected to defer to the black male ego. Many of us got out to salvage our own buffeted egos. However, most of the new feminists express only a general malaise they were never able to identify.

Nanette Rainone is twenty-seven, the wife of a newspaperman, the mother of a seven-month-old child, and a graduate of Queens College, where she studied English literature. She married while in graduate school, then quit before the year was out to become an office clerk at *Life* magazine. "I could have known the first day that I wasn't going to be promoted, but it took me eight months to find it out."

She spent the next five months idly at home, began doing volunteer public affairs interviews for WBAI radio, and now produces *Womankind,* a weekly program on the feminist movement.

"I always felt as though I was on a treadmill, an emotional treadmill. I thought it was neurotic, but it always focused on being a woman. Then I met another woman, who had two children. We talked about my pregnancy—my confusion about my pregnancy—and the problems she was having in caring for her children now that she was separated from her husband and wanted to work."

One evening Nanette Rainone's friend took her to a feminist meeting, and immediately she became part of the movement. "The child had been an escape. I was seeking a role I couldn't find on the outside," she says. "Then I became afraid my life would be overwhelmed, that I would never get out from under and do the things I had hoped to do.

"You struggle for several years after getting out of college. You know—what are you going to do with yourself? There's always the external discrimination, but somehow you feel you are talented and you should be able to project yourself. But you don't get a good job, you get a terrible job.

"I think I was typical of the average woman who is in the movement now, because the contradictions in the system existed in my life. My parents were interested in my education. I had more room to develop my potential than was required for the role I eventually was to assume.

"I don't put down the care of children. I just put down the fixated relationship that the mother has, the never-ending association, her urge that the child be something so that *she* can be something. People need objective projects. We all feel the need to actively participate in society, in something outside ourselves where we can learn and develop.

"The closest I've been able to come to what's wrong is that men have a greater sense of self than women have. Marriage is an aspect of men's lives, whereas it is the very center of most women's lives, the whole of their lives. It seemed to me that women felt they couldn't exist except in the eyes of men—that if a man wasn't looking at them or attending to them, then they just weren't there."

If women need more evidence, history books stand ready to assure
us that we have seldom existed except as shadows of men. We have
rarely been leaders of nations or industry or the great contributors to
art and science, yet very few sociologists, political leaders, historians, 16
and moral critics have ever stopped to ask why. Now, all around the
country, women are meeting in apartments and conference rooms and
coffee shops to search out the answers.

The sessions begin with accounts of personal problems and incidents. For years, we women have believed that our anger and frustration and unhappiness were "our problems." Suddenly, we discover that 17
we are telling *the same story!* Our complaints are not only common,
they are practically universal.

It is an exhilarating experience. Women's doubts begin to disappear and are replaced by new strength and self-respect. We stop
focusing on men, and begin to identify with other women and to analyze 18
the roots of our oppression. The conclusions that are drawn challenge
the legitimacy of the sex role system upon which our civilization is
based.

At the center of the feminist critique is the recognition that women
have been forced to accept an inferior role in society, and that we have
come to believe in our own inferiority. Women are taught to be passive,
dependent, submissive, not to pursue careers but to be taken care of 19
and protected. Even those who seek outside work lack confidence and
self-esteem. Most of us are forced into menial and unsatisfying jobs:
More than three-quarters of us are clerks, sales personnel, or factory
and service workers, and a fifth of the women with B.A. degrees are
secretaries.

Self-hatred is endemic. Women—especially those who have "made
it"—identify with men and mirror their contempt for women. The ap-
proval of women does not mean very much. We don't want to work 20
for women or vote for them. We laugh, although with vague uneasiness,
at jokes about women drivers, mothers-in-law, and dumb blondes.

We depend on our relationships with men for our very identities.
Our husbands win us social status and determine how we will be 21
regarded by the world. Failure for a woman is not being selected by
a man.

We are trained in the interests of men to defer to them and serve
them and entertain them. If we are educated and gracious, it is so we
can please men and educate their children. That is the thread that 22
runs through the life of the geisha, the party girl, the business executive's wife, and the First Lady of the United States.

Men define women, and until now most of us have accepted their
definition without question. If we challenge men in the world outside 23
the home, we are all too frequently derided as "aggressive" and "un-
feminine"—by women as readily as by men.

A woman is expected to subordinate her job to the interests of
her husband's work. She'll move to another city so he can take a pro-

motion—but it rarely works the other way around. Men don't take women's work very seriously, and, as a result, neither do most women. We spend a lot of time worrying about men, while they devote most of theirs to worrying about their careers.

We are taught that getting and keeping a man is a woman's most important job; marriage, therefore, becomes our most important achievement. One suburban housewife says her father started giving her bridal pictures cut from newspapers when she was six. "He said that was what I would be when I grew up."

Most feminists do not object to marriage per se, but to the corollary that it is creative and fulfilling for an adult human being to spend her life doing housework, caring for children, and using her husband as a vicarious link to the outside world.

Most people would prefer just about any kind of work to that of a domestic servant; yet the mindless, endless, repetitious drudgery of housekeeping is the central occupation of more than fifty million women. People who would oppose institutions that portion out menial work on the basis of race see nothing wrong in a system that does the same thing on the basis of sex. (Should black and white roommates automatically assume the Negro best suited for housekeeping chores?) Even when they work at full-time jobs, wives must come home to "their" dusting and "their" laundry.

Some insist that housework is not much worse than the meaningless jobs most people have today, but there is a difference. Housewives are not paid for their work, and money is the mark of value in this society. It is also the key to independence and to the feeling of self-reliance that marks a free human being.

The justification for being a housewife is having children, and the justification for children is—well, a woman has a uterus, what else would it be for? Perhaps not all feminists agree that the uterus is a vestigial organ, but we are adamant and passionate in our denial of the old canard that biology is destiny.

Men have never been bound by their animal natures. They think and dream and create—and fly, clearly something nature had not intended, or it would have given men wings. However, we women are told that our chief function is to reproduce the species, prepare food, and sweep out the cave—er, house.

Psychologist Bruno Bettelheim states woman's functions succinctly: "We must start with the realization that, as much as women want to be good scientists or engineers, they want first and foremost to be womanly companions of men and to be mothers."

He gets no argument from Dr. Spock: "Biologically and temperamentally, I believe women were made to be concerned first and foremost with child care, husband care, and home care." Spock says some women have been "confused" by their education. (Freud was equally reactionary on the woman question, but he at least had the excuse of his Central European background.)

The species must reproduce, but this need not be the sole purpose
of a woman's life. Men want children, too, yet no one expects them to
choose between families and work. Children are in no way a substitute
for personal development and creativity. If a talented man is forced
into a senseless, menial job, it is deplored as a waste and a personal 33
misfortune; yet, a woman's special skills, education, and interests are
all too often deemed incidental and irrelevant, simply a focus for hobbies
or volunteer work.

Women who say that raising a family is a fulfilling experience are
rather like the peasant who never leaves his village. They have never 34
had the opportunity to do anything else.

As a result, women are forced to live through their children and
husbands, and they feel cheated and resentful when they realize that
is not enough. When a woman says she gave her children everything,
she is telling the truth—and that is the tragedy. Often when she reaches 35
her late thirties, her children have grown up, gone to work or college,
and left her in a bleak and premature old age. Middle-aged women
who feel empty and useless are the mainstay of America's psychiatrists
—who generally respond by telling them to "accept their role."

The freedom to choose whether or not to have children has always
been illusory. A wife who is deliberately "barren"—a word that rein-
forces the worn-out metaphor of woman as Mother Earth—is considered 36
neurotic or unnatural. Not only is motherhood not central to a woman's
life, it may not be necessary or desirable. For the first time, some of
us are admitting openly and without guilt that we do not want children. And the population crisis is making it even clearer that as a symbol
for Americans motherhood ought to defer to apple pie.

The other half of the reproduction question is sex. The sexual revolution didn't liberate women at all; it only created a bear market for men. 37
One of the most talked-about tracts in the movement is a pamphlet
by Ann Koedt called "The Myth of the Vaginal Orgasm," which says
most women don't have orgasms because most men won't accept the
fact that the female orgasm is clitoral.

We are so used to putting men's needs first that we don't know
how to ask for what *we* want, or else we share the common ignorance 38
about our own physiology and think there is something wrong with
us when we don't have orgasms "the right way." Freudian analysts
contribute to the problem. The realization that past guilt and frustration have been unnecessary is not the least of the sentiments that draws
women to women's liberation.

Feminists also protest the general male proclivity to regard us as
decorative, amusing sex objects even in the world outside bed. We 39
resent the sexual sell in advertising, the catcalls we get on the street,
girlie magazines and pornography, bars that refuse to serve unescorted
women on the assumption they are prostitutes, the not very subtle
brainwashing by cosmetic companies, and the attitude of men who
praise our knees in miniskirts, but refuse to act as if we had brains.

Even the supposedly humanistic worlds of rock music and radical politics are not very different. Young girls who join "the scene" or "the movement" are labeled "groupies" and are sexually exploited; the flashy porno-sheets such as *Screw* and *Kiss* are published by the self-appointed advocates of the new "free," anti-Establishment life-style. "*Plus ça change. . . .*"

We are angry about the powers men wield over us. The physical power—women who study karate do so as a defense against muggers, not lovers. And the social power—we resent the fact that men take the initiative with women, that women cannot ask for dates but must sit home waiting for the phone to ring.

That social conditioning began in childhood when fathers went out to work and mothers stayed home, images perpetuated in schoolbooks and games and on television. If we were bright students, we were told, "You're smart—for a girl," and then warned not to appear *too* smart in front of boys—"Or you won't have dates."

Those of us who persisted in reaching for a career were encouraged to be teachers or nurses so we would have "something to fall back on." My mother told me: "You're so bright, it's a pity you're not a boy. You could become president of a bank—or anything you wanted."

Ironically, and to our dismay, we discovered that playing the assigned role is precisely what elicits masculine contempt for our inferiority and narrow interests. *Tooth and Nail,* a newsletter published by women's liberation groups in the San Francisco area, acidly points out a few of the contradictions: "A smart woman never shows her brains; she allows the man to think himself clever. . . . Women's talk is all chatter; they don't understand things men are interested in."

Or: "Don't worry your pretty little head about such matters. . . . A woman's brain is between her legs. . . Women like to be protected and treated like little girls. . . . Women can't make decisions."

The feminist answer is to throw out the whole simplistic division of human characteristics into masculine and feminine, and to insist that there are no real differences between men and women other than those enforced by culture.

Men say women are not inferior, we are just different; yet somehow they have appropriated most of the qualities that society admires and have left us with the same distinctive features that were attributed to black people before the civil rights revolution.

Men, for example, are said to be strong, assertive, courageous, logical, constructive, creative, and independent. Women are weak, passive, irrational, over-emotional, empty-headed, and lacking in strong superegos. (Thank Freud for the last.) Both blacks and women are contented, have their place, and know how to use wiles—flattery, and wide-eyed, open-mouth ignorance—to get around "the man." It is obviously natural that men should be dominant and women submissive. Shuffle, baby, shuffle.

Our "sexist" system has hurt men as well as women, forcing them
into molds that deny the value of sensitivity, tenderness, and sentiment.
Men who are not aggressive worry about their virility just as strong
women are frightened by talk about their being castrating females. The 49
elimination of rigid sex-role definitions would liberate everyone. And
that is the goal of the women's liberation movement.

Women's liberation groups, which have sprung up everywhere
across the country, are taking names like Radical Women or the
Women's Liberation Front or the Feminists. Most start as groups of
ten or twelve; many, when they get too large for discussion, split in a 50
form of mitosis. Sometimes they are tied to central organizations set
up for action, or they maintain communications with each other or
cosponsor newsletters with similar groups in their area.

Some are concerned with efforts to abolish abortion laws, a few
have set up cooperative day-care centers, others challenge the stereotypes of woman's image, and many are organized for "consciousness- 51
raising"—a kind of group therapy or encounter session that starts with
the premise that there is something wrong with the system, not the
women in the group.

The amorphousness and lack of central communication in the movement make it virtually impossible to catalogue the established groups, 52
let alone the new ones that regularly appear; many of the "leaders"
who have been quoted in newspapers or interviewed on television have
been anointed only by the press.

The one organization with a constitution, board members, and
chapters (some thirty-five) throughout the country is the National
Organization for Women. Its founding in 1966 was precipitated by the 53
ridicule that greeted the inclusion of sex in the prohibitions against job
discrimination in the 1964 Civil Rights Act. (A staff member in the
federal Equal Employment Opportunity Commission, which enforces
the act, said it took pressure from NOW to get the EEOC to take that
part of the law seriously.)

NOW members are not very different from women in other feminist groups, though they tend to include more professionals and older
women. In general, they eschew "consciousness-raising" in favor of
political action, and they are more likely to demonstrate for job equality 54
and child-care centers than for the abolition of marriage or the traditional family unit.

NOW's president is Betty Friedan, who in 1963 published *The
Feminine Mystique*, a challenge to the myth that a woman's place is
either in a boudoir in a pink, frilly nightgown, on her hands and knees
scrubbing the kitchen floor, or in a late model station wagon taking the 55
kids to music lessons and Cub Scout meetings. (An article that previewed
the theme of the book was turned down by every major women's magazine. "One was horrified and said I was obviously talking to and for
a few neurotic women." When the book came out, two of these mag-

azines published excerpts and several now have commissioned articles about the movement.)

Today, Betty Friedan says, the movement must gain political power by mobilizing the 51 per cent of the electorate who are women, as well as seeking elected offices for themselves. "We have to break down the actual barriers that prevent women from being full people in society, and not only end explicit discrimination but build new institutions. Most women will continue to bear children, and unless we create child-care centers on a mass basis, it's all talk."

Women are beginning to read a good deal about their own place in history, about the determined struggles of the suffragettes, the isolation of Virginia Woolf, and the heroism of Rosa Luxemburg. The Congress to Unite Women, which drew some 500 participants from cities in the Northeast, called for women's studies in high schools and colleges.

Present are all the accouterments of any social movement—feminist magazines such as *No More Fun and Games* in Boston, *Up from Under* in New York, and *Aphra,* a literary magazine published in Baltimore. (Anne Sexton wrote in the dedication, "As long as it can be said about a woman writer, 'She writes like a man' and that woman takes it as a compliment, we are in trouble.")

There are feminist theaters in at least New York and Boston, buttons that read "Uppity Women Unite," feminist poems and songs, a feminist symbol (the biological sign for woman with an equal sign in the center), and, to denounce specific advertisements, gum stickers that state, "This ad insults women."

With a rising feminist consciousness, everything takes on new significance—films, advertisements, offhand comments, little things that never seemed important before. A few women conclude that chivalry and flirting reduce women to mere sex objects for men. We stop feeling guilty about opening doors, and some of us experiment with paying our own way on dates.

Personal acts are matched by political ones. The National Organization for Women went to court to get a federal ruling barring segregated help-wanted ads in newspapers, and it regularly helps women file complaints before the EEOC and local human rights commissions.

A women's rights platform was adopted last year by the State Committee of the California Democratic Party, and the Women's Rights Committee of the New Democratic Coalition plans to make feminist demands an issue in New York politics. A women's caucus exists in the Democratic Policy Council, headed by Senator Fred Harris.

At Grinnell College in Iowa, students protested the appearance of a representative from *Playboy* magazine, and women from sixteen cities converged on Atlantic City to make it clear what they think of the Miss America Pageant. In New York, a group protested advertisements by toymakers that said "Boys were born to build and learn" and "girls were born to be dancers."

Women's caucuses have been organized in the American Political
Science, Psychological, and Sociological associations. At New York Uni- 64
versity, a group of law students won their fight to make women eligible
for a series of coveted $10,000 scholarships.

Pro-abortion groups have organized around the country to repeal
anti-abortion laws, challenge them in the courts, or openly defy them. 65
In Blooomington, Indiana, New York City, and elsewhere, women's
liberation groups have set up cooperative day-care centers, which are
illegal under strict state rules that regulate child care facilities.

Free child care is likely to become the most significant demand
made by the movement, and one calculated to draw the support of 66
millions of women who may not be interested in other feminist issues.
About four million working mothers have children under six years of
age, and only 2 per cent of these are in day-care centers.

Even Establishment institutions appear to reflect the new attitudes.
Princeton, Williams, and Yale have begun to admit women students, 67
though on an unequal quota basis—and not to the hallowed pine-
paneled halls of their alumni clubhouses.

Nevertheless, most people have only a vague idea of the significance of the new movement. News commentators on year-end analysis 68
shows ignored the question or sloughed it off uncomfortably. One said
the whole idea frightened him.

Yet, the women's movement promises to affect radically the life
of virtually everyone in America. Only a small part of the population
suffers because it is black, and most people have little contact with 69
minorities. Women are 51 per cent of the population, and chances are
that every adult American either is one, is married to one, or has close
social or business relations with many.

The feminist revolution will overturn the basic premises upon which
these relations are built—stereotyped notions about the family and the
roles of men and women, fallacies concerning masculinity and femininity, 70
and the economic division of labor into paid work and homemaking.

If the 1960s belonged to the blacks, the next ten years are ours. 71

15%

She tries to get things out of men
that she can't get because she's not
15% prettier.

Marlene Dixon

Why Women's Liberation?

The 1960s has been a decade of liberation; women have been swept up by that ferment along with blacks, Latins, American Indians and poor whites—the whole soft underbelly of this society. As each oppressed group in turn discovered the nature of its oppression in American society, so women have discovered that they too thirst for free and fully human lives. The result has been the growth of a new women's movement, whose base encompasses poor black and poor white women on relief, working women exploited in the labor force, middle class women incarcerated in the split level dream house, college girls awakening to the fact that sexiness is not the crowning achievement in life, and movement women who have discovered that in a freedom movement they 1
themselves are not free. In less than four years women have created a varity of organizations, from the nationally-based middle class National Organization of Women (NOW) to local radical and radical feminist groups in every major city in North America. The new movement includes caucuses within nearly every New Left group and within most professional associations in the social sciences. Ranging in politics from reform to revolution, it has produced critiques of almost every segment of American society and constructed an ideology that rejects every hallowed cultural assumption about the nature and role of women.

As is typical of a young movement, much of its growth has been underground. The papers and manifestos written and circulated would surely comprise two very large volumes if published, but this literature is almost unknown outside of women's liberation. Nevertheless, where even a year ago organizing was slow and painful, with small cells of six
or ten women, high turnover, and an uphill struggle against fear and 2
resistance, in 1969 all that has changed. Groups are growing up everywhere with women eager to hear a hard line, to articulate and express their own rage and bitterness. Moving about the country, I have found an electric atmosphere of excitement and responsiveness. Everywhere there are doubts, stirrings, a desire to listen, to find out what it's all about. The extent to which groups have become politically radical is

astounding. A year ago the movement stressed male chauvinism and psychological oppression; now the emphasis is on understanding the economic and social roots of women's oppression, and the analyses range from social democracy to Marxism. But the most striking change of all in the last year has been the loss of fear. Women are no longer afraid that their rebellion will threaten their very identity as women. They are not frightened by their own militancy, but liberated by it. Women's Liberation is an idea whose time has come.

The old women's movement burned itself out in the frantic decade of the 1920s. After a hundred years of struggle, women won a battle, only to lose the campaign: the vote was obtained, but the new millennium did not arrive. Women got the vote and achieved a measure of legal emancipation, but the real social and cultural barriers to full equality for women remained untouched.

For over 30 years the movement remained buried in its own ashes. Women were born and grew to maturity virtually ignorant of their own history of rebellion, aware only of a caricature of blue stockings and suffragettes. Even as increasing numbers of women were being driven into the labor force by the brutal conditions of the 1930s and by the massive drain of men into the military in the 1940s, the old ideal remained: a woman's place was in the home and behind her man. As the war ended and men returned to resume their jobs in factories and offices, women were forced back to the kitchen and nursery with a vengeance. This story has been repeated after each war and the reason is clear: women from a flexible, cheap labor pool which is essential to a capitalist system. When labor is scarce, they are forced onto the labor market. When labor is plentiful, they are forced out. Women and blacks have provided a reserve army of unemployed workers, benefiting capitalists and the stable male white working class alike. Yet the system imposes untold suffering on the victims, blacks and women, through low wages and chronic unemployment.

With the end of the war the average age at marriage declined, the average size of families went up, and the suburban migration began in earnest. The political conservatism of the '50s was echoed in a social conservatism which stressed a Victorian ideal of the woman's life: a full womb and selfless devotion to husband and children.

As the bleak decade played itself out, however, three important social developments emerged which were to make a rebirth of women's struggle inevitable. First, women came to make up more than a third of the labor force, the number of working women being twice the prewar figure. Yet the marked increase in female employment did nothing to better the position of women, who were more occupationally disadvantaged in the 1960s than they had been 25 years earlier. Rather than moving equally into all sectors of the occupational structure, they were being forced into the low paying service, clerical and semi-skilled categories. In 1940, women had held 45 per cent of all professional and

technical positions; in 1967, they held only 37 per cent. The proportion
of women in service jobs meanwhile rose from 50 to 55 per cent.

Second, the intoxicating wine of marriage and suburban life was
turning sour; a generation of women woke up to find their children
grown and life (roughly 30 more productive years) of housework and 7
bridge parties stretching out before them like a wasteland. For many
younger women, the empty drudgery they saw in the suburban life was
a sobering contradiction to adolescent dreams of romantic love and
the fulfilling role of woman as wife and mother.

Third, a growing civil rights movement was sweeping thousands
of young men and women into a moral crusade—a crusade which harsh
political experience was to transmute into the New Left. The American
Dream was riven and tattered in Mississippi and finally napalmed in 8
Viet-Nam. Young Americans were drawn not to Levittown, but to
Berkeley, the Haight-Ashbury and the East Village. Traditional political
ideologies and cultural myths, sexual mores and sex roles with them,
began to disintegrate in an explosion of rebellion and protest.

The three major groups which make up the new women's movement—working women, middle class married women and students—
bring very different kinds of interests and objectives to women's libera- 9
tion. Working women are most concerned with the economic issues of
guaranteed employment, fair wages, job discrimination and child care.
Their most immediate oppression is rooted in industrial capitalism and
felt directly through the vicissitudes of an exploitative labor market.

Middle class women, oppressed by the psychological mutilation and
injustice of institutionalized segregation, discrimination and imposed
inferiority, are most sensitive to the dehumanizing consequences of 10
severely limited lives. Usually well educated and capable, these women
are rebelling against being forced to trivialize their lives, to live vicariously through husbands and children.

Students, as unmarried middle class girls, have been most sensitized
to the sexual exploitation of women. They have experienced the frustration of one-way relationships in which the girl is forced into a "wife"
and companion role with none of the supposed benefits of marriage.
Young women have increasingly rebelled not only against passivity and 11
dependency in their relationships but also against the notion that they
must function as sexual objects, being defined in purely sexual rather
than human terms, and being forced to package and sell themselves as
commodities on the sex market.

Each group represents an independent aspect of the total institutionalized oppression of women. Their differences are those of emphasis
and immediate interest rather than of fundamental goals. All women
suffer from economic exploitation, from psychological deprivation, and 12
from exploitive sexuality. Within women's liberation there is a growing
understanding that the common oppression of women provides the basis
for uniting across class and race lines to form a powerful and radical
movement.

Racism and Male Supremacy

Clearly, for the liberation of women to become a reality it is necessary to destroy the ideology of male supremacy which asserts the biological and social inferiority of women in order to justify massive institutionalized oppression. Yet we all know that many women are as loud in their disavowal of this oppression as are the men who chant the litany of "a woman's place is in the home and behind her man." In fact, women are as trapped in their false consciousness as were the mass of blacks 20 years ago, and for much the same reason.

As blacks were defined and limited socially by their color, so women are defined and limited by their sex. While blacks, it was argued, were preordained by God or nature, or both, to be hewers of wood and drawers of water, so women are destined to bear and rear children, and to sustain their husbands with obedience and compassion. The Sky-God tramples through the heavens and the Earth-/Mother-Goddess is always flat on her back with her legs spread, putting out for one and all.

Indeed, the phenomenon of male chauvinism can only be understood when it is perceived as a form of racism, based on stereotypes drawn from a deep belief in the biological inferiority of women. The so-called "black analogy" is no analogy at all; it is the same social process that is at work, a process which both justifies and helps perpetuate the exploitation of one group of human beings by another.

The very stereotypes that express the society's belief in the biological inferiority of women recall the images used to justify the oppression of blacks. The nature of women, like that of slaves, is depicted as dependent, incapable of reasoned thought, childlike in its simplicity and warmth, martyred in the role of mother, and mystical in the role of sexual partner. In its benevolent form, the inferior position of women results in paternalism; in its malevolent form, a domestic tyranny which can be unbelievably brutal.

It has taken over 50 years to discredit the scientific and social "proof" which once gave legitimacy to the myths of black racial inferiority. Today most people can see that the theory of the genetic inferiority of blacks is absurd. Yet few are shocked by the fact that scientists are still busy "proving" the biological inferiority of women.

In recent years, in which blacks have led the struggle for liberation, the emphasis on racism has focused only upon racism against blacks. The fact that "racism" has been practiced against many groups other than blacks has been pushed into the background. Indeed, a less forceful but more accurate term for the phenomenon would be "social Darwinism." It was the opinion of the social Darwinists that in the natural course of things the "fit" succeed (i.e. oppress) and the "unfit" (i.e. the biologically inferior) sink to the bottom. According to this view, the very fact of a group's oppression proves its inferiority and the inevitable correctness of its low position. In this way each successive immigrant group coming to America was decked out in the garments of "racial" or biological inferiority until the group was sufficiently assimilated, whereupon Anglo-Saxon venom would turn on a new group filling up the space at the bottom. Now two groups remain, neither of which has been assimilated according to the classic American pattern: the "visibles"—blacks and women. It is equally true for both: "it won't wear off."

Yet the greatest obstacle facing those who would organize women
remains women's belief in their own inferiority. Just as all subject populations are controlled by their acceptance of the rightness of their own
status, so women remain subject because they believe in the rightness
of their own oppression. This dilemma is not a fortuitous one, for the
entire society is geared to socialize women to believe in and adopt as 19
immutable necessity their traditional and inferior role. From earliest
training to the grave, women are constrained and propagandized. Spend
an evening at the movies or watching television, and you will see a
grotesque figure called woman presented in a hundred variations upon
the themes of "children, church, kitchen" or "the chick sex-pot."

For those who believe in the "rights of mankind," the "dignity of
man," consider that to make a woman a person, a human being in her
own right, you would have to change her sex: imagine Stokely Carmichael "prone and silent"; imagine Mark Rudd as a Laugh-In girl;
picture Rennie Davis as Miss America. Such contradictions as these 20
show how pervasive and deep-rooted is the cultural contempt for
women, how difficult it is to imagine a woman as a serious human
being, or conversely, how empty and degrading is the image of woman
that floods the culture.

Countless studies have shown that black acceptance of white stereotypes lead to mutilated identity, to alienation, to rage and self-hatred.
Human beings cannot bear in their own hearts the contradictions of 21
those who hold them in contempt. The ideology of male supremacy
and its effect upon women merits as serious study as has been given
to the effects of prejudice upon Jews, blacks, and immigrant groups.

It is customary to shame those who would draw the parallel between women and blacks by a great show of concern and chest beating
over the suffering of black people. Yet this response itself reveals a
refined combination of white middle class guilt and male chauvinism,
for it overlooks several essential facts. For example, the most oppressed
group within the feminine population is made up of black women, many
of whom take a dim view of the black male intellectual's adoption of 22
white male attitudes of sexual superiority (an irony too cruel to require
comment). Neither are those who make this pious objection to the racial
parallel addressing themselves very adequately to the millions of white
working class women living at the poverty level, who are not likely to
be moved by this middle class guilt-ridden one-upmanship while having
to deal with the boss, the factory, or the welfare worker day after day.
They are already dangerously resentful of the gains made by the blacks,

and much of their "racist backlash" stems from the fact that they have been forgotten in the push for social change. Emphasis on the real mechanisms of oppression—on the commonality of the process—is essential lest groups such as these, which should work in alliance, become divided against one another.

White middle class males already struggling with the acknowledgment of their own racism do not relish an added burden of recognition: that to white guilt must soon be added "male." It is therefore understandable that they should refuse to see the harshness of the lives of most women—to honestly face the facts of massive institutionalized discrimination against women. Witness the performance to date: "Take her down off the platform and give her a good fuck," "Petty Bourgeois Revisionist Running Dogs," or in the classic words of a Berkeley male "leader," "Let them eat cock."

Among whites, women remain the most oppressed—and the most unorganized—group. Although they constitute a potential mass base for the radical movement, in terms of movement priorities they are ignored; indeed they might as well be invisible. Far from being an accident, this omission is a direct outgrowth of the solid male supremist beliefs of white radical and left-liberal men. Even now, faced with both fact and agitation, leftist men find the idea of placing any serious priority upon women so outrageous, such a degrading notion, that they respond with a virulence far out of proportion to the modest request of movement women. This only shows that women must stop wasting their time worrying about the chauvinism of men in the movement and focus instead on their real priority: organizing women.

Marriage: Genesis of Women's Rebellion

The institution of marriage is the chief vehicle for the perpetuation of the oppression of women; it is through the role of wife that the subjugation of women is maintained. In a very real way the role of wife has been the genesis of women's rebellion throughout history.

Looking at marriage from a detached point of view one may well ask why anyone gets married, much less women. One answer lies in the economics of women's position, for women are so occupationally limited that drudgery in the home is considered to be infinitely superior to drudgery in the factory. Secondly, women themselves have no independent social status. Indeed, there is no clearer index of the social worth of a woman in this society than the fact that she has none in her own right. A woman is first defined by the man to whom she is attached, but more particularly by the man she marries, and secondly by the children she bears and rears—hence the anxiety over sexual attractiveness, the frantic scramble for boyfriends and husbands. Having obtained and married a man the race is then on to have children, in order that their attractiveness and accomplishments may add more social worth. In a woman, not having children is seen as an incapacity somewhat akin to impotence in a man.

Beneath all of the pressures of the sexual marketplace and the
marital status game, however, there is a far more sinister organization
of economic exploitation and psychological mutilation. The housewife
role, usually defined in terms of the biological duty of a woman to
reproduce and her "innate" suitability for a nurturant and companionship role, is actually crucial to industrial capitalism in an advanced state 27
of technological development. In fact, the housewife (some 44 million
women of all classes, ethnic groups and races) provides, unpaid, absolutely essential services and labor. In turn, her assumption of all household duties makes it possible for the man to spend the majority of his
time at the workplace.

It is important to understand the social and economic exploitation
of the married woman, since the real productivity of her labor is denied
by the commonly held assumption that she is dependent on her husband, exchanging her keep for emotional and nurturant services. Margaret Benston, a radical women's liberation leader, points out: "In sheer
quantity, household labor, including child care, constitutes a huge
amount of socially necessary production. Nevertheless, in a society based
on commodity production, it is not usually considered even as 'real
work' since it is outside of trade and the marketplace. This assignment 28
of household work as the function of a special category 'women' means
that this group does stand in a different relationship to production. . . .
The material basis for the inferior status of women is to be found in
just this definition of women. In a society in which money determines
value, women are a group who work outside the money economy. Their
work is not worth money, is therefore valueless, is therefore not even
real work. And women themselves, who do this valueless work, can
hardly be expected to be worth as much as men, who work for money."

Women are essential to the economy not only as free labor, but also
as consumers. The American system of capitalism depends for its survival on the consumption of vast amounts of socially wasteful goods,
and a prime target for the unloading of this waste is the housewife. She
is the purchasing agent for the family, but beyond that she is eager 29
to buy because her own identity depends on her accomplishments as a
consumer and her ability to satisfy the wants of her husband and children. This is not, of course, to say that she has any power in the economy. Although she spends the wealth, she does not own or control it–
it simply passes through her hands.

In addition to their role as housewives and consumers, increasing
numbers of women are taking outside employment. These women leave
the home to join an exploited labor force, only to return at night to 30
assume the double burden of housework on top of wage work–that is,
they are forced to work at two full-time jobs. No man is required or
expected to take on such a burden. The result: two workers from one
household in the labor force with no cutback in essential female functions–three for the price of two, quite a bargain.

Frederick Engels, now widely read in women's liberation, argues that, regardless of her status in the larger society, within the context of the family the woman's relationship to the man is one of proletariat to bourgeoisie. One consequence of this class division in the family is to weaken the capacity of men and women oppressed by the society to struggle together against it.

In all classes and groups, the institution of marriage functions to a greater or lesser degree to oppress women; the unity of women of different classes hinges upon our understanding of that common oppression. The 19th century women's movement refused to deal with marriage and sexuality, and chose instead to fight for the vote and elevate the feminine mystique to a political ideology. That decision retarded the movement for decades. But 1969 is not 1889. For one thing, there now exist alternatives to marriage. The most original and creative politics of the women's movement has come from a direct confrontation with the issue of marriage and sexuality. The cultural revolution—experimentation with lifestyles, communal living, collective child-rearing—have all come from the rebellion against dehumanized sexual relationships, against the notion of women as sexual commodities, against the constriction and spiritual strangulation inherent in the role of wife.

Lessons have been learned from the failures of the earlier movement as well. The feminine mystique is no longer mistaken for politics, nor gaining the vote for winning human rights. Women are now all together at the bottom of the work world, and the basis exists for a common focus of struggle for all women in American society. It remains for the movement to understand this, to avoid the mistakes of the past, to respond creatively to the possibilities of the present.

Women's oppression, although rooted in the institution of marriage, does not stop at the kitchen or the bedroom door. Indeed, the economic exploitation of women in the workplace is the most commonly recognized aspect of the oppression of women.

Most women who enter the labor force do not work for "pin money" or "self-fulfillment." Sixty-two per cent of all women working in 1967 were doing so out of economic need (i.e., were either alone or with husbands earning less than $5000 a year). In 1963, 36 per cent of American families had an income of less than $5000 a year. Women from these families work because they must; they contribute 35 to 40 per cent of the family's total income when working full-time, and 15 to 20 per cent when working part-time.

Despite their need, however, women have always represented the most exploited sector of the industrial labor force. Child and female labor were introduced during the early stages of industrial capitalism, at a time when most men were gainfully employed in crafts. As industrialization developed and craft jobs were eliminated, men entered the industrial labor force, driving women and children into the lowest categories of work and pay. Indeed, the position of women and children industrial workers was so pitiful, and their wages so small, that the craft unions refused to organize them. Even when women organized themselves and engaged in militant strikes and labor agitation—from the shoemakers of Lynn, Massachusetts, to the International Ladies' Garment Workers and their great strike of 1909—male unionists continued to ignore their needs. As a result of this male supremacy in the unions, women remain essentially unorganized, despite the fact that they are becoming an ever larger part of the labor force.

The trend is clearly toward increasing numbers of women entering the work force: women represented 55 per cent of the growth of the
total labor force in 1962, and the number of working women rose from 37
16.9 million in 1957 to 24 million in 1962. There is every indication that the number of women in the labor force will continue to grow as rapidly in the future.

Job discrimination against women exists in all sectors of work, even in occupations which are predominantly made up of women. This discrimination is reinforced in the field of education, where women are being short-changed at a time when the job market demands higher educational levels. In 1962, for example, while women constituted 53 per cent of the graduating high school class, only 42 per cent of the entering college class were women. Only one in three people who received a B.A. or M.A. in that year was a woman, and only one in ten who received a Ph.D. was a woman. These figures represent a decline in educational achievement for women since the 1930s, when women
received two out of five of the B.A. and M.A. degrees given, and one 38
out of seven of the Ph.Ds. While there has been a dramatic increase in the number of people, including women, who go to college, women have not kept pace with men in terms of educational achievement. Furthermore, women have lost ground in professional employment. In 1960 only 22 per cent of the faculty and other professional staff at colleges and universities were women—down from 28 per cent in 1949, 27 per cent in 1930, 26 per cent in 1920. 1960 does beat 1919 with only 20 per cent—"you've come a long way, baby"—right back to where you started! In other professional categories: 10 per cent of all scientists are women, 7 per cent of all physicians, 3 per cent of all lawyers, and 1 per cent of all engineers.

Even when women do obtain an education, in many cases it does them little good. Women, whatever their educational level, are concentrated in the lower paying occupations. The figures in Chart A tell a story that most women know and few men will admit: most women are forced to work at clerical jobs, for which they are paid, on the average, $1600 less per year than men doing the same work. Working
class women in the service and operative (semi-skilled) categories, 39
making up 30 per cent of working women, are paid $1900 less per year on the average than are men. Of all working women, only 13 per cent are professionals (including low-pay and low-status work such as teaching, nursing and social work), and they earn $2600 less per year than do professional men. Household workers, the lowest category of all, are predominantly women (over 2 million) and predominantly black and third world, earning for their labor barely over $1000 per year.

Not only are women forced onto the lowest rungs of the occupational ladder, they are in the lowest income levels as well. The most constant and bitter injustice experienced by all women is the income differential. While women might passively accept low status jobs, limited opportunities for advancement, and discrimination in the factory, office and university, they choke finally on the daily fact that the male worker next to them earns more, and usually does less. In 1965 the median wage or salary income of year-round full-time women workers was only 60 per cent that of men, a 4 per cent loss since 1955. Twenty-nine per cent of working women earned less than $3000 a year as compared with 11 per cent of the men; 43 per cent of the women earned from $3000 to $5000 a year as compared with 19 per cent of the men; and 9 per cent of the women earned $7000 or more as compared with 43 per cent of the men. What most people do not know is that in certain respects, women suffer more than do non-white men, and that black and third world women suffer most of all.

Chart A. Comparative Statistics for Men and Women in the Labor Force, 1960

	PERCENTAGE OF WORKING WOMEN IN EACH OCCUPATIONAL CATEGORY	INCOME OF YEAR ROUND FULL TIME WORKERS		NUMBERS OF WORKERS IN MILLIONS	
OCCUPATION		WOMEN	MEN	WOMEN	MEN
Professional	13%	$4358	$7115	3	5
Managers, Officials and Proprietors	5	3514	7241	1	5
Clerical	31	3586	5247	7	3
Operatives	15	2970	4977	4	9
Sales	7	2389	5842	2	3
Service	15	2340	4089	3	3
Private Household	10	1156	—	2	—

Sources: U. S. Department of Commerce, Bureau of the Census: "Current Population Reports," P-60, No. 37, and U. S. Department of Labor, Bureau of Labor Statistics and U. S. Department of Commerce, Bureau of the Census.

Chart B. Median Annual Wages for Men and Women by Race, 1960

WORKERS	MEDIAN ANNUAL WAGE
Males, White	$5137
Males, Non-White	$3075
Females, White	$2537
Females, Non-White	$1276

Source: U. S. Department of Commerce, Bureau of the Census. Also see: President's Commission on the Status of Women, 1963.

Women, regardless of race, are more disadvantaged than are men,
including non-white men. White women earn $2600 less than white
men and $1500 less than non-white men. The brunt of the inequality 41
is carried by 2.5 million non-white women, 94 per cent of whom are
black. They earn $3800 less than white men, $1900 less than non-white
men, and $1200 less than the white women.

There is no more bitter paradox in the racism of this country than
that the white man, articulating the male supremacy of the white male
middle class, should provide the rationale for the oppression of black
women by black men. Black women constitute the largest minority in
the United States, and they are the most disadvantaged group in the 42
labor force. The further oppression of black women will not liberate
black men, for black women were never the oppressors of their men—
that is a myth of the liberal white man. The oppression of black men
comes from institutionalized racism and economic exploitation: from the
world of the white man. Consider the following facts and figures.

The percentage of black working women has always been propor-
tionately greater than that of white women. In 1900, 41 per cent of
black women were employed, as compared to 17 per cent for white
women. In 1963, the proportion of black women employed was still a
fourth greater than that of whites. In 1960, 44 per cent of black
married women with children under six years were in the labor force, 43
in contrast to 29 per cent for white women. While job competition requires ever higher levels of education, the bulk of illiterate women are
black. On the whole, black women—who often have the greatest need
for employment—are the most discriminated against in terms of opportunity. Forced by an oppressive and racist society to carry unbelievably
heavy economic and social burdens, black women stand at the bottom
of that society, doubly marked by the caste signs of color and sex.

The rise of new agitation for the occupational equality of women
also coincided with the re-entry of the "lost generation"—the housewives of the 1950s—into the job market. Women from middle class
backgrounds, faced with an "empty nest" (children grown or in school)
and a widowed or divorced rate of one-fourth to one-third of all marriages, returned to the workplace in large numbers. But once there 44
they discovered that women, middle class or otherwise, are the last
hired, the lowest paid, the least often promoted, and the first fired.
Furthermore, women are more likely to suffer job discrimination on
the basis of age, so the widowed and divorced suffer particularly, even
though their economic need to work is often urgent. Age discrimination
also means that the option of work after child-rearing is limited. Even
highly qualified older women find themselves forced into low-paid,
unskilled or semi-skilled work—if they are lucky enough to find a job
in the first place.

The realities of the work world for most middle class women—that they become members of the working class, like it or not—are understandably distant to many young men and women in college who have never had to work, and who tend to think of the industrial "proletariat" as a revolutionary force, to the exclusion of "bourgeois" working women. Their image of the "pampered middle class woman" is factually incorrect and politically naive. It is middle class women forced into working class life who are often the first to become conscious of the contradiction between the "American Dream" and their daily experience.

Faced with discrimination on the job—after being forced into the lower levels of the occupational structure—millions of women are inescapably presented with the fundamental contradictions in their unequal treatment and their massive exploitation. The rapid growth of women's liberation as a movement is related in part to the exploitation of working women in all occupational categories.

Male supremacy, marriage, and the structure of wage labor—each of these aspects of women's oppression has been crucial to the resurgence of the women's struggle. It must be abundantly clear that radical social change must occur before there can be significant improvement in the social position of women. Some form of socialism is a minimum requirement, considering the changes that must come in the institutions of marriage and the family alone. The intrinsic radicalism of the struggle for women's liberation necessarily links women with all other oppressed groups.

The heart of the movement, as in all freedom movements, rests in women's knowledge, whether articulated or still only an illness without a name, that they are not inferior—not chicks, nor bunnies, nor quail, nor cows, nor bitches, nor ass, nor meat. Women hear the litany of their own dehumanization each day. Yet all the same, women know that male supremacy is a lie. They know they are not animals or sexual objects or commodities. They know their lives are mutilated, because they see within themselves a promise of creativity and personal integration. Feeling the contradiction between the essentially creative and self-actualizing human being within her, and the cruel and degrading less-than-human role she is compelled to play, a woman begins to perceive the falseness of what her society has forced her to be. And once she perceives this, she knows that she must fight.

Women must learn the meaning of rage, the violence that liberates the human spirit. The rhetoric of invective is an equally essential stage, for in discovering and venting their rage against the enemy—and the enemy in everyday life is men—women also experience the justice of their own violence. They learn the first lessons in their own latent strength. Women must learn to know themselves as revolutionaries. They must become hard and strong in their determination, while retaining their humanity and tenderness.

There is a rage that impels women into a total commitment to women's liberation. That ferocity stems from a denial of mutilation; it is a cry for life, a cry for the liberation of the spirit. Roxanne Dunbar, surely one of the most impressive women in the movement, conveys

the feelings of many: "We are damaged—we women, we oppressed, we disinherited. There are very few who are not damaged, and they rule. . . . The oppressed trust those who rule more than they trust themselves, because self-contempt emerges from powerlessness. Anyway, few oppressed people believe that life could be much different. . . . We are damaged and we have the right to hate and have contempt and to kill and to scream. But for what? . . . Do we want the oppressor to
admit he is wrong, to withdraw his misuse of us? He is only too happy 50
to admit guilt—then do nothing but try to absorb and exorcize the new thought. . . . That does not make up for what I have lost, what I never had, and what all those others who are worse off than I never had. . . . Nothing will compensate for the irreparable harm it has done to my sisters. . . . How could we possibly settle for anything remotely less, even take a crumb in the meantime less, than the total annihilation of a system which systematically destroys half its people. . . ."

Walter Karp

The Feminine Utopia

The common features of human life have been with us for an immensely long time. Ever since humankind began to make a human world for his habitation, that world has been shared and divided along sexual lines. To the male half, by and large, has gone the responsibility for supporting and protecting females; to the female half, by and large, has gone the responsibility for nurturing children and for maintaining the households in which children are raised. Although we speak, in exalted moments, of "humanity," we see each other as males and females, as men and women, and not simply as fellow human beings. So enduring are these common features that they have come to seem natural, right, and unalterable, the permanent expression of our deepest human nature.

Today, for the first time, they are being attacked in the awesome name of liberty and justice. They are being shown to be not natural but contrived, not right but oppressive—and certainly not unalterable. This sharp and comprehensive attack is led by a protest movement known as Women's Liberation, the re-emergence after about a forty-year hiatus of what used to be called, more simply, the women's movement. It maintains that the common features of the human world are the basis of an ancient and radical injustice, which must now be swept away: the domination of females by males. It is a bold and comprehensive challenge, for if the movement is right, then much of what has passed for human wisdom is false. We would be forced to admit that humankind has been wrong just where we were most certain we were right: in the way we have ordered our most basic institutions to meet the elementary needs of human life. If, on the other hand, the women's movement is wrong, then we must recover half-forgotten fundamentals, fundamentals that have been obscured, I believe, by all that is modern in modern civilization, in order to understand why it is wrong.

The women's movement has a case, and it is a powerful one. That case begins with the simple acknowledgment of what anthropologists

have long since confirmed: the ascendancy of males over females is a
universal fact of life in every known human society. Virtually everything that a given society considers to be worthy and prestigious,
whether it be the making of laws or of wars, the conduct of politics,
religion, or business, or even, as Margaret Mead has observed, the 3
dressing of ceremonial dolls, is almost exclusively in the hands of
males. The male is the actor, the creator, the keeper of the cults, the
inventor of the taboos. He is concerned with most of what is specifically human in the human world, as opposed to what is merely natural,
merely biological, merely concerned with life itself.

The French existentialist Simone de Beauvoir pointed out in her
classic study, *The Second Sex*, that it is the males who create the values by which life in any society is justified: "At no time has (the female) ever imposed her own law." Even where men looked with awe
upon the reproductive powers of females and worshiped Earth Mothers in their image, it was the men who made the gods, as Sir James
Frazer, the pioneer student of pagan religion, observed a century ago. 4
In this male-dominated world, human achievement is so much a male
prerogative that we use the word "man" in speaking of humanity. It
made perfect sense for Aristotle to say, "we must look upon the female
character as a sort of natural deficiency"; for Roman law to put females
in the custody of males in recognition of feminine "imbecility"; for
Hebrew males to greet each day with the prayer, "Blessed be God . . .
that he has not made me a woman."

Yet this universal ascendancy of males did not just happen. This is
the crucial point. It was made possible by the most fundamental of all
mankind's social arrangements: the universal institution of the family,
the "patterned arrangement of the two sexes," in Dr. Mead's definition, "in which men play a role in the nurturing of women and children" within a "household shared by man or men and female partners
into which men bring food and women prepare it." This sexual divi- 5
sion of roles, however, is an unequal one. While females are largely
confined to the household sphere, males assume responsibility for most
of what takes place outside the home. As Mme de Beauvoir has emphasized, the male role in the family is individual, active, and open; the
female role, closed and far less individual. Her body, designed for childbearing, becomes within the family her "womanly" destiny, and to that
destiny she is asked to submit.

The family, however, is not a natural or a biological institution. It,
too, is a human contrivance, and it invites the question, which the
women's movement asks, why has the family division of roles been
drawn up the way it has? That women bear the children is a biological
fact; that those who bear children must carry the chief burden of tend- 6
ing them is not a biological necessity. It is certainly "convenient," as
Dr. Mead has pointed out, but convenience is not necessity. There is
even less reason for women to maintain the household simply because
they are female. Among the Todas of southern India, where women

may have more than one spouse, the men, interestingly enough, consider housekeeping too sacred for women.

To justify the sexual division of the human world, it was long supposed (by males) that women were allotted the household role because of their natural incapacity to do much else. They suffered, in Aristotle's phrase, a "natural deficiency" in the ability to think, to act, and to create. Yet there is no evidence, biological or psychological, of any such inherent incapacity in females (the anthropologist Ashley Montagu has even argued that women are "naturally superior"). If females are physically weaker than men, few human achievements require a great amount of muscular strength.

A justification less tainted with male chauvinism—in the women's movement phrase—has long been based on the presumed inherent temperament of females. According to this view, the female is naturally more passive, more tender, more inward-looking and private—in a word, more "feminine"—than the innately more active and aggressive male. It follows that the family division of roles is simply the reflection of this fixed fact of life. Sigmund Freud even constructed an elaborate theory, based on the female's discovery of her presumed anatomical deficiencies, to explain why females manifest a submissive feminine personality.

This theory has proved the most perishable portion of Freud's work because, as Margaret Mead demonstrated in her 1935 study *Sex and Temperament*, there are no innate female or male temperaments. Studying three New Guinea societies, she discoverd that in one, the Arapesh, women did indeed exhibit those temperamental traits of passivity, tenderness, and unaggressiveness that Western society has associated with the innately feminine. On the other hand, so did the men. In a neighboring tribe, the Mundugumor, the males exhibited the traits of egotism, boldness, and aggressiveness that we have long associated with the innately male. So, however, did the women. In the third society, the Tchambuli, the "masculine" traits were exhibited by the women and the "feminine" traits by the men. Dr. Mead drew from this the obvious conclusion: "Standardized personality differences between the sexes are . . . cultural creations to which each generation, male and female, is trained to conform."

It has been argued, more plausibly, that there is a natural link between mothers and their offspring, a maternal instinct or a natural sense of fulfillment in tending children that not only explains but justifies the female role within the family. If such a link exists, however, it can only be described as tenuous. There are societies in which hardly a trace of a maternal instinct appears. In one of the New Guinea tribes Dr. Mead studied, the women looked on their maternal role with unconcealed repugnance, and the rare woman who was motherly toward her children was treated with scorn. More striking yet are the Mbaya, studied by the greatest of modern anthropologists, Claude Lévi-Strauss. They look with such disfavor on motherhood that they employ a partial substitute for sexual reproduction: Mbaya warriors capture young prisoners and adopt them as children.

More telling than these isolated examples, however, is a universal fact: few human societies have considered the link between females and their offspring so natural or so fulfilling that they have neglected
to teach females that motherhood is their duty and their destiny. In- 11
deed, the more civilized a society becomes, the more insistent this training is likely to become; for the richer the human world grows in the range of its activities, the greater is the temptation of females to desert the household sphere.

In view of these considerations, many spokesmen for the women's movement conclude that males have deliberately confined females to the domestic sphere in a concerted effort to maintain their dominance. Employing an analogy with racism, many today speak of the present system of human life as "sexism"—"the definition of and discrimination
against half the human species by the other half," according to Robin 12
Morgan, editor of a recent collection of women's movement essays called *The Sisterhood is Powerful.* The most rigorous exponent of this view is Kate Millett, who has coined the term "sexual politics" (in a well-known book of that title) to designate the ways in which males contrive to keep females subordinate under what she calls "patriarchal government."

Miss Millett and other spokesmen for the movement are willing to admit that Western civilization—the United States in particular—is a "reformed patriarchal society." In this reformed system men and women are political equals, and have been since the general establishment of female suffrage. Most of the legal liabilities women once suffered—the prohibition against wives owning property, for example—have been repealed (though only within the past decade in France). If their opportunities still remain much more limited than those of men, women
have won the right to work at paid jobs other than domestic service, 13
to attend universities, and to establish careers. Yet females, in the view of the women's movement, remain subordinate, because they are still "economically dependent" on males, which is to say, husbands. Miss Millett views the entire "sexist" system as the means by which males prevent females from gaining "independence in economic life." As Mme de Beauvoir wrote twenty years earlier in Paris, the extent to which women are dominated is the extent to which they are kept "from assuming a place in productive labor." Only when all women are "raised and trained exactly like men . . . to work under the same conditions and for the same wages," will females ever be liberated.

What looms up as the giant barrier to such liberation is, of course, the primal institution of the family. It is the family that directly se-
cures the economic dependence of women, for within the family the 14
female is supported while she herself labors without pay—a point the women's movement finds particularly telling. It is by means of the family division of roles that females are assigned, in Miss Millett's

words, to "menial tasks and compulsory child-care," and thus are prevented from taking their place in the work force. It is by virtue of her training for the family that a female is brought up to be feminine, passive, compliant, and unaggressive, and so rendered unfit for winning independence through work.

The conclusion of the movement's argument is not easily avoided, though more moderate elements flinch from the logic of the case. The liberation of females, *all females,* can only come when the family is abolished as the primary unit of human life, to be supplanted, in the words of Miss Millett, by "collective, professional care of the young." With the end of the durable family-centered world, females would no longer have to be trained from birth to exhibit and admire domestic and maternal virtues. Legal distinctions, like that between legitimate and illegitimate children, and moral distinctions, like that between fidelity and adultery, would cease to have any meaning. The bond of marriage would be quite unnecessary and would be replaced by "voluntary associations."

In this familyless world females would enjoy "complete sexual autonomy," and their decision to bear children would become a purely voluntary one. Trained alike, sharing alike in the world's labor, men and women would be equals. Except for their differing roles in procreation, they would for the first time in human history be interchangeable, one with the other, as fellow human beings.

Those women's movement spokesmen who propose this "sexual revolution," as it has been called, do not expect that it lies in the immediate offing. What they do maintain is that this must be the ultimate goal of women in their struggle for liberation. They do not promise, in general, that humankind would be *happier* under this new dispensation. What they do say is that this new dispensation would be just and that only such a dispensation can liberate females from the age-old injustice of male domination.

And yet, something seems wrong, and very seriously wrong. At the base of the long and complicated argument propounded by spokesmen for the women's liberation movement lie two seminal assumptions, which deserve more scrutiny than the movement, to date, has given them. The first is the assumption that the family can be replaced successfully by a modern organization of experts, professionals, and salaried employees. The second is the assumption that human dignity is to be found in the organized wage-earning work force.

G. K. Chesterton put his finger on the first assumption in a short essay he wrote some fifty years ago, called "Marriage and the Modern Mind." What he asked, did the women's movement of his day think about children? The answer was that they did not think about them at all. They would "imitate Rousseau, who left his baby on the doorstep of the Foundling Hospital." They overlooked the problem of children, Chesterton implied, because they saw children not as a problem but merely as an obstacle. Yet every known human society has made the problem of children its primary concern, and has done so because the problem *is* primary.

The most important thing about children is that we must have
them. We must reproduce our kind in sufficient numbers to replace
those who die. This is so not because we are animals, who cannot
recognize, and will not mourn, the possible extinction of their species.
It is so because we are human and have made for ourselves a human
world whose essential attribute is its permanence. We die, yet it abides.
Without that assurance, human life would be unthinkable. But precisely because we inhabit a human world, not even the birth of chil- 20
dren is assured: as the women's movement has emphasized, there is no
maternal instinct and no natural fulfillment in bringing children into
the world. Just so. However, humankind must find some secure and
permanent means to ensure that females submit to motherhood, that
they continue to sacrifice a large portion of their individuality, for the
sake of the human world's survival.

To date, at least, this has been assured by the family. Because of
the personal bonds it establishes, the female is not asked to carry out an
abstract duty to the species and to the world. She bears children for
the sake of her spouse, or for the sake of her father, or for the sake of
her mother's clan, according to the form of the family system. By means
of the family, duty to the species becomes duty to known persons, to
persons united to females by abiding ties of loyalty and affection. But
what of the familyless world outlined by the women's movement? In
such a world the sexual training of females would be abolished and 21
bearing children would cease, of necessity, to be a deeply felt personal
virtue. Under such conditions reproduction would become a public
duty, as it was in the garrison state of Sparta, where women, as well
as men, were largely liberated from family ties. The personal voice of
the family would be replaced by mass exhortation—the voice of the
megaphone—urging females to bear children for the good of the State
or the Nation or the People.

Such a prospect can be looked on as merely repugnant, but more
is at stake than that. To make child rearing a public duty, and mothers
into state charges, it is worth remarking, was seen by the Nazis as a
perfect means to extend totalitarian control, which is why they exhorted females to bear children out of wedlock in sunny, luxurious
nursing homes. The Nazi effort to "liberate" females from the thralldom
of husbands was not done, however, for the sake of liberty. A society 22
compelled to make childbearing a public duty is one that puts into
the hands of its leaders a vast potential for tyranny and oppression.
The "purely voluntary" choice of bearing children might one day have
a very hollow ring.

But children pose another problem that the liberationists have not answered satisfactorily. Humankind is not born human, but must be made so through years of patient and watchful care. Yet making the newborn human and fit for the world is an immense and subtle task.

Teaching the newborn to speak, to discipline their spontaneous impulses, and to play their roles in adult life is only part of that task, and the most obvious part. In bringing children into the human world, we are bringing them into a moral world and a public world as well. The newborn must learn that modicum of trust in others and that sense of the permanence of things without which humans cannot act together to carry out their purposes. Only a saint need not trust in others or believe in the human world's permanence. In their rearing, too, the newborn must be provided with vivid models of personal loyalty, affection, and respect, or they will never know them at all, never know how to give or how to receive them. They would poison the world in their terrible innocence.

It is the institution of the family that has been assigned the chief role in making the newborn human. This, in truth, is its main purpose. It is the stability of the family, the fact that its members make a permanent home, that gives the newborn that primary sense of the durability and trustworthiness of things on which human action depends. It is because of the personal nature of the family, the fact that it can include within its sphere so many varieties of personal relationships, that the newborn can be endowed at all richly with personal attributes and a human personality.

But again, what of the familyless world of women's liberation? In describing possible family substitutes, spokesmen for the movement have not gone much beyond their cursory remarks about collective and professional child care. The details, however, do not matter as much as the essence of the thing. The care of children would be paid employment; the primary relation of adults to children would be the cash nexus. Child rearing would be an administrative function. That is the heart of the matter.

Certain consequences seem inevitable. From that primary experience of life the young would learn—could not help but learn—that the basic relation of one being to another is the relation of a jobholder to his job. Seeing that the paid functionaries who tended them could be replaced by any other paid functionaries, they would also learn that adults must be looked upon as interchangeable units, individually unique in no important way. Nor is it difficult to imagine the chief virtue the young would acquire should their care be turned into an administrative function. All our experience of bureaucracy tells us what it would be: the virtue of being quick to submit to standardized rules and procedures.

How would the human world appear to a child brought up in such a way? It would appear as a world whose inhabitants are jobholders and nothing more, where there is nothing else for a grownup to be except gainfully employed. What is more, the child would be perfectly raised, by the most basic lessons of his young life, to become another jobholder.

These last considerations touch on a final problem posed for humankind by the fact of birth. In making the newborn human, a way
must be found to preserve something of their spontaneity and newness,
for if the newness of the newborn is a danger, it is also the spring of
hope. A world capable only of duplicating itself in each new generation 28
is a doomed and oppressive one. It is in meeting this problem that the
institution of the family exhibits something more than its practicality.
It exhibits its one truly irreplaceable virtue, a virtue that lies wholly
in its private character.

Because the family is private, it is not quite of the world. It need
not share all the world's values, heed all its precepts, or embody all its
assumptions. As Dr. Mead has pointed out, it is the peculiar quality
of the modern family that no two families are alike. By virtue of its
privacy, the family is the primary shelter of human variety. In the very
process of preparing its newborn for the world the family can protect 29
them from the world. It can see to it that the world's standards do not
impinge too closely upon the defenseless young and so do not mold
them too precisely to the world's imperious demands. The young may
enter the world without being ignorant of any standard but the world's.
In this lies the human potentiality for freedom.

Here the contrast with the collective professionalized care of the
young is a stark one. Instead of protecting the young from the world,
such administrative child care would fasten the world's ways on the
newborn with a strangler's grip. In a society where cash is too often
the link between people, it would make cash the sole link between
adults and children. In a society where people are being reduced more
and more to mere jobholders and paid employees, it would make the
child's primary experience of life the experience of being someone's 30
job. In a society showing a remorseless capacity to standardize and
depersonalize, it would standardize and depersonalize the world in
which children are raised. The ideal world in which females would
be liberated for productive labor is a world that would tyrannize the
young, which means, in the end, it would tyrannize us all.

Paid labor is freedom and dignity: that is the axiom of the women's
movement today. It is not theirs alone. We hear it every day in a hundred different guises. We are told that the dignity of the citizen consists, not in being a free citizen, but in working on a job, that the dignity of the factory worker consists in working in a factory, and that
the dignity of the "hard-hat" comes from wearing a hard hat. When
an oppressed minority in America demands a citizen's share in power, 31
it is told that what it "really" needs are more and better jobs. That is
the common ideology, and if the dream of the women's movement is
monstrous, that ideology is its seedbed. The women's movement has
simply driven that ideology to its logical conclusion, and the ideal
"sexual revolution" is that conclusion.

We must turn, then, to the work world to see what it does offer in the way of human dignity, achievement, and freedom. The first and primary question is that of freedom and its relation to work. The relation is negative. To the Greeks it was axiomatic that those who must labor could not be free. To be free required leisure—even Karl Marx, the philosopher of productive labor, admitted in the end that freedom began when the workday ended. Without leisure, men could not take part in public affairs, could not speak and act in the polis, could not share in power, and thus could not be called free, for those subject to commands are not free. There is nothing abstruse about this, for quite obviously, people work and are paid for their labor even under conditions of abject tyranny and totalitarian domination. In the Soviet Union women play a far more prominent part in the work force than they do in America—most of the doctors in Russia, for example, are women—and thus, by the women's movement definition, are freer than women are here. Yet Russian women enjoy no freedom at all.

The liberationist's blindness to the nature of the work world may have been explained, inadvertently, by Mme de Beauvoir when she pointed out in *The Second Sex* that in comprehending men, women see little more than "the male." So, in looking at the realm of work, the women's movement sees that males, as such, are ascendant. But they have hardly begun to grasp the obvious: that some men are more ascendant than others. When movement spokesmen contrast the "male" role and "male" achievements with the monotonous tasks of the household, many men may well wonder which males they are talking about. According to a statement in *The Sisterhood is Powerful*, "a great many American men are not accustomed to doing monotonous, repetitive work which never ushers in any lasting, let alone important, achievement." It sounds like a typographical error. Most jobs *are* monotonous and do not usher in lasting or important achievements. The majority of jobs are narrow functions, dovetailing with other narrow functions, in large-scale organizations.

Because this is so, most jobs demand few of the moral qualities that mankind has found worthy of admiration. They demand our proficiency, patience, and punctuality, but rarely our courage, loyalty, generosity, and magnanimity, the virtues we mean when we speak of human dignity. The one honorable satisfaction that most men obtain from their labor is the satisfaction of providing for their families, and the women's liberation movement would sacrifice the family for the sake of performing such labors. A movement that began by asking for a fair share of dignity and human achievement can today think of no other source of dignity, no other source of achievement, than toiling at a job. It has looked on the modern mass society, a society in which more and more activities are in the hands of administrations and bureaucracies, a society in which more people are becoming, more and more, merely paid employees, and it has made this mass society its ideal for human life. That, in the end, is the failure of the women's movement.

This failure must be accounted a tragic one—for women *are* kept from their fair share of dignity and achievement; women's talents and moral qualities are too often wasted. A sense of inferiority still clings 35
to the position of women today. The question is, what can be done about it?

The history of the women's movement itself provides, I believe, the basis for an answer. The movement is less than two hundred years old. That some men had power—and women did not—that some men monopolized the privileges and achievements—and women did not—had never before given rise to a movement for female emancipation, or even to any articulate awareness that women were unfree. That 36
awareness did not come until the late eighteenth century, and it came with the rediscovery of political liberty as the Greeks understood it. Not until men asserted their right, as men, to the dignity of the citizen and their right to share in public power was it first borne in upon women that they, as females, were unequal and unfree.

The early leaders of the women's movement grasped this principle firmly. They saw that if men were equal insofar as they were citizens, men and women would be equal when women, too, were citizens. This is why the major struggle of the original women's movement was the fight for the franchise, that necessary condition for political equality between the sexes. The leaders of the movement, women like Susan B. Anthony, saw more in the vote than the simple act of voting. They saw that women would win their dignity—the citizen's dignity—by actively entering public life. They hoped that women by their political activity would help overthrow the political machines that corrupted— 37
and still corrupt—representative government and render the citizenry powerless in all but name. In this they grasped a profound political truth: that men and women would share equally in the dignity and freedom of the citizen only if the republic were truly a republic of self-governing citizens. In a republic where power is monopolized by a few, the very status of "citizen" is empty, and the equality of citizens —male and female—a phantom. In such a corrupted republic women might very well believe that "liberation" is paid labor.

It is often said that the old suffragists were wrong, because enfranchised women did not seize their opportunity. This only proves, however, that the opportunity was wasted. Today, that opportunity lies open as never before. From the point of view of public life women today might even be called privileged. Far more than men, they enjoy the precondition for public life, which is leisure, or at any rate the prerogative of managing their own time. The second advantage they 38
enjoy might be called a sense of locality. While men must shuttle back and forth between their homes and their places of work, it is women who live in local communities, who know what a community is, and it is in local communities that politics begins—at least in the American republic.

The opportunity to enter public life is there, and the will to do so is there as well. There are literally millions of women who thirst for public activity, though they are shunted by the established party machines into mere civic work or stultifying chores in the ranks of party bureaucracies. The old suffragists, however, were talking not of party politics but of nonparty politics, free republican politics that challenged party machines and their monopoly over power. This was—and still is—the crucial point, and there are tens of thousands of communities in which women can make a beginning. When they make that beginning, male ascendancy will near its end, for they would break the hold men still retain over human achievement.

As Susan B. Anthony said a hundred years ago, "they who have the power to make and unmake laws and rulers, are feared and respected." For those women whose gifts and ambitions turn them toward careers in the sphere of work, the public, political activity of women will open doors now shut. Who will be able to say that women are unfit to run a business when they share in that far more demanding activity of governing a community and a nation?

In playing their role as citizens, in helping to restore representative government by their free political activity, women would help restore to men and women alike the freedom and equality of the citizen, "our power and our glory," as Elizabeth Cady Stanton, another pioneer of woman's rights, reminded her audiences a century ago. In helping to do that—and what nobler venture can we undertake?—women would restore to motherhood itself its rightful and proper dignity. That dignity will not come from mass exhortations and mass propaganda, but from the knowledge that freedom bestows upon a free people the knowledge that it is indeed a grave and noble task to bring up children when we are bringing them up to live in freedom and independence.

This, I believe, is the path that women must take in their struggle for liberation—and because it is a true liberation, it means the enhancement of liberty for all.

Germaine Greer

Love: The Ideal

If the God who is said to be love exists in the imagination of men
it is because they have created Him. Certainly they have had a vision
of a love that was divine although it would be impossible to point out
a paradigm in actuality. The proposition has been repeated like a man-
tra in hate-filled situations, because it seemed a law of life. "God is
love." Without love there could have been no world. If all were Thanatos and no Eros, nothing could have come into being. Desire is the
cause of all movement, and movement is the character of all being.
The universe is a process and its method is change. Whether we call
it a Heraclitean dance or the music of the spheres or the unending
galliard of protons and neutrons we share an idea in all cultures of a 1
creative movement to and from, moved by desire, repressed by death
and the second law of thermodynamics. Various methods of formulation approximate knowledge of it at any time because the laws which
seek to control and formalize such dynamics for the reasoning mind
must be reformulated endlessly. Energy, creation, movement and harmony, development, all happen under the aegis of love, in the domain
of Eros. Thanatos trudges behind, setting the house in order, drawing
boundaries and contriving to rule. Human beings love despite their
compulsions to limit it and exploit it, chaotically. Their love persuades
them to make vows, build houses and turn their passion ultimately to
duty.

When mystics say that God is love, or when Aleister Crowley says
"Love is the law," they are not referring to the love that is woman's
destiny. Indeed many Platonists believed that women were not capable
of love at all, because they were men's inferiors physically, socially, 2
intellectually and even in terms of physical beauty. Love is not possible between inferior and superior, because the base cannot free their
love from selfish interest, as the desire either for security or social
advantage, and, being lesser, they themselves cannot comprehend the
faculties in the superior which are worthy of love. The superior being

on the other hand cannot demean himself by love for an inferior; his feeling must be tinged with condescension or else partake of perversion and a deliberate self-abasement. The proper subject for love is one's equal, seeing as the essence of love is to be mutual, and the lesser cannot produce anything greater than itself. Seeing the image of himself, man recognizes it and loves it, out of fitting and justifiable *amour propre*; such a love is based upon understanding, trust, and commonalty. It is the love that forms communities, from the smallest groups to the highest.[1] It is the only foundation for viable social structures, because it is the manifestation of common good. Society is founded on love, but the state is not because the state is a collection of minorities with different, even irreconcilable common goods. Like a father controlling siblings of different ages and sexes, the state must bring harmony among the warring groups, not through love, but external discipline. What man feels for the very different from himself is fascination and interest, which fade when the novelty fades, and the incompatibility makes its presence felt. Feminine women chained to men in our society are in this situation. They are formed to be artificially different and fascinating to men and end by being merely different, isolated in the house of a bored and antagonistic being.

From the earliest moments of life, human love is a function of narcissism. The infant who perceives his own self and the external world as the same thing loves everything until he learns to fear harm.[2] So if you pitch him into the sea he will swim, as he floated in his mother's womb before it grew too confining. The baby accepts reality, because he has no ego.

> The Angel that presided o'er my birth
> Said "Little creature, form'd of joy and mirth,
> Go love without the help of anything on Earth."[3]

Even when his ego is forming he must learn to understand himself in terms of his relationships to other people and other people in terms of himself. The more his self-esteem is eroded, the lower the opinion that he has of his fellows; the more inflated his self-esteem the more he expects of his friends. This interaction has always been understood, but not always given its proper importance. When Adam saw Eve in the Garden of Eden he loved her because she was of himself, bone of his bone, and more like him than any of the other animals created for his delectation. His movement of desire towards her was an act of love for his own kind. This kind of diffuse narcissism has always been accepted as a basis for love, except in the male-female relationship where it has been assumed that man is inflamed by what is different in women, and therefore the differences have been magnified until men have more in common with other men of different races, creeds and colors than they have with the women of their own environment. The principle of the brotherhood of man is that narcissistic one, for the grounds for that love have always been the assumption that we ought to realize that we are the same the whole world over.

The brotherhood of man will only become a reality when the consciousness of alien being corrects man's myopia, and he realizes that he has more in common with Eskimoes and Bengali beggars and black faggots than he has with the form of intelligent life on Solar System X. Nevertheless, we are discouraged from giving the name of love to relationships between people of common interests like footballers and musicians, especially if they are of the same sex. In denying such a description we ignore the testimony of bodies and behavior. If Denis 5
Law hugs Nobby Stiles on the pitch we tolerate it because it is *not* love. If Kenny Burell blows a kiss to Albert King on stage we congratulate ourselves on knowing how to take it. The housewife whose husband goes to the local every night does not tell herself that he loves his friends more than he loves her, although she resents it despite herself as an infidelity.

The arguments about the compatibility of marriageable people stem from a working understanding of the principle of parity in love, but it is very rarely seen that compatible interests at the level of hobbies and books and cinema do not make up for the enormous gulf which is kept open between the sexes in all other fields. We might note with horror those counsels which advise girls to take up their boyfriends' hobbies in order to seduce them by a feigned interest in something they like. In any event, the man's real love remains centered in his male peers, although his sex may be his woman's prerogative. Male bonding can be explained by this simple principle of harmony between *similes inter pares,* that is, love. On the other hand, female castration results in concentration of her feelings upon her male companion, and her impotence in confrontations with her own kind. Because all her love 6
is guided by the search for security, if not for her offspring then for her crippled and fearful self, she cannot expect to find it in her own kind, whom she knows to be weak and unsuitable. Women cannot love because, owing to a defect in narcissism, they do not rejoice in seeing their own kind. In fact the operation of female insecurity in undermining natural and proper narcissism is best summed up by their use of make-up and disguise, ruses of which women are infallibly aware. Those women who boast most fulsomely of their love for their own sex (apart from lesbians, who must invent their own ideal of love) usually have curious relations with it, intimate to the most extraordinary degree but disloyal, unreliable and tension-ridden, however close and longstanding they may be.

We can say the brotherhood of man, and pretend that we include the sisterhood of women, but we know that we don't. Folklore has it that women only congregate to bitch an absent member of their group, and continue to do so because they are too well aware of the consequences if they stay away. It's meant to be a joke, but like jokes about mothers-in-law it is founded in bitter truth. Women don't nip down to the local: they don't invent, as men do, pretexts like coin-collecting or old-schoolism or half-hearted sporting activities so that they can be together; on ladies' nights they watch frozen-faced while their men embrace and fool about commenting to each other that they are all overgrown boys. Of the love of fellows they know nothing. They cannot love each other in this easy, innocent, spontaneous way because they cannot love themselves. What we actually see, sitting at the tables by the wall, is a collection of masked menials, dressed up to avoid scrutiny in the trappings of the status symbol, aprons off, scent on, feigning leisure and relaxation where they feel only fatigue. All that can happen to make the evening for one of them is that she might disrupt the love affair around her by making her husband lavish attention on her or seeing that somebody else does. Supposing the men do not abandon their women to their own society, the conversation is still between man and man with a feminine descant. The jokes are the men's jokes; the activity and the anecdotes about it belong to the men. If the sex that has been extracted from the homosexual relationship were not exclusively concentrated on her, a woman would consider that she had cause for complaint. Nobody complains that she has sex without love and he has love without sex. It is right that way, appalling any other way.

Hope is not the only thing that springs eternal in the human breast. Love makes its appearance there unbidden from time to time. Feelings of spontaneous benevolence towards one's own kind still transfigure us now and then—not in relationship with the stakes of security and flattery involved, but in odd incidents of confidence and cooperation in situations where duty and compulsion are not considerations. This extraordinary case of free love appeared in the correspondence of the *People:*

> Eighteen years ago my husband and I moved into our first house. Two weeks later our neighbours arrived next door. We thought they were rather standoffish, and they, in return, were not too keen on us.
>
> But over the years we have blessed the day they came to live next door. We have shared happy times. They were godparents to our daughter. And when trouble was at its worst they were always at hand with help.
>
> Now they have paid us the biggest compliment ever. My husband recently changed his job and we had to move 200 miles. The parting was just too much. Rather than say goodbye, my neighbour's husband has changed his job, and they have moved with us.
>
> Although we are not neighbours, we are only five minutes away from each other. This is a friendship that really has stood the test of time.[4]

This remarkable situation is rare indeed, for it is the tendency of family relationships to work against this kind of extrafamilial affection. Every time a man unburdens his heart to a stranger he reaffirms the love that unites humanity. To be sure, he is unpacking his heart with words but at the same time he is encouraged to expect interest and sympathy, and he usually gets it. His interlocutor feels unable to impose his own standards on his confidant's behavior; for once he feels how

another man feels. It is not always sorrow and squalor that is passed on in this way but sometimes joy and pride. I remember a truck driver telling me once about his wife, how sexy and clever and loving she was, and how beautiful. He showed me a photograph of her and I blushed for guilt because I had expected something plastic and I saw a woman by trendy standards plain, fat and ill-clad. Half the point 9
in reading novels and seeing plays and films is to exercise the faculty of sympathy with our own kind, so often obliterated in the multifarious controls and compulsions of actual social existence. For, once we are not contemptuous of Camille or jealous of Juliet, we might even understand the regicide or the motherfucker. That is love.

The love of fellows is based upon understanding and therefore upon communication. It was love that taught us to speak, and death that laid its fingers on our lips. All literature, however vituperative, is an act of love, and all forms of electronic communication attest the possibility of understanding. Their actual power in girdling the global 10
village has not been properly understood yet. Beyond the arguments of statisticians and politicians and other professional cynics and deathmakers, the eyes of a Biafran child have an unmistakable message. But while electronic media feed our love for our own kind, the circumstances of our lives substitute propinquity for passion.

> His word pronounced "selfishness" blessed, the wholesome healthy selfishness that wells from a powerful soul—from a powerful soul to which belongs the high body, beautiful, triumphant, refreshing, around which everything becomes a mirror—the supple, persuasive body, the dancer whose parable and epitome is the self-enjoying soul.
>
> Nietzche, *Thus Spake Zarathustra*

If we could present an attainable ideal of love it would resemble the relationship described by Maslow as existing between self-realizing personalities. It is probably a fairly perilous equilibrium: certainly the forces of order and civilization react fairly directly to limit the possibilities of self-realization. Maslow describes his ideal personalities as having a better perception of reality—what Herbert Read called an innocent eye, like the eye of the child who does not seek to reject reality. Their relationship to the world of phenomena is not governed by their personal necessity to exploit it or be exploited by it, but a 11
desire to observe it and to understand it. They have no disgust; the unknown does not frighten them. They are without defensiveness or affectation. The only causes of regret are laziness, outbursts of temper, hurting others, prejudice, jealousy and envy. Their behavior is spontaneous but it corresponds to an autonomous moral code. Their thinking is problem-centered not ego-centered, and therefore they most often have a sense of commitment to a cause beyond their daily concerns. Their responses are geared to the present and not to nostalgia or anticipation. Although they do not serve a religion out of guilt or

fear or any other sort of compulsion, the religious experience, in Freud's term, the *oceanic feeling*, is easier for them to attain than for the conventionally religious. The essential factor in self-realization is independence, resistance to enculturation; the danger inherent in this is that of excessive independence or downright eccentricity; nevertheless, such people are more capable of giving love, if what Rogers said of love is to be believed, that "we can love a person only to the extent we are not threatened by him." Our self-realizing person might claim to be capable of loving everybody because he cannot be threatened by anybody. Of course circumstances will limit the possibility of his loving everybody, but it would certainly be a fluke if such a character were to remain completely monogamous. For those people who wanted to be dominated or exploited or to establish any other sort of compulsive symbiosis, he would be an unsatisfactory mate; as there are many fewer self-realizing personalities than there are other kinds, the self-realizer is usually ill-mated. Maslow has a rather unlooked-for comment on the sexual behavior of the self-realizer:

> Another characteristic I found of love in healthy people is that they have made no really sharp differentiation between the roles and personalities of the two sexes. That is, they did not assume that the female was passive and the male active, whether in sex or love or anything else. These people were so certain of their maleness or femaleness they did not mind taking on some of the aspects of the opposite sex role. It was especially noteworthy that they could be both passive and active lovers . . . an instance of the way in which common dichotomies are so often resolved in self-actualization, appearing to be valid dichotomies only because people are not healthy enough.[5]

What Maslow expresses may be little more than a prejudice in favor of a certain kind of personality structure, merely another way of compromising between Eros and civilization; nevertheless we are all involved in some such operative compromise. At least Maslow's terms indicate a direction in which we could travel and not merely a theoretical account of what personality might be like if psychoanalysis accomplished the aim which it has so far not even clearly declared itself or justified to the waiting world, "to return our souls to our bodies, to return ourselves to ourselves, and thus to overcome the human state of self-alienation."[6]

It is surprising but nevertheless it is true that Maslow included some women in his sample of self-realizing personalities. But after all it is foreseeable, even if my arguments about the enculturation of woman are correct. In some ways the operation of the feminine stereotype is so obvious and for many women entirely unattainable, that it can be easily reacted against. It takes a great deal of courage and independence to decide to design your own image instead of the one that society rewards, but it gets easier as you go along. Of course, a woman who decides to go her own way will find that her conditioning is ineradicable, but at least she can recognize its operation and choose to counteract it, whereas a man might find that he was being more subtly deluded. A woman who decided to become a lover without conditions might discover that her relationships broke up relatively easily because of her degree of resistance to efforts to "tame" her, and the opinion of her friends will usually be on the side of the man who was prepared to do the decent thing, who was in love with her, etcetera. Her promiscuity, resulting from her constant sexual desire, tenderness and interest in people, will not usually be differentiated from compulsive promiscuity or inability to say no, although it is fundamentally different. Her love may often be devalued by the people for whom she feels most tenderness, and her self-esteem might have much direct attack. Such pressures can never be utterly without effect. Even if a woman does not inhibit her behavior because of them, she will find herself reacting in some other way, being outrageous when she only meant to be spontaneous and so forth. She may limit herself to writing defenses of promiscuity, or even books about women. (Hm.)

For love's sake women must reject the roles that are offered to
them in our society. As impotent, insecure, inferior beings they can
never love in a generous way. The ideal of Platonic love, of Eros as a 14
stabilizing, creative, harmonizing force in the universe, was most fully
expressed in English in Shakespeare's abstract poem, "The Phoenix and
the Turtle," who

> . . . loved, as love in twain
> Had the essence but in one;
> Two distincts, division none:
> Number there in love was slain.
>
> Hearts remote, yet not asunder;
> Distance and no space was seen
> 'Twixt the turtle and his queen:
> But in them it were a wonder.

The poem is not a plea for suttee, although it describes the mutual
obsequies of the phoenix and the turtle. It states and celebrates the
concept of harmony, of fusion, melting together, neither sacrificed nor 15
obliterated, that nondestructive knowledge which Whitehead learned
to value from the writings of Lao-Tse.

> Property was thus appall'd
> That the self was not the same;
> Single nature's double name
> Neither two nor one was called.
>
> Reason in itself confounded,
> Saw division grow together;
> To themselves get either neither
> Simple were so well compounded.[7]

The love of peers is the spirit of commonalty, the unity of beauty and truth. The phoenix and the turtle do not necessarily cohabit, for they are the principle of sympathy which is not dependent upon familiarity. The phoenix renews itself constantly in its own ashes, as a figure of protean existence. The love of the phoenix and the turtle is not the lifelong coherence of a mutually bound couple but the principle of love that is reaffirmed in the relationship of the narcissistic self to the world of which it is a part. It is not the fantasy of annihilation of the self in another's identity by sexual domination, for it is a spiritual state of comprehension.

> Spirituality, by which I mean the purity of a strong and noble nature, with all the new and untried powers that must grow out of it—has not yet appeared on our horizon; and its absence is a natural consequence of a diversity of interests between man and woman, who are for the most part brought together through the attraction of passion; and who, but for that, would be as far asunder as the poles.[8]

In fact, men and women love differently, and much of the behavior that we describe by the term is so far from benevolence, and so antisocial, that it must be understood to be inimical to the essential nature of love. Our life-style contains more *Thanatos* than *Eros*, for egotism, exploitation, deception, obsession and addiction have more place in us than eroticism, joy, generosity and spontaneity.

THE IDEAL

1. In the Renaissance simple statements of the Platonic concept of love were disseminated as commonplace. To the basic arguments drawn from the *Convivium* and other dialogues were added the eulogies of Cicero and Plutarch and the theories of Heraclitus and Aristotle. The essence of this mixture can be found in many places, from the courtesy books like the *Cortigiano* and de la Primaudaye's *Academie* to the commonplace books and moral tracts for the consumption of the newly literate, e.g., Sir Thomas Elyot's *The Boke of the Governour* (1531), Section 31, *The Booke of Friendship of Marcus Tullius Cicero* (1550), John Charlton's *The Casket of Jewels* (1571), Baldwin's *Treatise of Moral Philosophy* (1550), Bodenham's *Politeuphuia* (1597) and Robert Allott's *Wits Theater of the little World* (1599). Possibly the most accessible and the most elegant formulation is Bacon's *Essay of Friendship.*
2. Schilder (*op. cit.*), p. 120; *cf.* Norman O. Brown, *Life Against Death* (*op. cit.*).
3. William Blake, Poems from MSS, *c.* 1810 (*Nonesuch,* p. 124); *cf.* Suttie (*op. cit.*), pp. 30-1.
4. *The People,* October 12, 1969.
5. A. H. Maslow, *Motivation and Personality* (New York, 1954), pp. 208-46; quotation from pp. 245-6.
6. Norman O. Brown, *Life Against Death.*
7. William Shakespeare, "The Phoenix and the Turtle" (*The Complete Works,* ed. W. J. Craig, Oxford, 1959, p. 1135).
8. S. E. Gay, *Womanhood in Its Eternal Aspect* (London, 1879), p. 4.

Edward Field

The Bride of Frankenstein

The Baron has decided to mate the monster,
to breed him perhaps,
in the interests of pure science, his only god.

So he goes up into his laboratory
which he has built in the tower of the castle
to be as near the interplanetary forces as possible,
and puts together the prettiest monster-woman you ever saw
with a body like a pin-up girl
and hardly any stitching at all
where he sewed on the head of a raped and murdered beauty queen.

He sets his liquids burping, and coils blinking and buzzing,
and waits for an electric storm to send through the equipment
the spark vital for life.
The storm breaks over the castle
and the equipment really goes crazy
like a kitchen full of modern appliances
as the lightning juice starts oozing right into that pretty corpse.

He goes to get the monster
so he will be right there when she opens her eyes,
for she might fall in love with the first thing she sees
as ducklings do.

That monster is already straining at his chains and slurping
ready to go right to it:
He has been well prepared for coupling
by his pinching leering keeper who's been saying for weeks,
"You gonna get a little nookie, kid."
or "How do you go for some poontang, baby."

All the evil in him is focused on this one thing now
as he is led into her very presence.

She awakens slowly,
she bats her eyes,
she gets up out of the equipment,
and finally she stands in all her seamed glory,
a monster princess with a hairdo like a fright-wig,
lightning flashing in the background
like a halo and a wedding veil,
like a photographer snapping pictures of great moments.

She stands and stares with her electric eyes,
beginning to understand that in this life too
she was just another body to be raped.

The monster is ready to go:
He roars with joy at the sight of her,
so they let him loose and he goes right for those knockers.
And she starts screaming to break your heart
and you realize that she was just born:
In spite of her big tits she was just a baby.

But her instincts are right—
rather death than that green slobber:
She jumps off the parapet.
And then the monster's sex drive goes wild.
Thwarted, it turns to violence, demonstrating sublimation crudely,
and he wrecks the lab, those burping acids and buzzing coils,
overturning the control panel so the equipment goes off like a bomb,
the stone castle crumbling and crashing in the storm
destroying them all . . . perhaps.

Perhaps somehow the Baron got out of that wreckage of his dreams
with his evil intact if not his good looks
and more wicked than ever went on with his thrilling career.

And perhaps even the monster lived
to roam the earth, his desire still ungratified,
and lovers out walking in shadowy and deserted places
will see his shape loom up over them, their doom—
and children sleeping in their beds
will wake up in the dark night screaming
as his hideous body grabs them.

William Carlos Williams

The Knife of the Times

1 AS THE YEARS PASSED the girls who had been such intimates as children still remained true to one another.

2 Ethel by now had married. Maura had married; the one having removed to Harrisburg, the other to New York City. And both began to bring up families. Ethel especially went in for children. Within a very brief period, comparatively speaking, she had three of them, then four, then five and finally six. And through it all, she kept in constant touch with her girlhood friend, dark-eyed Maura, by writing long intimate letters.

3 At first these had been newsy chit chat, ending always however in continued protestations of that love which the women had enjoyed during their childhood. Maura showed them to her husband and both enjoyed their full newsy quality dealing as they did with people and scenes with which both were familiar.

4 But after several years, as these letters continued to flow, there came a change in them. First the personal note grew more confidential. Ethel told about her children, how she had had one after the other —to divert her mind, to distract her thoughts from their constant brooding. Each child would raise her hopes of relief, each anticipated delivery brought only renewed disappointment. She confided more and more in Maura. She loved her husband; it was not that. In fact, she didn't know what it was save that she, Ethel, could never get her old friend Maura out of her mind.

5 Until at last the secret was out. It is you, Maura, that I want. Nothing but you. Nobody but you can appease my grief. Forgive me if I distress you with this confession. It is the last thing in this world that I desire. But I cannot contain myself longer.

6 Thicker and faster came the letters. Full love missives they were now without the least restraint.

7 Ethel wrote letters now such as Maura wished she might at some time in her life have received from a man. She was told that all these

years she had been dreamed of, passionately, without rival, without relief. Now, surely, Maura did not dare show the letters to her husband. He would not understand.

They affected her strangely, they frightened her, but they caused a shrewd look to come into her dark eyes and she packed them carefully away where none should ever come upon them. She herself was occupied otherwise but she felt tenderly toward Ethel, loved her in an old remembered manner—but that was all. She was disturbed by the turn Ethel's mind had taken and thanked providence her friend and she lived far enough apart to keep them from embarrassing encounters.

But, in spite of the lack of adequate response to her advances, Ethel never wavered, never altered in her passionate appeals. She begged her friend to visit her, to come to her, to live with her. She spoke of her longings, to touch the velvet flesh of her darling's breasts, her thighs. She longed to kiss her to sleep, to hold her in her arms. Franker and franker became her outspoken lusts. For which she begged indulgence.

Once she implored Maura to wear a silk chemise which she was sending, to wear it for a week and return it to her, to Ethel, unwashed, that she might wear it in her turn constantly upon her.

Then, after twenty years, one day Maura received a letter from Ethel asking her to meet her—and her mother, in New York. They were expecting a sister back from Europe on the *Mauretania* and they wanted Maura to be there—for old time's sake.

Maura consented. With strange feelings of curiosity and not a little fear, she stood at the gate of the Pennsylvania station waiting for her friend to come out at the wicket on the arrival of the Harrisburg express. Would she be alone? Would her mother be with her really? Was it a hoax? Was the woman crazy, after all? And, finally, would she recognize her?

There she was and her mother along with her. After the first stare, the greetings on all sides were quiet, courteous and friendly. The mother dominated the moment. Her keen eyes looked Maura up and down once, then she asked the time, when would the steamer dock, how far was the pier and had they time for lunch first?

There was plenty of time. Yes, let's lunch. But first Ethel had a small need to satisfy and asked Maura if she would show her the way. Maura led her friend to the Pay Toilets and there, after inserting the coin, Ethel opened the door and, before Maura could find the voice to protest, drew her in with herself and closed the door after her.

What a meeting! What a release! Ethel took her friend into her arms and between tears and kisses, tried in some way, as best she could, to tell her of her happiness. She fondled her old playmate, hugged her, lifted her off her feet in the eager impressment of her desire, whispering into her ear, stroking her hair, her face, touching

her lips, her eyes; holding her, holding her about as if she could never
again release her.

No one could remain cold to such an appeal, as pathetic to Maura
as it was understandable and sincere, she tried her best to modify its
fury, to abate it, to control. But, failing that, she did what she could
to appease her old friend. She loved Ethel, truly, but all this show was 16
beyond her. She did not understand it, she did not know how to return
it. But she was not angry, she found herself in fact in tears, her heart
touched, her lips willing.

Time was slipping by and they had to go. 17

At lunch Ethel kept her foot upon the toe of Maura's slipper. It
was a delirious meal for Maura with thinking of old times, watching
the heroic beauty of the old lady and, while keeping up a chatter of 18
small conversation, intermixed with recollections, to respond secretly
as best she could to Ethel's insistent pressures.

At the pier there was a long line waiting to be admitted to the en-
closure. It was no use—Ethel from behind constantly pressed her body
against her embarrassed friend, embarrassed not from lack of under- 19
standing or sympathy, but for fear lest one of the officers and Customs
inspectors who were constantly watching them should detect something
out of the ordinary.

But the steamer was met, the sister saluted; the day came to an
end and the hour of parting found Ethel still keeping close, close to 20
the object of her lifelong adoration.

What shall I do? thought Maura afterward on her way home, on
the train alone. Ethel had begged her to visit her, to go to her, to 21
spend a week at least with her, to sleep with her. Why not?

Questions and Quotations for Discussion and Writing Assignments

I

1. Is the consciousness-raising session described in the opening paragraphs of "The New Feminism" akin to the coffee klatsch? How are these conversations different from those held at any social gathering where the women are segregated from the men? Do you agree that women feel more free to discuss personal feelings and emotions than men? Does this suggest a need for male consciousness-raising?

2. What issues in the Women's Liberation Movement does everyone agree on?

3. Clichés are often based on sexual stereotypes, both male and female. Clichés entered the language, however, because they once seemed pithy, accurate. Can you destroy some clichés whose time has come?

4. Why do you feel so many women and men in America are threatened by/indifferent to/making fun of the Women's Liberation Movement? Is it because of the "bad press" the movement has gotten? What has

been the effect of newspaper coverage of bra-burnings? the news stories on W.I.T.C.H. (Women's International Terrorist Conspiracy from Hell) and S.C.U.M. (Society for Cutting Up Men)?

5. The Women's Movement in the 19th century concentrated on the right to vote. Do you agree with Marlene Dixon that this "retarded the movement for decades"? How can you explain the fact that, despite an increase in enrollment in colleges and universities, the proportion of women who graduate at every level of education has declined since 1930? Have women given up on education in the same way they have abrogated political power?

6. At the end of "Why Women's Liberation?" there is a long quotation from Roxanne Dunbar that supports Miss Dixon's contention that "the rhetoric of invective" is essential to total commitment to Women's Liberation. How has invective served radical groups in recent American history?

7. Walter Karp in his final paragraphs suggests that leisure and the sense of locality offer women the opportunity for wide participation in public life. Does this seem a promising direction for women? Does it consider the major areas of concern in the Women's Liberation Movement, the difficult trajectory from political equality to economic equality to social and cultural equality?

8. If "it is indeed a grave and noble task to bring up children when we are bringing them up to live in freedom and independence," why does Mr. Karp not mention fathers? In attempting to "restore to motherhood itself its rightful and proper dignity," at the same time would it not also be right and proper to encourage fatherhood? The marked absence of male prerogatives in these discussions of family and children bleakly reminds us of the limitations placed on men and on the contributions they can make within the realms of tenderness and love.

9. What is the significance of the title, "The Feminine Utopia"? Do you feel Mr. Karp's article does in fact describe what his title suggests? Examine his choice of words, his use of connotative detail in the piece. What does his diction reveal about his attitudes?

10. "The Feminine Utopia" stresses the consequences of failing to "ensure that females submit to motherhood, that they continue to sacrifice a large portion of their individuality, for the sake of the human world's survival." Is it reasonable that biological function (the bearing of children) should determine full life-sustaining responsibility? Contrast this idea, the concepts of *submission* and *sacrifice,* with Germaine Greer's analysis of "Altruism" (Section IV).

11. Are arguments against women's rights on the basis of "propagation of the species" legitimate during a crisis of overpopulation?

12. Germaine Greer in "Love: The Ideal" describes the character of a self-realizing woman, a woman who rejects the feminine stereotype, a woman who resists enculturation. What is the basis of the self-realizing character, male or female? What are the rewards of choosing this image?

13. If human love is a function of narcissism, how is the narcissism which Miss Greer describes denied to women? Is it impossible to love another until you love yourself?

14. Do you agree that women do not seem to have the "love of fellows," the sisterhood of women that parallels the brotherhood of man? Miss Greer describes the relationship in male bonding as love without sex; the relationship between men and women as sex without love. How is this accurate? Is this what women refer to when they characterize themselves as sex *objects*?
15. The evidence is sufficient: we do not care enough about people; we isolate ourselves from our fellows; we exploit others. Is the "principle of sympathy" with our own kind, the comprehension of others basic to love, so foreign to us that only a visitor from Solar System X can unite us, only "the consciousness of alien being" bring us together? This is a sweeping condemnation. Yet we have a tendency to reduce the ideal of love to a matter between men and women.
16. Women are beginning to reject the stereotypes that surround them. As an experiment in consciousness-raising, examine the image of women presented by media; or to be more personal, talk to the women and men you meet during a day, ask children about their feelings. See if a patterned response emerges. Bring your findings back to class for discussion; incorporate them into a paper; or just think about them.
17. In your class discussion of the Women's Liberation Movement, have reactions of either males or females been predictable in any way? Have some preferred to defer? Have there been snickers? Try to analyze your own conditioning. If your inner reactions and your outer behavior do not coincide, can you begin to deal with these problems in an open way?

II

1. We must endeavor to understand how it is that women's energy is systematically deflected from birth to puberty, so that when they come to maturity they have only fitful resource and creativity.

   GERMAINE GREER

2. It is the stretched soul that makes music, and souls are stretched by the pull of opposites—opposite bents, tastes, yearnings. Where there is no polarity—where energies flow in one direction—there will be much doing but no music.

   ERIC HOFFER

3. Why can't a woman be more like a man?

   (complaint)

4. A man has no need to cover his head, because man is the image of God and the mirror of his glory, whereas woman reflects the glory of man.

   I CORINTHIANS 11:7-8

5. Man swoops upon his prey like the eagle and the hawk; woman lies in wait like the carnivorous plant, the bog, in which insects and children are swallowed up.

   SIMONE DE BEAUVOIR

6. Men are what their mothers made them.

   RALPH WALDO EMERSON

7. I have all my life been dominated by the fear that my steed would flinch from beginning another race.

CASSANOVA

8. The only position for women in S.N.C.C. is prone.

STOKELY CARMICHAEL

9. If women are to cease producing cannon fodder for the final holocaust, they must rescue men from the perversities of their own polarization.

GERMAINE GREER

10. It is an odd paradox that the male inhabits a sensual world of sweetness, affection, gentleness, a feminine world, whereas woman moves in the male universe, which is hard and rough; her hands still long for contact with soft, smooth flesh: the adolescent boy, a woman, flowers, fur, the child; a whole region within her remains unoccupied and longs to possess a treasure like that which she gives the male.

SIMONE DE BEAUVOIR

11. There are no ugly women; there are only women who do not know how to look pretty.

LA BRUYERE

12. The romance in life consists in doing what you have to do decoratively.

DION CLAYTON CALTHORP

13. I'm sick of being a transvestite. I refuse to be a female impersonator. I am a woman, not a castrate.

GERMAINE GREER

14. Man has succeeded in enslaving woman; but in the same degree he has deprived her of what made her possession desirable. With woman integrated in the family and society, her magic is dissipated rather than transformed; reduced to the condition of servant, she is no longer that unconquered prey incarnating all the treasures of nature.

SIMONE DE BEAUVOIR

15. Woman's body *is* the woman.

AMBROSE BIERCE

16. The stereotype is the Eternal Feminine. She is the Sexual Object sought by all men, and by all women. She is of neither sex, for she herself has no sex at all.

GERMAINE GREER

17. Much of a young woman's identity is already defined in her kind of attractiveness and in the selectivity of her search for the man (or men) by whom she wishes to be sought.

ERIC ERIKSON

18. . . . as much as women want to be good scientists or engineers, they want first and foremost to be womanly companions of men and to be mothers.

BRUNO BETTELHEIM

19. Sex is just a commodity.

    ROXANNE DUNBAR

20. . . . most women will have to exercise their much denied but very much alive instincts for power through men for a while yet.

    GLORIA STEINEM

21. Women are unpredictable. You never know how they are going to get their own way.

    BEATRICE MANN

22. Trust in God: She will provide.

    EMMELINE PANKHURST

23. When a woman inclines to learning, there is usually something wrong with her sex apparatus.

    NIETZSCHE

24. Brooklyn's Shirley Chisolm, the first black woman ever elected to Congress, says that the feminist revolt has already begun. She herself, she feels, has been more discriminated against as a woman than as a Negro.

    Time

25. Feminine passivity is closely related to Negro apathy. In both cases, having restricted the participation of the group, the observer finds that inactivity is an innate group characteristic.

    MARY ELLMANN

26. If you changed rearing practices and stopped punishing people who depart from the accepted patterns, you'd have very minimal sex differences.

    ALICE ROSSI

27. In many ways the relaxation of sexual mores just makes a woman's life more difficult. If she is not cautious about sex, she is likely to get hurt; if she is too cautious, she will lose her man to more obliging women. Either way, her decision is based partly on fear and calculation, not on her spontaneous needs and desires.

    ELLEN WILLIS

28. You can't expect a man to give you your identity on a silver platter, which is what society would have us believe. That's dishonest, and it has produced a lot of bitter women.

    GLORIA STEINEM

29. When children are falsely presented to women as their only significant contribution, the proper expression of their creativity and their lives' work, the children and their mothers suffer for it.

    GERMAINE GREER

30. Homemaking is no longer belittled. It commands respect as a career requiring high intelligence plus devotion and especial sensitivity to the social and emotional needs of others.

    RHODA BACMEISTER

31. Can she bake a cherry pie, Billy Boy, Billy Boy?

    CHILDREN'S SONG

32. Giving birth and suckling are not *activities*, they are natural functions; no project is involved; that is why woman found in them no reason for a lofty affirmation of her existence—she submitted passively to her biological fate.

    SIMONE DE BEAUVOIR

33. As for myself, I do not hesitate to avow, that, although the women of the United States are confined within the narrow circle of domestic life, and their situation is in some respects one of extreme dependence, I have nowhere seen women occupying a loftier position; and if I were asked, now that I am drawing to the close of this work, in which I have spoken of so many important things done by the Americans, to what the singular prosperity and growing strength of that people ought mainly to be attributed, I should reply—the superiority of their women.

    ALEXIS DE TOCQUEVILLE

34. Tired of Bellowing and Rothing, Mailering and Malamuding, we looked around at the current literary scene and decided that, for whatever reasons of history and economics, it is still, or perhaps more than ever, dominated by the Judeo-Christian patriarchal ethos. Women have more to give the world than babies. Whole areas of life, of consciousness and feeling are crying for recording and interpretation from within. Too long have women been seen from outside and afar. Too long have we been brainwashed with male stereotypes of what they are like and what we are like. The view from the bottom may not be wide, but it is deep and upward, and for centuries women have had unique opportunities for practicing observation.

    ELIZABETH FISHER

35. One is not born, but rather becomes, a woman. No biological, psychological or economic fate determines the figure that the human female presents in society; it is civilization as a whole that produces this creature, intermediate between male and eunuch, which is described as feminine.

    SIMONE DE BEAUVOIR

36. What do women want? Dear God! What do they want.

    FREUD, age 77, to his diary

SECTION IV Love, Marriage, Family—Couples, Coupling, and Communes

The American Ideal, defined variously by groups both "left" and "right" of "center," has always embraced some important human relationships—love, marriage, family. Sanctified by religion, encouraged by society, people have come together, mated, and formed alliances. There is, however, a tendency by groups who hold any beliefs in common to stricture, to label, to find one kind of relationship acceptable, another deviant. If Sarah and her mother follow different paths to wisdom, Sarah's mother may somehow feel her own life invalidated by her daughter's choices. If Robert fails to commit himself to employment, marriage, and procreation, his father may be disturbed to have a son unlike other men's, may be truly puzzled to find that his son does not desire to live his father's choices.

Because there are bonds between people, because people do care passionately for *their* idea of the other person, discussions of alternative styles of love, marriage, and family abound in intolerance. In these discussions what seems clearly to be pigheadedness or brutal lack of concern is often the inability to cope with change. Germaine Greer speaks of the "enculturation" of women as incapacitating; Alvin Toffler suggests the outset of a crisis of adaptation. Social institutions—despite their bedrock status in the psyches of mankind—are in a process of regeneration.

The essays and poems in this section have been chosen to prepare students for these changes, to remove the fears that stem from shaking the cultural foundations of a society, to create an awareness of the possibilities the future holds. As Alvin Toffler indicates, "We have it in our power to shape change. We may choose one future over another. We cannot, however, maintain the past." When we divert the effort now being directed into preserving an image of the past, when we bypass codified norms of behavior, our energies will leap to reclaim the freedom of the American to deviate, to follow, legally and peacefully, his own inclination, to seek that which satisfies his individual conscience. Then we can settle into ourselves and get down to the business of living as common men.

MELINDA CARPENTER

The Garden of Love

I went to the Garden of Love,
And saw what I never had seen:
A Chapel was built in the midst,
Where I used to play on the green.

And the gates of this Chapel were shut,
And "Thou shalt not" writ over the door:
So I turned to the Garden of Love
That so many sweet flowers bore;

And I saw it was filled with graves,
And tomb-stones where flowers should be;
And Priests in black gowns were walking their rounds,
And binding with briars my joys and desires.

Rollo May

Paradoxes of Sex and Love

> Sexual intercourse is the human counterpart of the cosmic process.
>
> —Proverb of Ancient China

> A patient brought in the following dream: "I am in bed with my wife, and between us is my accountant. He is going to have intercourse with her. My feeling about this is odd—only that somehow it seemed appropriate."
>
> Reported by Dr. John Schimel

There are four kinds of love in Western tradition. One is *sex,* or what we call lust, libido. The second is *eros,* the drive of love to procreate or create—the urge, as the Greeks put it, toward higher forms of being and relationship. A third is *philia,* or friendship, brotherly love. The fourth is *agape* or *caritas* as the Latins called it, the love which is devoted to the welfare of the other, the prototype of which is the love of God for man. Every human experience of authentic love is a blending, in varying proportions, of these four.

We begin with sex not only because that is where our society begins but also because that is where every man's biological existence begins as well. Each of us owes his being to the fact that at some moment in history a man and a woman leapt the gap, in T. S. Eliot's words, "between the desire and the spasm." Regardless of how much sex may be banalized in our society, it still remains the power of procreation, the drive which perpetuates the race, the source at once of the human being's most intense pleasure and his most pervasive anxiety. It can, in its daimonic form, hurl the individual into sloughs of despond, and, when allied with eros, it can lift him out of his despondency into orbits of ecstasy.

The ancients took sex, or lust, for granted just as they took death for granted. It is only in the contemporary age that we have succeeded,

on a fairly broad scale, in singling out sex for our chief concern and
have required it to carry the weight of all four forms of love. Regardless of Freud's overextension of sexual phenomena as such—in which he
is but the voice of the struggle of thesis and antithesis of modern history
—it remains true that sexuality is basic to the ongoing power of the 3
race and surely has the *importance* Freud gave it, if not the extension.
Trivialize sex in our novels and dramas as we will, or defend ourselves
from its power by cynicism and playing it cool as we wish, sexual
passion remains ready at any moment to catch us off guard and prove
that it is still the *mysterium tremendum.*

But as soon as we look at the relation of sex and love in our time,
we find ourselves immediately caught up in a whirlpool of contradictions. Let us, therefore, get our bearings by beginning with a brief 4
phenomenological sketch of the strange paradoxes which surround sex
in our society.

Sexual Wilderness

In Victorian times, when the denial of sexual impulses, feelings,
and drives was the mode and one would not talk about sex in polite
company, an aura of sanctifying repulsiveness surrounded the whole
topic. Males and females dealt with each other as though neither possessed sexual organs. William James, that redoubtable crusader who was
far ahead of his time on every other topic, treated sex with the polite
aversion characteristic of the turn of the century. In the whole two
volumes of his epoch-making *Principles of Psychology*, only one page 5
is devoted to sex, at the end of which he adds, "These details are a
little unpleasant to discuss. . . ." But William Blake's warning a century before Victorianism, that "He who desires but acts not, breeds
pestilence," was amply demonstrated by the later psychotherapists.
Freud, a Victorian who did look at sex, was right in his description of
the morass of neurotic symptoms which resulted from cutting off so
vital a part of the human body and the self.

Then, in the 1920's, a radical change occurred almost overnight.
The belief became a militant dogma in liberal circles that the opposite
of repression—namely, sex education, freedom of talking, feeling, and
expression—would have healthy effects, and obviously constituted the
only stand for the enlightened person. In an amazingly short period
following World War I, we shifted from acting as though sex did not 6
exist at all to being obsessed with it. We now placed more emphasis on
sex than any society since that of ancient Rome, and some scholars believe we are more preoccupied with sex than any other people in all
of history. Today, far from not talking about sex, we might well seem,
to a visitor from Mars dropping into Times Square, to have no other
topic of communication.

And this is not solely an American obsession. Across the ocean in England, for example, "from bishops to biologists, everyone is in on the act." A perceptive front-page article in *The Times Literary Supplement*, London, goes on to point to the "whole turgid flood of post-Kinsey utilitarianism and post-Chatterley moral uplift. Open any newspaper, any day (Sunday in particular), and the odds are you will find some pundit treating the public to his views on contraception, abortion, adultery, obscene publications, homosexuality between consenting adults or (if all else fails) contemporary moral patterns among our adolescents."

Partly as a result of this radical shift, many therapists today rarely see patients who exhibit repression of sex in the manner of Freud's pre-World War I hysterical patients. In fact, we find in the people who come for help just the opposite: a great deal of talk about sex, a great deal of sexual activity, practically no one complaining of cultural prohibitions over going to bed as often or with as many partners as one wishes. But what our patients do complain of is lack of feeling and passion. "The curious thing about this ferment of discussion is how little anyone seems to be *enjoying* emancipation." So much sex and so little meaning or even fun in it.

Where the Victorian didn't want anyone to know that he or she had sexual feelings, we are ashamed if we do not. Before 1910, if you called a lady "sexy" she would be insulted; nowadays, she prizes the compliment and rewards you by turning her charms in your direction. Our patients often have the problems of frigidity and impotence, but the strange and poignant thing we observe is how desperately they struggle not to let anyone find out they don't feel sexually. The Victorian nice man or woman was guilty if he or she did experience sex; now we are guilty if we *don't*.

One paradox, therefore, is that enlightenment has not solved the sexual problems in our culture. To be sure, there are important positive results of the new enlightenment, chiefly in increased freedom for the individual. Most external problems are eased: sexual knowledge can be bought in any bookstore, contraception is available everywhere except in Boston where it is still believed, as the English countess averred on her wedding night, that sex is "too good for the common people." Couples can, without guilt and generally without squeamishness, discuss their sexual relationship and undertake to make it more mutually gratifying and meaningful. Let these gains not be underestimated. External social anxiety and guilt have lessened; dull would be the man who did not rejoice in this.

But *internal* anxiety and guilt have increased. And in some ways these are more morbid, harder to handle, and impose a heavier burden upon the individual than external anxiety and guilt.

The challenge a woman used to face from men was simple and direct—would she or would she not go to bed?—a direct issue of how she stood vis-à-vis cultural mores. But the question men ask now is no longer, "Will she or won't she?" but "Can she or can't she?" The challenge is shifted to the woman's personal adequacy, namely, her own capacity to have the vaunted orgasm—which should resemble a *grand*

mal seizure. Though we might agree that the second question places
the problem of sexual decision more where it should be, we cannot
overlook the fact that the first question is much easier for the person
to handle. In my practice, one woman was afraid to go to bed for fear
that the man "won't find me very good at making love." Another was 12
afraid because "I don't even know how to do it," assuming that her
lover would hold this against her. Another was scared to death of the
second marriage for fear that she wouldn't be able to have the orgasm
as she had not in her first. Often the woman's hesitation is formulated
as, "He won't like me well enough to come back again."

In past decades you could blame society's strict mores and preserve
your own self-esteem by telling yourself what you did or didn't do was
society's fault and not yours. And this would give you some time in
which to decide what you do want to do, or to let yourself grow into a 13
decision. But when the question is simply how you can perform, your
own sense of adequacy and self-esteem is called immediately into question, and the whole weight of the encounter is shifted inward to how
you can meet the test.

College students, in their fights with college authorities about hours
girls are to be permitted in the men's rooms, are curiously blind to the
fact that rules are often a boon. Rules give the student time to find
himself. He has the leeway to consider a way of behaving without
being committed before he is ready, to try on for size, to venture into
relationships tentatively—which is part of any growing up. Better to
have the lack of commitment direct and open rather than to go into 14
sexual relations under pressure—doing violence to his feelings by having
physical commitment without psychological. He may flaunt the rules,
but at least they give some structure to be flaunted. My point is true
whether he obeys the rule or not. Many contemporary students, understandably anxious because of their new sexual freedom, repress this
anxiety ("one should *like* freedom") and then compensate for the additional anxiety the repression gives them by attacking the parietal authorities for not giving them more freedom!

What we did not see in our short-sighted liberalism in sex was that
throwing the individual into an unbounded and empty sea of free choice 15
does not in itself give freedom, but is more apt to increase inner conflict. The sexual freedom to which we were devoted fell short of being
fully human.

In the arts, we have also been discovering what an illusion it was
to believe that mere freedom would solve our problem. Consider, for
example, the drama. In an article entitled "Is Sex Kaput?," Howard
Taubman, former drama critic of *The New York Times,* summarized 16
what we have all observed in drama after drama: "Engaging in sex was
like setting out to shop on a dull afternoon; desire had nothing to do
with it and even curiosity was faint." Consider also the novel. In the
"revolt against the Victorians," writes Leon Edel, "the extremists have
had their day. Thus far they have impoverished the novel rather than

enriched it." Edel perceptively brings out the crucial point that in sheer realistic "enlightenment" there has occurred a *dehumanization* of sex in fiction. There are "sexual encounters in Zola," he insists, "which have more truth in them than any D. H. Lawrence described—and also more humanity."

The battle against censorship and for freedom of expression surely was a great battle to win, but has it not become a new strait jacket? The writers, both novelists and dramatists "would rather hock their typewriters than turn in a manuscript without the obligatory scenes of unsparing anatomical documentation of their characters' sexual behavior. . . ." Our "dogmatic enlightenment" is self-defeating: it ends up destroying the very sexual passion it set out to protect. In the great tide of realistic chronicling, we forgot, on the stage and in the novel and even in psychotherapy, that imagination is the life-blood of eros, and that realism is neither sexual nor erotic. Indeed, there is nothing less sexy than sheer nakedness, as a random hour at any nudist camp will prove. It requires the infusion of the imagination (which I shall later call intentionality) to transmute physiology and anatomy into *interpersonal* experience—into art, into passion, into eros in a million forms which has the power to shake or charm us.

Could it not be that an "enlightenment" which reduces itself to sheer realistic detail is itself an escape from the anxiety involved in the relation of human imagination to erotic passion?

Salvation Through Technique

A second paradox is that *the new emphasis on technique in sex and love-making backfires.* It often occurs to me that there is an inverse relationship between the number of how-to-do-it books perused by a person or rolling off the presses in a society and the amount of sexual passion or even pleasure experienced by the persons involved. Certainly nothing is wrong with technique as such, in playing golf or acting or making love. But the emphasis beyond a certain point on technique in sex makes for a mechanistic attitude toward love-making, and goes along with alienation, feelings of loneliness, and depersonalization.

One aspect of the alienation is that the lover, with his age-old art, tends to be superseded by the computer operator with his modern efficiency. Couples place great emphasis on bookkeeping and timetables in their love-making—a practice confirmed and standardized by Kinsey. If they fall behind schedule they become anxious and feel impelled to go to bed whether they want to or not. My colleague, Dr. John Schimel, observes, "My patients have endured stoically, or without noticing, remarkably destructive treatment at the hands of their spouses, but they have experienced falling behind in the sexual time-table as a loss of love." The man feels he is somehow losing his masculine status if he does not perform up to schedule, and the woman that she has lost her feminine attractiveness if too long a period goes by without the man at least making a pass at her. The phrase "between men," which women use about their affairs, similarly suggests a gap in time like the *entr'acte*. Elaborate accounting- and ledger-book lists—how often this week have we made love? did he (or she) pay the right amount of attention to me during the evening? was the foreplay long enough?—make one wonder how the spontaneity of this most spontaneous act can possibly survive. The computer hovers in the stage wings of the drama of love-making the way Freud said one's parents used to.

It is not surprising then, in this preoccupation with techniques, that the questions typically asked about an act of love-making are not, Was there passion or meaning or pleasure in the act? but, How well did I perform? Take, for example, what Cyril Connolly calls "the tyranny of
the orgasm," and the preoccupation with achieving a simultaneous 21
orgasm, which is another aspect of the alienation. I confess that when people talk about the "apocalyptic orgasm," I find myself wondering, Why do they have to try so hard? What abyss of self-doubt, what inner void of loneliness, are they trying to cover up by this great concern with grandiose effects?

Even the sexologists, whose attitude is generally the more sex the merrier, are raising their eyebrows these days about the anxious overemphasis on achieving the orgasm and the great importance attached to "satisfying" the partner. A man makes a point of asking the woman if she "made it," or if she is "all right," or uses some other euphemism for an experience for which obviously no euphemism is possible. We men are reminded by Simone de Beauvoir and other women who try to interpret the love act that this is the last thing in the world a woman wants to be asked at that moment. Furthermore, the technical preoccupation robs the woman of exactly what she wants most of all, physi- 22
cally and emotionally, namely the man's spontaneous abandon at the moment of climax. This abandon gives her whatever thrill or ecstasy she and the experience are capable of. When we cut through all the rigmarole about roles and performance, what still remains is how amazingly important the sheer fact of intimacy of relationship is—the meeting, the growing closeness with the excitement of not knowing where it will lead, the assertion of the self, and the giving of self—in making a sexual encounter memorable. Is it not this intimacy that makes us return to the event in memory again and again when we need to be warmed by whatever hearths life makes available?

It is a strange thing in our society that what goes into building a
relationship—the sharing of tastes, fantasies, dreams, hopes for the 23
future, and fears from the past—seems to make people more shy and vulnerable than going to bed with each other. They are more wary of the tenderness that goes with psychological and spiritual nakedness than they are of the physical nakedness in sexual intimacy.

The New Puritanism

The third paradox is that our highly-vaunted sexual freedom has turned out to be a new form of puritanism. I spell it with a small "p" because I do not wish to confuse this with the original Puritanism. That, as in the passion of Hester and Dimmesdale in Hawthorne's *The Scarlet Letter*, was a very different thing. I refer to puritanism as it came down via our Victorian grandparents and became allied with industrialism and emotional and moral compartmentalization.

I define this puritanism as consisting of three elements. First, *a state of alienation from the body*. Second, *the separation of emotion from reason*. And third, *the use of the body as a machine*.

In our new puritanism, bad health is equated with sin. Sin used to mean giving in to one's sexual desires; it now means not having full sexual expression. Our contemporary puritan holds that it is immoral not to express your libido. Apparently this is true on both sides of the ocean: "There are few more depressing sights," the London *Times Literary Supplement* writes, "than a progressive intellectual determined to end up in bed with someone from a sense of moral duty. . . . There is no more high-minded puritan in the world than your modern advocate of salvation through properly directed passion. . . ." A woman used to be guilty if she went to bed with a man; now she feels vaguely guilty if after a certain number of dates she still refrains; her sin is "morbid repression," refusing to "give." And the partner, who is always completely enlightened (or at least pretends to be) refuses to allay her guilt by getting overtly angry at her (if she could fight him on the issue, the conflict would be a lot easier for her). But he stands broad-mindedly by, ready at the end of every date to undertake a crusade to assist her out of her fallen state. And this, of course, makes her "no" all the more guilt-producing for her.

This all means, of course, that people not only have to learn to perform sexually but have to make sure, at the same time, that they can do so without letting themselves go in passion or unseemly commitment—the latter of which may be interpreted as exerting an unhealthy demand upon the partner. *The Victorian person sought to have love without falling into sex; the modern person seeks to have sex without falling into love.*

I once diverted myself by drawing an impressionistic sketch of the attitude of the contemporary enlightened person toward sex and love. I would like to share this picture of what I call the new sophisticate:

> *The new sophisticate is not castrated by society, but like Origen is self-castrated. Sex and the body are for him not something to be and live out, but tools to be cultivated like a T.V. announcer's voice. The new sophisticate expresses his passion by devoting himself passionately to the moral principle of dispersing all passion, loving everybody until love has no power left to scare anyone. He is deathly afraid of his passions unless they are kept under leash, and the theory of total expres-*

> *sion is precisely his leash. His dogma of liberty is his repression; and his principle of full libidinal health, full sexual satisfaction, is his denial of eros. The old Puritans repressed sex and were passionate; our new puritan represses passion and is sexual. His purpose is to hold back the body, to try to make nature a slave. The new sophisticate's rigid principle of full freedom is not freedom but a new straitjacket. He does all this because he is afraid of his body and his compassionate roots in nature, afraid of the soil and his procreative power. He is our latter-day Baconian devoted to gaining power over nature, gaining knowledge in order to get more power. And you gain power over sexuality (like working the slave until all zest for revolt is squeezed out of him) precisely by the role of full expression. Sex becomes our tool like the caveman's bow and arrows, crowbar, or adz. Sex, the new machine, the Machina Ultima.*

This new puritanism has crept into contemporary psychiatry and psychology. It is argued in some books on the counseling of married couples that the therapist ought to use only the term "fuck" when discussing sexual intercourse, and to insist the patients use it; for any other word plays into the patients' dissimulation. What is significant here is not the use of the term itself: surely the sheer lust, animal but self-conscious, and bodily abandon which is rightly called fucking is not to be left out of the spectrum of human experience. But the interesting thing is that the use of the once-forbidden word is now made
into an *ought*—a duty for the moral reason of honesty. To be sure, it 29
is dissimulation to deny the biological side of copulation. But it is also dissimulation to use the term fuck for the sexual experience when what we seek is a relationship of personal intimacy which is more than a release of sexual tension, a personal intimacy which will be remembered tomorrow and many weeks after tomorrow. The former is dissimulation in the service of inhibition; the latter is dissimulation in the service of alienation of the self, a defense of the self against the anxiety of intimate relationship. As the former was the particular problem of Freud's day, the latter is the particular problem of ours.

The new puritanism brings with it a depersonalization of our whole language. Instead of making love, we "have sex"; in contrast to intercourse, we "screw"; instead of going to bed, we "lay" someone or (heaven help the English language as well as ourselves!) we "are laid." This alienation has become so much the order of the day that in some psychotherapeutic training schools, young psychiatrists and psychologists are taught that it is "therapeutic" to use solely the four-letter words 30
in sessions: the patient is probably masking some repression if he talks about making love; so it becomes our righteous duty—the new puritanism incarnate!—to let him know he only fucks. Everyone seems so intent on sweeping away the last vestiges of Victorian prudishness that we entirely forget that these different words refer to different kinds of human experience. Probably most people have experienced the different forms of sexual relationship described by the different terms and don't

have much difficulty distinguishing among them. I am not making a value judgment among these different experiences; they are all appropriate to their own kinds of relationship. Every woman wants at some time to be "laid"—transported, carried away, "made" to have passion when at first she has none, as in the famous scene between Rhett Butler and Scarlett O'Hara in *Gone with the Wind.* But if being "laid" is all that ever happens in her sexual life, then her experience of personal alienation and rejection of sex are just around the corner. If the therapist does not appreciate these diverse kinds of experience, he will be presiding at the shrinking and truncating of the patient's consciousness, and will be confirming the narrowing of the parent's bodily awareness as well as his or her capacity for relationship. This is the chief criticism of the new puritanism: it grossly limits feelings, it blocks the infinite variety and richness of the act, and it makes for emotional impoverishment.

It is not surprising that the new puritanism develops smoldering hostility among the members of our society. And that hostility, in turn, comes out frequently in references to the sexual act itself. We say "go fuck yourself" or "fuck you" as a term of contempt to show that the other is of no value whatever beyond being used and tossed aside. The biological lust is here in its *reductio ad absurdum.* Indeed, the word fuck is the most common expletive in our contemporary language to express violent hostility. I do not think this is by accident.

Motives of the Problem

In my function as a supervisory analyst at two analytic institutes, I supervise one case of each of six psychiatrists or psychologists who are in training to become analysts. I cite the six patients of these young analysts both because I know a good deal about them by now and also because, since they are not my patients, I can see them with a more objective perspective. Each one of these patients goes to bed without ostensible shame or guilt—and generally with different partners. The women—four of the six patients—all state that they don't feel much in the sex act. The motives of two of the women for going to bed seem to be to hang on to the man and to live up to the standard that sexual intercourse is "what you do" at a certain stage. The third woman has the particular motive of generosity: she sees going to bed as something nice you give a man—and she makes tremendous demands upon him to take care of her in return. The fourth woman seems the only one who does experience some real sexual lust, beyond which her motives are a combination of generosity to and anger at the man ("I'll force him to give me pleasure!"). The two male patients were originally impotent, and now, though able to have intercourse, have intermittent trouble with potency. But the outstanding fact is they never report getting much of a "bang" out of their sexual intercourse. Their chief motive for engaging in sex seems to be to demonstrate their masculinity. The specific purpose of one of the men, indeed, seems more to tell his analyst about his previous night's adventure, fair or poor as it may have been, in a kind of backstage interchange of confidence between men, than to enjoy the love-making itself.

Let us now pursue our inquiry on a deeper level by asking, What
are the underlying motives in these patterns? What drives people toward 33
the contemporary compulsive preoccupation with sex in place of their
previous compulsive denial of it?

The struggle to prove one's identity is obviously a central motive—
an aim present in women as well as men, as Betty Friedan in *The
Feminine Mystique* made clear. This has helped spawn the idea of
egalitarianism of the sexes and the *interchangeability* of the sexual
roles. Egalitarianism is clung to at the price of denying not only biological differences—which are basic, to say the least—between men and 34
women, but emotional differences from which come much of the delight
of the sexual act. The self-contradiction here is that the compulsive need
to prove you are identical with your partner means that you repress
your own unique sensibilities—and this is exactly what undermines your
own sense of identity. This contradiction contributes to the tendency
in our society for us to become machines even in bed.

Another motive is the individual's hope to overcome his own soli-
tariness. Allied with this is the desperate endeavor to escape feelings
of emptiness and the threat of apathy: partners pant and quiver hoping 35
to find an answering quiver in someone else's body just to prove that
their own is not dead; they seek a responding, a longing in the other
to prove their own feelings are alive. Out of an ancient conceit, this
is called love.

One often gets the impression, amid the male's flexing of sexual
prowess, that men are in training to become sexual athletes. But what
is the great prize of the game? Not only men, but women struggle to 36
prove their sexual power—they too must keep up to the timetable, must
show passion, and have the vaunted orgasm. Now it is well accepted in
psychotherapeutic circles that, dynamically, the overconcern with potency is generally a compensation for feelings of impotence.

The use of sex to prove potency in all these different realms has
led to the increasing emphasis on technical performance. And here we
observe another curiously self-defeating pattern. It is that the excessive
concern with technical performance in sex is actually correlated with
the reduction of sexual feeling. The techniques of achieving this ap- 37
proach the ludicrous: one is that an anesthetic ointment is applied to
the penis before intercourse. Thus feeling less, the man is able to postpone his orgasm longer. I have learned from colleagues that the pre-
scribing of this anesthetic "remedy" for premature ejaculation is not
unusual. "One male patient," records Dr. Schimel, "was desperate about
his 'premature ejaculations,' even though these ejaculations took place

after periods of penetration of ten minutes or more. A neighbor who was a urologist recommended an anesthetic ointment to be used prior to intercourse. This patient expressed complete satisfaction with the solution and was very grateful to the urologist." Entirely willing to give up any pleasure of his own, he sought only to prove himself a competent male.

A patient of mine reported that he had gone to physician with the problem of premature ejaculation, and that such an anesthetic ointment had been prescribed. My surprise, like Dr. Schimel's, was particularly over the fact that the patient had accepted this solution with no questions and no conflicts. Didn't the remedy fit the necessary bill, didn't it help him turn in a better performance? But by the time that young man got to me, he was impotent in every way imaginable, even to the point of being unable to handle such scarcely ladylike behavior on the part of his wife as her taking off her shoe while they were driving and beating him over the head with it. By all means the man was impotent in his hideous caricature of a marriage. And his penis, before it was drugged senseless, seemed to be the only character with enough "sense" to have the appropriate intention, namely to get out as quickly as possible.

Making one's self *feel less* in order to *perform better!* This is a symbol, as macabre as it is vivid, of the vicious circle in which so much of our culture is caught. The more one must demonstrate his potency, the more he treats sexual intercourse—this most intimate and personal of all acts—as a performance to be judged by exterior requirements, the more he then views himself as a machine to be turned on, adjusted, and steered, and the less feeling he has for either himself or his partner; and the less feeling, the more he loses genuine sexual appetite and ability. The upshot of this self-defeating pattern is that, in the long run, *the lover who is most efficient will also be the one who is impotent.*

A poignant note comes into our discussion when we remind ourselves that this excessive concern for "satisfying" the partner is an expression, however perverted, of a sound and basic element in the sexual act: the pleasure and experience of self-affirmation in being able to give to the partner. The man is often deeply grateful toward the women who lets herself be gratified by him—lets him give her an orgasm, to use the phrase that is often the symbol for this experience. This is a point midway between lust and tenderness, between sex and agapé—and it partakes of both. Many a male cannot feel his own identity either as a man or a person in our culture until he is able to gratify a woman. The very structure of human interpersonal relations is such that the sexual act does not achieve its full pleasure or meaning if the man and woman cannot feel they are able to gratify the other. And it is the other which often underlies the exploitative sexuality of the rape type and the compulsive sexuality of the Don Juan seduction type. Don Juan has to perform the act over and over again because he remains forever unsatisfied, quite despite the fact that he is entirely potent and has a technically good orgasm.

Now the problem is not the desire and need to satisfy the partner as such, but the fact that this need is interpreted by the persons in the sexual act in only a technical sense—giving physical sensation. What is omitted even from our very vocabulary (and thus the words may sound 41
"square" as I say them here) is the experience of giving feelings, sharing fantasies, offering the inner psychic richness that normally takes a little time and enables sensation to transcend itself in emotion and emotion to transcend itself in tenderness and sometimes love.

It is not surprising that contemporary trends toward the mechanization of sex have much to do with the problem of impotence. The distinguishing characteristic of the machine is that it can go through all the *motions* but it never *feels.* A knowledgeable medical student, one of whose reasons for coming into analysis was his sexual impotence, had a revealing dream. He was asking me in the dream to put a pipe in his head that would go down through his body and come out at the other end as his penis. He was confident in the dream that the pipe 42
would constitute an admirably strong erection. What was entirely missing in this intelligent scion of our sophisticated times was any understanding at all that *what he conceived of as his solution was exactly the cause of his problem,* namely the image of himself as a "screwing machine." His symbol is remarkably graphic: the brain, the intellect, is included, but true symbol of our alienated age, his shrewd system bypasses entirely the seats of emotions, the thalamus, the heart and lungs, even the stomach. Direct route from head to penis—but what is lost is the heart!

I do not have statistics on hand concerning the present incidence of impotence in comparison with past periods, nor does anyone else so far as I have been able to discover. But my impression is that impotence is increasing these days despite (or is it because of) the unrestrained freedom on all sides. All therapists seem to agree that more men are coming to them with that problem—though whether this represents a real increase in the prevalence of sexual impotence or 43
merely a greater awareness and ability to talk about it cannot be definitely answered. Obviously, it is one of those topics on which meaningful statistics are almost impossible to get. The fact that the book dealing with impotence and frigidity, *Human Sexual Response,* clung near the top of the best-seller lists for so many months, expensive and turgidly-written as it was, would seem to be plenty of evidence of the urge of men to get help on impotence. Whatever the reason, it is becoming harder for the young man as well as the old to take "yes" for an answer.

To see the curious ways the new puritanism shows itself, you have only to open an issue of *Playboy,* that redoubtable journal reputedly sold mainly to college students and clergymen. You discover the naked girls with silicated breasts side by side with the articles by reputable authors, and you conclude on first blush that the magazine is certainly on the side of the new enlightenment. But as you look more closely you see a strange expression in these photographed girls: detached, mechanical, uninviting, vacuous—the typical schizoid personality in the negative sense of that term. You discover that they are not "sexy" at all but that *Playboy* has only shifted the fig leaf from the genitals to the face. You read the letters to the editor and find the first, entitled "Playboy Priest," telling of a priest who "lectures on Hefner's philosophy to audiences of young people and numerous members of the clergy," that "true Christian ethics and morality are not incompatible with Hefner's philosophy" and—written with enthusiastic approbation—that "most clergymen in their fashionable parsonages live more like playboys than ascetics." You find another letter entitled "Jesus was a playboy," since he loved Mary Magdalene, good food, and good grooming, and castigated the Pharisees. And you wonder why all this religious justification and why people, if they are going to be "liberated," can't just enjoy their liberation?

Whether one takes the cynical view that letters to the editor are "planted," or the more generous one that these examples are selected from hundreds of letters, it amounts to the same thing. An image of a type of American male is being presented—a suave, detached, self-assured bachelor, who regards the girl as a "Playboy accessory" like items in his fashionable dress. You note also that *Playboy* carries no advertising for trusses, bald heads, or anything that would detract from this image. You discover that the good articles (which, frankly, can be bought by an editor who wants to hire an assistant with taste and pay the requisite amount of money) give authority to this male image. Harvey Cox concludes that *Playboy* is basically antisexual and that it is the "latest and slickest episode in man's continuing refusal to be human." He believes "the whole phenomenon of which *Playboy* is only a part vividly illustrates the awful fact of the new kind of tyranny." The poet-sociologist Calvin Herton, discussing *Playboy* in connection with the fashion and entertainment world, calls it the new sexual fascism.

Playboy has indeed caught on to something significant in American society: Cox believes it to be "the repressed fear of involvement with women." I go farther and hold that it, as an example of the new puritanism, gets its dynamic from a repressed anxiety in American men that underlies even the fear of involvement. This is the repressed anxiety about impotence. Everything in the magazine is beautifully concocted to bolster the *illusion of potency* without ever putting it to the test or challenge at all. Noninvolvement (like playing it cool) is elevated into the ideal model for the Playboy. This is possible because the illusion is airtight, ministering as it does to men fearful for their potency, and capitalizing on this anxiety. The character of the illusion is shown further in the fact that the readership of *Playboy* drops off significantly after the age of thirty, when men cannot escape dealing with real women. This illusion is illustrated by the fact that Hefner himself, a former Sunday-school teacher and son of devout Methodists, practically never goes outside his large establishment in North Chicago. Ensconced there, he carries on his work surrounded by his bunnies and amidst his nonalcoholic bacchanals on Pepsi-Cola.

The Revolt Against Sex

With the confusion of motives in sex that we have noted above —almost every motive being present in the act except the desire to make love—it is no wonder that there is a diminution of feeling and that passion has lessened almost to the vanishing point. This diminution of feeling often takes the form of a kind of anesthesia (now with
no need of ointment) in people who can perform the mechanical aspects 47
of the sexual act very well. We are becoming used to the plaint from the couch or patient's chair that "We made love, but I didn't feel anything." Again, the poets tell us the same things as our patients. T. S. Eliot writes in *The Waste Land* that after "lovely woman stoops to folly," and the carbuncular clerk who seduced her at tea leaves,

She turns and looks a moment in the glass
Hardly aware of her departed lover;
Her brain allows one half-formed thought to pass;
"Well now that's done: and I'm glad it's over."
When lovely woman stoops to folly and
Paces about her room again, alone,
She smoothes her hair with automatic hand,
And puts a record on the gramophone.

(III:249-256)

Sex is the "last frontier," David Riesman meaningfully phrases it in *The Lonely Crowd.* Gerald Sykes, in the same vein, remarks, "In a world gone grey with market reports, time studies, tax regulations and path lab analyses, the rebel finds sex to be the one green thing." It is surely true that the zest, adventure, and trying out of one's strength, the discovering of vast and exciting new areas of feeling and experience in one's self and in one's relations to others, and the validation
of the self that goes with these are indeed "frontier experiences." They 48
are rightly and normally present in sexuality as part of the psychosocial development of every person. Sex in our society did, in fact, have this power for several decades after the 1920's, when almost every other activity was becoming "other-directed," jaded, emptied of zest and adventure. But for various reasons—one of them being that sex by itself had to carry the weight for the validation of the personality in practically all other realms as well—the frontier freshness, newness and challenge become more and more lost.

For we are now living in the post-Riesman age, and are experiencing the long-run implications of Riesman's "other-directed" behavior, the radar-reflected way of life. The last frontier has become a teeming Las Vegas and no frontier at all. Young people can no longer get a bootlegged feeling of personal identity out of revolting in sexuality since there is nothing there to revolt against. Studies of drug addiction among young people report them as saying that the revolt against parents, the social "kick of feeling their own oats" which they used to get from sex, they now have to get from drugs. One such study indicates that students express a "certain boredom with sex, while drugs are synonymous with excitement, curiosity, forbidden adventure, and society's abounding permissiveness."

It no longer sounds new when we discover that for many young people what used to be called love-making is now experienced as a futile "panting palm to palm," in Aldous Huxley's predictive phrase; that they tell us that it is hard for them to understand what the poets were talking about, and that we should so often hear the disappointed refrain, "We went to bed but it wasn't any good."

Nothing to revolt against, did I say? Well, there is obviously one thing left to revolt against, and that is sex itself. The frontier, the establishing of identity, the validation of the self can be and not infrequently does become for some people, a revolt against sexuality entirely. I am certainly not advocating this. What I wish to indicate is that the very revolt against sex—this modern Lysistrata in robot's dress—is rumbling at the gates of our cities or, if not rumbling, at least hovering. The sexual revolution comes finally back on itself not with a bang but a whimper.

Thus it is not surprising that, as sex becomes more machinelike, with passion irrelevant and then even pleasure diminishing, the problem has come full circle. And we find, *mirabile dictu,* a progression from an *anesthetic* attitude to an *antiseptic* one. Sexual contact itself then tends to get put on the shelf and to be avoided. This is another and surely least constructive aspect of the new puritanism: it returns, finally, to a new asceticism. This is said graphically in a charming limerick that seems to have sprung up on some sophisticated campus:

The word has come down from the Dean
That with the aid of the teaching machine,
King Oedipus Rex
Could have learned about sex
Without ever touching the Queen.

Marshall McLuhan, among others, welcomes this revolt against sex. "Sex as we now think of it may soon be dead," write McLuhan and Leonard. "Sexual concepts, ideals and practices already are being altered almost beyond recognition. . . . The foldout playmate in *Playboy* magazine—she of outsize breast and buttocks, pictured in sharp detail—signals the death throes of a departing age." McLuhan and Leonard then go on to predict that eros will not be lost in the new sexless age but diffused, and that all life will be more erotic than now seems possible.

This last reassurance would be comforting indeed to believe. But as usual, McLuhan's penetrating insights into *present* phenomena are unfortunately placed in a framework of history—"pretribalism" with its so-called lessened distinction between male and female—which has no factual basis at all. And he gives us no evidence whatever for his optimistic prediction that new eros, rather than apathy, will suceed the demise of *vive la difference.* Indeed, there are amazing confusions in this article arising from McLuhan's and Leonard's worship of the new electric age. In likening Twiggy to an X-ray as against Sophia Loren 54
to a Rubens, they ask, "And what does an X-ray of a woman reveal? Not a realistic picture, but a deep, involving image. Not a specialized female, but a *human being.*" Well! An X-ray actually reveals not a human being at all but a depersonalized, fragmentized segment of bone or tissue which can be read only by a highly specialized technician and from which we could never in a thousand years recognize a human being or any man or woman we know, let alone one we love. Such a "reassuring" view of the future is frightening and depressing in the extreme.

And may I not be permitted to prefer Sophia Loren over Twiggy 55
for an idle erotic daydream without being read out of the New Society?

Our future is taken more seriously by the participants in the discussion on this topic at the Center for the Study of Democratic Institutions at Santa Barbara. Their report, called "The A-Sexual Society," frankly faces the fact that "we are hurtling into, not a bisexual or a multi-sexual, but an a-sexual society: the boys grow long hair and the girls wear pants. . . . Romance will disappear; in fact, it has almost disappeared now. . . . Given the guaranteed Annual Income and The Pill, will women choose to marry? Why should they?" Mrs. Eleanor Garth, a participant in the discussion and writer of the report, goes on
to point out the radical change that may well occur in having and 56
rearing children. "What of the time when the fertilized ovum can be implanted in the womb of a mercenary, and one's progeny selected from a sperm-bank? Will the lady choose to reproduce her husband, if there still are such things? . . . No problems, no jealousy, no love-transference. . . . And what of the children, incubated under glass? . . . Will communal love develop the human qualities that we assume emerge from the present rearing of children? Will women under these conditions lose the survival drive and become as death-oriented as the present generation of American men? . . . I don't raise the question in advocacy," she adds, "I consider some of the possibilities horrifying."

Mrs. Garth and her colleagues at the Center recognize that the real issue underlying this revolution is not what one does with sexual organs and sexual functions per se, but what happens to man's hu- 57
manity. "What disturbs me is the real possibility of the disappearance of our humane, life-giving qualities with the speed of developments in the life sciences, and the fact that no one seems to be discussing the alternative possibilities for good and evil in these developments."

The purpose of our discussion is precisely to raise the questions of the alternative possibilities for good and evil—that is, the destruction or the enhancement of the qualities which constitute man's "humane, life-giving qualities."

Germaine Greer

Altruism

"Love seeketh not Itself to please,
Nor for itself hath any care,
But for another gives its ease,
And builds a Heaven in Hell's despair."

So sung a little Clod of Clay,
Trodden with the cattle's feet . . .

I have talked of love as an assertion of confidence in the self, an extension of narcissism to include one's own kind, variously considered. And yet we are told, "Greater love hath no man than he lay down his life for his friend." At our school we were encouraged to deny ourselves in order to give to others. We ate no sweets and put our pennies in a red and yellow box with a pickaninny on the front for the missions, if we were holy that is. That understanding of love was that it was the negation by abnegation of the self, the forgetfulness of the self in humility, patience, and self-denial. The essential egotism of the practice was apparent to many of us in the demeanor of the most pious girls, for the aim of the exercise was ultimately to earn grace in the eyes of the Lord. Every such act had to be offered up, or else the heavenly deposit was not made to our account. And yet it was a seductive notion. It picked up on our masochistic tendencies and linked with fantasies of annihilation. This is the love, we were told, of the mother who flings her body across her child's when danger threatens, of the mother duck who decoys the hunters from her nest. Noble, instinctive and feminine. All our mothers had it, for otherwise they would not have dared pain and illness to bring us into the world. Nobody could tell the greatness of a mother's sacrifices for her children, especially for us who were not even getting free education. Every mother was a saint. The Commandment was of course to love thy neighbor as thyself, but the nuns were fired by the prospect of loving their neighbors more than themselves.

The ideal of altruism is possibly a high one, but it is unfortunately chimeric. We cannot be liberated from ourselves, and we cannot act in defiance of our own motivations, unless we are mother ducks and act as instinctive creatures, servants of the species. We, the children who were on the receiving end, knew that our mothers' self-sacrifice existed mostly in their minds. We were constantly exhorted to be grateful for the gift of life. Next to the redemption, for which we could never hope to be sufficiently grateful, although we had no very clear idea of why we needed anyone to die for us in the first place, we had to be grateful for the gift of life. The nuns pointed out that the Commandment to love our parents followed immediately upon the Commandments about loving God, and because they themselves were *in loco parentis* and living solely for God and their neighbor we ought to be grateful for that too. But children are pragmatic. We could see that our mothers blackmailed us with self-sacrifice, even if we did not know whether or not they might have been great opera stars or the toasts of the town if they had not borne us. In our intractable moments we pointed out that we had not asked to be born, or even to go to an expensive school. We knew that they must have had motives of their own for what they did with and to us. The notion of our parents' self-sacrifice filled us not with gratitude, but with confusion and guilt. We wanted them to be happy yet they were sad and deprived, and it was our fault. The cry of Portnoy's mother is the cry of every mother, unless she abandons the role of martyr absolutely. When we were scolded and beaten for making our mothers worry, we tried to point out that we did not ask them to concern themselves so minutely with our doings. When our school reports brought reproach and recrimination, we knew whose satisfaction the sacrifice was meant to entail. Was there no opportunity for us to be on the credit side in emotional transactions? As far as the nuns were concerned we were fairly sure that in giving up the world to devote their lives to God and to us they had not given up anything that they had passionately wanted, especially not for us whom they did not know.

But while boy-children might remain relatively detached and cynical about their parents' motivation little girls eventually recapitulate. Their concepts of themselves are so confused, and their cultivated dependency so powerful, that they begin to practice self-sacrifice quite early on. They are still expiating their primal guilt for being born when they bravely give up all other interests and concentrate on making their men happy. Somehow the perception of the real motivation for self-sacrifice exists alongside its official ideology. The public relations experts seek to attract girls to nursing by calling it the most rewarding job in the world, and yet it is the hardest and the worst paid. The satisfaction comes in the sensation of doing good. Not only will nurses feel good because they are relieving pain, but also because they are taking little reward for it; therefore they are permanent emotional creditors. Any patient in a public hospital can tell you what this exploitation of feminine masochism means in real terms. Anybody who has tossed all night in pain rather than ring the overworked and reproachful night nurse can tell you.

In sexual relationships, this confusion of altruism with love per-
verts the majority. Self-sacrifice is the leitmotiv of most of the marital
games played by women, from the crudest ("I've given you the best
years of my life") to the most sophisticated ("I only went to bed with
him so's he'd promote you"). For so much sacrificed self the expected
reward is security, and seeing that a reward is expected it cannot
properly speaking be called self-sacrifice at all. It is in fact a kind of
commerce, and one in which the female must always be the creditor.
Of course, it is also practiced by men who explain their failure to do
exciting jobs or risk insecurity because of their obligations to wife
and/or children, but it is not invariable, whereas it is hard to think of
a male-female relationship in which the element of female self-sacrifice was absent. So long as women must live vicariously, through men,
they must labor at making themselves indispensable and this is the
fulltime job that is generally wrongly called altruism. Properly speaking, altruism is an absurdity. Women are self-sacrificing in direct pro- 4
portion to their incapacity to offer anything but this sacrifice. They
sacrifice what they never had: a self. The cry of the deserted woman,
"What have I done to deserve this?" reveals at once the false emotional
economy that she has been following. For most men it is only in quar-
rels that they discover just how hypocritically and unwillingly their
women have capitulated to them. Obviously, spurious altruism is not
the monopoly of women, but as long as women need men to live by,
and men may take wives or not, and live just the same, it will be more
important in feminine motivation than it is in male. The misunderstood
commandment of Aleister Crowley to *do as thou wilt* is a warning not
to delude yourself that you can do otherwise, and to take full responsibility to yourself for what you do. When one has genuinely chosen a
course for oneself it cannot be possible to hold another responsible for
it. The altruism of women is merely the inauthenticity of the feminine
person carried over into behavior. It is another function of the defect
in female narcissism.

Richard Brautigan

As the Bruises Fade, the Lightning Aches

As the bruises fade, the lightning aches.
Last week, making love, you bit me.
Now the blue and dark have gone
and yellow bruises grow toward pale daffodils,
then paler to become until my body
is all my own and what that ever got me.

Richard Brautigan

The Moon Versus Us Ever Sleeping Together Again

I sit here, an arch-villain of romance,
thinking about you. Gee, I'm sorry
I made you unhappy, but there was nothing
I could do about it because I have to be free.
Perhaps everything would have been different
if you had stayed at the table or asked me
to go out with you to look at the moon,
instead of getting up and leaving me alone with her.

Walt Whitman

The Dalliance of the Eagles

Skirting the river road, (my forenoon walk, my rest,)
Skyward in air a sudden muffled sound, the dalliance of the eagles,
The rushing amorous contact high in space together,
The clinching interlocking claws, a living, fierce, gyrating wheel,
Four beating wings, two beaks, a swirling mass tight grappling,
In tumbling turning clustering loops, straight downward falling,
Till o'er the river pois'd, a twain yet one, a moment's lull,
A motionless still balance in the air, then parting, talons loosing,
Upward again on slow-firm pinions slanting, their separate diverse flight,
She hers, he his, pursuing.

Alvin Toffler

The Fractured Family

The flood of novelty about to crash down upon us will spread
from universities and research centers to factories and offices, from
the marketplace and mass media into our social relationships, from the 1
community into the home. Penetrating deep into our private lives, it
will place absolutely unprecedented strains on the family itself.

The family has been called the "giant shock absorber" of society
—the place to which the bruised and battered individual returns after
doing battle with the world, the one stable point in an increasingly flux- 2
filled environment. As the super-industrial revolution unfolds, this
"shock absorber" will come in for some shocks of its own.

Social critics have a field day speculating about the family. The
family is "near the point of complete extinction," says Ferdinand Lund-
berg, author of *The Coming World Transformation.* "The family is
dead except for the first year or two of child raising," according to 3
psychoanalyst William Wolf. "This will be its only function." Pessimists tell us the family is racing toward oblivion—but seldom tell us
what will take its place.

Family optimists, in contrast, contend that the family, having existed all this time, will continue to exist. Some go so far as to argue
that the family is in for a Golden Age. As leisure spreads, they theorize, 4
families will spend more time together and will derive great satisfaction from joint activity. "The family that plays together, stays together,"
etc.

A more sophisticated view holds that the very turbulence of tomorrow will drive people deeper into their families. "People will marry
for stable structure," says Dr. Irwin M. Greenberg, Professor of Psy- 5
chiatry at the Albert Einstein College of Medicine. According to this
view, the family serves as one's "portable roots," anchoring one against
the storm of change. In short, the more transient and novel the environment, the more important the family will become.

It may be that both sides in this debate are wrong. For the future is more open than it might appear. The family may neither vanish *nor* enter upon a new Golden Age. It may—and this is far more likely—break up, shatter, only to come together again in weird and novel ways. 6

The Mystique of Motherhood

The most obviously upsetting force likely to strike the family in the decades immediately ahead will be the impact of the new birth technology. The ability to pre-set the sex of one's baby, or even to "program" its IQ, looks and personality traits, must now be regarded 7
as a real possibility. Embryo implants, babies grown *in vitro*, the ability to swallow a pill and guarantee oneself twins or triplets or, even more, the ability to walk into a "babytorium" and actually purchase embryos —all this reaches so far beyond any previous human experience that one needs to look at the future through the eyes of the poet or painter, rather than those of the sociologist or conventional philosopher.

It is regarded as somehow unscholarly, even frivolous to discuss these matters. Yet advances in science and technology, or in reproductive biology alone, could, within a short time, smash all orthodox ideas about the family and its responsibilities. When babies can be grown 8
in a laboratory jar what happens to the very notion of maternity? And what happens to the self-image of the female in societies which, since the very beginnings of man, have taught her that her primary mission is the propagation of and nurture of the race?

Few social scientists have begun as yet to concern themselves with such questions. One who has is psychiatrist Hyman G. Weitzen, director of Neuropsychiatric Service at Polyclinic Hospital in New York. 9
The cycle of birth, Dr. Weitzen suggests, "fulfills for most women a major creative need . . . Most women are proud of their ability to bear children . . . The special aura that glorifies the pregnant woman has figured largely in the art and literature of both East and West."

What happens to the cult of motherhood, Weitzen asks, if "her offspring might literally not be hers, but that of a genetically 'superior' ovum, implanted in her womb from another woman, or even grown in a Petri dish?" If women are to be important at all, he suggests, it will no longer be because they alone can bear children. If nothing else, we are about to kill off the mystique of motherhood.

Not merely motherhood, but the concept of parenthood itself may be in for radical revision. Indeeed, the day may soon dawn when it is possible for a child to have more than two biological parents.

Dr. Beatrice Mintz, a developmental biologist at the Institute for Cancer Research in Philadelphia, has grown what are coming to be known as "multi-mice"—baby mice each of which has more than the usual number of parents. Embryos are taken from each of two pregnant mice. These embryos are placed in a laboratory dish and nurtured until they form a single growing mass. This is then implanted in the womb of a third female mouse. A baby is born that clearly shares the genetic characteristics of both sets of donors. Thus a typical multi-mouse, born of two pairs of parents, has white fur and whiskers on one side of its face, dark fur and whiskers on the other, with alternating bands of white and dark hair covering the rest of the body. Some 700 multi-mice bred in this fashion have already produced more than 35,000 offspring themselves. If multi-mouse is here, can "multi-man" be far behind?

Under such circumstances, what or who is a parent? When a
woman bears in her uterus an embryo conceived in another woman's 13
womb, who is the mother? And just exactly who is the father?

If a couple can actually purchase an embryo, then parenthood
becomes a legal not a biological matter. Unless such transactions are
tightly controlled, one can imagine such grotesqueries as a couple buying an embryo, raising it *in vitro*, then buying another in the name of 14
the first, as though for a trust fund. In that case, they might be regarded as legal "grandparents" before their first child is out of its
infancy. We shall need a whole new vocabulary to describe kinship ties.

Furthermore, if embryos are for sale, can a corporation buy one?
Can it buy ten thousand? Can it resell them? And if not a corporation,
how about a non-commercial research laboratory? If we buy and sell
living embryos, are we back to a new form of slavery? Such are the 15
nightmarish questions soon to be debated by us. To continue to think
of the family, therefore, in purely conventional terms is to defy all
reason.

Faced by rapid social change and the staggering implications of the
scientific revolution, super-industrial man may be forced to experiment
with novel family forms. Innovative minorities can be expected to try 16
out a colorful variety of family arrangements. They will begin by tinker-
ing with existing forms.

The Streamlined Family

One simple thing they will do is streamline the family. The typical
pre-industrial family not only had a good many children, but numerous
other dependents as well—grandparents, uncles, aunts, and cousins.
Such "extended" families were well suited for survival in slow-paced 17
agricultural societies. But such families are hard to transport or trans-
plant. They are immobile.

Industrialism demanded masses of workers ready and able to move
off the land in pursuit of jobs and to move again whenever necessary.
Thus the extended family gradually shed its excess weight and the
so-called "nuclear" family emerged—a stripped-down, portable family 18
unit consisting only of parents and a small set of children. This new
style family, far more mobile than the traditional extended family, became the standard model in all the industrial countries.

Super-industrialism, however, the next stage of eco-technological development, requires even higher mobility. Thus we may expect many among the people of the future to carry the streamlining process a step further by remaining childless, cutting the family down to its most elemental components, a man and a woman. Two people, perhaps with matched careers, will prove more efficient at navigating through education and social shoals, through job changes and geographic relocations, than the ordinary child-cluttered family. Indeed, anthropologist Margaret Mead has pointed out that we may already be moving toward a system under which, as she puts it, "parenthood would be limited to a smaller number of families whose principal functions would be childrearing," leaving the rest of the population "free to function—for the first time in history—as individuals."

A compromise may be the postponement of children, rather than childlessness. Men and women today are often torn in conflict between a commitment to career and a commitment to children. In the future, many couples will sidestep this problem by deferring the entire task of raising children until after retirement.

This may strike people of the present as odd. Yet once childbearing is broken away from its biological base, nothing more than tradition suggests having children at an early age. Why not wait, and buy your embryos later, after your work career is over? Thus childlessness is likely to spread among young and middle-aged couples; sexagenarians who raise infants may be far more common. The post-retirement family could become a recognized social institution.

Bio-Parents and Pro-Parents

If a smaller number of families raise children, however, why do the children have to be their own? Why not a system under which "professional parents" take on the childrearing function for others?

Raising children, after all, requires skills that are by no means universal. We don't let "just anyone" perform brain surgery or, for that matter, sell stocks and bonds. Even the lowest ranking civil servant is required to pass tests proving competence. Yet we allow virtually anyone, almost without regard for mental or moral qualification, to try his or her hand at raising young human beings, so long as these humans are biological offspring. Despite the increasing complexity of the task, parenthood remains the greatest single preserve of the amateur.

As the present system cracks and the super-industrial revolution rolls over us, as the armies of juvenile delinquents swell, as hundreds of thousands of youngsters flee their homes, and students rampage at universities in all the techno-societies, we can expect vociferous demands for an end to parental dilettantism.

There are far better ways to cope with the problems of youth, but professional parenthood is certain to be proposed, if only because it fits so perfectly with the society's overall push toward specialization. Moreover, there is a powerful, pent-up demand for this social innova-

tion. Even now millions of parents, given the opportunity, would happily
relinquish their parental responsibilities—and not necessarily through
irresponsibility or lack of love. Harried, frenzied, up against the wall,
they have come to see themselves as inadequate to the tasks. Given 25
affluence and the existence of specially-equipped and licensed professional parents, many of today's biological parents would not only gladly
surrender their children to them, but would look upon it as an act of
love, rather than rejection.

Parental professionals would not be therapists, but actual family
units assigned to, and well paid for, rearing children. Such families
might be multi-generational by design, offering children in them an
opportunity to observe and learn from a variety of adult models, as 26
was the case in the old farm homestead. With the adults paid to be
professional parents, they would be freed of the occupational necessity
to relocate repeatedly. Such families would take in new children as old
ones "graduate" so that age-segregation would be minimized.

Thus newspapers of the future might well carry advertisements
addressed to young married couples: "Why let parenthood tie you
down? Let us raise your infant into a responsible, successful adult.
Class A Pro-family offers: father age 39, mother, 36, grandmother, 67.
Uncle and aunt, age 30, live in, hold part-time local employment. Four- 27
child-unit has opening for one, age 6-8. Regulated diet exceeds government standards. All adults certified in child development and management. Bio-parents permitted frequent visits. Telephone contact allowed.
Child may spend summer vacation with bio-parents. Religion, art, music
encouraged by special arrangement. Five year contract, minimum. Write
for further details."

The "real" or "bio-parents" could, as the ad suggests, fill the role
presently played by interested godparents, namely that of friendly and 28
helpful outsiders. In such a way, the society could continue to breed
a wide diversity of genetic types, yet turn the care of children over
to mother-father groups who are equipped, both intellectually and
emotionally, for the task of caring for kids.

Communes and Homosexual Daddies

Quite a different alternative lies in the communal family. As transience increases the loneliness and alienation in society, we can anticipate increasing experimentation with various forms of group marriage.
The banding together of several adults and children into a single
"family" provides a kind of insurance against isolation. Even if one or 29
two members of the household leave, the remaining members have one
another. Communes are springing up modeled after those described by
psychologist B. F. Skinner in *Walden Two* and by novelist Robert
Rimmer in *The Harrad Experiment and Proposition* 31. In the latter
work, Rimmer seriously proposes the legalization of a "corporate fam-

ily" in which from three to six adults adopt a single name, live and raise children in common, and legally incorporate to obtain certain economic and tax advantages.

According to some observers, there are already hundreds of open or covert communes dotting the American map. Not all, by any means, are composed of young people or hippies. Some are organized around specific goals—like the group, quietly financed by three East Coast colleges—which has taken as its function the task of counseling college freshmen, helping to orient them to campus life. The goals may be social, religious, political, even recreational. Thus we shall before long begin to see communal families of surfers dotting the beaches of California and Southern France, if they don't already. We shall see the emergence of communes based on political doctrines and religious faiths. In Denmark, a bill to legalize group marriage has already been introduced in the Folketing (Parliament). While passage is not imminent, the act of introduction is itself a significant symbol of change.

In Chicago, 250 adults and children already live together in "family-style monasticism" under the auspices of a new, fast-growing religious organization, the Ecumenical Institute. Members share the same quarters, cook and eat together, worship and tend children in common, and pool their incomes. At least 60,000 people have taken "EI" courses and similar communes have begun to spring up in Atlanta, Boston, Los Angeles and other cities. "A brand-new world is emerging," says Professor Joseph W. Mathews, leader of the Ecumenical Institute, "but people are still operating in terms of the old one. We seek to re-educate people and give them the tools to build a new social context."

Still another type of family unit likely to win adherents in the future might be called the "geriatric commune"—a group marriage of elderly people drawn together in a common search for companionship and assistance. Disengaged from the productive economy that makes mobility necessary, they will settle in a single place, band together, pool funds, collectively hire domestic or nursing help, and proceed—within limits—to have the "time of their lives."

Communalism runs counter to the pressure for ever greater geographical and social mobility generated by the thrust toward super-industrialism. It presupposes groups of people who "stay put." For this reason, communal experiments will first proliferate among those in the society who are free from the industrial discipline—the retired population, the young, the dropouts, the students, as well as among self-employed professional and technical people. Later, when advanced technology and information systems make it possible for much of the work of society to be done at home via computer-telecommunication hookups, communalism will become feasible for larger numbers.

We shall, however, also see many more "family" units consisting of a single unmarried adult and one or more children. Nor will all of these adults be women. It is already possible in some places for unmarried men to adopt children. In 1965 in Oregon, for example, a thirty-

eight-year-old musician named Tony Piazza became the first unmarried
man in that state, and perhaps in the United States, to be granted
the right to adopt a baby. Courts are more readily granting custody to
divorced fathers, too. In London, photographer Michael Cooper, married at twenty and divorced soon after, won the right to raise his infant
son, and expressed an interest in adopting other children. Observing 34
that he did not particularly wish to remarry, but that he liked children,
Cooper mused aloud "I wish you could just ask beautiful women to
have babies for you. Or any woman you liked, or who had something
you admired. Ideally, I'd like a big house full of children—all different colors, shapes and sizes." Romantic? Unmanly? Perhaps. Yet attitudes like these will be widely held by men in the future.

Two pressures are even now softening up the culture, preparing
it for acceptance of the idea of childrearing by men. First, adoptable
children are in oversupply in some places. Thus, in Calilfornia, disc
jockeys blare commercials: "We have many wonderful babies of all
races and nationalities waiting to bring love and happiness to the right
families . . . Call the Los Angeles County Bureau of Adoption." At 35
the same time, the mass media, in a strange non-conspiratorial fashion,
appear to have decided simultaneously that men who raise children
hold special interest for the public. Extremely popular television shows
in recent seasons have glamorized womanless households in which men
scrub floors, cook, and, most significantly, raise children. *My Three
Sons, The Rifleman, Bonanza and Bachelor Father* are four examples.

As homosexuality becomes more socially acceptable, we may even
begin to find families based on homosexual "marriages" with the partners adopting children. Whether these children would be of the same
or opposite sex remains to be seen. But the rapidity with which homosexuality is winning respectability in the technosocieties distinctly
points in this direction. In Holland not long ago a Catholic priest "mar- 36
ried" two homosexuals, explaining to critics that "they are among the
faithful to be helped." England has rewritten its relevant legislation;
homosexual relations between consenting adults are no longer considered a crime. And in the United States a meeting of Episcopal clergymen concluded publicly that homosexuality might, under certain circumstances, be adjudged "good." The day may also come when a court
decides that a couple of stable, well educated homosexuals might make
decent "parents."

We might also see the gradual relaxation of bars against polygamy.
Polygamous families exist even now, more widely than generally believed, in the midst of "normal" society. Writer Ben Merson, after visiting several such families in Utah where polygamy is still regarded as 37
essential by certain Mormon fundamentalists, estimated that there are
some 30,000 people living in underground family units of this type in
the United States. As sexual attitudes loosen up, as property rights
become less important because of rising affluence, the social repression
of polygamy may come to be regarded as irrational. This shift may

be facilitated by the very mobility that compels men to spend considerable time away from their present homes. The old male fantasy of the Captain's Paradise may become a reality for some, although it is likely that, under such circumstances, the wives left behind will demand extramarital sexual rights. Yesterday's "captain" would hardly consider this possibility. Tomorrow's may feel quite differently about it.

Still another family form is even now springing up in our midst, a novel childrearing unit that I call the "aggregate family"—a family based on relationships between divorced and remarried couples, in which all the children become part of "one big family." Though sociologists have paid little attention as yet to this phenomenon, it is already so prevalent that it formed the basis for a hilarious scene in a recent American movie entitled *Divorce American Style.* We may expect aggregate families to take on increasing importance in the decades ahead.

Childless marriage, professional parenthood, post-retirement childrearing, corporate families, communes, geriatric group marriages, homosexual family units, polygamy—these, then, are a few of the family forms and practices with which innovative minorities will experiment in the decades ahead. Not all of us, however, will be willing to participate in such experimentation. What of the majority?

The Odds Against Love

Minorities experiment; majorities cling to the forms of the past. It is safe to say that large numbers of people will refuse to jettison the conventional idea of marriage or the familiar family forms. They will, no doubt, continue searching for happiness within the orthodox format. Yet, even they will be forced to innovate in the end, for the odds against success may prove overwhelming.

The orthodox format presupposes that two young people will "find" one another and marry. It presupposes that the two will fulfill certain psychological needs in one another, and that the two personalities will develop over the years, more or less in tandem, so that they continue to fulfill each other's needs. It further presupposes that this process will last "until death do us part."

These expectations are built deeply into our culture. It is no longer respectable, as it once was, to marry for anything but love. Love has changed from a peripheral concern of the family into its primary justification. Indeed, the pursuit of love through family life has become, for many, the very purpose of life itself.

Love, however, is defined in terms of this notion of shared growth. It is seen as a beautiful mesh of complementary needs, flowing into and out of one another, fulfilling the loved ones, and producing feelings of warmth, tenderness and devotion. Unhappy husbands often complain that they have "left their wives behind" in terms of social, educational or intellectual growth. Partners in successful marriages are said to "grow together."

This "parallel development" theory of love carries endorsement
from marriage counselors, psychologists and sociologists. Thus, says
sociologist Nelson Foote, a specialist on the family, the quality of the 44
relationship between husband and wife is dependent upon "the degree
of matching in their phases of distinct but comparable development."

If love is a product of shared growth, however, and we are to
measure success in marriage by the degree to which matched develop- 45
ment actually occurs, it becomes possible to make a strong and ominous
prediction about the future.

It is possible to demonstrate that, even in a relatively stagnant
society, the mathematical odds are heavily stacked against any couple
achieving this ideal of parallel growth. The odds for success positively
plummet, however, when the rate of change in society accelerates, as
it now is doing. In a fast-moving society, in which many things change, 46
not once, but repeatedly, in which the husband moves up and down
a variety of economic and social scales, in which the family is again
and again torn loose from home and community, in which individuals
move further from their parents, further from the religion of origin,
and further from traditional values, it is almost miraculous if two
people develop at anything like comparable rates.

If, at the same time, average life expectancy rises from, say, fifty
to seventy years, thereby lengthening the term during which this acro-
batic feat of matched development is supposed to be maintained, the
odds against success become absolutely astronomical. Thus, Nelson 47
Foote writes with wry understatement: "To expect a marriage to last
indefinitely under modern conditions is to expect a lot." To ask love
to last indefinitely is to expect even more. Transience and novelty
are both in league against it.

Temporary Marriage

It is this change in the statistical odds against love that accounts
for the high divorce and separation rates in most of the techno-societies. 48
The faster the rate of change and the longer the life span, the worse
these odds grow. Something has to crack.

In point of fact, of course, something has already cracked—and
it is the old insistence on permanence. Millions of men and women
now adopt what appears to them to be a sensible and conservative 49
strategy. Rather than opting for some offbeat variety of the family,
they marry conventionally, they attempt to make it "work," and then,
when the paths of the partners diverge beyond an acceptable point,
they divorce or depart. Most of them go on to search for a new partner
whose developmental stage, at that moment, matches their own.

As human relationships grow more transient and modular, the pursuit of love becomes, if anything, more frenzied. But the temporal expectations change. As conventional marriage proves itself less and less capable of delivering on its promise of lifelong love, therefore, we can anticipate open public acceptance of temporary marriages. Instead of wedding "until death do us part," couples will enter into matrimony knowing from the first that the relationship is likely to be short-lived.

They will know, too, that when the paths of husband and wife diverge, when there is too great a discrepancy in developmental stages, they may call it quits—without shock or embarrassment, perhaps even without some of the pain that goes with divorce today. And when the opportunity presents itself, they will marry again . . . and again . . . and again.

Serial marriage—a pattern of successive temporary marriages—is cut to order for the Age of Transience in which all man's relationships, all his ties with the environment, shrink in duration. It is the natural, the inevitable outgrowth of a social order in which automobiles are rented, dolls traded in, and dresses discarded after one-time use. It is the mainstream marriage pattern of tomorrow.

In one sense, serial marriage is already the best kept family secret of the techno-societies. According to Professor Jessie Bernard, a world-prominent family sociologist, "Plural marriage is more extensive in our society today than it is in societies that permit polygamy—the chief difference being that we have institutionalized plural marriage serially or sequential rather than contemporaneously." Remarriage is already so prevalent a practice that nearly one out of every four bridegrooms in America has been to the altar before. It is so prevalent that one IBM personnel man reports a poignant incident involving a divorced woman, who, in filling out a job application, paused when she came to the question of marital status. She put her pencil in her mouth, pondered for a moment, then wrote: "Unremarried."

Transience necessarily affects the durational expectancies with which persons approach new situations. While they may yearn for a permanent relationship, something inside whispers to them that it is an increasingly improbable luxury.

Even young people who most passionately seek commitment, profound involvement with people and causes, recognize the power of the thrust toward transience. Listen, for example, to a young black American, civil-rights worker, as she describes her attitude toward time and marriage:

"In the white world, marriage is always billed as 'the end'—like in a Hollywood movie. I don't go for that. I can't imagine myself promising my whole lifetime away. I might want to get married now, but how about next year? That's not disrespect for the institution [of marriage], but the deepest respect. In The [civil rights] Movement, you need to have a feeling for the temporary—of making something as good as you can, while it lasts. In conventional relationships, time is a prison.

Such attitudes will not be confined to the young, the few, or the
politically active. They will whip across nations as novelty floods into
the society and catch fire as the level of transience rises still higher. 57
And along with them will come a sharp increase in the number of
temporary—then serial—marriages.

The idea is summed up vividly by a Swedish magazine, *Svensk
Damtidning,* which interviewed a number of leading Swedish sociologists, legal experts, and others about the future of man-woman relation- 58
ships. It presented its findings in five photographs. They showed the
same beautiful bride being carried across the threshold five times—by
five different bridegrooms.

Marriage Trajectories

As serial marriages become more common, we shall begin to characterize people not in terms of their present marital status, but in terms
of their marriage career or "trajectory." This trajectory will be formed 59
by the decisions they make at certain vital turning points in their lives.

For most people, the first such juncture will arrive in youth, when
they enter into "trial marriage." Even now the young people of the
United States and Europe are engaged in a mass experiment with probationary marriage, with or without benefit of ceremony. The staidest
of United States universities are beginning to wink at the practice of 60
co-ed housekeeping among their students. Acceptance of trial marriage is
even growing among certain religious philosophers. Thus we hear the
German theologian Siegfried Keil of Marburg University urge what he
terms "recognized premarriage." In Canada, Father Jacques Lazure has
publicly proposed "probationary marriages" of three to eighteen months.

In the past, social pressures and lack of money restricted experimentation with trial marriage to a relative handful. In the future, both 61
these limiting forces will evaporate. Trial marriage will be the first step
in the serial marriage "careers" that millions will pursue.

A second critical life juncture for the people of the future will
occur when the trial marriage ends. At this point, couples may choose
to formalize their relationship and stay together into the next stage.
Or they may terminate it and seek out new partners. In either case,
they will then face several options. They may prefer to go childless. 62
They may choose to have, adopt or "buy" one or more children. They
may decide to raise these children themselves or to farm them out to
professional parents. Such decisions will be made, by and large, in the
early twenties—by which time many young adults will already be well
into their second marriages.

A third significant turning point in the marital career will come,
as it does today, when the children finally leave home. The end of 63
parenthood proves excruciating for many, particularly women who, once
the children are gone, find themselves without a *raison d'être.* Even

today divorces result from the failure of the couple to adapt to this traumatic break in continuity.

Among the more conventional couples of tomorrow who choose to raise their own children in the time-honored fashion, this will continue to be a particularly painful time. It will, however, strike earlier. Young people today already leave home sooner than their counterparts a generation ago. They will probably depart even earlier tomorrow. Masses of youngsters will move off, whether into trial marriage or not, in their mid-teens. Thus we may anticipate that the middle and late thirties will be another important breakpoint in the marital careers of millions. Many at that juncture will enter into their third marriage.

This third marriage will bring together two people for what could well turn out to be the longest uninterrupted stretch of matrimony in their lives—from, say, the late thirties until one of the partners dies. This may, in fact, turn out to be the only "real" marriage, the basis of the only truly durable marital relationship. During this time two mature people, presumably with well-matched interests and complementary psychological needs, and with a sense of being at comparable stages of personality development, will be able to look forward to a relationship with a decent statistical probability of enduring.

Not all these marriages will survive until death, however, for the family will still face a fourth crisis point. This will come, as it does now for so many, when one or both of the partners retires from work. The abrupt change in daily routine brought about by this development places great strain on the couple. Some couples will go the path of the post-retirement family, choosing this moment to begin the task of raising children. This may overcome for them the vacuum that so many couples now face after reaching the end of their occupational lives. (Today many women go to work when they finish raising children; tomorrow many will reverse that pattern, working first and childrearing next.) Other couples will overcome the crisis of retirement in other ways, fashioning both together a new set of habits, interests and activities. Still others will find the transition too difficult, and will simply sever their ties and enter the pool of "in-betweens"—the floating reserve of temporary unmarried persons.

Of course, there will be some who, through luck, interpersonal skill and high intelligence, will find it possible to make long-lasting monogamous marriages work. Some will succeed, as they do today, in marrying for life and finding durable love and affection. But others will fail to make even sequential marriages endure for long. Thus some will try two or even three partners within, say, the final stage of marriage. Across the board, the average number of marriages per capita will rise—slowly but relentlessly.

Most people will probably move forward along this progression, engaging in one "conventional" temporary marriage after another. But with widespread familial experimentation in the society, the more daring or desperate will make side forays into less conventional arrangements

as well, perhaps experimenting with communal life at some point, or going it alone with a child. The net result will be a rich variation in the types of marital trajectories that people will trace, a wider choice
of life-patterns, an endless opportunity for novelty of experience. Cer- 68
tain patterns will be more common than others. But temporary marriage will be a standard feature, perhaps the dominant feature, of family life in the future.

The Demands of Freedom

A world in which marriage is temporary rather than permanent, in which family arrangements are diverse and colorful, in which homosexuals may be acceptable parents and retirees start raising children —such a world is vastly different from our own. Today all boys and girls are expected to find life-long partners. In tomorrow's world, being single will be no crime. Nor will couples be forced to remain imprisoned, as so many still are today, in marriages that have turned rancid.
Divorce will be easy to arrange, so long as responsible provision is 69
made for children. In fact, the very introduction of professional parenthood could touch off a great liberating wave of divorces by making it easier for adults to discharge their parental responsibilities without necessarily remaining in the cage of a hateful marriage. With this powerful external pressure removed, those who stay together would be those who wish to stay together, those for whom marriage is actively fulfilling—those, in short, who are in love.

We are also likely to see, under this looser, more variegated family
system, many more marriages involving partners of unequal age. In- 70
creasingly, older men will marry young girls or vice versa. What will count will not be chronological age, but complementary values and interests and, above all, the level of personal development. To put it another way, partners will be interested not in age, but in stage.

Children in this super-industrial society will grow up with an ever enlarging circle of what might be called "semi-siblings"—a whole clan of boys and girls brought into the world by their successive sets of parents. What becomes of such "aggregate" families will be fascinating
to observe. Semi-sibs may turn out to be like cousins, today. They may 71
help one another professionally or in time of need. But they will also present the society with novel problems. Should semi-sibs marry, for example?

Surely, the whole relationship of the child to the family will be dramatically altered. Except perhaps in communal groupings, the family
will lose what little remains of its power to transmit values to the 72
younger generation. This will further accelerate the pace of change and intensify the problems that go with it.

Looming over all such changes, however, and even dwarfing them in significance is something far more subtle. Seldom discussed, there is a hidden rhythm in human affairs that until now has served as one of the key stabilizing forces in society: the family cycle.

We begin as children; we mature; we leave the parental nest; we give birth to children who, in turn, grow up, leave and begin the process all over again. This cycle has been operating so long, so automatically, and with such implacable regularity, that men have taken it for granted. It is part of the human landscape. Long before they reach puberty, children learn the part they are expected to play in keeping this great cycle turning. This predictable succession of family events has provided all men, of whatever tribe or society, with a sense of continuity, a place in the temporal scheme of things. The family cycle has been one of the sanity-preserving constants in human existence.

Today this cycle is accelerating. We grow up sooner, leave home sooner, marry sooner, have children sooner. We space them more closely together and complete the period of parenthood more quickly. In the words of Dr. Bernice Neugarten, a University of Chicago specialist on family development, "The trend is toward a more rapid rhythm of events through most of the family cycle."

But if industrialism, with its faster pace of life, has accelerated the family cycle, super-industrialism now threatens to smash it altogether. With the fantasies that the birth scientists are hammering into reality, with the colorful familial experimentation that innovative minorities will perform, with the likely development of such institutions as professional parenthood, with the increasing movement toward temporary and serial marriage, we shall not merely run the cycle more rapidly; we shall introduce irregularity, suspense, unpredictability—in a word, novelty—into what was once as regular and certain as the seasons.

When a "mother" can compress the process of birth into a brief visit to an embryo emporium, when by transferring embryos from womb to womb we can destroy even the ancient certainty that childbearing took nine months, children will grow up into a world in which the family cycle, once so smooth and sure, will be jerkily arhythmic. Another crucial stabilizer will have been removed from the wreckage of the old order, another pillar of sanity broken.

There is, of course, nothing inevitable about the developments traced in the preceding pages. We have it in our power to shape change. We may choose one future over another. We cannot, however, maintain the past. In our family forms, as in our economics, science, technology and social relationships, we shall be forced to deal with the new.

The Super-industrial Revolution will liberate men from many of the barbarisms that grew out of the restrictive, relatively choiceless family patterns of the past and present. It will offer to each a degree of freedom hitherto unknown. But it will exact a steep price for that freedom.

As we hurtle into tomorrow, millions of ordinary men and women
will face emotion-packed options so unfamiliar, so untested, that past
experience will offer little clue to wisdom. In their family ties, as in all 80
other aspects of their lives, they will be compelled to cope not merely
with transience, but with the added problem of novelty as well.

Thus, in matters both large and small, in the most public of conflicts and the most private of conditions, the balance between routine 81
and non-routine, predictable and non-predictable, the known and the
unknown, will be altered. The novelty ratio will rise.

In such an environment, fast-changing and unfamiliar, we shall
be forced, as we wend our way through life, to make our personal
choices from a diverse array of options. And it is to the third central 82
characteristic of tomorrow, *diversity,* that we must now turn. For it is
the final convergence of these three factors—transience, novelty and
diversity—that sets the stage for the historic crisis of adaptation that
is the subject of this book: future shock.

Interviews by
John Kronenberger

Is the Family Obsolete?

Depends on your definition, apparently. Five prominent Americans here suggest that something, at least, is on the way out. . . .

As the country goes through a spell of shooting the rapids, every familiar institution—the church, the Army, the city, the Government, the university— is being called into question, and the family has no exemption. LOOK sought prognoses on its future possibilities from several sources.

Alvin Toffler, Author, "Future Shock"

The family is in for a severe upheaval, and I think the reasons for this are twofold. First, there are a whole series of scientific developments, biological breakthroughs, that are likely to have a shattering impact on the family structure. America's only just beginning to feel the first impact of the pill, but the pill is like a popgun compared to the howitzers and nuclear weaponry that lie ahead in the field of biology: the notion that babies can be raised outside the womb, the possibility of creating what somebody has called "identi-groups"—tens of thousands of people with identical genetic characteristics—the possibilities of, in effect, pre-programming your own children and determining their characteristics. The striking thing about all of these developments is that they don't lie 50 years or a hundred years in the future; if you talk to scientists working on this, you get estimates of *ten years.*

Now, at the same time all that's happening, there are changes in the economy and the social structure that are putting pressure on for a much more mobile kind of family. We're moving toward a society based on temporary relationships rather than permanence. This already places an enormous premium on mobility and the nuclear family, which we accept as the norm: mother, father and child, but no encumbering

old folks, cousins, aunts, etc. We may find pressure to split the family
down further, and this could encourage a great deal of childlessness
in the society.

Seventy years ago, when people got married till death do us part,
that meant 30 years. Today, with the increased life-span, it means 50
years on the average. We are clinging to traditional assumptions in 3
the face of a fundamental change, and now expect people to make it
together for two generations instead of one—a rather astonishing bit
of optimism.

We forget that we've radically increased the rate of change in society, change in jobs, change in neighborhoods, changing sexual patterns, changing leisure-time pursuits, the change in the ratio between
alcohol and drugs, and all of these feed into society and make it more 4
difficult for two people in love to grow together. Each of them is
exposed to more and more experiences that are different from the
other's, with the consequence that the ideal of a couple's growing together through the years becomes increasingly remote.

My own hunch is that most people will try to go blindly through
the motions of the traditional marriage, and try to keep the traditional
family going, and they'll fail. And the consequence will be a subtle 5
but very significant shift to much more temporary marital arrangements, an intensification of the present pattern of divorce and remarriage and divorce and remarriage to the point at which we accept the
idea that marriages are not for life. I'm not endorsing it, but I think
it's likely to be the case.

Shirley MacLaine, Actress

Our problem is not whether the family's obsolete but whether the 6
autocratic family is obsolete, and I think, yes, that's so.

The idea of the father being the head of the family, whether you
think of him as a male figure or as a father, that he reigns supreme,
that he brings home the bacon while his wife brings up the children
and sees to their physical needs—*that* is obsolete, no question about it.
And the whole notion that children following their basic desires, their 7
tendencies to be curious about all sorts of things, should learn first thing
in their lives what *not* to do, instead of what they are able to do, what
is all right and permissible to do—that is the difference between an autocratic and a democratic family. An autocratic family produces repressed
individuals at adulthood, and a democratic family doesn't.

All this goes back as far as Christian culture, to what Mary and
Joseph started. It's got to do with monogamy, with the male being the
natural superior, with the belief that security comes in the form of 8
possessions, with hoeing your own little row of potatoes, that sort of
attitude. You *know* it's just a million things that have been handed
down with the Christian ethic, so when you begin to question the family,
you have to question all those things.

I don't think it's desirable to conform to having one mate, and for those two people to raise children. But everyone believes that's the ideal. They go around frustrated most of their lives because they can't find one mate. But who said that's the natural basic personality of man? To whom does monogamy make sense? To a muskrat, maybe. This is *not* the natural behavior pattern of a human individual—people who behave that way are operating out of repressive culture, out of Christian doctrine, out of Thou Shalt Not Commit Adultery, in one of the Ten Commandments.

When we get more into the figures on sexual behavior, I think we'll find that when the intensity of the love relationship goes past two and a half or three years, maybe five years (but at the outside five years), that's when the desire for monogamy wears off. Now, why is that so threatening?

If you have a male and a female who really have wonderful communication with each other, a really solid relationship, and they have children, and the intensity of the physical relationship wears off, which usually happens between two and five years (sometimes much sooner, of course, but I'm talking about real attraction), why should they then adhere to this state of monogamy? In a democratic family, individuals understand their natural tendencies, bring them out in the open, discuss them, and very likely follow them. And these tendencies are definitely *not* monogamous.

Erich Segal, Author, "Love Story"

Because I'm a pompous classics professor, I reached for the Latin dictionary to reassure myself that the word "family" means, in its Latin origins, "household," not the connotations of wife and husband and kids and dog, etc. I think with the new sort of romanticism around today, there are *new* concepts of family, one of which consists merely of man and wife. There are people for whom the commitment to one another is so great that, for reasons contributory to the quality of life on this planet, among others, they wish to form a family—household—that precludes increasing and multiplying, since that can mean increasing and multiplying the *population problem,* not merely children. So there's a lifetime of devotion to love, honor and cherish only one another.

Another sort of household is the commune, and I'm sorry for the connotations that Mr. Manson has given to the term. This is a viable concept for the future: the community as family. It's not going to be limited in the future to the eccentric fringe; it's going to be a new social institution. And you can see the large family, the tribe, as an obvious reaction to the dehumanization of the cities, against which the single family unit cannot compete. I admit, the notion of everybody's kids eating at one table and everybody's parents eating at another

is a little bit foreign to me, but only because I'm an uptight product
of the 1950's and not because I don't recognize the inherent humanity
of it all. There's the old cliché about two heads being better than one;
well, 12 hearts to love a child are better than two.

With Women's Lib, the dynamics of "standard" families will change.
The kind of family that doesn't differentiate between masculine and
feminine but emphasizes only that which is human, that's a *great* thing.
Kids will be enormously less hung-up about sexual identity, about their
thought processes, about their life's values—because their parents are 14
human beings, not Mothers and Fathers. What's it going to do to
romance? It will *remove* romance—and replace it with true love. Because, to me, romance implies a kind of sleight of hand, something of
an illusionary nature, and with illusion comes the ultimate disillusion—
and dissolution—of so many marriages.

Children of liberated marriages will seek the essence of life, which 15
is certainly not to live out a stereotype of gender. With this improvement in human values, there can't help but be a greater sensitivity,
which we all need.

Margaret Mead, Anthropologist

What Americans think is the American family is really the post-
World War II suburban family: totally isolated, desperately autonomous, unable to tolerate adolescent children at home, pushing its
children out into matrimony as rapidly as possible, no grandparents,
no cousins, no neighbors, no nothing—moving from place to place; it 16
started right after the war, and the average bride and groom didn't
unpack their wedding presents for ten years. They went from place to
place, with no ties, with husband and wife expected to be all things
to each other—so the husband has to take care of the children, help
with the cleaning, and even substitute for the mother's mother in the
delivery room.

This extraordinary over-domestication of men, and isolation of
women: this is what people think the American family is! But we've
just invented the kind of suburb where there are no sidewalks, where 17
children never walk. A good proportion of Americans lived very close
to where they grew up before World War II, so this whole isolation,
all of it, is new. It's a simply impossible form, and it's beginning to
run into difficulties.

The generation that grew up in that family—the kids that are now
entering college—they've had it; they don't want that kind of family. 18
They object to this scramble for what looks to them like material improvement and an emphasis on material things—though the people who
bought these suburbs thought they were doing the best thing for their
children. We have a demand for something different.

I think there will be more stringent conditions for parenthood—self-imposed, community-imposed, mass-media-imposed. Just as people were actually persecuted into marriage and having children in the 1950's and early 1960's, now they'll be harried into *not* having children. We're probably going to have a wave of adoption, which will be a liberal position; so if some people want to bring up ten children, they'll adopt at least five of them.

I don't think the whole country's going into day-care centers. If we get enough day-care centers for poor mothers who have to work, we'll be darned lucky. But I think we'll have a kind of living with the grandparent generation and adolescent kids around, so there'll be plenty of people to take care of the children. You'll put them in a pool in the center of the group, and you won't need a formal day-care center. In the whole of the period between the time my child was three and was old enough to be a baby-sitter herself, we had just one baby-sitting crisis in the group of people I lived among. We lived, not all in the same home, but in adjacent, nearby houses. Once, someone gave a party and idiotically invited everybody except the little ones, including the adolescents, and *then* there was a crisis. But there shouldn't be.

We had a great deal of what were substantially residential communes right after World War II among graduate students living in trailers, and they took care of each other's babies and did each other's shopping and worked together *nicely*. But the minute they got status, they all moved to the suburbs and never saw a friend again. Perhaps today's kids won't make that mistake.

Betty Friedan, Feminist

I think it's increasingly clear that the traditional nuclear family—Momma the housewife, Poppa the breadwinner, Junior and Janie—is in serious trouble. It's too confining a mold for the needs of people, for the very needs that people have sought to answer with the family. So there is going to be much more variety in the ways we live together.

There will be numbers of people who will continue to live at least part of their lives in something that *looks* like the American family today. But even that's not going to be identical with the structure of today. Even when Junior and Janie are still at home, and Momma and Poppa are still married, you already have 50 percent of all women working outside the home—so it isn't Momma the housewife, Poppa the breadwinner, any more, but both Momma and Poppa the breadwinners. In a certain sense, I object to any woman's being called a housewife, and yet up to now *all* women have been housewives, no matter what they did outside the home. Well, if the two-income family is needed to keep the family out of poverty, then you jointly share the burden and challenge of participation in society; so you should also share the responsibilities and joys of whatever home you choose to have, and of child-rearing. We're working out these new patterns.

You'll have people choosing forms of living together that meet the needs of intimacy, privacy and communality in a way that the isolated nuclear family of today doesn't. I'm speaking here of the needs of children, the needs of men, as well as the needs of women. One of the
reasons the family is in such trouble, perhaps, is that too much need 24
has been channeled to it—when you consider the rat-race associations that people have in their offices and places of work, and the equally competitive sort of country-club suburban kind of thing they have at home, or the simply alienating impersonality of so much city life today.

The point is, the *only place* that people are expected to meet their needs for intimacy, to assuage their loneliness, is in this single marital
situation. It's so heavily freighted with all this that it's almost *doomed* 25
to failure. So much is demanded. And then there are the inequities between the sexes today that sour the relationship and build hostilities in.

But even if we deal with those, and I think we are beginning to in our movement, even if we bring about the equality that is necessary, and a couple chooses to marry for only the right reasons (not just for
economic support or sex), I think that the years built around raising 26
children will be so few in a total life-span of 75 to 100 years that it isn't going to structure things any longer. We're going to see many different options. However, people will still need long-term intimacy, and that is most naturally built around the heterosexual relationship.

The ideal family doesn't exist in so many cases, yet there doesn't seem to be *any* other acceptable, non-deviant form that is recognized
by law and mortgage financing and all the rest. I think we're going 27
to have to have that, whether it's in terms of young people, old people, women, men, children. It's not, Down with Momma, Poppa, Junior and Janie—if they're happy, then *fine*. But if there are more choices, then so many people won't be straitjacketed into that form in a way that will make them unhappy.

Gary Snyder

Why Tribe

We use the term Tribe because it suggests the type of new society now emerging within the industrial nations. In America of course the word has associations with the American Indians, which we like. This new subculture is in fact more similar to that ancient and successful tribe, the European Gypsies—a group without nation or territory which maintains its own values, its language and religion, no matter what country it may be in.

The Tribe proposes a totally different style: based on community houses, villages and ashrams; tribe-run farms or workshops or companies; large open families; pilgrimages and wanderings from center to center. A synthesis of Gandhian "village anarchism" and I.W.W. syndicalism. Interesting visionary pamphlets along these lines were written several years ago by Gandhians Richard Gregg and Appa Patwardhan. The Tribe proposes personal responsibilities rather than abstract centralized government, taxes and advertising-agency-plus-Mafia type international brainwashing corporations.

In the United States and Europe the Tribe has evolved gradually over the last fifty years—since the end of World War I—in response to the increasing insanity of the modern nations. As the number of alienated intellectuals, creative types and general social misfits grew, they came to recognize each other by various minute signals. Much of this energy was channeled into Communism in the thirties and early forties. All the anarchists and left-deviationists—and many Trotskyites—were tribesmen at heart. After World War II, another generation looked at Communist rhetoric with a fresh eye and saw that within the Communist governments (and states of mind) there are too many of the same things as are wrong with "capitalism"—too much anger and murder. The suspicion grew that perhaps the whole Western Tradition, of which Marxism is but a (Millennial Protestant) part, is off the track. This led many people to study other major civilizations—India and China—to see what they could learn.

It's an easy step from the dialectic of Marx and Hegel to an interest
in the dialectic of early Taoism, the *I Ching,* and the yin-yang theories.
From Taoism it is another easy step to the philosophies and mythologies 4
of India—vast, touching the deepest areas of the mind, and with a view
of the ultimate nature of the universe which is almost identical with
the most sophisticated thought in modern physics—that truth, whatever
it is, which is called "The Dharma."

Next comes a concern with deepening one's understanding in an
experiential way: abstract philosophical understanding is simply not
enough. At this point many, myself included, found in the Buddha-
Dharma a practical method for clearing one's mind of the trivia, prejudices and false values that our conditioning had laid on us—and more 5
important an approach to the basic problem of how to penetrate to the
deepest non-self Self. Today we have many who are exploring the Ways
of Zen, Vajrayāna, Yoga, Shamanism, Psychedelics. The Buddha-Dharma
is a long, gentle, human dialog—2,500 years of quiet conversation—on the
nature of human nature and the eternal Dharma—and practical methods
of realization.

In the course of these studies it became evident that the "truth"
in Buddhism and Hinduism is not dependent in any sense on Indian 6
or Chinese culture; and that "India" and "China"—as societies—are as
burdensome to human beings as any others; perhaps more so. It became
clear that "Hinduism" and "Buddhism" as social institutions had long
been accomplices of the State in burdening and binding people, rather
than serving to liberate them. Just like the other Great Religions.

At this point, looking once more quite closely at history both East
and West, some of us noticed the similarities in certain small but
influential heretical and esoteric movements. These schools of thought
and practice were usually suppressed, or diluted and made harmless, 7
in whatever society they appeared. Peasant witchcraft in Europe, Tantrism in Bengal, Quakers in England, Tachikawa-ryū in Japan, Ch'an
in China. These are all outcroppings of the Great Subculture which runs
underground all through history. This is the tradition that runs without
break from Paleo-Siberian Shamanism and Magdalenian cave-painting;
through megaliths and Mysteries, astronomers, ritualists, alchemists and
Albigensians; gnostics and vagantes, right down to Golden Gate Park.

The Great Subculture has been attached in part to the official
religions but is different in that it transmits a community style of life,
with an ecstatically positive vision of spiritual and physical love; and 8
is opposed for very fundamental reasons to the Civilization Establishment.

It has taught that man's natural being is to be trusted and followed;
that we need not look to a model or rule imposed from outside in
searching for the center; and that in following the grain, one is being 9
truly "moral." It has recognized that for one to "follow the grain" it is
necessary to look exhaustively into the negative and demonic potentials

of the Unconscious, and by recognizing these powers—symbolically acting them out—one releases himself from these forces. By this profound exorcism and ritual drama, the Great Subculture destroys the one credible claim of Church and State to a necessary function.

All this is subversive to civilization: for civilization is built on hierarchy and specialization. A ruling class, to survive, must propose a Law: a law to work must have a hook into the social psyche—and the most effective way to achieve this is to make people doubt their natural worth and instincts, especially sexual. To make "human nature" suspect is also to make Nature—the wilderness—the adversary. Hence the ecological crisis of today.

We came, therefore, (and with many Western thinkers before us) to suspect that civilization may be overvalued. Before anyone says "This is ridiculous, we all know civilization is a necessary thing," let him read some cultural anthropology. Take a look at the lives of South African Bushmen, Micronesian navigators, the Indians of California; the researches of Claude Lévi-Strauss. Everything we have thought about man's welfare needs to be rethought. The tribe, it seems, is the newest development in the Great Subculture. We have almost unintentionally linked ourselves to a transmission of gnosis, a potential social order, and techniques of enlightenment, surviving from prehistoric times.

The most advanced developments of modern science and technology have come to support some of these views. Consequently the modern Tribesman, rather than being old-fashioned in his criticism of civilization, is the most relevant type in contemporary society. Nationalism, warfare, heavy industry and consumership, are already outdated and useless. The next great step of mankind is to step into the nature of his own mind—the real question is "just what is consciousness?"—and we must make the most intelligent and creative use of science in exploring these questions. The man of wide international experience, much learning and leisure—luxurious product of our long and sophisticated history—may with good reason wish to live simply, with few tools and minimal clothes, close to nature.

The Revolution has ceased to be an ideological concern. Instead, people are trying it out right now—communism in small communities, new family organization. A million people in America and another million in England and Europe. A vast underground in Russia, which will come out in the open four or five years hence, is now biding. How do they recognize each other? Not always by beards, long hair, bare feet or beads. The signal is a bright and tender look; calmness and gentleness, freshness and ease of manner. Men, women and children—all of whom together hope to follow the timeless path of love and wisdom, in affectionate company with the sky, winds, clouds, trees, waters, animals and grasses—this is the tribe.

Herbert A. Otto

Communes: The Alternative Life-Style

Angelina is a tall, striking blonde in her mid-forties, with a husky
voice and a motherly, forthright air about her. She had been a successful interior decorator in a well-known college town in Oregon. Follow- 1
ing her divorce, Angelina decided to rent some of the extra bedrooms
in her house to students.

"I was shocked seeing people dirty and with unwashed hair—until
I got to know them better and saw their soul reflected in their eyes.
They wanted country life and animals. They wanted to be creative and 2
to be themselves. At that time, I was attending a Unitarian church. I
talked to the minister about starting a commune. He said it wouldn't
work."

Angelina felt she needed new ideas and viewpoints, and she went 3
to the Esalen Institute at Big Sur, California. She stayed three months.
"I could see so much, feel so much, I thought I was really called."

Upon returning to her business, which she had left in competent
hands, Angelina decided to sell out and was able to do so at a favor-
able price. "I made up my mind I wanted the family feeling. At this 4
point, it was like Providence when I heard about the hundred and fifty
acres. The price was so reasonable. I thought there was something wrong
with the place. But when I saw it—with the half-dozen springs, three
streams, and mixed timber—I knew this was the spot for a nature commune."

Angelina started the commune two-and-a-half years ago with a
young couple she had met at Esalen. Today, there are thirty young
people and eight children in the community. Twelve of this group are 5
called "stable"; they have made a commitment to the commune. Median
age within the commune is in the mid-twenties. Sixty-five per cent of
the group are young men. There are many high school and college dropouts, but also a number of successful former businessmen and professionals, several teachers, and two engineers.

This commune, with Angelina as its prime mover and guiding spirit, is just one of many such living arrangements that have mushroomed around the country. Over the past few years, the commune movement has grown at an unprecedented and explosive rate, and there is every indication that this is only the initial phase of a trend that is bound to have far-reaching implications for the function and structure of our contemporary society. Some traditional institutions are already beginning to feel the impact of this explosive growth.

The commune movement has passed far beyond its contemporary origins in hippie tribalism and can no longer be described as a movement for youth exclusively. There are a rapidly growing number of communes composed of persons in their mid-twenties to upper thirties. A source at the National Institute of Health has estimated that more than 3,000 urban communes are now in operation. This figure closely corresponds to a recent *New York Times* inquiry that uncovered 2,000 communes in thirty-four states.

Certain common viewpoints, almost a *Weltanschauung,* are shared by members of the contemporary commune movement. First, there is a deep respect and reverence for nature and the ecological system. There is a clear awareness that 70 per cent of the population lives on 1 per cent of the land and that this 1 per cent is severely polluted, depressingly ugly, and psychologically overcrowded. Commune members generally believe that a very small but politically influential minority with no respect for the ecological system or the beauty of nature exploits all of the land for its own gain. Surpassing the credo of conservationist organizations, most commune members stress the rehabilitation of *all* lands and the conservation of *all* natural resources for the benefit of *all* the people.

Anti-Establishment sentiment is widespread, as is the conviction that a change in social and institutional structures is needed to halt man's dehumanization and to give him an opportunity to develop his potential. Considerable divergence of opinion exists on how social change is to be brought about, but there is general agreement that the commune movement contributes to change by bringing man closer to himself and to his fellow man through love and understanding.

Communes widely accept the idea that life is meant to be fundamentally joyous and that this is of the essence in doing, and enjoying, what you want to do—"doing your thing." Work in this context becomes a form of joyous self-expression and self-realization. Many commune members believe that existence can be an almost continuous source of joyous affirmation. They usually trace the absence of authentic joy in contemporary society to the confining nature of many of our social institutions, the stifling of spontaneity, and the preponderance of game-playing and of devitalized artificial ways of relating socially.

A strong inner search for the meaning of one's own life, an openness and willingness to communicate and encounter, coupled with a compelling desire for personal growth and development, are hallmarks

of the movement. A strong anti-materialistic emphasis prevails; it decries a consumption-oriented society. In many communes, what does
not fit into a room becomes commune property. A considerable number 11
of communes aim for the type of self-sufficiency through which they can exist independently of "the system."

There is a strong trend toward ownership of land and houses by communes. Leasing arrangements have not proved satisfactory; in too many instances, landlords have canceled leases when community pressures were exerted. The non-urban communes I have visited are strongly 12
aware of ecological factors, and, because of this, members usually had consulted with local health authorities concerning the construction and placement of sanitary facilities. Among the urban communes, toilet and bath facilities were in most cases short of the demand.

Marked preference for vegetarianism and for organically grown food are noticeable in the commune movement. Many individual members also experiment with different health diets. Roughly 40 per cent of the communes I visited were vegetarian; 20 per cent served both vegetarian and non-vegetarian meals. The remainder served meat when
available—usually two to six times a week. This third group, although 13
not vegetarian by choice, liked their vegetarian meals and expressed very little craving for meat. Whenever possible, communes concentrate on growing and raising their own food. An estimated 60 per cent of the urban communes are now purchasing some or most of their supplies from health-food stores or similar sources.

Not surprisingly, the commune has become the repository of repressed man's erotic fantasy. I was continuously told that visitors who
come not to learn and understand but to peek and ogle invariably ask 14
two questions: "Who sleeps with whom?" And, "Do you have group sex?" There appears to be much fantasizing by outsiders about the sex life in communes.

Although there is considerable sexual permissiveness, I found a high degree of pairing with a strong tendency toward interpersonal
commitment in a continuing relationship. Nudism is casual and accepted, 15
as is the development of a healthy sensuality, and natural childbirth, preferably within the commune, is encouraged. Group sex involving the whole commune occurs quite rarely, although there may be sexual experimentation involving two or more couples or combinations.

The research team of Larry and Joan Constantine has studied multilateral (group) marriage for the past three years. They have written and published more studies in this area than other behavioral
scientists, but have found only one commune practicing group marriage. 16
Most likely, there are others. About two dozen independent families are known to be engaged in multilateral marriage, taking as their model Bob Rimmer's novel *Proposition 31,* which presents a case for group marriage. Many others prefer to keep their arrangement totally secret for fear of reprisals. According to an article by the Constantines, entitled "Personal Growth in Multiple Marriages," failure rate is better

than one out of two, because "group marriage is a marathon that does not end—it takes a real commitment to genuine, substantial, and unrelenting personal growth to really make it function and work."

Interest in spiritual development is a dominant theme in most communes. Study of and acquaintance with Eastern and Western mystics and religious philosophies is widespread. Religiosity and denominationalism were seldom encountered. On the other hand, I was struck by the deep commitment to spiritual search of so many members in all the communes I visited. Many members were trying different forms of meditation, and books on Eastern religions and mysticism were prominent on shelves.

I find that although there is some overlapping of functions and categories, a number of distinct types of communes can be recognized and are found in operation.

- The Agricultural Subsistence Commune: The main thrust is to farm or till the soil (mostly organic farming) so that the land will provide most, if not all, needs and make the commune independent and self-supporting. Many of these communes cultivate such specialized crops as organically grown grain, vegetables, and other produce, which are then sold to health-food stores, health-food wholesalers, or supermarkets.
- The Nature Commune: Emphasis is on supporting the ecological system and on the enjoyment of nature. Buildings and gardening or farming plots are designed to fit into the landscape to preserve its natural beauty. Everyone "does his own thing," and economic support for subsistence usually comes from such varied sources as sale of produce and handicrafts, wages from part-time work, welfare support, etc.
- The Craft Commune: One or several crafts, such as weaving, pottery making, or carpentry (including construction or work on buildings outside the commune), occupy the interest of members. They often spend considerable blocks of time enjoying the exercise of their craft with the income contributed to the commune. Many of the craft communes sell directly to the consumer as a result of local, regional, or sometimes national advertisements and publicity. Profit margins vary since the vast majority of such communes do not subscribe to the amassing of profits as the primary aim of their enterprise. Included in this category are the multimedia communes that specialize in light shows, video tape, and film-making.
- The Spiritual/Mystical Commune: The ongoing spiritual development of members is recognized to be of primary importance. There may be adherence to a religious system, such as Buddhism, Sufism, or Zen, and a teacher or guru may be involved. Studies of various texts and mystical works, use of rituals, a number of forms of meditation (such as transcendental or Zen meditation), and spontaneous spiritual celebrations play key roles in the life of the commune. Several of these communes also describe themselves as Christian and have a strong spiritual, but not denominational, emphasis.

• The Denominational Commune: There is a religious emphasis
with membership restricted to those of a particular denomination. Ex- 23
amples are the Episcopalian Order of St. Michael, in Crown Point,
Indiana, and the Catholic Worker Farm, in Tivoli, New York.

• The Church-sponsored Commune: Such a commune may be
originated or sponsored by a church. There is usually a religious em- 24
phasis, but denominationalism is not stressed.

• The Political Commune: Members subscribe to or share a common ideology. They may identify themselves as anarchists, socialists,
pacifists, etc. Emphasis is on the communal living experience with others 25
sharing the same viewpoint. This is seen as fostering the individuals'
political development. The commune is rarely engaged in direct social
action in opposition to the Establishment.

• The Political Action Commune: Members are committed and
practicing political activists (or activists-in-training) for the purpose
of changing the social system. Classes are conducted, strategy formu- 26
lated and carried out. The commune may be identified with a minority
cause or be interested in organizing an industry, community, or ghetto
neighborhood. It often identifies itself by the single word "revolutionary."

• The Service Commune: The main goal is social service. Emphasis is on organizing communities, helping people to plan and carry
out community projects, offering professional or case-aide services, etc. 27
Some of these communes include members from the helping professions.
There are several such communes in the Philadelphia and New York
ghettos; another example is the Federation of Communities, which services several locations in the Appalachians.

• The Art Commune: Artists from different fields or the same
field come together to share in the stimulating climate of communal
artistic creativity. As compared with the craft commune, members of
the art commune are often painters, sculptors, or poets, who usually 28
sell their art works independently rather than collectively. There are
poetry and street theater communes in Berkeley and San Francisco.

• The Teaching Commune: Emphasis is on training and developing people who are able both to live and to teach others according to
a particular system of techniques and methods. Communes whose pur- 29
pose or mainstay is to conduct a school or schools also fall into this
category.

• The Group Marriage Commune: Although members may be
given the freedom to join in the group marriage or not, the practice
of group marriage plays an important and often central role in the 30
life of the commune. All adults are considered to be parents of the
members' children.

• The Homosexual Commune: Currently found in large urban
areas, with admission restricted to homophiles. The aim of these com- 31
munes is to afford individuals who share a common way of life an
opportunity to live and communicate together and to benefit from the

economies of a communal living arrangement. Some of the communes subscribe to the principles of the homophile liberation movement. From a recent ad in *Kaliflower,* the bi-weekly information journal for communes in the San Francisco Bay Area: "OUR GAY COMMUNE HAS ROOM FOR TWO MORE. CALL AND RAP."

• The Growth-centered Commune: The main focus is on helping members to grow as persons, to actualize their potential. There are ongoing group sessions; sometimes professionals are asked to lead these. The commune continues to seek out new experiences and methods designed to develop the potentialities of its members.

• The Mobile, or Gypsy, Commune: This is a caravan, usually on the move. Cars, buses, and trucks provide both transportation and living quarters. Members usually include artists, a rock group, or a light-show staff. The mobile commune often obtains contributions from "happenings" or performances given in communities or on college campuses.

• The Street, or Neighborhood, Commune: Several of these communes often are on the same street or in the same neighborhood. Ownership of property is in the hands of commune members or friendly and sympathetic neighbors. Basically the idea is of a free enclave or free community. For example, in a recent *New York Times* article, Albert Solnit, chief of advance planning for California's Marin County, was reported at work "on a city of 20,000 for those who wish to live communally." Several neighborhood or city communes are in the planning stage, but none to my knowledge has as yet been established.

Among the major problems faced by all communes are those involving authority and structure. Ideally, there is no one telling anyone else what to do; directions are given by those best qualified to do a job. In practice, strong personalities in the communes assume responsibility for what happens, and there is a tendency toward the emergence of mother and father figures. There are, however, a clear awareness of this problem and continuing efforts toward resolution. At present, opposition to any form of structure, including organizational structure, is still so strong that communes have found it almost impossible to cooperate with each other in joint undertakings of a major nature. Interestingly enough, communes with transcendent or spiritual values are the most stable and have the highest survival quotient. It is my conclusion that the weekly or periodic meetings of all commune members, which are often run as encounter groups, have a limited effectiveness in the resolution of interpersonal problems and issues. Although trained encounter leaders may be present as facilitators, their effectiveness is often considerably curtailed due to their own deep involvement in the issues that are the subject of confrontation. One answer to this dilemma might be to bring in a trained facilitator or for communes to exchange facilitators.

It is difficult to determine to what extent narcotics represent a problem for communes precisely because their consumption is as casual, widespread, and accepted as is the downing of alcoholic beverages in

the business community. Marijuana and hashish are widely enjoyed, while use of such hard drugs as heroin is seldom encountered, especially in the non-urban communes. In a number of communes where drug use was extensive, I noticed a general air of lassitude and a lack of vitality. I also had the distinct impression that "dropping acid" (LSD) was on the decline; among commune members there seemed to be a general awareness of the danger of "speed," or methedrine. A number of communes are totally opposed to the use of narcotics, especially those with
members who were former drug addicts. In most communes the sub- 36
ject of drugs periodically comes up for discussion so that changes in the viewpoint of the commune flow from the experience of the members. Similarly, problems of sexual possessiveness and jealousy appear to be less critical and are also handled by open group discussion. I noticed a tendency toward the maintenance of traditional sex roles, with the women doing the cooking and sewing, the men cutting lumber, etc. Upon questioning this, I repeatedly received the same answer: "Everyone does what they enjoy doing."

Another major problem in most communes is overcrowding and
the consequent lack of privacy and alone-time. Rarely does a member 37
enjoy the opportunity of having a room to himself for any length of time. The common practice is to walk off into the woods or fields, but this is an inadequate substitute for real privacy.

Community relations remains a major and critical problem since many communes are "hassled" by authorities or are located amid un-
friendly neighbors. As one member described it, the emotional climate 38
in a hassled commune is "full of not so good vibes—you don't know what they will try next, and you keep looking over your shoulder. That takes energy." Today's commune members generally have a clear awareness of the importance of establishing good community relations.

Many of the communes that have got under way this past year or are now being organized are beginning on a sound financial basis. This
trend appears to be related to the strong influx of people in their mid- 39
twenties, early or mid-thirties, and beyond. These individuals have financial reserves or savings and are, for the most part, successful professionals and businessmen with families.

One example is the Morehouse Commune, which now consists of thirteen houses in the San Francisco Bay Area, two in Hawaii, and another in Los Angeles; total assets are in excess of $2-million. Morehouse was founded a year and half ago by Victor Baranco, a former
attorney who is now head of the Institute of Human Abilities, in Oak- 40
land, California. There are several categories of membership or involvement in this commune. Members who belong to "the family" give all their assets to the commune, which then "takes care of them," although family members are expected to continue to make a productive contribution within their chosen fields. All income from family members goes into a general fund, but if a family member wishes to withdraw, his assets are returned, including a standard rate of interest for their having

been used. Each Morehouse commune in effect makes its own arrangements with members, who may be paid a salary or placed on an allowance system. All communes have a house manager, who assigns tasks or work on a rotating basis. In some Morehouse communes, certain categories of members pay in a fixed monthly sum (as much as $200) toward expenses.

About a third of the Morehouse couples are married and have children. According to one member, "There is no pressure to be married or unmarried. Nobody cares who lives with whom." Morehouse is a teaching commune built around a philosophy and way of life often described by group members as "responsible hedonism." The commune trains its own teachers and offers a considerable number of courses, such as Basic Sensuality, Advanced Sensuality, and Basic Communication.

The aim and credo of this group are taken from a description of the Institute of Human Abilities published in the commune journal *Aquarius*: "We offer the tools of deliberate living; we offer the techniques of successful communication on any level. We offer the knowledge of the human body and its sensual potential. And we offer love to a world that holds love to be suspect."

The rapid growth of the Morehouse communes is by no means an isolated example. A minister in Los Angeles founded a social-service and action-type commune that within a year grew to seven houses. Other instances can be cited. An unprecedented number of people want to join communes. In all but a few instances I was asked to conceal the name and location of the commune to make identification impossible. "We don't know what to do with all the people who come knocking on our door now," I was told repeatedly. In every commune, I heard of people who had recently left either to start a new commune or to join in the founding of one.

There is considerable mobility in communes, which is symptomatic of an endemic wanderlust and search. If people have to leave for any reason, once they have been exposed to communal living, they tend to return. They like the deep involvement with others in a climate of freedom, openness, and commitment. This feeling of belonging has been described as both "a new tribalism" and "a new sense of brotherhood." One young woman with whom I spoke had this to say about her commune experience: "When a white man walks into a room full of other whites, he doesn't feel he is among brothers like the black man does. In the communes, we are now beginning to feel that man has many brothers. . . . There is a new sense of honesty. You can say things to each other and share things like you never could in the family. I never had so much love in my whole life—not even in my own family." She also indicated, however, that commune living is highly intense and possibly not for everyone: "In the commune, there is nothing you can hide. Some people can't take it. They get sick or they leave."

Alvin Toffler in his recent book *Future Shock* notes that "most of today's 'intentional communities' reveal a powerful preference for the past, . . . but society as a whole would be better served by utopian experiments based on super- rather than pre-industrial forms. . . . In 45
short, we can use utopianism as a tool rather than as an escape, if we base our experiments on the technology and society of tomorrow rather than that of the past."

Although Toffler's observation is relevant, we must recognize that the commune movement, as with most other movements, is passing through certain developmental stages. At this stage, there is little readiness for communes to define themselves as laboratories for the exploration of alternative models that might benefit the society of the future. 46
Disenchantment with and opposition to science and technology are other impediments to the adoption of the laboratory concept. With today's communes, faith in the future of mankind appears to be at too low an ebb to produce any sustained interest in what Toffler calls "scientific future-sensing and the techniques of scientific futurism."

Although David Cooper, a colleague and disciple of British psychiatrist Ronald Laing, has sounded a death knell in his new book *The* 47
Death of the Family, I believe we are far from writing the epitaph. The traditional nuclear family will continue, although its form, to some extent, may change; in the years to come, possibly as high as 20 per cent of the population will explore alternative models of social living.

It would be a mistake to characterize the commune movement as a collection of dropouts who are content to exist like lilies in the field. A considerable number of successful people from all walks of life are now involved; they have merely shifted their sphere of interest and the nature of their creative contribution. We are dealing with a massive awakening of the awareness that life holds multiple options other than going from school to job to retirement. The commune movement has 48
opened a new and wide range of alternative life-styles and offers another frontier to those who have the courage for adventure. It is the test tube for the growth of a new type of social relatedness, for the development of an organization having a structure that appears, disappears, and reappears as it chooses and as it is needed. Communes may well serve as a laboratory for the study of the processes involved in the regeneration of our social institutions. They have become the symbol of man's new freedom to explore alternative life-styles and to develop deep and fulfilling human relationships through the rebirth and extension of our capacity for familial togetherness.

"Where Are the Parents of These Kids? Many of Them Come from Well-to-do Homes. Why Am I So Alone in This?"

The nature commune that Angelina started two years ago has a 49
reputation as one of the oldest and best run among the eight communes

located within a twenty-five-mile radius of a small town in southern Oregon. This is a hilly farm and lumber region where in winter it sometimes rains for weeks on end, after which the appearance of the sun is greeted with festivity.

I had arranged to first meet Angelina at a local coffee shop one afternoon. She was wearing a colorful dress, which, she explained, she had designed and sewn herself. She also explained that the couple she had met at Esalen and with whom she had founded the commune had since left. And that among the thirty-eight members presently living in the commune there are five individuals with exceptional skills as plumbers, mechanics, electricians, and carpenters. A stonemason is also in residence. Financial support of the commune derives from a number of sources, including member contributions, with Angelina—as owner of the property—playing a major role. Of the dozen members considered "stable," Angelina also explained: "They all have to split every once in a while, but they feel it's their home." We talked for about an hour over coffee, and then Angelina invited me to come to the commune for supper.

Located fifteen miles from town on a blacktop road, the commune is flanked by well-kept small farms. An elaborately carved and painted sign close to the road announces "The Good Earth Commune." Immediately behind the sign is an improvised parking field. It was filled with about two dozen cars and trucks and a bus, which obviously served as living quarters. Some of the cars had thick layers of dust and either were abandoned or had not been used for a long time. As we drove past, five boys and two girls, all deeply suntanned, were gathered around a pickup truck and were talking leisurely while watching two of their number work on the motor. They seemed like high school or college kids on a summer vacation.

Over a slight rise, hidden from the road and surrounded by old oak trees, stands the barn. This was the only building on the property when Angelina bought it and it now serves as the main gathering place of the commune. The interior of the barn has been rebuilt and there is a large kitchen with a long, well-scrubbed wooden table; this area also serves as the dining room. Next to this room is a communal quarter, with an improvised fireplace in the center of the dirt floor and barrels and pieces of logs or wooden blocks to sit on. Further construction is under way, but a well-stocked library can be reached by climbing a ladder. In the middle of the library's floor squats an old-fashioned wood-burning iron stove. There are pillows scattered around to sit on and a few old easy chairs that show signs of having been repaired with care.

Hal, who is one of the four left from the original group of fifteen that started the commune with Angelina, volunteered to act as guide. He is a slender, blond-haired man in his middle or upper twenties; he was dressed in clean, faded bluejeans, sandals, and a multihued shirt he had dyed himself. He was also wearing an ankh suspended from

a deceptively crude-looking, handmade brass chain around his neck. A dropout from a social science doctoral program at Yale, Hal has a habit of carefully forming his sentences. While dusk drew near, we walked together along paths through the wooded hillsides. More than a dozen single-room buildings have been so neatly fitted into the landscape that
they are hard to distinguish from their surroundings. Each is different 53
and has been constructed by the people who live in it from materials found on the land—old lumber and odds and ends. Some are built into the hillside and overlook the valley, and each structure is totally isolated, with no other neighbor visible. Only the sounds of birds could be heard; it was very peaceful.

Hal and I looked into several houses whose owners were away on trips. Most of these houses had one room dominated by a fireplace or an iron stove. There were mattresses on the floor, and chairs for the most part were improvised from lumber or were hand-hewn from logs.
Navajo rugs and colorful madras cloth and prints from India provided 54
decorative touches. Everything appeared neat and clean, and I was reminded of the outdoor shower and washing facilities near the barn, which we had investigated earlier and which had been shown with much pride.

On a different path back to the barn, we passed a tepee and a tent. A good-sized, intensively cultivated garden grows next to the barn; it furnishes the commune with most of the vegetables needed. Two nude girls with beautiful uniform tans were busy weeding. Hal explained that
those who want to, go nude whenever they feel like it. As we passed 55
the garden, we noticed Angelina walking along another path trying to join us. Although we slowed our pace so she could catch up with us, she had difficulty doing so, because out of nowhere would appear members who engaged her in intense conversations.

As we strolled on, I noticed several other people hovering in the background waiting. I asked Hal if Angelina functioned as guru or
leader and if she were directing the course of the commune. He was 56
emphatic—as were several others to whom I put the same question later—that Angelina is not in charge: "We all decide what we want to do."

Earlier, both Angelina and two of the other older members of the commune had made almost identical remarks: "We have lots of ideas and very little energy." Hal felt the reason was: "There is a lot of grass
around and people drop acid." Although he did add, philosophically, 57
"Everybody is into his own thing—each person is free to follow his own needs and interests. No one is forced to do anything. Everyone knows what needs to be done, and finally it gets done."

The commune has meetings once a week "to discuss everything that bothers us." There are seldom any major problems. Hal felt that
the commune's only significant problem was the lack of energy. Other 58
neighboring communes have factional disputes, hostile neighbors, suffer from lack of food and shelter, or are unable to pay their taxes. The

Good Earth Commune's relations with neighbors are friendly. As Angelina had put it at the coffee shop, "We live a very honest life." She had related a story of how one of the commune members had stolen a pump from a lumber company. This was discussed at one of the weekly meetings, and although the commune has definite strong feelings about lumber companies, the pump was returned.

During the weekly meetings, the group discusses what projects have priority; those members who want to, then volunteer for a particular project. To feed the commune, there is a kitchen list. Two members are chosen daily to provide the food and help prepare it. Farmers bring fruits and vegetables, which they barter for home-baked bread.

Eventually, Angelina caught up with us and led the way to her house. The second largest building on the grounds, it is almost circular in shape; members of the commune built it for her of field stones, hand-hewn timber, and used lumber. The large bedroom in the two-room dwelling has a fireplace and a double bed; placed here and there are many healthy-looking green plants in pots and on stands. An antique desk, a chest of drawers, a candelabra, and antique paintings and prints add richness to the room. The combination kitchen-living room was filled with young people reading, talking quietly, or playing the guitar and singing. Here also is the only phone in the commune. A young blonde girl was talking to her father. I could overhear snatches of her conversation: "No, Dad, I don't need any money. Just send me the plane ticket to Santa Barbara and I'll see you there at the house." Later, Angelina casually mentioned that the seventeen-year-old daughter of a two-star general is at the commune with the consent of her father. (She was not the girl using the telephone.)

The clanging of an old school bell called us to the barn for supper. Everyone formed a huge circle around the dinner table on which candles and kerosene lamps flickered. The room slowly grew quiet as the children scampered to their places in the circle. We all held hands. There was a long moment of silent communion, with heads bowed and eyes closed. The only sound was a dog barking in the distance. With no word spoken, the circle was broken. Conversation resumed, and we served ourselves buffet-style. The vegetarian meal consisted of a pea soup spiced with garden herbs; a combination entree of brown rice with onions, green peppers, and squash; a mixed green salad; freshly baked bread; and, for desert, bran muffins with nuts and dried fruit. Following supper, a fire was lighted in the large unfinished room next door and there was chanting, singing, and dancing.

As the evening progressed, Angelina told me that she would like to meet a warm, loving, sensitive type of man, maybe a minister—someone who knows how to counsel and work with young people. She said, "I haven't had a vacation for two years. I want to live in my house and get uninvolved. I want to travel. Older people point their finger at the commune instead of helping. I want some people with money to get involved. Where are the parents of these kids? Many of them come from well-to-do homes. Why am I so alone in this?"

As I prepared to leave, a phone call came from another commune
asking for advice. Going out the door, I could hear Angelina's husky 63
voice as she offered sympathy and suggestions. She was obviously very
much involved and perhaps not really as alone as she thought.

Questions and Quotations for Discussion and Writing Assignments

I

1. In "Paradoxes of Sex and Love" how do the elements of puritanism (with a small "p") combine to make a new definition based on sexual freedom? Does any statement which contains an "ought" contribute to a kind of puritanism?
2. Is it possible that in this age of sexual experimentation and discussion, we have lost the freedom to say *no* to sex? Are we so afraid of being thought "up-tight" about sex that we participate in sexual encounters that share only our bodies?
3. Can you support with illustrations May's idea that sexual freedom on stage, in movies, in literature falls short of being fully human? Have you felt that these fictional scenes prevent the exercise of imagination because they are so explicitly detailed, so graphic? Do you agree that *Playboy* is basically antisexual?
4. Altruism (from the Latin *alter*—other) is defined as concern for the welfare of others as opposed to egoism; selflessness. After reading "Altruism" by Germaine Greer, how should this definition be modified to convey her sense of the word?
5. Is self-denial a necessary part of love? Have you seen evidence of the "self-sacrifice motif" in your own families?
6. The fact that religious training promulgates the ideal of self-sacrifice makes denial of this "virtue" particularly difficult. Have we too willingly enlarged the spheres of the "thou shalt nots" into a series of "thou shalts"?
7. The enduring rhythm of human affairs (the family cycle: birth, childhood, maturity, which leads again to birth) in Alvin Toffler's view has been "one of the sanity-preserving constants of human existence." Is it possible to imagine such a permanent order outside the family structure? Is the structure in which the cycle takes place necessary to the continuation of the cycle?
8. Mr. Toffler says in "The Fractured Family" that "parenthood remains the greatest single preserve of the amateur" in an age when specialized training is required of almost everyone else. Yet Walter Karp in "The Feminine Utopia" feels that collective, professional child care (services provided by the pro-parents described in Toffler's essay) "would tyrannize the young, which means, in the end, it would tyrannize us all."

What evidence do you find that the nuclear family may not contain the rich variety of personal relationships Mr. Karp ascribes to it? Have you found "vivid models of personal loyalty, affection, and respect" outside your family? In short, how is your generation of human beings affected by the time-honored family structure?

9. Alvin Toffler defines love briefly as parallel development, shared growth, but believes that "transience and novelty are both in league against it." His prediction of the future for love involves "serial marriage" (consecutive relationships) plotted by the trajectory of personal development. Germaine Greer views love as possible only between "self-actualizing" human beings, two independent individuals who have successfully resisted enculturation, two psychic equals. This relationship "is not the lifelong coherence of a mutually bound couple, but the principle of love that is reaffirmed in the relationship of the narcissistic self to the world of which it is a part." Both views stress personal development, the changes that inevitably occur in active men and women during a lifetime. Is this lack of permanence in love threatening? Is the necessity to accept and act upon change in the personality a part of the individual's obligation to his lover, or is it destructive of the relationship? What are the criteria for the success or failure of love in these authors' views?
10. "Is the Family Obsolete?," a series of five short essays, contains five short samples of writing styles. If you did not know the authors' reputations, could you separate the professionals from the amateurs? Can you determine the tone (the author's attitude about his material and his audience) of each piece?
11. To what extent is the "tribal" movement described by Gary Snyder available to one unfamiliar with "The Dharma"? Much of the vocabulary in this essay is foreign to students educated in the western tradition, yet this language, these phrases have become the clichés of a subculture. Are you, as questing human beings, willing to check the accuracy of Snyder's contention that "small but influential heretical and esoteric movements . . . are all outcroppings of The Great Subculture which runs underground all through history"? Is such careful understanding necessary? If not, in what way is Gary Snyder then a father figure?
12. Alvin Toffler's *Future Shock* suggests that although "most of today's 'intentional communities' reveal a powerful preference for the past, . . . society as a whole would be better served by utopian experiments based on super- rather than pre-industrial forms." Do you feel that the "tribe" is a super-industrial experiment? Does exploring "just what is consciousness?" seem "the next great step of mankind"?
13. Communes may be defined as groups of human beings voluntarily linked by bonds of genuine similarity rather than accidents of birth; individuals who come together choosing a certain intellectual or emotional life style rather than accepting a familial or ethnic grouping. Herbert Otto's essay, "Communes: The Alternative Life Style" lists many distinct types of communes. Insofar as each has its general direction, its ideological bent, how is the commune essentially different from the variety of choices available within college fraternities, various fraternal orders (The Lions, The Elks), or religious denominations?

14. How is the interview with Angelina and the material devoted to her description in "Communes: The Alternative Life Style" used by the author? Can you suggest reasons for choosing her as a focal point for the essay (which appeared in *Saturday Review*)? Does Angelina herself prove Otto's point that although individual responsibility and capability are the ideal, in practice, "strong personalities in the communes assume responsibility for what happens, and there is a tendency toward the emergence of mother and father figures"?
15. One of the major problems in the communes (together with unclear lines of authority and the lack of privacy) is community relations, because the public view of the commune seems to be a stereotype leading generally to sexual fantasies. Do you find it ironic that within the communes, traditional sex roles are maintained while outside there is considerable agitation about the function of women? That within the commune there is still reverence for the family unit, flexible though it may be?

II

1. Love consists in this, that two solitudes protect and touch each other.

   RAINER MARIA RILKE

2. It destroys one's nerves to be amiable every day to the same human being.

   BENJAMIN DISRAELI

3. I can love her and her and you and you,/I can love any, so she be not true.

   JOHN DONNE

4. Love is just as much of a necessity as bread.

   HONORÉ DE BALZAC

5. . . . for it is better to marry than to be aflame with passion.

   I CORINTHIANS 7:9

6. Premarital continence is supposed to prepare for marriage. But the very same continence creates sexual disturbances and thus undermines marriage.

   WILHELM REICH

7. . . . It is well for a man not to touch a woman. But because of the temptation to immorality, each man should have his own wife and each woman her own husband. The husband should give to his wife her conjugal rights, and likewise the wife to her husband. For the wife does not rule over her own body, but the husband does; likewise the husband does not rule over his own body, but the wife does.

   I CORINTHIANS 7:1-4

8. Marriage is neither merely a matter of love, as claimed by some, nor merely an economic institution, as claimed by others. It is the form into which sexual needs were forced by the socioeconomic processes.

   WILHELM REICH

9. *It is not good for man to be alone.* Some would have the sense hereof to be in respect of procreation only; and *Austin* [Augustine] contests that manly friendship in all other regards had been a more becoming solace for *Adam* than to spend so many secret years in an empty world with one woman. But our writers severely reject this crabbed opinion; and defend that there is a peculiar comfort in the married state besides the genial bed, which no other society affords.

   JOHN MILTON

10. Don't make a hero of your husband, because you're sure to find him out. Make a comrade of him. It's far safer and lasts longer.

   PHILIP GIBBS

11. Every marriage sickens as a result of an ever increasing conflict between *sexual* and economic needs. The sexual needs can be satisfied with one and the same partner only for a limited period of time.

   WILHELM REICH

12. Probably the only place where a man can feel really secure is in a maximum security prison, except for the imminent threat of release.

   GERMAINE GREER

13. "What we have done this afternoon is to renounce happiness, renounce freedom, renounce tranquillity, above all renounce the romantic possibilities of an unknown future for the cares of a household and a family." —Jack Tanner announcing his marriage,

   GEORGE BERNARD SHAW,
   Man and Superman

14. A family is the best place in the world in which to learn how to live with other people.

   RHODA W. BACMEISTER

15. If we are to recover serenity and joy in living, we will have to listen to what our children are telling us in their own way, and not impose our own distorted image upon them in our crazy families.

   GERMAINE GREER

16. In my sex hygiene clinics, the fact became clear to me that *the function of the suppression of infantile and adolescent sexuality is that of facilitating for the parents the authoritarian submissiveness of the children.*

   WILHELM REICH

17. Patriarchal laws pertaining to culture, religion and marriage are essentially laws *against* sex.

   WILHELM REICH

18. . . . we still make love to organs and not to people: . . . so far from realizing that people are never more idiosyncratic, never more totally *there,* than when they make love, we are never more incommunicative, never more alone.

   GERMAINE GREER

19. What is needed for sexual harmony is not refinement in technique, rather, on the foundation of the moment's erotic charm, a mutual generosity of body and soul.

    SIMONE DE BEAUVOIR

20. "Did you know that a woman can now have children without a man?"
    "But what on earth for?"
    "You can apply ice to a woman's ovaries, for instance. She can have a child. Men are no longer necessary to humanity."
    At once Ella laughs, and with confidence. "But what woman in her senses would want ice applied to her ovaries instead of a man?"

    DORIS LESSING,
    The Golden Notebook

21. *Only the liberation of the natural capacity for love in human beings can master their sadistic destructiveness.*

    WILHELM REICH

22. Community, love, closeness . . . these must overcome the individualistic, rationalist man—the frontiersman who made his own way at the expense of others.

    ROLLO MAY

23. The challenge of marriage is the adventure of uncovering the depth of our love, the height of our humanity. It means risking ourselves physically and emotionally; leaving old habit patterns, and developing new ones; being able to express our desires fully, while sensitive to the needs of the other; being aware that each changes at his own rate, and unafraid to ask for help when needed.

    HERBERT A. OTTO

SECTION V A Place to Live—Sodom, Gomorrah, or the Hog Farm?

Most of the writers presented in this section fear man's almost suicidal propensity to create environments—*places to live*—that are hostile to the occupants, unsafe for human habitation. The ecologists and environmentalists have shouted warnings of the disastrous problems we are generating: industrial and municipal wastes, agricultural pesticides, automobile exhaust fumes, overpopulation, thermal destruction of lakes and rivers; and the list grows longer each day. These problems must be dealt with soon or we are headed for catastrophe. Dealing with them will require great sums of money, great sacrifice, and, ironically, the assistance of technology.

But what about the environments we create for our minds and spirits? How healthy are these places? We should not be surprised to know that the same individuals who contaminate the air they breathe and the water they drink also build cities, homes, schools, and offices that smother peoples' spirits and sap their humanity. In the rather prophetic, short poem, "London," William Blake pictures vividly the degradation of the human spirit, the "marks of weakness, marks of woe," the pain, fear, and disease of man living in his "chartered" cities. Man, as Blake sees him, is handcuffed by his own "mind-forged manacles"; man, in his lust to organize, explain, make rational, and legalize, demands that even the rivers be "chartered" rivers, not wild and mysterious, but mapped, plotted, controlled. As Robinson Jeffers says, perhaps we have become "A little to abstract, a little too wise"; we are "civilized, crying to be human again," but we don't know how.

We cut ourselves off from nature, and when we do, we suffer spiritual impoverishment. For primitive man nature was harsh, strange, wonderful, to be feared and even worshipped. But we, atom-age men, see ourselves as masters of the natural world, manipulators of nature for our own ends. We surround ourselves with asphalt, gas stations. apart-

Garbage Scow. Courtesy of Lester Lefkowitz.

ment buildings—cold structures that numb our ability to perceive, to feel as human beings. When we build superhighways, parking lots, hydroelectric dams, housing developments, we destroy the wilderness, the lakes, the forests. When we build department stores and shopping centers, we clutter our homes with mountains of "things" to make our lives easier, faster, more comfortable—hair dryers, electric toothbrushes, dishwashers, color televisions. . . . Like the Collyer brothers, we may be crushed by the weight of our acquisitions—and in our own homes!

Is there a way out? Can we make the places we live in healthy for our minds and bodies? Can we learn, as Ashley Montagu observes, that "our wholeness as human beings depends upon the depth of our awareness of the fact that we are part of the wholeness of nature"? This planet does not care what we do to it; some day it may expel us, but it will do so without consciously caring. Only we have the degree of consciousness to care about our living conditions; only we have to make commitments to places in which we live by an act of will. We have apparently cut ourselves off from whatever right instincts we may have had about place as we acquired more complicated intellects; but through this complicated intellect we can return to or recover the other parts of our natures and become whole.

President Nixon has said: "The great question of the 70's is: Shall we surrender to our surroundings or shall we make our peace with nature and begin to make reparations for the damage we have done to our air, to our land, and to our water?"

Subway Entrance. Courtesy of Lester Lefkowitz.

William Blake

London

I wander through each chartered street,
Near where the chartered Thames does flow,
And mark in every face I meet
Marks of weakness, marks of woe.

In every cry of every man,
In every infant's cry of fear,
In every voice, in every ban,
The mind-forged manacles I hear.

How the chimney-sweeper's cry
Every black'ning church appalls;
And the hapless soldier's sigh;
Runs in blood down palace walls.

But most through midnight streets I hear
How the youthful harlot's curse
Blasts the new-born infant's tear,
And blights with plagues the marriage hearse.

Robert Cowley

Does Your Room Look Like The Collyer Brothers'?

As I begin, I think of my cardboard boxes. There they are, crammed with the debris of a decade at least: childrens' drawings, aged desk calendars, a 1948 copy of *Life* with the stories of Truman's victory and the Donora smog, a guarantee for a long-defunct vacuum cleaner, letters and bank statements, an old Army Air Corps surplus map of Borneo, and—why?—a photo engraver's wood block with a picture of a gorilla. In my case, a move is rarely as good as a fire; the boxes not only travel with me but they multiply. Don't be disdainful. You, too, have your piled attic, your "hell corner," your Fibber McGee closet ready to trip its booby-trap freight of old Muriel cigar boxes and baseball mits with the Snuffy Sternweiss autograph imprint. We keep them, perhaps, because they are the closest representations that we have of our selves: these are the things that have formed the shape of *our* time, and it would take a revolution to get rid of them. And yet, there must be moments in our nightmares when the boxes or the stubborn roomful of junk seems to swell and we see ourselves engulfed by our own useless accumulations—our thing Triffids, our paper-and-metal Venus Flytraps.

How often do nightmares become real? There is the old story about the difference between a neurotic and a psychotic. The neurotic builds dream castles; the psychotic builds dream castles and lives in them—and the psychiatrist collects rent from both. In the home of Homer and Langley Collyer we find such a dream house, except that it is a Castle of Otranto in the middle of Harlem and its two inhabitants are uncomfortably real. For three weeks twenty-two years ago, we all took inventory of its contents, truckload after truckload; by the time the last of the Collyers' effects had been carted away and their house had fallen under the wrecker's ball, the obsession of two old men had permanently entered our language. For years my mother put it to me this way: "Aren't you ashamed? Your room looks like the Collyer brothers'."

The story broke on March 21, 1947. It was a typical first day of spring in New York City: a greymetal overcast, rain, and a temperature

that felt much colder than the 45 degrees on the thermometer. At about
ten that morning, a call came in to police headquarters. The voice of a
man who identified himself as "Charles Smith"—and no one ever
satisfactorily established who he was—announced, "There is a man dead
in the premises at 2078 Fifth Avenue." Here, for almost forty years, had
lived two legendary and mysterious recluses, Homer and Langley Collyer. Homer, paralyzed and, as *The New York Times* said, "blind as the
poet he was named for," had been seen only twice since 1934; Langley, 3
his younger brother (they were respectively sixty-five and sixty-one),
prowled the city at night, as furtive as one of the alley cats that made
their home in his basement. About the only people who had ever been
inside the house—and just once past the entrance hallway—were process
servers: the brothers did not believe in paying taxes. Occasionally
Langley would give an interview to the press; for all his anchoritic
ways, he seemed to delight in teasing the public with the details of his
life with Homer.

A newspaper picture of Langley taken in 1938 shows a man in
an oversized cloth cap peering down from a window. He has a long
nose with great nostrils, deep-set, dark-ringed eyes, and a scraggly
moustache that looks like a clump of grass growing from a crack in
the pavement. A man named Gruber had made an offer for some land
the brothers owned in Queens, and for the purpose of the legend the
picture caption is worth quoting. It alleged that Langley "never leaves 4
the house until dark" (true); that "he owns 17 grand pianos, one for
every room of the house" (he owned fourteen, some less than grand);
that "he has a Model T Ford in his basement" (he did, more or less
in pieces); that "he doesn't believe in banks" (he did, to the extent
that thirty-four bankbooks were later found, eleven of them cancelled);
that "there are 25,000 books in his library" (it was closer to five thousand); and that "he owns half of New York's waterfront" (the one
statement that was completely untrue).

When the enigmatic call came on that morning in March, a patrolman was dispatched to the Collyer house. He found himself pounding
at the front door of a weathered three-story brownstone on the north-
west corner of Fifth Avenue and 128th Street. Getting no response, he
summoned the emergency squad. With axes and crowbars they broke
down the door and were confronted, the *Herald Tribune* reported, 5
"with a wall of newspapers, folding chairs, broken boxes, part of a
wine press, half a sewing machine, folding beds, parts of a rocking
chair, and innumerable other pieces of junk." They tried the front basement door and again found their way barred by junk. It was the same
at the back: the areaway was piled to the ceiling with, among other
things, an old stove, umbrellas, wrapped packages of newspapers, a
broken scooter, and a gas mask canister.

A policeman climbed up on a fire ladder to one of the second-
floor windows. He could not even get a foot inside. By this time a

crowd of some six hundred people had gathered below, and they gaped at the things that came hurtling out of the window: a rake . . . a baby carriage frame . . . the New York *Evening Telegram* for November 24, 1918 (REDS KILL 500 WHILE RUSSIANS FIGHT FOR FOOD). At last the patrolman disappeared from view, only to return to the window a few moments later.

"There's a D.O.A. here," he called down.

Behind a stinking mountain of junk the beam of his flashlight had fallen on the body of a tiny old man sitting on the floor. His matted hair reached down to his shoulders, and he wore only a ragged bathrobe. Next to the corpse were a half-eaten Washington State apple, a leaking container of rancid milk, and a copy of the Philadelphia *Jewish Morning Journal* of Sunday, February 22, 1920. Homer Collyer, it first appeared, had been dead at least ten hours, though that estimate was later revised upward to from four days to a week; he had apparently succumbed to heart disease aggravated by starvation.

But what had become of Langley?

"That the collecting mania," writes A. A. Brill in *Fundamental Conceptions of Psychoanalysis,* "is a reaction to an unconscious need, to an inner feeling of voidness concerning some particular craving is best seen in the collections made by the insane." In the case of Langley and Homer Collyer we know of the void only through inferences. They were born in New York in the 1880's and grew up in the city.

Their father, Dr. Herman L. Collyer, was a prominent and wealthy gynecologist. This circumstance seems noteworthy, since neither of his sons ever married or had, as far as is known, any contact with women. At any rate, father and sons did not get along: their allegiances belonged all to their mother, a doting and possessive woman who was fond of reading the classics aloud to them in Greek. Homer went to the City College of New York, studied admiralty law, and practiced for a time. Langley majored in engineering at Columbia but never held a job. He aspired to become a concert pianist: "My last concert was in Carnegie Hall, a week before Paderewski's first. He got more notices than I, so I gave up. What was the use?" Whether the story was apocryphal or not is unimportant; it is the visible part of the iceberg—along with the pianos, the five violins, the several pipe organs, the cello with the phony "Stradivarius, 1727" imprint, the two cornets, the bugle, the trombone, and the musical clock weighing two hundred pounds.

When the family moved into the 128th Street house, Harlem was a neighborhood favored by the white middle class. But in the early 1900's Manhattan suffered one of its periodic real-estate collapses; Negroes began to migrate to Harlem, and a white exodus followed. Dr. Collyer himself moved to West 77th Street, but his sons could never bring themselves to leave the Harlem house. It was as if their own fear kept them there, these two frail, genteel men with their fine old New York accents, barricading themselves against a world that was in

every sense getting blacker and blacker. Police turned up four revolvers
and a hundred rounds of ammunition, a shotgun, two rifles, a cavalry
saber, and a twenty-four-inch French bayonet.

Dr. Collyer died in 1923. He must have been a little odd himself.
When his house was sold in the 1930's, the new owner found, to her
consternation, a Model T Ford in the basement. How had it got there?
Finding neither window nor door wide enough for it to pass through,
she paid a man $150 to take it apart and leave it out on the pavement.
Somehow Langley heard. He carted the car uptown, piece by dis- 13
assembled piece, chassis, engine, and all, and put it in his basement.
But that is going ahead of the story. In 1929, when the brothers were
in their late forties, their mother died. By this time their eccentricity
had already become marked. They cut off their utilities, used a kerosene stove for heat and cooking, carried water in demijohns from a
nearby park, and tried to generate their own electricity.

Homer started to go blind and in 1934 decided that he would never
go outside again. But Homer was seen outdoors one more time. Early
on New Year's morning, 1940, a policeman caught sight of the brothers 14
carrying the branch of a fallen elm tree across the street to the basement of their house.

Not long afterward Homer lost the use of his limbs as well as his
sight. He refused to see a doctor—or was it that Langley would not let
him? "You must remember we are sons of a doctor," Langley said.
"Homer eats 100 oranges a week— and is improving." Langley would
appear after dark, a wraith in a greasy cloth cap, pulling a cardboard 15
box on the end of a long rope. Sometimes he would walk as far as the
Williamsburg section of Brooklyn for whole-wheat bread. As for the
tons of newspapers in the house, he explained that he was saving them
for the day when Homer regained his sight: "He can catch up on the
news."

That was the only reason Langley ever gave for their collecting.
"A passion for collecting is frequently a direct surrogate for a sexual
desire," wrote the psychiatrist Karl Abraham. But there is something
monstrous about the Collyers that defies psychological explanation. One
thinks of the police officer who, on a day in 1942, decided to check
on a rumor that Homer was dead. After considerable hesitation, Lang- 16
ley let him in at the basement door and then led him up a pitch-black
stairway through precarious canyons of newsprint, under alarm systems
that would spew garbage and tin cans on the heads of the unwary and
the uninvited—delicately poised booby traps that would bring down a
suffocating edifice of junk. Did the policeman trip on the jawbone of
the horse? Did he collide with the chasis of the Model T or brush
against the skeletons used by the late Dr. Collyer? It took him half an
hour to reach the second-floor room, a small cleared section of which
Homer inhabited.

"I switched on my flashlight," the policeman related, "and there
was Homer sitting up like a mummy . . . 'I am Homer L. Collyer, 17

lawyer,' the old man says, in a deep voice. 'I want your name and shield number. I am not dead. I am blind and paralyzed.'"

Five years later Homer was buried in the family plot in Queens. The funeral was delayed in hope that Langley would miraculously show up, but he did not. An eleven-state alarm was sent out. He was variously reported in Atlantic City, in Asbury Park, New Jersey, where policemen rummaged through boarded-up summer cottages, on a subway in Brooklyn, and floating in a creek in the East Bronx. One old man was observed carrying a hand-lettered sign: "I am *not* Langley Collyer." Even Andrei Gromyko, the Russian delegate to the Security Council, looked up from his newspaper to comment, "Who knows, we might find out today where Langley Collyer is." As the headlines subsided and the story moved to the back pages, the *Daily News* wondered out loud: "We find ourselves wishing the New York policemen would just sweep Langley's place up a little more, and then quietly steal away, maybe leaving a little bowl of milk for him on his doorstep."

Meanwhile the clearing out of the house continued, day after day. In room after room junk was stacked to the ceiling, and Langley's alimentary burrows were the only way through. Nineteen tons were brought out one day . . . eighteen another . . . twelve tons, including five from a single six-foot area. By the time police and sanitation men were finished, 140 tons—280,000 thing-pounds—had been carted away. The search was becoming a "nightmare," the police said, and a hazardous one at that. Two detectives were almost buried by a booby trap on the stairs: "Close behind them," reported the *Herald Tribune,* "came two seventy-five pound chunks of concrete, two feet square, cardboard boxes containing tin cans, crowbars, and other inconceivable kinds of inutile material. . . ."

Then, on April 8, nineteen days after the search had begun, a detective rooting not ten feet from where Homer had died looked down and saw a hand. Langley Collyer had been crushed by one of his own booby traps as he carried food to his brother through a tunnel lined with a chest of drawers and an old bedspring. On the body there rested bundles of newspapers, a suitcase filled with metal, a sewing machine, and three breadboxes.

Robinson Jeffers

Return

A little too abstract, a little too wise,
It is time for us to kiss the earth again,
It is time to let the leaves rain from the skies,
Let the rich life run to the roots again.
I will go down to the lovely Sur Rivers
And dip my arms in them up to the shoulders.
I will find my accounting where the alder leaf quivers
In the ocean wind over the river boulders.
I will touch things and things and no more thoughts,
That breed like mouthless May-flies darkening the sky,
The insect clouds that blind our passionate hawks
So that they cannot strike, hardly can fly.
Things are the hawk's food and noble is the mountain, Oh noble
Pico Blanco, steep sea-wave of marble.

Signpost

Civilized, crying how to be human again: this will tell you how.
Turn outward, love things, not men, turn right away from humanity,
Let that doll lie. Consider if you like how the lilies grow,
Lean on the silent rock until you feel its divinity
Make your veins cold, look at the silent stars, let your eyes
Climb the great ladder out of the pit of yourself and man.
Things are so beautiful, your love will follow your eyes;
Things are the God, you will love God, and not in vain,
For what we love, we grow to it, we share its nature. At length
You will look back along the stars' rays and see that even
The poor doll humanity has a place under heaven.
Its qualities repair their mosaic around you, the chips of strength
And sickness; but now you are free, even to become human,
But born of the rock and the air, not of a woman.

Wendell Berry

Some Thoughts on Citizenship and Conscience in Honor of Don Pratt

I

The idea of citizenship in the United States seems to me to have
been greatly oversimplified. It has become permissible to assume that
all one needs to do to be a good citizen is to vote and obey and pay
taxes, as if one can be a good citizen without being a citizen either of 1
a community or of a place. As if citizenship is merely a matter of per-
functory dutifulness, a periodic deference to the organizations, beyond
which it is every man for himself.

Because several years ago I became by choice a resident of the
place I am native to, which I know intimately and love strongly, I
have begun to understand citizenship in more complex terms. As I have
come to see it, it requires devotion and dedication, and a certain inescapable bewilderment and suffering. It needs all the virtues, all of 2
one's attention, all the knowledge that one can gain and bring to bear,
all the powers of one's imagination and conscience and feeling. It is
the complete action. Rightly understood, its influence and concern per-
meate the whole society, from the children's bedroom to the capitol.

But it begins at home. Its meanings come clearest, it is felt most
intensely in one's own house. The health, coherence, and meaningful- 3
ness of one's own household are the measure of the success of the government, and not the other way around.

My devotion thins as it widens. I care more for my household than
for the town of Port Royal, more for the town of Port Royal than for
the County of Henry, more for the County of Henry than for the State 4
of Kentucky, more for the State of Kentucky than for the United States
of America. But I *do not* care more for the United States of America
than for the world.

I must attempt to care as much for the world as for my household.
Those are the poles between which a competent morality would balance and mediate: the doorstep and the planet. The most meaningful 5
dependence of my house is not the U. S. government, but on the

world, the earth. No matter how sophisticated and complex and powerful our institutions, we are still exactly as dependent on the earth as the earthworms.

To cease to know this, and to fail to act upon the knowledge, is to begin to die the death of a broken machine. In default of man's personal cherishing and care, now that his machinery has become so awesomely powerful, the earth must become the victim of his institutions, the violent self-destructive machinery of man-in-the-abstract. And so, conversely, the most meaningful dependence of the earth is not on the U. S. government, but on my household—how I live, how I raise my children, how I care for the land entrusted to me.

These two poles of life and thought offer two different points of view, perspectives that are opposite and complementary. But morally, because one is contained within the other and the two are interdependent, they propose the same consciousness and the same labor. To attempt to interpose another moral standard between these two, which I take to be absolute and ultimately the same, is to prepare the way for a power that is arbitrary and tyrannical. To assert that a man owes an allegiance that is antecedent to his allegiance to his household, or higher than his allegiance to the earth, is to invite a state of moral chaos that will destroy both the household and the earth.

Since there is no government of which the concern or the discipline is primarily the health either of households or of the earth, since it is in the nature of any state to be concerned first of all with its own preservation and only second with the cost, the dependable, clear response to man's moral circumstance is not that of law, but that of conscience. The highest moral behavior is not obedience to law, but obedience to the informed conscience even in spite of law. The government will be the *last* to see the moral implications of man's dependence on the earth, and the *last* to admit that wars can no longer be fought in behalf of some men but only against all men. Though these realizations have entered the consciences and the lives of certain persons, they have not yet superseded the self-interest of any government.

As law without conscience is hollow, so law that is not willingly preceded and shaped by conscience is tyrannical; the state is deified, and men are its worshipers, obeying as compulsively and blindly as ants. The law is no defense against the greatest ills of our time, for power, as always, subverts the law. Only the consciences of persons can be depended upon to take the stand that is unequivocally moral, and to make the clear, complete refusal.

I do not mean to support, and I do not respect, any act of civil disobedience that is violent, or that is obstructive of the rights of other people. Such overbearing zeal is as fearful to me in the service of peace and brotherhood as in the service of war and hate. But I do support and respect those peaceable acts of disobedience by which conscience withholds itself from the contamination of acts antithetical to it, as when

a believer in the sixth commandment refuses to kill or to support a
policy of killing even when legally required to do so. Such an act is
no mere vagary. It is the basis and essence of political liberty, defining
the true nature of government as only such acts can define it—assert- 10
ing, as it has been necessary time and again to assert in the history
both of our country and of our species, that the government governs
by the consent of the people, not by any divine or inherent right.

To hear the boasts and the claims of some of our political leaders,
one would think that we all *lived* in the government. The lower order
of our politicians no doubt do so, and they no doubt exhibit the effects.
But though I am always aware that I live in my household and in the
world, I wish to testify that in my best moments I am not aware of 11
the existence of the government. Though I respect and feel myself dignified by the principles of the Declaration and the Constitution, I do
not remember a day when the thought of the government made me
happy, and I never think of it without the wish that it might become
wiser and truer and smaller than it is.

II

Nothing in my education or experience prepared me even to expect
the horror and anxiety and moral bewilderment that I have felt during
these years of racism and disintegration at home and a war of unprecedented violence and senselessness abroad. The attempt to keep mean- 12
ing in one's life at such a time is a continuous strain, and perhaps
ultimately futile: there is undoubtedly a limit to how long private
integrity can hold out in the face of, and within, public disintegration.
The conflict is plainly seeded with madness and death.

Even in our sleep some critical part of our attention is held by the
descending roar of a machine bigger than the world—a society so automated and bureaucratized, so stuffed with the rhetoric of self-righteousness, that it is seemingly no longer capable of a moral or a human
response. With the world in our power and our power assigned to the 13
moral authority of those who will profit most by its misuse, we continue to bless and congratulate ourselves upon the boyhood honesty of
George Washington. And so the machine descends. We are already
suffocating in its fumes.

Slowly America wakens to the tragedy of her history, the unquieted
ghosts of her martyrs brooding over her in the night, her forfeited
visions, the plundered and desecrated maidenhood of her lands and
forests and rivers. I write a little more than a week after the death
of Martin Luther King, who lived as only the great live, in humble 14
obedience to the highest ideals, in proud defiance of men and laws that
would have required him to abide by a narrower vision and to dream
a narrower dream. He stood for the American hope in its full amplitude
and generosity. His martyrdom is the apparition of the death of that
hope in racism and violence.

And today I live with the sorrow and shame that one of the finest young men of the university where I teach is in jail. He is in jail because he refuses to co-operate in the prosecution of a war that he believes to be unjust and unnecessary and immoral, because he insists upon living by the sixth commandment and the Golden Rule, because he does not believe that a wrong is any less a wrong when committed with the government's sanction and by the government's order. He is in jail because he will not acknowledge, because he cannot see, any difference between public morality and private morality. This young man's name is Don Pratt, a citizen of Lexington, Kentucky, a student of the University of Kentucky, one of the exemplary men of Kentucky. I acknowledge myself deeply indebted to him. His sacrifice and his fate have become a clarifying pain in my consciousness. His nobility is one of the reasons I have—and they are not abundant—to continue to hope for the future of my species. He and the other young men who have taken the stand he has taken are among the most precious moral resources of our country. Because they have not only believed in our highest ideals, but have also acted as they believed, the world is whole before them, and they are whole before the world.

There is, as Thoreau said, a great shame in going free while good men are in jail because of their goodness. Perhaps there is also shame in only going to jail while innocent people are dying or burning alive by the "accidents" of our technological warfare. There is shame in the inheritance of ancestral wrong, in the realization of how deliberately for how many years we have lived by the exploitation and waste of the earth and of one another. To open one's consciousness to the world as we have made it is to receive the sleepless anguish of this shame. To feel it is one of the costs to our kind of being morally alive.

And so, the sense of shame deep in me, and full of craving for moral clarity, I ask myself why it is that *I* am not in jail. And I answer, with much uncertainty, that I have not yet been faced with going to jail as an inescapable obligation—an obligation, that is, which would cancel out such other obligations as that of keeping together my family and household.

My life, as I have made it and as I understand it, is turned against what I consider the evils of our society—its suicidal wish to become a machine, its lethargic assumption that a mythologized past can serve as some kind of moral goal that can effectively discipline the present. My aim is to imagine and live out a decent and preserving relationship to the earth. I am determined to cling to this effort as long as I can maintain some meaning in it. But I know, the events of recent years make it clear, that there may come a time when it will be necessary to give it up, when to hold to it will be more destructive of it than to let it go. If I should be required in the name of the law to place my life in the service of the machinery of man's destructiveness and hate, then I hope for the courage to refuse in the name of conscience.

III

But wait. I am about to cross over into too much solemnity, a useless shame. Let me step aside from crowds—even the crowd of those whose opinions I share—and stand up finally in the place, and among the concerns, of my own life. I wish to speak no further except out of the few acres of hillside and woods and riverbank near Port Royal, Kentucky, that I hope to have made mine for life. I accept the meanings of that place, for the time I will be there, as my meanings, accepting also that my life and its effects belong ineradicably to that place. I am occupied there with a small orchard, vines and berry bushes, henyard
and garden and pasture—with increasing the richness and the abun- 19
dance and the meaningfulness of that part of the earth for my family and myself, and for those who will live there after us. This effort has given me many hours of intense pleasure, both in itself and in the sense of what it means as a human possibility. It holds out to me in the most immediate way the hope of peace, the ideal of harmlessness, the redeeming chance that a man can live so as to enhance and enlarge the possibility of life in the world, rather than to diminish it. I do not acknowledge the pleasure I take in this part of my life with shame, though I know that while I have felt this pleasure much of the world has been miserable.

The solemnity and ostentatious grief of some implies that there is a mystical equation by which one man, by suffering enough guilt, by a denial of joy, can atone or compensate for the suffering of many men. The logical culmination of this feeling is self-incineration, which only removes one from the problem without solving it. Because so many are hungry, should we weep as we eat? No child will grow fat on our tears. But to eat, taking whatever satisfaction it gives us, and then to
turn again to the problem of how to make it possible for another to 20
eat, to undertake to cleanse ourselves of the great wastefulness of our society, to seek alternatives in our own lives to our people's thoughtless squandering of the world's goods—that promises a solution. That many are cold and the world is full of hate does not mean that one should stand in the snow for shame or refrain from making love. To refuse to admit decent and harmless pleasures freely into one's own life is as wrong as to deny them to someone else. It impoverishes and darkens the world.

My impression is that the great causes of peace and brotherhood are being served these days with increasing fanaticism, obsessiveness, self-righteousness, and anger. As if the aim is to turn the world into
a sort of Protestant heaven, from which all nonmembers have been 21
eliminated, and in which the principle satisfaction is to go around looking holy. In short, the supporters of these causes are becoming specialists, like preachers and generals, and I think that is a very bad sign. Such specialists, it seems to me, are the enemies of their cause. Too many are now expending themselves utterly in the service of political

abstractions, and my guess is that this is because of a growing sense of guilt and a growing belief that this guilt can be expiated in political action. I do not believe it, nor do I believe very much in the efficacy of political solutions. The political activist *sacrifices* himself to politics; though he has a cause, he has no life; he has become the driest of experts. And if he narrows and desiccates his life for the sake of the future of his ideals, what right has he to hope that the success of his ideals will bring a fuller life? Unsubstantiated in his own living, his motives grow hollow, puffed out with the blatant air of oratory.

What is happening now is that most public people, from government officials and political candidates to student activists, are involved in an ever-intensifying contest of self-righteous rhetoric. No one can feel certain he will be believed until he has said something more extreme than has been said before, and this both proceeds from and promotes the sense that the speaker is absolutely right and unimpeachably virtuous. There is no possibility of intelligence in it. And pacifists and peaceworkers especially should be aware of its enormous potential of violence. The problems of violence cannot be solved on public platforms, but only in people's lives. And to give the matter over to the processes of public rhetoric is to forego the personal self-critical moral intelligence that is essential to any hope for peace, and that can only function in the daily life of individuals. That I have abjured violence in principle does not mean that I have shrugged off the history of violence that I descend from, or the culture of violence that I have grown used to, or the habits and reflexes of violence in my body and mind, or the prejudices that preserve violence and justify it, or the love of violence. And this suggests to me that I can speak of my commitment to the cause of peace only with hesitance and with the greatest circumspection, and that I should avoid any rhetoric that might lead me to offer myself as a model.

IV

What one does can originate nowhere but in his life. If his life is organizational and abstract, dependent on the support and passion of crowds, full of the fervor of allegiance rather than the fervor of personal love and independence, then his love of peace is a hollow specialization. His hope is liable to be obscured by his cause. He is apt to find himself marching in protest against militarism and shouting or shoving in protest against force. The next step is only to join the militarists in making war in protest against war, soaring in self-righteousness, condemning and slurring all who do not agree. A tyranny of fanatical peace lovers is as credible to me as a tyranny of militarists, and I don't think there would be any difference.

It seems to me inescapable that before a man can usefully promote an idea, the idea must be implemented in his own life. If he is for peace he must have a life in which peace is possible. He must be peace-able.

To be a peaceable man is to be the hope of the world. To be only an
agitator for peace is to be a specialist, one in a swarm of random particles, destructive in implication, however pacific by intention. How
can a man hope to promote peace in the world if he has not made it
possible in his own life and his own household? If he is a peaceable 24
man, then he has assured a measure of peace in the world, though he
may never utter a public word.

I am struggling, amid all the current political uproar, to keep
clearly in mind that it is *not* merely because our policies are wrong
that we are so destructive and violent. It goes deeper than that, and
is more troubling. We are so little at peace with ourselves and our
neighbors because we are not at peace with our place in the world,
our land. American history has been to a considerable extent the history
of our warfare against the natural life of the continent. Until we end
our violence against the earth—a matter ignored by most pacifists, as
the issue of military violence is ignored by most conservationists—how 25
can we hope to end our violence against each other? The earth, which
we all have in common, is our deepest bond, and our behavior toward
it cannot help but be an earnest of our consideration for each other
and for our descendants. To corrupt or destroy the natural environment is an act of violence not only against the earth but also against
those who are dependent on it, including ourselves. To waste the soil
is to cause hunger, as direct an aggression as an armed attack; it is
an act of violence against the future of the human race.

The American disease is the assumption that when a man has exploited and used up the possibilities of one place, he has only to move
on to another place. This has made us a nation of transients, both
physically and morally, and as long as we remain so I think that we
will inhabit the earth like a plague, destroying whatever we touch.
It seems to me that our people are suffering terribly from a sort of 26
spiritual nomadism, a loss of meaningful contact with the earth and
the earth's cycles of birth, growth and death. They lack the vital
morality and spirituality that can come only from such contact: the
sense, for instance, of their dependence on the earth, and the sense
of eternal mystery surrounding life on earth, which is its ultimate and
most disciplining context.

As long as a man relates only to other men, he can be a specialist
with impunity; the illusion of the morality of "doing one's job," no
matter what the job, is still accessible to him. But if he would establish a satisfying relation to a place, the capsule of his specialization
must be broken and his commitments widen *perforce,* for the needs
of his place, his part of the earth, are not specialized, and are as far 27
as possible from the artificial, purely human contexts in which specialization is imaginable as a solution to any problem. Once he is joined
to the earth with any permanence of expectation and interest, his concerns ramify in proportion to his understanding of his dependence on
the earth and his consequent responsibility toward it. He realizes, be-

cause the demands of the place make it specific and inescapable, that his responsibility is not merely that of an underling, a worker at his job, but also moral, historical, political, aesthetic, ecological, domestic, educational, and so on.

V

What I am attempting to say is that what has come to be the common form of protest, in the anxiety and confusion of these times, is not the *only* form of protest, and that in the long run it is probably not the *best* form. I realize, of course, that there are some who have no alternative to public gestures of protest: demonstrations or draft refusal or exile. But for others there is the possibility of a protest that is more complex and permanent, public in effect but private in its motive and implementation: they can *live* in protest. I have in mind a sort of personal secession from the encroaching institutional machinery of destruction and waste and violence. Conscientious civil disobedience is the most familiar example of this, also the most dramatic, and surely all moral men must think of it as a possibility, and prepare themselves. But it is an extreme step, and in my opinion should be thought of only as a last resort. In addition to the personal sacrifice it demands, it removes one from other forms of protest; while one is involved in it, and in its consequences, one is by necessity a specialist of a sort.

Another possibility, equally necessary, and in the long run richer in promise, is to remove oneself as far as possible from complicity in the evils one is protesting, and to discover alternative possibilities. To make public protests against an evil, and yet live in dependence on and in support of the way of life that is the source of the evil, is an obvious contradiction and a dangerous one. If one disagrees with the nomadism and violence of our society, then one is under an obligation to take up some permanent dwelling place and cultivate the possibility of peace and harmlessness in it. If one deplores the destructiveness and wastefulness of the economy, then one is under an obligation to live as far out on the margin of the economy as one is able: to be economically independent of exploitive industries, to learn to need less, to waste less, to make things last, to give up meaningless luxuries, to understand and resist the language of salesmen and public relations experts, to see through attractive packages, to refuse to purchase fashion or glamour or prestige. If one feels endangered by meaninglessness, then one is under an obligation to refuse meaningless pleasure and to resist meaningless work, and to give up the moral comfort and the excuses of the mentality of specialization.

One way to do this—the way I understand—is to reject the dependences and the artificial needs of urban life, and to go into the countryside and make a home there in the fullest and most permanent sense: that is, live on and use and preserve and learn from and enrich and enjoy the land. I realize that to modern ears this sounds anachronistic and self-indulgent, but I believe on the ground of my experience that

it is highly relevant, and that it offers the possibility of a coherent and
particularized meaningfulness that is beyond the reach of the ways of
life of "average Americans." My own plans have come to involve an
idea of subsistence agriculture—which does not mean that I advocate 30
the privation and extreme hardship usually associated with such an
idea. It means, simply, that along with my other occupations I intend
to raise on my own land enough food for my family. Within the obvious limitations, I want my home to be a self-sufficient place.

But isn't this merely a quaint affectation? And isn't it a retreat
from the "modern world" and its demands, a way of "dropping out"?
I don't think so. At the very least, it is a way of dropping *in* to a concern for the health of the earth, which institutional and urban people
have had at second hand at best, and mostly have not had at all. But
the idea has other far-reaching implications, in terms of both private
benefits and public meanings. It is perhaps enough to summarize them
here by saying that when one undertakes to live fully on and from
the land the prevailing values are inverted: one's home becomes an 31
occupation, a center of interest, not just a place to stay when there is
no other place to go; work becomes a pleasure; the most menial task
is dignified by its relation to a plan and a desire; one is less dependent
on artificial pleasures, less eager to participate in the sterile nervous
excitement of movement for its own sake; the elemental realities of
seasons and weather affect one directly, and become a source of interest in themselves; the relation of one's life to the life of the world is
no longer taken for granted or ignored, but becomes an immediate
and complex concern. In other words, one begins to stay at home for
the same reasons that most people now go away.

I am writing with the assumption that this is only one of several
possibilities, and that I am obligated to elaborate this particular one
because it is the one that I know about and the one that is attractive
to me. Many people would not want to live in this way, and not want- 32
ing to seems the best reason not to. For many others it is simply not
a possibility. But for those with suitable inclinations and the necessary
abilities it is perhaps an obligation.

The presence of a sizable number of people living in this way
would, I think, have a profound influence on the life of the country and
the world. They would augment the declining number of independent
small landowners. By moving out into marginal areas abandoned by
commercial agriculture, they would restore neglected and impoverished
lands, and at the same time reduce the crowdedness of the cities. They
would not live in abject dependence on institutions and corporations, 33
hence could function as a corrective to the subservient and dependent
mentality developing among government people and in the mass life
of the cities. Their ownership would help to keep the land from being
bought up by corporations. Over a number of years, by trial and error,
they might invent a way of life that would be modest in its material
means and necessities and yet rich in pleasures and meanings, kind to

the land, intricately joined both to the human community and to the natural world—a life directly opposite to that which our institutions and corporations envision for us, but one which is more essential to the hope of peace than any international treaty.

VI

Though I have had many of these ideas consciously in mind for several years, I have found them extraordinarily difficult to write about. They are not new; other men have understood them better than I do. But there has not been much recent talk about them. Their language has been neglected, allowed to grow old-fashioned, so that in talking about them now one is always on the verge of sounding merely wishful or nostalgic or absurd. But they are ideas of great usefulness, and I am eager to have a hand in their revival. They have shown me a possibility and a promise beyond the dead end of going on as we are toward ever larger cities, in which ever more degraded and dependent and thwarted human beings stand in each other's way, breeding the fury of the world's end.

I am interested in the peace that is produced by politics because I believe that every day the holocaust is delayed gives the possibility that it will be delayed yet another day. But I am not exclusively interested in it, and I am not enthusiastic about it, because at best it is only temporary, and it is superficial, achieved always by expediency and always to the advantage of some and to the disadvantage of others. Political peace, like anything else political, is formed out of the collision of "interests," slogans, oversimplified points of view. And no matter how righteous the cause, it seems to me that a man is reduced by walking before the public with an oversimplification fastened to him. My evidence is that I have done it several times myself, and I never felt that I was doing what I was best able to do; I did not feel that there was any significant connection in what I was doing between my own life and the ideals and hopes I meant to serve. I was permitting shame to oversimplify what I thought and felt, so that I took too willingly to the crowd-comfort of slogans.

Political activity of any kind is doomed to the superficiality and temporariness of politics, able only to produce generalizations that will hold conflicting interests uneasily together for a time. But the life that attaches itself to the earth, to fulfill itself in the earth's meanings and demands, though it will certainly affect politics, will affect the earth and the earth's life even more. The land it has attached itself to will survive it, more whole for its sake. Its value will have the permanence of the earth, and be recorded in abundance.

Shame, like other hardships, must be borne. There is no handy expiation for the curious sense of guilt in having been born lucky, or in being well fed and warm and loved. To forsake life for the sake of life is to leave only a vacancy, all the old wrongs unchanged. Peaceableness and lovingness and all the other good hopes are exactly as difficult and complicated as living one's life, and can be most fully served in life's fullness.

VII

And so, difficult and troubling as the times are, I must not neglect to say that even now I experience hours when I am deeply happy and content, and hours when I feel the possibility of greater happiness and contentment than I have yet known. These times come to me when I am in the woods, or at work on my little farm. They come bearing the knowledge that the events of man are not the great events; that the
rising of the sun and the falling of the rain are more stupendous than 38
all the works of the scientists and the prophets; that man is more blessed and graced by his days than he can ever hope to know; that the wildflowers silently bloom in the woods, exquisitely shaped and scented and colored, whether any man sees and praises them or not. A music attends the things of the earth. To sense that music is to be near the possibility of health and joy.

Yet, though I know these things, I am still a member of the human race, and must share in its confusion and its fate. I cannot escape the knowledge that, though men are unable to attain the grace or the beauty of the merest flower, their destructiveness is now certainly equal to the world. Though I would only study the earth and serve it, I have
not learned to escape a hundred empty duties and distractions that 39
turn me against myself and implicate me in offenses against my own cause. Though I would sleep well and rise early, I lie awake in fear of evil. There is much of my life that I am not master of and that I see going to waste in bewilderment and subservience, lost in the driving storm of events and details.

What remains I commit to the earth. 40

Joseph Wood Krutch

Birds and Airplanes

Charles Lindbergh was recently quoted as saying that if he had to choose, he would rather have birds than airplanes. This makes a splendid addition to my list (*The American Scholar,* Spring, 1968) of pioneers in technology who lost enthusiasm for their inventions once they had been exploited: Alexander Graham Bell who wouldn't have a telephone in his house; Sloan who said he sometimes regretted that the internal combustion engine had ever been invented; and Vladimir Zworykin who, when asked his favorite TV program, replied comprehensively, "none."

Mr. Lindbergh's is a less sweeping statement. He still flies airplanes, and for us also the choice is not one we have to make. But it reminds us that there is a more general choice we do have to make, namely, that between some regard for the earth as nature made it and the determination to have faster airplanes, more development, reclamation, technology, and so forth, even though they are creating an environment more and more restricted to the mechanical and man-made along with the near extinction of every living thing except man—who flourishes (if that is the word) so exuberantly that he is on the point of trampling himself to death unless he starves or poisons himself first. How many of us would, in this symbolical sense, "choose birds"? A growing number certainly. Possibly enough, though at the present moment they do not seem to be. But at least there is no doubt that Mr. Lindbergh is among them.

When we were in the midst of our mafficking over the moon landing he was asked to comment and he chose to end with the following:

> Science and technology inform us that, after millions of years of successful evolution human life is now deteriorating genetically and environmentally at an alarming rate . . . that is why I have turned my attention from technological progress to life, from the civilized to the wild. In wildness there is a lens to the past, to the present, and to the future, offered to us for the looking—a direction, a successful selection, and an awareness of values that confronts us with the need

> for, and the means of, our salvation. Let us never forget that wildness has developed life, including the human species. By comparison, our own accomplishments are trivial.
>
> If we can combine our knowledge of science with the wisdom of wildness, if we can nurture civilization through roots in the primitive, man's potentialities appear to be unbounded. Through his evolving awareness, and his awareness of that awareness, he can merge with the miraculous—to which we can attach what better name than "God"? [*Life* Magazine, July 4, 1969]

Mr. Lindbergh's adjuration "Let us never forget that wildness has developed life, including the human species" together with his warning that "by comparison, our own accomplishments are trivial" reminds me that Thoreau used the word Wildness in this special sense and it led me to wonder if Mr. Lindbergh had chosen it for that reason. Part of
the relevant passage in Thoreau is as follows: "That West of which I 4
speak is but another name for the wild, and what I had been preparing to say is, that in wildness is the preservation of the world. Every tree sends its fibers forth in search of the wild. The cities import it at any price. Men plow and sail for it. From the forest and wilderness come the tonics and barks which brace mankind."

What I think Thoreau meant and what it is clear that Mr. Lindbergh means is that we are, after all, the creation of those forces which we know so little about that we are compelled to call them simply "Nature." Whatever else these forces may be they are not human intelligence, human contrivance, or human intentions; yet they have, nevertheless, brought us somehow from a beginning as some humble glob of macromolecular protein to the state where we are ready to
believe ourselves superior to that same "Nature," ready to cut ourselves 5
off from her entirely, and to direct evolution according to our own notions of what we should and can make ourselves become. Thoreau, again like Mr. Lindbergh, would believe now more strongly even than he did in his own rather simple society that man obviously does not know what is good for him. The American Academy of Arts and Sciences (to which I have the honor to belong) publishes a quarterly called *Daedalus* which, so I have sometimes thought, might more suggestively be entitled *Icarus.*

It is very important, I think, that the meaning of the word Nature as Thoreau and Mr. Lindbergh used it be distinguished from the more common one which refers simply to the animals, the plants, and the landscape which nature has created. And I think "trust in wildness" is a good substitute for the simple "love of nature" when we mean trust
in Nature as both the creator and sustainer of health, happiness and joy. 6
Outdoor recreation, interest in natural history, the desire to observe beauty spots are all worthy, even necessary concomitants to this deepest kind of love of Nature. But they are not in themselves enough to lead us back along the dangerous road we have been following to a more promising future.

Faith in Wildness or in Nature as a creative force has a deeper significance for our future. It is a philosophy, a faith; it is even, if you like, a religion. It puts our ultimate trust not in human intelligence but in whatever it is that created human intelligence and is, in the long run, more likely than we to solve our problems.

This is a modern version of ancient pantheism and therefore not wholly new. But it must not be confused with eighteenth- and nineteenth-century Romanticism which is, sometimes, even its antithesis. We no longer delude ourselves with the romantic notion of an all-wise and all-benevolent Nature upon whose bosom we should, but never have been willing, to rest. "Nature's kindly law" is, like that reaction against it—"Nature, red in tooth and claw," wholly inadequate to characterize that wildness which Thoreau celebrated. It is as often cruel as it is kind. No preexisting all-powerful intelligence could have conceivably planned the chaos of conflicting tendencies, problems and solutions which is the history of living things from the beginning down to the present. It is a history of frequently conflicting experiments, not the working out of any logical preconceived plan. Hence I at least cannot imagine it as directed by any intelligence superior to the outward manifestations of this evolutionary process.

And yet, in spite of the appearance of chaos and the constant conflict generated by what seem to be cross-purposes, Nature has (as even the most mechanical biologist will admit) "tended" although she never did and could not "intend." Something has been working itself out and to some of us, however difficult it may be to understand, Nature has tended towards something less simple than the so-called survival of the fittest—which after all means no more than the survival of those who survive. Reluctant as most biologists are to admit the fact, Nature has tended towards progress in two other directions. No creature met the test of mere survival more triumphantly than the sea squirt, but from the beginning of life onward the tendency has been towards a better and better chance for survival of the individual as opposed to that of the species. The higher you go in the scale, the less and less true it is that "So careful of the type she seems,/So careless of the single life." And no less significant is the fact that Nature has tended if not intended to increase the degree of consciousness in newly evolved forms and to make survival depend more and more upon conscious intelligence. How the strict theory of natural selection could account for either of these facts I do not understand, but that is no reason for refusing to acknowledge a tendency as plain as any of those which natural selection does account for. If a God did not create Nature then perhaps Nature is creating a God.

Another critical difference between the modern love of Nature and that of the Romantic poets has to do with the extent to which their celebration of Nature tends to be aesthetic rather than philosophical. Even Wordsworth's pantheism is fundamentally different from ours when he describes his God as "that being whose dwelling is the light

of setting suns" rather than, as a modern pantheist would be inclined
to say, "whose dwelling is in the mysterious proteins and even more 10
mysterious genes." But it is Coleridge who is furthest from what I take
to be the most characteristic modern view.

> O Lady! we receive but what we give
> And in our life alone does Nature live.

This makes the nature the Romantic poets celebrate a creation of man, not man's creator. A modern poet, Frost, makes the contrast in verses as clear as they are whimsical. The poem is called "Lucretius versus the Lake Poets" and is preceded by Walter Savage Landor's well-known: "Nature I loved; and next to Nature, Art."

> Dean, adult education may seem silly.
> What of it, though? I got some willy-nilly
> The other evening at your college deanery.
> And grateful for it (let's not be facetious!)
> For I thought Epicurus and Lucretius
> By Nature meant the Whole Goddam Machinery.
> But you say that in college nomenclature
> The only meaning possible for Nature
> In Landor's quatrain would be Pretty Scenery.
> Which makes opposing it to Art absurd
> I grant you—if you're sure about the word
> God bless the Dean and make his deanship plenary.*

Not long ago I had the pleasure of accompanying Mr. Lindbergh
on a short survey of Baja California, Mexico, in connection with his
work for the World Wildlife Fund, to which he now devotes his chief 11
attention. One of the things one could not help being aware of was the
fact that he is still, perhaps, the most widely known man in the whole
world and that his fame is based, not at all upon his career as a general
in the Air Force, but upon his lonely flight across the Atlantic Ocean
in 1927.

This pleasant experience of mine was before the landing on the
moon, but I doubt that the names of the astronauts are, even at this
moment, as well known as Lindbergh's, and I feel quite positive that
while the first landing on the moon will no doubt be long remembered 12
the names and personalities of the first men to make such a landing
will not.

If I am right in that guess then it raises an interesting question to
which I think the answer is rather simple: it was the man who was
most important when Lindbergh flew the ocean. And without subtract- 13
ing anything from the credit due to the extraordinary skill and daring
of the three astronauts it can hardly be denied that in their case the
relative importance of any single human being or any trio of human

*From "Lucretius versus the Lake Poets" from *The Poetry of Robert Frost,* edited by Edward Connery Lathem. Copyright 1947, © 1969, by Holt, Rinehart and Winston, Inc. Reprinted by permission of Holt, Rinehart and Winston, Inc.

beings was far less than that of science and technology. Lindbergh's flight attracted the admiration of the world because it was primarily an exhibition of human skill and of human resource, not something which depended upon advanced technology. He had an airplane but it was an ordinary airplane of the sort to which people were already accustomed. His triumph was the triumph of a man not the triumph of computers, of a large group of nearly anonymous specialists, plus the vast sums of money which had created hundreds of instruments and machines for this special purpose. Hence Lindbergh's flight made an appeal to the imagination which was so lasting that nearly fifty years later he never reveals his identity except when necessary and (as I can testify) is greeted by gasps when he is compelled to do so. Only human beings, not machines, can become heroes. Or at least that was true for my generation. Perhaps the generation now growing up has already developed an opposite reaction. Perhaps its members will admire computers and group technology more than human resource and courage. Perhaps its only hero will be those abstractions, Science and Technology, rather than human enterprise, but I hope not.

Smohalla Speaks

My young men shall never work. Men who work cannot dream, and wisdom comes in dreams.

You ask me to plow the ground. Shall I take a knife and tear my mother's breast? Then when I die she will not take me to her bosom to rest.

You ask me to dig for stone. Shall I dig under her skin for bones? Then when I die I cannot enter her body to be born again.

You ask me to cut grass and make hay and sell it, and be rich like white men. But how dare I cut off my mother's hair?

It is a bad law, and my people cannot obey it. I want my people to stay with me here. All the dead men will come to life again. We must wait here in the house of our fathers and be ready to meet them in the body of our mother.

From *The Nez Percé Indians* by Herbert J. Spinden, The American Anthropological Association, *Memoirs,* Vol. 2, part 3. Lancaster, 1908.

Crowded Signs. Courtesy of Lester Lefkowitz.

Edward Abbey

Episodes and Visions

Ranger, where is Arches National Monument?
I don't know, mister. But I can tell you where it was.

Labor Day. Flux and influx, the final visitation of the season, they
come in herds, like buffalo, down from The City. A veil of dust floats
above the sneaky snaky old road from here to the highway, drifting 1
gently downwind to settle upon the blades of the yucca, the mustard-
yellow rabbitbrush, the petals of the asters and autumn sunflowers,
the umbrella-shaped clumps of blooming wild buckwheat.

What can I tell them? Sealed in their metallic shells like molluscs
on wheels, how can I pry the people free? The auto as tin can, the
park ranger as opener. Look here, I want to say, for godsake folks get
out of them there machines, take off those fucking sunglasses and un-
peel both eyeballs, look around; throw away those goddamned idiotic
cameras! For chrissake folks what is this life if full of care we have
no time to stand and stare? eh? Take off your shoes for a while, unzip
your fly, piss hearty, dig your toes in the hot sand, feel that raw and
rugged earth, split a couple of big toenails, draw blood! Why not? Jesus
Christ, lady, roll that window down! You can't see the desert if you can't
smell it. Dusty? Of course it's dusty—this is Utah! But it's good dust, 2
good red Utahan dust, rich in iron, rich in irony. Turn that motor off.
Get out of that piece of iron and stretch your varicose veins, take off
your bassiere and get some hot sun on your old wrinkled dugs! You sir,
squinting at the map with your radiator boiling over and your fuel
pump vapor-locked, crawl out of that shiny hunk of GM junk and take
a walk—yes, leave the old lady and those squawling brats behind for
a while, turn your back on them and take a long quiet walk straight
into the canyons, get lost for a while, come back when you damn well
feel like it, it'll do you and her and them a world of good. Give the
kids a break too, let them out of the car, let them go scrambling over
the rocks hunting for rattlesnakes and scorpions and anthills—yes sir,
let them out, turn them loose; how dare you imprison little children in

your goddamned upholstered horseless hearse? Yes sir, yes madam, I entreat you, get out of those motorized wheelchairs, get off your foam rubber backsides, stand up straight like men! like women! like human beings! and walk—*walk*—WALK upon our sweet and blessed land!

"Where's the Coke machine?"

"Sorry lady, we have no Coke machine out here. Would you like a drink of water"? (She's not sure.)

"Say ranger, that's a godawful road you got in here, when the hell they going to pave it?" (They gather round, listening.)

"The day before I leave." (I say it with a smile; they laugh.)

"Well how the hell do we get out of here?"

"You just got here, sir."

"I know but how do we get out?"

"Same way you came in. It's a dead-end road."

"So we see the same scenery twice?"

"It looks better going out."

"Oh ranger, do you live in that little housetrailer down there?"

"Yes madam, part of the time. Mostly I live out of it."

"Are you married?"

"Not seriously."

"You must get awfully lonesome way out here."

"No, I have good company."

"Your wife?"

"No, myself." (They laugh; they all think I'm kidding.)

"Well what do you do for amusement?"

"Talk with the tourists." (General laughter.)

"Don't you even have a TV?"

"TV? Listen lady . . . if I saw a TV out here I'd get out my cannon and shoot it like I would a mad dog, right in the eye."

"Goodness! Why do you say that?"

"What's the principle of the TV, madam?"

"Goodness, I don't know."

"The vacuum tube, madam. And do you know what happens if you stick your head in a vacuum tube?"

"If you stick your head . . . ?"

"I'll tell you: *you get your brains sucked out.*" (Laughter!)

"Hey ole buddy, how far from here to Lubbock?"

"Where's Lubbock, sir?"

"Texas, ole buddy. Lubbock, Texas."

"Well sir, I don't know exactly how far that is but I'd guess it's not nearly far enough."

"Any dangerous animals out here, ranger?"

"Just tourists." (Laughter; tell the truth, they never believe you.)

"Where you keep these here Arches anyway?"

"What arches? All I see around here are fallen arches."

"Does it ever rain in this country, ranger?"

"I don't know, madam, I've only been here eleven years."

"Well you said yesterday it wasn't going to rain and it did rain."

"Did I? Well, that shows you can't ever trust the weather."

"You work out here all year round?"

"No sir, just for the summer."

"What do you do in the winter?"

"I rest."

"How much do you get paid for this kind of work?"

"Too much. But I give part of it back April 15th."

And then, after a brief and deadly dull lecture on the geology of
the Arches, I send them on to the campgrounds and picnic grounds—
"Be sure to let me know if you get lost"—relieved, happy and laughing. 3
It's a great country: you can say whatever you like so long as it is
strictly true—nobody will ever take you seriously.

In the evening, about suppertime, feeling somewhat guilty and
contrite—for they are, most of them, really good people and not actually
as simple-minded as they pretend to encourage me to pretend us all
to be—I visit them again around the fires and picnic tables, help them
eat their pickles and drink their beer, and make perhaps a trace of
contact by revealing that I, too, like most of them, come from that lost 4
village back in the hills, am also exiled, a displaced person, an internal
emigrant in this new America of concrete and iron which none of us
can quite understand or accept or wholly love. I may also, if I am lucky,
find one or two or three with whom I can share a little more—those
rumors from the underground where whatever hope we still have must
be found.

Among the visitors on this last big weekend are many Moabites
and other native Utahns: the Mormons, the Latter-Day Saints. Some
of my liberalized friends regard the LDS with disdain; they see in the
Church only a bastion of sectarian foolishness and political reaction 5
and in its adherents a voting bloc of Know-Nothings, racially prejudiced, religiously bigoted, opposed alike to the graduated income tax,
the United Nations, urban renewal, foreign aid, legislative reappor-
tionment, public welfare, Medicare and even free lunches for school-
children—actually or potentially a rabble of John Birchers.

What can you expect, they ask, of a sect which gave Utah a governor like J. Bracken Lee and Eisenhower a secretary of agriculture
like Ezra T. Benson? Which denies full church membership to Negroes
because they are believed to be the outcast sons of Ham? Whose patron
saint was an angel called Moroni? Whose founding father Joseph Smith
claimed to have carried about under his arms solid gold tablets which, 6
if they were the size he said they were (no one else ever saw them),
would have weighed about half a ton? (Gold a very heavy metal, specific gravity 19.3.) Whose official newspaper *The Desert News* solemnly proclaims on its masthead "We believe that the Constitution of the
United States was Divinely Inspired" but fails to explain why the Almighty changed His mind on the Eighteenth Amendment?

One can grant the accuracy of these charges without conceding that the Mormon religion is any more whimsical on points of doctrine than most other sects—the Baptists, for example, with their insistence on total immersion as a prerequisite to the salvation of the soul: All Christians must be totally immersed. (In what or for how long not being clearly specified.) Or the Jews, with their prepuce-collecting Yahweh, who created light on the first day and several days later, apparently as an afterthought, created the sun: "Six days He labored; on the seventh He was arrested." Or the Roman Catholics, with their dogmatic assertion of the physical Assumption of the Virgin Mary—launching her on a flat trajectory into outer space, like a shot off a shovel, without even a crash helmet or a pressure suit. Or the Hindus, with their sanctified ritual for nasal emunction: only one nostril may be discharged at a time, etc. Or the small-town atheist for that matter, with his Little Blue Books and sneering jokes against ancient and venerable institutions.

Leaving aside the comical aspects of their creed, one can argue that the Mormons in practice achieved a way of life in which there was much to admire, much worth saving. In addition to their pioneering migrations, full of unusual heroism and examples of fortitude (e.g., Brigham Young and his seventeen wives), the Mormons deserve respect for settling the most rugged, difficult as well as spectacular, terrain in the West. What was unusual, however, was their communitarian approach to the problems of settlement in an inhospitable environment. Their emphasis on mutual aid, cooperation and sharing was not unknown among other American communities—and indeed such qualities are vital to survival in a frontier situation—but the Mormons went about it in a far more deliberate, conscious manner, with more successful results. For example, in settling a given area they did not scatter themselves abroad over the landscape in isolated farms and ranches, each man for himself and the devil take the hindmost, but rather built small, rational, beautiful and durable towns in which all could live together, centered about the Church, which served not only as a religious center but also as a social and political focal point for the community (in this respect harking back to the model of New England). Irrigation systems were then built with the cooperative labor of all, the irrigable land divided fairly among the member families, and the back country —canyon and mesa—left open to all who might wish to engage in cattle raising, as well as farming. And nearly all did. (This formed the "open range" until the advent of large-scale fencing and the Taylor Grazing Act closed it off to all but an established few.) Each community, through the Church, also set up what we may call a public welfare service to provide sufficient and generous aid to those brought down by accident, illness, bad luck or other misfortune. In sum, the Mormons built coherent, self-sustaining communities with a vigorous common life in which all could participate, free of any great disparities in wealth, small enough to make each member important. There was even room for the dissenter and nonconformist—every town had a few jack-Mormons, those who smoked tobacco, drank tea or coffee or hard liquor, and perhaps even joined the Democratic Party.

Subsequently swamped by the new American mode, by industrialism, commercialism, urbanism, rugged and ragged individualism, the
old Mormon communities are now disappearing. But in such small
towns as Moab, Kanab, Boulder and Escalante we can still see the
handsome homes of hand-carved sandstone blocks, the quiet streets 9
lined with irrigation ditches and giant cottonwoods, the gardens and
irrigated pastures, the children riding their horses, which remind us on
the downhill side of the twentieth century of what life must have been
like back in the nineteenth. On its gentle side, that is.

As for the people themselves, at least those whom I have come
to know in and around Moab, they are generally very conservative in
their political opinions, yes, and old-fashioned in their morality, but
despite this or because of it have the usual virtues of country people:
are friendly, hospitable, honest, self-reliant and self-confident. Not very
interesting, perhaps, but good to know, good to have as friends and 10
neighbors. Capable of taking care of themselves, and with the means
to do it, it is not surprising that they question the justice of being
taxed by the Federal Government in order to help support the teeming
proletariat (literally and etymologically "the reproducers") of cities
which to some of these independent people seem as remote and foreign
as Calcutta or Cairo.

All of this is now under change, of course, and in the accelerating
process of urbanization the Mormons of Utah are already discovering
their interdependence with the rest of the nation and with the world.
Certainly in Salt Lake City itself there is no lack of intriguing social
problems—air pollution, traffic jams, angry adolescents, babies born 11
from sinlock and all the rest of it—and very soon the Latter-Day Saints
will be forced to confront directly the symptoms of discontent and
desperation with which most Americans are now familiar: from LDS
to LSD. Even unto the Land of Moab.

In the meanwhile the desert people persist in some of their quaint
and antiquated ways. Leslie McKee's wife, a sweet and kindly woman
and a pillar of the Church, tells me that she has unilaterally *bound* my
soul to hers, in accordance with the teaching of her faith, which has
provided this unusual technique for the salvation of souls which otherwise would obviously be lost and shoveled into Hell. This *binding*
means, if I understand her rightly, that when she goes to Heaven my 12
soul likewise will be dragged along like the tail of a kite, with or without my consent. And suppose she goes to Hell? She assures me that this
cannot happen, that she has already been saved and the place reserved
—for both of us. But I am not entirely set at ease; something might go
wrong. Furthermore she is a generation older than I—what about the
time factor? Is my soul to be prematurely and summarily unhouseled
in its prime, if as seems likely her demise precedes mine by some twenty

or thirty years? On this point she is uncomfortably vague. Perhaps it is all a sinister scheme to rid the world of the pagan Gentile without incurring suspicion.

However, it's too late now, Like it or not I am on my way:

We're marching to Zion,
To beautiful beautiful Zion,
We're marching upward to Zion,
The beautiful city of love.

It does not, after all, sound unpromising. God knows I have little to lose. But . . . let's not hurry. What's the rush?

Fresh snow on Tukuhnikivats and the other high peaks. They gleam like—like alabaster towers—under the noon sun and glow at evening in a soft, subtle shade of rosy pink, like mighty cones of strawberry ice cream. Very attractive. I prefer the desert.

Why? Because—there's something about the desert. Not much of an answer. There are mountain men, there are men of the sea, and there are desert rats. I am a desert rat. But why? And why, in precisely what way, is the desert more alluring, more baffling, more fascinating than either the mountains or the oceans?

The majority of the world's great spirits, from Homer to Melville and Conrad, have felt the call of the sea and responded to its power and mystery, its rhythm, antiquity and apparent changelessness. And the mountains, at least since Rousseau (anticipated by Petrarch) and that great expansion of human consciousness called the Romantic Movement, which opened up for men a whole new world of truth, have been explored and celebrated, strenuously if not adequately, by swarms of poets, novelists, scientists and frost-bitten inarticulate ("because it's there") mountain climbers. The desert, however, has been relatively neglected.

Not entirely, of course. There was T. E. Lawrence who liked the desert because, as he said, "it is clean," and another mad Englishman, C. M. Doughty—*Travels in Arabia Deserta*—who almost never came back. A few Americans have tried to understand the desert: Mary Austin in her book *Land of Little Rain*, John C. Van Dyke in an unjustly forgotten book *The Desert*, Joseph Wood Krutch with *The Voice of the Desert*, the contemporary novelists Paul Bowles and William Eastlake in part of their work (but only in an incidental way), and such obscure figures as the lad Everett Reuss, author of *On Desert Trails*, who disappeared at the age of twenty-six into the canyon country of southern Utah, never to return. This happened back in the late Thirties; his burros were found, part of his gear, but the young man himself, never. For all we know he is still down in there somewhere, living on prickly pear and wild onions, communing with the gods of river, canyon and cliff. Also deserving of mention, in this mere preliminary sketch of a desert bibliography, are the historical studies by Wallace Stegner—*Beyond the 100th Meridian* and *Mormon Country*—and of course the classic *Exploration of the Colorado River and Its Canyons* by Powell.

None of the works I have named attack directly the problem to
which I wish to address myself here: what is the peculiar quality or
character of the desert that distinguishes it, in spiritual appeal, from
other forms of landscape? In trying to isolate this peculiarity, if it
exists at all and is not simply an illusion, we must beware of a danger
well known to explorers of both the micro-and the macrocosmic—that
of confusing the thing observed with the mind of the observer, of
constructing not a picture of external reality but simply a mirror of 19
the thinker. Can this danger be avoided without falling into an opposite but related error, that of separating too deeply the observer and
the thing observed, subject and object, and again falsifying our view
of the world? There is no way out of these difficulties—you might as
well try running Cataract Canyon without hitting a rock. Best to launch
forth boldly, with or without life jackets, keep your matches dry and
pray for the best.

The restless sea, the towering mountains, the silent desert—what
do they have in common? and what are the essential differences? Gran-
deur, color, spaciousness, the power of the ancient and elemental, that
which lies beyond the ability of man to wholly grasp or utilize, these
qualities all three share. In each there is the sense of something ultimate, 20
with mountains exemplifying the brute force of natural processes, the
sea concealing the richness, complexity and fecundity of life beneath
a surface of huge monotony, and the desert—what does the desert
say?

The desert says nothing. Completely passive, acted upon but never
acting, the desert lies there like the bare skeleton of Being, spare,
sparse, austere, utterly worthless, inviting not love but contemplation. 21
In its simplicity and order it suggests the classical, except that the
desert is a realm beyond the human and in the classicist view only the
human is regarded as significant or even recognized as real.

Despite its clarity and simplicity, however, the desert wears at
the same time, paradoxically, a veil of mystery. Motionless and silent 22
it evokes in us an elusive hint of something unknown, unknowable,
about to be revealed. Since the desert does not act it seems to be waiting—but waiting for what?

In sailing the ocean we reach the other shore and find, as we
should have expected, everything much the same on either side. During
the voyage we see only the unvarying expanse of heaving green or
gray, and empty sky, and not very much of either—the horizon at sea
is only twelve miles away. In other words the journey is the central 23
thing, the expectation of what is to come; the ocean itself is merely a
medium of travel. (Only a trip by air or space is more abstract, more
synthetic, from the passenger's point of view. When and if our astronauts are actually launched off to the moon or Mars through the cold
black and white of space they will, I predict, be expertly drugged beforehand—how else could they endure the coffinlike confinement, the
static surroundings, of such a venture?) The most appealing part of

the sea, in fact, is its meeting with the land; it is the *seashore* which men love and not the ocean itself. (We are not writing here of the seafarer's trade, or of the underwater world.)

In climbing a mountain, if we persevere, we reach the summit; we get, you might say, to the point. Once on the mountaintop there is nothing to do but come down again; the weather up there is usually too hostile for delay; the situation is not suitable for reflection and meditation. Descending the mountain we enter by degrees into a friendlier, more comfortable, more human environment—forest, rushing streams, sunny meadows—and soon hear the cowbells, see the villages and roads, all that is familiar and reassuring.

The desert is different. Not so hostile as the snowy peaks, nor so broad and bland as the ocean's surface, it lies open—given adequate preparation—to leisurely exploration, to extended periods of habitation. Yet it can hardly be called a humane environment, what little human life there is will be clustered about the oases, natural or man-made. The desert waits outside, desolate and still and strange, unfamiliar and often grotesque in its forms and colors, inhabited by rare, furtive creatures of incredible hardiness and cunning, sparingly colonized by weird mutants from the plant kingdom, most of them as spiny, thorny, stunted and twisted as they are tenacious.

There is something about the desert that the human sensibility cannot assimilate, or has not so far been able to assimilate. Perhaps that is why it has scarcely been approached in poetry or fiction, music or painting; every region of the United States except the arid West has produced distinguished artists or has been represented in works of art which have agreed-upon general significance. Only the hacks rush in where genius hesitates to tread, and the baffling reality is lost behind the dust clouds thrown up by herds of Zane Greys and Ferde Grofés, by the anonymous painters of sugar-sweet landscapes and Roman-Indian portraits that clutter up certain galleries, and by those tough old humorous retired cowladies whose memoirs are so lovingly reprinted by the regional university presses—*No Life for a Lady, No High Adobe, No Time for Tea, No Sin in the Saddle,* etc. Behind the dust, meanwhile, under the vulture-haunted sky, the desert waits—mesa, butte, canyon, reef, sink, escarpment, pinnacle, maze, dry lake, sand dune and barren mountain—untouched by the human mind.

Even after years of intimate contact and search this quality of strangeness in the desert remains undiminished. Transparent and intangible as sunlight, yet always and everywhere present, it lures a man on and on, from the red-walled canyons to the smoke-blue ranges beyond, in a futile but fascinating quest for the great, unimaginable treasure which the desert seems to promise. Once caught by this golden lure you become a prospector for life, condemned, doomed, exalted. One begins to understand why Everett Reuss kept going deeper and deeper into the canyon country, until one day he lost the thread of labyrinth; why the oldtime prospectors, when they did find the common sort of gold, gambled, drank and whored it away as quickly as possible and returned to the burnt hills and the search. The search for what? They could not have said; neither can I; and would have muttered something about silver, gold, copper—anything as a pretext. And how could they hope to find this treasure which has no name and has never been seen? Hard to say—and yet, when they found it, they could not fail to recognize it. Ask Everett Reuss.

Where is the heart of the desert? I used to think that somewhere
in the American Southwest, impossible to say exactly where, all of
these wonders which intrigue the spirit would converge upon a climax
—and resolution. Perhaps in the vicinity of Weaver's Needle in the
Superstition Range; in the Funeral Mountains above Death Valley; in
the Smoke Creek Desert of Nevada; among the astonishing monoliths
of Monument Valley; in the depths of Grand Canyon; somewhere along 28
the White Rim under Grandview Point; in the heart of the Land of
Standing Rocks. Not so. I am convinced now that the desert has no
heart, that it presents a riddle which has no answer, and that the riddle
itself is an illusion created by some limitation of exaggeration of the
displaced human consciousness.

This at least is what I tell myself when I fix my attention on what
is rational, sensible and realistic, believing that I have overcome at
last that gallant infirmity of the soul called romance—that illness, that
disease, that insidious malignancy which must be chopped out of the
heart once and for all, ground up, cooked, burnt to ashes . . . con- 29
sumed. And for so long as I stay away from the desert, keep to the
mountains or the sea or the city, it is possible to think myself cured.
Not easy: one whiff of juniper smoke, a few careless words, one reck-
less and foolish poem—*The Wasteland,* for instance—and I become as
restive, irritable, brooding and dangerous as a wolf in a cage.

In answer to the original question, then, I find myself in the end
returning to the beginning, and can only say, as I said in the first 30
place: There is *something* about the desert . . . There is something
there which the mountains, no matter how grand and beautiful, lack;
which the sea, no matter how shining and vast and old, does not have.

Minor points on the same issue: I like horses. There is no place
for horses on the ocean; and in the mountains you will learn that mules,
generally speaking, are more useful. Also, of course, the people: though
rare as radium you find, if you can find them, a superior breed in the
deserts—consider the Bedouin, the Kazaks and Kurds, the Mongols, the 31
Apaches, the Kalahari, the Aborigines of Australia. Mountain people
tend to become inbred and degenerate and no one for a long time
has lived in the sea. As for those others, the wretched inhabitants of
city and plain, can we even think of them, to be perfectly candid, as
members of the same race?

Revealing my desert thoughts to a visitor one evening, I was accused of being against civilization, against science, against humanity. Naturally I was flattered and at the same time surprised, hurt, a little shocked.

He repeated the charge. But how, I replied, being myself a member of humanity (albeit involuntarily, without prior consultation), could I be against humanity without being against myself, whom I love—though not very much; how can I be against science, when I gratefully admire, as much as any man, Thales, Democritus, Aristarchus, Faustus, Paracelsus, Copernicus, Galileo, Kepler, Newton, Darwin and Einstein; and finally, how could I be against civilization when all which I most willingly defend and venerate—including the love of wilderness—is comprehended by the term?

We were not communicating very well. All night long we thrashed the matter out, burning up half a pinyon pine in the process, transforming its mass into energy, warmth, light, and toward morning worked out a rough agreement. With his help I discovered that I was not opposed to mankind but only to mancenteredness, anthropocentricity, the opinion that the world exists solely for the sake of man; not to science, which means simply knowledge, but to science misapplied, to the worship of technique and technology, and to that perversion of science properly called scientism; and not to civilization but to culture.

As an example of scientism he suggested the current superstition that science has lengthened the human life-span. One might as well argue that science, meaning technology, has actually reduced the average man's life expectancy to about fifteen minutes—the time it takes an ICBM to cover the distance between the U.S.S.R. and the U.S.A. The superstition, my visitor pointed out, is based on a piece of trickery, statistical sleight-of-hand: e.g., in a primitive culture without modern medical techniques, perhaps half of all the babies born die within the first year of infancy; the remainder survive and live for the normal, usual seventy years; taking the total born and dividing by the number of full-lived survivors, the statistician announces that the average life expectancy at birth for the members of this hypothetical society is thirty-five years. Confusing life expectancy with life-span, the gullible begin to believe that medical science has accomplished a miracle—lengthened human life! And persist in believing it, even though the Old Testament, written more than three thousand years ago, refers to "three score and ten" as being the typical number of years allotted to mortal man. The heroes, naturally, lived far longer, and not in that condition of medicated survival found in a modern hospital where the patient, technically still alive cannot easily be distinguished from the various machines to which he is connected. But this is now familiar stuff, common knowledge—why kick around a dead horse? Far more interesting is the distinction to be made between civilization and culture.

Culture, we agreed, means the way of life of any given human society considered as a whole. It is an anthropological term referring always to specific, identifiable societies localized in history and place, and includes all aspects of such organizations—their economy, their art, their religion. The U.S.A., for example, is not a civilization but a culture, as is the U.S.S.R., and both are essentially *industrial* cultures, the former in the mode of monopoly capitalism, the latter in the mode of state socialism or communism; if they seem to be competing against each other it is not because they are different but because they are basically so much alike; and the more they compete the more alike they become: MERGING TRAFFIC AHEAD.

Civilization on the other hand, while undoubtedly a product of various historical cultures, and as a category one which overlaps what we label culture, is by no means identical with culture. Cultures can exist with little or no trace of civilization; and usually do; but civilization while dependent upon culture for its sustenance, as the mind depends upon the body, is a semi-independent entity, precious and fragile, drawn through history by the finest threads of art and idea, a process or series of events without formal structure or clear location in time and space. It is the conscious forefront of evolution, the brotherhood of great souls and the comradeship of intellect, a *corpus mysticum,* The 36
Invisible Republic open to all who wish to participate, a democratic aristocracy based not on power or institutions but on isolated men—Lao-Tse, Chuang-Tse, Guatama, Diogenes, Euripides, Socrates, Jesus, Wat Tyler and Jack Cade, Paine and Jefferson, Blake and Burns and Beethoven, John Brown and Henry Thoreau, Whitman, Tolstoy, Emerson, Mark Twain, Rabelais and Villon, Spinoza, Voltaire, Spartacus, Nietzsche and Thomas Mann, Lucretius and Pope John XXIII, and ten thousand other poets, revolutionaries and independent spirits, both famous and forgotten, alive and dead, whose heroism gives to human life on earth its adventure, glory and significance.

To make the distinction unmistakably clear:

Civilization is the vital force in human history; culture is that inert mass of institutions and organizations which accumulate around and tend to drag down the advance of life;

Civilization is Giordano Bruno facing death by fire; culture is the Cardinal Bellarmino, after ten years of inquisition, sending Bruno to the stake in the Campo di Fiori;

Civilization is Sartre; culture Cocteau; 37

Civilization is Steinbeck in his youth and prime; culture is an old, soft man with the same name;

Civilization is mutual aid and self-defense; culture is the judge, the lawbook and the forces of Law & Ordure;

Civilization is uprising, insurrection, revolution; culture is the war of state against state, or of machines against people, as in Hungary and Vietnam;

Civilization is tolerance, detachment and humor, or passion, anger, revenge; culture is the entrance examination, the gas chamber, the doctoral dissertation and the electric chair;

Civilization is the Ukrainian peasant Nestor Makhno fighting the Germans, then the Reds, then the Whites, then the Reds again; culture is Stalin and the Fatherland;

Civilization is Jesus turning water into wine; culture is Christ walking on the waves;

Civilization is a youth with a Molotov cocktail in his hand; culture is the Soviet tank or the L.A. cop that guns him down;

Civilization is the wild river; culture, 592,000 tons of cement;

Civilization flows; culture thickens and coagulates, like tired, sick, stifled blood.

In the morning my visitor, whose name I didn't quite catch, crawled into his sack and went to sleep. I had to go to work. I went back to see him in the evening but he was gone, leaving behind only a forged signature in the registration book which wouldn't have fooled anybody —J. Prometheus Birdsong. He won't be back.

But don't get discouraged, comrades—Christ failed too.

Now here comes another clown with a scheme for the utopian national park: Central Park National Park, Disneyland National Park. Look here, he says, what's the matter with you fellows?—let's get cracking with this dump. Your road is bad; pave it. Better yet, build a paved road to every corner of the park; better yet, pave the whole damned place so any damn fool can drive anything anywhere—is this a democracy or ain't it? Next, charge a good stiff admission fee; you can't let people in free; that leads to socialism and regimentation. Next, get rid of all these homely rangers in their Smokey the Bear suits. Hire a crew of pretty girls, call them rangerettes, let them sell the tickets and give the campfire talks. And advertise, for godsake, advertise! How do you expect to get people in here if you don't advertise? Next, these here Arches—light them up. Floodlight them, turn on colored, revolving lights—jazz it up, man, it's dead. Light up the whole place, all night long, get on a 24-hour shift, keep them coming, keep them moving, you got two hundred million people out there waiting to see your product—is this a free country or what the hell is it? Next your campgrounds, you gotta do something about your campgrounds, they're a mess. People can't tell where to park their cars or which spot is whose —you gotta paint lines, numbers, mark out the campsites nice and neat. And they're still building fires on the ground with wood! Very messy, filthy, wasteful. Set up little grills on stilts, sell charcoal briquettes, better yet hook up with the gas line, install jets and burners. Better yet do away with the campgrounds altogether, they only cause delay and congestion and administrative problems—these people want to see America, they're not going to see it sitting around a goddamned campfire; take their money, give them the show, send them on their way—that's the way to run a business. . . .

I exaggerate. Slightly. Was he real or only a bad dream? Am I awake or sleeping? Will Tuesday never come? No wonder they call it Labor Day.

The holiday is over and a strange sweet stillness, better than any music, soars above the Arches. Gratefully I empty the overflowing garbage cans, read the soggy old newspapers—we believe that the Con-

stitution of the United States has finally expired—collect the scattered
beer cans and soda pop cans and burn them, along with the garbage,
in the dump. (Hastens oxidation.)

The magpies and jays squawk among the pinyon pines, which are
heavy-laden with clusters of light-green, rosin-sticky, fresh, fat cones—
we'll have a good crop of pine nuts this year. A variety of asters are
blooming along the road and among the dunes; with yellow centers
and vivid purple petals, the flowers stand out against their background 43
of rock and coral-red sand with what I can only describe as an existential assertion of life; they are almost audible. Heidegger was wrong, as
usual; man is *not* the only living thing that *exists*. He might well have
taken a tip from a fellow countryman: *Wovon man nicht spraechen
Kann, darueber muss man schweigen.*

Also the chamisa, bright and stinking as rancid butter; and the
mule-eared sunflowers, enjoying a great autumnal renascence; and the
wild buckwheat, the matchweed, the yellow borage, and on the mountain slopes a league away, the preliminary golden dying of the aspens. 44
Like a fire ignited in the spring, smoldering through the terrible summer, my desert world flares up briefly and brilliantly before the coming of cold and snow, the ashy winter, for the last time this season.

Even the night has changed. Over a late campfire, kept going now
for heat as well as liturgical requirements, I see new constellations 45
dominating the sky. Instead of Draco, Lyra, Sagittarius and vast Scorpio,
a different group is moving in and taking over:

Cassiopeia, the big "W," symbolizing—what? Who? In the year
1572 a temporary star appeared near this constellation bright enough
to be seen in full sunshine, throwing all the Christians of Europe into
uproar. With good reason; they had much to be fearful of, the swine.
Only seventeen years earlier they had burned alive Bishops Ridley and
Latimer at Oxenford; a year later Archbishop Cranmer and 277 other
religious leaders were also burned, also in Merrie England; only twelve
years earlier they had hanged twelve hundred Huguenots at Amboise; 46
ten years earlier an unrecorded number were massacred at Vassy, followed by more religious wars culminating in the St. Bartholomew's
Massacre of August 24, 1572. Something about trans-substantiation, con-
substantiation and whether or not infants are damned at birth or not
until later. *Gloria in Excelsis Deo*. . . . Now the high priests of nuclear
physics dispute about the number of electrons that can rotate on the
point of a pin—where will this lead? But their disputes are peaceful;
only the bystanders get burned nowadays.

Not far from Cassiopeia is Pegasus, for the Greeks a winged horse,
to the Phoenicians the emblem of a ship. According to some astronomers
the major stars of this constellation are approaching us at an inconceiv- 47
able speed. According to other astronomers, however, these same stars
are receding from us at an inconceivable speed. Opinions on the matter
are revised, exchanged, forgotten and revived with comforting regularity, just as in the other "hard" or exact sciences.

Linked to Pegasus by one star is Andromeda, the chained lady, low in the eastern sky. Within this constellation, visible to the naked eye, is a great nebula, the first to be discovered. Seen through my 7 by 50 binoculars it is a splendid sight—a cloud of glory.

And there is the Water Carrier, the Sea Goat, the Ram, the Whale and last, least and most obscure Musca the Fly, about halfway between Aries and the Pleiades, hard to see, scorned by the astrologers, neglected by all but me, a tiny group so far away that they may be already extinct, dead, extinguished, reminding us only by these last dim signals of their former existence.

So much for the stars. Why, a man could lose his mind in those incomprehensible distances. Is there intelligent life on other worlds? Ask rather, is there intelligent life on earth? There are mysteries enough right here in America, in Utah, in the canyons.

Had a letter today. Bob Waterman is coming from Aspen with his beard, his Land Rover and one hundred and fifty feet of new nylon rope. We are finally going to have a look into The Maze.

Paul Ehrlich

Eco-Catastrophe!

The end of the ocean came late in the summer of 1979, and it came
even more rapidly than the biologists had expected. There had been
signs for more than a decade, commencing with the discovery in 1968
that DDT slows down photosynthesis in marine plant life. It was announced in a short paper in the technical journal, *Science*, but to ecolo- 1
gists it smacked of doomsday. They knew that all life in the sea depends
on photosynthesis, the chemical process by which green plants bind the
sun's energy and make it available to living things. And they knew that
DDT and similar chlorinated hydrocarbons had polluted the entire
surface of the earth, including the sea.

But that was only the first of many signs. There had been the final
gasp of the whaling industry in 1973, and the end of the Peruvian
anchovy fishery in 1975. Indeed, a score of other fisheries had disappeared quietly from over-exploitation and various eco-catastrophes
by 1977. The term "eco-catastrophe" was coined by a California ecologist in 1969 to describe the most spectacular of man's attacks on the
systems which sustain his life. He drew his inspiration from the Santa
Barbara offshore oil disaster of that year, and from the news which 2
spread among naturalists that virtually all of the Golden State's seashore bird life was doomed because of chlorinated hydrocarbon inter-
ference with its reproduction. Eco-catastrophes in the sea became
increasingly common in the early 1970's. Mysterious "blooms" of previously rare microorganisms began to appear in offshore waters. Red
tides—killer outbreaks of a minute single-celled plant—returned to the
Florida Gulf coast and were sometimes accompanied by tides of other
exotic hues.

It was clear by 1975 that the entire ecology of the ocean was changing. A few types of phytoplankton were becoming resistant to chlorinated hydrocarbons and were gaining the upper hand. Changes in the 3
phytoplankton community led inevitably to changes in the community
of zooplankton, the tiny animals which eat the phytoplankton. These
changes were passed on up the chains of life in the ocean to the herring,

plaice, cod and tuna. As the diversity of life in the ocean diminished, its stability also decreased.

Other changes had taken place by 1975. Most ocean fishes that returned to fresh water to breed, like the salmon, had become extinct, their breeding streams so dammed up and polluted that their powerful homing instinct only resulted in suicide. Many fishes and shellfishes that bred in restricted areas along the coasts followed them as onshore pollution escalated.

By 1977 the annual yield of fish from the sea was down to 30 million metric tons, less than one-half the per capita catch of a decade earlier. This helped malnutrition to escalate sharply in a world where an estimated 50 million people per year were already dying of starvation. The United Nations attempted to get all chlorinated hydrocarbon insecticides banned on a worldwide basis, but the move was defeated by the United States. This opposition was generated primarily by the American petrochemical industry, operating hand in glove with its subsidiary, the United States Department of Agriculture. Together they persuaded the government to oppose the U. N. move—which was not difficult since most Americans believed that Russia and China were more in need of fish products than was the United States. The United Nations also attempted to get fishing nations to adopt strict and enforced catch limits to preserve dwindling stocks. This move was blocked by Russia, who, with the most modern electronic equipment, was in the best position to glean what was left in the sea. It was, curiously, on the very day in 1977 when the Soviet Union announced its refusal that another ominous article appeared in *Science*. It announced that incident solar radiation had been so reduced by worldwide air pollution that serious effects on the world's vegetation could be expected.

Apparently it was a combination of ecosystem destabilization, sunlight reduction, and a rapid escalation in chlorinated hydrocarbon pollution from massive Thanodrin applications which triggered the ultimate catastrophe. Seventeen huge Soviet-financed Thanodrin plants were operating in underdeveloped countries by 1978. They had been part of a massive Russian "aid offensive" designed to fill the gap caused by the collapse of America's ballyhooed "Green Revolution."

It became apparent in the early '70s that the "Green Revolution" was more talk than substance. Distribution of high yield "miracle" grain seeds had caused temporary local spurts in agricultural production. Simultaneously, excellent weather had produced record harvests. The combination permitted bureaucrats, especially in the United States Department of Agriculture and the Agency for International Development (AID), to reverse their previous pessimism and indulge in an outburst of optimistic propaganda about staving off famine. They raved about the approaching transformation of agriculture in the underdeveloped countries (UDCs). The reason for the propaganda reversal was never made clear. Most historians agree that a combination of utter ignorance of ecology, a desire to justify past errors, and pressure from agro-industry (which was eager to sell pesticides, fertilizers, and farm machinery to the UDCs and agencies helping the UDCs) was behind the campaign. Whatever the motivation, the results were clear. Many concerned people, lacking the expertise to see through the Green Revolution drivel, relaxed. The population-food crisis was "solved."

But reality was not long in showing itself. Local famine persisted in northern India even after good weather brought an end to the ghastly Bihar famine of the mid-'60s. East Pakistan was next, followed by a
resurgence of general famine in northern India. Other foci of famine 8
rapidly developed in Indonesia, the Philippines, Malawi, the Congo, Egypt, Colombia, Ecuador, Honduras, the Dominican Republic, and Mexico.

Everywhere hard realities destroyed the illusion of the Green Revolution. Yields dropped as the progressive farmers who had first accepted the new seeds found that their higher yields brought lower prices—effective demand (hunger plus cash) was not sufficient in poor countries to keep prices up. Less progressive farmers, observing this, refused to make the extra effort required to cultivate the "miracle" grains. Transport systems proved inadequate to bring the necessary fertilizer to the fields where the new and extremely fertilizer-sensitive grains were being grown. The same systems were also inadequate to move produce to markets. Fertilizer plants were not built fast enough,
and most of the underdeveloped countries could not scrape together 9
funds to purchase supplies, even on concessional terms. Finally, the inevitable happened, and pests began to reduce yields in even the most carefully cultivated fields. Among the first were the famous "miracle rats" which invaded Philippine "miracle rice" fields early in 1969. They were quickly followed by many insects and viruses, thriving on the relatively pest-susceptible new grains, encouraged by the vast and dense plantings, and rapidly acquiring resistance to the chemicals used against them. As chaos spread until even the most obtuse agriculturists and economists realized that the Green Revolution had turned brown, the Russians stepped in.

In retrospect it seems incredible that the Russians, with the American mistakes known to them, could launch an even more incompetent program of aid to the underdeveloped world. Indeed, in the early 1970's there were cynics in the United States who claimed that outdoing the stupidity of American foreign aid would be physically impossible. Those critics were, however, obviously unaware that the 10
Russians had been busily destroying their own environment for many years. The virtual disappearance of sturgeon from Russian rivers caused a great shortage of caviar by 1970. A standard joke among Russian scientists at that time was that they had created an artificial caviar which was indistinguishable from the real thing—except by taste. At any rate the Soviet Union, observing with interest the progressive deterioration of relations between the UDCs and the United States, came up with a solution. It had recently developed what it claimed was the

ideal insecticide, a highly lethal chlorinated hydrocarbon complexed with a special agent for penetrating the external skeletal armor of insects. Announcing that the new pesticide, called Thanodrin, would truly produce a Green Revolution, the Soviets entered into negotiations with various UDCs for the construction of massive Thanodrin factories. The USSR would bear all the costs; all it wanted in return were certain trade and military concessions.

It is interesting now, with the perspective of years, to examine in some detail the reasons why the UDCs welcomed the Thanodrin plan with such open arms. Government officials in these countries ignored the protests of their own scientists that Thanodrin would not solve the problems which plagued them. The governments now knew that the basic cause of their problems was overpopulation, and that these problems had been exacerbated by the dullness, daydreaming, and cupidity endemic to all governments. They knew that only population control and limited development aimed primarily at agriculture could have spared them the horrors they now faced. They knew it, but they were not about to admit it. How much easier it was simply to accuse the Americans of failing to give them proper aid; how much simpler to accept the Russian panacea.

And then there was the general worsening of relations between the United States and the UDCs. Many things had contributed to this. The situation in America in the first half of the 1970's deserves our close scrutiny. Being more dependent on imports for raw materials than the Soviet Union, the United States had, in the early 1970's, adopted more and more heavy-handed policies in order to insure continuing supplies. Military adventures in Asia and Latin America had further lessened the international credibility of the United States as a great defender of freedom—an image which had begun to deteriorate rapidly during the pointless and fruitless Viet-Nam conflict. At home, acceptance of the carefully manufactured image lessened dramatically, as even the more romantic and chauvinistic citizens began to understand the role of the military and the industrial system in what John Kenneth Galbraith had aptly named "The New Industrial State."

At home in the USA the early '70s were traumatic times. Racial violence grew and the habitability of the cities diminished, as nothing substantial was done to ameliorate either racial inequities or urban blight. Welfare rolls grew as automation and general technological progress forced more and more people into the category of "unemployable." Simultaneously a taxpayers' revolt occurred. Although there was not enough money to build the schools, roads, water systems, sewage systems, jails, hospitals, urban transit lines, and all the other amenities needed to support a burgeoning population, Americans refused to tax themselves more heavily. Starting in Youngstown, Ohio in 1969 and followed closely by Richmond, California, community after community was forced to close its schools or curtail educational operations for lack of funds. Water supplies, already marginal in quality and quantity in many places by 1970, deteriorated quickly. Water rationing occurred in 1723 municipalities in the summer of 1974, and hepatitis and epidemic dysentery rates climbed about 500 per cent between 1970-1974.

Air pollution continued to be the most obvious manifestation of environmental deterioration. It was, by 1972, quite literally in the eyes of all Americans. The year 1973 saw not only the New York and Los Angeles smog disasters, but also the publication of the Surgeon General's massive report on air pollution and health. The public had been partially prepared for the worst by the publicity given to the U.N. pollution conference held in 1972. Deaths in the late '60s caused by smog were well known to scientists, but the public had ignored them because they mostly involved the early demise of the old and sick
rather than people dropping dead on the freeways. But suddenly our 14
citizens were faced with nearly 200,000 corpses and massive documentation that they could be the next to die from respiratory disease. They were not ready for that scale of disaster. After all, the U.N. conference had not predicted that accumulated air pollution would make the planet uninhabitable until almost 1990. The population was terrorized as TV screens became filled with scenes of horror from the disaster areas. Especially vivid was NBC's coverage of hundreds of unattended people choking out their lives outside of New York's hospitals. Terms like nitrogen oxide, acute bronchitis and cardiac arrest began to have real meaning for most Americans.

The ultimate horror was the announcement that chlorinated hydrocarbons were now a major constituent of air pollution in all American cities. Autopsies of smog disaster victims revealed an average chlorinated hydrocarbon load in fatty tissue equivalent to 26 parts per million of DDT. In October, 1973, the Department of Health, Education and Welfare announced studies which showed unequivocally that increasing death rates from hypertension, cirrhosis of the liver, liver cancer and a series of other diseases had resulted from the chlorinated hydrocarbon load. They estimated that Americans born since 1946 (when DDT usage began) now had a life expectancy of only 49 years, and predicted that if current patterns continued, this expectancy would reach 42 years by
1980, when it might level out. Plunging insurance stocks triggered a 15
stock market panic. The president of Velsicol, Inc., a major pesticide producer, went on television to "publicly eat a teaspoonful of DDT" (it was really powdered milk) and announce that HEW had been infiltrated by Communists. Other giants of the petrochemical industry, attempting to dispute the indisputable evidence, launched a massive pressure campaign on Congress to force HEW to "get out of agriculture's business." They were aided by the agro-chemical journals, which had decades of experience in misleading the public about the benefits and dangers of pesticides. But by now the public realized that it had been duped. The Nobel Prize for medicine and physiology was given to Drs. J. L. Radomski and W. B. Deichmann, who in the late 1960's had pioneered in the documentation of the long-term lethal effects of

chlorinated hydrocarbons. A Presidential Commission with unimpeachable credentials directly accused the agro-chemical complex of "condemning many millions of Americans to an early death." The year 1973 was the year in which Americans finally came to understand the direct threat to their existence posed by environmental deterioration.

And 1973 was also the year in which most people finally comprehended the indirect threat. Even the president of Union Oil Company and several other industrialists publicly stated their concern over the reduction of bird populations which had resulted from pollution by DDT and other chlorinated hydrocarbons. Insect populations boomed because they were resistant to most pesticides and had been freed, by the incompetent use of those pesticides, from most of their natural enemies. Rodents swarmed over crops, multiplying rapidly in the absence of predatory birds. The effect of pests on the wheat crop was especially disastrous in the summer of 1973, since that was also the year of the great drought. Most of us can remember the shock which greeted the announcement by atmospheric physicists that the shift of the jet stream which had caused the drought was probably permanent. It signalled the birth of the Midwestern desert. Man's air-polluting activities had by then caused gross changes in climatic patterns. The news, of course, played hell with commodity and stock markets. Food prices skyrocketed, as savings were poured into hoarded canned goods. Official assurances that food supplies would remain ample fell on deaf ears, and even the government showed signs of nervousness when California migrant field workers went out on strike again in protest against the continued use of pesticides by growers. The strike burgeoned into farm burning and riots. The workers, calling themselves "The Walking Dead," demanded immediate compensation for their shortened lives, and crash research programs to attempt to lengthen them.

It was in the same speech in which President Edward Kennedy, after much delay, finally declared a national emergency and called out the National Guard to harvest California's crops, that the first mention of population control was made. Kennedy pointed out that the United States would no longer be able to offer any food aid to other nations and was likely to suffer food shortages herself. He suggested that, in view of the manifest failure of the Green Revolution, the only hope of the UDCs lay in population control. His statement, you will recall, created an uproar in the underdeveloped countries. Newspaper editorials accused the United States of wishing to prevent small countries from becoming large nations and thus threatening American hegemony. Politicians asserted that President Kennedy was a "creature of the giant drug combine" that wished to shove its pills down every woman's throat.

Among Americans, religious opposition to population control was very slight. Industry in general also backed the idea. Increasing poverty in the UDCs was both destroying markets and threatening supplies of raw materials. The seriousness of the raw material situation had been brought home during the Congressional Hard Resources hearings in

1971. The exposure of the ignorance of the cornucopian economists had been quite a spectacle—a spectacle brought into virtually every American's home in living color. Few would forget the distinguished geologist from the University of California who suggested that economists be legally required to learn at least the most elementary facts of geology. Fewer still would forget that an equally distinguished Harvard economist added that they might be required to learn some economics, too. 18
The overall message was clear: America's resource situation was bad and bound to get worse. The hearings had led to a bill requiring the Departments of State, Interior, and Commerce to set up a joint resource procurement council with the express purpose of "insuring that proper consideration of American resource needs be an integral part of American foreign policy."

Suddenly the United States discovered that it had a national consensus: population control was the only possible salvation of the underdeveloped world. But that same consensus led to heated debate. How could the UDCs be persuaded to limit their populations, and should not the United States lead the way by limiting its own? Members of the intellectual community wanted America to set an example. They pointed out that the United States was in the midst of a new baby boom: her birth rate, well over 20 per thousand per year, and her growth rate of over one per cent per annum were among the very highest of the developed countries. They detailed the deterioration of the Ameri- 19
can physical and psychic environments, the growing health threats, the impending food shortages, and the insufficiency of funds for desperately needed public works. They contended that the nation was clearly unable or unwilling to properly care for the people it already had. What possible reason could there be, they queried, for adding any more? Besides, who would listen to requests by the United States for population control when that nation did not control her own profligate reproduction?

Those who opposed population controls for the U. S. were equally vociferous. The military-industrial complex, with its all-too-human mixture of ignorance and avarice, still saw strength and prosperity in numbers. Baby food magnates, already worried by the growing nitrate pollution of their products, saw their market disappearing. Steel manufacturers saw a decrease in aggregate demand and slippage for that 20
holy of holies, the Gross National Product. And military men saw, in the growing population-food-environment crisis, a serious threat to their carefully nurtured Cold War. In the end, of course, economic arguments held sway, and the "inalienable right of every American couple to determine the size of its family," a freedom invented for the occasion in the early '70s, was not compromised.

The population control bill, which was passed by Congress early in 1974, was quite a document, nevertheless. On the domestic front, it authorized an increase from 100 to 150 million dollars in funds for "family planning" activities. This was made possible by a general feeling in the country that the growing army on welfare needed family planning. But the gist of the bill was a series of measures designed to impress the need for population control on the UDCs. All American aid to countries with overpopulation problems was required by law to consist in part of population control assistance. In order to receive any assistance each nation was required not only to accept the population control aid, but also to match it according to a complex formula. "Over-population" itself was defined by a formula based on U. S. statistics, and the UDCs were required not only to accept aid, but also to show progress in reducing birth rates. Every five years the status of the aid program for each nation was to be re-evaluated.

The reaction to the announcement of this program dwarfed the response to President Kennedy's speech. A coalition of UDCs attempted to get the U. N. General Assembly to condemn the United States as a "genetic aggressor." Most damaging of all to the American cause was the famous "25 Indians and a dog" speech by Mr. Shankarnarayan, Indian Ambassador to the U. N. Shankarnarayan pointed out that for several decades the United States, with less than six per cent of the people of the world had consumed roughly 50 per cent of the raw materials used every year. He described vividly America's contribution to worldwide environmental deterioration, and he scathingly denounced the miserly record of United States foreign aid as "unworthy of a fourth-rate power, let alone the most powerful nation on earth."

It was the climax of his speech, however, which most historians claim once and for all destroyed the image of the United States. Shank-arnarayan informed the assembly that the average American family dog was fed more animal protein per week than the average Indian got in a month. "How do you justify taking fish from protein-starved Peruvians and feeding them to your animals?" he asked. "I contend," he concluded, "that the birth of an American baby is a greater disaster for the world than that of 25 Indian babies." When the applause had died away, Mr. Sorensen, the American representative, made a speech which said essentially that "other countries look after their own self-interest, too." When the vote came, the United States was condemned.

This condemnation set the tone of U.S.-UDC relations at the time the Russian Thanodrin proposal was made. The proposal seemed to offer the masses in the UDCs an opportunity to save themselves and humiliate the United States at the same time; and in human affairs, as we all know, biological realities could never interfere with such an opportunity. The scientists were silenced, the politicians said yes, the Thanodrin plants were built, and the results were what any beginning ecology student could have predicted. At first Thanodrin seemed to offer excellent control of many pests. True, there was a rash of human fatalities from improper use of the lethal chemical, but, as Russian technical advisors were prone to note, these were more than compen-sated for by increased yields. Thanodrin use skyrocketed throughout the underdeveloped world. The Mikoyan design group developed a dependable, cheap agricultural aircraft which the Soviets donated to the effort in large numbers. MIG sprayers became even more common in UDCs than MIG interceptors.

Then the troubles began. Insect strains with cuticles resistant to Thanodrin penetration began to appear. And as streams, rivers, fish culture ponds and onshore waters became rich in Thanodrin, more fisheries began to disappear. Bird populations were decimated. The sequence of events was standard for broadcast use of a synthetic pesticide: great success at first, followed by removal of natural enemies and development of resistance by the pest. Populations of crop-eating insects in areas treated with Thanodrin made steady comebacks and soon became more abundant than ever. Yields plunged, while farmers in their desperation increased the Thanodrin dose and shortened the time between treatments. Death from Thanodrin poisoning became common. The first violent incident occurred in the Canete Valley of Peru, where 25
farmers had suffered a similar chlorinated hydrocarbon disaster in the mid-'50s. A Russian advisor serving as an agricultural pilot was assaulted and killed by a mob of enraged farmers in January, 1978. Trouble spread rapidly during 1978, especially after the word got out that two years earlier Russia herself had banned the use of Thanodrin at home because of its serious effects on ecological systems. Suddenly Russia, and not the United States, was the *bête noir* in the UDCs. "Thanodrin parties" became epidemic, with farmers, in their ignorance, dumping carloads of Thanodrin concentrate into the sea. Russian advisors fled, and four of the Thanodrin plants were leveled to the ground. Destruction of the plants in Rio and Calcutta led to hundreds of thousands of gallons of Thanodrin concentrate being dumped directly into the sea.

Mr. Shankarnarayan again rose to address the U.N., but this time it was Mr. Potemkin, representative of the Soviet Union, who was on the hot seat. Mr. Potemkin heard his nation described as the greatest mass killer of all time as Shankarnarayan predicted at least 30 million 26
deaths from crop failures due to overdependence on Thanodrin. Russia was accused of "chemical aggression," and the General Assembly, after a weak reply by Potemkin, passed a vote of censure.

It was in January, 1979, that huge blooms of a previously unknown variety of diatom were reported off the coast of Peru. The blooms were accompanied by a massive die-off of sea life and of the pathetic remainder of the birds which had once feasted on the anchovies of the area. Almost immediately another huge bloom was reported in the Indian ocean, centering around the Seychelles, and then a third in the 27
South Atlantic off the African coast. Both of these were accompanied by spectacular die-offs of marine animals. Even more ominous were growing reports of fish and bird kills at oceanic points where there were no spectacular blooms. Biologists were soon able to explain the phenomena: the diatom had evolved an enzyme which broke down Thanodrin; that enzyme also produced a breakdown product which interfered with the transmission of nerve impulses, and was therefore

lethal to animals. Unfortunately, the biologists could suggest no way of repressing the poisonous diatom bloom in time. By September, 1979, all important animal life in the sea was extinct. Large areas of coastline had to be evacuated, as windrows of dead fish created a monumental stench.

But stench was the least of man's problems. Japan and China were faced with almost instant starvation from a total loss of the seafood on which they were so dependent. Both blamed Russia for their situation and demanded immediate mass shipments of food. Russia had none to send. On October 13, Chinese armies attacked Russia on a broad front. . . .

A pretty grim scenario. Unfortunately, we're a long way into it already. Everything mentioned as happening before 1970 has actually occurred; much of the rest is based on projections of trends already appearing. Evidence that pesticides have long-term lethal effects on human beings has started to accumulate, and recently Robert Finch, Secretary of the Department of Health, Education and Welfare expressed his extreme apprehension about the pesticide situation. Simultaneously the petrochemical industry continues its unconscionable poison-peddling. For instance, Shell Chemical has been carrying on a high-pressure campaign to sell the insecticide Azodrin to farmers as a killer of cotton pests. They continued their program even though they know that Azodrin is not only ineffective, but often *increases* the pest density. They've covered themselves nicely in an advertisement which states, "Even if an overpowering migration [sic] develops, the flexibility of Azodrin lets you regain control fast. Just increase the dosage according to label recommendations." It's a great game—get people to apply the poison and kill the natural enemies of the pests. Then blame the increased pests on "migration" and sell even more pesticide!

Right now fisheries are being wiped out by over-exploitation, made easy by modern electronic equipment. The companies producing the equipment know this. They even boast in advertising that only their equipment will keep fishermen in business until the final kill. Profits must obviously be maximized in the short run. Indeed, Western society is in the process of completing the rape and murder of the planet for economic gain. And, sadly, most of the rest of the world is eager for the opportunity to emulate our behavior. But the underdeveloped peoples will be denied that opportunity—the days of plunder are drawing inexorably to a close.

Most of the people who are going to die in the greatest cataclysm in the history of man have already been born. More than three and a half billion people already populate our moribund globe, and about half of them are hungry. Some 10 to 20 million will starve to death *this year.* In spite of this, the population of the earth will increase by 70 million souls in 1969. For mankind has artificially lowered the death rate of the human population, while in general birth rates have remained high. With the input side of the population system in high gear

and the output side slowed down, our fragile planet has filled with people at an incredible rate. It took several million years for the population to reach a total of two billion people in 1930, while a *second two billion will have been added by 1975!* By that time some experts feel 31
that food shortages will have escalated the present level of world hunger and starvation into famines of unbelievable proportions. Other experts, more optimistic, think the ultimate food-population collision will not occur until the decade of the 1980's. Of course more massive famine may be avoided if other events cause a prior rise in the human death rate.

Both worldwide plague and thermonuclear war are made more probable as population growth continues. These, along with famine, make up the trio of potential "death rate solutions" to the population problem—solutions in which the birth rate-death rate imbalance is redressed by a rise in the death rate rather than by a lowering of the birth rate. Make no mistake about it, *the imbalance will be redressed.* 32
The shape of the population growth curve is one familiar to the biologist. It is the outbreak part of an outbreak-crash sequence. A population grows rapidly in the presence of abundant resources, finally runs out of food or some other necessity, and crashes to a low level or extinction. Man is not only running out of food, he is also destroying the life support systems of the Spaceship Earth. The situation was recently summarized very succinctly: "It is the top of the ninth inning. Man, always a threat at the plate, has been hitting Nature hard. It is important to remember, however, that Nature bats last."

Questions and Quotations for Discussion and Writing Assignments

I

1. How does our garbage symbolize our values? How is the automobile a fitting symbol of American romanticism and values?
2. What, more than anything else, stands in the way of solving the problem of getting rid of wastes and garbage?
3. In his article on the Collyer brothers, Robert Cowley quotes from two authorities who attempt to explain "collecting mania." Which explanation seems most suited to the Collyer brothers' behavior? Are the Collyer brothers neurotic extensions of some quality found in lesser degrees in most men—the desire to surround themselves with things?
4. What does the death of the Collyer brothers signify about man and his possessions?
5. What is the meaning of the famous quotation from Emerson, "Things are in the saddle,/And ride mankind"?
6. In the next to last paragraph, Cowley, describing the "junk" brought from the Collyers' apartment, remarks that the tunnels in the rooms had become "alimentary burrows." Is this an apt metaphor?

7. How do possessions enrich our lives? How can they impoverish our lives? How rich and fulfilling were the lives of the Collyer brothers? Is it possible that possessions can cut man off from human contacts? What kinds of weapons were found in the Collyer brothers' house?
8. How, as Wendell Berry insists, does citizenship begin at home? What is the difference between the dependence of a man's household on the U. S. government and its dependence on the earth? Why is it wrong "to assert that a man owes an allegiance that is antecedent to his allegiance to his household, or higher than his allegiance to the earth"?
9. Berry believes that man's informed conscience provides a better response to moral circumstances than the law does. Why? Law is a tool of government. What are Berry's attitudes toward government?
10. Wendell Berry links our national acts of violence abroad and at home to "our warfare against the natural life of the continent." How, in his opinion, are these two kinds of violence related? Do you agree that they are related?
11. Berry's essay is complex and subtle, the work of a man who has thought long and hard about ways to live a moral, fulfilling life. Even though he has found a way on a small farm in Kentucky, he is still troubled by fears that in seeking his own contentment he may be turning his back on the larger community to which he has a responsibility. He is torn between his desire for a private life and his strong social conscience. How does he resolve this dilemma?
12. Berry believes that public protests against the machine called government can become as stiff and inflexible as the machine itself. What kinds of private protest does he advocate for concerned people? Is his own life style a protest? How? Against what?
13. Describe the joys and pleasures Berry finds in his life on the farm. He writes that "the presence of a sizable number of people living in this way [on the land] would . . . have a profound influence on the life of the country and the world." What form would this influence take? Is Berry realistic in his view or is he a romantic dreamer? Is he advocating a return to a preindustrial, agricultural economy? Does the life he lives and recommends appeal to you?
14. In Berry's opinion "the great causes of peace and brotherhood are being served these days with increasing fanaticism, obsessiveness, self-righteousness, and anger." Do you agree? Berry worries that the supporters of causes "are becoming specialists, like preachers and generals." Why does Berry dislike "specialists" and "experts"?
15. The following statement seems to summarize many of the points Wendell Berry wishes to make about private conscience and public responsibility: "It seems to me inescapable that before a man can usefully promote an idea, the idea must be implemented in his own life." How does Berry implement his beliefs in his own life? What examples can you give of people who promote an idea but do not live by it?
16. One of the chief "diseases" in America, Berry says, is "nomadism"; Americans are transients who move from place to place without making commitments to the places in which they live. Do you agree? Can people

who live in "mobile homes" or people who move from apartment to apartment ever develop a sense of place? Are they cut off from the realities and strengths of the earth?

17. Do you agree with Berry's theory that, as they have moved into the cities and from place to place, Americans have lost a vital source of morality and inner peace? Would the nation be healthier and morally stronger if more people followed Berry's advice and returned to the land? If life on the land, on the farm, is so good, why have so many people left the farms and gone to the cities?
18. How is Wendell Berry's attitude toward the earth different from that of the "nature lover" who takes long walks in the woods and knows the names of birds, flowers, and trees?
19. To Joseph Wood Krutch man has come to the point where he will have to choose, symbolically, between birds and airplanes. Are there any indications that man will choose birds?
20. What is the meaning of Charles Lindbergh's adjuration, "Let us never forget that wildness has developed life, including the human species"?
21. Man is a product of Nature's evolutionary forces; his human intelligence is also a product of that process. Has our intelligence made us, as Krutch says, "ready to believe ourselves superior to that same 'Nature,' ready to cut ourselves off from her entirely, and to direct evolution according to our own notions of what we should and can make ourselves become"? Is anything created by man's intelligence "unnatural"? If man's intelligence itself is a natural development, then how can it conceive of anything that is not natural? How would you define "unnatural"?
22. Krutch writes that "Nature has tended towards progress in two directions." What are they? Explain Krutch's statement that "If a God did not create Nature then perhaps Nature is creating a God." What evidence does Krutch offer to explain why he personally does not believe in a creator of the universe, a creator with superior intelligence. What is the difference between saying that Nature "tends" to do something and that Nature "intends" to do it?
23. What are Edward Abbey's attitudes toward tourists and automobiles as revealed in "Episodes and Visions"?
24. Even though he laughs at certain aspects of the Mormon religion, Abbey admires "their communitarian approach to the problem of settlement in an inhospitable environment." What in their "approach" attracts him and wins his admiration?
25. Edward Abbey loves the desert. Why does he love it? Why does he love it better than the mountains or the oceans? He says that the desert is a giant riddle beyond the comprehension of human consciousness. How might this mysterious quality of the desert be like a magnet in its attraction?
26. Explain in your own words the distinction between "culture" and "civilization."
27. A careful reading of "Episodes and Visions" reveals that it has more coherence than at first appears. It begins with a discussion of the crowds

that come to Arches National Monument on Labor Day and ends with their departure at the close of the holiday weekend. How do the middle sections of the essay relate to the beginning and the end of it? How does the dialogue between the tourists and the ranger make almost the same point as the later list of differences between culture and civilization? How does the section on the Mormon culture tie in with the section on culture and civilization? How does the desert as a symbol bring together the qualities of life that Abbey admires? What kind of people does he like?

28. "The end of the ocean came late in the summer of 1979," writes Paul Ehrlich. What evidence suggests that his prediction is coming true? Is there evidence to the contrary?
29. What roles do Russia and the U. S. play in Ehrlich's scenario of ecological catastrophe? How do political decisions by these world powers affect the ecology of the rest of the world? What does Ehrlich think of governments in general?
30. In Ehrlich's picture of eco-catastrophe, politics and human greed seem to be the great enemies of the earth. How, in his scenario, do economic interests insure the continued use of DDT after it is proved harmful, even fatal? How, in your opinion, do politics and greed contribute to environmental imbalance?
31. Is there any evidence that Ehrlich's prophecies will not come true? Is overpopulation a real threat? Has it been checked?
32. How effective is Ehrlich's scenario? What makes it effective? Is he just another man walking down the street carrying a sign saying "YE ARE DOOMED," or does he seem credible?

II

1. As a rule of thumb, the bigger a city gets, the less livable it is. . . .

   BOB PACKWOOD

2. We need the tonic of wilderness, to wade sometimes in the marshes where the bittern and the meadow hen lurk, and hear the booming of the snipe. . . .

   HENRY DAVID THOREAU

3. If you've seen one redwood tree, you've seen them all.

   RONALD REAGAN

4. The significance of the natural areas that environmentalists endeavor to preserve in countryside, public forests, national parks, and wild life refuges does not lie in any function of these places as resorts, playgrounds, or meccas for tourists. It lies in their vital contribution to man's understanding of himself as a being essentially related to his fellow men, to all the other forms of life, to the transgalactic universe, and to reality as a whole.

   ANTHONY WAYNE SMITH

5. There is no beast on earth nor fowl that flieth, but the same are a people like unto you, and to God they shall return.

   THE KORAN

6. Ask now the beasts and they shall teach thee; and the fowls of the air, and they shall teach thee:
   Or speak to the earth, and it shall teach thee and the fishes of the sea shall teach thee.
   Who knoweth not in all these that the hand of the Lord hath wrought this?
   In whose hand is the soul of every living thing, and the breath of all mankind.

   BOOK OF JOB

7. An apology to an already overpopulated society for our third, and final, child.

   BIRTH ANNOUNCEMENT

8. To anyone who thinks in biological as well as in economic, political and sociological terms, it is self-evident that a society that practices death control must at the same time practice birth control—that the corollary of hygiene and preventive medicine is contraception.

   ALDOUS HUXLEY

9. For the vital question, in the end, is not simply how many stomachs the earth can feed, but how mankind is going to live—the quality of life.

   ROLF EDBERG

10. American house pets are fed, each day, a diet that is nutritionally better balanced than the diet of almost half of the world's human population.

    TONY WAGNER

11. One generation plants the trees—another gets the shade.

    CHINESE PROVERB

12. We know now that a generation has risked posterity for the sake of prosperity.

    ADLAI E. STEVENSON III

13. Have we become a nation of people who would sell the sunset if someone would put a price on it?

    ROBERT AND LEONA TRAIN RIENOW

14. . . . . growth for the sake of growth is the ideology of the cancer cell.

    EDWARD ABBEY

15. It is my belief that only the flat rejection of war-as-usual, profits-as-usual, comforts-as-usual, and politics-as-usual thinking will save this planet from its quickening slide into environmental disaster. . . .

    SENATOR VANCE HARTKE

16. And God blessed them, and God said unto them, Be fruitful, and multiply, and replenish the earth, and subdue it: and have dominion over the fish of the sea, and over the fowls of the air, and over every living thing that moveth upon the earth.

    GENESIS I: 28

17. For that which befalleth the sons of men befalleth the beast; even one thing befalleth them: as the one dieth, so dieth the other; yea, they have all one breath; so that a man hath no preeminence above a beast; for all is vanity.

    ECCLESIASTES III: 19

18. The earth does not care what we do to it. Some day it may expel us, but pollution exists only in our minds.

    JACK CARPENTER

19. What we need, actually is a revolution in consciousness. The ecological crisis stems from a lack of reverence for life, and that goes a long way back.

    STEPHANIE MILLS

20. The physical environment of our nation is not only the reflection of our aspirations as a people, it is our human habitat. If we fail to sustain it, it is an inexorable law of nature that it will fail to sustain us.

    STEWART L. UDALL

21. Empty space does not necessarily mean room for population expansion.

    PAUL R. EHRLICH

22. . . . perhaps there is more hope now. We sense that our continued failure to control ourselves has placed man, himself, on the endangered species list. We fear that if we do not go out with a bang or a whimper, it may be with a cough. We have reached for the moon and beyond, and looking back through space we have been confronted by the insignificance of the planet which sustains us. . . .

    ADLAI E. STEVENSON III

SECTION VI Doors of Education, Doors of Perception

Something is wrong with our schools! We learned that from the hard lessons of the last few years. Critics have enumerated specific grievances against the school system, many of which are justified. To make the schools responsive to the needs of the students and the nation, reforms are necessary; or, for those to whom "reforms" seems a soft, mushy word, let us concede that radical changes may be necessary. Before we radically alter the schools, however, we should perhaps ask ourselves what citizens of a democracy need and want to learn. Or better: What does the human organism need to learn in order to thrive and grow to full maturity? If we think seriously about these questions, we have already begun to change the schools.

For the slave, Frederick Douglass, learning to read was the first step toward freedom from bondage. Both he and his master knew that learning to read would "unfit him to be a slave" and that knowledge abolishes the "white man's power to perpetuate the enslavement of the black man." Douglass's experience provides a clue to what people *need* to learn—whatever will make them politically, socially, and personally free.

Any society generates the controls necessary for it to run smoothly; the governmental machine "socializes" people for the purposes of control, exploitation, or merely to make them acquiescent. A bureaucratized society tends to socialize its citizens by giving them roles to play; these roles are those required for maintaining or perpetuating the bureaucracy. Individual consciousness and the state's assigned roles can become one and the same if the citizens allow it. Learning and education, however, can prevent the rigid socialization of individuals by teaching them to think for themselves and by encouraging them to say exactly what they think, even if they wish only to criticize the system. If people are to reason for themselves, they will need to develop what Neil Postman and Charles Weingartner call a shockproof "crap detector," a sensitive instrument that will free them from slavery to lies, slogans, superstitions, bureaucratic double-talk, and related "crap." A free society must be a community of adults, independent in spirit, responsible for their moral decisions, capable of making choices; these adults must have the skills of social, political, and cultural criticism. Only when they learn these skills will they cease to "venerate crap," as Postman and Weingartner put it, and begin to seek something better.

Learning, then, has a profoundly important public or social dimension. It also has what we might call a personal, subjective dimension. One idea that emerged from the struggles of the 1960's is that many students *want* to learn things about themselves and their personal relationships with others that are not discussed in textbooks and classrooms. To these students much of what is taught in the schools is irrelevant to their personal needs and life styles. Classes are fifty-minute hours that range in interest from the soporific to the scintillating, while college is a safe community in which to experiment with alternative ways of knowing, learning, and perceiving—through the use of drugs, meditation, the study of mysticism, nonverbal communication, and group encounters.

Some call these experiments fads and insist that what students want to learn is of little importance. What they need to know, these critics reason, is how to perform well in a job: education as job training. Students do, of course, fall for fads, and perhaps they do need to acquire job skills. (Where should they acquire these skills is the important question.) Nevertheless, the desire to expand one's knowledge of one's inner self, one's feelings, or one's perceptions is not mere fashion: to the ancient Greeks, "Know thyself" was a maxim to live by. The young, perhaps more than most, are self-obsessed because they are at an age when self is not well defined, and a place where the boundaries of the ego are not sharply delineated. The only escape from this self-obsession is self-knowledge.

But there is a world of difference between the dizzying, kaleidoscopic, exhileration of the drug "high" and the serious exploration of the landscapes of consciousness. Carlos Castaneda learned from the Yaqui sorcerer Don Juan what many men have learned before him: To know oneself is not easy; it requires discipline, diligence, and even a sense of ritual. True self-knowledge, awareness, or expanded consciousness should manifest itself in what Peter Marin calls "intelligent activity" and even provide the energy source for the crap detector we discussed above. Unless one retreats into a private sanctuary away from the society of men in order to meditate, or into the private, cartoon world of the drug freak, one must test the validity and value of self-knowledge in personal confrontation with the people and the institutions of the community. For finally, one cannot meditate social change; and the "Oh! Wow!" of the tripper will not eliminate poverty and injustice.

Neil Postman
and Charles Weingartner

Crap Detecting

"In 1492, COLUMBUS DISCOVERED AMERICA. . . ." Starting from this disputed fact, each one of us will describe the history of this country in a somewhat different way. Nonetheless, it is reasonable to assume that most of us would include something about what is called the "democratic process," and how Americans have valued it, or at least have said they valued it. Therein lies a problem: one of the tenets of a democratic society is that men be allowed to think and express themselves freely on any subject, even to the point of speaking out against the idea of a democratic society. To the extent that our schools are instruments of such a society, they must develop in the young not only an awareness of this freedom but a will to exercise it, and the intellectual power and perspective to do so effectively. This is necessary so that the society may continue to change and modify itself to meet unforeseen threats, problems, and opportunities. Thus, we can achieve what John Gardner calls an "ever-renewing society."

So goes the theory.

In practice, we mostly get a different story. In our society, as in others, we find that there are influential men at the head of important institutions who cannot afford to be found wrong, who find change inconvenient, perhaps intolerable, and who have financial or political interests they must conserve at any cost. Such men are, therefore, threatened in many respects by the theory of the democratic process and the concept of an ever-renewing society. Moreover, we find that there are obscure men who do *not* head important institutions who are similarly threatened because they have identified themselves with certain ideas and institutions which they wish to keep free from either criticism or change.

Such men as these would much prefer that the schools do little or nothing to encourage youth to question, doubt, or challenge any part of the society in which they live, especially those parts which are most vulnerable. "After all," say the practical men, "they are *our* schools,

and they ought to promote *our* interests, and *that* is part of the democratic process, too." True enough; and here we have a serious point of conflict. Whose schools are they, anyway, and whose interests should they be designed to serve? We realize that these are questions about which any self-respecting professor of education could write several books, each one beginning with a reminder that the problem is not black or white, either/or, yes or no. But if you have read our introduction, you will not expect us to be either professorial or prudent. We are, after all, trying to suggest strategies for survival as they may be
developed in our schools, and the situation requires emphatic responses. 4
We believe that the schools must serve as the principal medium for developing in youth the attitudes and skills of social, political, and cultural criticism. No. That is not emphatic enough. Try this: In the early 1960s, an interviewer was trying to get Ernest Hemingway to identify the characteristics required for a person to be a "great writer." As the interviewer offered a list of various possibilities, Hemingway disparaged each in sequence. Finally, frustrated, the interviewer asked, "Isn't there any one essential ingredient that you can identify?" Hemingway replied, "Yes, there is. In order to be a great writer a person must have a built-in, shockproof crap detector."

It seems to us that, in his response, Hemingway identified an essential survival strategy and the essential function of the schools in today's world. One way of looking at the history of the human group is that it has been a continuing struggle against the veneration of "crap." Our intellectual history is a chronicle of the anguish and suffering of men
who tried to help their contemporaries see that some part of their 5
fondest beliefs were misconceptions, faulty assumptions, superstitions, and even outright lies. The mileposts along the road of our intellectual development signal those points at which some person developed a new perspective, a new meaning, or a new metaphor. We have in mind a new education that would set out to cultivate just such people—experts at "crap detecting."

There are many ways of describing this function of the schools, and many men who have. David Riesman, for example, calls this the "counter-cyclical" approach to education, meaning that schools should stress values that are not stressed by other major institutions in the culture. Norbert Wiener insisted that the schools now must function as "anti-entropic feedback systems," "entropy" being the word used to
denote a general and unmistakable tendency of all systems—natural 6
and man-made—in the universe to "run down," to reduce to chaos and uselessness. This is a process that cannot be reversed but that can be slowed down and partly controlled. One way to control it is through "maintenance." This is Eric Hoffer's term, and he believes that the quality of maintenance is one of the best indices of the quality of life in a culture. But Wiener uses a different metaphor to get at the same idea. He says that in order for there to be an anti-entropic force, we

must have adequate feedback. In other words, we must have instruments to tell us when we are running down, when maintenance is required. For Wiener, such instruments would be people who have been educated to recognize change, to be sensitive to problems caused by change, and who have the motivation and courage to sound alarms when entropy accelerates to a dangerous degree. This is what we mean by "crap detecting." It is also what John Gardner means by the "ever-renewing society," and what Kenneth Boulding means by "social self-consciousness." We are talking about the schools' cultivating in the young that most "subversive" intellectual instrument—the anthropological perspective. This perspective allows one to be part of his own culture and, at the same time, to be out of it. One views the activities of his own group as would an anthropologist, observing its tribal rituals, its fears, its conceits, its ethnocentrism. In this way, one is able to recognize when reality begins to drift too far away from the grasp of the tribe.

We need hardly say that achieving such a perspective is extremely difficult, requiring, among other things, considerable courage. We are, after all, talking about achieving a high degree of freedom from the intellectual and social constraints of one's tribe. For example, it is generally assumed that people of other tribes have been victimized by indoctrination from which our tribe has remained free. Our own outlook seems "natural" to us, and we wonder that other men can perversely persist in believing nonsense. Yet, it is undoubtedly true that, for most people, the acceptance of a particular doctrine is largely attributable to the accident of birth. They might be said to be "ideologically interchangeable," which means that they would have accepted any set of doctrines that happened to be valued by the tribe to which they were born. Each of us, whether from the American tribe, Russian tribe, or Hopi tribe, is born into a symbolic environment as well as a physical one. We become accustomed very early to a "natural" way of talking, and being talked to, about "truth." Quite arbitrarily, one's perception of what is "true" or real is shaped by the symbols and symbol-manipulating institutions of his tribe. Most men, in time, learn to respond with fervor and obedience to a set of verbal abstractions which they feel provides them with an ideological identity. One word for this, of course, is "prejudice." None of us is free of it, but it is the sign of a competent "crap detector" that he is not completely captivated by the arbitrary abstractions of the community in which he happened to grow up.

In our own society, if one grows up in a language environment which includes and approves such a concept as "white supremacy," one can quite "morally" engage in the process of murdering civil-rights workers. Similarly, if one is living in a language environment where the term "black power" crystallizes an ideological identity, one can engage, again quite "morally," in acts of violence against any nonblack persons or their property. An insensitivity to the unconscious effects of our "natural" metaphors condemns us to highly constricted perceptions of how things are and, therefore, to highly limited alternative modes of behavior.

Those who *are* sensitive to the verbally built-in biases of their "natural" environment seem "subversive" to those who are not. There is probably nothing more dangerous to the prejudices of the latter than a man in the process of discovering that the language of his group is
limited, misleading, or onesided. Such a man is dangerous because he 9
is not easily enlisted on the side of one ideology or another, because he sees beyond the words to the processes which give an ideology its reality. In his *May Man Prevail?*, Erich Fromm gives us an example of a man (himself) in the process of doing just that:

> The Russians believe that they represent socialism because they talk in terms of Marxist ideology, and they do not recognize how similar their system is to the most developed form of capitalism. We in the West believe that we represent the system of individualism, private initiative, and humanistic ethics, because we hold on to *our* ideology, and we do not see that our institutions have, in fact, in many ways become more and more similar to the hated system of communism.

Religious indoctrination is still another example of this point. As Alan Watts has noted: "Irrevocable commitment to any religion is not only intellectual suicide; it is positive unfaith because it closes the mind to any new vision of the world. Faith is, above all, openness—an act of trust in the unknown." And so "crap detecting" requires a perspective
on what Watts calls "the standard-brand religions." That perspective 10
can also be applied to knowledge. If you substitute the phrase "set of facts" for the word "religion" in the quotation above, the statement is equally important and accurate.

The need for this kind of perspective has always been urgent but never so urgent as now. We will not take you again through that painful catalogue of twentieth-century problems we cited in our Introduction. There are, however, three particular problems which force us to
conclude that the schools must consciously remake themselves into 11
training centers for "subversion." In one sense, they are all one problem but for purposes of focus may be distinguished from each other.

The first goes under the name of the "communications revolution," or media change. As Father John Culkin of Fordham University likes to say, a lot of things have happened in this century and most of them plug into walls. To get some perspective on the electronic plug, imagine that your home and all the other homes and buildings in your neighborhood have been cordoned off, and from them will be removed all the
electric and electronic inventions that have appeared in the last 50 12
years. The media will be substracted in reverse order, with the most recent going first. The first thing to leave your house, then, is the television set—and everybody will stand there as if they are attending the funeral of a friend, wondering, "What are we going to do tonight?"

After rearranging the furniture so that it is no longer aimed at a blank space in the room, you suggest going to the movies. But there won't be any. Nor will there be LP records, tapes, radio, telephone, or telegraph. If you are thinking that the absence of the media would only affect your entertainment and information, remember that, at some point, your electric lights would be removed, and your refrigerator, and your heating system, and your air conditioner. In short, you would have to be a totally different person from what you are in order to survive for more than a day. The chances are slim that you could modify yourself and your patterns of living and believing fast enough to save yourself. As you were expiring, you would at least know something about how it was before the electric plug. Or perhaps you wouldn't. In any case, if you had energy and interest enough to hear him, any good ecologist could inform you of the logic of your problem: a change in an environment is rarely only additive or linear. You seldom, if ever, have an old environment *plus* a new element, such as a printing press or an electric plug. *What you have is a totally new environment requiring a whole new repertoire of survival strategies.* In no case is this more certain than when the new elements are technological. Then, in no case will the new environment be more radically different from the old than in political and social forms of life. When you plug something into a wall, someone is getting plugged into you. Which means you need new patterns of defense, perception, understanding, evaluation. You need a new kind of education.

It was George Counts who observed that technology repealed the Bill of Rights. In the eighteenth century, a pamphlet could influence an entire nation. Today all the ideas of the Noam Chomskys, Paul Goodmans, Edgar Friedenbergs, I. F. Stones, and even the William Buckleys, cannot command as much attention as a 30-minute broadcast by Walter Cronkite. Unless, of course, one of them were given a prime-time network program, in which case he would most likely come out more like Walter Cronkite than himself. Even Marshall McLuhan, who is leading the field in understanding media, is having his ideas transformed and truncated by the forms of the media to fit present media functions. (One requirement, for example, is that an idea or a man must be "sensational" in order to get a hearing; thus, McLuhan comes out not as a scholar studying media but as the "Apostle of the Electronic Age.")

We trust it is clear that we are not making the typical, whimpering academic attack on the media. We are not "against" the media. Any more, incidentally, than McLuhan is "for" the media. You cannot reverse technological change. Things that plug in are here to stay. But you can study media, with a view toward discovering what they are doing to you. As McLuhan has said, there is no inevitability so long as there is a willingness to contemplate what is happening.

Very few of us have contemplated more rigorously what is happening through media change than Jacques Ellul, who has sounded

some chilling alarms. Without mass media, Ellul insists, there can be no effective propaganda. With them, there is almost nothing but. "Only through concentration of a large number of media in a few hands can one attain a true orchestration, a continuity, and an application of scientific methods of influencing individuals." That such concentration is occurring daily, Ellul says, is an established fact, and its results may
well be an almost total homogenization of thought among those the 15
media reach. We cannot afford to ignore Norbert Wiener's observation of a paradox that results from our increasing technological capability in electronic communication: as the number of messages increases, the amount of information carried decreases. We have more media to communicate fewer significant ideas.

Still another way of saying this is that, while there has been a tremendous increase in media, there has been, at the same time, a decrease in available and viable "democratic" channels of communication because the mass media are entirely one-way communication. For example, as a means of affecting public policy, the town meeting is dead. Significant community action (without violence) is increasingly rare. A small printing press in one's home, as an instrument of social change, is absurd. Traditional forms of dissent and protest seem impractical, e.g., letters to the editor, street-corner speeches, etc. No one can reach many people unless he has access to the mass media. As this is written, for example, there is no operational two-way communication possible with respect to United States policies and procedures in Vietnam. The communication is virtually all one way: from the top down,
via the mass media, especially TV. The pressure on everyone is to sub- 16
scribe without question to policies formulated in the Pentagon. The President appears on TV and clearly makes the point that anyone who does not accept "our policy" can be viewed only as lending aid and comfort to the enemy. The position has been elaborately developed in all media that "peaceniks" are failing in the obligation to "support our boys overseas." The effect of this process on all of us is to leave no alternative but to accept policy, act on orders from above, and implement the policy without question or dialogue. This is what Edgar Friedenberg calls "creeping Eichmannism," a sort of spiritless, mechanical, abstract functioning which does not allow much room for individual thought and action.

As Paul Goodman has pointed out, there are many forms of censorship, and one of them is to deny access to "loudspeakers" to those with dissident ideas, or even *any* ideas. This is easy to do (and not
necessarily conspiratorial) when the loudspeakers are owned and oper- 17
ated by mammoth corporations with enormous investments in their proprietorship. What we get is an entirely new politics, including the possibility that a major requirement for the holding of political office be prior success as a show-business personality. Goodman writes in *Like a Conquered Province:*

> The traditional American sentiment is that a decent society cannot be built by dominant official policy anyway, but only by grassroots resistance, community cooperation, individual enterprise, and citizenly vigilance to protect liberty. . . . *The question is whether or not our beautiful libertarian, pluralist, and populist experiment is viable in modern conditions.* If it's not, I don't know any other acceptable politics, and I am a man without a country.

Is it possible that there are millions becoming men without a country? Men who are increasingly removed from the sources of power? Men who have fewer and fewer ideas available to them, and fewer and fewer ways of expressing themselves meaningfully and effectively? Might the frustration thus engendered be one of the causes of the increasing use of violence as a form of statement?

We come then to a second problem which makes necessary a "subversive" role for the schools. This one may appropriately be called the "Change Revolution." In order to illustrate what this means, we will use the media again and the metaphor of a clock face. Imagine a clock face with 60 minutes on it. Let the clock stand for the time men have had access to writing systems. Our clock would thus represent something like 3,000 years, and each minute on our clock 50 years. On this scale, there were no significant media changes until about nine minutes ago. At that time, the printing press came into use in Western culture. About three minutes ago, the telegraph, photograph and locomotive arrived. Two minutes ago: the telephone, rotary press, motion pictures, automobile, airplane, and radio. One minute ago, the talking picture. Television has appeared in the last ten seconds, the computer in the last five, and communications satellites in the last second. The laser beam—perhaps the most potent medium of communication of all—appeared only a fraction of a second ago.

It would be possible to place almost any area of life on our clock face and get roughly the same measurements. For example, in medicine, you would have almost no significant changes until about one minute ago. In fact, until one minute ago, as Jerome Frank has said, almost the whole history of medicine is the history of the placebo effect. About a minute ago, antibiotics arrived. About ten seconds ago, open-heart surgery. In fact, within the past ten seconds there probably have been more changes in medicine than is represented by all the rest of the time on our clock. This is what some people call the "knowledge explosion." It is happening in every field of knowledge susceptible to scientific inquiry.

The standard reply to any comment about change (for example, from many educators) is that change isn't new and that it is easy to exaggerate its meaning. To such replies, Norbert Wiener had a useful answer: the difference between a fatal and a therapeutic dose of strychnine is "only a matter of degree." In other words, change isn't new; what is new is the *degree of change.* As our clock-face metaphor was intended to suggest, about three minutes ago there developed a qualitative difference in the character of change. Change changed.

This is really quite a new problem. For example, up until the last generation it was possible to be born, grow up, and spend a life in the United States without moving more than 50 miles from home, without ever confronting serious questions about one's basic values, beliefs, and patterns of behavior. Indeed, without ever confronting serious challenges to anything one knew. Stability and consequent predictability—within "natural cycles"—was the characteristic mode. But now, in just the last 22
minute, we've reached the stage where change occurs so rapidly that each of us in the course of our lives has continuously to work out a set of values, beliefs, and patterns of behavior that are viable, or *seem* viable, to each of us personally. And just when we have identified a workable system, it turns out to be irrelevant because so much has changed while we were doing it.

Of course, this frustrating state of affairs applies to our education as well. If you are over twenty-five years of age, the mathematics you were taught in school is "old"; the grammar you were taught is obsolete and in disrepute; the biology, completely out of date, and the 23
history, open to serious question. The best that can be said of you, assuming that you *remember* most of what you were told and read, is that you are a walking encyclopedia of outdated information. As Alfred North Whitehead pointed out in *The Adventure of Ideas:*

> Our sociological theories, our political philosophy, our practical maxims of business, our political economy, and our doctrines of education are derived from an unbroken tradition of great thinkers and of practical examples from the age of Plato . . . to the end of the last century. The whole of this tradition is warped by the vicious assumption that each generation will substantially live amid the conditions governing the lives of its fathers and will transmit those conditions to mould with equal force the lives of its children. *We are living in the first period of human history for which this assumption is false.*

All of which brings us to the third problem: the "burgeoning bureaucracy." We are brought there because bureaucracies, in spite of their seeming indispensability, are by their nature highly resistant to change. The motto of most bureaucracies is, "Carry On, Regardless."
There is an essential mindlessness about them which causes them, in 24
most circumstances, to accelerate entropy rather than to impede it. Bureaucracies rarely ask themselves Why?, but only How? John Gardner, who as President of the Carnegie Corporation and (as of this writing) Secretary of Health, Education, and Welfare has learned about bureaucracies at first hand, has explained them very well:

> To accomplish renewal, we need to understand what prevents it. When we talk about revitalizing a society, we tend to put exclusive emphasis on finding new ideas. But there is usually no shortage of

> new ideas; the problem is to get a hearing for them. And that means breaking through the crusty rigidity and stubborn complacency of the *status quo*. The aging society develops elaborate defenses against new ideas—"mind-forged manacles," in William Blake's vivid phrase. . . . As a society becomes more concerned with precedent and custom, it comes to care more about how things are done and less about *whether* they are done. The man who wins acclaim is not the one who "gets things done" but the one who has an ingrained knowledge of the rules and accepted practices. Whether he accomplishes anything is less important than whether he conducts himself in an "appropriate" manner.
>
> The body of custom, convention, and "reputable" standards exercises such an oppressive effect on creative minds that new developments in a field often originate outside the area of respectable practice.

In other words, bureaucracies are the repositories of conventional assumptions and standard practices—two of the greatest accelerators of entropy.

We could put before you a volume of other quotations—from Machiavelli to Paul Goodman—describing how bureaucratic structures retard the development and application of new survival strategies. But in doing so, we would risk creating the impression that we stand with Goodman in yearning for some anarchistic Utopia in which the Army, the Police, General Motors, the U. S. Office of Education, the Post Office, et al. do not exist. We are not "against" bureaucracies, any more than we are "for" them. They are like electric plugs. They will probably not go away, but they do need to be controlled if the prerogatives of a democratic society are to remain visible and usable. This is why we ask that the schools be "subversive," that they serve as a kind of antibureaucracy bureaucracy, providing the young with a "What is it good for?" perspective on its own society. Certainly, it is unrealistic to expect those who control the media to perform that function. Nor the generals and the politicians. Nor is it reasonable to expect the "intellectuals" to do it, for they do not have access to the majority of youth. But schoolteachers do, and so the primary responsibility rests with them.

The trouble is that most teachers have the idea that they are in some other sort of business. Some believe, for example, that they are in the "information dissemination" business. This was a reasonable business up to about a minute or two ago on our clock. (But then, so was the horseshoe business and the candle-snuffer business.) The signs that their business is failing are abundant, but they keep at it all the more diligently. Santayana told us that a fanatic is someone who redoubles his efforts when he has forgotten his aim. In this case, even if the aim has not been forgotten, it is simply irrelevant. But the effort has been redoubled anyway.

There are some teachers who think they are in the "transmission of our cultural heritage" business, which is not an unreasonable business if you are concerned with the whole clock and not just its first 57 minutes. The trouble is that most teachers find the last three minutes

too distressing to deal with, which is exactly why they are in the wrong business. Their students find the last three minutes distressing—and confusing—too, especially the last 30 seconds, and they need *help.* While they have to live with TV, film, the LP record, communication satellites, and the laser beam, their teachers are still talking as if the only medium on the scene is Gutenberg's printing press. While they have to understand psychology and psychedelics, anthropology and anthropomor- 27
phism, birth control and biochemistry, their teachers are teaching "subjects" that mostly don't exist anymore. While they need to find new roles for themselves as social, political, and religious organisms, their teachers (as Edgar Friedenberg has documented so painfully) are acting almost entirely as shills for corporate interests, shaping them up to be functionaries in one bureaucracy or another.

Unless our schools can switch to the right business, their clientele will either go elsewhere (as many are doing) or go into a severe case of "future shock," to use a relatively new phrase. Future shock occurs when you are confronted by the fact that the world you were educated to believe in doesn't exist. Your images of reality are apparitions that disappear on contact. There are several ways of responding to such a condition, one of which is to withdraw and allow oneself to be overcome by a sense of impotence. More commonly, one continues to act *as if* his apparitions were substantial, relentlessly pursuing a course of action that he knows will fail him. You may have noticed that there are scores of political, social, and religious leaders who are clearly suffering from advanced cases of future shock. They repeat over and over
again the words that are supposed to represent the world about them. 28
But nothing seems to work out. And then they repeat the words again and again. Alfred Korzybski used a somewhat different metaphor to describe what we have been calling "future shock." He likened one's language to a map. The map is intended to describe the territory that we call "reality," i.e., the world outside of our skins. When there is a close correspondence between map and territory, there tends to be a high degree of effective functioning, especially where it relates to survival. When there is little correspondence between map and territory, there is a strong tendency for entropy to make substantial gains. In this context, the terrifying question What did you learn in school today? assumes immense importance for all of us. We just may not survive another generation of inadvertent entropy helpers.

What is the necessary business of the schools? To create eager consumers? To transmit the dead ideas, values, metaphors, and information of three minutes ago? To create smoothly functioning bureaucrats? *These* aims are truly subversive since they undermine our chances
of surviving as a viable, democratic society. And they do their work in 29
the name of convention and standard practice. We would like to see the schools go into the anti-entropy business. Now, that is subversive, too. But the purpose is to subvert attitudes, beliefs, and assumptions that foster chaos and uselessness.

Peter Marin

The Open Truth and Fiery Vehemence of Youth: A Sort of Soliloquy

It is midnight and I am sitting here with my notes, enough of them to make two books and a half and a volume of posthumous fragments, trying to make some smaller sense of them than the grand maniacal design I have in my mind. I don't know where to begin. Once, traveling in summer across the country with a friend from Hollywood and my young son in a battered green Porsche, I stopped for lunch somewhere in Kansas on a Sunday morning. As we walked into the restaurant, bearded, wearing dark glasses and strange hats, and followed by my long-haired boy, one Kansas matron bent toward another and whispered: "I bet those two men have kidnapped that little girl." I took a deep breath and started to speak, but I did not know where to begin or how to explain just how many ways she was mistaken. Now, trying to write clearly about education and adolescence, I feel the same way.

For that reason I have chosen an eccentric method of composition, one that may seem fragmentary, jumpy, and broken. This article will be more like a letter, and the letter itself is an accumulation of impressions and ideas, a sampling of thoughts at once disconnected but related. There is a method to it that may disappear in its mild madness, but I do not know at this juncture how else to proceed. Shuffling through my notes I feel like an archeologist with a mass of uncatalogued shards. There is a pattern to all this, a coherence of thought, but all I can do here is assemble the bits and pieces and lay them out for you and hope that you can sense how I get from one place to another.

An entire system is hiding behind this, just beginning to take form, and these notes are like a drawing, a preliminary sketch. I feel comfortable with that notion, more comfortable than with the idea of forcing them together, cutting and pasting, to make a more conventional essay. I can perceive in myself at this moment what I also see in the young: I am reluctant to deal in sequence with my ideas and

experience, I am impatient with transition, the habitual ways of getting "from here to there." I think restlessly; my mind, like the minds
of my students, works in flashes, in sudden perceptions and brief extended clusters of intuition and abstraction—and I have stuck stubbornly to that method of composition. There is still in me the ghost
of an apocalyptic adolescent, and I am trying to move it a few steps
toward the future.

One theme, as you will see, runs through what I have written or
thought: we must rethink our ideas of childhood and schooling. We
must dismantle them and start again from scratch. Nothing else will
do. Our visions of adolescence and education confine us to habit, rule
perception out. We make do at the moment with a set of ideas inherited
from the nineteenth century, from an industrial, relatively puritanical,
repressive, and "localized" culture; we try to gum them like labels to
new kinds of experience. But that won't do. Everything has changed.
The notions with which I began my job as a high-school director have 4
been discarded one by one. They make no sense. What emerges through
these children as the psyche of this culture is post-industrial, relatively
unrepressed, less literate and local: a new combination of elements,
almost a new strain. Adolescents are, each one of them, an arena in
which the culture transforms itself or is torn between contrary impulses; they are the victims of a culture raging within itself like man
and wife, a schizoid culture—and these children are the unfinished and
grotesque products of that schism.

They are grotesque because we give them no help. They are
forced to make among themselves adjustments to a tension that must
be unbearable. They do the best they can, trying, in increasingly eccentric fashions, to make sense of things. But we adults seem to have
withdrawn in defeat from that same struggle, to have given up. We
are enamored, fascinated, and deluded by adolescence precisely be- 5
cause it is the last life left to us; only the young rebel with any real
passion against media, machines, the press of circumstance itself. Their
elders seem to have no options, no sense of alternative or growth. Adult
existence is bled of life and we turn in that vacuum toward children
with the mixed repulsion and desire of wanton puritans toward life
itself.

As for me, an adult, I think of myself as I write as an observer
at a tribal war—an anthropologist, a combination of Gulliver and a
correspondent sending home news by mule and boat. By the time you
hear of it, things will have changed. And that isn't enough, not enough 6
at all. Somebody must step past the children, must move into his own
psyche or two steps past his own limits into the absolute landscape of
fear and potential these children inhabit. That is where I am headed.
So these ideas, in effect, are something like a last message tacked to
a tree in a thicket or tucked under a stone. I mean: we cannot *follow*
the children any longer, we have to step ahead of them. Somebody has
to mark a trail.

Adolescence: a few preliminary fragments . . .

(FROM MY STUDENT, V): *yr whole body moves in a trained way & you know that youve moved this way before & it contains all youve been taught its all rusty & slow something is pushing under that rusted mesh but STILL YOU CANNOT MOVE you are caught between 2 doors & the old one is much closer & you can grab it all the time but the other door it disappears that door you cant even scratch & kick (like the early settlers were stung by the new land) but this new land doesnt even touch you & you wonder if youre doing the right thing to get in*

(FROM FRANZ KAFKA): *He feels imprisoned on this earth, he feels constricted; the melancholy, the impotence, the sicknesses, the feverish fancies of the captive afflict him; no comfort can comfort him, since it is merely comfort, gentle headsplitting comfort glazing the brutal fact of imprisonment.* But if he is asked what he wants he cannot reply. . . . He has no conception of freedom.

(FROM TAPES RECORDED IN PACIFIC PALISADES, 1966, SEVERAL BOYS AND GIRLS AGED 12-14):—*Things are getting younger and younger. Girls twelve will do it now. One guy said I fuck a girl every Friday night. What sexual pleasure do you get out of this (he's very immature you know) and he would say, I don't know I'm just going to fuck.*

or

—How old are you? —*Twelve.* —Will you tell us your first experience with drugs, how you got into it?—*Well, the people I hung around with were big acid-heads. So one day my friend asked me if I wanted to get stoned and I said yes. That was about five months ago and I've been getting on it ever since. Started taking LSD about one month ago. Took it eleven times in one month. I consider it a good thing. For getting high, smoking grass is better, or hashish—it's about six times stronger than marijuana.*

(FROM PAUL RADIN: Primitive Man As Philosopher): *It is conceivably demanding too much of a man to whom the pleasures of life are largely bound up with the life of contemplation and to whom analysis and introspection are the self-understood prerequisites for a proper understanding of the world, that he appreciate . . . expressions which are largely non-intellectual—where life seems, predominatingly, a discharge of physical vitality, a simple and naive release of emotions or an enjoyment of sensations for their own sake. Yet . . . it is just such an absorption in a life of sensations that is the outward characteristic of primitive peoples.*

Can you see where my thought leads? It is precisely at this point, adolescence, when the rush of energies, that sea-sex, gravitation, the thrust of the ego up through layers of childhood, makes itself felt, that the person is once more like an infant, is swept once more by energies that are tidal, unfamiliar, and unyielding. He is in a sense born again, a fresh identity beset inside and out by the rush of new experience. It is at this point, too—when we seem compelled by a persistent lunacy to isolate him—that what is growing within the adolescent demands expression, requires it, and must, in addition, be received by the world and given form—or it will wither or turn to rage. Adolescence is a second infancy. It is then that a man desires solitude and at the same time contact with the vivid world; must test within social reality the new power within himself; needs above all to discover himself for the first time as a bridge between inner and outer, a maker of value, a vehicle through which culture perceives and transforms itself. It is now, ideally, that he begins to understand the complex and delicate nature of the ego itself as a thin skin between living worlds, a synaptic jump, the self-conscious point at which nature and culture combine.

In this condition, with these needs, the adolescent is like a primitive man, an apocalyptic primitive; he exists for the moment in that
state of single vision in which myth is still the raw stuff of being, he
knows at first hand through his own energies the possibilities of life—
but he knows these in muddled, sporadic, contradictory ways. The rush 9
of his pubescent and raw energy seems at odds with public behavior,
the *order* of things, the tenor of life around him, especially in a culture
just emerging—as is ours—from a tradition of evasion, repression, and
fear.

The contradictions within the culture itself intensify his individual
confusion. We are at the moment torn between future and past: in the
midst of a process of transformation we barely understand. The development of adolescent energy and ego—difficult at any time—is complicated in our own by the increase in early sexuality, the complicated
messages of the media, and the effects of strong and unfamiliar drugs.
These three elements are, in themselves, the salient features of a culture
that is growing more permissive, less repressive. They are profound,
complex, and strong: heavy doses of experience demanding changes in
attitude, changes in behavior. The direction and depth of feeling responds accordingly; the adolescent tries—even as a form of self-defense 10
against the pressure of his own energies—to move more freely, to change
his styles of life, to "grow." But it is then that he finds he is locked into
culture, trapped in a web of ideas, law, and rituals that keep him a
child, deprive him of a chance to test and assimilate his newer self.
It is now that the culture turns suddenly repressive. His gestures are
evaded or denied; at best he is "tolerated," but even then his gestures,
lacking the social support of acknowledgment and reward, must seem
to him lacking in authenticity—more like forms of neurosis or selfishness than the natural stages in growth.

He is thrust back upon himself. The insistent natural press within
him toward becoming whole is met perpetually by unbudging resistance. Schools, rooted as they are in a Victorian century and seemingly
suspicious of life itself, are his natural enemies. They don't help, as
they might, to make that bridge between his private and the social 11
worlds; they insist, instead, upon their separation. Indeed, family, community, and school all combine—especially in the suburbs—to isolate
and "protect" him from the adventure, risk, and participation he needs;

the same energies that relate him at this crucial point to nature result in a kind of exile from the social environment.

Thus the young, in that vivid confrontation with the thrust of nature unfolding in themselves, are denied adult assistance. I once wrote that education through its limits denied the gods, and that they would return in the young in one form or another to haunt us. That is happening now. You can sense it as the students gather, with their simplistic moral certainty, at the gates of the universities. It is almost as if the young were once more possessed by Bacchanalian gods, were once again inhabited by divinities whose honor we have neglected. Those marvelous and threatening energies! What disturbs me most about them is that we lack rituals for their use and balance, and the young—and perhaps we ourselves—now seem at their mercy. The young have moved, bag and baggage, into areas where adults cannot help them, and it is a scary landscape they face, it is crowded with strange forms and faces, and if they return from it raddled, without balance and pitched toward excess, who can pretend to be surprised—or blameless?

At times they seem almost shell-shocked, survivors of a holocaust in which the past has been destroyed and all the bridges to it bombed. I cannot describe with any certainty what occurs in their minds, but I do know that most adults must seem to the young like shrill critics speaking to them in an alien language about a Greek tragedy in which they may lose their lives. The words we use, our dress, our tones of voice, the styles of adult lives—all of these are so foreign to that dramatic crisis that as we approach them we seem to increase the distance we are trying to cross. Even our attention drives them further away, as if adolescents perceived that adults, coming closer, diminish in sense and size.

The inner events in an adolescent demand from what surrounds him life on a large scale, in a grand style. This is the impulse to apocalypse in the young, as if they were in exile from a nation that does not exist—and yet they can sense it, they know it is there—if only because their belief itself demands its presence. Their demand is absolute and unanswerable, but it exists and we seem unable at this point in time to suppress or evade it. For one reason or another, massive shifts in cultural balances, the lessening of repression for whatever reasons—economic, technological, evolutionary—those energies, like gods, have appeared among us again. But what can we make of them? The simple problem is that our institutions are geared to another century, another set of social necessities, and cannot change quickly enough to contain, receive, or direct them—and as we suppress or refuse them they turn to rage.

Primitive cultures dealt with this problem, I think, through their initiation rites, the rites of passage; they legitimized and accepted these energies and turned them toward collective aims; they were merged with the life of the tribe and in this way acknowledged, honored, and

domesticated—but not destroyed. In most initiation rites the participant
is led through the mythical or sacred world (or a symbolic version)
and is then returned, transformed, to the secular one as a new person,
with a new role. He is introduced through the rites to a dramatic reality
coexistent with the visible or social one and at its root; he is put in
direct touch with the sources of energy, the divinities of the tribe. In
many cultures the symbolic figures in the rites are unmasked at the 15
end, as if to reveal to the initiate the interpenetration of the secular
and sacred worlds. Occasionally the initiate is asked at some point to
don the ritual mask himself—joining, as he does, one world with another
and assuming the responsibility for their connection. This shift in status,
in *relation*, is the heart of the rite; a liturgized merging of the individual with shared sources of power.

Do you see what I am driving at? The rites are in a sense a social
contract, a binding up; one occurring specifically, profoundly, on a
deep psychic level. The individual is redefined in the culture by his
new relation to its mysteries, its gods, to one form or another of nature.
His experience of that hidden and omnipotent mythical world is the
basis for his relation to the culture and his fellows, each of whom has 16
a similar bond—deep, personal, and unique, but somehow shared, in-
visibly but deeply. These ritualized relationships of each man to the
shared gods bind the group together; they form the substance of culture: an invisible landscape that is real and felt, commonly held, a
landscape which resides in each man and in which, in turn, each man
resides.

I hope that makes sense. That is the structure of the kaleidoscopic
turning of culture that Blake makes in "The Crystal Cabinet," and it
makes sense too, in America, in relation to adolescents. What fascinates
me is that our public schools, designed for adolescents—who seem, as
apocalyptic men, to demand this kind of drama, release, and support
—educate and "socialize" their students by depriving them of everything the rites bestow. They manipulate them through the repression
of energies; they isolate them and close off most parts of the community; they categorically refuse to make use of the individual's private 17
experience. The direction of all these tendencies is toward a cultural
schizophrenia in which the student is forced to choose between his own
relation to reality or the one demanded by the institution. The schools
are organized to weaken the student so that he is forced, in the absence
of his own energies, to accept the values and demands of the institution. To this end we deprive the student of mobility and experience;
through law and custom we make the only legal place for him the
school, and then, to make sure he remains dependent, manipulable, we
empty the school of all vivid life.

We appear to have forgotten in our schools what every primitive
tribe with its functional psychology knows: allegiance to the tribe can 18
be forged only at the deepest levels of the psyche and in extreme circumstance demanding endurance, daring, and awe; that the participant

must be given *direct* access to the sources of cultural continuity—by and in himself; and that only a place in a coherent community can be exchanged for a man's allegiance.

I believe that it is precisely this world that drugs replace; adolescents provide for themselves what we deny them: a confrontation with some kind of power within an unfamiliar landscape involving sensation and risk. It is there, I suppose, that they hope to find, by some hurried magic, a new way of seeing, a new relation to things, to discard one identity and assume another. They mean to find through their adventures the *ground* of reality, the resonance of life we deny them, as if they might come upon their golden city and return still inside it: at home. You can see the real veterans sometimes on the street in strange costumes they have stolen from dreams: American versions of the Tupi of Brazil, who traveled thousands of miles each year in search of the land where death and evil do not exist. Theirs is a world totally alien to the one we discuss in schools; it is dramatic, it enchants them; its existence forms a strange brotherhood among them and they cling to it—as though they alone had been to a fierce land and back. It is that which draws them together and makes of them a loose tribe. It is, after all, some sort of shared experience, some kind of foray into the risky dark; it is the best that they can do. When you begin to think about adolescence in this way, what sense can you make of our schools? None of the proposed changes makes sense to me: revision of curriculum, teaching machines, smaller classes, encounter groups, redistributions of power—all of these are stopgap measures, desperate attempts to keep the young in schools that are hopelessly outdated. The changes suggested and debated don't go deeply enough; they don't question or change enough. For what needs changing are not the methods of the school system but its aims, and what is troubling the young and forcing upon their teachers an intolerable burden is the *idea* of childhood itself; the ways we think about adolescents, their place in the culture itself. More and more one comes to see that changes in the schools won't be enough; the crisis of the young cuts across the culture in all its areas and includes the family and the community. The young are displaced; there seems no other word for it. They are trapped in a prolonged childhood almost unique.

In few other cultures have persons of fifteen or eighteen been so uselessly isolated from participation in the community, or been deemed so unnecessary (in their elders' eyes), or so limited by law. Our ideas of responsibility, our parental feelings of anxiety, blame, and guilt, all of these follow from our curious vision of the young; in turn, they concretize it, legitimize it so that we are no longer even conscious of the ways we see childhood or the strain that our vision puts upon us. That is what needs changing: the definitions we make socially and legally of the role of the young. They are trapped in the ways we see them, and the school is simply one function, one aspect, of the whole problem. What makes real change so difficult in the schools is only in part their natural unwieldiness; it is more often the difficulty we have in escaping our preconceptions about things.

In general the school system we have inherited seems to me based upon three particular things:

1. What Paul Goodman calls the idea of "natural depravity": our
puritanical vision of human nature in which children are perceived as 21
sinners or "savages" and in which human impulse or desire is not to
be trusted and must therefore be constrained or "trained."

2. The necessity during the mid-nineteenth century of "Americanizing" great masses of immigrant children from diverse backgrounds and creating, through the schools, a common experience and character.

3. The need in an industrialized state for energy and labor to run the machines: the state, needing workers, educates persons to be technically capable but relatively dependent and responsive to authority so that their energies will be available when needed.

These elements combine with others—the labor laws that make
childhood a "legal" state, and a population explosion that makes it
necessary now to keep adolescents off both the labor market and the
idle street—to "freeze" into a school system that resists change even as 22
the culture itself and its needs shift radically. But teachers can't usually
see that, for they themselves have been educated in this system and
are committed to ideas that they have never clearly understood. Time
and again, speaking to them, one hears the same questions and anguish:

"But what will happen to the students if they don't go to school?"
"How will they learn?" "What will they do without adults?" 23

What never comes clear, of course, is that such questions are, at
bottom, statement. Even while asking them teachers reveal their unconscious and contaminating attitudes. They can no longer imagine
what children will do "outside" schools. They regard them as young
monsters who will, if released from adult authority or help, disrupt
the order of things. What is more, adults no longer are capable of
imagining learning or child-adult relationships outside the schools. But
mass schooling is a recent innovation. Most learning—especially the 24
process of socialization or acculturation—has gone on outside schools,
more naturally, in the fabric of the culture. In most cultures the passage from childhood to maturity occurs because of social necessity, the
need for responsible adults, and is marked by clear changes in role.
Children in the past seem to have learned the ways of the community
or tribe through constant contact and interchange with adults, and it
was taken for granted that the young learned continually through their
place close to the heart of the community.

We seem to have lost all sense of that. The school is expected to
do what the community cannot do and that is impossible. In the end,
we will have to change far more than the schools if we expect to create 25
a new coherence between the experiences of the child and the needs
of the community. We will have to rethink the meaning of childhood;
we will begin to grant greater freedom *and* responsibility to the young;

we will drop the compulsory-schooling age to fourteen, perhaps less; we will take for granted the "independence" of adolescents and provide them with the chance to live alone, away from parents and with peers; we will discover jobs they can or want to do in the community—anything from mail delivery to the teaching of smaller children and the counseling of other adolescents. At some point, perhaps, we will even find that the community itself—in return for a minimum of work or continued schooling—will provide a minimal income to young people that will allow them to assume the responsibility for their own lives at an earlier age, and learn the ways of the community outside the school; finally, having lowered the level of compulsory schooling, we will find it necessary to provide different *kinds* of schools, a wider choice, so that students will be willing voluntarily to continue the schooling that suits their needs and aims.

All these changes, of course, are aimed at two things: the restoration of the child's "natural" place in the community and lowering the age at which a person is considered an independent member of the community. Some of them, to be sure, can be made in the schools, but my sense of things, after having talked to teachers and visited the schools, is that trying to make the changes in schools *alone* will be impossible.

One problem, put simply, is that in every school I have visited, public or private, traditional or "innovational," the students have only these two choices: to drop out (either physically or mentally) or to make themselves smaller and smaller until they can act in ways their elders expect. One of my students picked up a phrase I once used, "the larger and smaller worlds." The schools we visit together, he says, are always the smaller world: smaller at least than his imagination, smaller than the potential of the young. The students are asked to put aside the best things about themselves—their own desires, impulses, and ideas—in order to "adjust" to an environment constructed for children who existed one hundred years ago, if at all. I wonder sometimes if this condition is simply the result of poor schooling; I am more inclined to believe that it is the inevitable result of mass compulsory schooling and the fabrication of artificial environments by adults for children. Is it possible at all for adults to understand what children need and to change their institutions fast enough to keep up with changes in culture and experience? Is it possible for children to grow to their full size, to feel their full strength, if they are deprived of individual volition all along the line and forced to school? I don't know. I know only that during the Middle Ages they sometimes "created" jesters by putting young children in boxes and force-feeding them so that, as they grew, their bones would warp in unusual shapes. That is often how the schools seem to me. Students are trapped in the boxes of pedagogic ideas, and I am tempted to say to teachers again and again: more, much more, you must go further, create more space in the schools, you

must go deeper in thought, create more resonance, a different feeling,
a different and more human, more daring style.

Even the best teachers, with the best intentions, seem to diminish
their students as they work through the public-school system. For that
system is, at bottom, designed to produce what we sometimes call good
citizens but what more often than not turn out to be good soldiers; it
is through the schools of the state, after all, that we produce our armies.
I remember how struck I was while teaching at a state college by the
number of boys who wanted to oppose the draft but lacked the courage or strength to simply say no. They were trapped; they had always 28
been taught, had always tried, to be "good." Now that they wanted
to refuse to go, they could not, for they weren't sure they could bear
the consequences they had been taught would follow such refusal: jail,
social disgrace, loss of jobs, parental despair. They could not believe
in institutions, but they could not trust themselves and their impulse
and they were caught in their own impotence: depressed and resentful,
filled with self-hatred and a sense of shame.

That is a condition bred in the schools. In one way or another
our methods produce in the young a condition of pain that seems very
close to a mass neurosis: a lack of faith in oneself, a vacuum of spirit
into which authority or institutions can move, a dependency they feed
on. Students are encouraged to relinquish their own wills, their freedom of volition; they are taught that value and culture reside outside 29
oneself and must be acquired from the institution, and almost everything in their education is designed to discourage them from activity,
from the wedding of idea and act. It is almost as if we hoped to discourage them from thought itself by making ideas so lifeless, so hopeless, that their despair would be enough to make them manipulable
and obedient.

The system breeds obedience, frustration, dependence, and fear:
a kind of gentle violence that is usually turned against oneself, one that
is sorrowful and full of guilt, but a violence nonetheless, and one
realizes that what is done in the schools to persons is deeply connected
to what we did to the blacks or are doing now in Vietnam. That is: 30
we don't teach hate in the schools, or murder, but we do isolate the
individual; we empty him of life by ignoring or suppressing his impulse
toward life; we breed in him a lack of respect for it, a loss of love—
and thus we produce gently "good" but threatened men, men who will
kill without passion, out of duty and obedience, men who have in
themselves little sense of the vivid life being lost nor the moral strength
to refuse.

From first to twelfth grade we acclimatize students to a fundamental deadness and teach them to restrain themselves for the sake of
"order." The net result is a kind of pervasive cultural inversion in which 31
they are asked to separate at the most profound levels their own experience from institutional reality, self from society, objective from

subjective, energy from order—though these various polarities are precisely those which must be made coherent during adolesence.

I remember a talk I had with a college student.

"You know what I love to do," he said. "I love to go into the woods and run among the trees."

"Very nice," I said.

"But it worries me. We shouldn't do it."

"Why not?" I asked.

"Because we get excited. It isn't *orderly*."

"Not orderly?"

"Not orderly."

"Do you run into the trees?" I asked.

"Of course not."

"Then it's orderly," I said.

In a small way this exchange indicates the kind of thinking we encourage in the schools: the mistaking of rigidity and stillness for order, of order as the absence of life. We try to create and preserve an order which depends upon the destruction of life both inside and out and which all life, when expressed, must necessarily threaten or weaken.

The natural process of learning seems to move naturally from experience through perception to abstraction in a fluid continuous process that cannot be clearly divided into stages. It is in that process that energy is somehow articulated in coherent and meaningful form as an act or thought or a made object. The end of learning is wisdom and wisdom to me, falling back as I do on a Jewish tradition, is, in its simplest sense, "intelligent activity" or, more completely, the suffusion of activity with knowledge, a wedding of the two. For the Hassidic Jews every gesture was potentially holy, a form of prayer, when it was made with a reverence for God. In the same way a gesture is always a form of wisdom—an act is wisdom—when it is suffused with knowledge, made with a reverence for the truth.

Does that sound rhetorical? I suppose it does. But I mean it. The end of education is intelligent activity, *wisdom*, and that demands a merging of opposites, a sense of process. Instead we produce the opposite: immobility, insecurity, an inability to act without institutional blessing or direction, or, at the opposite pole, a headlong rush toward motion without balance or thought. We cut into the natural movement of learning and try to force upon the students the end product, abstraction, while eliminating experience and ignoring their perception. The beginning of thought is in the experience through one's self of a particular environment—school, community, culture. When this is ignored, as it is in schools, the natural relation of self and knowledge is broken, the parts of the process become polar opposites, antitheses, and the young are forced to choose between them: objectivity, order, and obedience as against subjectivity, chaos, and energy. It doesn't really matter which they choose; as long as the two sets seem irreconcilable their learning remains incomplete. Caught between the two, they suffer our intellectual schizophrenia until it occupies them, too. They wait. They sit. They listen. They learn to "behave" at the expense of themselves. Or else—and you can see it happening now—they turn against it with a vengeance and may shout, as they did at Columbia, "Kill all adults," for they have allied themselves with raw energy against reason and balance—our delicate, hard-won virtues—and we should not be surprised. We set up the choices ourselves, and it is simply that they have chosen what we hold to be the Devil's side.

If this is the case, what are the alternatives? I thought at one time that changes in schooling could be made, that the school itself could become at least a microcosm of the community outside, a kind of halfway house, a preparatory arena in which students, in semi-protective surroundings, would develop not only the skill but the character that would be needed in the world. But more and more, as I have said, it seems to me impossible to do that job in a setting as isolated and restrictive as our schools. Students don't need the artificiality of schools; they respond more fully and more intelligently when they make direct contact with the community and are allowed to choose roles that have
some utility for the community and themselves. What is at stake here, 36
I suppose, is the freedom of volition, for this is the basic condition with which people must learn to deal, and the sooner they achieve within that condition wit, daring, and responsibility the stronger they will be. It seems absurd to postpone the assumption of that condition as long as we do. In most other cultures, and even in our own past, young people have taken upon themselves the responsibility of adults and have dealt with it as successfully as most adults do now. The students I have seen can do that, too, when given the chance. What a strain it must be to have that capacity, to sense in one's self a talent for adventure or growth or meaning, and have that sense continually stifled or undercut by the role one is supposed to play.

Thus, it seems inescapably clear that our first obligation to the young is to create a place in the community for them to act with volition and freedom. They are ready for it, certainly, even if we aren't. Adolescents seem to need at least some sense of risk and gain "out there" in the world: an existential sense of themselves that is vivid to the extent that the dangers faced are "real." The students I have worked with seem strongest and most alive when they are in the mountains of
Mexico or the Oakland ghetto or out in the desert or simply hitch- 37
hiking or riding freights to see what's happening. They thrive on distance and motion—and the right to solitude when they want it. Many of them want jobs; they themselves arrange to be teachers in day-care centers, political canvassers, tutors, poolroom attendants, actors, governesses, gardeners. They returned from these experiences immeasurably brightened and more sure of themselves, more willing, in that new assurance, to learn many of the abstract ideas we had been straining to teach them. It was not simply the experience in itself that brought this about. It was also the feeling of freedom they had, the sense that

they could come and go at will and make any choice they wanted—no matter how absurd—if they were willing to suffer what real consequences followed. Many wanted to work and travel and others did not; they wanted to sit and think or read or live alone or swim or, as one student scrawled on my office wall, "ball and goof." What they finally came to understand, of course, was that the school made no pretense at either limiting or judging their activities; we considered them free agents and limited our own activities to advice, to what "teaching" they requested, and to support when they needed it in facing community, parents, or law.

What we were after was a *feeling* to the place: a sense of intensity and space. We discarded the idea of the microcosm and replaced it with an increased openness and access to the larger community. The campus itself became a place to come back to for rest or discussion or thought; but we turned things inside out to the extent that we came to accept that learning took place more naturally elsewhere, in any of the activities that our students chose, and that the school was in actuality wherever they were, whatever they did. What students learned at the school was simply the feel of things; the sense of themselves as makers of value; the realization that the environment is at best an extension of men and that it can be transformed by them into what they vitally need.

What we tried to create was a flexible environment, what a designer I know has called permissive space. It was meant to be in a sense a model for the condition in which men find themselves, in which the responsibility of a man was to make connections, value, and sense. We eliminated from the school all preconceptions about what was proper, best, or useful; we gave up rules and penalties; we refused at all levels to resort to coercive force and students were free to come and go at will, to do anything. What we were after was a "guilt-free" environment, one in which the students might become or discover what they were without having to worry about preconceived ideas of what they had to be.

What we found was that our students seemed to need, most of all, relief from their own "childhood"—what was expected of them. Some of them needed merely to rest, to withdraw from the strange grid of adult expectation and demand for lengthy periods of introspection in which they appeared to grow mysteriously, almost like plants. But an even greater number seemed to need independent commerce with the world outside the school: new sorts of social existence. Nothing could replace that. The simple fact seemed to be that our students grew when they were allowed to move freely into and around the adult community; when they were not, they languished.

We came to see that learning is natural, yes, but it results naturally from most things adolescents do. By associating learning with one particular form of intellection and insisting upon that in school we make a grave error. When students shy away from that kind of intellection

it doesn't mean they are turning away forever from learning or abstractions; it means simply that they are seeking another kind of learning
momentarily more natural to themselves. That may be anything from 41
physical adventure or experimental community work to withdrawn
introspection and an exploration of their fantasies and dreams.

Indeed, it is hard for them to do anything without some kind of
learning, but that may be what we secretly fear—that those other forms
of learning will make them less manageable or less like ourselves. That,
after all, may be one reason we use all those books. Levi-Strauss insists
on the relation of increased literacy and the power of the state over
the individual. It may well be that dependence on print and abstraction
is one of the devices we use to make students manipulable, as if we
meant to teach them that ideas exist in talk or on the page but rarely 42
in activity. We tried to avoid that. When we permitted students the
freedom of choice and gave them easy access to the community, we
found that ideas acquired weight and value to the extent that students
were allowed to try them out in action. It was in practical and social
situations that their own strength increased, and the merging of the
two—strengthened self and tested knowledge—moved them more quickly
toward manhood than anything else I have seen.

One might make a formula of it: to the extent that students had
freedom of volition and access to experience knowledge became important. But volition and access were of absolute value; they took
precedence over books or parental anxiety; without them, nothing
worked. So we had to trust the students to make their own choices,
no matter what we thought of them. We learned to take their risks 43
with them—and to survive. In that sense we became equals, and that
equality may in the end be more educational for students than anything else. That, in fact, may be the most important thing we learned.
New ways in seeing them were more effective than changes in curriculum, and without them nothing made much difference. But we
must understand too that the old way of seeing things—the traditional
idea of childhood—is in some way baked into the whole public-school
system at almost every level and also hidden in most pedagogy.

In some ways it is compulsory schooling itself which is the problem, for without real choice students will remain locked in childhood
and schools, away from whatever is vivid in life. But real choice, as 44
we know, includes dominion over one's own time and energies, and
the right to come and go on the basis of what has actual importance.
And I wonder if we will ever get round, given all our fears, to granting
that privilege to students.

One thing alone of all I have read has made recent sense to me
concerning adolescents. That is the implicit suggestion in Erik Erikson's 45
Young Man Luther that every sensitive man experiences in himself the
conflicts and contradictions of his age. The great man, he suggests, is
the man who articulates and resolves these conflicts in a way that has
meaning for his time; that is, he is himself, as was Luther, a victim of

his time and its vehicle and, finally, a kind of resolution. But all men, not only the great, have in some measure the capacity to experience in themselves what is happening in the culture around them. I am talking here about what is really shared among the members of a particular culture is a condition, a kind of internal "landscape," the psychic shape that a particular time and place assumes within a man as the extent and limit of his perceptions, dreams, and pleasure and pain.

If there is such a shared condition it seems to me a crucial point, for it means that there is never any real distance between a man and his culture, no real isolation or alienation from society. It means that adolescents are not in their untutored state cut off from culture nor outside it. It means instead that each adolescent is an arena in which the contradictions and currents sweeping through the culture must somehow be resolved, must be resolved by the person himself, and that those individual resolutions are, ideally, the means by which the culture advances itself.

Do you see where this leads? I am straining here to get past the idea of the adolescent as an isolate and deviant creature who must be joined—as if glued and clamped—to the culture. For we ordinarily think of schools, though not quite consciously, as the "culture" itself, little models of society. We try to fit the student into the model, believing that if he will adjust to it he will in some way have been "civilized." That approach is connected to the needs of the early century, when the schools were the means by which the children of immigrant parents were acculturated and moved from the European values of their parents toward more prevalent American ones. But all of that has changed now. The children in our schools, all of them, are little fragments of *this* culture; they no longer need to be "socialized" in the same ways. The specific experiences of every adolescent—his fears, his family crises, his dreams and hallucinations, his habits, his sexuality—all these are points at which the general culture reveals itself in some way. There is no longer any real question of getting the adolescent to "adjust" to things.

The problem is a different one: What kind of setting will enable him to discover and accept what is already within him; to articulate it and perceive the extent to which it is shared with others; and, finally, to learn to change it within and outside himself? For that is what I mean when I call the adolescent a "maker of value." He is a trustee, a trustee of a world that already exists in some form within himself—and we must both learn, the adolescent and his teachers, to respect it.

In a sense, then, I am calling for a reversal of most educational thought. The individual is central; the individual, in the deepest sense, *is* the culture, not the institution. His culture resides in him, in experience and memory, and what is needed is an education that has at its base the sanctity of the individual's experience and leaves it intact.

What keeps running through my mind is a line I read twelve years ago in a friend's first published story: *The Idea in that idea is: there*

is no one over you. I like that line: *There is no one over you.* Perhaps
that signifies the gap between these children and their parents. For
the children it is true, they sense it: there is no one over them; be-
lievable authority has disappeared; it has been replaced by experience.
As Thomas Altizer says, God is dead; he is experienced now not as
someone above or omnipotent or omniscient or "outside," but inwardly,
as conscience or vision or even the unconscious or Tillich's "ground of
being." This is all too familiar to bother with here, but this particular 50
generation is a collective dividing point. The parents of these children,
the fathers, still believe in "someone" over them, insist upon it; in fact,
demand it for and from their children. The children themselves cannot
believe it; the idea means nothing to them. It is almost as if they are
the first real Americans—suddenly free of Europe and somehow father-
less, confused, forced back on their own experience, their own sense
of things, even though, at the same time, they are forced to defy their
families and schools in order to keep it.

This is, then, a kind of Reformation. Arnold was wrong when he
said that art would replace religion; education replaced it. Church
became School, the principal vehicle for value, for "culture," and just
as men once rebelled against the established Church as the mediator
between God and man, students now rebel against the *public* school
(and its version of things) as the intermediary between themselves and
experience, between themselves and experience and the making of
value. Students are expected to reach "reality" (whether of knowledge
or society) through their teachers and school. No one, it is said, can
participate in the culture effectively without having at one time passed
through their hands, proven his allegiance to them, and been blessed.
This is the authority exercised by priests or the Church. Just as men 51
once moved to shorten the approach to God, they are moved now to
do the same thing in relation to learning and to the community. For
just as God was argued to appear within a man—unique, private, and
yet shared—so culture is, in some way, grounded in the individual; it
inhabits him. The schools, like the Church, must be the expression of
that habitation, not its exclusive medium. This is the same reformative
shift that occurred in religion, a shift from the institutional (the external) to the individual (the internal), and it demands, when it occurs,
an agony, an apocalyptic frenzy, a destruction of the past itself. I believe it is happening now. One sees and feels it everywhere: a violent
fissure, a kind of quake.

I remember one moment in the streets of Oakland during the draft
demonstrations. The students had sealed off the street with overturned
cars and there were no police; the gutters were empty and the students
moved into them from the sidewalks, first walking, then running, and 52
finally almost dancing in the street. You could almost see the idea
coalesce on their faces: The street is ours! It was as if a weight had
been lifted from them, a fog; there was not at that moment any fury
in them, any vengefulness or even politics; rather, a lightness, delight,

an exhilaration at the sudden inexplicable sense of being free. George Orwell describes something similar in *Homage to Catalonia*: that brief period in Barcelona when the anarchists had apparently succeeded and men shared what power there was. I don't know how to describe it, except to say that one's inexplicable sense of invisible authority had vanished: the oppressive father, who is not really there, was gone.

That sudden feeling is familiar to us all. We have all had it from time to time in our own lives, that sense of "being at home," that ease, that feeling of a Paradise which is neither behind us nor deferred but is around us, a natural household. It is the hint and beginning of Manhood: a promise, a clue. One's attention turns to the immediate landscape and to one's fellows: toward what is there, toward what can be felt as a part of oneself. I have seen the same thing as I watched Stokely Carmichael speaking to a black audience and telling them that they must stop begging the white man, like children, for their rights. They were, he said, neither children nor slaves, no, they were—and here they chanted, almost cried, in unison—a beautiful people: *yes our noses are broad and our lips are thick and our hair is kinky . . . but we are beautiful, we are beautiful, we are black and beautiful.* Watching, you could sense in that released joy an emergence, a surfacing of pride, a refusal to accept shame or the white man's dominance—and a turning to one another, to their own inherent value.

But there is a kind of pain in being white and watching that, for there is no one to say the same things to white children; no "fathers" or brothers to give them that sense of manhood or pride. The adolescents I have seen—white, middle-class—are a long way from those words *we are beautiful, we are beautiful.* I cannot imagine how they will reach them, deprived as they are of all individual strength. For the schools exist to deprive one of strength. That is why one's own worth must be proven again and again by the satisfaction of external requirements with no inherent value or importance; it is why one must satisfy a set of inexplicable demands; it is why there is a continual separation of self and worth and the intrusion of a kind of institutional guilt: failure not of God but of *the system,* the nameless "others," the authority that one can never quite see; and it explains the oppressive sense of some nameless transgression, almost a shame at Being itself.

It is this feeling that pervades both high schools and college, this Kafkaesque sense of faceless authority that drives one to rebellion or withdrawal, and we are all, for that reason, enchanted by the idea of the Trial, that ancient Socratic dream of confrontation and vindication or martyrdom. It is then, of course, that Authority shows its face. In the mid-fifties I once watched Jack Kerouac on a television show and when the interviewer asked him what he wanted he said: to see the face of God. How arrogant and childish and direct! And yet, I suppose, it is what we all want as children: to have the masks of authority, all its disguises, removed and to see it plain. That is what lies in large part behind the riots in the schools. Their specific grievances are incidental; their real purpose is to make God show his face, to have whatever pervasive and oppressive force makes us perpetual children reveal itself, declare itself, commit itself at last. It is Biblical; it is Freudian; it reminds me in some way of the initiation rites: the need to unmask the gods and assume their power, to become an equal—and to find in that the manhood one has been denied.

The schools seem to enforce the idea that there *is* someone over
you; and the methods by which they do it are ritualized, pervasive.
The intrusion of guilt, shame, alienation from oneself, dependence,
insecurity—all these feelings are not the accidental results of schools;
they are intentional, and they are used in an attempt to make children 56
manipulable, obedient, "good citizens" we call it, and useful to the
state. The schools are the means by which we deprive the young of
manhood—that is what I mean to say—and we must not be surprised
when they seek that manhood in ways that must of necessity be childish and violent.

But I must admit this troubles me, for there is little choice between mindless violence and mindless authority, and I am just enough
of an academic, an intellectual, to want to preserve much of what will
be lost in the kind of rebellion or apocalypse that is approaching. And
yet, and yet . . . the rapidity of events leaves me with no clear idea,
no solution, no sense of what will be an adequate change. It may be
that all of this chaos is a way of breaking with the old world and that
from it some kind of native American will emerge. There is no way
of knowing, there no longer seems any way of estimating what is necessary or what will work. I know only that the problem now seems to
be that our response to crisis is to move away or back rather than
forward, and that we will surely, for the sake of some imagined order, 57
increase in number and pressure the very approaches that have brought
us to this confusion. I don't know. I believe that the young must have
values, of course, be responsible, care, but I know too that most of the
violence I have seen done to the young has been done in the name of
value, and that the well-meaning people who have been so dead set
on making things right have had a hand in bringing us to where we
are now. The paradox is a deep and troubling one for me. I no longer
know if change can be accomplished—for the young, for any of us,
without the apocalyptic fury that seems almost upon us. The crisis of
youth and education is symptomatic of some larger, deeper fault in
our cities and minds, and perhaps nothing can be done consciously in
those areas until the air itself is violently cleared one way or another.

So I have no easy conclusions, no startling synthesis with which
to close. I have only a change in mood, a softening, a kind of sadness.
It may be, given that, that the best thing is simply to close with an 58
unfinished fragment in which I catch for myself the hint of an alternative:

. . . *I am trying to surround you, I see that, I am trying to make with these words a kind of city so natural, so familiar, that the other world, the one that appears to be, will look by comparison absurd and flat, limited, unnecessary. What I am after is liberation, not my own, which comes often enough these days in solitude or sex, but yours, and that is arrogant, isn't it, that is presumptuous, and yet that is the function of art: to set you free. It is that too which is the end of education: a liberation from childhood and what holds us there, a kind of midwifery, as if the nation itself were in labor and one wanted to save both the future and the past—for we are both, we are, we are the thin bridge swaying between them, and to tear one from the other means a tearing of ourselves, a partial death.*

And yet it may be that death is inevitable, useful. It may be. Perhaps, as in the myth, Aphrodite can rise only where Cronos' testicles have fallen into the sea. It may be that way with us. The death of the Father who is in us, the death of the old authority which is part of us, the death of the past which is also our death; it may all be necessary: a rending and purgation. And yet one still seeks another way, something less (or is it more) apocalyptic, a way in which the past becomes the future in ourselves, in which we become the bridges between: makers of culture.

Unless from us the future takes place, we are Death only, *said Lawrence, meaning what the Chassids do: that the world and time reside within, not outside, men; that there is no distance, no "alienation," only a perpetual wedding to the world. It is that—the presence in oneself of Time—that makes things interesting, is more gravid and interesting than guilt. I don't want to lose it, don't want to relinquish that sense in the body of another dimension, a distance, the depth of the body as it extends backward into the past and forward, as it contains and extends and transforms.*

What I am after is an alternative to separation and rage, some kind of connection to things to replace the system of dependence and submission—the loss of the self—that now holds sway, slanted toward violence. I am trying to articulate a way of seeing, of feeling, that will restore to the young a sense of manhood and potency without at the same time destroying the past. That same theme runs through whatever I write: the necessity for each man to experience himself as an extension and maker of culture, and to feel the whole force of the world within himself, not as an enemy—but as himself:

. . . An act of learning is a meeting, and every meeting is simply the discovery in the world of a part of oneself that had previously been unacknowledged by the self. It is the recovery of the extent of one's being. It is the embrace of an eternal but elusive companion the shadowy "other" in which one truly resides and which blazes, when embraced, like the sun.

Jerzy Kosinski

Children of TV*

During the last four years, I have taught at Wesleyan, Princeton,
and at Yale University. I have often lectured at many schools throughout the country. I am appalled by what I think emerges as the dominant trait of the students of today—their short span of attention, their
inability to know or believe anything for more than half an hour. I
feel it was television which turned them into spectators, since by comparison with the world of television, their own lives are slow and un- 1
eventful. When they first believed that what they saw on TV was real,
they overreacted, only to feel cheated when the next program demanded
a new emotion. Later, they felt simply manipulated by whatever drama
they witnessed. By now, they have become hostile, and so they either
refuse to watch the TV altogether or they dissect the medium and
throw out all that upsets them.

It was from the daily log of TV that they accepted the world as
single-faceted and never complex. After all, if it was accessible to TV
cameras, it couldn't possibly be otherwise. It was digestible and motion-
lessly marching in front of them. From TV's comic cartoons they first 2
deducted that death is not final, since their hero, no matter how dead,
would rise. It was TV that taught them that they need not be experienced but avoid it. Hence, they remain at the mercy of the pain reliever
commercials.

It was TV that first convinced them that drugs were to be trusted
and that with their help there was no suffering, no need to be tensed—
indeed, unhappy. As a professor of prose I am constantly reminded of
television's legacy. The students don't describe. They announce, as if 3
an ever-present screen orchestrated their meaning for everyone. In hundreds of essays, none of them approached killing, illness, passion. All
this was dismissed by shorthand, mutilated, suffered, feeling bad. A
lover throbs innocence. The recipient sweats sweetness.

During their scholarly and leisure pursuits, they switch with exactly the same intensity and staying power from subject to subject, as
if changing TV channels. Fifteen minutes is all a teacher can hope for,

* Editor's title.

assuming the classroom is freezing and the students' chairs are very uncomfortable. Whether discussing Vietnam or what's for lunch or a film, they seem incapable of reflecting. Even though their stomachs are full like exotic fishes of the Amazon, they swallow indiscriminately, quickly ejecting all as waste.

Reading, however, is solitary, requiring effort and imagination to translate a symbol into reality. Hence, the youngsters don't venture beyond required reading texts or worse, limit themselves to condensed aids. And so, at the campuses, the novel is not dead. Its readers are dying fast. The students never seem to be alone for more than a few hours. To them, solitude means feeling lonely. When awake, if they ever are, they join the group. Others provide a stage for being turned on, but no more than a TV set can they turn themselves on. This requires assistance and moviemakers, music pushers, encounter group merchants, fashion promoters, and television are there to keep the young plugged in.

Another myth of this greening of America is the young are using drugs to create mystic experience and self-discovery. A drug, whether soft or hard, is the crudest do-it-yourself identity kit remedy. Using it, many young miss their identity in the same way so many of their elders who are engaged in the socalled sexual revolution miss the meaning of love in the guise of being free.

Rock is another safely collective rite. At best, they can claim it a shared situation. They listen to music in a group. Deafening sound effectively rules out every exchange and permits each of them to escape direct contact with the others. They barely retain the memory of the lyrics and the beat. The students' political revolution has been no more than another football trip. There are the momentary heroes, the cheerleaders, the spectators, a bit of virility and of machismo. In ten years, the white young rebels of this country have not sustained any ideology, one effective group or party. Politics, after all, is for them another channel to turn to and be turned by.

Those of you who feel that what I have just said is valid, make no mistake. To the young who watch me now, it is nothing but a billboard, temporarily occupied by a public-health message of sorts. They are ready for the next program. Why, therefore, you ask, do I still teach at universities? Because, as with television, there's always a chance for a better program, a different generation, or at least, for a few profound specials.

Carlos Castaneda

From the Teachings of Don Juan: A Yaqui Way of Knowledge

1

My notes on my first session with don Juan are dated June 23,
1961. That was the occasion when the teachings began. I had seen him
several times previously in the capacity of an observer only. At every
opportunity I had asked him to teach me about peyote. He ignored 1
my request every time, but he never completely dismissed the subject,
and I interpreted his hesitancy as a possibility that he might be inclined
to talk about his knowledge with more coaxing.

In this particular session he made it obvious to me that he might
consider my request provided I possessed clarity of mind and purpose
in reference to what I had asked him. It was impossible for me to fulfill such a condition, for I had asked him to teach me about peyote only
as a means of establishing a link of communication with him. I thought 2
his familiarity with the subject might predispose him to be more open
and willing to talk, thus allowing me an entrance into his knowledge
on the properties of plants. He had interpreted my request literally,
however, and was concerned about my purpose in wishing to learn
about peyote.

Friday, June 23, 1961

"Would you teach me about peyote, don Juan?"

"Why would you like to undertake such learning?"

"I really would like to know about it. Is not just to want to know a good reason?"

"No! You must search in your heart and find out why a young
man like you wants to undertake such a task of learning." 3

"Why did you learn about it yourself, don Juan?"

"Why do you ask that?"

"Maybe we both have the same reasons."

"I doubt that. I am an Indian. We don't have the same paths."

"The only reason I have is that I *want* to learn about it, just to know. But I assure you, don Juan, my intentions are not bad."

"I believe you. I've smoked you."

"I beg your pardon!"

"It doesn't matter now. I know your intentions."

"Do you mean you saw through me?"

"You could put it that way."

"Will you teach me, then?"

"No!"

"Is it because I'm not an Indian?"

"No. It is because you don't know your heart. What is important is that you know exactly why you want to involve yourself. Learning about 'Mescalito' is a most serious act. If you were an Indian your desire alone would be sufficient. Very few Indians have such a desire."

Sunday, June 25, 1961

I stayed with don Juan all afternoon on Friday. I was going to leave about 7 P.M. We were sitting on the porch in front of his house and I decided to ask him once more about the teaching. It was almost a routine question and I expected him to refuse again. I asked him if there was a way in which he could accept just my desire to learn, as if I were an Indian. He took a long time to answer. I was compelled to stay because he seemed to be trying to decide something.

Finally he told me that there was a way, and proceeded to delineate a problem. He pointed out that I was very tired sitting on the floor, and that the proper thing to do was to find a "spot" (*sitio*) on the floor where I could sit without fatigue. I had been sitting with my knees up against my chest and my arms locked around my calves. When he said I was tired, I realized that my back ached and that I was quite exhausted.

I waited for him to explain what he meant by a "spot," but he made no overt attempt to elucidate the point. I thought that perhaps he meant that I should change positions, so I got up and sat closer to him. He protested my movement and clearly emphasized that a spot meant a place where a man could feel naturally happy and strong. He patted the place where he sat and said it was his own spot, adding that he had posed a riddle I had to solve by myself without any further deliberation.

What he had posed as a problem to be solved was certainly a riddle. I had no idea how to begin or even what he had in mind. Several times I asked for a clue, or at least a hint, as to how to proceed in locating a point where I felt happy and strong. I insisted and argued that I had no idea what he really meant because I couldn't conceive the problem. He suggested I walk around the porch until I found the spot.

I got up and began to pace the floor. I felt silly and sat down in front of him.

He became very annoyed with me and accused me of not listening,
saying that perhaps I did not want to learn. After a while he calmed
down and explained to me that not every place was good to sit or be
on, and that within the confines of the porch there was one spot that 9
was unique, a spot where I could be at my very best. It was my task
to distinguish it from all the other places. The general pattern was that
I had to "feel" all the possible spots that were accessible until I could
determine without a doubt which was the right one.

I argued that although the porch was not too large (12 x 8 feet),
the number of possible spots was overwhelming, and it would take me
a very long time to check all of them, and that since he had not specified the size of the spot, the possibilities might be infinite. My arguments were futile. He got up and very sternly warned me that it might
take me days to figure it out, but that if I did not solve the problem, 10
I might as well leave because he would have nothing to say to me. He
emphasized that he knew where my spot was, and that therefore I could
not lie to him; he said this was the only way he could accept my desire
to learn about Mescalito as a valid reason. He added that nothing in
his world was a gift, that whatever there was to learn had to be learned
the hard way.

He went around the house to the chaparral to urinate. He returned 11
directly into his house through the back.

I thought the assignment to find the alleged spot of happiness was
his own way of dismissing me, but I got up and started to pace back
and forth. The sky was clear. I could see everything on and near the
porch. I must have paced for an hour or more, but nothing happened
to reveal the location of the spot. I got tired of walking and sat down; 12
after a few minutes I sat somewhere else, and then at another place, until
I had covered the whole floor in a semisystematic fashion. I deliberately
tried to "feel" differences between places, but I lacked the criteria for
differentiation. I felt I was wasting my time, but I stayed. My rationalization was that I had come a long way just to see don Juan, and I
really had nothing else to do.

I lay down on my back and put my hands under my head like a
pillow. Then I rolled over and lay on my stomach for a while. I repeated 13
this rolling process over the entire floor. For the first time I thought I
had stumbled upon a vague criterion. I felt warmer when I lay on my
back.

I rolled again, this time in the opposite direction, and again covered
the length of the floor, lying face down on all the places where I had
lain face up during my first rolling tour. I experienced the same warm 14
and cold sensations, depending on my position, but there was no difference between spots.

Then an idea occurred to me which I thought to be brilliant: don
Juan's spot! I sat there, and then lay, face down at first, and later on 15
my back, but the place was just like all the others. I stood up. I had

had enough. I wanted to say good-bye to don Juan, but I was embarrassed to wake him up. I looked at my watch. It was two o'clock in the morning! I had been rolling for six hours.

At that moment don Juan came out and went around the house to the chaparral. He came back and stood at the door. I felt utterly dejected, and I wanted to say something nasty to him and leave. But I realized that it was not his fault; that it was my own choice to go through all that nonsense. I told him I had failed; I had been rolling on his floor like an idiot all night and still couldn't make any sense of his riddle.

He laughed and said that it did not surprise him because I had not proceeded correctly. I had not been using my eyes. That was true, yet I was very sure he had said to feel the difference. I brought that point up, but he argued that one can feel with the eyes, when the eyes are not looking right into things. As far as I was concerned, he said, I had no other means to solve this problem but to use all I had —my eyes.

He went inside. I was certain that he had been watching me. I thought there was no other way for him to know that I had not been using my eyes.

I began to roll again, because that was the most comfortable procedure. This time, however, I rested my chin on my hands and looked at every detail.

After an interval the darkness around me changed. When I focused on the point directly in front of me, the whole peripheral area of my field of vision became brilliantly colored with a homogeneous greenish yellow. The effect was startling. I kept my eyes fixed on the point in front of me and began to crawl sideways on my stomach, one foot at a time.

Suddenly, at a point near the middle of the floor, I became aware of another change in hue. At a place to my right, still in the periphery of my field of vision, the greenish yellow became intensely purple. I concentrated my attention on it. The purple faded into a pale, but still brilliant, color which remained steady for the time I kept my attention on it.

I marked the place with my jacket, and called don Juan. He came out to the porch. I was truly excited; I had actually seen the change in hues. He seemed unimpressed, but told me to sit on the spot and report to him what kind of feeling I had.

I sat down and then lay on my back. He stood by me and asked me repeatedly how I felt; but I did not feel anything different. For about fifteen minutes I tried to feel or to see a difference, while don Juan stood by me patiently. I felt disgusted. I had a metallic taste in my mouth. Suddenly I had developed a headache. I was about to get sick. The thought of my nonsensical endeavors irritated me to a point of fury. I got up.

Don Juan must have noticed my profound frustration. He did not laugh, but very seriously stated that I had to be inflexible with myself
if I wanted to learn. Only two choices were open to me, he said: either 24
to quit and go home, in which case I would never learn, or to solve the riddle.

He went inside again. I wanted to leave immediately, but I was too tired to drive; besides, perceiving the hues had been so startling
that I was sure it was a criterion of some sort, and perhaps there were 25
other changes to be detected. Any way, it was too late to leave. So I sat down, stretched my legs back, and began all over again.

During this round I moved rapidly through each place, passing don Juan's spot, to the end of the floor, and then turned around to cover the outer edge. When I reached the center, I realized that another change in coloration was taking place, again on the edge of my field of vision. The uniform chartreuse I was seeing all over the area turned,
at one spot to my right, into a sharp verdigris. It remained for a mo- 26
ment and then abruptly metatmorphosed into another steady hue, different from the other one I had detected earlier. I took off one of my shoes and marked the point, and kept on rolling until I had covered the floor in all possible directions. No other change of coloration took place.

I came back to the point marked with my shoe, and examined it. It was located five to six feet away from the spot marked by my jacket,
in a southeasterly direction. There was a large rock next to it. I lay 27
down there for quite some time trying to find clues, looking at every detail, but I did not feel anything different.

I decided to try the other spot. I quickly pivoted on my knees and was about to lie down on my jacket when I felt an unusual apprehension. It was more like a physical sensation of something actually pushing on my stomach. I jumped up and retreated in one movement. The 28
hair on my neck pricked up. My legs had arched slightly, my trunk was bent forward, and my arms stuck out in front of me rigidly with my fingers contracted like a claw. I took notice of my strange posture and my fright increased.

I walked back involuntarily and sat down on the rock next to my shoe. From the rock, I slumped to the floor. I tried to figure out what
had happened to cause me such a fright. I thought it must have been 29
the fatigue I was experiencing. It was nearly daytime. I felt silly and embarrassed. Yet I had no way to explain what had frightened me, nor had I figured out what don Juan wanted.

I decided to give it one last try. I got up and slowly approached the place marked by my jacket, and again I felt the same apprehension.
This time I made a strong effort to control myself. I sat down, and 30
then knelt in order to lie face down, but I could not lie in spite of my will. I put my hands on the floor in front of me. My breathing accelerated; my stomach was upset. I had a clear sensation of panic,

and fought not to run away. I thought don Juan was perhaps watching me. Slowly I crawled back to the other spot and propped my back against the rock. I wanted to rest for a while to organize my thoughts, but I fell asleep.

I heard don Juan talking and laughing above my head. I woke up.

"You have found the spot," he said.

I did not understand him at first, but he assured me again that the place where I had fallen asleep was the spot in question. He again asked me how I felt lying there. I told him I really did not notice any difference.

He asked me to compare my feelings at that moment with what I had felt while lying on the other spot. For the first time it occurred to me that I could not possibly explain my apprehension of the preceding night. He urged me in a kind of challenging way to sit on the other spot. For some inexplicable reason I was actually afraid of the other place, and did not sit on it. He asserted that only a fool could fail to see the difference.

I asked him if each of the two spots had a special name. He said that the good one was called the *sitio* and the bad one the enemy; he said these two places were the key to a man's well-being, especially for a man who was pursuing knowledge. The sheer act of sitting on one's spot created superior strength; on the other hand, the enemy weakened a man and could even cause his death. He said I had replenished my energy; which I had spent lavishly the night before, by taking a nap on my spot.

He also said that the colors I had seen in association with each specific spot had the same overall effect either of giving strength or of curtailing it.

I asked him if there were other spots for me like the two I had found, and how I should go about finding them. He said that many places in the world would be comparable to those two, and that the best way to find them was by detecting their respective colors.

It was not clear to me whether or not I had solved the problem, and in fact I was not even convinced that there had been a problem; I could not avoid feeling that the whole experience was forced and arbitrary. I was certain that don Juan had watched me all night and then proceeded to humor me by saying that wherever I had fallen asleep *was* the place I was looking for. Yet I failed to see a logical reason for such an act, and when he challenged me to sit on the other spot I could not do it. There was a strange cleavage between my pragmatic experience of fearing the "other spot" and my rational deliberations about the total event.

Don Juan, on the other hand, was very sure I had succeeded, and, acting in accordance with my success, let me know he was going to teach me about peyote.

"You asked me to teach you about Mescalito," he said. "I wanted to find out if you had enough backbone to meet him face to face.

Mescalito is not something to make fun of. You must have command
over your resources. Now I know I can take your desire alone as a 39
good reason to learn."

"You really are going to teach me about peyote?"

"I prefer to call him Mescalito. Do the same."

"When are you going to start?"

"It is not so simple as that. You must be ready first."

"I think I am ready."

"This is not a joke. You must wait until there is no doubt, and then you will meet him."

"Do I have to prepare myself?"

"No. You simply have to wait. You may give up the whole idea after a while. You get tired easily. Last night you were ready to quit as soon as it got difficult. Mescalito requires a very serious intent."

2

Monday, August 7, 1961

I arrived at don Juan's house in Arizona about seven o'clock on
Friday night. Five other Indians were sitting with him on the porch
of his house. I greeted him and sat waiting for them to say something.
After a formal silence one of the men got up, walked over to me, and
said, "Buenas noches." I stood up and answered, "Buenas noches." Then 40
all the other men got up and came to me and we all mumbled "buenas
noches" and shook hands either by barely touching one another's finger-
tips or by holding the hand for an instant and then dropping it quite
abruptly.

We all sat down again. They seemed to be rather shy—at a loss 41
for words, although they all spoke Spanish.

It must have been about half past seven when suddenly they all
got up and walked toward the back of the house. Nobody had said a
word for a long time. Don Juan signaled me to follow and we all got
inside an old pickup truck parked there. I sat in the back with don 42
Juan and two younger men. There were no cushions or benches and
the metal floor was painfully hard, especially when we left the highway and got onto a dirt road. Don Juan whispered that we were going
to the house of one of his friends who had seven mescalitos for me.

I asked him, "Don't you have any of them yourself, don Juan?"

"I do, but I couldn't offer them to you. You see, someone else has to do this."

"Can you tell me why?"

"Perhaps you are not agreeable to 'him' and 'he' won't like you, 43
and then you will never be able to know 'him' with affection, as one
should; and our friendship will be broken."

"Why wouldn't he like me? I have never done anything to him."

"You don't have to *do* anything to be liked or disliked. He either takes you, or throws you away."

"But, if he doesn't take me, isn't there anything I can do to make him like me?"

The other two men seemed to have overheard my question and laughed.

"No I can't think of anything one can do," don Juan said.

He turned half away from me and I could not talk to him anymore.

We must have driven for at least an hour before we stopped in front of a small house. It was quite dark, and after the driver had turned off the headlights I could make out only the vague contour of the building.

A young woman, a Mexican, judging by her speech inflection, was yelling at a dog to make him stop barking. We got out of the truck and walked into the house. The men mumbled "Buenas noches" as they went by her. She answered back and went on yelling at the dog.

The room was large and was stacked up with a multitude of objects. A dim light from a very small electric bulb rendered the scene quite gloomy. There were quite a few chairs with broken legs and sagging seats leaning against the walls. Three of the men sat down on a couch, which was the largest single piece of furniture in the room. It was very old and had sagged down all the way to the floor; in the dim light it seemed to be red and dirty. The rest of us sat in chairs. We sat in silence for a long time.

One of the men suddenly got up and went into another room. He was perhaps in his fifties, dark, tall, and husky. He came back a moment later with a coffee jar. He opened the lid and handed the jar to me; inside there were seven odd-looking items. They varied in size and consistency. Some of them were almost round, others were elongated. They felt to the touch like the pulp of walnuts, or the surface of cork. Their brownish color made them look like hard, dry nutshells. I handled them, rubbing their surfaces for quite some time.

"This is to be chewed [*esto se masca*]," don Juan said in a whisper.

I had not realized that he had sat next to me until he spoke. I looked at the other men, but no one was looking at me; they were talking among themselves in very low voices. This was a moment of acute indecision and fear. I felt almost unable to control myself.

"I have to go to the bathroom," I said to him. "I'll go outside and take a walk."

He handed me the coffee jar and I put the peyote buttons in it. I was leaving the room when the man who had given me the jar stood up, came to me, and said he had a toilet bowl in the other room.

The toilet was almost against the door. Next to it, nearly touching the toilet, was a large bed which occupied more than half of the room. The women was sleeping there. I stood motionless at the door for a while, then I came back to the room where the other men were.

The man who owned the house spoke to me in English: "Don Juan says you're from South America. Is there any mescal there?" I told him that I had never even heard of it.

They seemed to be interested in South America and we talked
about the Indians for a while. Then one of the men asked me why I 55
wanted to eat peyote. I told him that I wanted to know what it was like.
They all laughed shyly.

Don Juan urged me softly, "Chew it, chew it [*Masca, masca*]." 56

My hands were wet and my stomach contracted. The jar with the
peyote buttons was on the floor by the chair. I bent over, took one at
random, and put it in my mouth. It had a stale taste. I bit it in two and
started to chew one of the pieces. I felt a strong, pungent bitterness; in
a moment my whole mouth was numb. The bitterness increased as I
kept on chewing, forcing an incredible flow of saliva. My gums and
the inside of my mouth felt as if I had eaten salty, dry meat or fish, 57
which seems to force one to chew more. After a while I chewed the
other piece and my mouth was so numb I couldn't feel the bitterness
anymore. The peyote button was a bunch of shreds, like the fibrous
part of an orange or like sugarcane, and I didn't know whether to
swallow it or spit it out. At that moment the owner of the house got
up and invited everybody to go out to the porch.

We went out and sat in the darkness. It was quite comfortable 58
outside, and the host brought out a bottle of tequila.

The men were seated in a row with their backs to the wall. I was
at the extreme right of the line. Don Juan, who was next to me, placed 59
the jar with the peyote buttons between my legs. Then he handed me
the bottle, which was passed down the line, and told me to take some
of the tequila to wash away the bitterness.

I spit out the shreds of the first button and took a sip. He told
me not to swallow it, but to just rinse out my mouth with it to stop 60
the saliva. It did not help much with the saliva, but it certainly helped
to wash away some of the bitterness.

Don Juan gave me a piece of dried apricot, or perhaps it was a
dried fig—I couldn't see it in the dark, nor could I taste it—and told me 61
to chew it thoroughly and slowly, without rushing. I had difficulty
swallowing it; it felt as if it would not go down.

After a short pause the bottle went around again. Don Juan handed
me a piece of crispy dried meat. I told him I did not feel like eating. 62

"This is not eating," he said firmly. 63

The pattern was repeated six times. I remember having chewed
six peyote buttons when the conversation became very lively; although
I could not distinguish what language was spoken, the topic of the conversation, in which everybody participated, was very interesting, and I 64
attempted to listen carefully so that I could take part. But when I tried
to speak I realized I couldn't; the words shifted aimlessly about in my
mind.

I sat with my back propped against the wall and listened to what
the men were saying. They were talking in Italian, and repeated over 65
and over one phrase about the stupidity of sharks. I thought it was a
logical, coherent topic. I had told don Juan earlier that the Colorado

River in Arizona was called by the early Spaniards "el rio de los tizones [the river of charred wood]"; and someone misspelled or misread "ti-zones," and the river was called "el rio de los tiburones [the river of the sharks]." I was sure they were discussing that story, yet it never occurred to me to think that none of them could speak Italian.

I had a very strong desire to throw up, but I don't recall the actual act. I asked if somebody would get me some water. I was experiencing an unbearable thirst.

Don Juan brought me a large saucepan. He placed it on the ground next to the wall. He also brought a little cup or can. He dipped it into the pan and handed it to me, and said I could not drink but should just freshen my mouth with it.

The water looked strangely shiny, glossy, like a thick varnish. I wanted to ask don Juan about it and laboriously I tried to voice my thoughts in English, but then I realized he did not speak English. I experienced a very confusing moment, and became aware of the fact that although there was a clear thought in my mind, I could not speak. I wanted to comment on the strange quality of the water, but what followed next was not speech; it was the feeling of my unvoiced thoughts coming out of my mouth in a sort of liquid form. It was an effortless sensation of vomiting without the contractions of the diaphragm. It was a pleasant flow of liquid words.

I drank. And the feeling that I was vomiting disappeared. By that time all noises had vanished and I found I had difficulty focusing my eyes. I looked for don Juan and as I turned my head I noticed that my field of vision had diminished to a circular area in front of my eyes. This feeling was neither frightening nor discomforting, but, quite to the contrary, it was a novelty; I could literally sweep the ground by focusing on one spot and then moving my head slowly in any direction. When I had first come out to the porch I had noticed it was all dark except for the distant glare of the city lights. Yet within the circular area of my vision everything was clear. I forgot about my concern with don Juan and the other men, and gave myself entirely to exploring the ground with my pinpoint vision.

I saw the juncture of the porch floor and the wall. I turned my head slowly to the right, following the wall, and saw don Juan sitting against it. I shifted my head to the left in order to focus on the water. I found the bottom of the pan; I raised my head slightly and saw a medium-size black dog approaching. I saw him coming toward the water. The dog began to drink. I raised my hand to push him away from my water; I focused my pinpoint vision on the dog to carry on the movement, and suddenly I saw him become transparent. The water was a shiny, viscous liquid. I saw it going down the dog's throat into his body. I saw it flowing evenly through his entire length and then shooting out through each one of the hairs. I saw the iridescent fluid traveling along the length of each individual hair and then projecting out of the hairs to form a long, white, silky mane.

At that moment I had the sensation of intense convulsions, and in a matter of instants a tunnel formed around me, very low and narrow, hard and strangely cold. It felt to the touch like a wall of solid tinfoil. I found I was sitting on the tunnel floor. I tried to stand up, but hit my head on the metal roof, and the tunnel compressed itself until it
was suffocating me. I remember having to crawl toward a sort of round 71
point where the tunnel ended; when I finally arrived, if I did, I had forgotten all about the dog, don Juan, and myself. I was exhausted. My clothes were soaked in a cold, sticky liquid. I rolled back and forth trying to find a position in which to rest, a position where my heart would not pound so hard. In one of those shifts I saw the dog again.

Every memory came back to me at once, and suddenly all was clear in my mind. I turned around to look for don Juan, but I could not distinguish anything or anyone. All I was capable of seeing was the dog becoming iridescent; an intense light radiated from his body. I saw again the water flowing through him, kindling him like a bonfire. I got to the water, sank my face in the pan, and drank with him. My hands were in front of me on the ground and, as I drank, I saw the fluid running through my veins setting up hues of red and yellow and green. I drank more and more. I drank until I was all afire; I was all aglow. I drank until the fluid went out of my body through each pore, and projected out like fibers of silk, and I too acquired a long, lustrous,
iridescent mane. I looked at the dog and his mane was like mine. A 72
supreme happiness filled my whole body, and we ran together toward a sort of yellow warmth that came from some indefinite place. And there we played. We played and wrestled until I knew his wishes and he knew mine. We took turns manipulating each other in the fashion of a puppet show. I could make him move his legs by twisting my toes, and every time he nodded his head I felt an irresistible impulse to jump. But his most impish act was to make me scratch my head with my foot while I sat; he did it by flapping his ears from side to side. This action was to me utterly, unbearable funny. Such a touch of grace and irony; such mastery, I thought. The euphoria that possessed me was indescribable. I laughed until it was almost impossible to breathe.

I had the clear sensation of not being able to open my eyes; I was looking through a tank of water. It was a long and very painful state filled with the anxiety of not being able to wake up and yet being awake. Then slowly the world became clear and in focus. My field of
vision became again very round and ample, and with it came an ordi- 73
nary conscious act, which was to turn around and look for that marvelous being. At this point I encountered the most difficult transition. The passage from my normal state had taken place almost without my realizing it: I was aware; my thoughts and feelings were a corollary of that awareness; and the passing was smooth and clear. But this second change, the awakening to serious, sober consciousness, was gen-

uinely shocking. I had forgotten I was a man! The sadness of such an irreconcilable situation was so intense that I wept.

Saturday, August 5, 1961

Later that morning, after breakfast, the owner of the house, don Juan, and I drove back to don Juan's place. I was very tired, but I couldn't go to sleep in the truck. Only after the man had left did I fall asleep on the porch of don Juan's house.

When I woke up it was dark; don Juan had covered me up with a blanket. I looked for him, but he was not in the house. He came later with a pot of fried beans and a stack of tortillas. I was extremely hungry.

After we had finished eating and were resting he asked me to tell him all that had happened to me the night before. I related my experience in great detail and as accurately as possible.

When I finished he nodded his head and said, "I think you are fine. It is difficult for me to explain now how and why. But I think it went all right for you. You see, sometimes he is playful, like a child; at other times he is terrible, fearsome. He either frolics, or he is dead serious. It is impossible to know beforehand what he will be like with another person. Yet, when one knows him well—sometimes. You played with him tonight. You are the only person I know who has had such an encounter."

"In what way does my experience differ from that of others?"

"You're not an Indian; therefore it is hard for me to figure out what is what. Yet he either takes people or rejects them, regardless of whether they are Indians or not. That I know. I have seen numbers of them. I also know that he frolics, he makes some people laugh, but never have I seen him play with anyone."

"Can you tell me now, don Juan, how does peyote protect . . ."

He did not let me finish. Vigorously he touched me on the shoulder.

"Don't you ever name him that way. You haven't seen enough of him yet to know him."

"How does Mescalito protect people?"

"He advises. He answers whatever questions you ask."

"Then Mescalito is real? I mean he is something you can see?"

He seemed to be baffled by my question. He looked at me with a sort of blank expression.

"What I meant to say, is that Mescalito . . ."

"I heard what you said. Didn't you see him last night?"

I wanted to say that I saw only a dog, but I noticed his bewildered look.

"Then you think what I saw last night was him?"

He looked at me with contempt. He chuckled, shook his head as though he couldn't believe it, and in a very belligerent tone he added, "A poco crees que era tu—mamá [Don't tell me you believe it was your—mama]?" He paused before saying "mamá" because what he meant to say was "tu chingada madre," an idiom used as a disrespect-

ful allusion to the other party's mother. The word "mamá" was so
incongruous that we both laughed for a long time.

Then I realized he had fallen asleep and had not answered my
question. 80

Sunday, August 6, 1961

I drove don Juan to the house where I had taken peyote. On the
way he told me that the name of the man who had "offered me to
Mescalito" was John. When we got to the house we found John sitting
on his porch with two young men. All of them were extremely jovial. 81
They laughed and talked with great ease. The three of them spoke
English perfectly. I told John that I had come to thank him for having
helped me.

I wanted to get their views on my behavior during the hallucino-
genic experience, and told them I had been trying to think of what I
had done that night and that I couldn't remember. They laughed and
were reluctant to talk about it. They seemed to be holding back on 82
account of don Juan. They all glanced at him as though waiting for
an affirmative cue to go on. Don Juan must have cued them, although
I did not notice anything, because suddenly John began to tell me what
I had done that night.

He said he knew I had been "taken" when he heard me puking.
He estimated that I must have puked thirty times. Don Juan corrected 83
him and said it was only ten times.

John continued: "Then we all moved next to you. You were stiff,
and were having convulsions. For a very long time, while lying on your
back, you moved your mouth as though talking. Then you began to
bump your head on the floor, and don Juan put an old hat on your
head and you stopped it. You shivered and whined for hours, lying on 84
the floor. I think everybody fell asleep then; but I heard you puffing
and groaning in my sleep. Then I heard you scream and I woke up.
I saw you leaping up in the air, screaming. You made a dash for the
water, knocked the pan over, and began to swim in the puddle.

"Don Juan brought you more water. You sat quietly in front of the
pan. Then you jumped up and took off all your clothes. You were
kneeling in front of the water, drinking in big gulps. Then you just sat
there and stared into space. We thought you were going to be there 85
forever. Nearly everybody was asleep, including don Juan, when suddenly you jumped up again, howling, and took after the dog. The dog
got scared and howled too, and ran to the back of the house. Then
everybody woke up.

"We all got up. You came back from the other side still chasing
the dog. The dog was running ahead of you barking and howling. I
think you must have gone twenty times around the house, running in 86
circles, barking like a dog: I was afraid people were going to be curious.
There are no neighbors close, but your howling was so loud it could
have been heard for miles."

One of the young men added, "You caught up with the dog and brought it to the porch in your arms."

John continued: "Then you began to play with the dog. You wrestled with him, and the dog and you bit each other and played. That, I thought, was funny. My dog does not play usually. But this time you and the dog were rolling on each other."

"Then you ran to the water and the dog drank with you," the young man said. "You ran five or six times to the water with the dog."

"How long did this go on?" I asked.

"Hours," John said. "At one time we lost sight of you two. I think you must have run to the back. We just heard you barking and groaning. You sounded so much like a dog that we couldn't tell you two apart."

"Maybe it was just the dog alone," I said.

They laughed, and John said, "You were barking there, boy!"

"What happened next?"

The three men looked at one another and seemed to have a hard time deciding what happened next. Finally the young man who had not yet said anything spoke up.

"He choked," he said, looking at John.

"Yes, you certainly choked. You began to cry very strangely, and then you fell to the floor. We thought you were biting your tongue; don Juan opened your jaws and poured water on your face. Then you started shivering and having convulsions all over again. Then you stayed motionless for a long time. Don Juan said it was all over. By then it was morning, so we covered you with a blanket and left you to sleep on the porch."

He stopped there and looked at the other men who were obviously trying not to laugh. He turned to don Juan and asked him something. Don Juan smiled and answered the question. John turned to me and said, "We left you here on the porch because we were afraid you were going to piss all over the rooms."

They all laughed very loudly.

"What was the matter with me?" I asked. "Did I . . ."

"Did you?" John sort of mimicked me. "We were not going to mention it, but don Juan says it is all right. You pissed all over my dog!"

"What did I do?"

"You don't think the dog was running because he was afraid of you, do you? The dog was running because you were pissing on him."

There was general laughter at this point. I tried to question one of the young men, but they were all laughing and he didn't hear me.

John went on: "My dog got even though; he pissed on you too!"

This statement was apparently utterly funny because they all roared with laughter, including don Juan. When they had quieted down, I asked in all earnestness, "Is it really true? This really happened?"

Still laughing, John replied: "I swear my dog really pissed on you."

Driving back to don Juan's place I asked him: "Did all that really happen, don Juan?"

"Yes," he said, "but they don't know what you saw. They don't realize you were playing with 'him.' That is why I did not disturb you."

"But is this business of the dog and me pissing on each other true?"

"It was not a dog! How many times do I have to tell you that? This is the only way to understand it. It's the only way! It was 'he' who played with you."

"Did you know all this was happening before I told you about it?"

He vacillated for an instant before answering.

"No, I remembered, after you told me about it, the strange way you looked. I just suspected you were doing fine because you didn't seem scared."

"Did the dog really play with me as they say?"

"Goddammit! It was not a dog!"

Gary Snyder

Passage to More Than India

> "It will be a revival, in higher form, of the liberty, equality, and fraternity of the ancient gentes."
>
> —LEWIS HENRY MORGAN

The Tribe

The celebrated human Be-In in San Francisco, January of 1967, was called "A Gathering of the Tribes." The two posters: one based on a photograph of a Shaivite sadhu with his long matted hair, ashes and beard; the other based on an old etching of a Plains Indian approaching a powwow on his horse—the carbine that had been cradled in his left arm replaced by a guitar. The Indians, and the Indian. The tribes were Berkeley, North Beach, Big Sur, Marin County, Los Angeles, and the host, Haight-Ashbury. Outriders were present from New York, London and Amsterdam. Out on the polo field that day the splendidly clad ab/originals often fell into clusters, with children, a few even under banners. These were the clans.

Large old houses are rented communally by a group, occupied by couples and singles (or whatever combinations) and their children. In some cases, especially in the rock-and-roll business and with light-show groups, they are all working together on the same creative job. They might even be a legal corporation. Some are subsistence farmers out in the country, some are contractors and carpenters in small coast towns. One girl can stay home and look after all the children while the other girls hold jobs. They will all be cooking and eating together and they may well be brown-rice vegetarians. There might not be much alcohol or tobacco around the house, but there will certainly be a stash of marijuana and probably some LSD. If the group has been together for some time it may be known by some informal name, magical and natural. These house-holds provide centers in the city and also out in the country for loners and rangers; gathering places for the scattered smaller hip families and havens for the questing adolescent children of

the neighborhood. The clan sachems will sometimes gather to talk
about larger issues—police or sheriff department harassments, busts,
anti-Vietnam projects, dances and gatherings.

All this is known fact. The number of committed total tribesmen
is not so great, but there is a large population of crypto-members who
move through many walks of life undetected and only put on their
beads and feathers for special occasions. Some are in the academies,
others in the legal or psychiatric professions—very useful friends in- 3
deed. The number of people who use marijuana regularly and have
experienced LSD is (considering it's all illegal) staggering. The impact
of all this on the cultural and imaginative life of the nation—even the
politics—is enormous.

And yet, there's nothing very new about it, in spite of young hippies just in from the suburbs for whom the "beat generation" is a kalpa
away. For several centuries now Western Man has been ponderously
preparing himself for a new look at the inner world and the spiritual 4
realms. Even in the centers of nineteenth-century materialism there were
dedicated seekers—some within Christianity, some in the arts, some
within the occult circles. Witness William Butler Yeats. My own opinion
is that we are now experiencing a surfacing (in a specifically "American" incarnation) of the Great Subculture which goes back as far perhaps as the late Paleolithic.

This subculture of illuminati has been a powerful undercurrent in
all higher civilizations. In China it manifested as Taoism, not only Lao- 5
tzu but the later Yellow Turban revolt and medieval Taoist secret
societies; and the Zen Buddhists up till early Sung. Within Islam the
Sufis; in India the various threads converged to produce Tantrism. In
the West it has been represented largely by a string of heresies starting
with the Gnostics, and on the folk level by "witchcraft."

Buddhist Tantrism, or Vajrayana as it's also known, is probably the
finest and most modern statement of this ancient shamanistic-yogic-
gnostic-socioeconomic view: that mankind's mother is Nature and
Nature should be tenderly respected; that man's life and destiny is 6
growth and enlightenment in self-disciplined freedom; that the divine
has been made flesh and that flesh is divine; that we not only should
but *do* love one another. This view has been harshly suppressed in the
past as threatening to both Church and State. Today, on the contrary,
these values seem almost biologically essential to the survival of humanity.

The Family

Lewis Henry Morgan (d. 1881) was a New York lawyer. He was
asked by his club to reorganize it "after the pattern of the Iroquois
confederacy." His research converted him into a defender of tribal 7
rights and started him on his career as an amateur anthropologist. His
major contribution was a broad theory of social evolution which is still
useful. Morgan's *Ancient Society* inspired Engels to write *Origins of*

the Family, Private Property and the State (1884, and still in print in both Russia and China), in which the relations between the rights of women, sexuality and the family, and attitudes toward property and power are tentatively explored. The pivot is the revolutionary implications of the custom of matrilineal descent, which Engels learned from Morgan; the Iroquois are matrilineal.

A schematic history of the family:

Hunters and gatherers—a loose monogamy within communal clans usually reckoning descent in the female line, i.e., matrilineal.

Early agriculturalists—a tendency toward group and polyandrous marriage, continued matrilineal descent and smaller-sized clans.

Pastoral nomads—a tendency toward stricter monogamy and patrilineal descent; but much premarital sexual freedom.

Iron-Age agriculturalists—property begins to accumulate and the family system changes to monogamy or polygyny with patrilineal descent. Concern with the legitimacy of heirs.

Civilization so far has implied a patriarchal, patrilineal family. Any other system allows too much creative sexual energy to be released into channels which are "unproductive." In the West, the clan, or gens, disappeared gradually, and social organization was ultimately replaced by political organization, within which separate male-oriented families compete: the modern state.

Engels' Marxian classic implies that the revolution cannot be completely achieved in merely political terms. Monogamy and patrilineal descent may well be great obstructions to the inner changes required for a people to truly live by "communism." Marxists after Engels let these questions lie. Russia and China today are among the world's staunchest supporters of monogamous, sexually turned-off families. Yet Engels' insights were not entirely ignored. The Anarcho-Syndicalists showed a sense for experimental social reorganization. American anarchists and the I.W.W. lived a kind of communalism, with some lovely stories handed down of free love—their slogan was more than just words: "Forming the new society within the shell of the old." San Francisco poets and gurus were attending meetings of the "Anarchist Circle"—old Italians and Finns—in the 1940's.

The Redskins

In many American Indian cultures it is obligatory for every member to get out of the society, out of the human nexus, and "out of his head," at least once in his life. He returns from his solitary vision quest with a secret name, a protective animal spirit, a secret song. It is his "power." The culture honors the man who has visited other realms.

Peyote, the mushroom, morning-glory seeds and Jimson-weed are some of the best-known herbal aids used by Indian cultures to assist in the quest. Most tribes apparently achieved these results simply through yogic-type disciplines: including sweat-baths, hours of dancing, fasting and total isolation. After the decline of the apocalyptic fervor

of Wovoka's Ghost Dance religon (a pan-Indian movement of the 1880's
and 1890's which believed that if all the Indians would dance the Ghost
Dance with their Ghost shirts on, the Buffalo would rise from the
ground, trample the white men to death in their dreams, and all the
dead game would return; America would be restored to the Indians),
the peyote cult spread and established itself in most of the western
American tribes. Although the peyote religion conflicts with pre-existing
tribal religions in a few cases (notably with the Pueblo), there is no
doubt that the cult has been a positive force, helping the Indians main- 12
tain a reverence for their traditions and land through their period of
greatest weakness—which is now over. European scholars were investigating peyote in the twenties. It is even rumored that Dr. Carl Jung
was experimenting with peyote then. A small band of white peyote
users emerged, and peyote was easily available in San Francisco by
the late 1940's. In Europe some researchers on these alkaloid com-
pounds were beginning to synthesize them. There is a karmic connection between the peyote cult of the Indians and the discovery of lysergic
acid in Switzerland.

Peyote and acid have a curious way of tuning some people in to
the local soil. The strains and stresses deep beneath one in the rock,
the flow and fabric of wildlife around, the human history of Indians
on this continent. Older powers become evident: west of the Rockies,
the ancient creator-trickster, Coyote. Jaime de Angulo, a now-legendary 13
departed Spanish shaman and anthropologist, was an authentic Coyote-
medium. One of the most relevant poetry magazines is called *Coyote's
Journal*. For many, the invisible presence of the Indian, and the heart-
breaking beauty of America work without fasting or herbs. We make
these contacts simply by walking the Sierra or Mohave, learning the
old edibles, singing and watching.

The Jewel in the Lotus

At the Congress of World Religions in Chicago in the 1890's two
of the most striking figures were Swami Vivekananda (Shri Ramakrish-
na's disciples) and Shaku Soyen, the Zen Master and Abbot of Engaku-
ji, representing Japanese Rinzai Zen. Shaku Soyen's interpreter was a
college student named Teitaro Suzuki. The Ramakrishna-Vivekananda 14
line produced scores of books and established Vedanta centers all
through the Western world. A small band of Zen monks under Shaku
Sokatsu (disciple of Shaku Soyen) was raising strawberries in Hayward, California, in 1907. Shigetsu Sasaki, later to be known as the
Zen Master Sokei-an, was roaming the timberlands of the Pacific North-
west just before World War I, and living on a Puget Sound Island with
Indians for neighbors. D. T. Suzuki's books arc to be found today in
the libraries of biochemists and on stone ledges under laurel trees in
the open-air camps of Big Sur gypsies.

A Californian named Walter Y. Evans-Wentz, who sensed that the
mountains on his family's vast grazing lands really did have spirits in

them, went to Oxford to study the Celtic belief in fairies and then to Sikkim to study Vajrayana under a lama. His best-known book is *The Tibetan Book of the Dead.*

Those who do not have the money or time to go to India or Japan, but who think a great deal about the wisdom traditions, have remarkable results when they take LSD. The *Bhagavad-Gita,* the Hindu mythologies, *The Serpent Power,* the *Lankavatara-sūtra,* the *Upanishads,* the *Hevajra-tantra,* the *Mahanirvana-tantra*—to name a few texts—become, they say, finally clear to them. They often feel they must radically reorganize their lives to harmonize with such insights.

In several American cities traditional meditation halls of both Rinzai and Soto Zen are flourishing. Many of the newcomers turned to traditional meditation after initial acid experience. The two types of experience seem to inform each other.

The Heretics

"When Adam delved and Eve span,
Who was then a gentleman?"

The memories of a Golden Age—the Garden of Eden—the Age of the Yellow Ancestor—were genuine expressions of civilization and its discontents. Harking back to societies where women and men were more free with each other; where there was more singing and dancing; where there were no serfs and priests and kings.

Projected into future time in Christian culture, this dream of the Millennium became the soil of many heresies. It is a dream handed down right to our own time—of ecological balance, classless society, social and economic freedom. It is actually one of the possible futures open to us. To those who stubbornly argue "it's against human nature," we can only patiently reply that you must know your own nature before you can say this. Those who have gone into their own natures deeply have, for several thousand years now, been reporting that we have nothing to fear if we are willing to train ourselves, to open up, explore and grow.

One of the most significant medieval heresies was the Brotherhood of the Free Spirit, of which Hieronymus Bosch was probably a member. The Brotherhood believed that God was immanent in everything, and that once one had experienced this God-presence in himself he became a Free Spirit; he was again living in the Garden of Eden. The brothers and sisters held their meetings naked, and practiced much sharing. They "confounded clerics with the subtlety of their arguments." It was complained that "they have no uniform . . . sometimes they dress in a costly and dissolute fashion, sometimes most miserably, all according to time and place." The Free Spirits had communal houses in secret all through Germany and the Lowlands, and wandered freely among them. Their main supporters were the well-organized and affluent weavers.

When brought before the Inquisition they were not charged with witchcraft, but with believing that man was divine, and with making

love too freely, with orgies. Thousands were burned. There are some
who have as much hostility to the adepts of the subculture today. This
may be caused not so much by the outlandish clothes and dope, as by
the nutty insistence on "love." The West and Christian culture on one 21
level deeply wants love to win—and having decided (after several sad
tries) that love can't, people who still say it will are like ghosts from
an old dream.

Love begins with the family and its network of erotic and responsible relationships. A slight alteration of family structure will project
a different love-and-property outlook through a whole culture . . . 22
thus the communism and free love of the Christian heresies. This is a
real razor's edge. Shall the lion lie down with the lamb? And make
love even? The Garden of Eden.

White Indians

The modern American family is the smallest and most barren
family that has ever existed. Each newly-maried couple moves to a 23
new house or apartment—no uncles or grandmothers come to live with
them. There are seldom more than two or three children. The children
live with their peers and leave home early. Many have never had the
least sense of family.

I remember sitting down to Christmas dinner eighteen years ago
in a communal house in Portland, Oregon, with about twelve others
my own age, all of whom had no place they wished to go home to.
That house was my first discovery of harmony and community wtih
fellow beings. This has been the experience of hundreds of thousands
of men and women all over America since the end of the World War
II. Hence the talk about the growth of a "new society." But more; 24
these gatherings have been people spending time with each other—
talking, delving, making love. Because of the sheer amount of time
"wasted" together (without TV) they know each other better than most
Americans know their own family. Add to this the mind-opening and
personality-revealing effects of grass and acid, and it becomes possible
to predict the emergence of groups who live by mutual illumination—
have seen themselves as of one mind and one flesh—the "single eye"
of the heretical English Ranters; the meaning of sahajiya, "born together"—the name of the latest flower of the Tantri community tradition in Bengal.

Industrial society indeed appears to be finished. Many of us are,
again, hunters and gatherers. Poets, musicians, nomadic engineers and
scholars; fact-diggers, searchers and re-searchers scoring in rich foun- 25
dation territory. Horse-traders in lore and magic. The super hunting-
bands of mercenaries like Rand or CIA may in some ways belong to
the future, if they can be transformed by the ecological conscience, or
acid, to which they are very vulnerable. A few of us are literally hunters and gatherers, playfully studying the old techniques of acorn flour,
seaweed-gathering, yucca-fiber, rabbit snaring and bow hunting. The

densest Indian population in pre-Columbian America north of Mexico was in Marin, Sonoma and Napa Counties, California.

And finally, to go back to Morgan and Engels, sexual mores and the family are changing in the same direction. Rather than the "breakdown of the family" we should see this as the transition to a new form of family. In the near future, I think it likely that the freedom of women and the tribal spirit will make it possible for us to formalize our marriage relationships in any way we please—as groups, or polygynously or polyandrously, as well as monogamously. I use the word "formalize" only in the sense of make public and open the relationships, and to sacramentalize them; to see family as part of the divine ecology. Because it is simpler, more natural, and breaks up tendencies toward property accumulation by individual families, matrilineal descent seems ultimately indicated. Such families already exist. Their children are different in personality structure and outlook from anybody in the history of Western culture since the destruction of Knossos.

The American Indian is the vengeful ghost lurking in the back of the troubled American mind. Which is why we lash out with such ferocity and passion, so muddied a heart, at the black-haired young peasants and soldiers who are the "Viet Cong." That ghost will claim the next generation as its own. When this has happened, citizens of the USA will at last begin to be Americans, truly at home on the continent, in love with their land. The chorus of a Cheyenne Indian Ghost dance song—"hi-niswa' vita'ki'ni"—"We shall live again."

> "Passage to more than India!
> Are thy wings plumed indeed for such far flights?
> O Soul, voyagest thou indeed on voyages like those?"

Questions and Quotations for Discussion and Writing Assignments

I

1. According to Neil Postman and Charles Weingartner, there are men who "would much prefer that the schools do little or nothing to encourage youth to question, doubt, or challenge any part of the society in which they live. . . ." Do such men exist? Why should they wish to squash free inquiry and discussion?
2. What are the attributes of a competent "crap detector"?
3. What is "entropy"? How are "conventional assumptions and standard practices two of the greatest accelerators of entropy"? (Postman and Weingartner)
4. Postman and Weingartner stress that schools should cultivate in the young "that most 'subversive' intellectual instrument—the anthropological perspective." What is an "anthropological perspective"? How can it free us from the prejudices of our tribe or social unit? How does the language we learn condemn "us to highly constricted perceptions of how things are and, therefore, to highly limited alternative modes of behavior"?

5. "Adolescence is a second infancy," writes Peter Marin. What does this statement mean? What characteristics of adolescence does Marin describe?
6. What are initiation rites, sometimes called "rites of passage"? How, according to Marin, do these rites secure the allegiance of individuals to the community or tribe?
7. How are the schools the "natural enemies" of adolescents? In your view, do schools "isolate and protect" you from "adventure, risk, and participation"? (Marin)
8. Peter Marin is deeply concerned that America offers no rites of passage for its young people, no chance for them to participate in the community. Do you agree with this idea? Are you "trapped in a prolonged childhood" as he suggests?
9. What, in Marin's opinion, happens to the energies and passions of adolescents when they are not allowed to expand within the social system?
10. Marin writes that our present, restrictive school system is "based upon three particular things." What are they? Do your experiences in various schools support Marin's idea or disprove it?
11. Over and over Marin suggests that our view of childhood is restrictive and harmful. He feels that young people should be given greater freedom and responsibility, greater independence. Do you think that adolescents should be given greater independence and more responsibility? What kinds of responsibility? How are responsibilities and risks related?
12. Marin compares schools to the boxes into which children were put in the Middle Ages so that they would grow into unusual shapes. Is this analogy fair and accurate? Is it an overstatement?
13. Describe Marin's idea of a "perfect" school. What would students do in this school?
14. When Carlos Castaneda asks Don Juan, the Yaqui sorcerer, to teach him about peyote, Don Juan puts him off. Why?
15. Don Juan poses a problem for Castaneda to solve in preparation for his peyote experiences. What is this problem? How does Castaneda at first try to solve it? How does he succeed in solving it? This experiment suggests that there are at least two ways of solving problems. What are they? What did Castaneda learn from this all-night experience? In your own words, describe Castaneda's sensations during the night of search.
16. Later Castaneda has his first peyote experience. What are his subjective sensations during his meeting with Mescalito? What was the objective reality of the experience as the others saw it? Which is more significant or meaningful to Castaneda, the subjective or the objective experience? Which is more real?
17. Gary Snyder's essay "Passage to More than India" could have been included in other sections of this book because in it he discusses family structures, Indians, the occult, sex, women's roles, tribal communes as well as consciousness expansion. Yet it also belongs in this section on "learning" and "knowing" for in it Snyder catalogs the ways men have studied to know their natures, to open their minds, and, as a consequence,

to form new social structures and ways of living together. What are some of the ways men have tried to expand their perceptions? What new social structures does Snyder desire?

18. Snyder writes that "Industrial society indeed appears to be finished." On what evidence can he make this startling statement? Many other writers in this book—especially Peter and Brigitte Berger, Alvin Toffler, and Isaac Asimov—consider such an idea naïve and outlandish. Why?
19. What kind of society, in Snyder's view, will replace industrial society when it collapses? Why are "monogamy and patrilineal descent" threats to the ideal society Snyder envisions?

II

1. I know that I know not.

   SOCRATES

2. As long as you live, keep learning how to live.

   SENECA

3. The first step in the acquisition of wisdom is silence, the second listening, the third memory, the fourth practice, the fifth teaching others.

   HEBREW PROVERB

4. When you understand all about the sun and all about the atmosphere and all about the rotation of the earth, you may still miss the radiance of the sunset. There is no substitute for the direct perception of the concrete achievement of a thing in its actuality.

   ALFRED NORTH WHITEHEAD

5. I can never understand how anything can be known *for truth* by a process of abstract reasoning.

   JOHN KEATS

6. The intellectual life of man consists almost wholly in his substitutions of a conceptual order for the perceptual order in which his experiences originally come.

   WILLIAM JAMES

7. The only thing I would whip schoolboys for is not knowing English.

   WINSTON CHURCHILL

8. The spontaneous wish to learn, which every normal child possesses, as shown in his efforts to walk and talk, should be the driving force in education. The substitution of this force for the rod is one of the great advances of our time.

   BERTRAND RUSSELL

9. What we call education and culture is for the most part nothing but the substitution of reading for experience, of literature for life . . . of obsolete fictions for contemporary experience.

   GEORGE BERNARD SHAW

10. I find that the three major administrative problems on a campus are sex for the students, athletics for the alumni, and parking for the faculty.

    CLARK KERR

11. The eye may see for the hand, but not for the mind.

    HENRY DAVID THOREAU

12. Age is no better, hardly so well, qualified for an instructor as youth, for it has not profited so much as it has lost.

    HENRY DAVID THOREAU

13. The roots of education are bitter, but the fruit is sweet.

    ARISTOTLE

14. Reading maketh a full man, conference a ready man, and writing an exact man.

    FRANCIS BACON

15. Every man who rises above the common level has received two educations: the first from his teachers; the second, more personal and important, from himself.

    EDWARD GIBBON

16. Education has really only one basic factor, a *sine qua non*—one must want it.

    GEORGE EDWARD WOODBERRY

17. Our visions of adolescence and education confine us to habit, rule perception out.

    PETER MARIN

18. . . . An act of learning is a meeting, and every meeting is simply the discovery in the world of a part of oneself that had previously been unacknowledged by the self. It is the recovery of the extent of one's being. It is the embrace of an eternal but elusive companion, the shadowy "other" in which one truly resides and which blazes, when embraced, like the sun.

    PETER MARIN

19. To return the word to the flesh. To make knowledge carnal again; not by deduction, but immediate by perception or sense at once; the bodily senses.

    NORMAN O. BROWN

20. . . . families, schools, churches are the slaughter-houses of our children; colleges and other places are the kitchens. As adults in marriages and business, we eat the product.

    R. D. LAING

21. Meaning is in people. Without people there are no meanings.

    NEIL POSTMAN AND CHARLES WEINGARTNER

22. Observing is a function of the symbol systems the observer has available to him. The more limited the symbol systems, in number and kind, the less one is able to "see."

    POSTMAN AND WEINGARTNER

23. Facts are statements about the world as perceived by human beings. They are, therefore, as tentative as all human judgments.

    POSTMAN AND WEINGARTNER

24. Since the concepts people live by are derived only from perceptions and from language and since the perceptions are received and interpreted only in light of earlier concepts, man comes pretty close to living in a house that language built.

    RUSSELL F. W. SMITH

25. Every language is a special way of looking at the world and interpreting experience. . . . One sees and hears what the grammatical system of one's language has made one sensitive to, has trained one to look for in experience. This bias is insidious because everyone is so unconscious of his native language as a system.

    C. KLUCKHOHN

26. When the mind is thinking, it is talking to itself.

    PLATO

27. The purpose of Newspeak was not only to provide a medium of expression for the world-view and mental habits proper to the devotees of Ingsoc, but to make all other modes of thought impossible.

    GEORGE ORWELL

28. Thus the task of education is to make children fit to live in a society by persuading them to learn and accept its codes—the rules and conventions of communication whereby the society holds itself together. . . . For the child has to be taught not only what words are to stand for what things, but also the way in which his culture has tacitly agreed to divide things from each other, too mark out the boundaries within our daily experience.

    ALAN WATTS

29. Supposedly if we had no words, we should still be able to think. But it is the nature of human brains that they think so much better with words than with any other medium—with mental pictures, for instance—that, words being available, we learn to think with them, and rely upon them so much that for practical purposes most people think only about things for which they have words and can think only in the directions for which they have words.

    C. LAIRD

30. "When *I* use a word," Humpty Dumpty said, in a rather scornful tone, "it means just what I choose it to mean—neither more nor less."

    "The question is," said Alice, "whether you *can* make words mean so many different things."

"The question is," said Humpty Dumpty, "which is to be master—that's all."

LEWIS CARROLL

31. Unless I was going to become an academic, a lawyer, a C.P.A., or some other carefully defined careerist, school was a liability. So I began to treat it as a part-time job. By no means was I a dropout, I still took my courses and passed. But like my friends I shifted my commitment outside the classroom.

ROGER RAPOPORT (class of '68)

32. One cannot, therefore, on looking at these young people in all the glory of their defiant rags and hairdos, always just say, with tears in one's eyes: "There goes a tragically wayward youth, striving romantically to document his rebellion against the hypocrisies of the age." One has sometimes to say, and not without indignation: "There goes a perverted and willful and stony-hearted youth by whose destructiveness we are all, in the end, to be damaged and diminished."

GEORGE KENNAN

33. For it is in the ideal of a community of concerned persons who share a common interest in the life of the mind and the quality of human experience that the genius of the university lies.

HAROLD TAYLOR

34. . . . the purpose of universities like Berkeley and Columbia is to train the technicians who will administer our society. . . . Within this university factory, students are manipulated and channeled, stripped of creativity and energy, ready at the end of the assembly line to take their places in death-like offices of still more educational factories.

MARK RUDD

35. You never know what is enough unless you know what is more than enough.

WILLIAM BLAKE

36. We need to get kids out of the school buildings, give them a chance to learn about the world at first hand. It is a very recent idea, and a crazy one, that the way to teach our young people about the world they live in is to take them out of it and shut them up in brick boxes.

JOHN HOLT

37. It is nothing short of a miracle that the modern methods of instruction have not yet entirely strangled the holy curiosity of inquiry; for this delicate little plant, aside from stimulation, stands mainly in need of freedom; without this it goes to wrack and ruin without fail.

ALBERT EINSTEIN

Related Readings:

WATTS, ALAN, "The Future of Ecstasy," page 426.

SECTION VII The Good Life—Making It with Style

Do we have any living national heroes? Any exceptional individuals through whom the nation projects its ideals? Any human symbols of the "good life"? As a nation we have admired rich men, sports figures, daring, brave men, and men who have risen from humble origins in log cabins. Now we seem to want quantity; we consume heroes the way we consume kleenex: hero today, goon tomorrow. (Sorry.) Perhaps we value quantity because in almost every part of our lives we have so little quality. We have so much of the bogus and the trivial that we cannot decide what the standards of success and excellence are any more. In this age of confusion about basic human values the quest for the good life is frantic because the meaning and symbols of it are ambiguous and difficult to identify. Though we want meaningful work to do, good things to own, refreshing recreation, in our restlessness we cannot seem to find them; we seem almost addicted to the inferior and the disposable. Is it possible that we have simply grown too cynical to believe wholeheartedly in heroes or that we have grown so small, settled for so little, that we do not want them around reminding us of what we have become?

Once, when the land of plenty was not, a man could measure his success by the things he owned, and if not by his possessions, at least by the status accorded him because of his job. But how can we measure success and the good life in terms of things owned when the things we own are shoddy and, in truth, own us? It is becoming obvious that when a man acquires many of the things he has lusted for—cars, a boat, a color TV, an American Express Money Card—he hasn't got much, especially if he got them by working at a job he detested. Too many of our jobs force us to compromise some part of ourselves and make us value things more than we value self. Finding no fulfillment in work, we project onto the objects we work for a symbolic importance great enough to compensate for the negative feelings we have about our accomplishments. It is no wonder that we cry for law and order and live in terror of losing everything to a thief. If a thief takes our things, he has also taken our lives. "Things are in the saddle/ And ride mankind," Emerson said. Things tyrannize man before he owns them by driving him to obtain them and after he has obtained them by requiring that he spend his time using, repairing, and guarding them. A color TV must be watched.

Increased leisure time has not brought the good life or the contentment many expected; it merely created another void, this time to be filled by hobbies, travel, and chasing after new experiences, new things to do, new roles to play. Again the confusion of quantity and quality. If we measure the good life by counting the things we do, then we trivialize doing. *Doings* become proud possessions. ("What do you do?" "Oh, I sail, ski, surf, fly a little, play the guitar, and take pictures." "What do you do well?" "Excuse me. I think I'll get another drink.") Why do one thing well when it is so easy to do a little bit of everything? Leisure combined with affluence creates the possibility of learning about new life styles and actually trying them out. So why be a spectator? Be a flamenco dancer this week, a movie maker the next; be a skin diver or a skier during the appropriate seasons; and if all else fails to satisfy, become a Jesus freak on Sundays. The proper costumes and tools can be purchased at any large department store or sports shop. So what if you don't develop skill or grace or style in these new roles; accomplishment requires practice, discipline, and rigor. And who has time?

For growing numbers of people the good life no longer means two cars and a four-bedroom house stuffed with furniture. It may mean instead a small farm where one grows some of one's food, or simply the freedom to be eccentric, or time to make pottery, music, and love. "Making it" may be working at a job one believes important, regardless of the pay, or working at a job that carries with it no status (thus no headaches), a job requiring no white-shirt uniform. A romantic dream? Maybe. Certainly not everyone is chasing this ideal; for every man or woman who drops out of the money-success-status game, another takes his place at the gaming table. But in quiet moments that we would like extended, some of us do yearn for the genuine, the intense experience. We hear a voice from our past saying, "simplify, simplify." We want to be human, but we have just about forgotten how.

Instead of moaning about how dehumanized and conforming we have become, let us return to the subject of heroes.

Bo Diddley, Willie Mays,* Erich Segal, Rod McKuen, Peter Fonda, and Dennis Hopper are cats who have "made it" with style. America likes what they do and rewards them for doing it with fame and money—still yardsticks for "success." But what does it mean to be at the top? What price must be paid to get there? In a society that eschews excellence and almost demands inferior pleasures, what does it mean to be a source of great pleasure to many?

America likes its arts thin and popular, and it creates POP-HEROES out of its entertainers. Perhaps these POP-HEROES are our human contribution to the conforming, computerized world in which true heroism and individuality are almost as extinct as dinosaurs. Science and technology have robbed us of many of our myths and have not replaced them as yet; nonetheless, we still believe that only human beings can become heroes. So through some show-biz magic, our POP-HEROES symbolize our desires to be special, mostly because STARS are naive and innocent and thus believe in their own myths, in their own greatness. And they have style—sometimes garrish and neon, but they are never drab as we are. No one really believes that Erich Segal is a great novelist—no one, that is, except Erich Segal. The rest of us are not sure about our greatness anymore, so perhaps we don't want magnificent men— true heroes—reminding us of our weakness and insignificance. POP-HEROES do not make many demands on us.

*(As Peter Schrag notes, Willie Mays may belong to another age, an age that was more innocent than ours and believed in its myths and its heroes.)

Michael Lydon

The Second Coming of Bo Diddley

> "A person is an individual, and being an individual person is a gas. I have my own way of expressing my soulful feelings. I never wanted to be like anybody else and I can't copy anybody else. I got my own bag of tricks."
>
> *Everything I know I taught myself.*
>
> —Bo Diddley

[I]

Bo Diddley, a Protean genius and as great an artist as any who
has graced American shores, lives in exile in California's San Fernando
Valley. His house, a medium-to-large tan ranch-style, is on the 17500
block of a winding street in that suburban nation. It is surrounded by
cars. In front is the orange Dodge he bought for his wife's birthday
because he had a lot of work in August. Beside it is a Ford LTD
limousine he got cheap from a chauffeur service a few years ago. In 1
the side drive are four more cars, all flashy Detroit numbers Bo sal-
vaged from junkyards and then transformed. He works on them in his
spare time (of which in exile he has a lot) to keep his mind off money
worries and his hands busy. He could quit the music business any
time—he's been threatening to for years—or, he adds, he could lose a
finger; in either case he hopes car work could be his living.

A big tree with small, shimmering leaves shades the house prettily.
On the stoop beside the screen door, which hangs limp from countless
bangings, are cases and cases of RC Cola empties. To the left, seen
through a window, hangs a picture of Bo so big that only his glasses
and one ear are visible. There are always kids on the stoop—one of 2
Bo's own four or his two grandchildren, or almost any kid in the neighborhood: Bo's house is the hangout for the whole block. Scattered under-
foot are dozens of cancelled checks; when Bo noticed them, he first
said the hell with 'em, then figured he'd better clean them up because
some might be important for business.

His exile is not complete, nor is it entirely bitter. Indeed, it could be said not to exist. Bo Diddley does play what jobs he can get; last winter he recorded an LP, *The Black Gladiator.* Everybody calls him "the great Bo Diddley" and awards him place as a founder of rock 'n' roll. Yet in a perfectly simple way he is without honor in his own land. 3
The return to him, in any form, has not been commensurate with what he's given, and he knows it. He wants what he deserves, but he's too proud to beg. So he's biding his time, looking for work and fixing up his cars.

In the kitchen his wife Kay, a tall and beautiful woman, is making dinner. Tan, Bo's oldest daughter, is helping; her husband, who works in a Valley styrofoam plant (night shift), and two kids are in the living room, kept dark in the late afternoon for the TV. Walter Brennan is on in some crummy serial—another underrated artist doing time. Two 4
white teenie-boppers from the block are watching from the sofa. Connie, who writes songs and plays rhythm guitar in Bo's band, is giving her chihuahua, Poopsie, a good scratch; Bambi, Kay's chihuahua, is looking on jealously.

Spider, Bo's shaggy mutt, is asleep under the carved Japanese chair, and Bo himself is seated at the card table, half an eye on the tube, the other eye and a half on the life around him. He's washed up from his day underneath the Chevy van, but he's still in a T-shirt and baggy corduroy jeans. Ricky McMillan, an old friend who is temporarily 5
living in a room beside the studio out back, walks in with a stack of shrimp cocktails and some Slim Jim sausage sticks. Bo takes four of the shrimp tins for himself and orders one of the kids to put the Slim Jims beside his bed. The kid goes. Bo is Daddy in his house.

He digs into the shrimp methodically, from time to time scratching his chin with the plastic fork. It's tiny in his hands, which are huge and hook-like, cracked like a laborer's. His arms are thick beams and his shoulders are rounded like the great Marciano's. Bo Diddley is a small black mountain, mobile but immovable. The peak is his hard, round head, and from it, through glistening glasses, beam eyes whose 6
fire he can hood but never quench. When he laughs, his mouth falls way open, baring wide gaps between his teeth; his eyes almost spark.

Bo shrugs. His shrimp are gone. Spider is nosing around the fake bonzai tree beside the fireplace. "Spider!" Bo calls, his voice booming with reproach. "What you doin', dog? Tammi, take Spider out before he lets go." Spider, as woebegone as I ever saw a dog, trails out in disgrace.

"Kay, d'you see what Spider tryin' to do? *Spider,* messing around that bush, hah, he know better than that."

Bo looks down his nose at tiny Poopsie, yapping at all the commotion. "*That dog,* hah! Hey, somebody throw that joker down the garbage disposal." He laughs at his own joke.

"As I was saying," he continues, "I started out doing my thing. I did my thing, am still doing my thing and plan to keep doing my thing;

but see, where I lost a lot of my stepping ground is right here: I had
the doorknob in my hand. I opened the door—everybody's *gone*. Are 10
you ready for that?" His eyes are burning.

[II]

Americans have always divided their response to creativity into
two bags, one for Art and one for entertainment. Proud of their Art,
they have enjoyed their entertainment not because all entertainment
is art, but because the greatest artists in America have in their own
times been considered entertainers. There are good writers, architects
and painters who have always been "taken seriously," but the bulk of
the heavies have, like Raymond Chandler, Buster Keaton and Billie
Holiday, been out there to please the people. Their art is the work
they do. They either get paid for it or they don't, but they are not
"supported" as "artists" are. Their self-effacement tends to make their 11
art invisible; their generosity puts their audience so at ease that the
masses are quick to make the proffered gifts their own—the admission
fee means you don't have to say thank you. Those masses have been
more beloved than loving; after success's first and only honeymoon,
many popular artists have had long struggles to keep alive the romance
on which their livelihood and means of expression depended. Though
famous, they have often been lonely, and their rewards have been so
mixed with abuse that it's hard to tell them apart.

With these artists in popular media, Bo Diddley stands in the first
rank. His lifework evidences a cohesive and profound vision, sustained
by a confident personality and driven home with a power dark as voo-
doo. His values, drawn directly from his own life, are universally human, and he makes them convincing, even overpowering. A master of
his craft, he has made major innovations within it. He is a fine musician, 12
a singer of great gusto and, rare indeed, a devoted teacher. He's more
funky than primitive, and funky can be sophisticated too. Inadmissible
fare for honky TV, he is too large a presence for the modern stage.
Though the rock industry is not sure it wants him, the only art that
can contain him today is rock 'n' roll music.

To the same extent that Bo is under-appreciated, so is this music.
"I don't want any more of that 'great Bo Diddley' b. s.," says Bo; rock
'n' roll doesn't need it either. In the news since its inception, it has,
since the Beatles, been one of the most important things happening on 13
the planet. It's not often that music has such a prominent place in world
affairs; when it does, it is usually at a moment important also to music's
own history.

In the early 1950s, music in America was in healthy shape—a lot
of different bags, and good people working in all of them. Jazz was
cooling off after a period of intense innovation. Pop was insipid, but 14
blues and country were gaining: blues was becoming rhythm and blues,
and Hank Williams was a rivival by himself. Modern classical music
was only slowly making headway against the overwhelming popularity

of works from the 19th century and before. A few composers were going electronic, and John Cage was circling about. Yet in one sense all was stagnant, for music had not yet boldly crossed its latest frontier: electricity, the only absolutely new addition to music-making for generations.

Electricity had been available to music for decades in three forms —the creation of sound in electric instruments, the storing of it on records, and the broadcasting of it by amplification and radio. All three had been used by musicians but to a degree far below their revolutionary potential; none had *become* music. Radio, with its Make-Believe Ballrooms, was still trying to "take you there" instead of *bringing* you something new. The fact that no one style of music dominated the medium indicates that no one had found "radio music." The same is true for records, on which editing was still primitive and which in no case were considered an art form on their own. Except for the tentative experiments of the electronicists, it was the same again for electric instruments—they mostly made the sound a little louder.

Electricity was up for grabs, and the question (which I doubt anyone asked) was, who would get it? Who would find that music to make records music, not copies of it; to make radio a medium, not a transmitter? Who could make beautiful music on electrical instruments? There was quite a prize for the winner, for that musician who could put electricity in the service of his art might bring down walls higher than Jericho's.

Who got it? The niggers, they got it. Not the whole story, but pretty close. A bunch of musicians in their twenties, either black or else whites in love with black American music, started playing in a way indefinably but definitely new. It got called rock 'n' roll, achieving consciousness of itself as a unique genre almost immediately. Founded on blues, it was a patchwork of many musics, but at least two things set it apart.

First, electricity was indispensable to it. Rock 'n' roll energy could survive, even thrive, on electronic storage and dispersal; it was a music as used to the speed of light as the speed of sound. Almost always played with some electric instruments, it made radio and records its secondary instruments. It took over radio in a few years (rescuing it from its prophesied murder by TV), and has by now almost completed its victory in recording. Producer Ralph Bass dates rock from his "Open the Door, Richard" of 1946, not only because it was an R&B hit that crossed over to pop, but because he faded the end. Rock 'n' roll has been the inspiration for, or used best, many of the breakthroughs in recording technology of the past 15 years.

Second, rock 'n' roll had a feeling, an indelibly vivid something *more*; in the beat but more than the beat; that intensity that made non-believers call it noisy when played low, but made believers know it had to be played *loud*. That feeling—not one emotion, but from a new emotional level—was energy released by the discovery of the possibility

of freedom. Nothing less than that could have made electricity its ally. Rock 'n' roll was black American liberation music (a tune quickly taken up by young whites); its creators were black heralds. Though there hadn't been much "progress," "Negroes" were recovering from the traumas of captivity and enslavement. Rock 'n' roll occurred at that moment 19
in the healing when the patient, if not well, first gets back on his feet. More blacks had confidence in their own worth and were eager to assert it. The story of that attitude growing into a movement and then a revolution is as well known as rock n' roll's, and the two are clearly linked in parallel.

Even within the black musical tradition rock 'n' roll was a brash development. By the early '50s, black musicians, though often in a favored position, had been only slightly more aggressive socially than
black people at large. They stuck to their own and tried to please (or 20
at least certainly not to offend) when in the white world. Much truth was said in irony and understatement, but the involuted style and language of the '40s bebop (a re-bop) movement was as outrageous as black musicians had dared get.

Rock 'n' roll stars were relatively wild men. Flamboyant to the point of eccentricity, they wrote songs, all crisp and short, as up-to-date as their cars and flashy clothes. Technically less intricate than their jazz contemporaries and less subtle than their blues predecessors,
they had as compensation a genius for stagecraft. They played their 21
blues with a heavier beat, wrote gaudier lyrics, and reached beyond the blues to take ideas from pop, country and gospel. They avoided blues' hard life themes, concentrating instead on the joys of dancing; the sexual metaphors of the blues they extended into cocksure statements of total male potency. Their aim was to get the message of "feeling good" across by any means necessary—and they did.

Of the many black creators of rock 'n' roll, four stand pre-eminent: Little Richard, Fats Domino, Chuck Berry and Bo Diddley. Little
Richard is an "ecstatic" more than an artist; what he does, by his own 22
admission, is up to God more than to himself. Antoine Domino's music rolls on as surely as the Mississippi through his native New Orleans. Chuck Berry, an angry and accurate prophet, makes rock 'n' roll about rock 'n' roll. Bo is their Prometheus. His songs are hymns to himself. Not that he is vain—the reverse—but he is one black boy who made 21, and that is a discovery worth a thousand songs.

[III]

I'm a Man
I spell it
M, A, N,
MAN

Ellas McDaniel (Bo Diddley is a childhood nickname that stuck) was born on December 30, 1929, in Magnolia, Mississippi, which makes him nominally a Delta-born bluesman. But his mother, then only 16, moved downstate to McComb when Bo was a baby. He never saw his father, and after age six was raised not by his mother but by her cousin, Mrs. Gussie McDaniel, who took him with her children when she moved to Chicago in about 1934.

"My real mother is a high-spirited and wonderful woman," he said at the start of three days of talking about his life, "and I always dug that she couldn't raise me. About my father, I don't think he and my mother were ever really together. I never cried over not seeing him, but I do feel he could have been a man and come by once to say hi. Even if he didn't have nothing to give, just say hi. It would have been the greatest thing in the world.

"Know something? I'm classed as a Negro but I'm not: I'm what you call a black Frenchman, a Creole. All my people are from New Orleans, the bayou country. Just like Fats. French, African, Indian, all mixed up. I like gumbo, dig? Hot sauces, too. That's where my music come from, all the mixture. Some peoples are known for this, some for that. Mix 'em and it can get weird, hah!"

Listening to Bo was an experience; he'd talk in wide-ranging circles, pausing for great chunks of his philosophy in between the facts of his life, which he had little interest in organizing in sequential patterns. He could get serious about memories dear to him, but his chief attitude was the rough-and-ready logic of a man who keeps a wry eye on everything that's going down and isn't afraid to speak his mind. A few times he approached things he thought he shouldn't discuss, then he'd go ahead; "I'm not a person to lie about anything" was his explanation.

He remembers being lonely as a little boy—"I think that's why I like people around now"—but in Chicago there were plenty of cousins to play with on the sidewalks of the South Side around 47th and Drexel. Racially nothing had changed. "Where I was living, it was just like Mississippi. We could cross Drexel Boulevard and be in *trouble.* There was a mass stupid confusion goin' on all the time, and even as a child I called it what I call it now: stupid. I was never taught to hate people but 'Do unto others as you would have them do unto you.' That is beautiful.

"I got a paper route across Drexel, man. Me and my cousin. I was about 12 years old. We had made three or four deliveries the first day, and we had to cut it loose or get half *hung* over there. This is the way things were and I just couldn't see why people had to be this way."

Home was strict and proper. Bo wasn't supposed to leave the block without permission; his uncle, who still works at a meat packing plant, and his adopted mother were regular members of the Ebeneezer Baptist Church. Another uncle (his mother's brother) is the pastor of several churches in Biloxi, Mississippi, and Bo calls himself a very religious man, "even though I play rock 'n' roll." But the Ebeneezer Baptist, with its big organ, robed choir, and Sunday school, was never his bag. When he was seven he made the mistake of saying one day that he

wanted a violin like the man in church. His parents couldn't afford
one, so the church scraped together $30 and bought him one. That was
his first instrument and he labored at it, instructed by Professor O. W.
Frederick, for 12 years. Today he remembers he played music by "those
German guys, Heichhof or something, I could pronounce 'em when I
was into it."

The music he yearned for was "down home." "I used to stand
around and listen at the sanctified church. Break off from home and
stand on the sidewalk and look in the door. Or they'd leave a window
open and I'd climb on a milk crate and peep in at 'em dancing and
shaking their tambourines, and I'd say, 'One day I'm gonna get me
something that sounds like that.' A thing I used to hum was a thing 30
they used to play all the time." He turned to a piano, fiddled, then
played a gospel chorus, the chords ascending, falling, going up to a
climax, then falling back to rest. In them, partly disguised by the
religious flavor, was the Bo Diddley beat. Chink-a-chink-chink, ca-chink-
chink. Chink-a-chink-chink, ca-chink-chink. Steady as a rock. Bo turned
back.

"And that always stuck with me. The Baptist church was all stately
and calm, but in the sanctified church, everything was rockin'! This is 31
where I got part of my rhythm; my music is really based around a
religious beat."

He was 13 when his half-sister gave him his first guitar, to the
horror of his adopted mother. She wanted him to be a concert violinist,
but for Bo the violin faded into the background, and by 15 he and his 32
guitar were out on the streetcorner with a cousin on washboard, picking
up nickels and dimes. By that time he was out of school and had started
boxing, then as important as music to him; a four-eyes had to look out
for himself.

"I was trying to figure out about growing up and molding myself
to manhood, and since I knew I had to walk this dirt road alone, I
might as well learn not to be scared. Boxing was it. I was a light-heavy,
one of those hard-hitting dudes, hah! Used to go to a neighborhood
gym or over to Eddie Nichol's gym at 48th and Michigan. It wasn't that 33
I wanted to be tough, but I think you should like something rough, to
be a *man.* I figure 'man' means more than being male. Like the word
'woman.' What does a woman do? She bears children. This is something
great, so she has a title: woman. *Man,* that's a *word,* looks like to me.
'Man' means to me a cat is supposed to protect himself as well as his
family, put his life on the line for them. Having the opportunity to be
a husband, father and provider is a good title, if you live up to it."

By the time he was 16 his streetcorner group had progressed to the point where it had a name, the Langley Avenue Jive Cats (sometimes it was the Hipsters): Roosevelt Jackson on washtub bass, Jerome Green on maracas, and Bo on guitar. Jerome, of "Bring It to Jerome" fame, joined by accident. "When I met Jerome, he was a jazz cat, played a tuba that was bigger than he was. One day when we had nothing to do I brought him some maracas and taught him how to shake 'em. I said, 'Hey, why don't you come down to the corner and pass the hat for us?' He said he couldn't; that was begging. Begging? Hah! It was *work*. But he came in his Buick—a real smoker, made five gallons to 20 blocks—and passed the hat, saw the dollars falling in, and asked me next day, 'Bo, when you gonna play that corner again?'

"We was then playing behind a cat named Samuel Johnson; he could sing like Billy Eckstine and he sanded, too." I looked blank. "Sanding? Oh, he was terrific. He'd carry a bag of sand around and a piece of board. We'd play 'Tea for Two' or something, and he'd get up on a board and do a thing, his feet *gliding*. That cat cracked up. I thought he was beautiful, but he was no Casanova-looking dude, and people telling him he was ugly broke him. Don't know what happened to him, but he was something else.

"Music I liked was Louis Jordan and Nat Cole. John Lee Hooker, too. I tried to catch his strange guitar sounds, but at first I couldn't understand him. My main man was Muddy Waters. He and Little Walter used to play at a place—man, I got throwed out of there enough times 'cause I was under age. They had a jukebox near the door. I'd get in the corner between the juke and the cigarette machine where I could split when I saw the man coming. One night I got slapped upside the head." But Muddy was only a few steps from playing on the street himself, and when Bo and the Jive Cats had a few sides up, they started hustling for club dates.

"Man, we played some *smokey* holes, bars under the El station, in storefront clubs, and it was hard, so hard you was looking for the *worm* to pull the *robin* into the ground, you dig? You ask cats like Muddy and Willie Dixon and J. B. Lenoir, you ask 'em how hard it was to get five dollars or six dollars together on a weekend. When you worked a club you *worked* it. Sometimes I'd make less than I would on the street, because on the street they'd say, 'How cute that boy is,' and put in 50 cents; but in a club you had to have it together or be *cut*."

Blues couldn't pay the bills or even come close; off stage, Bo was just one more black man looking for work. "I was on relief when my oldest daughter Tan was nine months old. I couldn't get a job noplace. I knew how to run a whole lot of different machines but no use. Back in 1951, '52, '53, I'm talking about. I went to get some welfare and I told the people my kid was hungry and sick *right now*, and they told me I had to make one more trip down there before I could get any money. What was I supposed to do—turn off a valve to stop her from crying because she was hungry? The next step was to stick somebody up, and I didn't want to do that.

"When a cat dedicated to his family gets so his hind parts is dragging and he can't get work— I have been this way. I ain't just sitting here talkin'. Every morning I'd get up and walk from my home on 47th Street down to 12th Street, trying to find a job. Get on the streetcar 'til the conductor saw me, then jump off and wait on the next one. I was

looking for anything, plain labor, but you'd go into a place and they're
talking 35-40 cents an hour. That's no money; that's about $29 a week.
Are you ready for that? You wouldn't believe it existed in the '50s, but
I worked on some of 'em. I unloaded boxcars, and then I drove dump
trucks. Truck driving wasn't so bad, but there was discrimination against 39
black drivers. I'd drive to the stone quarry and couldn't get no stone.
Everybody was told a black dude's bad business; a black dude ain't
even supposed to *be* there. I just told people, 'Hey, man, I'm a *man.*
I don't give a damn what color I am, I didn't ask to come into this
world no way.'

"If you got no money in this country, you is out of it. 'Land of the
free and home of the brave'—hah! Ain't *nobody* free in America without money." When Bo gets talking about money he gets angry. With
those who've worked a lifetime without ever feeling financially secure,
he can become obsessed with money, licking wounds long open. He
doesn't like to harp on the subject, but has decided not to avoid it. He
does try to be fair. "One thing: a lot of black people don't want to 40
see nothing but that they've been mistreated for 350 years or whatever
it is they are screaming about, but there is whites who've been in as
much hard luck as the black man. Down in Mississippi the only difference between us and some white folks was that they could go in the
front door of a restaurant and sit down and eat, and the black cat had
to go in the back and stand. But we was *all* scratching, you dig?"

In 1954 he was 26; he had quit boxing because he saw no future
in it except getting punchdrunk, and he was working regularly as a
bluesman. He was still driving trucks, and when he made his first record
it was not because he had plans of becoming a full-time professional.
"I went in to Chess Records 'cause I finally realized it was right around
the corner from where I lived. Went in, did my thing, signed a mess 41
of papers and went out, feelin' no different. I heard I had a hit in a
couple of weeks. Scared me to death; I didn't know what was happening. I had never been nowhere in my life, and they told me I'd have
to go on the road.

"My first contract was for $800. Two nights in New Orleans, me
and Howlin' Wolf on the same show. I had never seen $800 in one pile
in my life. I took off for New Orleans and got lost, taking the road for
St. Louis instead. I played the job and made it back home with 35
cents. We had blowouts, breakdowns, tickets from the Southern police, 42
in and out of jail once, and paying the musicians—oh, man, was I green,
I didn't know nothing. But I went to school and I *learned,* man, the
hard way. They graduated me—put me from kindergarten right through
college!

"Then I quit driving, but it wasn't because of the record really.
I was gonna quit anyway. A few months before, my daughter had been
sick, and the boss told me that if I took a day off to take her to the 43
hospital he'd make me take four days off without pay. So I did what
he would have done if it had been his kid sick. I said, 'Crazy, you get

the four days ready, 'cause I'm going.' 'You *need* a rest,' he said. Man, it was a bad scene for a black dude then.

"A while later I made the record. I walked up to him one day and said, 'Here's your keys, baby.' He looked at me and said, 'What's this?' 'I ain't going this morning,' I said. He says, 'Mac, did you make a record?' I said, 'Yeah, how you like it—pretty nice, huh?' He said, 'This record got anything to do with it?' I says, 'Not really, but remember the day you threatened me a few months ago? About how I needed a rest? Well, now I'm taking a rest, a long rest, man.'"

The record he had made was "Bo Diddley" and "I'm a Man," two roughly hewn self-portraits. "Bo Diddley" is in the form of an old folk round ("Daddy's gonna buy you a looking-glass; if that looking-glass should break," etc.). But Bo slips in a few jokes ("If that diamond ring don't shine, I'm gonna take it to a private eye; if that private eye can't see, he ain't gonna get that ring from me"), boasts of catching a bear-cat, and floats out on a piece of nonsense—"Hey, Bo Diddley, have you heard, my pretty baby says she's a bird." His beat is there, fully realized, Bo setting it with his guitar, maracas and drums played like congas underpinning it. That beat has often been described as "shave and a haircut, two bits," the joke rhythm you beep on your car horn at the drive-in. Nothing is further from the truth. Bo's beat is his own pulse made art. More than a signature, it is his ultimate statement, the stable matrix from which his music flows.

Yet the beat, a four-four shoved off center, is complex and changing. Bo can and does syncopate it any way he wants to. His physical strength makes it profoundly sensual, and the maracas evoke a past (African or Haitian?) that came before the blues. On one hand dense, its ambiguity of shadings opens it up and keeps it moving. It is the Bo Diddley beat; "Everybody from New Orleans," Louis Armstrong once said, "got that thing."

"I'm a Man" is a more standard blues, Bo's obvious tribute to his idol Muddy Waters and "Hootchie-Kootchie Man," a Willie Dixon blues that had become Waters's trademark. But it is just the difference between "Hootchie-Kootchie Man" and "I'm a Man" (and between Muddy and Bo) that marks the difference between the blues and rock 'n' roll. Bo's song is good imitation Muddy until the refrain, then Bo delivers his "I'm a Man" bit. Spelling it out to avoid any mistake, Bo rings the consonants like tolling bells. The refrain stands as an independent entity in the song; the sureness of its voicing makes the Muddy-style choruses that surround it, with their magic and exaggerations, seem boasting. But "Bo Diddley" was the "A" side, the novelty hit which established Bo as a jokester, a "rock 'n' roller," less serious than the "bluesmen" who preceded him. In "I'm a Man" Bo's continuity with and development from the blues is expressed. Bo was a good pupil, with good teachers. "We knew at the time there was a difference between me and Chuck on one hand, and Muddy and those cats on the other; but it wasn't no generation gap," said Bo, "we were just younger, that's all."

"The same thing is true today with the cats that are younger than
me," Bo went on. "But, man, I don't know what we're gonna do now 48
that Jimi Hendrix copped out on us. He took *my* thing one step further.
He was the only black cat who could play psychedelic."

[IV]

At a break in talking on the first day, Bo gave me a tour of the
house. "As you can see, I have a family and we don't live fancy," he
said; "I don't believe in living beyond my means." True enough; Bo's
place is a family-worn home. In the breezeway there are old toys, bikes
with one wheel, and folded patio chairs. The pool is empty; Bo will 49
sandblast it one day, but now the kids use it for baseball. Past that
is the cinderblock studio he built, a two-track job with a darkroom in
one corner. It's mostly used as a rehearsal hall for the teenage bands
Bo coaches for free. By the garage are scattered tools and a pile of
sand left over from cement work.

Inside, the few decorator items, like the carved Japanese chairs,
don't disrupt the calm of the wall-to-wall and the drapes. On a wall
near the bathroom is a gold record for the "Outstanding Album Sales
in 1962" of *Bo Diddley's a Gunslinger*; Bo paid for it himself. The
kitchen door is the only door anybody uses and the kitchen is the 50
center of the house. It's Kay's room. Kay tries to stay out of Bo's public
life because she knows some fans like to think of him as single, and
because she knows people are prejudiced. Kay is white and from
Georgia.

"The first time I met Ellas," she said, in a soft twang, "I drove 250
miles to see him and 250 miles back. He and Jackie Wilson were the
only ones I'd drive that far to see. It was 1960. My girl friend was
going with a guy in the show, and before it started, Bo sent a girl out
with the message, 'Come to me.' I played it cool and said, 'He knows 51
where to find me.' But later we went up to the dressing room. He was
sitting there like King Tut, aiming at playing around, here tonight, gone
tomorrow, like the rock 'n' roll star he was. But I had some money to
follow him, and time—I wasn't doing anything else. He wasn't figuring
on that. Tried to avoid me for a while, then he gave up."

Partners in business and song writing as well as family life, Bo
and Kay get along extremely well. The bedroom is their room and they
are proud of it. You enter to face a trellis covered with a jungle of
plastic plants; all is dark until you get accustomed to the glow of indirect red lights along the ceiling. The long-tufted carpet is black and
very deep; the walls are black, too, and there are more plastic jungles 52
along the baseboards. One wall is walk-in closets. At one end of it are
Bo's old show clothes, including the few ruffled shirts left of the 175
he once owned. His guitar is in one corner. The center of the room is
a low platform, also carpeted, and in the center of that is a king-size
mattress covered with comforters and colored pillows. A TV hangs on a
platform from the ceiling at its foot, and at one side of the head is a

record player-cassette-radio console. At the far corners, hidden by and rising from the jungles, are the speakers.

Bo designed the whole bedroom, but the speakers are creations. The technique is standard do-it-yourself plaster over chicken wire and wood frame, the inspiration pure Diddley. The plaster was slapped on in massive gobs and roughly molded by powerful hands. They are about three feet high, the same width, and shaped like crumpled sea anemones, or the suction pads of octopi, or something else oozily subaqueous. Spray-painted black and gold, they are arresting sculpture, startlingly sexual and strange. Bo likes them. "Whatever I'm doing, I do my thing."

In the store-room behind the studio there are a few more speakers, but those are lost behind boxes of old tapes, appliances and toys; one of the boxes has turbans Bo made his band wear a long time ago. Some have plain junk. "You ask, you just ask Daddy what his favorite hobby is," Tan had said before, laughing, "and there's only one thing he can say truly, and that's digging in the dump. After music he likes dirt best." Like a true junkster, Bo didn't bother to defend himself, just reached into a cabinet and pulled out a beautiful antique cast-iron pot he had found. One recent find was a third-grader's spelling test from the 1930s—Bo just dug it.

There are scrapbooks, too, ill-kept but bulging. Pictures of Bo smiling with d.j.'s at nightclub tables; pictures of his name on the Apollo marquee; on stage with Jerome and the Duchess (his younger half-sister, Norma Jean); beside an airport limousine which he once owned and painted up weird. One picture included the amp he built for himself in the '50s; "I was the first cat I know to make amps bigger than what the companies would give you." There was a picture he had taken of himself a couple of years ago. In it he is standing beside a burnt-out stove and other trash; he is in raggedy overalls, no shirt, and his guitar is at his feet. A pitchfork is in one hand, the other is outstretched. "Took that on the ashes of my mother's house in McComb a few years back. The title is: 'Where do we go from here?' "

There were pictures, too, of other stars: Arthur Prysock, the Moonglows, Clyde McPhatter. "I got a few of Jackie Wilson," said Bo, leafing through the stacks; "he was a favorite of mine—he sure had a thing with those girls. And here are the Shirelles—now, they were beautiful, and nice to work with. Just did a job with them in Boston, one of those revival shows, and they're still great. Man, it's funny, here I am with all these stars, and now look at me. I been there with all the greatest, and I can't see why I didn't get further than I did."

[V]

From "Bo Diddley" in 1955 and the LP *Bo Diddley's a Gunslinger,* Bo was a star. He and Chuck Berry were Chess Records' gold-dust twins, though Bo was never as big as Chuck. Chuck was a more clever hit-maker than Bo, his lyrics snappier and his touch a trifle more pop-

oriented. Bo's audience was smaller but perhaps more fanatical: once
you had connected with Bo, it was hard to get loose. At the time some
talked of a feud, but Bo says it's nonsense. "I never had no envious 57
feelings toward Chuck. I never got too close to him. He was quiet back
then just like he is now. I admit he's a strange dude, but I can get along
with anybody."

Once established, Bo started working at the rock 'n' roll business,
hard work indeed. It had a lot more flash and a little more money than
blues club jobs, but it also included endless travelling and the psychological strain of having to "stay on top." Like Berry and dozens of 58
others, Bo toured, wrote and recorded for seven straight years. There
was no time for vacations and no premium for development; you were
only as good as your latest hit. It was not a way to get rich; on this
point Bo is adamant.

"After my first record I started getting $250 a gig, and I never got
much more than that, even when I had the hottest record in the country.
I had a band to pay, a car to run, and I was trying to send about a 59
hundred bucks a week back to my family. Managers, hah! I used to
wouldn't ask questions, because I figured the manager cat was in my
corner, he was gonna do everything in his power to do my thing for
me. No way!

"A guy would tell me, 'I got you covered, you play your axe, man,
I'll do the rest.' So I say, 'Crazy,' and there I am, going down the road,
two, three, four in the morning, sleeping on the road, doing my thing 60
at gigs every night. Then I look for my money, and the man say, 'Oh,
everything's all right, man.' And I say, 'Sure, it's fine for you, at home
every night with your wife and kids, but when I get home I'm broke
again.'

"I'm not gonna tell no lie and say, 'Yeah, because I'm Bo Diddley
I got a whole lot of money.' I ain't got a *quarter*—by that I mean I ain't
got the couple of hundred thousand in the bank I should have. Right 61
now I'm not really in debt, but I wouldn't say I was out of debt either.
I'm putting food on the table and that's all. I have been robbed of
what was really mine because I worked for it. I have been robbed from
styles and arrangements, *sounds*, and I don't know who is getting the
money, but I ain't. They told me once you can't copyright a beat. Hah!

"It was hard, man, it was hard. I wouldn't have the problems I have
today if the record company had taken care of business and given me
what was due. The record companies have got ways of getting around 62
you, of b.s.-ing you. They say, 'Oh, man, you ain't but sold 9000 records,' but they want to sign you again. Now why they keep signing me
if I ain't making them no business? Would you go out and pick up
rotten apples if you can't sell 'em? But I took it. What else could I
do? You danced to the tune they was playing, or you didn't dance at
all."

Yet a few sentences later Bo could talk of Leonard and Phil Chess as
"beautiful cats." By all accounts Chess Records was run like many ghetto

businesses; the brothers (Phil is still alive; Leonard died in October 1969) were tyrants and exploiters, but their own tough Jewish soul kept them close to the artists whom, on some level, they truly loved. What other white man but Leonard Chess could call Sonny Boy Williamson "motherfucker" and get away with it? Chess is probably the best record company in America; their vaults will some day be recognized as a national treasure.

Bo has made over a dozen LPs for Chess, ranging from classics like *Bo Diddley Is a Lover* and *Have Guitar, Will Travel* to topically titled jobs like *Bo Diddley's a Twister, Surfin' with Bo Diddley,* and even *Bo Diddley's Beach Party.* As with all such albums, there is some repetition —*Roadrunner,* for instance, is a mixture of old and new material. But that was not Bo's doing, and in all the hours of music he made there is not one dull minute. *Bo Diddley's 16 All-Time Greatest Hits,* 45 minutes of stunning rock 'n' roll music, is probably the best introduction to his music, but why stop there? On some tracks done to fill up albums, he really relaxes and gets *strange.* He wrote some of the most beautiful ballads in rock ("Come On, Baby" on *Gunslinger* and "Love Is a Secret" on *Bo Diddley Is a Lover*), some lovely guitar instrumentals (like "Spanish Guitar" on *Have Guitar*) that almost sound Arabic, and even did a tune called "Mr. Krushchev" that is a showstopper on the *Bo Diddley* album, one of his very best. His introduction to "Congo" on the *Lover* LP sounds like Jimi Hendrix ten years early.

Bo's musical gestures are so bold that on hearing them on record one feels that it was not so much that the microphones overheard his music, but that, like a painter working in plastic, Bo personally stamped his image on the vinyl discs. Every track is inimitably Bo's, not because they all sound the same—there is a wide stylistic variation—but because Bo's artistic vision is founded on a belief in his own uniqueness. "A person is an individual, and being an individual person is a gas," he said. "I have my own way of expressing my soulful feelings. I never wanted to be like anybody else and I can't copy anybody else. I got my own bag of tricks."

All Bo's songs express that radical humanism. Sometimes called the Originator, he finds his creative energy not in his environment or other musicians but within himself. That crude energy, coming from levels too mysterious for self-conscious control, vitalizes everything he makes. His power is *shaman* power, and like the devil, he gives himself many names: the Puffessor, Doctor Diddley, Diddley Daddy, the Man Who Knows Everything, and, of course, Bo Diddley. Roadrunner, and gunslinger, too, he can take on any guise because he knows who he is.

His exulting in himself is both comic and cosmic. In "Hey, Bo Diddley," he's like Old McDonald with "women here, women there, women, women everywhere"; in "Gunslinger" he's got "a gun on his hip and a rose on his chest." In "Who Do You Love," one of his masterpieces (he also wrote "Love Is Strange"), he lets it all out:

I got 47 miles of barbwire,
I use a cobra snake as a necktie
I got a brand new house on the roadside,
Made of rattlesnake hide,
I got a brand new chimney made on top,
Made out of human skulls,
Now, c'mon, take a little walk with me, Arlene, 67
An' tell me, who do you love. . . .
Got a tombstone hand and a graveyard mind,
Just 22 and I don't mind dying,
Who do you love,
Yeah,
Who do you love?

If his preening were vanity, he would not be sexy; as it is, Bo is
one of the sexiest men in music. He loves women more than himself,
and establishes his manhood only to prove the power of his feelings. 68
"She's Alright" has almost no structure as a song; it's just Bo shouting
about his "Mary Lou." "Dearest Darling" is a crooner's song with lyrics
to match:

I once had a heart so good and true,
But now it's gone from me to you,
For you have two hearts and I have none.

But Bo sings it with such unaffected simplicity, and adds so many grunts, moans and mammalian pleasure noises that there's no mistaking what he's talking about. "I'm Sorry" is a perfect rock 'n' roll ballad with that stately pace that groups like the Penguins and the Moonglows were so good at. Bo's compression of his inchoate emotions into the song's ordered progress fills what could have been a banal tune with passion.

All his work is filled with good humor. "Say, Man," which is Bo
and Jerome trading insults ("You'se so ugly your mother had to put
a sheet over your head so sleep could slip up on you"), is all jokes and 69
ends with a joke on itself: an unidentified third party (in fact Bo) sticks
his head in and agrees with either one or both. When Bo laughs in
"Roadrunner" after saying, "Gonna put some dirt in our eye!" you
know he means it. The humor is not just the jokes; it is Bo's whole
stance. He obviously enjoys making records, and that enjoyment comes
through the music. So much of Bo comes through that he feels free to
talk directly to the listener: in Willie Dixon's "You Can't Judge a Book
by the Cover," he commands, "You got your radio turned down too low.
Turn it up!"

Bo's music is, however, more in his rhythm than his words or
melodies; most of the latter are skeletal or nonexistent. "The Bo Diddley Beat" suggests a formula; it is rather a tribute to him, one of the
few great rhythm-makers in rock 'n' roll. Bo can play fine solo blues 70
guitar, but mostly he plays rhythm. Playing on the neck, below the pick-
ups, along the strings, and even tapping the body, he gets an astonishing dynamic range to his beats. He starts almost every song himself;

their drive is always his. Bo Diddley's many beats cannot be described in words by me; besides saying his beat is infectious, joyous, and strong as the man himself, I can only hope you dig it.

Bo called it his "thing" and doesn't underestimate its importance in communicating his art. "It's my rhythm that makes my music penetrate to the followers I have. What you do has got to *penetrate.* You can be a good speaker and know what to say, but if you ain't shooting it out right, it just ain't gonna do right. You almost gotta write it on a piece of paper and sing it at the same time, just so as to make sure people don't misunderstand. You got to get it out there, *produce* it, make the people feel it, and if they like it, well, you got something going."

[VI]

If Bo's peak was in 1962, his fall came swiftly on its heels. One effect of the Beatles' arrival on the scene was to make stars of the '50s memories instead of contemporary performers. Bo was a hit in England —where he became close friends with the Rolling Stones—but in America the kids wanted the English boys who idolized and imitated Bo. With every year Bo's old fans grew further from their record-buying teenage years. Bo, no longer riding the crest, had to check his finances more closely. That inevitably led to run-ins at Chess.

"The minute I started speaking up, right away the cats are saying, 'Well, it looks like this black boy is getting smart.' Man, do you know I've never gotten a check in the mail from Chess Records? Royalties—a joke. Ever since I been there it seems like *I owe Chess.*" He rummaged through a stack of old mail and found a letter from Chess (now part of the GRT Corporation) he got a few months ago. It was a bill for studio time, instrument rental, hotel rooms and other miscellaneous charges; it added up to $39,000. "Are you ready for that?" asked Bo. He threw the paper down.

"I got rid of my last Cadillac years ago; I let it go back to the collection people. Chess, they wanted me to have it. What for? My *car* don't play nothing. A cat with a big car is showing off his equipment; the cat who pulls up with a raggedy car and his instruments falling out—watch him, he's dangerous. I decided I wasn't falling for that flashy trick bag no more. When I stopped taking those new Cadillacs, the Chess brothers they got worried. They knew they had nothing to bribe me with no more."

By the mid-'60s his relations with Chess were so bad that Bo made the crucial decision: to stop recording, stop hoping that one more record would break the cycle. He moved his family to California from Chicago, beginning the exile he is still living. Two years ago, when I first thought of interviewing Bo, Chess representatives discouraged me, saying Bo was a "difficult cat" who had inexplicably hidden himself away. To Chess, Bo's decision probably was inexplicable: who ever heard of a black artist rejecting Cadillacs and going on strike?

Idleness has been hard on Bo. For weeks at a time he does not
know when his next gig will be. He makes calls, trying to get work,
but has to watch that he doesn't wear out his welcome where one is
extended. He's done time stewing in his own juices, and though he
has nothing to do with politics, he has a mordant view of the American
Way. Americans, he says, "are great believers in b.s. They love to listen
to it; the truth—they don't want to hear." He's never liked cops—"I've
been shoved up against the wall a few times, in jail for stuff I didn't
know about, and that created a little dislike"—and he has little respect 76
for the Establishment in general. "Those judges and lawyers and people
who have already had their day, they is sitting on top of their money,
they is got the keys, and is keeping the top *securely* fastened. They
have everything they want, and if they ain't got it, they's probably
stealing it through some way a bookkeeper is doing for them. I know
the whole scene. Look how it works for us musicians: everybody likes
our records, even the people who owns the banks, but nobody wants
to give us credit. We is well loved, but we is bad risks. Hah!"

Fortunately, the bitterness is balanced by deep religious faith. The
Bible is *the* book for Bo, and as he gets his beat from the sanctified
church, he draws his world-view from his Baptist upbringing. "Some
things in the Bible I don't understand. I shake my head and say, 'Maybe
I'll come across somebody one day with better answers,' but until then
I'll let it be." One thing he does know is that he is a man because he 77
is a son of Adam. "We are all sons and daughters of him and Eve—
the Bible don't mention anybody else getting it all started—so we are
all sisters and brothers. Man has got to get it together for himself. Do
you know we are the only animal that kills for the hell of it? We preach
love and practice hate; we preach peace and practice war. Harmony,
man, people getting along with themselves and each other, it would be
so beautiful."

Those sentiments put him foursquare behind "the kids"; of course,
he's seen it coming for a while. "The white kids started digging what
we were laying down because finally it was time for a change. They 78
got tired of listening to Tchaikovsky and all them cats that their mom-
mies and daddies were throwing at them. Tired of always playing the
music real *low* so you could carry on a conversation while the music
is in the background. The kids decided they wanted to use the record
players for all the power they had. Pops and Moms still don't understand what's happening."

From exile he watched the spread of rock 'n' roll after the Beatles,
the success of his friends the Rolling Stones, the growth of the long-
hair culture, and he dug it. "When the Beatles came out with that 79
'Yeah, yeah, yeah' stuff, 'It's been a hard day's night,' " he sang with a
big smile, "the old folks said, 'How cute.' Then a few weeks later they
look around and there's Junior, and they say, 'Junior, when you gonna
get a haircut?' And pretty soon Junior's hair is down to *here!* Hah! *Man,
if I could grow my hair long, I'd grow it down to the ground!*

"All this talk about a generation gap? It's the parents who created it. The kids are trying to tell 'em what's happening in words, music, dress and all, but the parents won't understand. They slam the door; they is belligerent. I've seen it happen at these festivals; the cops call it a riot, but it's the cops who start it. They call one off saying there is *gonna* be a riot—how can they know that unless it's them who makes 'em?"

Bo knows he has a place in this musical and social movement, but he hasn't known how to get it. He wears home tie-dyed jeans on stage now, and would like to organize with other musicians to do low-cost cooperative gigs—"We could play schoolyards Saturday afternoons and make it a buck a head or something." The much-publicized "rock 'n' roll revival" of a year ago did get his name around a bit more, but it put him in an "oldie but goldie" bag he doesn't like at all. To combat that, he finally did go back to Chess studios last winter and made *Black Gladiator.* Phil Chess was the producer—Bo would deal with no one else. It was released at the same time as Chuck Berry's *Home Again,* his first record on Chess for six years, and together they got the old-home-week treatment. *Home Again* is brilliant in parts, but the band, Chess studio men, is unsympathetic, and some tracks seem like throwaways; Chuck's anger has become frozen rage.

Black Gladiator, on the other hand, is a totally fresh record, bursting, exploding and just plain rocking with Bo's energy. The title and theme are in direct line with "I'm a Man"; as Bo explains it, "Man is supposed to be built. Look at the gladiators back in Roman days. These cats could walk up and hit a mule, deck a horse by cracking him on the jaw. Man is getting out of that; try it today and you break your hand. We are living too fast. We are using the knowledge box more, doing less of a physical thing. Like my wife says, and she makes sense, 'We're gonna be all head and no body after a while.' I believe it should be more balanced than that." Or, as he sometimes sings, "Don't write a check with your mouth you can't cash with your tail."

The record starts with "Elephant Man" and that sets the pace; two other songs are "Power House" and "You, Bo Diddley" (as in, "Who's the greatest man in town? You, Bo Diddley"). Everything sounds the way the back jacket photo looks: Bo, guitar in hand, his head back, singing, mouth open wide, his bare chest and arms in studded leather belts—a suit he designed for himself and had made by a tailor in Montreal.

Side two opens with "I've Got a Feeling," and that feeling is that Bo's "gonna be happy for once in his life." The old "Hush Your Mouth" has become "Shut Up, Woman," in which Bo gives his woman an epic talking-to, but only because he knows that "I'm yours, and you'se mine. . . . We *love* one another." "I Don't Like You" is funnier than the original "Say, Man." "If you don't watch out, you is gonna play mountain and get climbed on," warns Bo's antagonist. "*Start climbing, baby,"* Bo grunts back. It also introduces Bo the opera singer, a side of himself he had concealed until now. "But I've always had that voice. In Sunday school choir, even when I was in the back row, when I got to *singing,* the teacher would stop everything and tell me to hush up."

Black Gladiator is Bo Diddley at his very best, not a revived memory but a revitalized artist at the very height of his powers. In person,
too, he is better than ever, in full command of the stage and audience 85
from the moment he steps to the mike ("The only person I ever feared
on stage is Ray Charles"). He has hopes that his days in exile are close
to over; he'd much rather be making music than fixing cars.

* * *

At the Fillmore a few months ago, he looked out, a hand shading
his eyes against the spotlights. "Hey, everybody," he said, "I'm Doctor 86
Diddley, the Puffessor—what you got on your mind?—I got the answer."
There was a ripple of laughter.

"Have mercy. But there's one thing I want you to know, one thing
you gotta dig with Bo: I *understand.*" Silence greeted that; maybe Bo's 87
eyes were burning too brightly. He pulled back a bit.

"And I remember, too, that without you who are so beautiful I
wouldn't have made it at all with what you might call the rock 'n' 88
roll music. Thank you, thank you, thank you, from the bottom of my
heart. You see, I'm always *your* Bo Diddley."

The hall responded with a murmur and scattered clapping. Bo
smiled, hit a chord, and called the next tune to the band. He looked 89
back at the audience. "I thank you in advance for the great round of
applause I am about to get."

Peter Schrag

The Age of Willie Mays

Time is of the essence. The shadow moves
From the plate to the box, from the box to second base,
From second to the outfield, to the bleachers.
Time is of the essence. The crowd and players
Are the same age always, but the man in the crowd
*Is older every season. Come on, play ball!**

It was always a game of myth and memory. The ritual transcended
the moment of play, tested performance against immortality, and allowed otherwise ordinary men to place themselves in something larger
than conventional time. Each spring brought its own renewal and each
summer its moments of truth. The word came from Vero Beach and
St. Pete and Scottsdale, where the big leaguers trained before the season: new faces and new ballyhoo, and new predictions of who would
be greater (someday) than Mantle, who could throw like Koufax, and 1
who could run like Cobb. But there was more; there was the man in
the crowd, his memories, his moments, his brush with greatness, and,
above all, his return, year after year, to the places where the idols of
the past, the anticipated glory of the future, and the remembrance of
youth came together against the clipped green grass of the field in the
afternoon sun, against the crowd, and against a ritual that, despite its
historical brevity, seemed as old as time.

Those of us who came to know baseball when there was little television and no big-time professional football or basketball talked its
language, heard its lore, and were taken with its special sense before
we had ever played an organized game or pondered its beautiful mys- 2
tery. There were giants on the field, men of legend whose voices we
had never heard, whose faces we knew only from newspaper photographs or from the murky images on our bubblegum cards, and whose
records—batting average, home runs, runs batted in—suggested meaning

beyond anything we understood. "Facts" supported myth, and myth magnified the facts on which it was supposed to be based.

It was always a game of argument. The action on the field was
never sufficient to fill the time, and it therefore required of its spectators something more than catcalls and cheers. After every play we
confronted not only the opportunity but the necessity for discussion,
analysis, and comparison, and it was in those long moments of inaction 3
—when the teams changed sides, when the relief pitchers ambled in from
the bullpen (in the days before they rode on golf carts), in the winter
hiatus, in the stretches when nothing might ever happen again—that
we, the fans, chose our idols and elected our heroes.

*Time is of the essence. The crowd and players are the same age
always, but the man in the crowd is older every season.* Perhaps it will
always be that way; perhaps the ritual will survive conditions that have
destroyed other American perennials, and will live a charmed life into
eternity. And yet something has changed: The crowd, too, is getting
older; it is losing its small-town innocence and its capacity to believe 4
without ambivalence, and the half-life of demigods becomes shorter
with each passing year. We make and discard them according to the
requirements of the television schedule; we demand action—violent
action—to fill the anxious moments, and we seem no longer capable of
creating idols in our idleness.

There is nothing new in the argument that something is destroying
baseball—avaricious major league club owners buying and selling fran-
chises, moving teams, abandoning old fans, and wooing new ones with
cast-off bush league players who should be selling sporting goods or
life insurance; mounting expenses; the competition of other activities;
and the influence of television itself. But these things—though they
are, for some of us, matters of concern—are hardly as significant as the
fate of the hero himself. Each generation likes to say that there will 5
never be another Ruth, another DiMaggio, another Ted Williams, con-
gratulating itself (as mythology must have it) that it lived in the last
great age of heroism and achievement. Ask any big league manager
and he will remind you that the eclipse of one generation of stars
always heralds the rise of another. It is only the man in the crowd
who is older every season. The players are more skilled—are larger,
faster, stronger—than any in history.

And yet this time they are wrong. We will have great players, but
we have left the age of the mythic hero. The immortals were forged
in innocence, products of the belief that this was one nation with a
single set of values, that any boy might succeed, of the ability to say
"Wow" without embarrassment, and of the nearly magical capacity of 6
big league baseball to preserve its small-town qualities within the secure
confines of big-city stadiums. Once we walked through the turnstiles,
we all became boys again, breathed a little easier, and enjoyed the
protection of the ritual, the memories, the immersion in another dimension of time.

For many of us who came to our baseball in those more innocent days, only one great man is left, and his name is Willie Mays. This week—on May 6—he became forty years old, and he should, therefore, be well past his prime, an aging star dogged by fragile legs, trick knees, fatigue, and the other assorted aches and pains that the flesh of annuating athletes is supposed to suffer. But Mays moves with the grace of memory, defying time, defying the inexorable erosion of fantasies, defying age itself. He remains unequivocally our man. To see him now is like watching the instant replay of a generation, the crowds of twenty years, the old ball parks with their erratic dimensions and their even more erratic fans, Hilda Chester and the Dodger Symphony at Ebbets Field, the short right field foul line in the Polo Grounds, where Mel Ott, among others, once hit his "Chinese" home runs. And, of course, there is the image of Mays himself: the unbelievable catches, the 3,000 base hits, the 630-odd home runs (second only to Babe Ruth's lifetime total), the elegance that, when we first saw it in 1951, could hardly be comprehended. Mays always moved differently from other players, started instinctively toward the place where the ball was hit—moving from his center field position almost, it seemed, before the batter swung—and he caught fly balls against his belt with the palm of his glove turned up, playing with a casual defiance of error, a disdain for security, and with an emphasis on style that repudiated mere professional competence.

When Mays came to the Giants in 1951, Jackie Robinson, who broke the color line in major league baseball, already had been with the Dodgers for four years; in the meantime, moreover, a handful of other Negro players had been signed, and they were being cautiously accepted by the fans and players. But Mays brought with him something that I imagine the game rarely enjoyed before, and that can only be described as aristocratic class. Despite his notorious disregard for the official causes of civil rights (for which he was later attacked by Robinson himself), Mays was not merely a ballplayer who happened to be Negro; he was a black athlete. He ran black, swung black, and caught black. He did not play the man's game but his own, and his every move disparaged the tight-assed honkies who did things by the book. William Goldman, in a book about the theater, recalled what Mays had done for him: "It was about time he arrived on my horizon, because during all those years of being bored by baseball, of sitting on bleacher seats for pitchers' battles, or dying from the heat while the manager brought in some slow reliever, I'd been waiting for Willie. He was what it was all about." There are countless thousands of us who felt the same way. Mention Mays now and you find more people who claim to have seen his first game with the Giants than could ever have squeezed into the Polo Grounds that day; more who remember his impossible catch of Vic Wertz's 440-foot drive in the 1954 World Series than ever attended a Series game. Of such stuff are legends made.

This spring, for the first time, I made the pilgrimage, a forty-year-old man pursuing another forty-year-old who was the idol of the boy. Instant replay—what every kid used to dream about, and what many still do—sitting in the Arizona sun, or leaning against the batting cage to feel the intensity of the pitch and the opposing concentration of the hitter, or, again, standing in the locker room to watch the man who preserves the fantasy. Spring training. The symbols of time come together, old players and young, Hall of Famers and rookies, welding a continuity
that goes back beyond remembrance: Carl Hubbell, Hall of Fame 9
pitcher who won 253 games between 1928 and 1943, the man who struck out Ruth, Gehrig, Foxx, Simmons, and Cronin—one after another—in the 1934 All-Star game (now director of the Giants' farm system) sitting by the dugout; Wes Westrum, who managed the Mets in leaner days, hitting ground balls to the infield; Larry Jansen, who helped pitch the Giants into the World Series in 1951, watching the young pitchers warming up—kids just up from Fresno and Amarillo and St. Cloud.

Around the field the sports writers are trying to grab a few crumbs for tomorrow's paper, looking for another rookie of promise, escalating every solid drive into a slugger's future, and in the bleachers people with memories longer than mine are discussing games played twenty years before I was born. Juan Marichal, another player of supreme
elegance, is pitching batting practice. (High kick, the left foot higher 10
than the head, the ball coming from some deep recess of motion, the glove brushing the knee as the ball is thrown, and turning an ordinary man of six feet into a fantastic engine of power.) Mays, his right foot dug in at the rear of the batter's box, hits a couple to the fence in left center, then takes a pitch low and away.

"I can't hit that," he says to Marichal. "Can't hit that no way."

Marichal pitches another, again low and a little outside, and Mays 11
smokes it on a line over the head of the shortstop.

"That was the same pitch," Marichal says. "The same pitch."

"I had to hit it," Mays answers, his voice rising and, at the same
time, a little resigned. Logic loses to performance, and Charlie Fox, the 12
Giants' manager, turns from his position behind the batting cage with an expression of futile amazement: What can you say when you are supervising a genius?

Mays still plays the same game. After the first two weeks of the 1971 season, he led the league in runs batted in and was among the leaders in batting average and home runs. Twenty years and three
thousand games later the style hasn't changed. He will run a little less 13
this year, steal fewer bases, skip—with Charlie Fox's blessings—the fatiguing Tuesday and Friday night games at Candlestick Park, the Giants' home field in San Francisco, but the moves are all the same, and the virtuosity is unblemished. He protects himself in a dozen different ways: He does not drink or smoke; throws underhand whenever possible to protect the arm and shoulder; takes his meals in his room

when the team is on the road; walks onto the Arizona practice field wearing a warmup jacket so the autograph hunters, failing to recognize his face, won't swarm to his number; melts away from practice before the other players and slips into his pink Imperial, license number SAY HEY, to drive to lunch and then to a round of golf. "He never stands when he can sit," says Fox, "and he never sits when he can lie down."

In the locker room he is a person—or, better, a kid, shifting moods from highpitched exuberance to petulance—and in the stadium he is a demigod, but between them he becomes an apparition that materializes and evaporates according to its own impulse. Perhaps, you say, he is hurting, suffering the anguish of exploitation, of too many games, too many pitchmen, too many sellers of clothes, bats, gloves, buttons, pictures, and causes, too many journalists asking questions—how much did he sign for? how much does he want?—too much pressure, but he has no intention of thinking about himself as a man of complexity or as the aging star (like Mantle) whose every painful move becomes a heroic act. His public role is to remain a player only—a man who plays —because he seems incapable of any other part.

And yet it is hard for anyone to tell how much is man, how much boy, and how much the distillation of idolatry. We are sitting in the team dining room at the Francisco Grande, an Arizona hotel owned by the Giants: Mays, wearing asparagus-green trousers, a green turtleneck shirt, and a green cardigan sweater; Sy Berger of New York, the king of the bubble-gum cards—which, he explains, are bigger than ever with the kids—and the boy from New York. Somewhere else another presence of Mays is negotiating a new contract with the Giants—he has asked for $75,000 a year for ten years, but the reporters, after the contract is signed, guess $165,000 a year for two years—and he is clearly concerned about something that other people would call the future. But here at lunch Mays talks only about playing ball—"I'm not thinking about five years from now"—and complaining about the old photographs that Berger uses on his bubble-gum cards. Berger answers that Mays looks the same as ever, and Mays screws up his face and says sheeit. . . . Somehow, I tell myself, he seems to make it possible to contemplate the old days without confronting the matter of age itself, but I am not really sure. Which one of us is the kid, and which one the man of maturity? (A good businessman, say the flacks around the field—investments, endorsements, he's got a bundle—but the speculation in the swamp between myth and reality is so rank that anything goes.) I do not know, therefore, just how the fantasies lodge between us, but I do sense some regret (mine, perhaps; yet possibly his) about the past.

Before the Giants moved from New York to San Francisco, Mays spent part of his free time playing stickball with the kids in Harlem, going from the Polo Grounds to the streets not as an act of charity but as an activity of natural joy. (Although he was good there, too, he was not the best; but that may indeed have been an act of charity.) He

does not do such things anymore—they don't play stickball in California,
he said—nor has he ever become the idol in San Francisco that he had
been in New York. They have a show-me attitude out there, one of the
sports writers explained, very sophisticated compared to the hayseeds
in New York, and that, too, seems a pity. How can one tell them—for 16
the sake of everything, for Mays, for the game, for the nation—that the
height of baseball sophistication is exuberance and the instinct to understand the subtle line between the ingenuous and the hyperbolic, and
between the serious and the comic?

You leave your reservations and ambivalence at the gate. This is a
conservative game that sometimes oozes with unbounded chauvinism—
about the country, the flag, and itself—and that cannot tolerate even
the most minimal expressions of dissent. There are players—Joe Pepi-
tone of the Cubs, for example—who wear their hair long, and others
who have associated themselves with the peace movement, or who read
Dostoevsky, but most clubs and players regard every manifestation of
independent thought with suspicion. In this monopolistic business where 17
athletes are chattel, the image of the well-dressed, well-groomed, politically benign player is regarded as a matter of importance. The in-
junction to regard ballplayers as interesting human beings is therefore
self-defeating: What they do in their moments off the field is the same
sort of thing that might interest any ordinary man whose means outrun
his imagination. They play cards, watch television, go hunting, and
discuss their sexual exploits.

At the Francisco Grande one night, the Giant management showed
a film of the team's 1970 season to a crowd of balding boosters and
their wives, people who spend much of their time in VIP lounges and
not in the bleachers. On the screen there was flash and glamour—Gay-
lord Perry winning twenty-three games; Marichal striking out the side;
Willie McCovey, described by the film narrator as the most feared 18
hitter in baseball, lining one over the fence in right while the crowd
cheered and the background orchestra played a few measures of Beethoven. Just outside the room where the film was shown, Marichal and
McCovey, in sports shirts and slacks, were watching a John Wayne
film on television while Perry was beginning the sixth hour of a card
game that had been in progress since early afternoon—ordinary men
attempting to fill tedious moments in lonely cities.

You leave your ambivalence at the gate. It does not matter what
kind of person Willie Mays "really" is, nor does the question mean
very much. He is what he does, a ballplayer and then something more,
a man who has—like most highly talented performers in other fields— 19
transcended his trade. In the locker room he is one of the boys, needling
other players, denying any knowledge about who might have placed
Tito Fuentes's missing socks into his locker, tossing a football down
the aisle, lending a couple of bats to Bobby Bonds, discussing his golf
scores. And beyond the locker room there are endless theories, each of
them fit for a moment: that he has dollar signs in his eyes, that he is

supremely generous ("There was this sick kid in the hospital . . ."), that he is interested in nothing but baseball and women, that he will play two more years and then become the first black manager in baseball, that he expects too much of other players to manage a club. . . .

Mays never has been even remotely political, and if you ask him what he has done for the cause of racial justice—where he has marched or what organizations he supports—he will tell you (if he answers at all) that he does things his own way, without publicity and without making himself a politically marked man. Long ago his ebullience earned him the nickname Say Hey (which by contemporary sensibilities, might suggest something just this side of "boy"), but in recent years he has become more cautious, a man who seems to have learned that everything has its price and that he himself (as the highest paid player in the game, as an endorser of bats, automobiles, clothes, and cosmetics) is a highly valuable piece of property.

But none of that matters. The "contribution" is more subtle and profound, a contribution of style. Mays has become a sports hero by doing things his own way, and if few other athletes can do that, it is all the more a tribute to his skill. One morning in Phoenix, at Charlie Fox's request, he took a group of young outfielders to a corner of the ball park to work on some of the finer points. Although Mays always has been comfortable with kids, it is not something he does very often, and it turned into an extended disquisition on style. (All of them were black, which may have added to the urgency, however subtle, of the message.) "You don't play it by the book," he said. "You play it opposite; you come up with the ball on the side you're going to throw. . . ." (Going through the motions now, picking up a ball from the grass, always moving, the bare hand sweeping the ball out of the glove, the arm cocking. . . .) "Don't get directly in front of it; if you want to make money, get the ball on the side; if you get in front of it you're playing it safe. You have to move everything, your arm, your legs, your body, keep it all moving; you're like a ballet dancer out there; don't short-arm it, don't be afraid to let it go, and don't ever figure the ball's going to get by you."

One of them asked a question about a play last year in which the crowd in San Francisco hooted its disapproval. "Don't worry about the fans, fuck the fans. They don't know anything about what you're trying to do." They all watch him again, the legs moving, the glove, the hand, the arm, the whole dance that we have seen a thousand times on the field performed in slow motion. (You can remember it all, hear the announcers, the crowd, see the fielder going back, back to a forgotten fence, taking the ball with his back to the plate, driving his spikes against the wall, putting his shoulder against it, throwing on a line toward the infield if there are runners on base, or if there are none heaving it underhand, nonchalantly, and walking back to retrieve his cap where it had fallen during the chase.) "I've studied the game," he is saying to them now, trying to explain his imposition on them, "but nobody ever showed me. My father started me, but nobody showed me." Later in the day I will see one of them, George Foster, carrying a baseball through the lobby of the motel, practicing the two-fingered, across-the-seams grip that Mays had explained that morning.

Mays was nineteen when the Giants bought his contract from the
Birmingham Barons, a Negro team, and brought him up to the white
man's big game. He played one season of minor league ball at Trenton
and part of another at Minneapolis before arriving at the Polo Grounds.
Harry Truman was President, Joe DiMaggio was still playing for the 23
Yankees, and the presence of Negro players in the major leagues was,
on the one hand, a matter of caution (whom would they room with?
how would they travel? could they take the pressure?) and, on the
other, an occasion for liberal self-congratulation.

Every black player, therefore, was something of a secret agent; a
man had to express himself on the field and nowhere else. Mays arrived
in New York in the same year that Mantle started his career with the
Yankees, and comparisons were therefore inevitable: who was the better
hitter? who was faster? who could hit more home runs? Mantle was,
in every respect, the hero of tradition—a big, strong, attractive kid from 24
a small town in Oklahoma, the kind of player about whom they write
books for boys. But what was Mays? The myth had no place for him;
all it offered was the possibility of limited integration—the hope that
he might become one of the boys, might be good, and might be liked.
The one chance of transcending those limitations was style itself, and
the style became like a signature.

If you want to make money, don't play it safe. He runs out every
hit, the legs flowing, long smooth strides, the feet slightly pigeon-toed
(Dr. Spock says somewhere that pigeon-toed babies are more likely
than others to be athletes), making the turn at first as if he might go
for two—the convincing performance—making the fielder throw, making
him think, and adding a beat to a play that might otherwise be routine. 25
At such moments you feel the possibilities, the suspended tremor, the
delicacy of time in the balance. Time is of the essence: The difference
between a single and a double is a fraction of a second and a cloud of
dust; the difference between an infield out and a single is the blink of
an umpire's eye.

When Mays first came up, he said a great deal about learning from
Joe DiMaggio—the ritual probably demanded it, especially of an athlete
playing in New York at the time—but he owed more to talent than to
any coach or player. In Arizona this spring, Leo Durocher, who managed the Giants in Mays's first season, observed that he didn't teach 26
Mays anything: "He could do it all." The ability, Durocher said, pointing a bat at the heavens, came from *there.* But the triumph exceeded
competence. Just at the moment when everything in America was going
corporate, when the old idols of Americanism were entering their declining years, and when baseball itself seemed to be dulled by tepid
professionalism, he appeared to us as the new romantic individualist,

a man of the ritual, but a man who also enriched it. He brought jazz to the game.

In the decade that followed there would be others, Henry Aaron of the Braves, Bob Gibson of the Cardinals, Ernie Banks of the Cubs —all of them suffering the misfortune of having to play outside the New York limelight—but Mays was the symbol. He expressed on the field what James Baldwin and others would later try to say in words: If you would retrieve your humanity from the fear of death, the fear of defeat, the fear of vulnerability, you need us as much as we need you, need to learn something again about joy and suffering, about risk, and about those possibilities of uninhibited expression without which neither life nor art can survive. "Something very sinister happens to the people of a country," Baldwin wrote, "when they distrust their own reactions as deeply as they do here, and become as joyless as they have become."

The tragedy lies in our own limitations. We loved the player but failed too often to appreciate the message, did not understand the significance of the play. We missed the lesson of improvisation—"all human effort beyond the lowest level of the struggle for animal existence," wrote Albert Murray, "is motivated by the need to live in style"—and thus Mays may himself become a transitory kind of figure. There will never be—not for many years, at any rate—a black Babe Ruth or a black Charles Lindbergh, men who can lead the celebration of national achievement, because our racism still runs too deep and because—in any case—we have outgrown our hope and innocence. At the very moment when Mays became the greatest player in baseball the game was diminished; even as he enriched it, and thereby promised to enrich us all, it lost its symbolic pre-eminence, ceased to be the intimate common possession it once had been, and became just another big-time sport. Black players now dominate professional sports—basketball, football, and baseball—but we switch channels too fast to permit them to become our own; after this game there will be another, and another, people jumping, tackling, blocking, running, throwing, catching. Everything is taken with a touch of detachment—a little "sophistication"; we are here and they are out there, and we thus create barriers against fantasy and destroy the ability to identify without equivocation. Every black kid may understand, but the rest of us have reservations.

The game, of course, goes on, but the possibility that we will ever again have common, integrating heroes seems more remote than ever. The people we admire now are, almost without exception, symbols of particularism—baseball stars, football stars, track stars, heroes of the black, heroes of the young, heroes of division: Muhammad Ali, César Chavez, John Lennon, the Berrigans, people of style and distinction in an age that lacks the rituals and values of community. We failed in the great effort to syntheticize a national adventure in the space program because it required (for technical and political reasons) a group of courageous, proficient, but totally indistinguishable individuals, men with nearly identical profiles, styles, and personalities. They took risks, too, but the risk was in trusting someone else's technology, in betting on the competence of thousands of anonymous technicians on the ground. They could not possibly transcend their medium or play it opposite from the book, and no one will ever turn to his neighbor in front of the television set and say "Conrad? [Or Cooper or Glenn or Schirra or Shepard?] Conrad? He *stinks.*" No one will ever stand on the sidelines pointing at the heavens to explain where they got their phenomenal talents.

Perhaps it was appropriate that I saw Mays at close range in that Arizona setting of retired cardiac cases, development houses, and plastic. On the field the dream was preserved—if you play ball you must continue to believe in the permanence of the ritual—but in the surroundings something had gone sour. The world was threatening to come through the turnstiles in pursuit of the fans, and not even the reveries that flourish in the sunshine seemed quite secure anymore. Every day the old people came to the field to sit in the warm sun,
watch practice, and collect autographs, but even the autograph collect- 30
ing was indiscriminate. Anything in uniform would do, and when they saw a face they remembered from television—the face of an actor or an announcer—they asked for his autograph, too. Only the kids knew better; they wanted Mays and Marichal and McCovey. (One elderly man got Mays's signature on a ball, but didn't recognize the face or the number, and couldn't read the writing: "I just got number 24," he said to his friend, "do you know who he is?") Here in the sunshine of the Southwest, the dream was coming to an end and people were gathering its remains like squirrels before the winter.

But what the head observes the heart resists. We are still in the presence of a beautiful mystery; style always defies time, and all the sociology in the world isn't worth a moment of poetry. In the hotel the old players and the coaches tell stories about athletes and games most
of us have long forgotten or never knew, and on the field young men 31
create the fantasies out of which new stories may someday be told. It is a good time to be forty—old enough to remember and young enough to believe—a good time to sit in the sun with someone you love. If the ritual is no longer for everyone, one can only regret what others are missing. For me the game goes on; Willie Mays is still playing.

Peter Fonda
and Dennis Hopper

Are We All Pushers?

Interviewed by David Frost

FROST: Welcome, Peter, very good to have you with us.

FONDA: I'm very happy to be here. I've watched my father now on this show, and I think, My God, if I can get that together as well as he did! I've never seen him so open on a show.

FROST: Delighted you say that.

FONDA: There's something about the way you don't say anything that just brings it right out.

(*Laughter*)

FROST: And he feels there's a silence there and must fill it in some way.

FONDA: He's a professional. He's got to keep it going.

FROST: Tell me. We've never had a chance to talk about *Easy Rider*. The film has become a sort of *cause célèbre*. Are you at all surprised by that? Or did you have a sort of germ of a thought that you were going to become a prophet—P-H-E-T, as well as P-R-O-F-I-T?

FONDA: Profit I-T, we figured, because the price was so low. Prophet the other way I wasn't so sure of. But Dennis, he knew all the way.

FROST: What do you hope people come away from *Easy Rider* thinking?

FONDA: I hope they just think. Or rather, I hope we stimulate them to question. I feel we've left them holding the bag.

I remember the phone call that I made to Dennis from Torado. I was very insecure. Thank God Dennis answered the phone. I said, "Listen, listen to this idea, you know, these guys, they score some dope, and they sell it, and they make some money, and they split. They're going to retire to Florida, you know that gig, and maybe do something in Florida. And they get killed before they get there. They get ripped off by some duck hunters."

He says, "Yeah, right, that's perfect," you know. "That'll make a great film." I said, "Oh, whew."

FROST: Was there a reason why you made them drug pushers at the outset of the film?

FONDA: Well, it's a reason after the fact. I mean, I'll say it's after the fact, although we discussed it while were were writing the story. It's an immoral act, and illegal, dealing in narcotics. Cocaine is what we say it was, but we didn't dare identify it in the script. It could have been heroin. Whatever the worst thing is possible for anybody to think of.

And we take this money that we've earned dealing in hard and split to Florida to retire. Part of the great American dream is to make a lot of money no matter who goes down, and go and retire. So we make a moral problem for an audience. People will have to identify with us, especially when we bring Jack Nicholson in. He's such a lovable, understandable character. Kill him, where do they go? They have to go to us.

Now we're a bunch of dope pushers. So at the end, when we get killed by a couple of other guys who just don't like the way we look. You know, "Let's pull alongside there, I'm going to scare the hell out of them," you know, and pow. Well, the audience has to decide. And they can't make the decision. It's a moral impossibility for most of the people I know, or the great silent majority who will eventually see the film. They know their kids have. And the audience has to decide: how can we like dope pushers? How can we feel sorry for them at their demise? Are we the people in the truck? Do we do that? Are we so blind that we don't see ourselves pushing dope?

Because all the people are pushing dope. Whether they're pushing it across the camera with lies, or propaganda of any sort. Or whether they're pushing it in Wall Street, as Dennis says, where eighty percent of your energies are spent trying to cheat the government, and twenty percent trying to be creative within the market. All these things manifest. You know, the farmers who burn the potato crop to demonstrate something, whether people are starving, or dump the milk on the ground to demonstrate a rise of prices. Or what happened a while ago at Kent University.

These are all manifestations of fear, instinctual fear of hard problems. And when something occurs within the herd that has no precedent, people react violently.

FROST: And so you were really wanting people to come away from the picture torn.

FONDA: Oh, yes.

FROST: And it would be disturbing to you if they came away with a clear idea?

FONDA: It disturbed me that so many young people came away thinking, "Oh yeah, those people are free, you know, and they got everything together." And they didn't have it together. I turned to Hopper at the end of the flick, and said, "We blew it." He says, "What do you mean? We're rich, we made it, we retired in Florida." Well, we blew it.

Without explanation the people have to go out, the people who are interested, and say, "What does he mean, 'We blew it'?"

FROST: In addition to the content of the picture, what is there about the style that you think has caught people's imaginations? I mean, it's very lyrical about America.

FONDA: Well, that's Dennis as a director. He has a great style. As we were putting the story together, we discussed having a lyrical kind of a thing, utilizing rock and roll songs a bit at a time to emphasize our rides, and showing America the beautiful.

FROST: Yes, some of that journey was marvelous and beautiful.

Do you think the people who are afraid of the direction young people are taking today have got anything to be afraid of?

FONDA: Well, I went to the Pleasure Fair, which is here in Los Angeles.

FROST: What's that?

FONDA: This is a gathering of people who get it on in kind of a Renaissance flavor. And I was sitting having lunch with my two children and my lady, and we were dressed appropriately. I wasn't, I was more like this. But my lady had a peasant's outfit on from the time, and my children looked groovy. And this guy came up to me, and he said, "Oh, man, we're in a lot of trouble up in Berkeley," you know, "and we need arms."

And I'm at this Pleasure Fair, and this guy's hitting me up for money to buy arms, because these people there are uptight, and they're fighting one another in a reactive sense.

Well, we have a President who one hour says one thing; an hour later we announce a totally different aspect. And we have a Congress that's been unable to enact the Bill of Rights. And we have a people who remain silent. And we have a group of young people saying "Power to the people." Well, they've got that power, and that's what's happening.

And there's too much to even begin to talk about. I'm too wiped out about the past events. Not only in Indochina, but this country, the Mideast, the stock market, the whole thing.

FROST: Now let's talk with Dennis Hopper. I understand there is a deep personal family relationship between you and Mr. Fonda, on your left there. Is that correct?

HOPPER: Yes, well, Peter's father was married to my ex-wife's mother, and Peter's—Now wait, wait, I'm going the wrong way. But I'm close to it. Wait . . . Peter's father was married to my ex-wife's mother for the first time, right? But when Peter . . . I'm getting it confused.

FONDA: I'll take it.

HOPPER: You can take it with Marin and try to work it out from there, baby.

FONDA: I'll never get it straight with Marin. Marin is *your* daughter.

Hopper: Give it from Brook's point of view. Brook is my ex-wife. That's the easiest.

Fonda: Yes, Brook Hayward.

Hopper: We were married for eight years, and we have a beautiful young daughter eight years old.

Fonda: Anyway, Brook's mother was Maggie Sullavan, a great actress here. Maggie was married to my father the first time out for both, 1932, or '31, or something like that. Married nine months, hung right in there.

Hopper: Boy, were they lucky I was married—

Fonda: My father was married to his wife's mother when his wife's father was my father's agent.

Hopper: "It's Hollywood, da-da-da-da, Hollywood."

Fonda: My associate producer on *Easy Rider*, and my partner now, is Bill Hayward, his wife's brother, who was the son of my father's first wife and my father's agent, while she was my father's first wife. But, you know, we could have had a nice Italian family.

Hopper: I tell you, I'm a Mick. The Micks and Italians made it together, and here we are.

Frost: That's the ending of that story?

Hopper: Wasn't it touching? Very happy ending.

Frost: Really some tears, look at that.

Hopper: Oh, if the audience only knew. I don't know how much more of this I can smoke.

Fonda: I'll take a hit. No, go ahead.

(*Crosstalk*)

Hopper: It's Marlboro. Oh, Marlboro, I shouldn't say that coast to coast, should I?

Frost: Peter, are you sure you're comfortable there, because you know you can sit here.

Fonda: His horse ran away, and he's—

Hopper: I gave you my horse.

Fonda: You did not, I don't take horse. I'm soft.

Hopper: They shoot horse, don't they? I don't believe in any needles, babe. Needles are out. I take vitamin B occasionally, but I don't dig it. No, really, I swear to God. I think anyone who uses needles is totally insane. And marijuana is ridiculous if it isn't legal. I think heroin and cocaine should be legalized, because we don't need larger law enforcement agencies to take care of that kind of thing.

We need to be able to watch them, and have doctors and be able to, like, take care of it the same way they do in England.

Frost: In England heroin and cocaine are illegal, and they ought to be.

Hopper: Sure, but you go to a drugstore and buy it, if you can prove that you're an addict.

FROST: You've got to somehow absolutely destroy the traffic in heroin, surely.

HOPPER: Well, I would hope so. But if you're not going to do that, like you're giving the underworld a tremendous amount of money by making it illegal. If a guy can prove he's an addict, let him go to a drugstore and pick it up. Then you can have a doctor and a psychiatrist there, and then you can treat the problem, and it's not an abstraction any more.

We don't need more policemen. We need to be able to take care of the people that way. We don't need them stealing that way. An addict should be able to go and get it.

FROST: It's not as available as that in England. You can't nip into a drugstore and get it.

HOPPER: Sorry. If you can prove that you're an addict.

FROST: You may know of a private drugstore.

HOPPER: I don't use it.

FROST: No, I know you don't.

HOPPER: I smoke marijuana and take LSD occasionally, though.

FROST: In England it's only someone who's unfortunate enough to have become hooked on heroin or cocaine who after going through a lot of tests can then get supplies gradually lessened and lessened hopefully to a cure.

HOPPER: Great!

FROST: But surely you've got to press with every force in the world ruthlessly to stamp out that traffic.

HOPPER: Yeah, but an addict is a sick person. Anybody that's sticking a needle in their arm is sick.

FROST: Of course they're sick.

HOPPER: Well, then, like, have doctors. Have it available for them. Don't, like, make them have to go out and steal. An addict has to get a hundred and fifty dollars a day. You know, *I* can't even afford that. You're making a criminal of him, so you're enlarging your police force to find him, arresting people. I mean, it's crazy.

FROST: Of course you've got to do something about people who are addicts. But how do you stop them becoming addicts?

HOPPER: Once you see who the addicts are, then you can start. First of all, the underworld's going to lose a lot of money. And, like, I think that's important. I don't think we should give them tax-free dollars.

FROST: But explain more how you stop people from becoming addicted in the first place.

HOPPER: First of all, you let the people see the addicts lined up at the drugstore, and you let the doctors and the psychiatrists see them. You expose them, so they're no longer criminals and no longer stealing out of your houses. Because eighty percent of our crimes in our cities are by people who are addicted and have to steal to get their addiction taken care of.

Legalize it, let us see it, let us deal with the problem when it's out in the open. Why do we keep pushing everything down, pushing everything down?

FROST: You seem to be saying something that you're not saying you're saying. Legalizing it is a different thing from providing limited supplies, available on medical prescription.

HOPPER: I said it about twice now. If a person can prove that they're addicted to heroin or any of those drugs, let them go to the drugstore and be able to purchase it. Let them see a doctor. Let them see a psychiatrist. They're sick. And, like, they're a problem to the society.

FROST: But you would make a criminal out of the pusher if heroin became available by prescription only, wouldn't you?

HOPPER: Well, if it was legalized. I see no difference between the man who pushes cocaine at the beginning of *Easy Rider* and a man on Wall Street who's involved in defense plants who takes all of his money and puts it in a Swiss bank. It's tax-free.

FROST: Dennis, you keep switching between the two definitions. You'd rather switch than fight. (*Laughter*) You say that the person who pushes heroin or cocaine should go to jail, I think.

HOPPER: The person who pushes it?

FROST: Yes.

HOPPER: No, I don't believe that any more than the man who is involved in defense plants should go to jail. I think they're both criminals.

FROST: He's not making a total bodily wreck of a man.

HOPPER: Yes, he is. He's sending people over to Indochina and to China and to Russia, wherever they're going to be sending them soon.

FROST: Metaphorically, but—

HOPPER: He's not only making a wreck of them. He's killing them personally.

FROST: Do you think that the person who pushes heroin or cocaine should be regarded as a criminal? Because I certainly do.

HOPPER: Well, I do too. But I'm saying he's no less a criminal than the other man.

FROST: But he would be a criminal.

HOPPER: Of course.

FROST: Peter, let's turn to the difficult subject of what one says to one's children. What sort of advice about life do you give your children? How have you decided to bring them up? How *are* you bringing them up?

FONDA: Well, that's a better question. Deciding how to bring them up is a deadly thing. You know, it's very hard to say. My six-year-old daughter picked up *Life* magazine and saw the My Lai massacre and asked me why. Today, fortunately, she doesn't know about what's happened recently with the students at Kent State and the students at

Berkeley and the students all over the place, and all the other people. She's unaware of the implications of Cambodia or the elections in this country, and she does know other things. I don't try to protect her from that.

The only way I can relate to bringing her up is taking her out. That's a really depressing thought, to remove from this country the people who will run the country, who will be the country, to take them out before they're destroyed by the country.

FROST: Destroyed?

FONDA: Destroyed. Well, you know, on many levels it'll be very general and very light and very easy and nonpolitical and easy for this whole country to take on. What is my daughter going to breathe in ten years? People can go without food, if they're trained, for a certain amount of time. Maybe ninety days on sugar and water. They can go without water for five or six days. They can go without breath for four or five minutes. On what order is importance laid out? There won't be anything for her to breathe, let alone think about, whether it's a political society or whether people are shooting each other on the street or not. That's all going to happen. It's all happening right now, whether we would wish to expose it or not. That's going on in everybody's mind, left and right. The whole reactive syndrome. What's my daughter going to breathe in ten years? If she'll be able to survive this reactive syndrome within the society, this violence which we have bred, which we are conditioned to respond with and so forth, what's she going to breathe in ten years?

FROST: How about what's she going to hear in ten years from you? I mean, as compared with the way your generation was brought up, how do you think she'll be brought up differently?

FONDA: Well, she's going to hear, as she hears now, that I love her. And she feels that I love her, and she sees that I love her. And she knows that I talk to her, and she knows that I want her to talk to me and that I appreciate her expression of herself, as does my son, and my wife. That's my family.

(*Applause*)

Nora Ephron

Mush

> *". . . there may be a new trend gathering momentum. It is a return to romanticism, a yearning for years past, when life was simpler and values stronger."*
>
> —TIME MAGAZINE

The media have been calling it a return to romance, but of course the return is only on the part of the media. The rest of the country never went away. The poems of Kahlil Gibran and books like *A Friend Is Someone Who Likes You* and *Happiness Is A Warm Puppy* have
been selling hundreds of thousands of copies in recent years. Heart- 1
shaped satin boxes of chocolate candy, single red American Beauty roses, record albums by Mantovani and the George Melachrino Strings, rhinestone hearts on silver chains—all of it sells to the multitudes out there.

What has changed, however, is that sentimentality is now being peddled by people who seem to lend it an aura of cultural respectability. Take Rod McKuen and Erich Segal. Both of them have hit the jackpot in the romance business: one is a poet, the other a professor. And each thinks of himself as much more than the mushhuckster he is. McKuen, the author of five slim volumes of sentimental poetry and countless songs, is the fastest-selling poet in America; Segal is the
author of *Love Story,* which has sold almost 500,000 copies in hard 2
cover, had the largest paperback first printing (4,350,000 copies) in history, and is on the way to being the weepiest and most successful film ever made. All of it is treacle, pure treacle, with a message that is perfect escapism to a country in the throes of future shock: the world has not changed, the old values prevail, kids are the same as ever, love is just like they told us in the movies. This optimism comes in nice small packages that allow for the slowest reader with the shortest concentration span and the smallest vocabulary.

To lump Segal and McKuen together here is not to say that they know each other—they don't—or that their work is alike. But there are some disarming similarities. Both appeal primarily to women and teen-age girls. Both are bachelors who enjoy referring to themselves as loners. Both belong to professions that rarely lead to commercial success. Both have the habit of repeating compliments others have paid them, and both do it in a manner that is so blatant it almost seems ingenuous. Segal, for instance, speaking on the prototype of his book's heroine: "Jenny exists and knows she is the inspiration for one of the strongest feminine figures in modern literature—honest to God, that's really what one critic wrote." Or McKuen: "There are a lot of people who take potshots at me because they feel I'm not writing like Keats or Eliot. And yet I've been compared to both of them. So figure that out."

More important, both of them have hit on a formula so slick that it makes mere sentimentality have the force of emotion. Their work is instantly accessible and comprehensible; and when the reader is moved by it, he assumes that it must be art. As a result, Segal and McKuen, each of whom started out rather modest about his achievement, have become convinced that they must be doing something not just right but important. Can you blame them? The money rolls in. The mail arrives by the truckload. The critics outside New York are enthusiastic. And to those who aren't, Segal and McKuen fall back on sheer numbers. Millions of people have read and loved their work. The stewardess on American Airlines Flight No. 2 from Los Angeles to New York loves every bit of it. "I'm so sick of all the crap in the world," she says. "All the killings, the violence, the assassinations. This one getting it. That one getting it. I don't want to read any more about that kind of thing. Romanticism is here to stay." She really said it. Honest.

I am a big crybaby. I want to tell you that before I tell you anything at all about Erich Segal. I cry at almost everything. I cry when I watch *Marcus Welby, M.D.* on television or when I see movies about funny-looking people who fall in love. Any novel by Dickens sets me off. Dogs dying in the arms of orphans, stories of people who are disabled but ultimately walk/see/hear or speak, having something fall on my foot when I am in a hurry, motion pictures of President Kennedy smiling, and a large number of very silly films (particularly one called *The West Point Story*) will work me into a regular saltwater dither.

One other thing about me before I begin. I love trash. I have never believed that kitsch kills. I tell you this so you will understand that my antipathy toward *Love Story* is not because I am immune either to sentimentality or garbage—two qualities the book possesses in abundance. When I read *Love Story* (and I cried, in much the same way that I cry from onions, involuntarily and with great irritation), I was deeply offended—a response I never have, for example, with Jacqueline Susann novels. It was not just that the book was witless, stupid and manipulative. It was that I suspected that unlike Miss Susann, Segal knew better. I was wrong to think that, as it happened. I was fooled by his academic credentials. The fact is that *Love Story* is Erich Segal at the top of his form; he knows no better and can do no better. I know that now. I know that I should no longer be offended by the book. And I'm not. What is it that I'm offended by? Perhaps you will begin to see as we go along.

"Dear Mr. Segal: I realize that you are a busy man but I must tell you something that will probably make you inspired and honored. This past summer a very dear friend of mine passed away. She was seventeen and hardly ever unhappy or sad. Leslie had read your book. Not once but three times. She loved it so much. It was funny but everyone related Love Story with Leslie. She cried and said the story was so
beautiful and realistic. When she was buried a copy of your book was 7
placed next to her. . . . I wish you knew her. She was so unpredictable. That's what life is. She had an instant heart failure, and thank G-d she didn't suffer. I hope you don't think I'm a foolish college kid. I felt any person who could capture young hearts and old must be sensitive to life."

That is a typical letter plucked out of a large pile of mail on Erich Segal's desk. There are thousands more, from old ladies who say they haven't cried that hard since the Elsie Dinsmore books, from young girls who want to interview Erich for their high-school papers, from young men who have read the book and want to go to Harvard and play hockey and marry a girl who has leukemia. The mail has been
coming in in sacks since about Valentine's Day, 1970 (*Love Story* was 8
published ten days before). The reviews of the book were exultant. The movie is now on the way to being the biggest film in history. And what has happened to Erich Segal as a result of all this? "I always was the way I am," he says, "only I was less successful at it. The difference being that people used to think I was an idiot ass-hole dilettante and now—you can find a nice adjective." Yes, Erich was always this way, only now he is more so. You can find a nice adjective.

"Erich, Erich, you're so pale," shouts Mrs. Jessie Rhine, a lady from Brooklyn, as Erich Segal, the rabbi's son, signs an autograph for her and rumples his curly black hair and stubs his toe and rolls his big brown eyes. His aw-shucks thing. Mrs. Rhine loves it, loves Erich, loves his book, and she would very much like to slip him the name of her niece except that there is this huge group of ladies, there must be
a hundred of them, who are also surrounding Erich and trying to slip 9
him the names of *their* nieces. The ladies have just heard Erich give a speech to eleven hundred New York women at the Book and Author Luncheon at the Waldorf-Astoria. Robert Ardrey, the anthropologist, who also spoke at the luncheon, is hanging around Erich trying to soak up some of the attention, but it does him no good. The ladies want Erich and they are all asking him where they can get a copy of his speech.

Erich's speech. Erich has been giving his speech for months on the book-and-author circuit and he has found that it works. The audience especially responds to the way Erich's speech praises *Love Story* at the expense of *Portnoy's Complaint* and then rises to a crescendo in a condemnation of graphic sex in literature. "Have you any doubt," Segal asks the ladies, "what happened between Romeo and Juliet on their wedding night?" The ladies have no doubt. "Would you feel any better if you had seen it?" No, eleven hundred heads shake, no. "Fortunately," Segal concludes, "Shakespeare was neither curious nor yellow." Wild applause. Everyone loves Erich's speech. Everyone, that is, but Pauline Kael, the film critic, who heard an earlier version of Erich's speech at a book-and-author luncheon in Richmond, Virginia, and told him afterward that he was knocking freedom of speech and sucking up to his audience. To which Erich replied, "We're here to sell books, aren't we?"

The phenomenon of the professor as performer is not a new one: many teachers thrive on exactly the kind of idolatry that characterizes groupies and middle-aged lady fans. Still, there has never been an academician quite as good as Erich at selling books, quite as . . . you can find a nice adjective. He checks in with his publicists once or twice a day. Is everything being done that could be? What about the Carson show? What about running the Canby review again? What about using Christopher Lehmann-Haupt's quote in the ad? Is this anecdote right for Leonard Lyons? "I've been in this business fourteen years and Erich is the closest thing to what a publicist's dream would be," says Harper & Row's Stuart Harris. "All authors feel they have to make a publicity tour, but they don't know how to do it. Erich knows. He knows how to monopolize the time on a talk show without being obvious. *I* would know he's obvious, *you* would know he's obvious, but millions listening in don't know. So many authors don't know how to say anything about their books. They're shy. Erich knows how to do it without being blatant. He had to make a speech the week he was number one on the *Time* magazine best-seller list. He wanted to get that over to the audience, that it was number one, so he got up and began, 'I just flew down and made three stops. Every time the plane landed, I got off and went to the newsstand and bought *Time* magazine to see if I was still number one on the best-seller list.' The audience adored it."

We're here to sell books, aren't we? Yes indeed. And Erich knows that every book counts. One night in a restaurant, an out-of-town couple shyly approached Segal and asked him to autograph a menu for a neighbor who had loved his book. "Why a menu?" Segal asked. Because, the couple explained, it was all they had. "I'll tell you what," said Segal. "There's a bookstore around the corner that's still open. Go in and buy a copy of *Love Story*, bring it back, and I'll autograph that."

Erich has been around the country several times, giving his speech, talking about his book, never letting the conversation wander away from its proper focus. "My novel, *Love Story*, and Paramount's film of it mark, I believe, the turning point in the morals of the younger generation." Erich said that in New York several weeks after publication. Note how it is self-aggrandizing, but in the cause of public morality. Note how it is reassuring to older people. Note the way the name of the book is plunked into the sentence, along with a plug for the film and a plug for the film studio. Erich got so carried away with slipping these little factual details into his sentences that Jacqueline Susann, who is no slouch herself in the self-aggrandizement department, felt called upon to advise him against it. "Every time you mention the book's name," she told him, "you don't really have to add that it's number one on the best-seller list."

Exactly what has made *Love Story* so phenomenally successful is something of a mystery. There are theories, but none of them fully explains what happened. Yes, it makes readers cry. Yes, it has nothing whatsoever to do with life today and encourages people to believe the world has not changed. Yes, as Segal points out, the book has almost no description; people tend to read themselves into it. And yes, it has come at a time when young people are returning to earlier ways. As the critic for Yale's *New Journal* pointed out:

"Segal has perceived that the revolution we all talk of being in the midst of is in large part a romantic one, a movement not so much forward as backward, away from technology and organization and toward nature and people. . . . *Love Story* is a trick, a joke, a pun on those among us to whom an alliance with the fortyish-matron set would be anathema. Segal has tricked us into reading a novel about youth today that has little sex, no drugs, and a tear-jerking ending; and worse, he has made us love it, ponder it, and feel it to be completely contemporary. We are, deep down, no better than the sentimental slobs who sit under the hair dryers every Friday afternoon. It's all the same underneath. Segal has our number."

When *Love Story* was first published, Segal himself seemed to possess a measure of self-deprecation. He admitted that his book was banal and cliché-ridden. But as time went on, he began to relax, the self-deprecation turned to false humility, and he took his success seriously. He acknowledged in a recent interview that he might well be the F. Scott Fitzgerald of his generation. He says that he has been compared to Dostoevsky. He claims that his novel is in the tradition of the *roman nouveau* developed in France by Alain Robbe-Grillet and Nathalie Sarraute. He implies that people who hate his book are merely offended by its success. When *Love Story* took off in France, he called an associate long distance and said, "We are no longer a movement. We are a religion."

Can you blame him? Can you honestly say that you would have reacted any differently to such extraordinary success? Three, four years ago Erich Segal was just another academic with show-biz connections. "I lived for the day I would see my name in *Variety*," he recalled. He was born in Brooklyn in 1937, the eldest son of a well-known New York rabbi who presided over a Reform synagogue but kept a kosher home. "He dominated me," said Segal. "From the time I was the littlest boy I wanted to be a writer. My mother says that when I was two I used to dictate epic dramas to her. I believe her. I used to dictate tunes to my music teacher. I was that kind of spoiled child. But I came from a nice Jewish family. What kind of job was it being a writer? There was no security. My father wanted me to be a professional person." Rabbi Segal sent his son to Yeshiva, made him take Latin, and insisted he attend night classes at the Jewish Theological Seminary in Manhattan after he finished track practice at Midwood High School in Brooklyn. "I was always odd man out," said Segal. "It is true that I ended Midwood as president of the school and won the Latin prize, but those were isolated. What kind of social life could I have had? I spent my life on the subway."

At Harvard, which he attended because his father told him to, Erich was salutatorian and class poet. He ran every year in the Boston marathon and ran every day to keep in shape—a practice he continues. He also wrote two musicals, one of which had a short run Off-Broadway, and performed in the Dunster Dunces, a singing group that often sang a Segal original, *Winter is the Time to Snow Your Girl.* Despite his activity, he always reminded his friends not of Larry Hart but of Noel Airman. (The influence of *Marjorie Morningstar* on Jewish adolescents in the 1950's has yet to be seriously acknowledged.)

Segal got his Ph.D. in comparative literature and began teaching at Yale, where no one took his show-business talk much more seriously than they had at Harvard. Yes, Erich was collaborating with Richard Rodgers, but the show never got off the ground. Yes, Erich had a credit on *Yellow Submarine,* but how much of that was writing anyway? And then came *Love Story.* Script first. Erich's agents didn't even want to handle it. Howard Minsky, who decided to produce it, received rejections from every major studio. Then Ali MacGraw committed herself to it, Paramount bought it, and Erich started work on the novel, the slender story of a poor Catholic girl named Jenny who marries a rich Wasp named Oliver and dies after several idyllic, smart-talking, poverty-stricken years.

Not a single eye was dry, everybody had to cry. Even Erich Segal burst into tears when he wrote it. "In this very room," Segal said one day in his living room at Yale, "in that very chair at that very typewriter. When I got to the end of the book, it really hit me. I said, 'Omigod,' and I came and sat in that very chair and I cried and I cried and I cried. And I said to myself, 'All right, Segal, hold thyself. Why are you crying? I don't understand why you are crying. When was the last time you cried? And I said, 'The only time I've cried in my adult life was at my father's funeral.' Now it's stretching a lot to make any kind of connection whatsoever. So I finally concluded, after all the honesty I could muster after forty-five minutes of crying and introspection, that I was crying for Jenny. I mean, I really was crying for Jenny. I got up and wiped my face and finished the thing."

Segal's apartment, in a Saarinen-designed dormitory, is a simply furnished, messy one filled with copies of *Variety,* unopened mail, and half-packed suitcases—Segal is rarely at Yale more than three or four

days a week. He spends the rest of his time on promotion tours or in
conference in Hollywood. (Two other Segal scripts have been produced:
The Games, about marathon runners, and *R.P.M.,* about a campus
revolt.) His icebox has nothing in it but yogurt, and Segal is relaxing
in his living room, eating a container of the stuff and saying that he
is happy with the lecture on *Phaedra* he delivered that morning because
it convinced one of the students that Hippolytus was in fact a tragic
hero. Student opinion of Segal at Yale ranges from those who dislike 21
his book and his huckstering to those who rather like it and envy him
for his success in what is referred to in cloistered environments as the
real world. But most agree that whatever failings Segal has as a personality are overcome by his ability as a teacher. He teaches classics
with great verve—in suede pants, he paces back and forth onstage,
waves his hands, speaks quickly, gulps down a cup of coffee a student
has given him, and generates enormous excitement. Segal has written
several scholarly works, one a book on Plautus called *Roman Laughter.*

"It's a tremendous relief to be able to walk into a classroom and
speak freely," Segal is saying. "I don't mean your mind. I mean your
vocabulary. I don't go in for Buckleyish sesquipedalian terms, but I
do go in for *le mot juste.* Even to be able to say, 'Aristotelian cathar-
sis'. . . . On a podium, if I said that, they'd say who is this pompous 22
bastard. This to me is a normal way of speaking. This is the existence
whence I emanate. This is the way I really am." But if this is the way
you really are, Erich, who is traveling around the country delivering
those speeches? And why?

"What am I going to say to them?" he replies. "I don't know. I
had to sell books. I mean, do you know what I mean? I'm embarrassed
but I'm not sorry, because the end justifies the means, you know. Three
or four *yentas* who buy the book will get it to the readers who have 23
never bought a book before, and get the readership I really cherish,
which is the readership of the young people." He paused. "Do you
think I was pandering to them?"

No. Not really. Because Erich Segal really believes in what he is
saying, is really offended by sex in literature, is really glad he wrote
Love Story instead of *Portnoy's Complaint,* thinks that—however acci-
dentally—he has stumbled onto something important. Don't be fooled
by the academic credentials: a man who can translate Ovid cannot be
expected to know better—or know anything at all, for that matter—when
it comes to his own work. "You see, I wrote the book in a kind of 24
faux naïf style," Segal explained. "And if you think it's easy to write
as simply as that, well, you're wrong. But little did I know that I was
creating a whole style that's perfect for the Seventies. Let's face it.
Movies are the big thing now, and this is the style that's right for the
age of—as McLuhan called it—electronic literature. Writing should be
shorthand, understated, no wasting time describing things. I had no
idea that I was solving the whole problem of style this way. But I like
it. I'm going to keep it for all my other novels." Can you blame him?

It is a well-dressed, well-behaved group, this crowd of young men and women, lots of young women, who are waiting patiently in Constitution Hall in Washington, D. C., for the concert to begin. You won't see any of your freaks here, no sir, any of your tie-dye people, any of your long-haired kids in jeans lighting joints. This is middle America. The couples are holding hands, nuzzling, sitting still, waiting like well-brought-up young people are supposed to, and here he is, the man they've been waiting for, Rod McKuen. Let's have a nice but polite round of applause for Rod, in his Levi's and black sneakers. You won't see any of your crazy groupies here, squealing and jumping onstage and trying for a grab at the performer's parts. No sir. Here they are not groupies but fans, and they carry Instamatics with flash attachments and line up afterward with every one of Rod's books for him to autograph. The kids you never hear about. They love The Beatles, they love Dylan, but they also love Rod. "He's so sensitive," one young man explains. "I just hope that he reads a lot of his poetry tonight."

They want to hear the poetry. They gasp in expectation when he picks up a book and flips it open in preparation. And onstage, about to give them what they want in his gravelly voice ("It sounds like I gargle with Dutch Cleanser," he says), is America's leading poet and Random House's leading author. "I've sold five million books of poetry since 1967," says Rod, "but who's counting?" As a matter of fact, Random House is counting and places the figure at three million. Nevertheless, it is a staggering figure—and the poetry is only the beginning. There are records of Rod reciting his poetry, records of Rod's music, records of Rod singing Rod's lyrics to Rod's music, records of Rod's friends singing Rod's songs—much of this on records produced by Rod's record company. There are the concerts, television specials, film sound tracks and a movie company formed with Rock Hudson. There are the Stanyan Books, a special line of thirty-one books Rod publishes and Random House distributes, with *Caught in the Quiet* its biggest seller, followed by *God's Greatest Hits,* compiled from the moments He speaks in the Bible. McKuen's income can be conservatively estimated at $3,000,000 a year.

That literary critics and poets think nothing whatsoever of McKuen's talent as a poet matters not a bit to his followers, who are willing to be as unabashedly soppy as their bard and are not, in any event, at all rigid in their distinctions between song lyrics and poetry. "I'm often hit by critics and accused of being overly sentimental," Rod is saying to his concert audience. "To those critics I say tough. Because I write about boys and girls and men and women and summer and spring and winter and fall and love and hate. If you don't write about those things there isn't much to write about." And now Rod will read a poem. "This poem," he says, "is about a marvelous cat I once knew. . . ."

McKuen's poetry also covers—in addition to the subjects he lists above—live dogs, lost cats, freight trains, missed connections, one-

night stands, remembered loved ones and remembered streets, and
loneliness. The poem about the cat, which is among his most famous,
concerns a faithful feline named Sloopy who deserted McKuen after
he stayed out too late one night with a woman. Her loss brings the
poet to the following conclusion: *"Looking back/ perhaps she's been/*
the only human thing/ that ever gave back love to me." McKuen's poetry,
which he reads to background instrumental accompaniment, is a kind 28
of stream-of-consciousness free verse filled with mundane images
("raped by Muzak in an elevator," for example) and with adjectives
used as nouns ("listen to the warm," "caught in the quiet," etc.). A
recent McKuen parody in the *National Lampoon* sums up his style as
well as anything; it begins, *"The lone$ome choo choo of my mind/*
i$ warm like drippy treacle/ on the wind$wept beach."

Occasionally McKuen can be genuinely piquant and even witty.
"I wrote Paul this morning/ after reading his poem,/ I told him, it's
okay to drop your pants/ to old men sometimes/ but I wouldn't recom-
mend it/ as a way of life. *I didn't mail the letter."* But for the most part, 29
McKuen's poems are superficial and platitudinous and frequently silly.
"It is irrelevant to speak of McKuen as a poet," says Pulitzer prize winning poet Karl Shapiro.

There was a time when Rod McKuen might modestly have agreed
with Shapiro. Ten years or so ago, when he was scrounging in New York,
living on West Fifty-fifth Street with Sloopy the cat and trying to make
ends meet, McKuen might gladly have admitted to being just a song-
writer. Even recently, after only two of his books had appeared, he told
a reporter, "I'm not a poet—I'm a stringer of words." But then it happened: the early success mushroomed. "I don't think it's irrelevant to 30
speak of me as a poet," McKuen says today. "If I can sell five million
books of poetry, I must be a poet." Three million, Rod. "If my poetry
can be taught in more than twenty-five hundred colleges, seminaries
and high schools throughout the United States, if it can be hailed in
countries throughout the world as something important, I must be a
poet. In France, one newspaper wrote, 'Rod McKuen is the best poet
America has to offer and we should listen to him and mark him well.'"

The saga of Rod McKuen and his rise to the top is a story so full
of bad times and hard knocks that it almost serves as a parody of such
tales. Rodney Marvin John Michael James McKuen was born in 1933
in a Salvation Army Hospital in Oakland, California. His mother was a 31
dime-a-dance girl; his father deserted her just before their son was
born and McKuen has never met him. *"I remember hearing children/*
in the streets outside. . . . / They had their world/ I had my room/
I envied them only/ for the day long sunshine/ of their lives/ and their
fathers./ Mine I never knew."

McKuen's mother Clarice worked as a barmaid, scrubbed floors
and operated a switchboard to pay bills. Then she married his stepfather, who drove tractors to level dirt for highways; the family moved
from one construction site to the next in California and Nevada. "My

stepfather used to get drunk and come home in the middle of the night and yank me out of bed and beat me up," McKuen recalled. "That 32
was kind of traumatic."

At eleven, McKuen dropped out of school and went to work as a lumberjack, ditchdigger, ranch hand, shoe salesman and cookie puncher. At fifteen, he received his first serious rejection from a young lady. At eighteen, he became a disc jockey with San Francisco's station KROW, dispensing advice to the lovelorn. After a stint in Korea writing psychological-warfare material for radio, he returned to San Francisco and was booked into the Purple Onion. A screen test followed and in 33
the mid-fifties he worked at Universal on such films as *Rock, Pretty Baby* and *Summer Love*. In what must have been a move of some distinction, he walked out on the filming of *The Haunted House on Hot Rod Hill*. For his film career, McKuen had a dermabrasian, which partially removed his adolescent acne scars; he also has a long scar across his chin, the result of an automobile accident.

In 1959 McKuen moved to New York and before beginning to compose music for the CBS Television Workshop, he sold blood for money and crashed parties for food. Then in 1961, after the CBS job folded, he helped compose a rock song called *Oliver Twist,* which was noteworthy mainly in that it rhymed "chickens" with "Dickens." When no one famous could be found to record it, Rod did it himself; when the record took off, he began touring the country with a backup group (he does not play a musical instrument and has only recently learned formal composition). As Mr. Oliver Twist he played Trude Heller's, 3
the Copacabana lounge, and did a twelve-week tour of bowling alleys around the country. "He was a pretty big act," said his then-manager Ron Gittman. "He wasn't your Ricky Nelson or your Everly Brothers, but he pulled people." The constant performing six nights a week proved too much for McKuen's voice: his vocal chords swelled, he could not speak, and after six weeks in bed the old tenor voice was gone and a new froggy one had emerged.

McKuen moved back to Los Angeles, played the Troubadour, and continued to set his lyrics to the simple music he composed in his head. In 1965 he opened at The Bitter End and was praised by The New York *Times* and compared to Charles Aznavour and Jacques Brel. Eddy Arnold, Johnny Cash and Glenn Yarbrough began to record his songs of love and loneliness. The market had changed. "In the Fifties and early Sixties there were formulas," said rock publicist Connie de 3
Nave, who handled Rod when he was doing the *Oliver Twist*. "Your group wore certain colors, sweaters over pants, their hair had to be well-groomed, no smoking or drinking onstage. In the mid-Sixties suddenly the individual could wear what he wanted. He didn't have to spend $18,000 on arrangements for nightclub acts. All the outlets where Rod had to do the *Oliver Twist* died. The college market began. The change made things ripe for Rod. Before lyrics had been simple and

uncomplicated. Now they wanted depth. No one could come out and go, 'Oo, wa, oo wa.' You came out with your stool and you sang, and you didn't even have to sing that great. You just had to feel. And as Rod was growing, the market came around."

Stanyan Street and Other Sorrows, McKuen's first book of poetry and songs, was an accidental by-product of a Glenn Yarbrough recording. When requests about the song began to pour into the record company, McKuen decided to publish a book containing it. With his own money, he paid for the printing, stored the books in his garage, and put the covers on and mailed them out in Jiffy bags. "I was very unsophisticated about it," McKuen recalled. "I didn't know what sort of
discount you gave bookstores. I made them all pay cash and pay in 36
advance. We had no salesmen, so I called the telephone company and got the yellow pages of all the major cities. We sent mailers to every bookstore. I knew people were asking for it and it wasn't listed in *Publishers' Weekly* or the guide to books. No one knew where it was from or how to get it." In a year, *Stanyan Street* sold 60,000 copies—about 120 times what the average book of poetry sells in a lifetime. Random House took over the distribution, signed McKuen to his next book, and gave him a Mercedes Benz.

Today Rod McKuen lives in a thirty-room house on a hill facing Beverly Hills, which has a pool, orange trees, four in help, several sheepdogs and cats, and a barbershop for Rod and his streaky blond hair. He spends about half the year on the road and in Europe; he has an
illegitimate son in France whom he sees frequently. When he is in Los 37
Angeles, he rarely leaves his house except for a recording session or a trip to his office on Sunset Boulevard. "I have about fifteen people who work for me there," said McKuen. "I don't like to think they work *for* me. They work *with* me."

McKuen is sitting now in the music room of his house. He is wearing a yellow pullover sweater and the ever-present sneakers and Levi's and he is talking about the return to romance he feels the country is in the midst of. "I paved the way for Erich Segal," he says. "It's been my strange lot to have preceded all sorts of things for some time now.
I told everybody that folk music was going to come in very big three 38
years before it happened and nobody believed me and of course it did happen. And I went around telling people there was going to be a romantic revival and nobody believed that either. I think it's a reaction people are having against so much insanity in the world. I mean, people are really all we've got. You know it sounds kind of corny and I suppose it's a cliché, but it's really true, that's just the way it is."

It is not entirely easy to interview McKuen, you see. Not that he isn't open and garrulous—but for one thing, most of his thoughts seem
to end up in statements he supposes are clichés; and for another he 39
tends to ramble. Ask him about his childhood and within seconds he will be off on a ramble about prejudice and the Army. Ask him whether his poetry paints too sanguine a picture of the world and before you

know it he will be telling you about capital punishment. Ask him about his new book:

"My new book has its roots in my childhood and in how I feel
now, about getting back to basics. You notice in this house, I like lumber. I like wood. Frank Lloyd Wright was my favorite architect because everything he did sprang out of the ground. And even though 40
you see a lot of gadgets and stuff like that I like them because they
are gadgets. They don't try to be anything else. I don't like artificial
flowers, for instance. . . ." Like that.

In any case, it really doesn't matter to Rod McKuen how the interview goes, because he is sick and tired of being written about and
criticized for what he is doing. Rod McKuen, who in the old days would
talk to *Stamp World Magazine* if they wanted to profile him, has now
become what he calls "gun-shy." Writers describe him as a guru and
he hates it. Critics confuse his songs with his poetry and criticize him 41
unfairly and he hates it. Everyone is out to get him. "You know, it's
pretty fashionable to knock me down," he says. "There's something
criminal, apparently, about being a successful poet. Too many writers
take umbrage at that. It's not fair. I don't think poets should starve. I
don't think anyone should starve. That's another problem we have in
this country that should be changed. . . ." And off he goes on a ramble
about poverty in America, leaving the reporter to wonder about it all.

What does it mean?

What does it signify?

What is McKuen trying to say?

And the answer is probably best put in a poem McKuen himself 42
wrote: *"If you had listened hard enough/you might have heard/what I
meant to say. Nothing."*

Questions and Quotations for Discussion and Writing Assignments

I

1. Why does Michael Lydon call Bo Diddley the "Prometheus" of rock 'n' roll?
2. In presenting his picture of Bo Diddley, Lydon packs his article with details about Bo Diddley's house, his cars, his family, his hands, his music, etc. From these details what kind of man emerges? In other words, can you describe Bo Diddley's character and his personality? What are his attitudes toward "The American Way"? How do his house, his cars, his hands, etc., reveal what kind of man he is?
3. How does Bo Diddley feel about the white musicians who have borrowed much of their style and energy from him? How does he feel about white kids who rebel against the old order?
4. Can it be said that Bo Diddley has "made it" as an artist and as a man? What is the significance of his refusal to accept any more Cadillacs from Chess Records?

5. Bo Diddley sings about being a MAN. How does he define the word? Is he an example of a male chauvinist?
6. In the first six paragraphs of "The Age of Willie Mays," Mays' name does not appear; instead of writing about the central figure of the essay, Peter Schrag writes about baseball itself. Or, to be more exact, he writes about what baseball once meant to him and thousands of other fans. What qualities of the game does he fondly recall? What does he mean by his statement, "we have left the age of the mythic hero"? What outside forces have changed baseball and the fans' attitudes toward the game and the players?
7. Schrag writes that Willie Mays is a black athlete who "ran black, swung black, and caught black." Schrag does not intend to sound condescending in this remark; actually he is trying to describe the unique quality of Mays' consummate skills as a ball player. How does Schrag clarify his remark? Might he simply have said that Mays plays with "soul" (see the article by Al Calloway)?
8. In Schrag's view Willie Mays' great contribution to the game is a sense of "style." Drawing on your reading and on your experiences of having seen Mays play in person or on television, describe his style.
9. To Peter Schrag baseball is losing its sense of myth, symbol, and ritual. No longer can a baseball player become a hero of people's fantasies, a mythic hero with whom thousands of fans can identify. "We have," he writes, "outgrown our hope and innocence." Why does Schrag think "we will never again have common, integrating heroes"?
10. What is a hero? Who are some of the potential heroes with style and distinction that Schrag names? Are they heroes? Why can the astronauts never be great heroes, in spite of their courage, their risks? Who first stepped on the moon?
11. What is personal style? Schrag says, "style always defies time, and all the sociology in the world isn't worth a moment of poetry."
12. After reading both the essay about Bo Diddley and the one about Willie Mays, consider this question: Which man did you learn most about? Or, to state the question another way, are Schrag and Lydon concerned with telling about these two great men, or do they want to explain their feelings about these men?
13. Is the public worship of a great sports figure defensible in our desperate age? To avoid making your answer or essay ambiguous and general, you may wish to point to specific sports heroes or heroines who have importance, either literal or symbolic, to the public; or you may wish to illustrate your argument by citing examples of athletes who have failed to safeguard the public trust in them. (Aside: Joe Dimaggio smoked for years, but he would not do a cigarette commercial because of his image to kids.)
14. The interview does not provide the ideal format for probing deeply into issues, especially with Dennis Hopper. What kind of person does Hopper seem to be? What are his views on the legalization of heroin?

15. Peter Fonda seems more willing to be interviewed than Dennis Hopper and tries to answer several questions seriously. What is his explanation of the famous line in the movie *Easy Rider*, "We blew it"?
16. Fonda states that "all the people are pushing dope." What examples does he give to support this statement? Are farmers who burn crops as guilty of an immoral act as the guy who pushes to ten-year olds? Is there no difference "between the man who pushes cocaine at the beginning of *Easy Rider* and a man on Wall Street who's involved in defense plants and who transfers all his money to a Swiss bank," as Hopper says?
17. Interviews are becoming part of our ordinary reading materials. Interviews with rock stars appear in *Rolling Stone*; Hollywood actors are interviewed in *McCalls*; political figures are interviewed in *The New York Review of Books*. As an interesting experiment try conducting an interview with someone—a teacher, a musician visiting your campus, a student leader, a famous politician. If you have a tape recorder, you can make great use of it; if not, you will have to write the dialogue down in shorthand or note form and fill in the blanks later from memory. To insure that the interview has some direction and coherence, you may wish to write out some of your questions ahead of time.
18. In "Mush" Nora Ephron writes, "The media have been calling it a return to romance." What is the meaning of the word "romance" as she uses it? In her opinion "romance" has never been far from the center of many people's lives. What evidence does she give for this opinion? Can you cite additional evidence?
19. Why does Miss Ephron call Erich Segal and Rod McKuen "mush-hucksters"?
20. Miss Ephron states that Segal and McKuen appeal primarily to teenage girls and women. What are some of the implications of this idea? Why should girls and women fall more easily for these writers than male readers? Judging from your experience, is Miss Ephron correct about the Segal-McKuen appeal?
21. What is Miss Ephron's opinion of *Love Story* and Rod McKuen's poetry? Is her opinion justified?
22. In her view what characteristics of these literary works make them sell?
23. What is Miss Ephron's opinion of Erich Segal's talent?
24. Miss Ephron calls herself a "crybaby" and a lover of "trash." What is her purpose in making these admissions? How do these admissions strengthen her attack on *Love Story*?
25. What sort of people, according to Nora Ephron, attend a Rod McKuen concert?
26. Throughout her essay Miss Ephron refrains from making explicit judgments about Segal and McKuen; yet by using irony and by carefully arranging her evidence, she makes it quite clear that she has little respect for either man. How does she reveal her attitudes toward Rod McKuen's intelligence (see especially the last few paragraphs of the essay)? What is the effect of the last sentence of her essay, a quotation from a McKuen poem?

27. What is meant by the phrase "personal integrity"? Which of the personalities discussed in this section seems to have the most personal integrity? Which of these men could be said to have "sold out"?

II

1. How frighteningly few are the persons whose death would spoil our appetite and make the world seem empty.

   ERIC HOFFER

2. The fame of great men ought always to be estimated by the means used to acquire it.

   LA ROCHEFOUCAULD

3. The traditional hero in epics, in mythology, was always representative of the community from which he emerged. He was the person who did things for the community, who did things that the community could not do by itself.

   IHAM HASSAN

4. When a man dies he clutches in his hands only that which he has given away in his lifetime.

   JEAN JACQUES ROUSSEAU

5. SEVERAL DEFINITIONS OF SUCCESS:

   Self-expression at a profit.

   MARCELENE COX

   To write your name high upon the outhouse of a country tavern.

   ELBERT HUBBARD

   Nothing more than doing what you can do well; and doing well whatever you do, without a thought of fame.

   HENRY WADSWORTH LONGFELLOW

   Success is that old ABC—ability, breaks, and courage.

   CHARLES LUCKMAN

6. I can understand the anguish of the younger generation. They lack models, they have no heroes, they see no great purpose in the world.

   HENRY A. KISSINGER

7. How can they say my life isn't a success? Have I not for more than sixty years got enough to eat and escaped being eaten?

   LOGAN PEARSALL SMITH

8. There is only one success—to be able to spend your whole life in your own way.

   CHRISTOPHER MORLEY

9. The mass of men lead lives of quiet desperation.

   HENRY DAVID THOREAU

10. Students are approaching the Establishment, trying to discover if they can chart their own destiny, if they can have greater control over it. One

of the themes on our campus might be termed "impotent outrage." We want so badly to have an impact on the society in which we live.

KIRK HANSON, student at Stanford

11. Beware of all enterprises that require new clothes.

THOREAU

12. How dreary to be somebody!

EMILY DICKINSON

13. The final test of fame is to have a crazy person imagine that he is you.

ANON.

14. Wherever you want to go everything revolves around profit and private property. Those are the premises, and you can't question the logic. The logic is consistent. . . . But there's a passion for religious meaning, for spirituality that's just been squelched for so long: people are dying for spirituality. *Me I'm* dying.

PETER COHEN

15. That man is richest whose pleasures are the cheapest.

THOREAU

16. The theory seems to be that so long as a man is a failure he is one of God's chillun, but that as soon as he has got any luck he owes it to the Devil.

H. L. MENCKEN

17. To burn always with this hard, gemlike flame, to maintain this ecstasy, is success in life.

WALTER PATER

18. Doth not even nature itself teach you, that, if a man have long hair, it is a shame unto him.

ST. PAUL

19. The only criterion of wisdom to vulgar judgments—success.

EDMUND BURKE

20. The history of what man has accomplished in this world, is at bottom the History of Great Men who have worked here.

THOMAS CARLYLE

Related Readings:

KRUTCH, JOSEPH WOOD, "Birds and Airplanes," page 258.

SECTION VIII Utopia or Apocalypse?

Paper Cup Man. Courtesy of Lester Lefkowitz.

Gerald Clarke

Putting the Prophets in Their Place

Some societies are dominated by the past; America seems obsessed
by the future. No sooner is a President elected than commentators
begin to estimate his chances next time around. Hours after the discovery of a trend, someone is predicting how and when it will end
and what will take its place. Why so much compulsive eagerness to
read history before it happens? Perhaps it is an escape from an un- 1
satisfactory present. Perhaps, also, Americans—and 20th century men
generally—are deluded by the Faustian illusion that by predicting the
future, they can control it. If all this seems occasionally oppressive, if
the arrogance of the prophets begins to irritate the layman, there is
one consolation: the forecasters are usually wrong, since predicting is
a loser's game.

It is unlikely that any major enterprise was ever undertaken without an expert arguing conclusively that it would not succeed. At the
behest of King Ferdinand and Queen Isabella, a panel of Spanish sages
looked at Columbus' plan for a voyage to the Indies, and in 1490 came
up with six good reasons why it was impossible. So many centuries
after the creation, they concluded triumphantly, it was unlikely that 2
anyone could find hitherto unknown lands of any value. This negative
reaction was similar to the learned argument that greeted Galileo when
he reported that Jupiter had moons. "Jupiter's moons are invisible to
the naked eye," said a group of Aristotelian professors, "and therefore
can have no influence on the earth, and therefore would be useless,
and therefore do not exist.

The "therefores" continued into the 19th century, when several
experts asserted that a new invention known as the railroad would kill
all of its passengers. Anyone traveling at 30 m.p.h., they reasoned, 3
could not breathe and would die of suffocation. This was only a fore-
taste of the dire warnings that awaited the inventors of the airplane.
"The demonstration that no possible combination of known substances,
known forms of machinery and known forms of force can be united
in a practical [flying] machine seems to the writer as complete as it

is possible for the demonstration of any physical fact to be," one scientist wrote about the turn of the century. One week before the Wright brothers took off at Kitty Hawk, the New York *Times* editorially advised Samuel Langley, one of the Wright brothers' chief competitors, to turn his talents to "more useful employment."

All Time to Come

The rocket was launched with similar expert predictions of failure. In 1940 the editor of the *Scientific American* wrote Willy Ley, prophet of space travel, that the notion of a rocket bomb was "too farfetched to be considered." In December 1945, even though Germany's V-1s and and V-2s had already terrorized London, Dr. Vannevar Bush, head of the Office of Scientific Research and Development, said that intercontinental missiles would not be possible for a "very long period of time." The American public, he impatiently contended, should not even think about them. Only last December, Dr. Bentley Glass, a geneticist and the retiring president of the American Association for the Advancement of Science, added his name to the list of doubters. The basic laws of science are all now known, he said. "For all time to come these [laws] have been discovered, here and now, in our own lifetime."

Such naysaying led Arthur Clarke, the science and science-fiction writer, to lay down what he calls Clarke's Law: "When a distinguished but elderly scientist states that something is possible, he is almost certainly right. When he states that something is impossible, he is very probably wrong." Most erroneous predictions, Clarke believes, stem from one of two causes: a failure of imagination or a failure of nerve. His law holds up in science, at least, where knowledge seems almost a barrier to drawing an accurate picture of the future. Far better as prophets have been the science-fiction writers, who usually have limited scholarly credentials but who are abundantly endowed with both nerve and imagination. Almost everybody knows about Jules Verne, who foresaw both submarines and voyages to the moon. Just as prophetic, however, was the late Hugo Gernsback, the first American science-fiction writer (*Ralph 124C 41 Plus*), who predicted, among other things, radar, television, night baseball, rocket planes and communications satellites.

With a few exceptions, the record of the social forecasters is even more dismal than that of their brethren in the physical sciences. In 1784 the Marquis de Condorcet, a leading mathematician and philosopher of the Enlightenment, saw a placid present and looked forward to an even more placid future. "The great probability," he said, "is that we will have fewer great changes and fewer large revolutions to expect from the future than from the past. The prevailing spirit of moderation and peace seems to assure us that henceforth wars will be less frequent." Reverse everything and Condorcet would have been right on target. Five years later, France was convulsed by revolution; eight years later, Condorcet himself called his country to war; ten years later, he was a victim of the Reign of Terror. At least he lived, if only briefly, to acknowledge his error.

Condorcet was not alone in trying to build the future on the present. Writing in an era of late 19th century tranquillity, French Historian Emile Faguet looked forward to an even more serene, albeit somewhat bland 20th century. "The chances are that from now on history will be
less filled with vicissitudes, less colorful, and less dramatic," he wrote. 7
"The great conqueror, the great reformer, and the great statesman will become increasingly rare." So much for Lenin, Mussolini, Stalin, Hitler, Wilson, Gandhi, Churchill and Franklin Roosevelt—not to mention such colorful vicissitudes as two world wars.

That Overrated Bore

While Condorcet and Faguet erred in being too optimistic about the future, some modern social prophets have been proved wrong by being too pessimistic. Two widespread predictions of the early '60s, for example, have turned out to be incorrect, at least up till now. Automation, which a large number of Cassandras, from Michael Harrington
to Linus Pauling, thought would put millions out of work, seems to 8
have created more jobs than it abolished. Worldwide famine, which seemed mandated by exploding populations, has been forestalled by the "green revolution," the development of new wonder grains. Probably fewer people are hungry today than ten years ago.

Leaving aside that overrated bore Nostradamus, whose predictions were so gnomic that they could be interpreted to suit events, there have been a few prescient souls who have shrewdly guessed the future of society and relations among nations. Although wrong about some things—including the imminent decline and fall of capitalism—Lenin in 1918 foresaw "an inevitable conflict" between the U. S. and Japan over
control of the Pacific. Six years later, General Billy Mitchell, one of 9
the few military leaders to predict the potential of airpower in warfare, told how the Japanese would begin the conflict some morning with an attack on Pearl Harbor. Shortly before the Six-Day War in 1967, Charles de Gaulle announced almost exactly how long the war would last, who would win, and what kind of peace would follow. (He was only slightly less accurate in saying, before her marriage to Aristotle Onassis, that Jackie Kennedy would wind up on the yacht of an oilman.)

For sheer weight of accurate prediction, few can match another Frenchman, Alexis de Tocqueville, whose *Democracy in America* is still
an amazingly accurate portrayal of the U. S. and its people. Writing at 10
a time when the U. S. and Russia were hardly thought of as great powers, Tocqueville projected an inevitable American-Russian rivalry. "Their starting point is different and their courses are not the same," he wrote. "Yet each of them seems marked out by the will of Heaven to sway the destinies of half the globe."

What separates a Tocqueville from a Condorcet? The difference is not so much in nerve as in imagination. As the French futurist Bertrand de Jouvenel points out in his book *The Art of Conjecture,* it is impossible for most men to visualize a reversal of an existing trend. The early 1780s, when Condorcet was writing, and the late 1890s, when Faguet made his predictions, were quiet and the world seemed civilized. Neither could conceive of a revolution or a global war that would change the foundations of society.

Lessons from the Past

In an attempt to discern just such unexpected reversals, some prophets have searched the past for clues to the future. There are, after all, lessons in history, aren't there? Not always. Looking back to the English Civil War of the 17th century and the Restoration of Charles II, French royalists, for example, expected an early return of the Bourbons after their own revolution. They got Napoleon instead. Some social prophets today have suggested that the sexual permissiveness of the 1960s will be followed by a puritanical reaction during the '70s. That, after all, is what happened in England after the licentiousness of the Restoration, and in the U. S. after the giddiness of the '20s. Perhaps it will happen again, but don't take any bets.

Quite often, predictors have been right and wrong at the same time. They have correctly discerned the beginning of a trend or movement, but they have failed to anticipate its effects, which frequently are just as important. In 1899, a writer for *Scientific American* accurately foresaw the triumph of the automobile over the horse. He then made the mistake of adding: "The improvement in city conditions can hardly be overestimated. Streets clean, dustless and odorless would eliminate a greater part of the nervousness, distraction and strain of modern metropolitan life." A few minutes' application of imagination and arithmetic, putting together the collective impact of cars, people, noise and exhausts (even if many cars were then powered by steam or electricity), would have shown that if the first part of his projection was right, the second could not possibly be.

In recent years, the art of prediction has gained from sophisticated new analytic techniques and the computer. A half-scientific school of predictors known as futurists—men like De Jouvenel and Herman Kahn—has come into vogue. Will they prove to be more accurate than their less scientific, more intuitive predecessors?

The futurists, together with other leading thinkers, seem to be in general agreement that there is little likelihood of a third World War and that the population explosion (in most of the world, at least) will continue unchecked. "In the indigent two-thirds of the human race," asserts Historian Arnold Toynbee, "family planning will be long delayed. The surplus population will live miserably, without hope, on

dole from the productive minority." The futurists also believe that the
prosperity of the industrial countries will reach even greater heights,
that Japan will be the No. 1 power of the 21st century, and that the
revolution in mores and social values—"redesigning a way of life" in
the words of Harvard Psychologist B. F. Skinner—will go right on. Although the professional seers have generally not descended to such 15
trivialities, almost everyone seems to think that marijuana will be
legalized before very long. Many experts meanwhile are convinced that
pollution will make all the above forecasts irrelevant. Civilization will
end within a generation, says George Wald, Harvard's Nobel-prize-
winning biochemist, unless drastic and immediate steps are taken to
reverse the despoliation of man's environment.

All these predictions seem so plausible that they have already
taken on the color of conventional wisdom. The contemporary prophets
may well turn out to be right. But there are some factors that ultimately might make the forecasts look foolish indeed. At least part of
the Japanese economic miracle, for instance, is the product of Japan's
desire to imitate and beat the West. If the West decided that prosperity
was no longer its goal, would Japan run so fast? Or, all by itself, might
affluence dull the Japanese dedication to work? In other industrial 16
countries, changing social attitudes that put less value on work might
very well slow or stop the growth of prosperity. The population explosion, at the same time, might be defused by nothing more profound
than a truly cheap, effective and uncomplicated method of birth control. As for pot, its legalization might be forestalled by medical proof
that long-term use leads to as yet unsuspected side effects. World War
III? One can only hope—and add unhappily that few people in January
1914 predicted World War I.

The best that can be said for the futurists, and for prophets of
all kinds, is that their predictions force men to examine the likely out-
come of what they are doing, and then add a little to the limited choice
and control men have over events. "I would willingly say," declares 17
Bertrand de Jouvenel, "that forecasting would be an absurd enterprise
were it not inevitable. We have to make wagers about the future; we
have no choice in the matter."

Isaac Asimov

The Next 100 Years

The world's population is increasing quickly, and each year the World Almanac will be presenting its population statistics with a sharper sense of urgency. But population will level off. By 2000, when the world's population will have reached six billion, scientists expect 1 that birth control will be well-established over most of the world. A plateau will have been reached and the main talk of the Twenty-first Century will be to keep it from being exceeded.

By 2068, a major factor will be in progress to increase the quality of the human population. Gene-analysis will be the technique used. Each child as born will have its gene content checked as routinely as its footprints are taken. This gene-analysis will be an essential part of 2 the medical records, since it will give information as to possible physical and mental weak points. The attempt will be to encourage only the birth of those children who may be expected to have a gene pattern that predisposes them toward excellence.

Increasingly, there will be a tendency to control not only the number of births but the right to parenthood. Perhaps the greatest 3 social controversy of 2068 will be between those who favor an absolute right on the part of society to dictate who may or may not have children, and those who dispute man's understanding of what constitutes "excellence" and who advocate the "right-to-have-children."

Each side in the dispute may have to take into account the rapid development of "ectogenesis"; that is, the development of fetuses outside the human body. This will have several advantages. Women will 4 be freed of the biological task of actual child-bearing. Embryos can be nurtured under optimum conditions, something not always available in the natural womb. Genic analysis can be carried through before birth, thus allowing a more liberal policy on conception, since checks would be possible afterward. The techniques involved in ectogenesis will be delicate and space-consuming, and even in 2068 the process will not be common. It will have become important enough, however,

so that the World Almanac of the time may well list numbers of births
in two columns: "natural" and "ectogenetic."

The goal of controlling quantity and quality of population would
be quite impossible without some international agency making full use
of computerized equipment. In fact, the computer, as it develops stead- 5
ily over the next century, will make the present division of the planet
obsolete. The necessary controls that will keep six billion human beings
alive and comfortable in 2068 can only be planet-wide in scope.

We will still be a world of nations in 2068, for tradition and self-
esteem will keep us "national" in feeling. But the computers that alone
will be able to guide the world economy and make the necessary
decisions will transcend the nations, which will, in real importance,
be at about the level of our county governments of today. Since computers are designed to solve problems on a rational basis, the com- 6
puterization of the world will be its rationalization as well. Decisions,
for instance, will be directed that will alter conditions that give rise
to social friction, thus minimizing the danger of national wars or internal rioting. This will be done not because wars or riots are immoral,
but because they are irrational. And society will, by and large, obey
the decisions of computers because to avoid doing so will bring disaster.

By 2068, the active desire to raise human intuition above the
complex computer-driven calculations will be gone. There will still be
"intuitionist" parties and societies in various parts of the globe that will
refuse to use computers and will carry on anti-computer activities, but 7
they will have no influence. In fact, the computer will be an integral
part of the domestic scene by 2068. The home computer that keeps
tabs on bills, makes out checks, organizes shopping and menus, turns
on appliances, keeps tabs on the family pet, and controls the cooking,
will solve the servant problem.

There will even be a tendency to use self-contained mobile computers (or "robots") as a kind of literal servant-substitute. These, however, will still be a luxury in 2068. The tendency in that year will be
in the other direction, instead; toward consolidation. More and more
households will be tied in to a large community computer for the sake 8
of greater efficiency. And, of course, the Central Planetary Computer
will keep track of all statistics, down to the minutest, for instant recall.
The statistical contents of a reference book like the World Almanac
will be largely computer-prepared and computer-checked, though it
will still require the active and agile intelligence of the human personnel to decide *which* statistics and *how* the whole is to be organized.

Energy will not be a problem in 2068. The key breakthrough into
the practical use of fusion power will have been made at least a half-
century before. The oceans will then offer a supply of deuterium as 9
an energy fuel that will last in copious quantity for millions of years.
By 2068, man will have gone beyond that. There will be space stations
circling Earth that will be capable of absorbing and transmitting solar

energy to Earth, a source that will last for billions of years. The world of 2068 will be one of infinite energy, and therefore one in which we can control the environment easily. For instance, the difficulty today in obtaining fresh water from the sea or metals from low-content slag, or in removing pollutants from air and water, is not any lack in understanding but is a matter of expense only. In 2068, with infinite energy at our disposal and very advanced techniques, expense will be no factor, and the world's resources can be mobilized with ease and efficiency to support six billion in far greater affluence than we can now support three billion, and without the accumulation of waste or pollution.

Food supply will be crucial, of course. The last decades of the twentieth century will see a greater and more intelligent use of the ocean as a food source. In the twenty-first century, the great age of ocean-farming and ocean-herding will begin. Plants will be grown underwater and sea-life will be "domesticated"; that is, bred and cared for, so that the annual increase may be exploited without danger of overuse.

But the great trend in 2068 will be the use of microorganisms as food for mankind. Yeasts and algae can be grown far more rapidly and efficiently than the higher forms of life can. They can be flavored to suit and eventually can be prepared in varieties of forms, textures and tastes that will outshine more common classes of foods. They will also be carefully designed to supply optimal nutritional needs. Food will become the product of gigantic laboratories and the percentage of space on land and sea which must be devoted to food will be decreasing in 2068. More and more of the Earth's surface can be turned into amusement resorts, parkland and wildlife refuges.

Even Earth's surface load of cities will be declining in 2068. The twenty-first century will see man burrowing underground. The process will only be underway in 2068; the majority of mankind will still be living above ground; but the future will be clear. Every city will already have its underground portion; many newer suburbs will be entirely underground.

The underground city will have as its chief advantage an utter freedom from weather vicissitudes or day-night change. Temperature will be equable the year round and there will be neither wind nor rain nor snow. Well-lit and well-ventilated, the underground cities will be computer-designed from the start for rationality and comfort. With the day-night cycle gone, the entire planet can eventually be put on a single "planet-time."

Nor will the underground dweller be deprived of the touch of nature. Quite the contrary. Where the modern city dweller may have to travel twenty miles to get out "in the country," the underground dweller will merely have to rise a few hundred feet in an elevator, for once a city is completely underground, the area above can be made into parkland.

With abundant energy and advanced computers lifting from the shoulders of mankind all forms of routinized and unrewarding labor, there will be room and scope for fun and creation. In this endeavor, human beings will compete freely and with an increasing feeling of social equality. As the planet becomes a computer-guided community, the sense of "foreigner" will diminish. Ghettos and slums will disappear as copious energy makes affluence possible for all and as computerized 15
decisions modify conditions that would otherwise be brought about by irrational feelings of bigotry. Some people may still choose to be selective in their social and intimate associations, but there will be no great gaps in living standards or opportunity between one loose association and another; no economic barriers between them; and therefore no burning fears or hatreds.

With the declining birth-rate, the rise in ectogenesis, the disappearance of routine housework, and the conversion of all work into a low-muscle, high-brain endeavor that can be performed by either sex, it is clear that the woman of 2068 will be completely equal to man economically and socially. The family will no longer be an essential 16
economic unit and sex will no longer be tied to child-birth. Sexual associations will be looser in 2068 and more casual. The sorrows of unrequited love and of jealousy will not disappear, but perhaps they can more easily be recovered from in the casual atmosphere of the time.

In 2068's world of leisure and comfort, the greatest industry will be that of supplying what may be called "amusement." Sports and shows of all sorts will still be popular, but there will be entirely new outlets. One-man reaction motors can place individuals in the air, so that the sensation of scuba-diving can become air-borne. Trips to the Moon may 17
be common and large space-stations may be established in orbit about the Earth for the chief purpose of supplying vacationers with no-gravity fun. The casual life will allow greater individual tastes in style and manner of behavior. There probably will be chemicals to supply a world of inner illusion without adverse side-effects, and large sections of the population may choose to withdraw into themselves.

Matching the emphasis on amusement will be that on education. By 2068, a substantial percentage of the human race will be seriously devoting the major portion of their lives to a continuing program of education in a variety of fields. Education will be quite comfortable and amusing in 2068. Closed-circuit television and microfilms will offer dramatic ways of transferring information. Computers will design courses in any subject to match the capacity and temperament of the individual. 18
The central library of the planet will be open to everybody and anything in it available on demand through a computerized copying service.

Those who choose education as their goal will have a chance to develop what creativity they possess and to participate in the important work of the world of 2068, the further increase and refinement of knowledge. Those groups who, in 2068, will be pushing hard for controlling the quality of births will undoubtedly have as their goal the increase in the percentage of those who would be so constituted, temperamentally, as to choose continuing education over passive amusement.

Space will still offer an outstanding technological adventure in progress in 2068. A successful, self-supporting colony on the Moon will be celebrating more than half a century of existence. It will be a sizable community, increasing quickly in numbers and drawing a large immigration from Earth. Also the development of rational underground towns on the Moon and the discoveries by the Lunar colonists of techniques for the proper utilization of microorganisms for food will have stimulated similar changes on Earth. Nor will the Moon serve merely as a human residential community. The greatest astronomical observatory will be established on its far side and huge research complexes will be working on chemical and physical techniques that utilize hard vacuums. A Lunar-based computer will analyze data from probes that circle the Sun at closer-than-Mercury distances and from satellites that circle the Earth, watching its atmospheric changes. Weather-forecasting on Earth will become a science and so will another kind of weather-forecasting: that of predicting changes in the Solar wind, necessary, if space travel is to be safe.

By 2068, there will also be a small colony on Mars and manned probes will have swept across the neighborhood of Venus and Mercury. Temporary landings will have been made on Ceres, the largest of the asteroids. But the outer planets will still remain to be explored. In 2068, the news headlines will feature the preparation for manned flights to the moons of Jupiter. (These headlines, by the way, can be on television screens, called for at will, with any news item or feature reproduced on paper for your records, as desired, at the push of a button. Many, however, will wish to obtain printed newspapers, complete with comics and feature columns, for leisure reading and for absorption in depth—and that will be available, too.) Unmanned probes will have preceded the flight, both to the neighborhood of Jupiter and to the planets beyond. It will be clear that by 2100 man will have explored to the limits of the Solar system.

Are there any great unsolved problems that will face the world of 2068? In the fields of science and technology, two overriding ones will remain.

In the first place, the gap between the Solar system and other planets circling other stars will still be unbridgeable in 2068. Is the gap permanently unbridgeable, or can there exist techniques undreamed of, even in 2068, by which the distance can be crossed, without unbearable expenditure of energy and of time? The importance of reaching the stars is that somewhere out there are other life forms and even, in all likelihood, other intelligences. To study other forms of life or to make contact with other intelligences would represent a chance at a monumental advance of knowledge.

Second, the thorough understanding of the human brain will still be an unattained goal in 2068. The biochemistry of other tissues will be solved in considerable detail by then and it will be possible to "create life" in the test-tube—that is, to synthesize nucleic acid molecules capable of reproducing themselves. But the big problem will remain; the intricate interrelationships of the human brain will still be 24
out of sight. A major push in this direction will be in progress in 2068. After all, a true understanding of what makes us tick will make it possible for mankind to guide itself all the better in a further rational advance that will, by 2168, make the world of 2068 seem, by comparison, nothing more than a collection of cavemen huddled about a brushfire.

Alan Watts

The Future of Ecstasy

It wasn't until 30 years ago, in the 1960's, that there began to be any widespread realization that ecstasy is a legitimate human need—as essential for mental and physical health as proper nutrition, vitamins, rest and recreation. Though the idea had been foreshadowed by Freud and stressed by Wilhelm Reich, there had never been anything particularly ecstatic about psychoanalysts, or their patients. They seemed, on the whole, emotionally catharticized and drearily mature. Ecstasy, in the form of mystical experience, had also been the objective of a growing minority that, since the beginning of the century, had been fascinated with yoga, Tibetan Buddhism, Zen, Vedanta and other forms of Oriental meditation; and these people were always rather serious and demure.

But in the Sixties, everything blew up. Something almost like a mutation broke out among people from 15 to 25, to the utter consternation of the adult world. From San Francisco to Katmandu, there suddenly appeared multitudes of hippies with hair, beards and costumes that disquietingly reminded their elders of Jesus Christ, the prophets and the apostles—who were all at a safe historical distance. At the peak of our technological affluence, these young people renounced the cherished values of Western civilization—the values of property and status. Richness of experience, they maintained, was far more important than things and money, in pursuit of which their parents were miserably and dutifully trapped in squirrel cages.

Scandalously, hippies did not adopt the ascetic and celibate ways of traditional holy men. They took drugs, held sexual orgies and substituted freeloving communities for the hallowed family circle. Those who hoped that all this was just an adolescent quest for kicks that would soon fade away were increasingly alarmed, for it appeared to be in lively earnest. The hippies moved on from marijuana and LSD to Hindu chants and yoga, hardly aware that mysticism, in the form of realizing that one's true self is the Godhead, is something Western society would not tolerate. After all, look what happened to Jesus. Mysticism, or democracy in the kingdom of God, seemed arrant subversion and blasphemy to people whose official image of God had always been monarchical—the cosmic counterpart of the Pharaohs and Cyruses of the ancient world. Mysticism was therefore persecuted alike by church and state and the taboo still continued—with assistance from the psychiatric inquisition. Admittedly, the hippies were credulous, undiscriminating and immoderate in their spiritual explorations. But if the approach was fumbling, the goal was clear. I have before me a faded copy of the summer 1969 bulletin of what was then California's revolutionary Midpeninsula Free University (now the world-respected Castalia University of Menlo Park), which bluntly affirms that "The natural state of man is ecstatic wonder; we should not settle for less."

Looking back from 1990, all this is very understandable, however inept. The flower children knew what their parents hardly dared contemplate: that they had no future. At any moment, they might suffer instant cremation by the H-bomb or the slower and grislier dooms of chemical and biological warfare. The history of man's behavior warned them that armaments which exist are almost invariably used and may 4
even go off by themselves. By the end of 1970, their protests against the power structure of the West (which from their standpoint included Russia), combined with the black-power movement, had so infuriated the military-industrial-police-labor-union-Mafia complex known as the establishment that the U. S. was close to civil war.

Happily, it was just then that the leading scientists, philosophers and responsible statesmen of the world abruptly called factionists and politicians to their senses. They solemnly proclaimed an ecological crisis and put it so bluntly that the world almost went into panic. Ideological, national and racial disputes were children's tiffs in comparison with the many-headed menace of overpopulation, totally inadequate food production, shortage of water, erosion of soil, pollution of air and water, deforestation, poisoned food and utter chemical imbalance of nature. By 1972, no one could refuse to see that all extravagant military and 5
space projects must forthwith be canceled and every energy diverted to feeding and cleansing the world. Had this not happened, I could not be writing to you. Civilization would not have endured beyond 1980 and certainly would not have taken its present direction. For we have gone a long way in persuading people that "the natural state of man is ecstatic wonder."

Because ecstasy was rare, crude and brief in your day, I should perhaps try to define it. Ecstasy is the sensation of surrendering to vibrations and sometimes to insights, that take you out of your so-called self. By and large, "self" as a direct sensation is nothing more than chronic neuromuscular tension—a habitual resistance to the pulsing of life; which may explain why nonecstatic people are correctly described

as uptight. They are what Freud called anal-retentive types and commonly suffer from impotence and frigidity, being afraid to let themselves go to the spontaneous rhythms of nature. They conceive man as
something apart from and even *against* nature, and civilization as an 6
architecture of resistance to spontaneity. It was, of course, this attitude,
aided by a powerful technology, that brought about the ecological
crisis of the early Seventies and, having seen the mistake, we now
cultivate ecstasy as we once cultivated literacy or morality.

Do not suppose, however, that we are merely a society of lotus-
eaters, lolling on divans and cuddling lovely women. Ecstasy is something higher, or further out, than ordinary pleasure, and few hippies
realized that its achievement requires a particular discipline and skill
that is comparable to the art of sailing. We do not resist the vibrations, 7
pulses and rhythms of nature, just as the yachtsman does not resist the
wind. But he knows how to manage his sails and, therefore, can use
the wind to go wherever he wishes. The art of life, as we see it, is
navigation.

Ecstasy is beyond pleasure. Ordinarily, one thinks of the rainbow
spectrum of light as a band having red at one end and violet at the
other, thus not seeing that violet is the mixture of red and blue. The
spectrum could therefore be displayed as a ring or concentric circles
instead of a band, but its eye-striking central circle would be where
pale, bright yellow comes nearest to white light. This would represent
ecstasy. But it can be approached in two ways, starting from violet: 8
through the blues and greens of pleasure or the reds and oranges of
pain. This explains why ecstasy can be achieved in battle, by ascetic
self-torture and through the many variations of sadomasochistic sexuality. This we call the left-hand, or negative, approach. The right-hand,
or positive, approach is through activities that are loving and life-
affirming. Since both approaches reach the same point, it must be noted
that ecstasy is always a pleasure/pain experience, as when one weeps
for joy or as when there is a certain hurt in intense sexual orgasm.

Pure ecstasy cannot, therefore, be long endured, for, as the Bible says, "No man can see God and live." But frequent plunges into ecstasy transform one's normal consciousness. The everyday world becomes luminous and transparent. The chronic neuromuscular tension against the world disappears, and thus one loses the sensation of carrying one's body around like a load. You feel light, almost weightless, realizing that you are one with a planet that is just falling at ease through space. It's something like the happy, released, energetic feeling one gets after a splendid experience of love-making in the middle of the day.

Continuing the story, you will remember that even as early as 1968, the hippie style of life was, in a superficial form, becoming fashionable in society at large. Beards and longish hair were increasingly noted upon stockbrokers, doctors, professors and advertising men. Men and women alike began to sport sensuous and psychedelic fabrics and free-form new styles were observed in the highest levels of society. Less publicized was the fact that in these same circles, there was a great deal of experimentation with marijuana and LSD and a surprising number of successful businessmen became dropouts, fed up with the strain and the dubious rewards of maintaining the uptight posture.

At the same time, various aspects of hippie life and the vaguer, more generalized revolution of youth against the uptight culture began to interest a new generation of film makers and dramatists—young men and women who had already acquired mastery of the techniques of camera and stage and, therefore, brought imaginative discipline into the quest for ecstasy. Fully realizing that their ever-growing market was a population under 30, they gave a rich and precise articulation to the ambiguous aspirations of the young. They began to replace the 11
old-fashioned, leering style of bawdy film with elegant masterpieces of erotic art. Studying all the new disciplines of sensitivity training and encounter groups (which, by the beginning of 1969, had spread from California and New York to some 40 centers all over the United States and Canada), they distinguished truly spontaneous behavior from merely forced imitation of how people might be expected to behave when relieved of all inhibitions.

This point needs some expansion. The encounter group, as it evolved in your time, was a situation in which the participants were encouraged to express their genuine feelings about themselves and one another, barring only physical violence. A variation was the encounter marathon, in which the group stayed together for 48 hours, sometimes in the nude to encourage the act of total exposure of oneself to others. But in early experiments, it was soon realized that certain people would fake openness and naturalness, often affecting hostility as the sure sign of being genuine. The problem was that, because very few people really 12
knew how they felt naturally, they would act out their preconceptions of natural and unrestricted behavior, and act merely crudely and lewdly. The encounter group was therefore augmented by sensitivity training, which is the art of abandoning all conceptions of how one *should* feel in order to discover how one actually *does* feel—to get down to pure experience, free from all prejudices and preconceptions of what it is "supposed" to be. The focus is simply on what is now. This is, of course, extremely disconcerting to the habitual role player whose social intercourse is restricted to a finite repertoire of well-rehearsed acts.

The new generation of film makers and dramatists took the experiences of sensitivity training and encounter out onto screen and stage, broke down the barrier of the proscenium arch, made the theater less and less a spectacle and more and more a participatory experience.
In film, they produced highly sophisticated versions of the primitive 13
light shows of the Sixties, so that audiences became totally immersed in pulsations of sound, light and pattern. In the early Eighties, they used geodesic domes to cover the audience with the screen and get them to dancing with and in paradisiacal films that surrounded the spectator with patterns of iridescent bubbles, animations of Persian

miniatures and arabesques, vast enlargements of diatoms and Radiolaria, interior views of intricately cut jewels with landscapes beyond, tapestries of ferns, flowers and foliage, gigantic butterfly wings, Tibetan mandalas, visions of the world as seen by flies, and fantasies of their own which, though anything but vague in form or wishy-washy in color, escaped all possible identification. Such involving presentations were hypnotic and irresistible; even the solidest squares became like those Ukrainian peasants of the Ninth Century who, on visting the cathedral of St. Sophia in Byzantium, thought they had arrived in heaven.

The new theater, above all, had everyone rocking with laughter at the attitudes and postures of the uptight world—so much so that, quite outside the theater, it became totally impossible to preach, orate, moralize or platitudinize before any young audience. One was met with derision or, even more unsettling, with smiling eyes that said, "You've *got* to be putting us on." These developments of screen and stage had much to do with a subsequent advance in psychotherapy: it became the real foundation of an art-science of ecstasy which—not that I like the word—we now call Ecstatics.

Early in 1972, two psychiatrists—Roseman of Los Angeles and Kotowari of Tokyo, then working at UCLA—came up with what we now know as Vibration Training. Like most honest psychiatrists, they felt that their techniques were only scratching the surface and that they were burdened with obsolete maps, assumptions and procedures based largely on the scientific world view of the late 19th Century, which looked at the mind in terms of Newtonian mechanics. Roseman and Kotowari reasoned that the foundation of all experience is a complex of interwoven vibrations of many wave lengths, dimensions and qualities. As white light manifests the seven-hued spectrum, so the total spectrum of vibrations has behind it the mysterious E (which $= MC^2$). In their view, a child emerging into the world is the vibration spectrum becoming aware of itself in a particular and partial way, since human senses are by no means responsive to all known vibrations. (We do not see infrared or gamma rays.) To the baby, these vibrations make neither sense nor nonsense. They are simply what is there. He has no problem about giggling at some or crying at others, since no one has yet taught him which vibrations are good and which are bad. He just goes along uncritically with the whole buzz, without the slightest notion that it is one thing and he another.

But as time goes on, his mother and father, brothers and sisters teach him how to make sense of the show. By gestures, attitudes and words, they point out what is baby and what is kitty. When he throws up or soils his diapers, they say, "Ugh!" When he sucks on his bottle or swallows Pablum, they say, "Good baby!" They show delight if he smiles, annoyance if he cries and anxiety if he runs a fever or bleeds from a cut. In due course, he has learned all the rudiments of *their* interpretation of what the vibrations are doing and has taken note of their extreme resistance to interpreting them in any other way. Thus,

when he asks the name for what is, to him, a clearly shaped area of
dry space in a puddle of milk on the table, they say, "Oh, that's nothing." They are very insistent upon what is worth noticing and what
isn't, upon wiggles allowed and wiggles forbidden, upon good smells
and bad smells (most are bad). The baby has no basis for arguing with
this interpretation of the vibrations and, as he grows up, he becomes
as fixated on the system of interpretation as his instructors.

But have they given him the correct, or the only possible, interpretation of the system? After all, they got it from their parents, and
so on down the line, and who has seriously bothered to check it? We
might ask such basic questions as whether the past or the future *really*
exists, whether it's really all that important to go on living, whether
voluntary and involuntary behavior are genuinely different (what about
breathing?) or whether male and female behavior, in gesture and 17
speech, are necessarily distinct in the ways that we suppose. To what
extent is the real world simply our own projection upon the vibrations?
You have lain in bed looking at some chintz drapes adorned with dauby
roses and, all at once, a face appears in the design. As you go on looking, the area surrounding the face begins, if you don't force the process,
to form a logical pattern; and the longer you look, the more the whole
scene becomes as clear as a photograph. Could we, then, through all
our senses, be making some collective projection upon the vibrations,
passing it on to our children as the sober truth?

Roseman and Kotowari did not carry their ideas quite that far.
Their point was simply that our conceptions of the world are much too
rigid and our neuromuscular responses to the vibrations extremely in-
elastic; that, in other words, we are exhausting and frustrating ourselves with unnecessary defensiveness. They constructed an electronic
laboratory where vibrations of all kinds could be simulated, then began
to expose themselves and some selected volunteers to various forms
of low-energy vibration that would ordinarily be annoying. They tried
tickling sensations on various sensitive areas of the skin, the rocking
motion of a ship in rough weather, slowly dripping water on the forehead, sounds of fingernails scratching on a blackboard and of squeaky 18
wheels, discordant combinations of musical tones, irritating and incomprehensible melodies, toilet noises, rasping voices with terrible
accents, voices that were unctuously insincere, going on to groans,
weeping, screams and maniacal laughter and, finally, all kinds of electronically produced shudders, needles and pins and nameless sounds.
At the beginning of each session, the subject was put into a mild hypnotic state with the one suggestion that he simply give in to whatever
vibration is aroused, letting his organism respond freely in whatever
way seemed natural. If, for example, a stimulus made him feel like
squirming, he was encouraged to squirm as much as he liked and really
get with it.

As might be expected, people began to acquire a taste for these
formerly taboo vibrations and their now uninhibited and often convul-

sive responses began to take on an erotic and sometimes ecstatic quality. The doctors supplemented sonic and tactile vibrations with video: strobe lights, vivid color movies of falling through space, of revolting messes accompanied with appropriate smells, of explosions, approaching tornadoes, monstrous spiders, hideous human faces and of people running through endless crystalline corridors as if totally lost in the 19
mazes of the brain. They then tried low degrees of electronically induced pain, following Grantley Dick-Reid's discovery that labor pains could be reinterpreted as orgiastic tensions, and found that, with a little practice, subjects could tolerate relatively intense degrees of this stimulus—even though writhing and screaming quite unashamedly, yet without giving the doctor any signal to stop.

The researchers also worked with a 24-speaker, 360-degree sound system that surrounded the subject with stereo music of the strongest emotional impact played from 24-track tapes. They had mechanisms for atomizing all kinds of perfume, incense, natural flower scents and the beneficent aromas of gardens, fields and forests. They used exquisite and innocently performed erotic movies, filmed kaleidoscopic patterns of jewels and of iridescent whorls of weaving smoke and mock-ups of unbelievably vast temples and palaces rich with fretted screens and polychrome sculpture. The subject would be visually, aurally, olfactorily 20
and kinesthetically led through their enormous courtyards, gardens, galleries, naves and sanctuaries to the accompaniment of angelic choirs, sonorous trumpets, double-bass-throated bells and gongs and unearthly chants and hymns, until the journey reached its climax in a holy of holies where he might be confronted with a remarkably beautiful goddess or a colossal aureole of rich and brilliant light into which he would be finally absorbed—to find himself soaring bodilessly in clear-blue sky, like a sea gull. Sometimes they accompanied this climax with electrical stimulation of the pleasure centers of the brain.

It should be noted that, through all this, the gadgetry was, as far as possible, installed in a separate room, away from the subject, who lay in a spacious neutral chamber with walls that could be decorated in any way desired by light projection. Those who volunteered for a course of this treatment discovered that their responses to the ordinary, 21
everyday vibration system were radically changed. Almost all uptightness had disappeared, for they had learned how to reinterpret and actually dig the vibratory sensations hitherto called anxiety, fear, grief, depression, shame, guilt and a considerable degree of what they had known as pain.

It was as if the science of electronics had thus far just been waiting for something important to do. From every continent, electronic buffs got in touch with Roseman and Kotowari with suggestions and requests 22
for information and it was only a few months before similar laboratories were set up in cities all over the world. Shortly afterward, such corporations as Bell Telephone and Varian Associates began to design miniaturized versions of the equipment, which could be mass-produced,

so that by 1979 it had become the major technique for psychotherapy and a large research center for the two doctors was established at Castalia University.

The general effect was that uptightness came to be recognized as a sickness, like alcoholism or paranoia, so that more and more people began to be increasingly comfortable in a world where truth and reality were far less rigidly defined. They stopped looking for rocks on which to stand and foundations for building their lives, dropping all such metaphors of fortification and stony solidity. They realized that the world, the vibration system, is more airy and liquid than solid and they reacted to it as swimmers, sailors and airmen rather than as landlub- 23
bers. They found security in letting go rather than in holding on and, in so doing, developed an attitude toward life that might be called psychophysical judo. Nearly 25 centuries ago, the Chinese sages Lao-tzu and Chuang-tzu had called it *wu wei*, which is perhaps best translated as "action without forcing." It is sailing in the stream of the Tao, or course of nature, and navigating the currents of *li* (organic pattern) —a word that originally signified the natural markings in jade or the grain in wood.

As this attitude spread and prevailed in the wake of Vibration Training, people became more and more indulgent about eccentricity in life style, tolerant of racial and religious differences and adventurous in exploring unusual ways of living. Present time became more important than future time, on the reasoning that there is no point in making plans for the future if you can't fully enjoy their results when they, in turn, become part of the present. By and large, we stopped rushing and found that with less haste, we had more speed, since rushing sets up a whole multitude of antagonistic vibrations. We got out of uptight
clothes—trousers, girdles, neckties, hard shoes and other contraptions 24
for trussing and binding the body, as if to say, "Now you really exist and will not fall apart." We shifted into every variety of colorful sarong, kimono, sari, caftan, burnoose and poncho and wore them on the streets and for business. We equipped our homes with spacious Japanese bathtubs or saunas, where we all sat and relaxed after the day's work. These tubs were made so that six people could sit with hot water up to their necks; and, of course, one did not wash in the tub itself but took a shower first. Several of my friends in California had them back in 1968, but now they're everywhere.

Absence of rush gave us a very new and different approach to sexual relations. You must understand that despite the ecological crisis of the Seventies, technology gave us an enormous amount of leisure. By 1985, there were no longer nine-to-five jobs. The whole world be- 25
gan to run on Greenwich mean time and work hours today are staggered throughout each 24-hour period, amounting in all to about ten hours a week—unless, of course, one is an enthusiast for doctoring, engineering, scientific research or carpentry, in which case he can work as long as he likes. Under these circumstances, we no longer speak of

sexual relations as sleeping or going to bed with someone. After all, why wait until you're tired? Furthermore, late-night or early-morning sex in bed tends to restrict the relationship to simple fucking, so that the whole thing is over in from two to twenty minutes. Men in a hurry to prove—what?

We take our time. The man and the woman take turns to manage the occasion, the one acting as servant of the other (although this is no rigid pattern and the arrangement may also be mutual). One begins by serving his beloved a light but exquisite meal, which is usually eaten from a low table surrounded with large floor cushions. It should be explained that today most men know how to cook and that for many years people have been keeping their legs limber by sitting on the floor. For the meal, the couple wear loose and luscious clothes and often the cooking is done at the table over an electric Permacoal or ordinary charcoal fire. As is now customary (and, I should add, quite legal), a water pipe is brought to the table after the meal for the smoking of marijuana or hashish, since it is now recognized that any alcohol other than light wine or beer is not conducive to sexual ecstasy.

So as not to interfere with conversation during the meal, music is not played until the pipe is brought. Vibration Training has abolished mere background music and it is now considered extremely bad taste not to listen whenever music is played. The music may be recorded, but sometimes one or two friends, or even the children of the couple, come in at this time with instruments and play for an hour or so while the pipe is smoked; and, after the serving partner clears the table, the couple adjourn to the bath for showers and a half-hour soak in the big tub. The serving partner then gives his or her companion a complete massage on a special pad provided in the bathroom. (Toilet facilities, I should note, are always in a separate room.) While the one who has received the massage takes a short rest, the other lays out a thick, fold-up floor pad by the table, setting beside it a basket of flowers, a box of jewels and a make-up kit. Sometimes a pair of tall candlesticks is placed at each end of the pad and incense, in a burner with a long wooden handle, is set on the table.

The other person is then escorted, naked, from the bathroom and seated on the pad, and he or she is then adorned with jewels—usually an elaborate (but nonscratchy) necklace with matching wrist and ankle bracelets. The incense burner is lifted by its handle and used to perfume the hair and, thereafter, make-up is applied decoratively and imaginatively to the eyes, lips and forehead, and often to other parts of the body. The forehead, for example, is usually adorned with a small "third eye" design such as is used among Hindu dancers. Flowers are then set in the hair and, perhaps, hung around the neck in the form of a *lei.* The serving partner usually puts on his or her own adornments immediately after the massage, during the rest.

Both are now seated on the pad, facing each other. One of the benefits of Vibration Training is that it allows almost everyone to have

a good singing voice, for the blocks against producing a clear tone have
been removed. Therefore, it is now quite usual for lovers to sing to
each other, with a hummed chant or with articulate words, sometimes
using a guitar or a lute. It is thus that, before bodily contact begins,
they caress each other with their eyes while singing. Some people prefer, at this time, to play such games as checkers, dominoes or ten-
second chess, the winner having the privilege of proposing any form
of sexplay desired. From this point on, almost anything goes, though
the mood established by the preparations is often conducive to a long, 29
slow form of sexual intercourse wherein the couple remain joined for
an hour or more with very little motion, keeping the pre-orgasmic
tension as high as possible without aiming at the release of climax.
I realize that, back in 1970, most men would consider this ritual affected and ridiculous and term the whole business a good honest fuck
spoiled. Looking back, it is amazing to realize how unconscious we
were of our barbarity, our atrocious manners, our slipshod cooking, our
uncomfortable clothes and our absurdly graceless and limited sex acts.

Something more should be said about our use of psychedelics.
Today these substances are given the same kind of respect that has
always been accorded to the very finest French wines. Anyone, for
example, who smokes them throughout the day is regarded as a crude
guzzler incapable of appreciating their benefits. They are not used at
ordinary parties amid chitchat and gossip but only under circumstances 30
in which the fullest attention may be given to the changes in consciousness that they confer. Thus, they are taken more as religious sacraments
than as kicks, though today our religious attitudes are not pious or sanc-
timonious, since only very ignorant people now think of God as the
cosmic stuffed shirt in whose presence no laughter is allowed.

I well remember the first great hemp shop that was opened in
San Francisco around 1976. It was essentially a long wooden bar with
stools for the customers. On the bar itself were a few large crocks containing the basic and cheaper forms of the weed—Panama Red, Aca-
pulco Gold, Indian Ganja and Domestic Green. But against the wall
behind the bar stood a long cabinet furnished with hundreds of small
drawers that a local guitar maker had decorated with intricate ivory
inlays in the Italian style. Each drawer carried a label indicating the 31
precise field and year of the product, so that one could purchase all
the different varieties from Mexico, Lebanon, Morocco, Egypt, India
and Vietnam, as well as the carefully tended plants of devout Canna-
binologists here at home. Business was conducted with leisure and
courtesy and the salesmen offered small samples for testing at the
bar, along with sensitive and expert discussion of their special effects.
I might add that the stronger psychedelics, such as LSD, were coming
to be used only rarely—for psychotherapy, for retreats in religious institutions and in our special hospitals for the dying.

These latter became common after about 1978, when some of the
students of Roseman and Kotowari realized that the sensation of dying

could be reinterpreted ecstatically as total self-release. As a result, death became an occasion for congratulations and rejoicing. After all, "You only die once" (as the slogan went), and if death is as proper and natural as birth, it is absurd not to make the most of it. Even today, the science of geriatrics is far from conferring physical immortality, though it is increasingly common for people to pass their 100th
or even 150th birthdays. Our hospitals for the dying are the work of 32
our most imaginative architects and are set about with orchards and flower gardens, fountains and spas, and we have utterly forsaken the grisly and hollow rituals of mid-century morticians. Even the young have been taught to contemplate without creeps and shudders the prospect of their annihilation, by means of exposure—in the course of Vibration Training—to intense light and sound, followed by total darkness and silence.

And we now have something *completely* new. You will remember that in 1969, Dr. Joseph Weber of the University of Maryland discovered and measured gravity waves. This led, in 1982, to a method for polarizing the force of gravity that has revolutionized transportation, abolished smog and so redistributed population that densely crowded cities no longer exist. Three physicists—Conrad, Schermann and Grodzinski—found a way of polarizing a material similar to lead so as to give it a negative weight in proportion to its positive, or normal, weight. This material can be attached to the back of a strong,
wide belt, carrying also the requisite electronic equipment, plus direc- 33
tional and volume controls, thus enabling the wearer to float off the ground or shoot high into the air. At low volume, one can take enormous strides, a mile long and 50 feet high at the peak, or float gently through valleys and over the tops of trees without rush or noise. At high volume and dressed in a space suit, one can soar into outer space or travel easily at 300 miles an hour at 4000 feet. Needless to say, every such outfit is equipped with a radar device that brings one to a hovering halt the moment there is any danger of collision. Much larger units of the leadlike material are attached to freight and passenger aircraft, and the silent ease of vertical ascent and descent has freed us from all the hassle and inconvenience of the old airports.

But we are not in a hurry. As a result, negative gravitation has given us everything for which we envied the birds and it is much used for the sport of lolling about in the air, for sky-diving and dancing, for
"sitting" on clouds and for reaching homes now built on otherwise in- 34
accessible mountaintops and in secluded valleys. You will remember the reports of the ecstasy of weightlessness given long ago by spacemen, sky and skindivers. Now this is available for everyone and we literally float about our business. As Toynbee foresaw, civilization has become etherealized; grass grows on the highways and earth has been relieved of all its concrete belts and patches.

Of course, the main problem of the ecstatic life is comparable to fatigue in metals: It is impossible to remain at a peak of ecstasy for a

long time, even when the types of ecstasy are frequently varied. Furthermore consciousness tends to repress or ignore a perpetual stimulus —such as the sea-level pressure of air on the skin. This has given us a new respect for mild asceticism. Since the ecological crisis, enormous numbers of people have taken to gardening and we cultivate fruits and vegetables on every scrap of arable land, using large Fuller domes as hothouses in winter, which itself is much milder than it used to be, thanks to world-wide climate control. Millions are therefore up by six in the morning (your time), digging, hoeing, weeding and pruning. At
the same time, we eat much less in bulk and no longer expect disgust- 35
ingly overloaded plates in restaurants. Not only is our food more nutritive but we also find our stamina and muscle tone much better for lack of stuffing ourselves. Despite the advantages of negative gravitation, we walk and hike almost religiously, for with our wealth of gardens, the landscape is worth seeing and the unpaved ground is easy on the feet. Ample time and absence of rush likewise encourage patient and highly skilled work in all types of art and craft. You would, I suppose, call us fanatical hobbyists—a world of experts in whatever one loves to do, from athletics to zoology.

We are much aware of *little* ecstasies—the sensation of carving wood with a really sharp chisel, timeless absorption in making carpets as glowing as the finest Orientals, laying down and polishing parquet floors in various natural colors of wood, bottling dried herbs from the garden, unraveling tangled string, listening to wind bells made of sonor (a new and marvelously resonant metal), selecting and arranging painted tiles for a chessboard, expertly boning a fish, roasting chestnuts
over charcoal in the evening, combing a woman's hair or washing and 36
massaging a friend's feet. As soon as we freed ourselves from the mirage of hurrying time—which was nothing more than the projection of our own impatience—we were alive again, as in childhood, to the miracles and ecstasies of ordinary life. You would be astounded at the beauty of our homes, our furniture, our clothes and even our pots and pans, for we have the time to make most of these things ourselves, and the sense of reality to see that they—rather than money—constitute genuine wealth.

We also cultivate something oddly known as the ecstasy of ordinary consciousness—related, it would seem, to the Zen principle that "Your usual consciousness is Buddha," meaning here the basic reality of life. We have become accustomed to living simultaneously on several levels of reality, some of which appear to be in mutual contradiction—
as your physicists could regard the nucleus as both particle and wave. 37
In your time, the overwhelmingly orthodox view of the world was objective; you took things to be just as scientists described them, and we still give due weight to this point of view. Taken by itself, however, it degrades man to a mere object: It defines him as he is seen from outside and so screens out his own inside vision of things. Therefore we also take into account the subjective, naïve and childlike way of

seeing life and give it at least equal status. It was, I think, first shown by a British architect, Douglas Harding, writing in the early Sixties, that from this point of view, one has no head. The only directly perceptual content of the head, he wrote, especially through the eyes and ears—which are directed outward from the head—is everything *except* the head. Once this obvious but overlooked fact becomes clear, you no longer regard your head as the center of consciousness: you cease to be a central *thing* upon which experience is banging, scratching and being recorded. Thus, the center of awareness becomes one with all it perceives. You and the world become identical and this disappearance of oneself is, to say the least, a blissful release.

This way of interpreting reality does not contradict the scientific way any more than the colorlessness of a lens rejects the colors of flowers. On the contrary, it restores a whole dimension of value to life which your passion for objectivity neglected and, by comparison, your exclusively scientific universe seems a desiccated, rattling and senseless 38
mechanism. Though it was *self*-centered, in the largest sense, it left out man himself. We have put him back—not as a definable object but as the basic and supreme mystery. And as the Dutch philosopher Aart van der Leeuw once put it, "The mystery of life is not a problem to be solved but a reality to be experienced."

Kurt Vonnegut, Jr.

Harrison Bergeron

The year was 2081, and everybody was finally equal. They weren't only equal before God and the law. They were equal every which way. Nobody was smarter than anybody else. Nobody was better looking than anybody else. Nobody was stronger or quicker than anybody else. All this equality was due to the 211th, 212th, and 213th Amendments to the Constitution, and to the unceasing vigilance of agents of the United States Handicapper General.

Some things about living still weren't quite right, though. April, for instance, still drove people crazy by not being springtime. And it was in that clammy month that the H-G men took George and Hazel Bergeron's fourteen-year-old son, Harrison, away.

It was tragic, all right, but George and Hazel couldn't think about it very hard. Hazel had a perfectly average intelligence, which meant she couldn't think about anything except in short bursts. And George, while his intelligence was way above normal, had a little mental handicap radio in his ear. He was required by law to wear it at all times. It was tuned to a government transmitter. Every twenty seconds or so, the transmitter would send out some sharp noise to keep people like George from taking unfair advantage of their brains.

George and Hazel were watching television. There were tears on Hazel's cheeks, but she'd forgotten for the moment what they were about.

On the television screen were ballerinas.

A buzzer sounded in George's head. His thoughts fled in panic, like bandits from a burglar alarm.

"That was a real pretty dance, that dance they just did," said Hazel.

"Huh?" said George.

"That dance—it was nice," said Hazel.

"Yup," said George. He tried to think a little about the ballerinas. They weren't really very good—no better than anybody else would have been, anyway. They were burdened with sash-weights and bags of birdshot, and their faces were masked, so that no one, seeing a free and graceful gesture or a pretty face, would feel like something the cat drug in. George was toying with the vague notion that maybe dancers shouldn't be handicapped. But he didn't get very far with it before another noise in his ear radio scattered his thoughts.

George winced. So did two out of the eight ballerinas.

Hazel saw him wince. Having no mental handicap herself, she had to ask George what the latest sound had been.

"Sounded like somebody hitting a milk bottle with a ball peen hammer," said George.

"I'd think it would be real interesting, hearing all the different sounds," said Hazel, a little envious. "All the things they think up."

"Um," said George.

"Only, if I was Handicapper General, you know what I would do?" said Hazel. Hazel, as a matter of fact, bore a strong resemblance to the Handicapper General, a woman named Diana Moon Glampers. "If I was Diana Moon Glampers," said Hazel, "I'd have chimes on Sunday—just chimes. Kind of in honor of religion."

"I could think, if it was just chimes," said George.

"Well—maybe make 'em real loud," said Hazel. "I think I'd make a good Handicapper General."

"Good as anybody else," said George.

"Who knows better'n I do what normal is?" said Hazel.

"Right," said George. He began to think glimmeringly about his abnormal son who was now in jail, about Harrison, but a twenty-one-gun salute in his head stopped that.

"Boy!" said Hazel, "that was a doozy, wasn't it?"

It was such a doozy that George was white and trembling, and tears stood on the rims of his red eyes. Two of the eight ballerinas had collapsed to the studio floor, were holding their temples.

"All of a sudden you look so tired," said Hazel. "Why don't you stretch out on the sofa, so's you can rest your handicap bag on the pillows, honeybunch." She was referring to the forty-seven pounds of birdshot in a canvas bag, which was padlocked around George's neck. "Go on and rest the bag for a little while," she said. "I don't care if you're not equal to me for a while."

George weighed the bag with his hands. "I don't mind it," he said. "I don't notice it any more. It's just a part of me."

"You been so tired lately—kind of wore out," said Hazel. "If there was just some way we could make a little hole in the bottom of the bag, and just take out a few of them lead balls. Just a few."

"Two years in prison and two thousand dollars fine for every ball I took out," said George. "I don't call that a bargain."

"If you could just take a few out when you came home from work," said Hazel. "I mean—you don't compete with anybody around here. You just set around."

"If I tried to get away with it," said George, "then other people'd get away with it—and pretty soon we'd be right back to the dark ages again, with everybody competing against everybody else. You wouldn't like that, would you?"

"I'd hate it," said Hazel.

"There you are," said George. "The minute people start cheating on laws, what do you think happens to society?"

If Hazel hadn't been able to come up with an answer to this question, George couldn't have supplied one. A siren was going off in his head.

"Reckon it'd fall all apart," said Hazel.

"What would?" said George blankly.

"Society," said Hazel uncertainly. "Wasn't that what you just said?"

"Who knows?" said George.

The television program was suddenly interrupted for a news bulletin. It wasn't clear at first as to what the bulletin was about, since the announcer, like all announcers, had a serious speech impediment. For about half a minute, and in a strong state of high excitement, the announcer tried to say, "Ladies and gentlemen—"

He finally gave up, handed the bulletin to a ballerina to read.

"That's all right"—Hazel said of the announcer, "he tried. That's the big thing. He tried to do the best he could with what God gave him. He should get a nice raise for trying so hard."

"Ladies and gentlemen—" said the ballerina, reading the bulletin. She must have been extraordinarily beautiful, because the mask she wore was hideous. And it was easy to see that she was the strongest and most graceful of all the dancers, for her handicap bags were as big as those worn by two-hundred-pound men.

And she had to apologize at once for her voice, which was a very unfair voice for a women to use. Her voice was a warm, luminous, timeless melody. "Excuse me—" she said, and she began again, making her voice absolutely uncompetitive.

"Harrison Bergeron, age fourteen," she said in a grackle squawk, "has just escaped from jail, where he was held on suspicion of plotting to overthrow the government. He is a genius and an athlete, is under-handicapped, and should be regarded as extremely dangerous."

A police photograph of Harrison Bergeron was flashed on the screen—upside down, then sideways, upside down again, then right side up. The picture showed the full length of Harrison against a background calibrated in feet and inches. He was exactly seven feet tall.

The rest of Harrison's appearance was Halloween and hardware. Nobody had ever borne heavier handicaps. He had outgrown hindrances faster than the H-G men could think them up. Instead of a little ear radio for a mental handicap, he wore a tremendous pair of earphones, and spectacles with thick wavy lenses. The spectacles were intended to make him not only half blind, but to give him whanging headaches besides.

Scrap metal was hung all over him. Ordinarily, there was a certain symmetry, a military neatness to the handicaps issued to strong people, but Harrison looked like a walking junkyard. In the race of life, Harrison carried three hundred pounds.

And to offset his good looks, the H-G men required that he wear at all times a red rubber ball for a nose, keep his eyebrows shaved off, and cover his even white teeth with black caps at snaggle-tooth random.

"If you see this boy," said the ballerina, "do not—I repeat, do not—try to reason with him."

There was the shriek of a door being torn from its hinges.

Screams and barking cries of consternation came from the television set. The photograph of Harrison Bergeron on the screen jumped again and again, as though dancing to the tune of an earthquake.

George Bergeron correctly identified the earthquake, and well he might have—for many was the time his own home had danced to the same crashing tune. "My God—" said George, "that must be Harrison!"

The realization was blasted from his mind instantly by the sound of an automobile collision in his head.

When George could open his eyes again, the photograph of Harrison was gone. A living, breathing Harrison filled the screen.

Clanking, clownish, and huge, Harrison stood in the center of the studio. The knob of the uprooted studio door was still in his mind. Ballerinas, technicians, musicians, and announcers cowered on their knees before him, expecting to die.

"I am the Emperor!" cried Harrison. "Do you hear? I am the Emperor! Everybody must do what I say at once!" He stamped his foot and the studio shook.

"Even as I stand here—" he bellowed, "crippled, hobbled, sickened—I am a greater ruler than any men who ever lived! Now watch me become what I *can* become!"

Harrison tore the straps of his handicap harness like wet tissue paper, tore straps guaranteed to support five thousand pounds.

Harrison's scrap-iron handicaps crashed to the floor.

Harrison thrust his thumbs under the bar of the padlock that secured his head harness. The bar snapped like celery. Harrison smashed his headphones and spectacles against the wall.

He flung away his rubber-ball nose, revealed a man that would have awed Thor, the god of thunder.

"I shall now select my Empress!" he said, looking down on the cowering people. "Let the first woman who dares rise to her feet claim her mate and her throne!"

A moment passed, and then a ballerina arose, swaying like a willow.

Harrison plucked the mental handicap from her ear, snapped off her physical handicaps with marvellous delicacy. Last of all, he removed her mask.

She was blindingly beautiful.

"Now—" said Harrison, taking her hand, "shall we show the people the meaning of the word dance? Music!" he commanded.

The musicians scrambled back into their chairs, and Harrison stripped them of their handicaps, too. "Play your best," he told them, "and I'll make you barons and dukes and earls."

The music began. It was normal at first—cheap, silly, false. But Harrison snatched two musicians from their chairs, waved them like batons as he sang the music as he wanted it played. He slammed them back into their chairs.

The music began again and was much improved.

Harrison and his Empress merely listened to the music for a while—listened gravely, as though synchronizing their heartbeats with it.

They shifted their weights to their toes.

Harrison placed his big hands on the girl's tiny waist, letting her sense the weightlessness that would soon be hers.

And then, in an explosion of joy and grace, into the air they sprang!

Not only were the laws of the land abandoned, but the law of gravity and the laws of motion as well.

They reeled, whirled, swiveled, flounced, capered, gamboled, and spun.

They leaped like deer on the moon.

The studio ceiling was thirty feet high, but each leap brought the dancers nearer to it.

It became their obvious intention to kiss the ceiling.

They kissed it.

And then, neutralizing gravity with love and pure will, they remained suspended in air inches below the ceiling, and they kissed each other for a long, long time.

It was then that Diana Moon Glampers, the Handicapper General, came into the studio with a double-barreled ten-gauge shotgun. She fired twice, and the Emperor and the Empress were dead before they hit the floor.

Diana Moon Glampers loaded the gun again. She aimed it at the musicians and told them they had ten seconds to get their handicaps back on.

It was then that the Bergerons' television tube burned out.

Hazel turned to comment about the blackout to George. But George had gone out into the kitchen for a can of beer.

George came back in with the beer, paused while a handicap signal shook him up. And then he sat down again. "You been crying?" he said to Hazel.

"Yup," she said.

"What about?" he said.

"I forget," she said. "Something real sad on television."

"What was it?" he said.

"It's all kind of mixed up in my mind," said Hazel.

"Forget sad things," said George.

"I always do," said Hazel.

"That's my girl," said George. He winced. There was the sound of a rivetting gun in his head.

"Gee—I could tell that one was a doozy," said Hazel.

"You can say that again," said George.

"Gee—" said Hazel, "I could tell that one was a doozy."

Frederik Pohl

Day Million

On this day I want to tell you about, which will be about ten 1
thousand years from now, there were a boy, a girl and a love story.
Now, although I haven't said much so far, none of it is true. The
boy was not what you and I would normally think of as a boy, because
he was a hundred and eighty-seven years old. Nor was the girl a girl,
for other reasons. And the love story did not entail that sublimation
of the urge to rape, and concurrent postponement of the instinct to 2
submit, which we at present understand in such matters. You won't
care much for this story if you don't grasp these facts at once. If, however, you will make the effort you'll likely enough find it jampacked,
chockful and tip-top crammed with laughter, tears and poignant sentiment which may, or may not, be worthwhile. The reason the girl was
not a girl was that she was a boy.

How angrily you recoil from the page! You say, who the hell wants
to read about a pair of queers? Calm yourself. Here are no hot-breath-
ing secrets of perversion for the coterie trade. In fact, if you were to 3
see this girl you would not guess that she was in any sense a boy.
Breasts, two; reproductive organs, female. Hips, callipygean; face hair-
less, supra-orbital lobes non-existent. You would term her female on
sight, although it is true that you might wonder just what species she
was a female of, being confused by the tail, the silky pelt and the gill
slits behind each ear.

Now you recoil again. Cripes, man, take my word for it. This is a
sweet kid, and if you, as a normal male, spent as much as an hour in
a room with her you would bend heaven and Earth to get her in the sack.
Dora—We will call her that; her "name" was omicron-Dibase seven- 4
group-totter-oot S Doradus 5314, the last part of which is a colour
specification corresponding to a shade of green—Dora, I say, was feminine, charming and cute. I admit she doesn't sound that way. She was,
as you might put it, a dancer. Her art involved qualities of intellection
and expertise of a very high order, requiring both tremendous natural
capacities and endless practice; it was performed in null-gravity and

I can best describe it by saying that it was something like the performance of a contortionist and something like classical ballet, maybe resembling Damilova's dying swan. It was also pretty damned sexy. In a symbolic way, to be sure; but face it, most of the things we call "sexy" are symbolic, you know, except perhaps an exhibitionist's open clothing. On Day Million when Dora danced, the people who saw her panted, and you would too.

About this business of her being a boy. It didn't matter to her
audiences that genetically she was male. It wouldn't matter to you, if
you were among them, because you wouldn't know it—not unless you
took a biopsy cutting of her flesh and put it under an electron-micro-
scope to find the XY chromosome—and it didn't matter to them because
they didn't care. Through techniques which are not only complex but
haven't yet been discovered, these people were able to determine a
great deal about the aptitudes and easements of babies quite a long 5
time before they were born—at about the second horizon of cell-division,
to be exact, when the segmenting egg is becoming a free blastocyst—
and then they naturally helped those aptitudes along. Wouldn't we?
If we find a child with an aptitude for music we give him a scholarship
to Julliard. If they found a child whose aptitudes were for being a
woman, they made him one. As sex had long been dissociated from
reproduction this was relatively easy to do and caused no trouble and
no, or at least very little, comment.

How much is "very little"? Oh, about as much as would be caused
by our own tampering with Divine Will by filling a tooth. Less than
would be caused by wearing a hearing aid. Does it still sound awful?
Then look closely at the next busty babe you meet and reflect that she
may be a Dora, for adults who are genetically male but somatically 6
female are far from unknown even in our own time. An accident of
environment in the womb overwhelms the blueprints of heredity. The
difference is that with us it happens only by accident and we don't
know about it except rarely, after close study; whereas the people of
Day Million did it often, on purpose, because they wanted to.

Well, that's enough to tell you about Dora. It would only confuse
you to add that she was seven feet tall and smelled of peanut butter. 7
Let us begin our story.

On Day Million, Dora swam out of her house, entered a transportation tube, was sucked briskly to the surface in its flow of water 8
and ejected in its plume of spray to an elastic platform in front of her
—ah—call it her researsal hall.

"Oh, hell!" she cried in pretty confusion, reaching out to catch her
balance and finding herself tumbled against a total stranger, whom we 9
will call Don.

They met cute. Don was on his way to have his legs renewed. Love
was the farthest thing from his mind. But when, absentmindedly taking 10
a shortcut across the landing platform for submarinites and finding
himself drenched, he discovered his arms full of the loveliest girl he

had ever seen, he knew at once they were meant for each other. "Will
you marry me?" he asked. She said softly, "Wednesday," and the promise was like a caress.

Don was tall, muscular, bronze and exciting. His name was no
more Don than Dora's was Dora, but the personal part of it was Adonis
in tribute to his vibrant maleness, and so we will call him Don for
short. His personality colour-code, in Angstrom units, was 5,290, or only 11
a few degrees bluer than Dora's 5,314—a measure of what they had
intuitively discovered at first sight; that they possessed many affinities
of taste and interest.

I despair of telling you exactly what it was that Don did for a
living—I don't mean for the sake of making money, I mean for the sake
of giving purpose and meaning to his life, to keep him from going off
his nut with boredom—except to say that it involved a lot of travelling.
He travelled in interstellar spaceships. In order to make a spaceship
go really fast, about thirty-one male and seven genetically female human beings had to do certain things, and Don was one of the thirty-
one. Actually, he contemplated options. This involved a lot of exposure 12
to radiation flux—not so much from his own station in the propulsive
system as in the spillover from the next stage, where a genetic female
preferred selections, and the sub-nuclear particles making the selections
she preferred demolished themselves in a shower of quanta. Well, you
don't give a rat's ass for that, but it meant that Don had to be clad at
all times in a skin of light, resilient, extremely strong copper-coloured
metal. I have already mentioned this, but you probably thought I
meant he was sunburned.

More than that, he was a cybernetic man. Most of his ruder parts
had been long since replaced with mechanisms of vastly more permanence and use. A cadmium centrifuge, not a heart, pumped his blood.
His lungs moved only when he wanted to speak out loud, for a cascade
of osmotic filters rebreathed oxygen out of his own wastes. In a way,
he probably would have looked peculiar to a man from the 20th century, with his glowing eyes and seven-fingered hands. But to himself,
and of course to Dora, he looked mighty manly and grand. In the course
of his voyages Don had circled Proxima Centauri, Procyon and the
puzzling worlds of Mira Ceti; he had carried agricultural templates to 13
the planets of Canopus and brought back warm, witty pets from the
pale companion of Aldebaran. Blue-hot or red-cool, he had seen a
thousand stars and their ten thousand planets. He had, in fact, been
travelling the starlanes, with only brief leaves on Earth, for pushing
two centuries. But you don't care about that, either. It is people who
make stories, not the circumstances they find themselves in, and you
want to hear about these two people. Well, they made it. The great
thing they had for each other grew and flowered and burst into fruition
on Wednesday, just as Dora had promised. They met at the encoding
room, with a couple of well-wishing friends apiece to cheer them on,
and while their identities were being taped and stored they smiled and

whispered to each other and bore the jokes of their friends with blushing repartee. Then they exchanged their mathematical analogues and went away, Dora to her dwelling beneath the surface of the sea and Don to his ship.

It was an idyll, really. They lived happily ever after—or anyway,
until they decided not to bother any more and died. 14

Of course, they never set eyes on each other again. 15

Oh, I can see you now, you eaters of charcoal-broiled steak, scratching an incipient bunion with one hand and holding this story with the
other, while the stereo plays d' Indy or Monk. You don't believe a word 16
of it, do you? Not for one minute. People wouldn't live like that, you
say with a grunt as you get up to put fresh ice in a drink.

And yet there's Dora, hurrying back through the flushing com-
muter pipes toward her underwater home (she prefers it there; has
had herself somatically altered to breathe the stuff). If I tell you with
what sweet fulfillment she fits the recorded analogue of Don into the
symbol manipulator, hooks herself in and turns herself on . . . if I try
to tell you any of that you will simply stare. Or glare; and grumble,
what the hell kind of love-making is this? And yet I assure you, friend,
I really do assure you that Dora's ecstasies are as creamy and passionate
as any of James Bond's lady spies', and one hell of a lot more so than
anything you are going to find in "real life." Go ahead, glare and grumble. Dora doesn't care. If she thinks of you at all, her thirty-times-great-
great-grandfather, she thinks you're a pretty primordial sort of brute.
You are. Why, Dora is farther removed from you than you are from
the australopithecines of five thousand centuries ago. You could not
swim a second in the strong currents of her life. You don't think prog- 17
ress goes in a straight line, do you? Do you recognize that it is an
ascending, accelerating, maybe even exponential curve? It takes hell's
own time to get started, but when it goes it goes like a bomb. And you,
you Scotch-drinking steak-eater in your relaxacizing chair, you've just
barely lighted the primacord of the fuse. What is it now, the six or seven
hundred thousandth day after Christ? Dora lives in Day Million, the mil-
lionth day of the Christian Era. Ten thousand years from now. Her
body fats are polyunsaturated, like Crisco. Her wastes are haemodi-
alysed out of her bloodstream while she sleeps—that means she doesn't
have to go to the bathroom. On whim, to pass a slow half-hour, she
can command more energy than the entire nation of Portugal can spend
today, and use it to launch a weekend satellite or remould a crater on
the Moon. She loves Don very much. She keeps his every gesture, man-
nerism, nuance, touch of hand, thrill of intercourse, passion of kiss
stored in symbolic-mathematical form. And when she wants him, all
she has to do is turn the machine on and she has him.

And Don, of course, has Dora. Adrift on a sponson city a few hundred yards over her head, or orbiting Arcturus fifty light-years away, Don has only to command his own symbol-manipulator to rescue Dora from the ferrite files and bring her to life for him, and there she is;

and rapturously, tirelessly they love all night. Not in the flesh, of course; but then his flesh has been extensively altered and it wouldn't really be much fun. He doesn't need the flesh for pleasure. Genital organs feel nothing. Neither do hands, nor breasts, nor lips; they are only receptors, accepting and transmitting impulses. It is the brain that feels;
it is the interpretation of those impulses that makes agony or orgasm, 18
and Don's symbol manipulator gives him the analogue of cuddling, the analogue of kissing, the analogue of wild, ardent hours with the eternal, exquisite and incorruptible analogue of Dora. Or Diane. Or sweet Rose, or laughing Alicia; for to be sure, they have each of them exchanged analogues before, and will again.

Rats, you say, it looks crazy to me. And you—with your aftershave
lotion and your little red car, pushing papers across a desk all day and 19
chasing tail all night—tell me, just how the hell do you think you would look to Tiglath-Pileser, say, or Attila the Hun?

Questions and Quotations for Discussion and Writing Assignments

I

1. Isaac Asimov predicts that within the next one hundreds years the quantity and the quality of the population will be controlled. How? By whom? Should a computer, a committee, or even an individual be empowered to decide who can have children?
2. What roles will computers play in the year 2068? What effects will they have on wars and internal violence?
3. What important areas of life does Asimov fail to make predictions about?
4. What, according to Asimov, will education be like in 2068? Does the education he predicts for the future sound attractive to you? Would you prefer a computer to design courses to match your "capacity and temperament"? Who would decide your capacity?
5. According to Asimov, what two great problems will be still unsolved in 2068?
6. In Alan Watts' description of the events leading to the future life of ecstasy, he remarks that one world-shaking crisis made the future possible—near ecological disaster. How could this problem force history to turn in a new direction?
7. What is Watts' definition of ecstasy? What is the opposite of ecstasy? How is ecstasy related to pleasure and to pain? Watts writes that ecstasy requires both "discipline" and "skill." Why should it? What kinds of discipline and skill?
8. Watts says that many people were once "against nature" and that these people "brought about the ecological crisis of the early seventies." Explain this cause and effect relationship.
9. How does Watts explain the difference between "encounter groups" and "sensitivity training"?

10. Watts devotes more than two paragraphs to a discussion of how children are made to see the world in a certain way by their parents. His point is that our perceptions of the world are learned and limited. He raises two intriguing questions: "To what extent is the real world simply our own projection upon the vibrations?" and "Could we, then, through all our senses, be making some collective projection upon the vibrations, passing it on to our children as sober truth?" Well, what do you think? (Before you can answer these questions, you will probably have to define the word "vibrations" as Watts uses it.)

11. What is the difference between *objective* and *subjective*? Can man ever be totally objective in his way of looking at the world?

12. What is the meaning of "up-tight"? What, in Watts' view, happens to people when they stop being "up-tight"?

13. Beginning with a description of "a light but exquisite meal," Watts lovingly details the love-making of a couple in the year 1990. Why does he linger on the details? What parts of this ritual experience seem most appealing? Does any of it seem silly?

14. What effects does Watts achieve by telling us about the future from the point of view of someone who is already there? Notice that in his article Isaac Asimov looks ahead one hundred years and speculates. Is it fair to say that whereas Asimov wants to suggest what the future *might* be, Watts wants to persuade us of what the future *should* be? In others words, isn't Watts selling something—a philosophy or a life style? If he is selling an idea, how has he made it look attractive? Has he presented more than one side of the picture?

15. Watts admits that "it is impossible to remain at a peak of ecstasy for a long time." What, then, do people do in their free, non-ecstatic time in Watts' future? What is "asceticism"?

16. It is fashionable in some groups to condemn competition because it inevitably forces comparisons and makes people feel inferior or superior —weaker-stronger, dull-bright, homely-beautiful. These groups would abolish such harmful comparisons. Would you? In his humorous story, Kurt Vonnegut, Jr. creates a world of the future in which everyone is equal, made so by the United States Handicapper General. Does the Handicapper General already function in our lives?

17. What happens to the arts as a result of forced equality in "Harrison Bergeron"?

18. Is Vonnegut's story a parable about the evils of forced equality? What bad effects does forced equality have on the characters and on human relationships? How do George and Hazel react to the death of their son?

19. Is there a difference between "equal" and "average"?

20. The most beautiful, strongest, most talented person in the story is Harrison Bergeron, and he declares himself "Emperor." Is Vonnegut saying that gifted people demand position, fame, recognition, and even the subservience of others? If so, and if forced equality is bad, what other alternatives are there?

21. What are the advantages to the kind of marriage Don and Dora have in "Day Million"?

22. Both Alan Watts and Frederik Pohl write about love-making in the future. How are their visions of futuristic intercourse similar? How different? In Pohl's story the flesh has been so altered that it is not needed for pleasure; after all, "it is the brain that feels." Is this idea merely an extension of the vibration-sensitivity training done by Roseman and Kotowari in 1972 that Watts describes? Would Watts agree with the idea that the flesh some day will no longer be needed for pleasure?

23. Pohl projects his story ten thousand years into the future. Do the characters, Don and Dora, reveal any human traits that we in this century can recognize? How is their love story conventional—i.e., like the fictional love stories we know? How different?

24. a. Most of us, no matter how involved we are with living each moment fully, think about our futures. We feel that we can predict tomorrow on the basis of what we know about the past. For this assignment let your imaginations run free. Make ten predictions about life in the year 2001. As you make your list, the following questions may help spring your mind free: What new inventions will we use in our daily lives? How will we determine our values? Will we live in family units? Will marriage exist in any form in the year 2001? Will religions continue to influence people's lives? If so, what will these religions be like? You may also wish to consider these aspects of future life: transportation, food, sex, recreation, work, health, fashions, energy sources, communication, language, and education.

    b. From your list of predictions choose one and write a short essay about it. In your essay you should explain the basis for your prediction and the effects your prediction, if it came true, would have on our lives in the year 2001.

II

1. To complain of the age we live in, to murmur at the present possessors of power, to lament the past, to conceive extravagant hopes of the future, are the common dispositions of the greatest part of mankind.

   EDMUND BURKE

2. Hear the voice of the Bard!
   Who present, past, and future sees.

   WILLIAM BLAKE

3. You can never plan the future by the past.

   EDMUND BURKE

4. The future cannot be predicted, but futures can be invented. It was man's ability to invent which has made human society what it is. The mental processes of invention are still mysterious. They are rational, but not logical, that is to say deductive. The first step of the technological or social inventor is to visualize by an act of imagination a thing or state of things which does not yet exist and which appears to him in some

way desirable. He can then start rationally arguing backwards from the invention and forward from the means at his disposal, until a way is found from one to the other.

DENNIS GABOR

5. If history teaches anything with complete clarity, it is that a society which fails to act and plan for the future is already doomed.

MARCUS GOODALL

6. The crucial question confronting us now is not whether we can change the world but what kind of world we want, as well as how to turn our choices into realities; for nearly everything even slightly credible is becoming possible, in both man and society, once we decide what and why it should be.

RICHARD KOSTELANETZ

7. The need . . . seems to me to be for an attitude toward change, an attitude which views change as something not to be opposed, and not just to be met, but to be seized upon with enthusiasm, an attitude which views change as the essential quality of growth, which thinks of growth as the essential meaning of life, and which thinks that the future is a good idea, which I do.

W. WILLARD WIRTZ

8. Future shock is the head-on collision between an accelerative push forever pressing us to live faster, to adapt more quickly, to make or break our environmental ties more frequently, to make speedier decisions, and the equally powerful counter-pressures of novelty and diversity which demand that we process more data, that we break out of our old, carefully honed routines, that we examine each situation anew before we make a decision.

ALVIN TOFFLER

9. . . . the coming generation will be the last generation to seize control over technology before technology has irreversibly seized control over it. A generation is not much time, but it is *some* time. . . .

ROBERT L. HEILBRONER

10. When the mad professor of fiction blows up his laboratory and then himself, that's O.K., but when scientists and decision-makers act out of ignorance and pretend it is knowledge, they are using the biosphere, the living space, as an experimental laboratory. The whole world is put in hazard.

LORD RITCHIE-CALDER

11. Children of the future age,
Reading this indignant page,
Know that in a former time,
Love, sweet love, was thought a crime.

WILLIAM BLAKE

12. One of the most gripping historical dilemmas facing mankind at the moment is that at a time when one generation has accumulated a vast

battery of intellectual and instrumental power whereby it can reshape the global environment almost at whim, its successor is adamantly rejecting the principles of living upon which that accumulation is based.

RICHARD KEAN

13. The control of human behavior by artificial means will have become by the year 2000 a frightening possibility. Government—"big brother"—might use tranquilizers, or hallucinogens like L.S.D., to keep the population from becoming unruly or overindependent. More and more subtle forms of conditioning will lead people to react in predictable ways desired by government or by commercial interests without people quite knowing how they are hoodwinked. . . .

    BENTLEY GLASS

14. The best hope space exploration offers is that this colossal perversion of energy, thought and other precious human resources may awaken a spontaneous collective reaction sufficient to bring us down to earth again. Any square mile of inhabited earth has more significance for man's future than all the planets in our solar system. . . .

    LEWIS MUMFORD

Related Readings:

EHRLICH, PAUL, "Eco-Catastrophe," page 279.

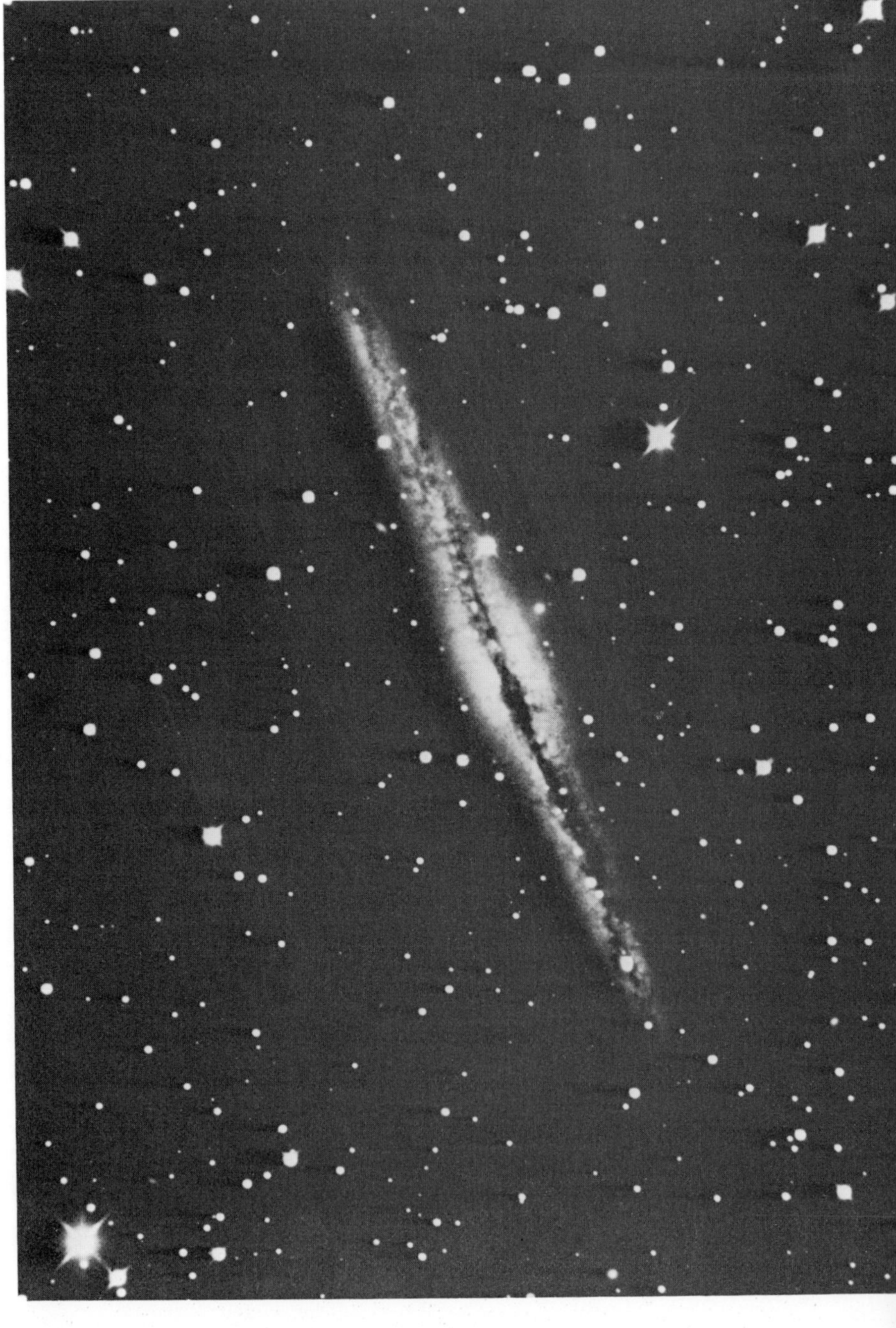